Contents

5 Map of principal sights
9 Map of touring programmes
14 Places to stay
17 Introduction
18 Description of the country
24 Historical table and notes
28 Traditions and folklore
31 The Breton language
33 Evolution and regionalism
34 Learning and literature in Brittany
36 Art
48 Breton food and drink
51 Sights
297 Practical information
312 Regional nature parks
313 Calendar of events
316 Admission times and charges
344 Useful French words and phrases
346 Index

The Michelin maps you will need with this guide are:

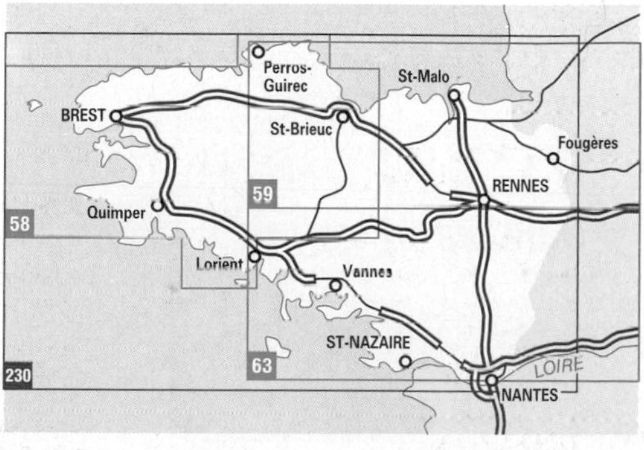

Vieille Lighthouse, Pointe du Raz

L. Salou/EXPLORER

A FEW IDEAS FOR THE FAMILY...

Sun (not guaranteed!), sea and sand

(see Places to stay map)

La Baule☼☼☼
Beg-Meil☼
Bénodet☼☼
Corniche bretonne (Pink Granite Coast)★★
Carantec☼
Carnac☼
Concarneau★★
Le Croisic★
Dinard☼☼☼
Douarnenez Bay
Côte d'Émeraude★★★
Fouesnant★
Loctudy (Île-Tudy)
Quiberon☼
Trégastel☼☼
Le Val-André☼☼

Fins, fur or feathers

Audierne Fish Farm
Binic (Trégomeur): Brittany Zoo
Bourbansais Château Zoo and Gardens
Brest Océanopolis★★
Cancale Oyster and Shellfish Museum
Cornouaille: Cap Sizun Bird Sanctuary★
Grande Brière: Nature Reserve
Lorient: Pont Scorff Zoo
La Roche-Bernard: Branféré Zoological Park
Roscoff Charles-Pérez Aquarium★ *and Fish Farm*
Tinténiac Zooloisirs
Vannes Aquarium★ *and Live Butterfly Centre*

Science and technology

Douarnenez Port Museum (Boats)★★
Lohéac Motor Museum★★
Nantes Maillé Brézé Ship
Pleumeur-Bodou Radar Dome★ *and Planetarium*★
St-Nazaire Espadon Submarine
Ouessant (Ushant) Lighthouse Museum

Places to stay

This map illustrates a selection of holiday destinations which are particularly to be recommended for the accommodation and leisure facilities they offer, and for their pleasant setting.

Accommodation

Consult the **Michelin Red Guide France** for hotels and restaurants and the **Michelin Guide Camping Caravaning France** for camp sites. Both are compiled with the help of regular on-the-spot visits and enquiries. Hotels and camp sites are classified according to the degree of comfort and range of amenities they offer.
Tourist offices *(syndicats d'initiative)* offer different types of accommodation (country cottages, guest rooms etc.) as well as providing information on local open-air activities, cultural or traditional events, and sports. The address and telephone number of the larger tourist offices is given in the Admission Times and Charges section at the end of the guide.

Michelin maps at a scale of 1: 200 000 *(see p 3)* help you to see at a glance the sort of surroundings in which your holiday destination is located and indicate not only road information but also places where you can swim, or play golf, or go to the races etc.

Use the ***Map of principal sights*** *to plan a special itinerary.*

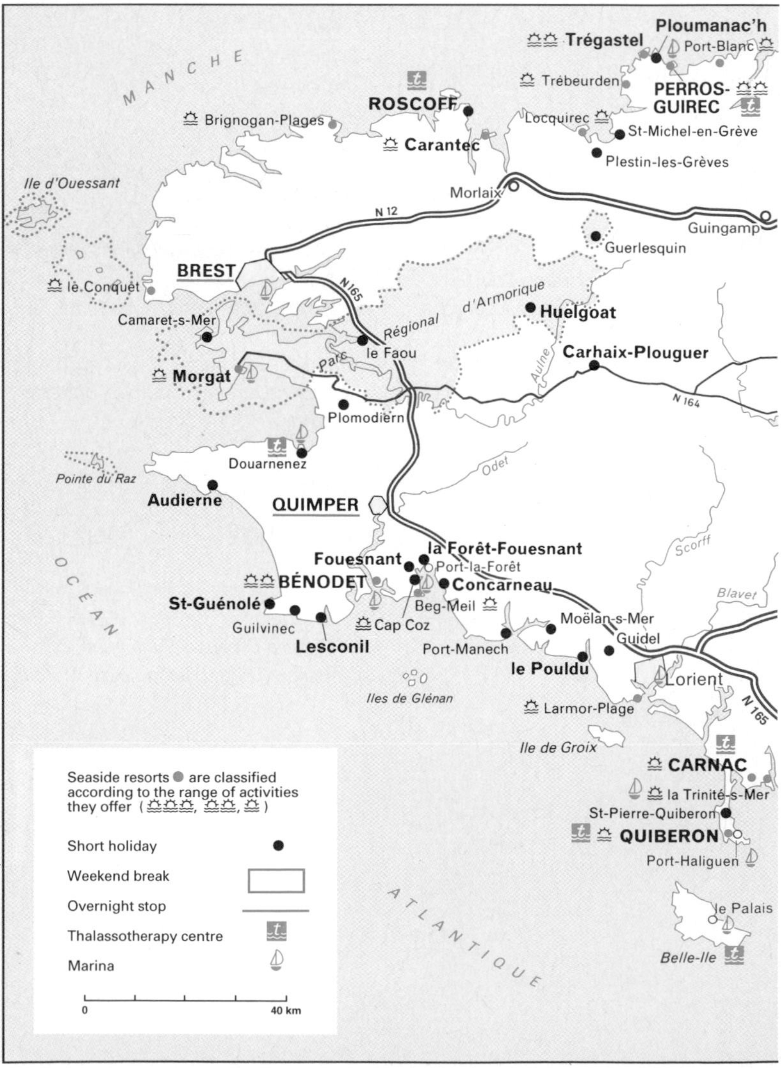

Choosing where to stay

The Places to stay map shows **overnight stops,** fairly large towns which should be visited and which have good accommodation facilities. Besides **seaside resorts,** of which there are many, the map indicates traditional destinations for a **short break,** which combine accommodation, charm and a peaceful setting. As far as Rennes, Vannes, Nantes and St-Malo are concerned, the influence they exert in the region and the wealth of monuments, museums and other sights to which they are home make them the ideal setting for a **weekend break.**
Finally the map mentions **marinas** and **thalassotherapy centres.** Brittany is excellently endowed with facilities of this type, which are all located where the beauty of their setting best combines with the health- and pleasure-giving properties of the sea.

With this guide use Michelin Maps *nos 58, 59 and 63.*

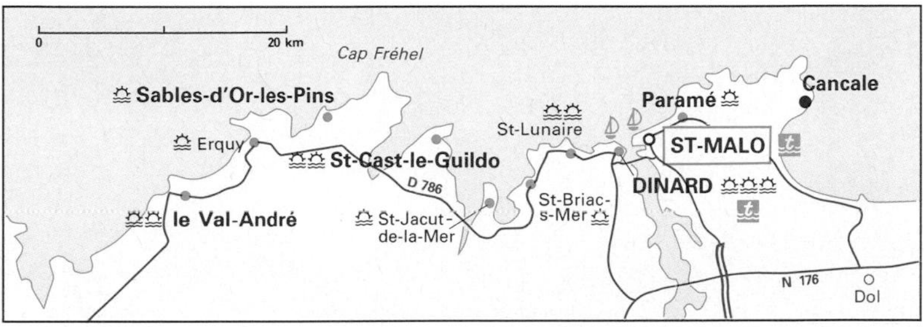

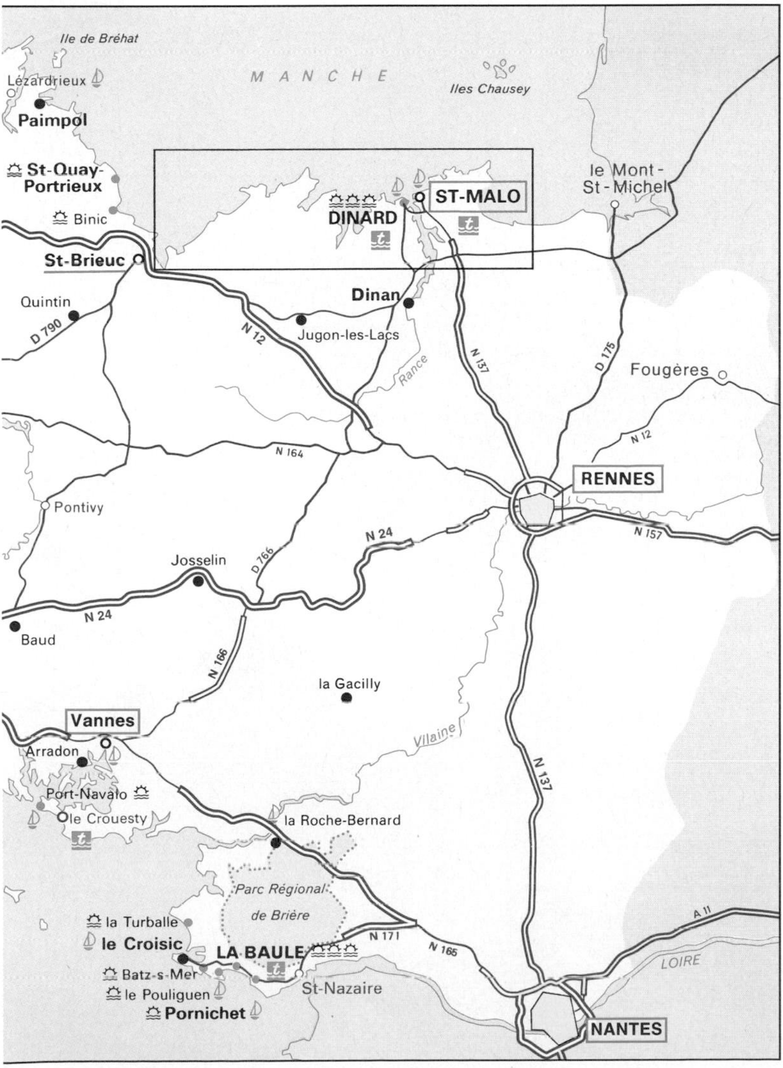

Camaret – Pointe du Toulinguet

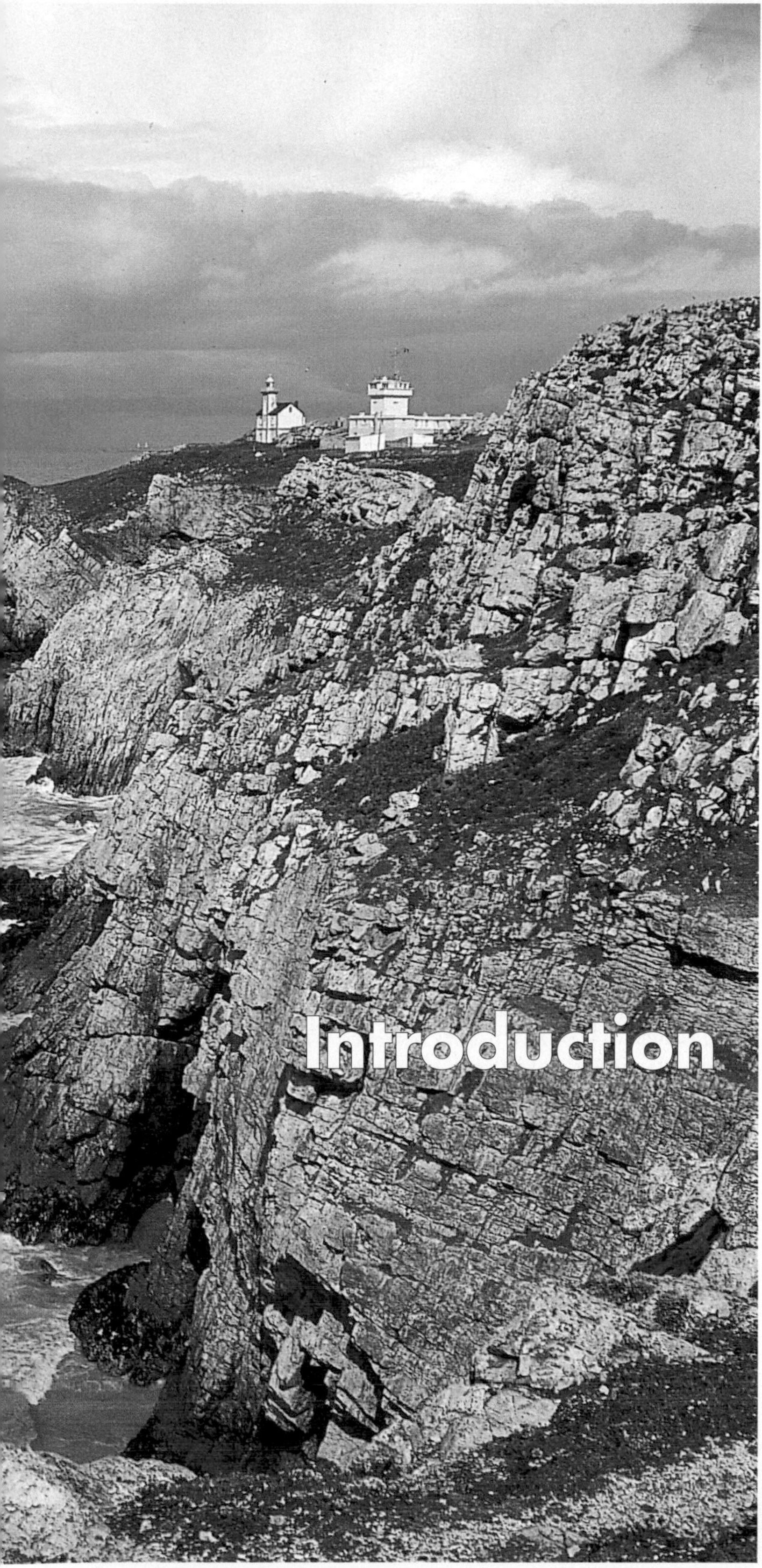

Introduction

G. Thouvenin/EXPLORER

Description of the country

LAND FORMATION

The relief of Brittany is the result of an evolutionary process which has taken place over millions of centuries. The planet earth, a fiery globe, is thought to have detached itself from the sun over four thousand million years ago. This period is divided into eras.

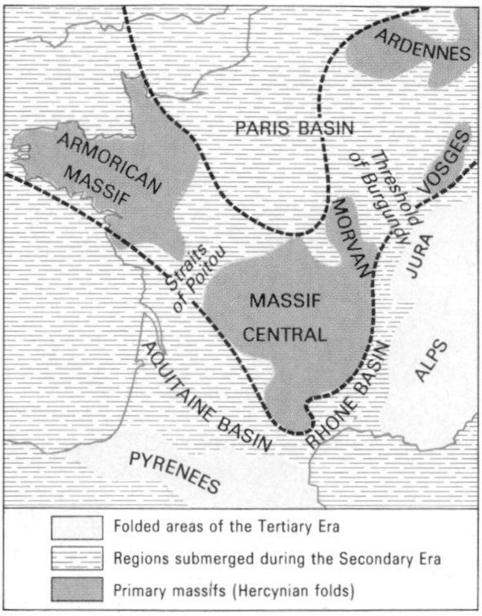

Primary Era – This began about 600 million years ago. Water covered the entire area of what is now France. It was in this era that the earth's crust underwent a tremendous upheaval; this upheaval or folding movement, known as the "Hercynian fold", whose V-shaped appearance is shown by dotted lines on the map opposite, resulted in the emergence of a number of high-mountainous areas (the Armorican and Central Massifs, the Vosges and the Ardennes). These mountains of impermeable, crystalline rock – granite, gneiss and mica-schist mixed with volcanic rock such as porphyry – appeared in Brittany as two massive chains stretching from east to west and separated by a central furrow.

Secondary Era – This began about 200 million years ago. From the beginning of this era, the Hercynian relief was levelled by erosion forming the Armorican peneplain. Erosion, or the constant destruction of the soil by alternating rain, sun, frost and the action of running water, wore away rocks as hard as granite or sandstone.

Tertiary Era – This began about 60 million years ago. The altitude of the Armorican Massif rose only slightly. The highest point is the Toussaines Beacon – Tuchenn Gador – in the Monts d'Arrée (alt 384m - 1 288ft). The deep cuts into the coastline were formed by rocking movements of the earth.

Quaternary Era – This, the present era, began about 2 million years ago. It is the age during which the evolution of man has taken place.
Changes in the sea level, due to the waters freezing over during the Ice Age followed by a rise in water level as the ice melted, brought about the flooding of valleys, thus forming the deep estuaries known in Breton as **abers.** The inland mountains became steep cliffs (Cap Fréhel, Pointe du Penhir, Pointe du Raz) and the hills turned into islands (Batz, Ouessant, Sein, Groix, Belle-Ile, etc.).

THE LAND, THE SEA AND THEIR HARVEST

The Armor

The name **Armor,** which means "country near the sea", was given to the coastal region by the Gauls; the interior was Argoat, "country of the wood" *(see below).*
The Breton coast is extraordinarily indented; this makes it 1 200 km - 750 miles long whereas it would be half that without its saw-teeth. The jagged nature of this coastline with its islands, islets and reefs is due only in part to the action of the sea and is one of the characteristics of Brittany.
The most typical seascapes are to be found at the western tip of the peninsula. Sombre cliffs, rugged capes 50-70m - 160-224ft high, islands, rocks and reefs give the coastline a grimness which is reflected in sinister local names: the Channel of Fear (Fromveur), the Bay of the Dead (Baie des Trépassés), the Hell of Plogoff (Enfer de Plogoff).
There are many other impressive features, too: piles of enormous blocks of pink granite sometimes rising as much as 20m - 64ft as at Ploumanach and Trégastel; the red sandstone promontory of Cap Fréhel standing 57m - 182ft above the sea; the brightly coloured caves of Morgat. The Brest roadstead, the Bay of Douarnenez, the Golfe du Morbihan and its islands are unforgettable. The successive estuaries between the Rance and the Loire offer magnificent views at high tide as one crosses the impressive bridges that span them (Pont Albert-Louppe and Pont de Térénez).
Some low-lying sections of the coast contrast with the more usual rocks. In the north, Mont-St-Michel Bay is bordered by a plain reclaimed from the sea; in the south, the inhospitable Bay of Audierne, the coast between Port-Louis and the base of the Presqu'île de Quiberon, and the beach at La Baule give a forestaste of the great expanses of sand which predominate south of the Loire.

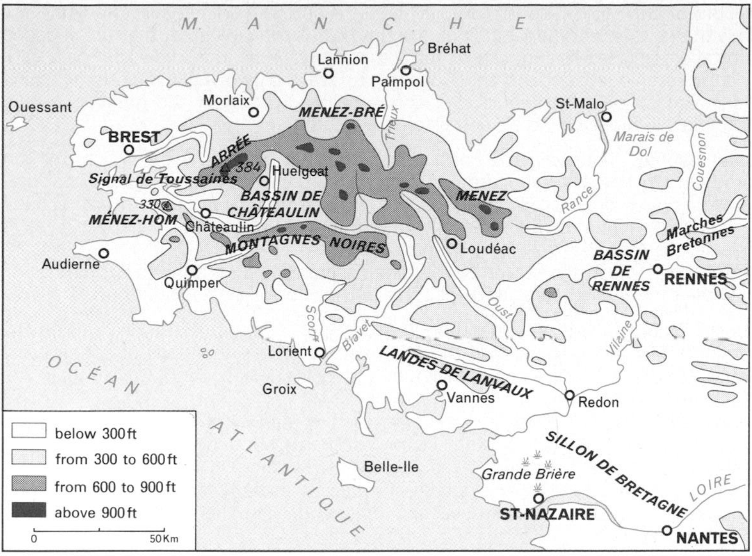

Wherever the coast is directly open to the sea winds, it is completely barren. This is so on the points and on the summits of the cliffs; the salt with which the winds are impregnated destroys the vegetation. But in sheltered spots there are magnificent profusely flowering shrubs. Arum lilies, camellias, hydrangeas and rhododendrons, which would be the pride of many a skilled gardener, grace the smallest gardens.
The climate is so mild that plants which grow in hot countries flourish in the open, e.g. mimosa, agave, pomegranate, palm, eucalyptus, myrtle, oleander and fig trees.

The tides – Visitors should first learn the rhythm of the tides, a division of time as regular as that of the sun. Twice every twenty-four hours the sea advances on the coast – this is the rising tide. It reaches high water mark, where it stays for a while, and then drops back – this is the falling or ebb tide – until it reaches low water mark. It remains at this low level for a while, and then the cycle begins again.
The timetables for the tides are displayed in hotels, on quays and in local papers. Look at them before planning a trip, as they may affect the timing of your programme.
It is at high tide that the coast of Brittany is most beautiful. The waves advance on the coast, break on the rocky outspurs and surge in parallel crests into the bays; a shining liquid carpet fills the estuaries. This is the time when a journey along a coast road or a walk to the harbour is the most rewarding. At low tide the uncovered rocks, stained with algae and seaweed, are often dirty and can be disappointing. At the mouths of the great coastal rivers there is only a poor thread of water winding between mudflats. The greater the tide and the gentler the slope, the greater is the expanse of shore uncovered; in Mont-St-Michel Bay the sea retreats 15-20km – 9-12 miles. On the other hand, low tide is the joy of anyone fishing for crab, shrimp, clams, mussels, etc.
On the north coast, the tide sweeps in, in exceptional cases to a height of 13.50m - 43ft in the Bay of St-Malo and 15m - 49ft in Mont-St-Michel Bay. When the wind blows, the battering-ram effect of the sea is tremendous. Sometimes the shocks given to the rocks off Penmarch are felt as far off as Quimper, 30km – 18 miles away. Attacking the softest parts of the cliffs, the sea makes fissures and brings down slabs of rock. In this way, caves (Morgat), tunnels and arches (Dinan "Château") are formed. Peninsulas joined to the mainland by strips of softer material are turned gradually into islands.
The waves do not only destroy; they also have a constructive effect. The sand they carry, added to the alluvial deposits brought down by the rivers, forms beaches, gradually silts up the bays (Mont-St-Michel Bay is a striking example), and connects islands with the mainland; this is the case at Quiberon and it will also be the same, in due course, at Bréhat.

The waves – Waves are an undulating movement produced by the wind. Even after the wind has dropped, the movement continues; this is the swell. The impression that the water moves forward is an optical illusion: by watching a floating cork one can see that the up and down movement does not displace the water.
Near the shore the undulation of the waves, which may reach heights of up to 30m - 100ft, is impeded by the sea bottom. The rhythmic balance is upset and the crest collapses, thus forming rollers of foam and giving out a dull, rhythmic sound: this is the surf. When the wave meets a steep obstacle, such as rocks or cliffs, it seems to recoil, shoots up, flinging spray into the air, and then falls with all its weight. On stormy days the spectacle can be awe-inspiring.

A people of the sea – The Bretons, if one is to believe a well-known proverb, "are born with the waters of the sea flowing round their hearts". Whether they are engaged in coastal or deep-sea fishing, fishing for cod or crustaceans, they have kept pace with the latest techniques. Lorient and Concarneau are the two most important fishing ports in France after Boulogne, and consequently Brittany is the greatest fishing region, both in monetary value and size of the catch.

Coastal fishing – All along the coast there is inshore fishing. Boats which sail and return with the tide bring in fresh fish such as sole, mullet, turbot, skate, bass, sea-bream, mackerel, crustaceans, scallops, etc. Even so the catch is not nearly enough for local needs, and a town like St-Brieuc on the north side of the peninsula receives supplementary supplies from Lorient in the south.

On the Atlantic coast, the season for sardine fishing lasts from June to September. In winter the sardine boats are used for trawling, lobster or crab fishing.

Deep-sea fishing – Trawlers operating in the Bay of Biscay, the Irish Sea and off the coasts of Iceland bring in most of the fresh fish, especially the kinds of fish in great demand. Trawling is the main activity of big ports like Lorient, Concarneau and Douarnenez.

For **tunny** fishing both live bait and nets are used in the Bay of Biscay and seine nets along the African coasts. The white tunny is fished from June to October: starting somewhere between Portugal and the Azores, the season ends in the Bay of Biscay. Tropical or albacore tunny is the quarry of a fleet of some thirty boats with refrigerated holds, equipped at Concarneau and operating from the ports of West Africa during the season.

B. Stichelbaut/CEDRI

Unloading the catch at Guilvinec

Cod fishing – The **cod-fishing** fleets operate in the fisheries of Newfoundland, Labrador and Greenland. Paimpol and St-Malo were once renowned for their cod fleets but now only St-Malo has connections with cod fishing. The fleets are currently undergoing reorganisation since public preference has shifted from salted to frozen cod. The trawlers are almost factories, with mechanical filletting and freezing equipment on board. St-Malo is the leading port for frozen cod and third in importance for the salted product.

Oceanology and marine fish breeding – The decline in natural resources, which is affecting the most common breeds of fish, has compelled researchers at **IFREMER** (Institut Français de Recherche pour l'Exploitation de la Mer) to seek new solutions to the problem. It is quite probable that fishing will one day be linked with fish breeding. There are already fish farms successfully breeding salmon and turbot. Oceanology is pursued most actively in the Finistère.

Crustaceans – Most crustacean fishing takes place along the rocky coasts using lobster pots and traps, but long-distance fishing using modern equipment is also common. Lobster boats with refrigeration plants leave from Camaret, Audierne and Douarnenez for the coast of Mauritania for several months at a time. The boats are equipped with tanks as well as freezing plants. When the boats return to harbour, part of the catch is put into storage beds. These are situated at many points round the coast, the most important lying between Primel and Audierne.

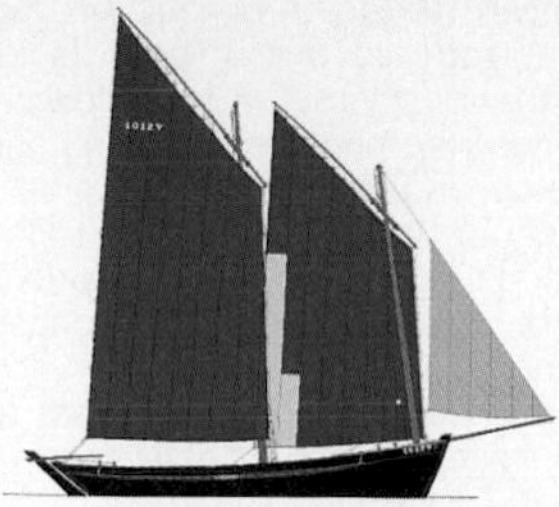

Morbihan *sinago*
(oyster fishing boat)

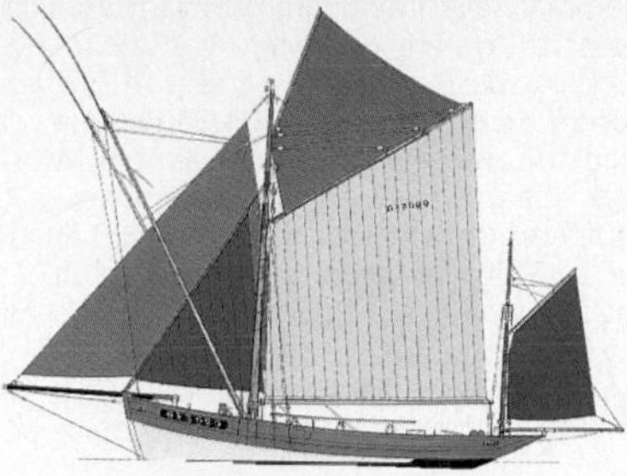

Île de Groix tunny boat

Quimper coasting lugger

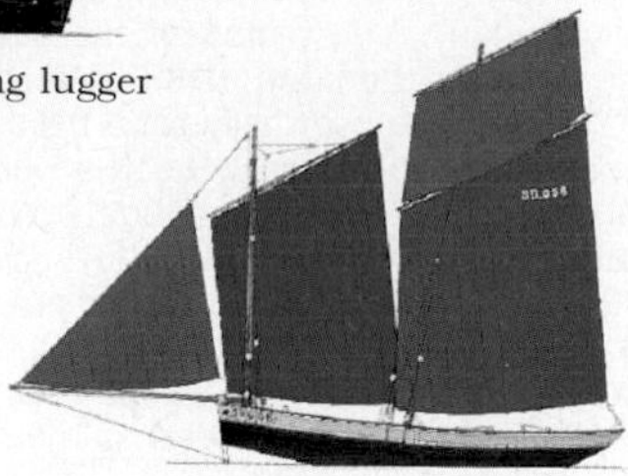

Légué lugger

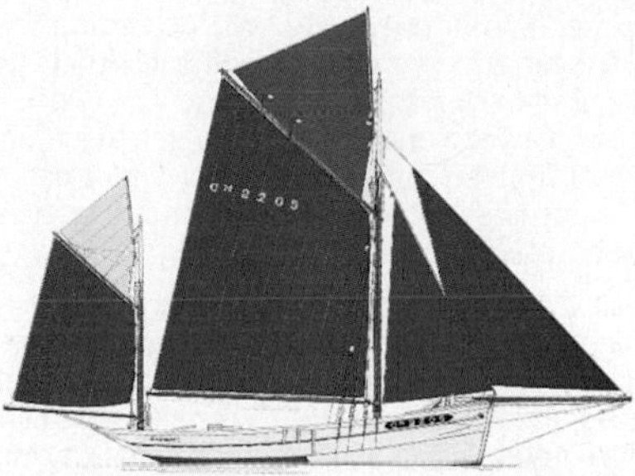

Camaret Dundee lobster boat

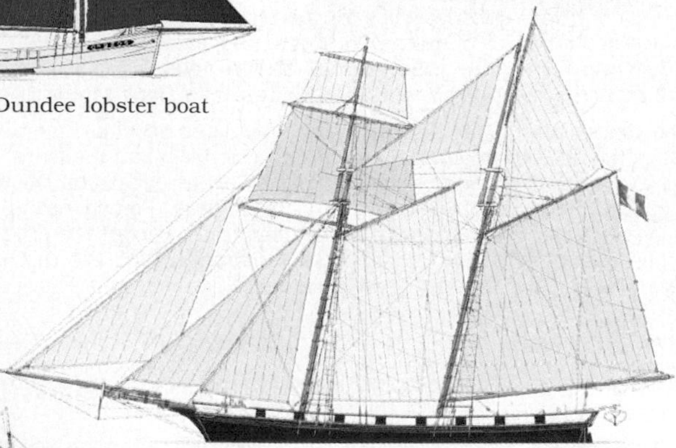

Brest schooner

Dahouët *chaloupe*
(lugger)

Paimpol schooner

H. Kérisit – Éditions Chasse-Marée/Armen

Oysters and shellfish – Conchyliculture – or oyster and mussel breeding – has become commercially important. Brittany, which has long been the great production region for flat oysters *(Belons)*, has also developed its Portuguese oyster beds (sold as *Creuses de Bretagne* or *Fines de Bretagne*). There are considered to be a dozen different excellent types of Breton oyster. The biggest maturing beds lie between Cancale and the Abers passing by Paimpol, Morlaix Bay, Peuzé and Brest river estuaries; on the Atlantic coast from Audierne to Le Croisic, mainly in the Étel and Pénerf Rivers, Quiberon Bay and Golfe du Morbihan. Brittany's annual oyster production amounts, in 9 000ha of breeding pools, to 30 000 tonnes of *creuses* and 2 000 tonnes of *plates*, which is a quarter of France's national production.
Mussel breeding on poles known as "*bouchots*" is carried out along the coast from Mont-St-Michel Bay to St-Brieuc Bay and in the Vilaine estuary. Mussel farms are found all along the southern coast.

Fish processing – Sardines, mackerel, white and albacore tunny are all canned in the factories round the coast, particularly in the Penmarch region, at Douarnenez, Concarneau, Étel and Nantes. Brittany produces two-thirds of the national total.

Algae and algae-processing – Harvested and used as fertiliser for many years, then as raw materials for the chemical industry (soda from the 18C, iodine in the 19C, discovery of gelling properties in the early 20C), the various types of algae are as likely nowadays to be found in bathrooms as on restaurant tables or in thalassotherapy centres. Both sea wrack and seaweed found on the shore used to be collected and used for fertiliser, however harvesting is now subject to regulations. The cultivation of sea tangle (laminaria) as a crop is authorised, using boats specially equipped with a "skoubidou". The region of the **Abers** is the main centre of this activity. The first harvest was gathered in 1983 on Ouessant, thanks to the efforts of **IFREMER**.
The Bretons also use shelly sand from beaches, sea mud and maërl (sand from banks containing calcified algae, found around Paimpol) to improve the soil. According to a local saying, these sands change "gorse to clover and rye grass to wheat"; they can be used either in their natural form or as a processed product.
Vast plants (the largest is at Pleubian) process seaweed and alginates which are found in a diverse range of products such as foodstuffs (biscuits), cosmetics and plastics. Other plants along the coast manufacture iodine and soda, refine maërl and process fish offal for use in fertilisers, animal feed and pharmaceutical products.

Naval dockyards – Half of all the ships built in France come from the Breton yards: the Atlantic Dockyards at St-Nazaire for merchant vessels and battleships and Brest and Lorient Dockyards for ships for the French Navy. The Atlantic Dockyards, capable of dealing with ships of up to 500 000 tonnes, have had to come to terms with falling orders and turn to the production of smaller items, such as container ships, oil rigs and cruisers. Naval repair work also represents a significant part of their activity.

The Golden Belt – In addition to the sea-related activities, market gardening in the sheltered, rich alluvial coastal area between St-Malo and the Loire, which is known as the Golden Belt *(Ceinture Dorée)*, makes an essential contribution to the Breton economy. Potatoes, cauliflower, artichokes, peas, French beans, carrots, cabbage, onions and garlic are all grown in the open fields. Part of the production supplies the large consumer markets, notably the Paris region, and the rest is sent to the local canneries and exported to Great Britain and Germany.

The Argoat

Inland Brittany, the Argoat, has its own beauty and appeals strongly to those who enjoy the bucolic charms of the countryside.

The plateaux – Plains cover most of the country, although you must not expect to find great expanses extending without a break to far horizons. Instead you cross a series of rises without any clear idea of their general direction. Between these uplands flow deeply sunken rivers with brown, rushing waters. The land is usually cut up into a chequerboard pattern by banks and dry-stone walls which form the boundaries of fields and pastures. Pollarded oaks grow on most of the banks and it is these which make the countryside, seen from a distance, seem heavily wooded.

The mountains – Mountains! The word rather overpowers the Breton hills. But this is what the coast dwellers call the central part of Brittany. It must be said that in many places the barrenness and loneliness of the heights, the saw-toothed crests contrasting with the undulating plains that they overshadow and the strong wind give an impression of high altitude.
In clear weather a vast expanse can be seen from the Roc Trévezel (384m - 1 229ft), the Ménez-Hom (330m - 1 056ft) and the Menez Bré (302m - 966ft).
The rivers flowing down from the hills to the Channel or the Atlantic offer pretty scenery. The fresh vegetation in their valleys contrasts with the barren lands of the heights.

Forests and moors – Brittany once had immense forests of oak and beech. Successive generations since the Romans have wielded the axe in these woods, and there are now only scattered strips of woodland: the forests of Paimpont, Loudéac, Huelgoat,

Quénécan, etc. These woodlands are very hilly and intersected by gorges, ravines and tumbled rocks. A perfect example of this type of country is to be seen at Huelgoat. Unfortunately most of the woodlands would appear to be neglected and brushwood predominates. The fine forests are rare and these Breton woodlands owe their picturesque quality more to their relief than to their trees.
Untilled moors succeeded the forests. Near the summits they still form great empty stretches whose gloom is relieved for a time only when the gorse wears its golden cloak and the heather spreads a purple carpet on the hills. Elsewhere, moors have yielded to the efforts of the peasants and have become tilled fields. Such are the Landes de Lanvaux, where the visitor, misled by the name and expecting rough ground, finds reclaimed land, rich in promise for the future.
The terrible storm of 15 and 16 October 1987 caused such serious damage that in some areas it is feared that reforestation will take several decades.

Economic activity – For a long time the Argoat was essentially an agricultural and stock-rearing region but a great stimulus has been given to its industrial development as a result of a decentralisation policy adopted by many large firms.

Agriculture – Although Brittany is said to be a harsh and poor land, it is, nevertheless, one of France's foremost agricultural regions.
Nearly one-third of the land under cultivation is given over to cereal production together with fodder crops (mainly corn) reserved as cattle feed.
There are still many apple orchards in Ille-et-Vilaine and in the south of the Finistère but a certain decline is noticeable in Morbihan. The apples are used in the making of cider, apple juice and concentrate.

Stock rearing – The Argoat has a reputation in particular for its dairy cattle, which produce about 20% of French dairy products. Large dairies are located throughout the region. Pig rearing has been industrialised and represents half of France's production. It supplies national markets and the many firms which produce fresh, canned or salted pork products.
Poultry farming is suitable for small holdings and has been increasingly successful. The Côtes d'Armor, which has a poultry research centre at Plougrafan, and the Finistère head the list in the production of chickens and eggs. Morbihan is the principal turkey producer.

Industry – Processing industries, employing some 200 000 people, consist of two major sectors: food processing and service industries.
Food processing (30% of the workforce) includes pork and beef and their by-products, milk products, animal foodstuffs and vegetable and fish canning. These industries are branching out more and more into such areas as pre-cooked, frozen and diet foods.
Service industries (34% workforce) include motor vehicles and parts, telecommunications, electronics and office automation.
To expand, **consumer industries** (19% workforce), made up of traditional activities (woodworking, furnishings, clothing and footwear, printing) must rely largely on new sectors such as pharmaceuticals and cosmetics.
Processing industries (17% of the workforce), once based on building materials and iron and steel works, must nowadays depend on chemical fertilisers, paper products, rubber and plastics.

SEASONS

Brittany's climate is both mild and invigorating.

Spring is the time when gorse and broom flare golden. The countryside is brightly coloured and scented with flowers, and alive with the song of birds of every species.
A characteristic of the Breton **summer** is its moderate warmth (average 17°C - 64°F), due to the bracing sea breeze which blows from the ocean.
Occasional showers keep the fields green, the foliage fresh and the mosses flourishing. Intermittent spells of heat are heralded by infrequent light winds from the east. The hazy light has a special quality unique to this region.
In **autumn**, the russet tints of the trees can make a splendid picture at sunset. Northwesterly and southwesterly gales are frequent; for those who like to watch rough seas, however, the gales provide a wonderful spectacle!
The **winter** is mild, with the same mean temperature as the Mediterranean coast. A bitter wind may come from the east, but not too often. During these "dark months", as they are known locally, northwesterlies and southwesterlies often unleash their fury in sudden storms.

Historical table and notes

Events in italics indicate milestones in history.

Ancient Armor

BC	**6C**	The Celts arrive in the peninsula and name it Armor (country of the sea). A little-known people who set up many megaliths were there before them.
	56	Caesar destroys the fleet of the Veneti, the most powerful tribe in Armor *(see Golfe du MORBIHAN)*, and conquers the whole country.
AD		For four centuries Roman civilization does its work. Then the barbarian invasions wreck Armor, which returns almost to savagery.

Armor becomes Brittany

460	Arrival of the Celts from Britain, driven out by the Angles and Saxons. Immigration continues for two centuries. These colonists revive and convert Armor and give it a new name, Little Britain, later shortened to Brittany. The Breton people make saints of their religious leaders, who become the patrons of many towns in the peninsula. The political state, made up of innumerable parishes, remains anarchic.
799	Charlemagne subjugates all Brittany.

The Duchy of Brittany

826	Louis the Pious makes Nominoé *(qv)*, a noble of Vannes, Duke of Brittany.
845	Nominoé throws off Frankish suzerainty by defeating Charles the Bald, near Redon. He brings all of Brittany under his authority and founds an independent ducal dynasty which lasts for more than a century.
851	Erispoë, son of Nominoé, takes the title, King of Brittany. He is later assassinated by his cousin Salomon who reigns from 857.
874	Salomon (the Great, or St Salomon) assassinated. During his reign the Kingdom of Brittany reached its zenith, embracing Anjou and Cotentin.
919	Great invasion of Norsemen. Violent robbery and pillage.
939	King Alain Barbe-Torte drives out the last Norsemen.
952	Death of Alain, the last King of Brittany. In the fortresses built all over the country to resist the Norsemen, the nobles defy the successors of Barbe-Torte. There follows a period of disorder and poverty which lasts until nearly the end of the 14C.
1066	*William the Conqueror lands in England.*
1215	*Magna Carta.*
1337	Start of the Hundred Years War ending in 1453.
1341	The War of Succession begins on the death of Duke Jean III. His niece, Jeanne de Penthièvre, wife of Charles of Blois, supported by the French, fights her brother Jean of Montfort, ally of the English, for the Duchy.
1351	Battle of the Thirty *(qv)*.
1364	Charles of Blois, though aided by Du Guesclin *(qv)*, is defeated and killed at Auray *(qv)*. Brittany emerges ruined from this war.

Du Guesclin

Bertrand Du Guesclin, born at La Motte-Broons Castle, near Dinan, was one of France's greatest warriors.
Entering the King's service (in 1356), he was dubbed knight at the Château de Montmuran *(qv)*, on the capture of Rennes. Subsequent victories brought further titles and honours: Governor of Pontorson (1360), Count of Longueville (1364), Duke of Molina and Transtamarre (1366), King of Granada (1369), High Constable of France (1370). His campaigns *(see map below)*, waged mostly against the English and their allies, had brought about considerable expansion of the crown lands by his death in 1380 *(see DINAN)*.

Musée de Bretagne, Rennes

Du Guesclin

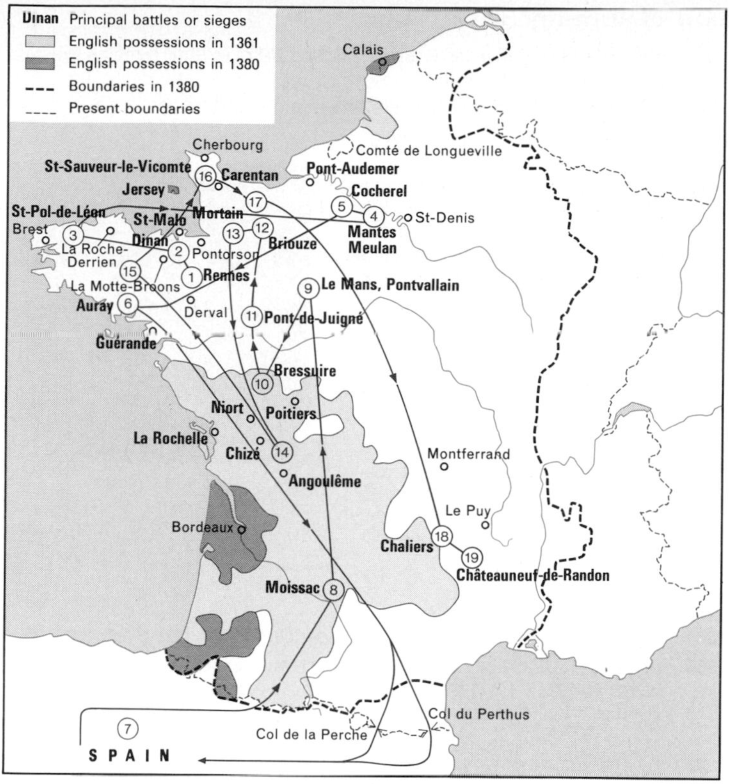

①	1356	Capture of Rennes.
②	1359	Liberation of Dinan.
③	1363	Capture of Breton towns. From St-Pol, Du Guesclin sends ships against the English.
④	1364	Capture of Mantes and Meulan.
⑤	–	(May 16) Victory of Cocherel.
⑥	–	(Sept 29) Defeat of Auray. Du Guesclin taken prisoner.
⑦	1366	"The Great Companies", commanded by Du Guesclin, march into Spain. A series of victories over Peter the Cruel and the English brings the French to Seville.
	1367	(April 3) Defeat of Najera: Du Guesclin taken prisoner and taken to Bordeaux.
	1369	(Jan 17) Du Guesclin ransomed and returns to Spain. (March) Siege of Montiel Castle; Peter the Cruel killed; Du Guesclin returns to France.
⑧	1370	Capture of Moissac and liberation of Périgord.
⑨		Liberation of Le Mans. Victory of Pontvallain. Liberation of Maine and Anjou.
⑩		Capture of Bressuire.
⑪		Defeat of Pont-de-Juigné. Du Guesclin taken prisoner.
⑫	1371	Capture of Briouze.
⑬	1372	Victory of Mortain. The Norman Bocage is freed.
⑭	1372-1373	Capture of towns in Poitou, Saintonge and Angoumois.
⑮	1373	All Brittany conquered except Brest and Derval.
⑯	1374	Capture of St-Sauveur-le-Vicomte.
⑰	1378	All Normandy conquered except Cherbourg.
⑱	1380	(June 27) Capture of Chaliers.
⑲		(July 13-14) Capture of Châteauneuf-de-Randon. Death of Du Guesclin.

The Montforts

1364-1468 The Dukes of the House of Montfort restore the country. This is the most brilliant period of its history. The arts reach their highest development. The dukes are the real sovereigns and pay homage only in theory to the King of France. Constable de Richemont *(see VANNES)*, the companion-in-arms of Joan of Arc, succeeds his brother in 1457 as Duke of Brittany.

1488 Duke François II, who has entered into the federal coalition against the Regent of France, Anne of Beaujeu, is defeated at St-Aubin-du-Cormier and dies. His daughter, Anne of Brittany, succeeds him.

Reunion of Brittany with France

1491 Anne of Brittany marries Charles VIII *(see RENNES)* but remains Duchess and sovereign of Brittany.

1492 *Christopher Columbus discovers America on 12 October.*

1498 Charles VIII dies accidentally. Anne returns to her Duchy.

1499 Anne again becomes Queen of France by marrying Louis XII, who had hastily repudiated his first wife. The Duchy remains distinct from the Crown *(see VANNES)*.

1514 Anne of Brittany dies. Her daughter, Claude of France, inherits the Duchy. She marries François of Angoulême, the future François I.

1532 Claude cedes her Duchy to the Crown. François I has this permanent reunion of Brittany with France ratified by the Parliament at Vannes.

Anne of Brittany

Musée de Bretagne, Rennes

French Brittany

1534 Jacques Cartier discovers the St Lawrence estuary *(see ST-MALO)*.

1588 Brittany rebels against its governor, the Duke of Mercœur, who wants to profit from the troubles of the League to seize the province. Bandits like the famous La Fontenelle ravage the country *(see DOUARNENEZ)*.

1598 By the *Edict of Nantes*, Henri IV puts an end to religious strife *(see NANTES)*.

1675 The "Stamped Paper" Revolt *(see PONT-L'ABBÉ)* develops into a peasants' rising.

1711 Duguay-Trouin *(qv)* takes Rio de Janeiro.

1764 The Rennes Parliament and its Public Prosecutor, La Chalotais, oppose Governor Aiguillon *(qv)*. The authority of the Crown is much weakened. The Revolution is near.

1765 Arrival on Belle-Île of many Acadian families of French origin from Nova Scotia *(qv)*.

1773 Birth of Surcouf *(qv)*, the Breton pirate.

1776 *American Declaration of Independence.*

1789 The Bretons welcome the Revolution with enthusiasm.

1793 Carrier has thousands drowned in the Loire near Nantes *(qv)*.

Surcouf

Musée de St-Malo

1793-1804 The Laws against the priests and the mass levies give rise to the *Chouannerie* (revolt of Breton Royalists).

1795 A landing by Royalist exiles is defeated at Quiberon *(qv)*.

1804 Cadoudal *(qv)*, who tried to revive the *Chouannerie*, is executed.

1826 René Laënnec *(qv)*, the great physician, dies.

1832 Another attempted revolt, organised by the Duchess of Berry *(qv)*, fails. This is the last uprising.

1861 *Start of the American Civil War.*

1909 Strikes and riots among the Concarneau cannery workers.

1914-8 Brittany pays a heavy toll in loss of life during the First World War.

1927-8	The Morbihan aviator Le Brix, accompanied by Costes, is the first to fly round the world.
1940	The islanders of Sein *(qv)* are the first to rally to General de Gaulle's call.
1942	An Anglo-Canadian commando raids the St-Nazaire *(qv)* submarine base.
1944-5	The end of the German Occupation leaves in its wake a trail of destruction, especially at Brest, Lorient and St-Nazaire.
1951	Formation of the organisation Comité d'Études et de Liaison des Intérêts Bretons (CELIB), to safeguard Breton interests, is an initial step towards the rejuvenation of the local economy.
1962	First transatlantic transmission by satellite of a television programme by the station at Pleumeur-Bodou *(qv)*.
1966	The opening of the Rance *(qv)* tidal power scheme and the Monts d'Arrée nuclear station near Brennilis.
1967	The *Torrey Canyon* disaster off the English coast causes great oil slicks to contaminate the beaches of Brittany.
1969	Creation of the Parc naturel régional d'Armorique *(qv)*.
1970	Creation of the Parc naturel régional de Brière *(qv)*.
1975	First search for oil in the Iroise Sea off the Finistère coast.
1978	Establishment of a charter and council to safeguard the Breton cultural heritage. *Amoco Cadiz* oil spill on Brittany beaches.
1985	Introduction of bilingual road signs in French and Breton.
1994	The Law Courts at Rennes, home to the Breton Parliament, are burned to the ground by rioting French farmers.
1994	The opening of the Pont de l'IROISE spanning the Eloen.
1996	Inauguration of the La Roche-Bernard bridge.
	John Paul II leads a pilgrimage to Ste-Anne-d'Auray.

Historical routes

Since 1975, the Demeure Historique and the Caisse Nationale des Monuments Historiques et des Sites (CNMHS) have set up over 80 historical routes covering France. These signposted routes explore architectural, archaeological, botanical or geological heritage within a historical context.
Five historical routes run through Brittany, on: Châteaubriand, the regions of Léon and Tréguier, the Painters of Cornouaille, the Dukes of Brittany and the Breton Marches. Most tourist information offices have leaflets on these routes, otherwise contact the Centre d'information de la CNMHS, Hôtel de Sully, 62 Rue St-Antoine, 75004 Paris, ☎ 01 44 61 21 42.

Fountain at St-Nicolas-du-Pélem

Traditions and folklore

A LAND OF LEGENDS

The Breton soul has always been inclined to the dreamy, the fantastic and the supernatural. This explains the astonishing abundance and persistence of legends in the Armor country.

The Round Table – After the death of Christ, Joseph of Arimathea, one of His disciples, left Palestine, carrying away a few drops of the divine blood in the cup from which the Redeemer drank during the Last Supper. He landed in Britain according to some legends, in Brittany according to others, where he lived for some time in the Forest of Brocéliande (now the Forêt de Paimpont) before vanishing without trace.
In the 6C King Arthur and fifty knights set out to find this precious cup. For them it was the Holy Grail, which only a warrior whose heart was pure could win. Percival (Wagner's Parsifal) was such a man. In the Middle Ages the search for the Grail gave rise to the endless stories of adventure which formed the Cycle of the Round Table. The most famous versions of the tale in English are, of course, Sir Thomas Malory's *Morte d'Arthur* (1471) and Alfred Lord Tennyson's *Idylls of the King* (1859).

Merlin and Viviane – One of King Arthur's companions, Merlin the sorcerer, came to the Forest of Brocéliande to live in seclusion. But he met the fairy Viviane, and love inflamed them both. To make sure of keeping Merlin, Viviane enclosed him in a magic circle. It would have been easy for him to escape, but he joyfully accepted this romantic captivity for ever.

Tristan and Isolde – Tristan, Prince of Lyonesse, was sent to Ireland by his Uncle Mark, King of Cornouaille, to bring back Isolde, whom Mark was to marry. On board their ship, Tristan and Isolde accidentally drank a philtre which was intended to bind Isolde to her husband in eternal love. Passion stronger than duty sprang up in both their hearts. There are several versions of the end: sometimes Tristan is slain by Mark, furious at his betrayal; sometimes he marries and dies in his castle in Brittany. But Isolde always follows him to the grave. Wagner's opera has made the love story famous.

The town of Is – At the time of good **King Gradlon**, about the 6C, Is was the capital of Cornouaille; finds in Trépassés and Douarnenez Bays and off the Presqu'île de Penmarch are said to have come from Is. The town was protected from the sea by a dike, opened by locks to which the King always carried the golden key.
The King had a beautiful but dissolute daughter, **Dahut**, also known as Ahès, who was seduced by the Devil in the form of an attractive young man. To test her love he asked her to open the seagate. Dahut stole the key while the King was asleep, and soon the sea was rushing into the town.
King Gradlon fled on horseback, with his daughter on the crupper. But the waves pursued him and were about to swallow him up. At this moment a celestial voice ordered him, if he would be saved, to throw the demon who was riding behind him into the sea. With an aching heart the King obeyed, and the sea withdrew at once, but Is was destroyed.

D. Taulin-Hommell

Pardon at Ste-Anne-la-Palud

For his new capital Gradlon chose Quimper, this is why his statue stands between the two towers of the cathedral. He ended his days in the odour of sanctity, guided and sustained by St Corentine. As for Dahut, she turned into a mermaid, who is known as **Marie-Morgane** and whose beauty still lures sailors to the bottom of the sea. This state of affairs will persist until the Good Friday when Mass is celebrated in one of the churches of the drowned city. Then Is will cease to be accursed, and Marie-Morgane will no longer be a siren.

THE PARDONS

The Breton *pardons* are above all a manifestation of popular religious fervour. They take place in the churches and chapels which may be consecrated by the tradition of a thousand years. There the faithful come to seek forgiveness, fulfil a vow or beg for grace.
The great *pardons* are most impressive, while the smaller events, though they may be less spectacular, are often more fervent. It is well worth tourists' while to arrange their trip so that they may be present at one of them *(see the Calendar of events at the end of the guide)*. It is also one of the rare occasions when they will see the old costumes, perhaps slightly modernised.

THE SAINTS OF BRITTANY

Brittany, with its magicians, spirits, fairies and demons – both male and female – has also claimed more haloes than any other part of France. Its saints number in hundreds and are represented by painted wooden statues adorning chapels and churches. Truth to tell, those who were canonised by the Vatican authorities (St Yves for example) can be counted on one's fingers. The most "official" among them were simply recognised by the bishops; the people themselves adopted others. Their fame goes no further than the borders of the province, or even the limits of the villages where they are venerated. (For the purposes of this guide, the names of saints revered in a particular region have been left in their local form).

Patrons of towns – The Celtic religious leaders who landed from the British Isles in the 5C *(see Celtic Exodus)* were adopted as the patron saints of the seven former bishoprics: St-Malo, St-Brieuc, (St Brioch), St-Pol-de-Léon (St Paul the Aurelian), Dol (St Samson), Tréguier (St Tugdual), Quimper (St Corentine) and Vannes (St Patern). This applies to many other localities: St-Efflam, St-Lunaire, St-Briac, St-Gildas, etc.

The "healing saints" – The Bretons have always been on trusting, friendly and even familiar terms with their saints.
There are saints who are invoked on all occasions. Innumerable others are invoked against specified aliments: rheumatism, baldness, etc. For centuries they took the place of doctors. Horses and oxen also have their appointed saints (St Cornely and St Herbot).

The "Tro Breiz"

Until the 16C, tradition demanded that every Breton should make a pilgrimage at least once in their lifetime to the seven cathedrals of Brittany. The **"Tro Breiz"**, or "Tour of Brittany", as it was known, drew people in their thousands during the 12C to the 16C, with its popularity reaching a peak in the 14C; estimates suggest that crowds numbering up to 30 000 to 40 000 pilgrims were taking to the roads! The tour covered nearly 700km - 435 miles, and it enabled the faithful to pay homage to the holy relics of the founding saints of Brittany; St Brieuc and St Malo at the town of those names, St Samson at Dol-de-Bretagne, St Patern at Vannes, St Corentine at Quimper, St Paul the Aurelian at St-Pol-de-Léon and St Tugdual at Tréguier. Whoever failed to carry out this duty was supposed to have to undertake the pilgrimage after their death, advancing by the length of their coffin every seven years!
Nowadays, ever increasing numbers of individuals continue to make this journey, in groups or alone, retracing the steps of the earlier pilgrims.
For further details, contact: "Les Chemins du Tro Breiz", Maison Prébendale, 29250 St-Pol-de-Léon, ☎ 02 98 69 16 53.

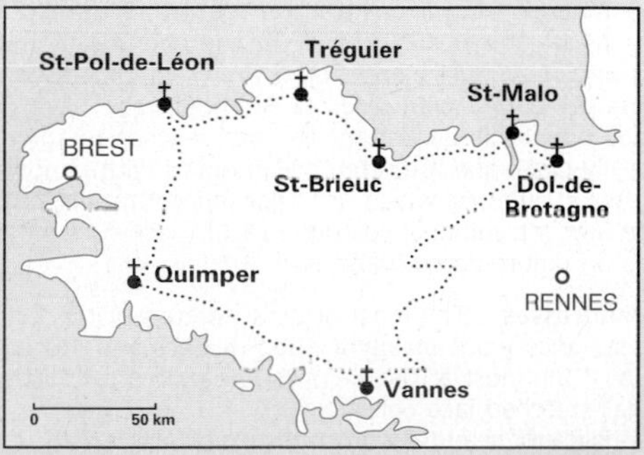

Saint Yves – "Monsieur Saint Yves" is the most popular saint in Brittany. He is the righter of all wrongs and the comforter of the poor.
Yves Helori, the son of a country gentleman, was born at Minihy-Tréguier *(qv)* in 1253. When quite young he developed a taste for the ascetic life. He came to Paris to study law, and unravelled its subtleties for thirteen years. On his return to Brittany he became a priest, and at the bishop's palace of Tréguier acted as a magistrate in one court and as an advocate in others.
He won unheard-of popularity by his spirit of justice and conciliation, the rapidity of his judgments and the brevity of his pleas. One day a bourgeois summoned before him a beggar who came every day to the grating of his kitchen to enjoy the smell of cooking. Yves took a coin, made it ring on the bench and dismissed the plaintiff, saying: "The sound has paid for the smell."
In order not to "cut out" the barristers, Yves always chose the most wretched cases, and thus became known as the "poor man's counsel". In fact, he was a precursor of free legal aid. He was canonised in 1347.
As the patron saint of advocates and men of law, his cult has spread all over Europe and even to America. And within the last few years delegations of barristers from many foreign countries have joined the unceasing stream of pilgrims who attend the blessing of the poor *(pardon des pauvres)* at Tréguier *(qv)*.

The calendar saints – Mystical Brittany has made a place among its innumerable saints for the great figures of the Church.
Statues of the Apostles line church porches and stand on Calvaries; St Michael is the patron of high places; St James that of sailors; St Fiacre of gardeners. St Barbara, who is invoked in stormy weather, is the patroness of corporations which handle explosives (her father, who had her martyred, was killed by lightning). St Apolline protects people from toothache, and many others have an established cult. The Virgin Mary and her mother, St Anne, are the most fervently invoked of the saints.

Saint Anne – The cult of Saint Anne was brought to western Europe by those returning from the Crusades. Her eager adoption by the Bretons was in part due to the popularity of the Duchess, Anne of Brittany and her later renown. Patroness of Brittany and mother of the Virgin Mary, Saint Anne was originally invoked for a good harvest.
The most famous *pardon* in Brittany, that of Ste-Anne-d'Auray, is dedicated to her, as is the very important one of Ste-Anne-la-Palud *(photograph p28)*. These colourful events, which express Breton religious fervour, have given rise to the local saying, "Whether dead or alive, every Breton goes at least once to Saint-Anne".
A doubtful legend makes St Anne a Cornouaille woman of royal blood who was taken to Nazareth by angels to save her from her husband's brutality. After having given birth to the Virgin Mary she returned to Brittany and lived there till her death. It was Jesus who, when visiting his grandmother, called forth the sacred spring of Ste-Anne-la-Palud.
The statues usually portray her alone or teaching Mary to read, very often wearing a green cloak symbolising hope for the world.

COSTUMES AND HEADDRESSES

Costumes – Brittany possesses costumes of surprising richness and variety. The fine clothes passed down from one generation to another were to be seen at every family festivity. It was customary for a girl at her marriage to acquire a costly and magnificent outfit that would last many years. Nowadays the traditional costumes are brought out only on great occasions such as *pardons*, and sometimes High Mass on feast days.
In spite of attempts to modernise the dress, and the efforts of regional societies over the last few years – and they have had some success – to make the young appreciate the old finery, the tourist who travels quickly through Brittany is not likely to see many of the rich, traditional dresses made familiar by picture postcards and books on the subject.
The most striking and attractive feature of the women's traditional costumes is their aprons which reveal how well off the family is by the richness of their decoration. The aprons, of every size and shape, are made of satin or velvet and are brocaded, embroidered or edged with lace: at Quimper they have no bib, at Pont-Aven they have a small one, while at Lorient the bib reaches to the shoulders. Ceremonial dresses are usually black and are often ornamented with bands of velvet. The finest examples are those of Quimper which are adorned with multi-coloured embroidery.
The men's traditional costume, rarely seen nowadays, includes a felt hat with ribbons and an embroidered waistcoat.

Headdresses – The most original feature of the Breton costume is the **coiffe** or headdress, once worn mainly in the Finistère and Morbihan.
One of the most attractive is the headdress of **Pont-Aven** which has, as an accessory, a great starched lace collar.
The **Bigouden** headdress from the **Pont-l'Abbé** area is one of the most curious; it used to be quite small but since 1930 has become very tall.

Pont-Aven headdress

Bigouden headdresses

In **Quimper** the headdress is much smaller and is worn on the crown of the head; in **Plougastel**, where tradition is still strong, it has a medieval appearance with ribbons tied on the side.
In **Tréguier** the plainest of materials is allied with the most original of shapes. The **Douarnenez** headdress is small and fits tightly round the bun on the back of the head, that of **Auray** shades the forehead and that of **Huelgoat** is almost like a lace hair net.

In order to get a complete picture of the richness and variety of Breton costume, the tourist should visit the museums of Quimper, Guérande, Rennes, Nantes, Dinan, Pont l'Abbé, etc, all of which have fine collections of traditional dress.

THE BRETON LANGUAGE

Modern Breton *(brezhoneg)*, derived from Brythonic, belongs to the Celtic languages and manifests itself in four main dialects: *cornouaillais* (south Finistère), *léonard* (north Finistère), *trégorrois* (Tréguier and the Bay of St-Brieuc) and *vannetais* (Vannes and the Golfe du Morbihan). *Vannetais* distinguishes itself from the other three, which are closely related, for example by replacing "z" with "h"; thus *Breiz (Brittany)* becomes *Breih.* In an attempt to overcome such differences, the use of "zh" has been introduced for the relevant words, thus *Breizh.*

Place names – In Brittany, as in other French provinces, the meaning of place names is often easy to find. Most names are formed from a root to which the name of a saint or local character has been added.

The original term **ploue**, from the Latin *plebs* (people), came to mean "church" in the Middle Ages and, by extension, "parish". **Pleu, plou, plo** and **pl** are all derived from **ploue** and, combined with suffixes, give rise to names like: Ploudaniel (parish of St Daniel), Plogoff (parish of St Cof), Ploërmel (parish of St Armel), Plounevez (new parish), Pleumeur (large parish), Pleubian (bishop's parish), Ploudiry (oak parish), etc.

Tré, trèv or **tref**, meaning "parish subdivision", give rise to: Tréboul (place of the pool), Trégastel (place of the castle), Trémeur (large place), etc.

Loc (holy place) gives: Locmaria (place of Mary Mother of God), Locronan (place of St Ronan), Locminé (place of monks), etc.

Lann or **lan** (sanctuary or church) give: Lannion (church of St Yon), Lampaul (church of St Paul), Landerneau (church of St Ternoc), etc.

Ker, kear, car, cré, quer, all unique to Breton (meaning village or house), often appear in the names of places off the beaten track: Kermaria (Mary's village), Kermeur (big house), Kerfeunteun (village of the fountain), etc.

Gwik, from the Latin vicus, then **gui** (hamlet) give: Guimiliau (town of St Méliau), Guisseny (town of St Seny), etc.

Bleiz, bleid, blaid, blaye (wolf): although wolves disappeared from Brittany more than a century ago, names such as Boblaye (wolf's lair), Kerbleiz (wolf's village), Poulbleizi (wolves' pool), etc bear witness to their passage.

Traon, traou, tro (valley) give: Tromelin (valley of the mill), Tromeur (great valley), etc.

Koad, coat, goat, goët, hoet (wood) appears in Huelgoat (tall wood), Penhoët (end of the wood), Toulgoët (clearing in the wood), etc.

Baud headdresses

Double toponymy – Place names appear on road signs in both French and Breton, e.g., Châteauneuf-du-Faou/Kastel-Nevez-Ar-Faou, Guérande/Gwenrann, Lorient/An Oriant, Morlaix/Montroulez, Nantes/Naoned, Pontivy/Pondivi, Port-Launay/Meilh-ar-Wern, Quimper/Kemper, Rennes/Roazhon, St-Brieuc/Sant-Brieg, St-Paul-de-Léon/Kastell-Paol, Tréguier/Landreger, Vannes/Gwened.

Family names – Many are formed from Ker (house) followed by a variation of a Christian name: Kerber (house of Peter), Kerbol (house of Paul), etc.
Other names indicate professions: Le Barazer (cooper), Le Goff (blacksmith), Le Quéméneur (tailor), Le Tocquer (hatter), etc., and others reflect nicknames: Le Bihan (little), Le Braz (big), Le Bail (marked on the forehead), Le Fur (wise), Galloüédec (powerful), Le Moigne (one-armed), Le Troadec (big feet), Le Guen (white), Le Dantec (toothy), Pennec (stubborn), etc.

Common Christian names include: Alan, Anna, Aziliz, Arzhel or Armel, Edern, Erwan or Iwan, Fañch, Goulven, Gweltaz, Gwenn, Gwenole, Jakez, Jezequel, Kaourintin, Loeiz, Maloù, Marzhin, Per and Tangi.

The Breton variations for "**grenouille*** *" (frog) have given rise to some memorable place names, such as Poulrian (Frog Pond) and Riantec (The Froggery) – from* **rian/réan** *– or, more simply Glesquer (Frog) from* **glesker** *– or Le Grand Signan (The Big Frog) – from* **chignan***.*

EVOLUTION AND REGIONALISM

The **two Brittanies** – The map below delimits **Upper Brittany** (Haute-Bretagne), or the "Gallo" country, and **Lower Brittany** (Basse-Bretagne), or the Breton-speaking country. French is spoken in the first, French and Breton in the second. Lower Brittany has four regions, each of which has its customs and brings shades of diversity to the Breton language. These are: the district of Tréguier or Trégorrois, the district of Léon, the district of Cornouaille and the district of Vannes or Vannetais.
Apart from the language, these limits conform with tradition. It is in Lower Brittany that one is more likely to find the old customs; in Upper Brittany they have hardly left a trace. And the delimitation has not remained fixed.

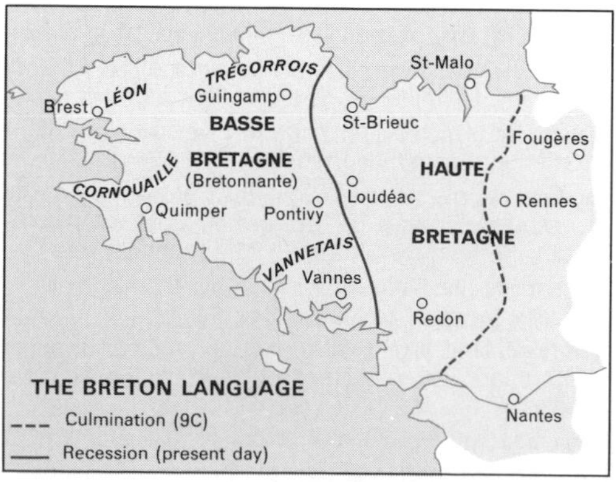

The two Brittanies

The Breton language – From the ethnic and linguistic point of view, the Bretons are nearer to the Irish and Welsh than to the French.

This is because from the 4-7C, Armorica (present day Brittany) offered asylum to Britons driven from Britain (present-day Great Britain) by the Anglo-Saxon invasion. Brittany was founded, and the Breton language opposed the French language, derived from Low Latin.
In the 9C, the dynasty of Nominoé *(qv)* marked the apogee of the Breton nation and the furthest advance of its language. The Viking invasions that followed and feudal rule harmed the unity of Brittany.
The annexation of the province to France in the 15C and the French Revolution enhanced the trend in favour of French.
An association called U.D.B. (Union for the Defence of the Breton Language), after a vigorous campaign for the optional teaching of Breton in Lower Brittany, secured this in the secondary and teachers' training schools. For further information contact: DIWAN-ZA – Saint-Ernel BP 156 – 26411 – Landerneau Cedex. ☎ 02 98 21 33 69.

Brittany's rapid development – Brittany changed more in the first half of the 20C than in the two previous centuries. Contacts of Breton soldiers with men from other provinces, and especially the return to their homeland of men who had held administrative or executive posts in the navy, the civil service, commerce and industry, hastened the evolution started by the tourists.
The distinctive character of customs, dress and furniture has faded away. Villages no longer keep alive a mass of traditional customs and traditional beliefs. Less than half the population still know their own language.

Regionalism and Celtic Clubs – Brittany cultivates regionalism. There are more than 250 Celtic Clubs, which revive and bring fame to all that is Breton – dances, music, and costume... The traditional bagpipe *(cornemuse écossaise)* and bombard *(biniou)* players, for example, are in great demand at parties, festivals, etc.

The Breton flag – The current flag is called Gwenn ha du (white and black) and was designed by Morvan Marchal in 1925. The five black stripes represent the five original bishoprics of Upper Brittany (Rennes, Nantes, Dol, St-Malo and St-Brieuc); the four white stripes represent those of Lower Brittany (Léon, Cornouaille, Vannes and Tréguier); the field of ermine evokes the Duchy of Brittany.

A. Dauzat

The Triskell – This ornament takes the form of a revolving cross with three arms or vortexes symbolising earth, fire and water. It is Celtic in origin, and has been found on Celtic coins, in the British Isles, Denmark, even in South and North America.

Learning and literature in Brittany

The Middle Ages and the Renaissance – Learning was centred in the monasteries; the language used was Latin; the subjects studied were concerned, for the most part, with the history of the Church or of Brittany, moral philosophy and the lives of the saints. A life of St Guénolé was written by Wurdistein, Abbot of Landévennec, in the 9C, and a life of St Pol by Wromonoc, a monk from the same abbey.
Authors are rarely known by name, but there are some exceptions such as, in the 12C: the philosopher **Pierre Abélard**, one of the most brilliant figures of the Middle Ages, who was born at Le Pallet near Nantes and became Abbot of St-Gildas-de-Rhuys *(qv)*. He wrote an account of the hardships he endured.
Étienne de Fougères, who was named bishop of Rennes in 1168, wrote *Livre des manières*, a Book of Manners, which gave him free rein to lecture his contemporaries on moral issues. **Guillaume Le Breton** was poet and historian at the court of Philippe-Auguste, whose reign he patriotically eulogised.
Students from Brittany first went to the Paris University, and then to Nantes when that establishment was founded in the 15C. Schools were established to supplement the teaching provided by the churches and monasteries in out of the way parishes. However, it was not until the 15 and 16C that one began hearing of names such as those of the historians Pierre Le Baud, Alain Bouchard and Bertrand d'Argentré, of the poet Meschinot from Nantes who wrote a series of ballads entitled *Les Lunettes des princes* (The Princes' Spectacles), which became well known in his own time, of Noël du Fail, Councillor of the Rennes Parliament, who depicted the world around him so well, and of the Dominican Albert Legrand, who wrote *Vie des Saints de la Bretagne armoricaine* (Life of the Saints of Armorican Brittany).

17 and 18C – The best-known figures of the 17 and 18C are **Mme de Sévigné** – Breton by marriage – who addressed many of her letters from her residence, the Rochers-Sévigné Chateau *(qv)* and wrote vivid descriptions of Rennes, Vitré, Vannes and Port-Louis, **Lesage**, the witty author of *Gil Blas* who came from Vannes, and Duclos, moralist and historian, who was Mayor of Dinan.
There was also **Élie Fréron** *(qv)*, who became known only through his disputes with Voltaire and who was the director of a literary journal published in Paris and, finally, the Benedictines Dom Lobineau and Dom Morice, historians of Brittany.

The Romantics and contemporary writers – Three figures dominated literature in the 19C in Brittany:
François-René de Chateaubriand *(qv)*, who had an immense influence on French literature. The effect he had over his contemporaries arose from his sensitivity, his passionate eloquence, his fertile imagination, all of which were displayed with brilliant and powerful style; in his *Mémoires D'Outre-Tombe* (Beyond the Tomb), he recounts his childhood at St-Malo and his youth at Combourg Castle.
Lamennais *(qv)*, fervent apologist of theocracy who became a convinced democrat, reflected in his philosophical works the evolution of his thought.
Ernest Renan *(qv)*, philologist, historian and philosopher, was a thinker who maintained that he had faith only in science. He wrote many books in an easy and brilliant prose and in one, *Souvenirs d'enfance et de jeunesse* (Recollections of Childhood and Youth), described his native Brittany. Less important but, nevertheless, true interpreters of the native soil and turn of mind of Brittany are the sensitive poet **Auguste Brizeux** (1803-58), author of *Marie* and the poems *Telen Arvor;* Émile Souvestre, who wrote such stories as *Les derniers Bretons* (The Last Bretons); Hersart de la Villemarqué, who published a collection of poems, based on popular folk songs; Frédéric Le Guyader, a poet who sang the praises of cider; **Anatole Le Braz** (1859-1926) the folklorist; **Charles Le Goffic** (1863-1932) the novelist; and **Théodore Botrel** (1868-1925) the song writer.
Others who came from Brittany and should be noted though they did not write in praise of their native province are: the Symbolist poets **Villiers-de-l'Isle-Adam** and Tristan Corbière; the novelists **Paul Féval**, author of *Bossu;* **Jules Verne** (1828-1905, *qv)*, precursor of modern scientific discoveries; Zénaïde Fleuriot, whom young people

ROGER VIOLLET
Henri Queffélec

still read; **Louis Hémon** who became known through his *Maria Chapdelaine*, and finally **Pierre Loti** with his *Pêcheur d'Islande* and *Mon frère Yves*.
Alphonse de Chateaubriant (1877-1951), depicted the Brière, **Jean-Pierre Calloc'h**, a lyrical poet, native of the île de Groix *(qv)*, wrote in the Breton language. The Surrealist poet Saint-Pol-Roux (1861-1940), Marseilles-born but an undying lover of Brittany, wrote works graced with Romanticism, *Les Féeries intérieures; Bretagne est univers* was published posthumously. **René-Guy Cadou** (1920-51), also a poet, sang praise of his home region.
Henri Queffélec (1910-1992) is one of the contemporary authors who has most lauded Brittany in *Le Recteur de l'île de Sein, Un homme d'Ouessant, Au bout du monde, Franche et secrète Bretagne* and *Promenades en Bretagne*. Another contemporary author, **Pierre-Jakez Hélias** (b1917), recounts vividly in *Cheval d'orgueil* the traditions of the Pont-l'Abbé region (Claude Chabrol made a memorable film from the work).
Unfortunately, few Breton authors have been translated into English.

Brittany and Painters

The harsh rocky landscape, the deeply indented coastlines, the melancholy succession of rainfall and stormy weather, the play of light and reflections in sea, lake or river and sky, the lively atmosphere of the ports, the strongly upheld traditions and enduring legends have all played a part in drawing numerous painters to Brittany, from the pioneering journey by the famous Turner in 1826 to the time spent there by contemporary artists. A particularly captivating setting, a hospitable or influential artist or a friendly inn have frequently provided sufficient encouragement for the blossoming of a picturesque, buzzing colony in just the space of a few months or years. Cornouaille, with Douarnenez, Concarneau and Pont-Aven, as well as Quimper, Audierne and le Pouldu, was the favourite among artists, but the Presqu'Île de Guérande, Camaret, le Faou and Belle-Ile attracted talent in their turn.
Some of the time spent in Brittany by these artists was to give rise to new departures in the art of painting, which were of great significance for the history of this art. In this way the important work done by Eugène Boudin at le Faou, Camaret and Plougastel was to pave the way for the Impressionist revolution; the no less important meeting of Paul Gauguin and Emile Bernard at Pont-Aven in 1888 was to give birth to Symbolism, itself to throw wide the gate to Abstract art. Corot, Monet, Renoir, Vuillard, Matisse, Marquet, Derain, Robert Delaunay, to name but a few of the better-known examples, honed their talent on Brittany's soil.
The arrival of masters such as these and the intensity of their research had a profound effect on certain Breton artists. Lemordant and Méheut were the first to seek a means of combining modernism and being Breton; many others were to follow in their footsteps, for example the great Surrealist painter Yves Tanguy, or Pierre de Belay from Quimper, who modelled himself on Picasso.

ABC OF ARCHITECTURE

To assist readers unfamiliar with the terminology employed in architecture, we describe below the most commonly used terms, which we hope will make their visits to ecclesiastical, military and civil buildings more interesting.

Ecclesiastical architecture

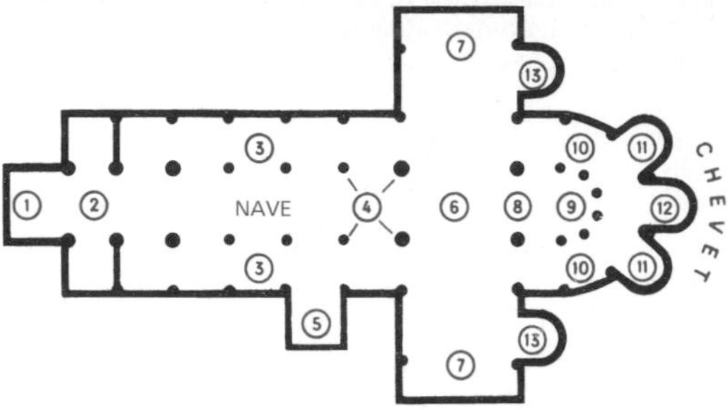

illustration I ▶

Ground plan: The more usual Catholic form is based on the outline of a cross with the two arms of the cross forming the transept: ① Porch - ② Narthex - ③ Side aisles (sometimes double) - ④ Bay (transverse section of the nave between 2 pillars) - ⑤ Side chapel (often predates the church) - ⑥ Transept crossing - ⑦ Arms of the transept, sometimes with a side doorway - ⑧ Chancel, nearly always facing east towards Jerusalem; the chancel often vast in size was reserved for the monks in abbatial churches - ⑨ High altar - ⑩ Ambulatory: in pilgrimage churches the aisles were extended round the chancel, forming the ambulatory, to allow the faithful to file past the relics - ⑪ Radiating or apsidal chapel - ⑫ Axial chapel. In churches which are not dedicated to the Virgin this chapel, in the main axis of the building, is often consecrated to the Virgin (Lady Chapel) - ⑬ Transept chapel.

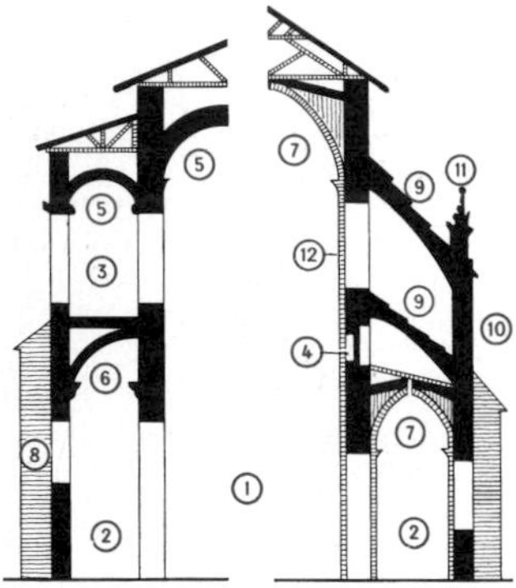

Romanesque Gothic

◀ illustration II

Cross-section: ① Nave - ② Aisle - ③ Tribune or gallery - ④ Triforium - ⑤ Barrel vault - ⑥ Half-barrel vault - ⑦ Pointed vault - ⑧ Buttress - ⑨ Flying buttress - ⑩ Pier of a flying buttress - ⑪ Pinnacle - ⑫ Clerestory window.

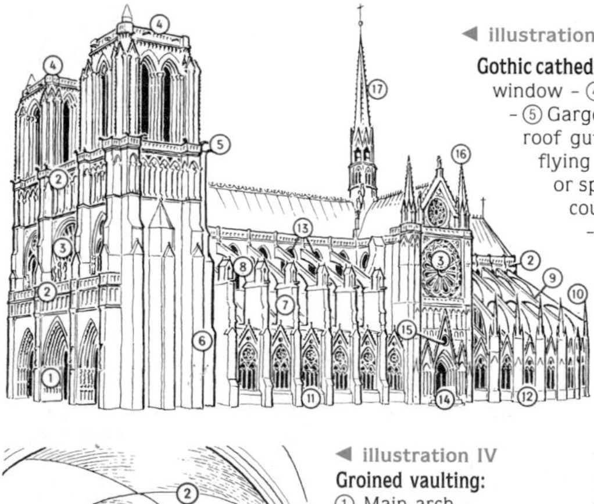

◀ illustration III

Gothic cathedral: ① Porch - ② Gallery - ③ Rose window - ④ Belfry (sometimes with a spire) - ⑤ Gargoyle acting as a waterspout for the roof gutter - ⑥ Buttress - ⑦ Pier of a flying buttress (abutment) - ⑧ Flight or span of flying buttress - ⑨ Double-course flying buttress - ⑩ Pinnacle - ⑪ Side chapel - ⑫ Radiating or apsidal chapel - ⑬ Clerestory windows - ⑭ Side doorway - ⑮ Gable - ⑯ Pinnacle - ⑰ Spire over the transept crossing.

◀ illustration IV

Groined vaulting:
① Main arch -
② Groin -
③ Transverse arch.

illustration V ▶

Oven vault: termination of a barrel vaulted nave.

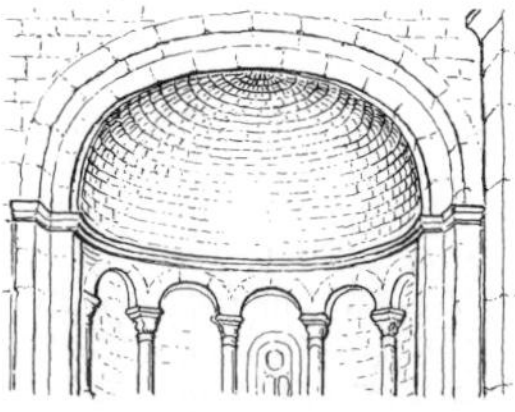

illustration VI

Lierne and tierceron vaulting: ① Diagonal - ② Lierne - ③ Tierceron - ④ Pendant - ⑤ Corbel.

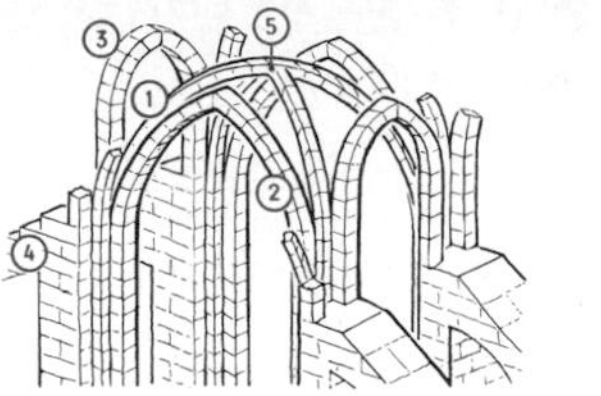

illustration VII

Quadripartite vaulting: ① Diagonal - ② Transverse - ③ Stringer - ④ Flying buttress - ⑤ Keystone.

▼ illustration VIII

Doorway: ① Archivolt. Depending on the architectural style of the building this can be rounded, pointed, basket-handled, ogee or even adorned by a gable - ② Arching, coving (with string courses, mouldings, carvings or adorned with statues). Recessed arches or orders form the archivolt - ③ Tympanum - ④ Lintel - ⑤ Archshafts - ⑥ Embrasures. Arch shafts, splaying sometimes adorned with statues or columns - ⑦ Pier (often adorned by a statue) - ⑧ Hinges and other ironwork.

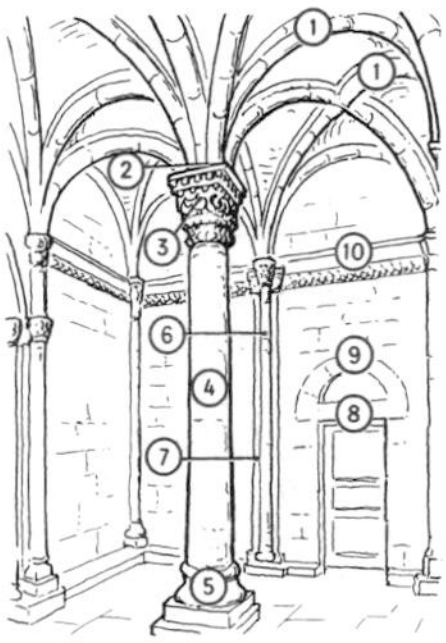

illustration IX ►

Arches and pillars: ① Ribs or ribbed vaulting - ② Abacus - ③ Capital - ④ Shaft - ⑤ Base - ⑥ Engaged column - ⑦ Pier - ⑧ Lintel - ⑨ Discharging or relieving arch - ⑩ Frieze.

Military architecture

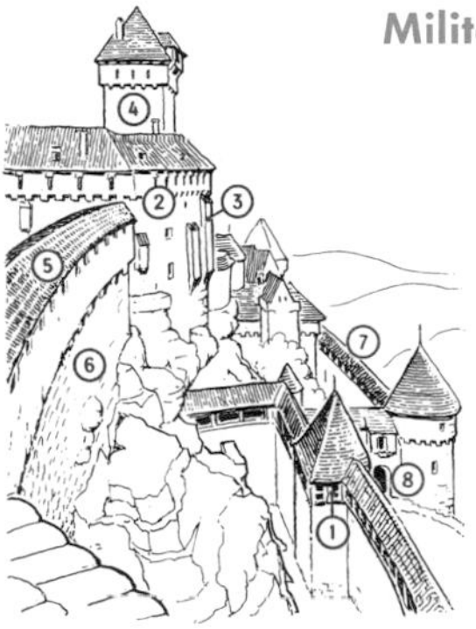

illustration X

Fortified enclosure: ① Hoarding (projecting timber gallery) - ② Machicolations (corbelled crenellations) - ③ Barbican - ④ Keep or donjon - ⑤ Covered watchpath - ⑥ Curtain wall - ⑦ Outer curtain wall - ⑧ Postern.

illustration XI

Towers and curtain walls: ① Hoarding - ② Crenellations - ③ Merlon - ④ Loophole or arrow slit - ⑤ Curtain wall - ⑥ Bridge or drawbridge.

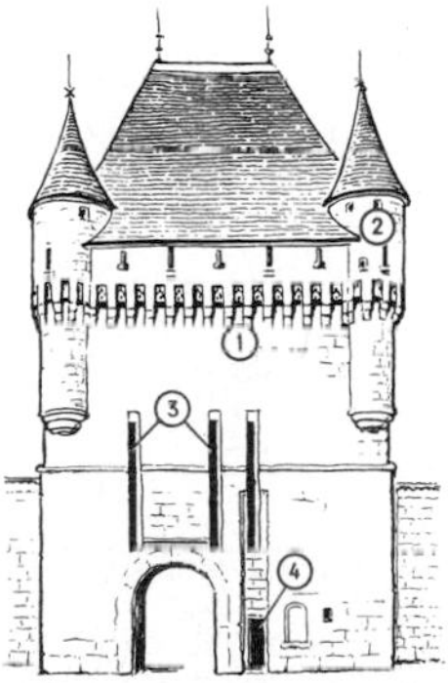

◄ illustration XII

Fortified gatehouse: ① Machicolations - ② Watch turrets or bartizan - ③ Slots for the arms of the drawbridge - ④ Postern.

illustration XIII ►

Star fortress: ① Entrance - ② Drawbridge - ③ Glacis - ④ Ravelin or half-moon - ⑤ Moat - ⑥ Bastion ⑦ Watch turret - ⑧ Town - ⑨ Assembly area.

ART AND ARCHITECTURAL TERMS USED IN THE GUIDE

Aisle: illustration I.
Ambulatory: illustration I.
Apsidal or radiating chapel: illustration I.
Archivolt: illustration VIII.
Axial or Lady Chapel: illustration I.
Bailey: open space or court of stone built castle.
Barrel vaulting: illustration II.
Basket-handled arch: depressed arch (late medieval and Renaissance architecture).
Bay: illustration I.
Bracket: small supporting piece of stone or timber to carry a beam or cornice.
Buttress: illustration II.
Capital: illustration IX.
Chevet: French term for the east end of a church; illustration I.
Coffered ceiling: vault or ceiling decorated with sunken panels.
Conical roof: sometimes pepperpot roof.
Corbel: see bracket.
Credence: side table, shelf or niche for eucharistic elements.
Crypt: underground chamber or chapel.
Curtain wall: illustration XI.
Depressed arch: three-centred arch sometimes called a basket-handled arch.
Diagonal ribs: illustration VII.
Dome: illustrations XIV and XV.
Flamboyant: last phase (15C) of French Gothic architecture; name taken from the undulating (flame-like) lines of the window tracery.
Fresco: mural painting executed on wet plaster.
Gable: illustration III.
Gallery: illustration II.
Gargoyle: illustration III.
Glory: luminous nimbus surrounding the body; mandorla: an almond-shapedglory.
Groined vaulting: illustration IV.
Hammerbeam: illustration XVII.
High relief: haut-relief; sculpted relief figures which are proud of their background by more than half their thickness.
Jetty: overhanging upper storey.
Keep or donjon: illustration X.
Keystone: middle and topmost stone in an arch or vault: illustration VII.
Lintel: illustrations VIII and IX.
Lombard arcades: decorative blind arcading composed of small arches and intervening pilaster strips; typical of Romanesque art in Lombardy.
Loophole or arrow slit: illustration XI.
Low relief: bas relief; carved or sculpted figures which are slightly proud of their background.
Machicolations: illustration X.
Misericord: illustration XIX.
Moat: a trench surrounding a castle or town, generally water-filled.
Modillion: small console supporting a cornice.
Oven vaulting: illustration V.
Pampre: vine-leaf and grape decoration in a moulding.
Parapet wall: see watchpath; illustration X.
Parclose screen: screen separating a chapel or the choir from the rest of the church.
Parish close: *see Breton Art: Parish Closes (below) and Parish Closes, in main body of guide.*
Pepperpot roof: conical roof.
Pier: illustration VIII.
Pietà: Italian term designating the Virgin Mary with the dead Christ on her knees.
Pilaster: engaged rectangular column.
Pilaster strip: decorative feature characteristic of Romanesque architecture in Lombardy consisting of shallow projecting pilasters and blind arcading.
Pinnacle: illustrations II and III.
Piscina: basin for washing the sacred vessels.
Pointed arch: illustrations VI and VII.
Porch: covered approach to the entrance to a building.
Postern: illustrations X and XII.
Purlin: horizontal beams; in Brittany they are decorated with running carved ornamentation; illustration XVI.
Quadripartite vaulting: illustration VII.
Recessed arches: illustration VIII.

Rood-beam: sometimes tref; illustration XVIII.
Rood screen: illustration XX.
Rose window: illustration III.
Sacristy: room in a church for sacred vessels and vestments.
Semicircular arch: round-headed arch.
Spire: illustration III.
Squinches, dome on: illustration XIV.
Stalls: illustration XIX.
Tie-beam: beam connecting two slopes of a roof at the height of wall-plate; in Brittany tie-beams are often carved into monstrous heads and painted.
Tracery: interesting stone ribwork in the upper part of a window.
Transept: illustration I.
Transverse arch: arch separating one bay of the nave from the next; illustration IV.
Tref: see rood-beam.
Triptych: three panels hinged together, chiefly used as an altarpiece.
Tunnel vaulting: see barrel vaulting.
Twinned or paired: columns or pilasters grouped in twos.
Wall walk: see watchpath.
Watchpath: illustration X.
Wheel window: see rose window.

◀ illustration XIV

Dome on squinches:
① Octagonal dome – ② Squinch – ③ Arches of transept crossing

illustration XV ▶

Dome on pendentives:
① Circular dome – ② Pendentive – ③ Arches of transept crossing

illustration XVI

Purlin with carved decoration

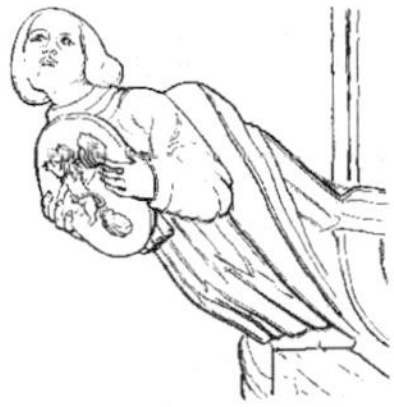

illustration XVII

End of hammerbeam

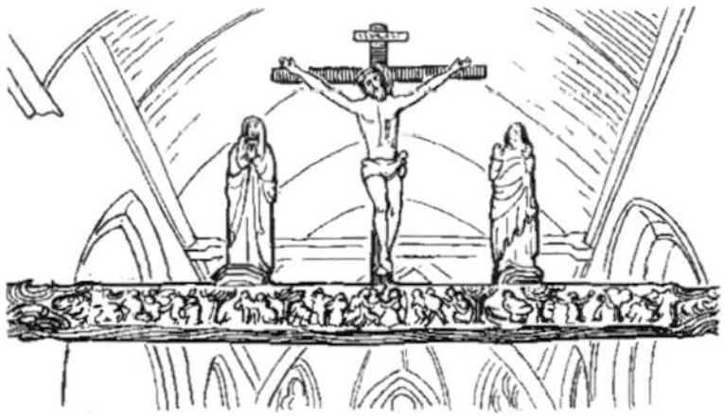

◀ illustration XVIII

Rood-beam or tref: This supports the triumphal (chancel or rood) arch at the entrance to the chancel. The rood carries a Crucifix flanked by statues of the Virgin and St John and sometimes other personages from the Calvary.

illustration XIX ▼

Stalls: ① High back – ② Elbow rest – ③ Cheek-piece – ④ Misericord.

illustration XX

Rood screen: This replaces the rood-beam in larger churches, and may be used for preaching and reading of the Epistles and Gospel. Many disappeared from the 17C onwards as they tended to hide the altar.

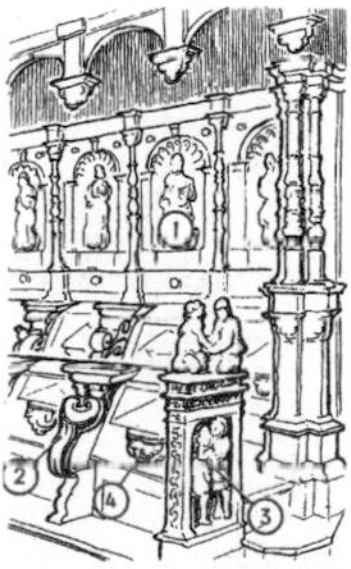

BRETON ART

Prehistoric monuments

The megaliths or "great stones" – More than 3 000 "great stones" are still to be found in the Carnac district alone. These monuments were set up between 5000 and 2000 BC by the little-known race who preceded the Gauls. They must have had a certain degree of civilization to be able to move and set upright stones which weigh up to 350 tons. To give a simple comparison, the Luxor obelisk in the Place de la Concorde in Paris weighs only 220 tons.

The **menhir**, or single stone, was set up at a spring, near a tomb and more often on a slope. It must have had a symbolic meaning. In Brittany there are about twenty menhirs over 7m - 23ft high; the biggest is at Locmariaquer *(qv)*.

The **alignments** or lines of menhirs are probably the remains of religious monuments associated with the worship of the sun or moon. Most are formed by only a few menhirs set in line (many of the menhirs now isolated are the remains of more complicated groups). There are, however, especially in the Carnac area *(see CARNAC: Megalithic Monuments)*, fields of menhirs arranged in parallel lines running from east to west and ending in a semicircle or **cromlech.** In the Lagatjar *(qv)* area the lines intersect. The lines of the menhirs appear also to be astronomically set, with an error of a few degrees, either by the cardinal points of the compass, or in line with sunrise and sunset at the solstices, from which it has been concluded that sun worship had something to do with the purpose of the monuments. As for the **dolmens** (the best-known is the Table des Marchands Table at Locmariaquer), these are considered to have been burial chambers. Some are preceded by an ante-chamber or corridor. Originally all were buried under mounds of earth or dry stones called **tumuli** but most of them have been uncovered and now stand in the open air. The round tumuli found in the interior are of more recent date than the tumuli with closed chambers like the one of St-Michel at Carnac and the former were probably built up to 1000 BC. **Cairns** are tumuli composed entirely of stones such as the ones at Barnenez *(qv)*, which dates back to over 5000 BC and at Gavrinis *(qv)*, which is not so old. Some tumuli without burial chambers probably served as boundary markers.

In northern Brittany **gallery graves** or **covered alleyways** are formed of a double row of upright stones with flat slabs laid on them, sometimes engraved.

Although the tumuli have never been fully excavated, some have been found to contain beautiful artefacts: polished axes made of rare stone (jadeite), or jewellery and marvellous necklaces made of "callaïs". The museums at Carnac and Vannes contain particularly good collections of these early works of art.

Mystical tradition – For many centuries the menhirs were connected with the mystic life of the people of Brittany. The Romans adapted some to their rites, carving pictures of their gods upon them. When the Christian religion became established, it acknowledged many raised stones that people still venerated by crowning them with a cross or cutting symbols on them.

Société Polymathique du Morbihan, Vannes

"Callaïs" necklace (variscite) – Musée archéologique de Vannes

Churches and chapels

Nine cathedrals or former cathedrals, about twenty large churches and thousands of country churches and chapels make up an array of religious buildings altogether worthy of mystical Brittany.

The edifices were built by the people and designed by artists who transmitted to them an inspired faith. This faith appeared in a richness that was sometimes excessive – the exaggeratedly decorated altarpieces are an example – and a realism that was at times almost a caricature – as, for instance, the carvings on certain capitals and many purlins *(qv)*. Only affected in part by outside influences, the artists always preserved their individuality and remained faithful to their own traditions.

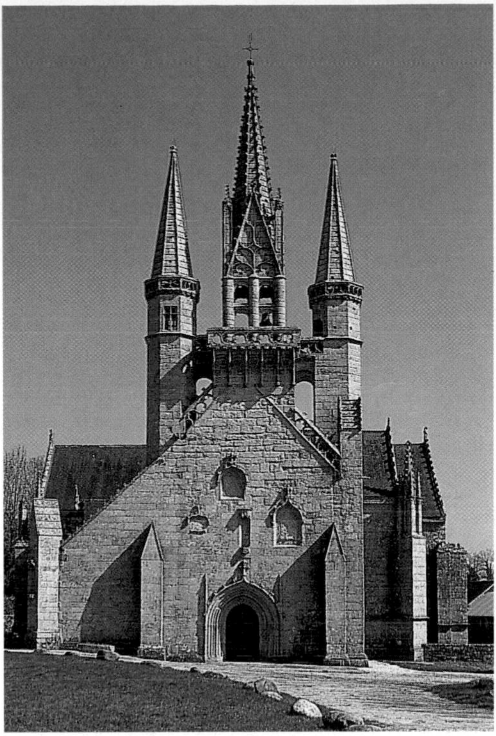

Chapelle St-Fiacre

Cathedrals – These are inspired by the great buildings in Normandy and Ile-de-France, although they do not rival their prototypes either in size or ornamentation. The small towns that built them had limited means. Moreover, their erection was influenced by the use of granite, a hard stone, difficult to work. The builders had to be content with rather low vaulting and simplified decoration. Financial difficulties dragged out the work for three to five centuries. As a result, every phase of Gothic architecture is found in the buildings, from the bare and simple arch of early times to the wild exuberance of the Flamboyant style; the Renaissance often added the finishing touches.

The most interesting cathedrals are those of St-Pol-de-Léon, Tréguier, Quimper, Nantes and Dol-de-Bretagne.

The corresponding Gothic period in England lasted until the end of the 13C and included in whole or in part the cathedrals of Wells (1174), Lincoln (chancel and transept: 1186), Salisbury (1220-58), Westminster Abbey (c1250) and Durham (1242).

Country churches and chapels – In the Romanesque period (11 and 12C) Brittany was miserably poor. Buildings were few and small. Most of them were destroyed or transformed in the following centuries.

It was during the Gothic and the Renaissance periods, under the Dukes and after the union with France, that the countryside saw the growth of churches and chapels.

Buildings constructed before the 16C are usually rectangular, though one also frequently sees the disconcerting T-plan in which the nave, usually without side aisles, ends in a chancel flanked by often disproportionately large chapels. The chevet is flat; there are no side windows – light comes through openings pierced right at the east end of the church.

Stone vaulting is rare and is nearly always replaced by wooden panelling, often painted, whose crocodile headed tie beams (cross beams dividing the roof timbers), wooden cornices at the base of the vaulting and hammerbeams are frequently carved and painted. When there is no transept, a great stone arch separates the chancel from the nave.

From the 16C onwards there was a complete transformation in architectural design; it became necessary to include a transept which, inevitably, gave rise to the Latin Cross outline. The central arch disappeared; the east end became three sided; the nave was lit by windows in the aisles.

The tourist will be surprised to find in hamlets, and even in dreary wastes, chapels of which large towns might be proud (Notre-Dame-du-Folgoët, Kernascléden, Notre-Dame-du-Crann, St-Fiacre-du-Faouët, etc). The faith of the Breton communities has worked miracles.

Nevertheless, there are many chapels where services are held only, perhaps, once a year on the occasion of a *pardon* or local festival, which leave a marked impression of spiritual as well as material neglect.

Belfries – The Bretons take great pride in their belfries. The towers did not serve only to hold bells; they were also symbolic of both religious and civic life. In olden days the people prized them greatly, and it was a terrible punishment for them when an angry king had them laid low.
The belfries are usually square in outline and their position on the building varies considerably.
Small churches and chapels were often given the lighter and less costly gable tower in preference to a belfry. The tower was placed either on the west front gable or on the roof itself, at the intersection of the chancel and the nave. It is reached by outside steps or by stairs in the turrets that flank it and are linked to it by a gallery.
Sometimes these little belfries become so reduced as only to be walls in gable form, pierced by arcades. This form of architecture, while fairly widespread in southwest France, is somewhat rare in Brittany.

Porches – Breton churches have a large porch on the south side.
For a long period the porch was used as a meeting place for the parish notables, who were seated on stone benches along the walls.
A double row of Apostles often decorates the porch. They can be recognised by their attributes: St Peter holds the key of Heaven; St Paul, a book or a sword; St John, a chalice; St Thomas, a set square; St James the Elder, a pilgrim's staff. Others carry the instruments of their martyrdom: St Matthew, a hatchet; St Simon, a saw; St Andrew, a cross; St Bartholomew, a knife.

Fountains

There are innumerable fountains associated with the worship of water in Lower Brittany. Most of them are deemed to have healing virtues. Nearly all places where *pardons* are held have a fountain situated by the chapel where pilgrims come to drink. It is placed under the protection of a saint or of the Virgin, whose statues are set in small sanctuaries which range from being simple to very ornate.
In important places of pilgrimage, like that of Ste-Anne-d'Auray, the fountain has been arranged in modern fashion, with basins, troughs and staircases.
Many of these fountains which were once venerated are now used for domestic purposes.

Religious furnishings

Sculpture – From the 15 to the 18C an army of Breton sculptors working in stone and more particularly in wood supplied the churches with countless examples of religious furnishings: pulpits, organ casings, baptisteries and fonts, choir screens, rood screens, rood-beams, altarpieces, triptychs, confessionals, niches with panels, Holy Sepulchres, statues, etc.
These works are, as a general rule, more highly developed than the figures carved on the Calvaries, since it is much easier to work in oak, chestnut or alabaster than in granite.
Visits to the churches and chapels of Guimiliau, Lampaul-Guimiliau, St-Thégonnec, St-Fiacre near Le Faouët and Tréguier Cathedral (stalls) will give a good general idea of Breton religious furnishings.
The many **rood screens** *(jubés)* to be found in the churches of Brittany are often of unparalleled richness. Some are cut in granite, as in the church at Le Folgoët, but most are carved in wood which makes them peculiar to Brittany.
Their decoration is very varied and is different on both sides.
The rood screen serves two purposes: it separates the chancel from the part of the church reserved for worshippers and completes the side enclosures of the chancel; the upper gallery may also be used for preaching and reading prayers. (The name derives from the first word of a prayer sung from the gallery.)
The screen is usually surmounted by a large Crucifix flanked by statues of the Virgin and St John the Divine facing the congregation.
The **rood-beam** or *tref*, which supported the main arch of the church, was the origin of the rood screen.
To prevent the beam from bowing it had to be supported by posts which were eventually

Musée départemental breton, Quimper

Holy Trinity (15C) (Musée départemental breton, Quimper)

Rood screen, Chapelle St-Fiacre

replaced by a screen carved to a greater or lesser degree. It is to be seen mostly in the small chapels and churches where it serves as a symbolic boundary for the chancel; it is usually decorated with scenes from the Passion and always carries a group of Jesus Christ, the Virgin and St John.

Renaissance works are numerous and very elaborate. **Fonts** and **pulpits** are developed into richly decorated monuments.

Altarpieces, or retables, show an interesting development which can be traced through many stages in Breton churches. Originally the altar was simply a table: as the result of decoration it gradually lost its simplicity and reached a surprising size. In the 12 and 14C altars were furnished with a low step and altarpiece, the same length as the altar. Sculptors took possession of the feature and added groups of figures in scenes drawn from the Passion. From the 15C onwards, the altarpiece became a pretext for twisted columns, pediments, niches containing statues and sculpted panels, which reached their highest expression in the 17C.

Finally the main subject was lost in decoration consisting of angels, garlands, etc. and the altarpiece occupied the whole of the chapel reserved for the altar, and sometimes even, joined to the retables of side altars, decorated the whole wall of the apse as is the case at Ste-Marie-de-Ménez-Hom *(qv)*.

It is curious to find in 15C Breton altarpieces the influence of the Flemish craftsmen who excelled in this type of decorative carving, producing tiny figures in the minutest detail.

Devotion to the Rosary, which was promoted in the 15C by Alain de la Roche, a Breton Friar of the Dominican Order, gave rise from 1640 onwards to the erection of several altarpieces in which Our Lady is shown giving the chaplet to St Dominic and St Catherine of Siena.

Of less importance but equally numerous are the niches which, when the two panels are open, reveal a **Tree of Jesse.** Jesse, who was a member of the tribe of Judah, had a son, David, from whom the Virgin Mary was descended. Jesse is usually depicted lying on his side; from his heart and his body spring the roots of the tree whose branches bear the figures, in chronological order, of the kings and prophets who were Christ's forebearers. In the centre the Virgin is portrayed representing the branch which bears the flower: Jesus Christ.

Among the many statues ornamenting the churches, such as the Trinity of St Anne and the Virgin and Child, portraits of real people and items of great importance in the study of the history of costume in Brittany are often to be found. Such representation, seen frequently in Central Europe, is rare in France.

The Entombment – The Entombment, which is often shown as part of a Calvary group in other parts of France, is not common in Brittany. The best depictions of the Entombment or Holy Sepulchre with the group of seven round the dead Christ are at Lampaul-Guimiliau and St-Thégonnec.

Funerary statuary is magnificently represented by the tombs of François II at Nantes and Olivier de Clisson at Josselin.

Stained-glass windows – Whereas the altarpieces, friezes and statues were often coloured, paintings and frescoes, as such, were rare; almost the only exception are those at Kernascléden. In contrast there are a great many stained-glass windows, often Italian or Flemish inspired, but always made in Brittany. Some are really fine: the Cathedral at Dol has a beautiful 13C window.

The workshops at Rennes, Tréguier and Quimper produced stained glass between the 14 and 16C which should be seen; the most remarkable windows from these workshops are in the churches of Notre-Dame-du-Crann, La Roche and St-Fiacre near Le Faouët.

In the 20C, the restoration and building of numerous churches and chapels has offered the possibility of decorating these edifices with colourful non-figurative stained-glass windows. The cathedral at St-Malo is a good example.

Gold and silver church plate – In spite of considerable losses, Brittany still possesses many wonderful pieces of gold and silver church plate. This was made by local craftsmen, most of them from Morlaix. Though fine chalices and shrines may be hidden away for security, magnificent reliquaries, chalices, richly decorated patens and superb processional crosses may be seen at Carantec, St-Jean-du-Doigt, St-Gildas-de-Rhuys, Paimpont and Locarn.

Parish closes

The parish close *(enclos paroissial)* is the most typical monumental grouping in Breton communities.

The tourist should not leave Brittany without having seen a few examples, and we therefore describe a tour of parish closes *(qv)* taking in the most interesting.

The centre of the close was the cemetery which was very small and with gravestones of uniform size. Nowadays this is tending to disappear. Around the cemetery, which is often reached through a **triumphal arch**, are grouped the **church** with its small square *(placître)*, the **Calvary**, and the **charnel house** or ossuary. Thus the spiritual life of the parish is closely linked with the community of the dead. Death, *Ankou*, was a familiar idea to the Bretons who often depicted it *(illustration under La ROCHE-MAURICE)*.

The extraordinary rivalry between neighbouring villages explains the richness of the closes which were built in Lower Brittany at the time of the Renaissance and in the 17C. Competition between Guimiliau and St-Thégonnec went on for two centuries: a Calvary answered a triumphal arch, a charnel house a porch, a tower replied to a belfry, a pulpit to a font, an organ loft to a set of confessionals, an Entombment to chancel woodwork. The two finest closes in Brittany sprang from this rivalry.

Triumphal arch – The entrance to a cemetery is often ornamented with a monumental gateway. This is treated as a triumphal arch to symbolise the accession of the Just to immortality.

Some arches built during the Renaissance, like those of Sizun and Berven, are surprisingly reminiscent of the triumphal arches of antiquity.

Charnel house or ossuary – In the tiny Breton cemeteries of olden days, bodies had to be exhumed to make room for new dead. The bones were piled in small shelters with ventilation openings, built against the church or cemetery wall. The skulls were placed there separately in special "skull caskets". Then these charnel houses became separate buildings, larger and more carefully built and finally reliquaries, which could be used as funerary chapels.

Calvary – In these small granite monuments, episodes of the Passion are represented around Christ on the Cross. Many of them were built to ward off, as in 1598, a plague epidemic, or to give thanks after it ended. They served for religious teaching in the parish. The priest preached from the dais, pointing out with a wand the scenes which he described to his congregation.

The distant forerunners of the Calvaries were Christianised menhirs *(qv)*, which were still fairly common, and their immediate predecessors were the crosses, plain or ornate. Crosses along roads in this countryside are countless; there have been tens of thousands. In the 16C a Bishop of Léon boasted that he alone had had 5 000 put up. Ornate crosses were common in the 14C; many were destroyed. The oldest remaining Calvary is that of Tronoën, which dates from the end of the 15C. They were being erected as late as the end of the 17C. The most famous are those of Guimiliau with 200 figures, Plougastel-Daoulas with 180 and Pleyben.

The sculpture is rough and naïve – the work of a village stonemason – but it shows a great deal of observation and is often strikingly lifelike and expressive. Many figures, notably soldiers, wear the costumes of the 16 and 17C.

Langelano/DIAF

Guimiliau Calvary (detail)

A lesson in sacred history – Walking round a large Calvary, we see the history of the Virgin and Christ pass before our eyes: the Virgin's marriage, the Annunciation, the Visitation, the Nativity in the Adoration of the Shepherds, the Adoration of the Magi, the Presentation the Temple, the Circumcision, the Flight into Egypt, the Baptism of Jesus, the Entry into Jerusalem, the Last Supper, the Washing of Feet, the Mount of Olives, the Kiss of Judas, the Arrest of Jesus, Jesus before Caiaphas, Jesus before Herod, Pilate washing his hands, the Scourging, the Crown of Thorns, the Carrying of the Cross, Jesus falling beneath the Cross, the Descent from the Cross, the Embalming, the Entombment, the Resurrection and the Harrowing of Hell.
No Calvary has all these scenes. The sculptor chose those that inspired him most, and arranged them without any regard for chronological order. Some can be recognised at a glance while others have been damaged to some degree or treated too sketchily.

① Cross of Christ. This is sometimes alone or flanked by one thief's cross.
② Thieves' crosses. Usually T-shaped and on either side of the Crucifix.
③ Horsemen (Roman guards) or the Holy Women, or St Peter, St John or St Yves.
④ Virgin of Pity (Mary holding the body of Jesus removed from the Cross) or angels catching His Blood in chalices.
⑤ and ⑥ Dais and frieze encircling the base of the Cross. They carry many figures, either isolated (Apostles, saints and holy women) or in scenes from the Passion. The four Evangelists are usually set in niches at the corners.
⑦ Altar on which is the statue of the saint to whom the Calvary is dedicated.

Catell-Gollet – The story of Catell-Gollet (Catherine the Lost) appears on several Calvaries (Plougastel-Daoulas, Guimiliau). Catherine, a young servant girl, has concealed her misbehaviour at confession and steals a consecrated Host to give it to the Devil, who appears in the guise of her lover. The culprit is condemned to eternal fire. She is seen above (at the corner of the platform, below the right-hand cross) in the jaws of Hell: devils hold her neck with a fork and tear her naked body with their claws.

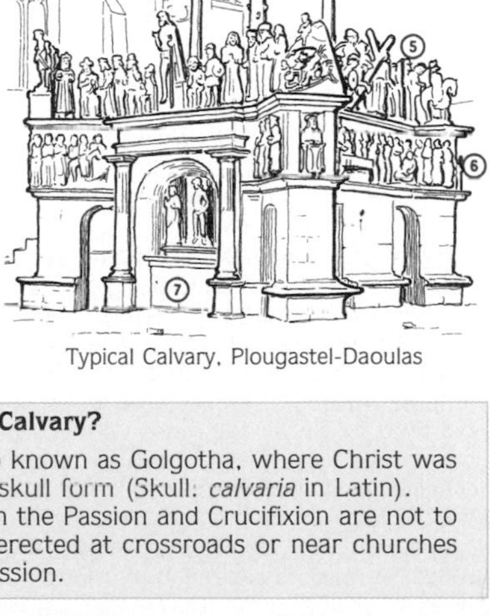

Typical Calvary, Plougastel-Daoulas

What is a Calvary?

Calvary is the name given to the hill, also known as Golgotha, where Christ was crucified. The hill took its name from its skull form (Skull: *calvaria* in Latin). Breton Calvaries representing scenes from the Passion and Crucifixion are not to be confused with wayside crosses often erected at crossroads or near churches to mark the site of a pilgrimage or procession.

Breton domestic furniture

For centuries Breton artisans made box beds, chests, sideboards, dressers, wardrobes and clock cases. Repetition of the same models, differing only in small ornamental details, gave rise to true mastery of them.
The **box bed,** an essential characteristic of Breton furnishing, afforded protection against the cold as well as privacy in the large common room. It sometimes has two storeys or bunks, one above the other, and two sliding doors, replaced by one large door in Léon and thick curtains in the Audierne and Morbihan regions. There is also a bench-chest for easy access and storage. The façade of the bed and the chest are richly decorated with lunes, garlands, religious designs sometimes including the monogram of Christ, interlaced or adjoining geometrical figures, known as compass decoration. Wardrobes are decorated in a similar style. In Upper Brittany the box bed is replaced by the four poster bed with a canopy and curtains. As in most regions of France, the chest plays an important part. It is used to store linen or grain for everyday use.
The two-door wardrobe is also an important piece of Breton furniture. It is usually topped by a flat overhanging cornice or sometimes by a twin-arched one as in the Rennes basin.
Dressers are large with five doors and two drawers and some designs are picked out in copper studs as in the case of wardrobes.
Tables are large chests with sliding panels and are accompanied by carved seats.
Fine furniture and reconstructions of old interiors are to be seen in the museums of Nantes, Pont-l'Abbé, St-Brieuc, Rennes and Quimper and the Château de Kerjean.

Castles and fortresses

Breton granite is somewhat daunting to the tourist coming to Brittany for the first time. Clean cut and hard, it does not age or weather and it would, therefore, not be possible to give a date to the grey buildings that blend perfectly into the landscape were it not for the architectural design and methods employed in construction. With the exception of the fortresses, most of which stood guard on the eastern border in fear of the kings of France or along the coast to ward off the raids of English invaders, there are few great castles in Brittany. This lack conveys perfectly the Breton character that turned all its artistic endeavour to the service of religion.

D'après photo Dupont/EXPLORER

Breton interior

Nevertheless, it is easy to imagine Brittany in the Middle Ages. Few regions, in fact, had such fortresses and though many were destroyed or have fallen into ruin, a number are still standing. Before these walls the problems of war in the Middle Ages can be imagined. Although some fortresses fell at once to a surprise attack, it was not unusual for a siege to go on for several months. The attacker then sapped the ramparts, brought up machines which could hurl stones weighing over 100kg-200lbs, and tried to smash the gates with battering-rams before launching the final assault.
In the middle of the 15C, artillery brought about new methods of attack and changes in military architecture.
At St-Malo and at Guérande, the stone walls that encircled these towns can be seen in their entirety. Remains of ramparts of varying extent can be seen in many other places. Vannes, Concarneau and Port-Louis have ramparts that are almost complete.

Vitré – Entrance gateway of the castle

There are many fortresses: those of Fougères and Vitré are among the finest in France. Dinan and Combourg have fortified castles still standing; Suscinio, Tonquédec, etc, have impressive ruins; La Hunaudaye, of lesser importance, the towers of Elven, Oudon and Châteaugiron still stand proudly upright. Fort la Latte, standing like a sentinel, boasts a magnificent site.
Buildings, half fortress and half palace, like Kerjean, Josselin and the Château des Ducs de Bretagne at Nantes, are interesting to see, but there are few of them. The fact is that the Breton nobility, except for the Duke and a few great families, were poor. They included many country gentlemen who lived in very simple manors, which nevertheless retained their watch tower defences. They cultivated their own land, like the peasants, but they did not give up their rank and they continued to wear the sword. In some places these manor farms add a great deal of character to the Breton countryside. This is the case in Léon where they are numerous and where Kergonadéac'h, Kerouzéré, Kergroadès and Traonjoly together form a background setting to Kerjean, pride of the province. Certain other châteaux, such as Rocher-Portail, were built later, and lack all appearance of being fortresses, but impress by their simplicity of outline and the grouping of the buildings; at such places as Lanrigan and La Bourbansais, on the other hand, it is the detail that charms the visitor. Landal is one of those that gain enormously from their surroundings; others take great pride in a well laid-out garden or a fine park – these include Bonne-Fontaine, Caradeuc and Rosanbo.

Old streets and old houses

One of the charms of travelling in Brittany is to stroll in the old quarters of the towns. There is hardly a town or village which has not kept and had beautifully restored whole streets, or at least a few single houses, just as they were 300 or 400 years ago. Some picturesque old streets include Dinan: Rue du Jerzual (p 114), Guingamp: Place du Centre (p 147), Morlaix: Grand'Rue (p 192), Pontivy: Rue du Fil (p 223), Quimper: Rue Kéréon (p 234), Quimperlé: Rue Dom-Morice (p 239) and Vitré: Rue de la Baudrairie (p 294).

Modern towns

It is difficult to find any basis of comparison between the old towns with their historical associations and the modern towns. Nonetheless, while Dinan, Locronan, Vitré, Morlaix and Quimper, to name but a few, as well as the marvellously reconstructed St-Malo, have an undeniable appeal, it is impossible not to be struck also by the planning and grouping of buildings in such towns as Brest and Lorient. The wide streets and huge, airy squares are elegant and have obviously been built to achieve harmony and unity. Visitors may well be surprised by certain buildings, but they will find something to admire in the upward sweep of a tall bell tower, the simple lines of a concrete façade, the successful decorative effect of stone and cement combined. Above all, if they have some slight appreciation of colour harmony and go inside any building, they will be struck by the contemporary artist's skill in lighting.

Breton food and drink

Breton cooking is characterised by the high quality and freshness of the ingredients used, many of which will have been plucked from land or sea and brought almost directly to table after the briefest of interventions in the kitchen.

Seafood, crustaceans and fish – Shellfish, crustaceans and fish are all excellent. Particularly outstanding are the spiny lobsters, grilled or stuffed clams, scallops, shrimp, crisp batter-covered fried fish morsels and crab pasties.

Belon oysters, Armorican oysters from Concarneau, La Forêt and Île-Tudy, and Cancale oysters are all well known in France, but are not at their best until the end of the tourist season.

Lobster is served grilled or with cream and especially in a *coulis*, the rich hot sauce which makes the dish called "Armoricaine" or "à l'Américaine" (the latter name is due to a mistake made in a Paris restaurant).

Try also *cotriade* (a Breton fish soup like *bouillabaisse)*, conger-eel stew, the Aulne or Élorn salmon, trout from the Monts d'Arrée and the Montagnes Noires, or pike and shad served with "white butter" in the district near the Loire. This is a sauce made from slightly salted butter, vinegar and shallots, and its preparation requires real skill. Finally, there are *civelles* (elvers), which are a speciality of Nantes.

Meat, vegetables and fruit – The salt pasture sheep *(prés-salés)* of the coast are famous. Breton leg of mutton (with white beans) is part of the great French gastronomic heritage. Grey partridges and heath hares are tasty as are the chickens from Rennes and Nantais ducks. Pork butchers' meat is highly flavoured: Morlaix ham, bacon, black pudding, smoked sausage from Guéméné-sur-Scorff and chitterlings from Quimperlé. Potatoes, artichokes, cauliflowers and green peas are the glory of the Golden Belt *(qv)*. There are also strawberries and melons from Plougastel, cherries from Fouesnant and many other fruits.

Crêpes, cakes and sweetmeats – Most towns have *crêperies* (pancake shops) where these very flat pancakes, called *crêpes*, made either of wheat or buckwheat, are served with cider or yoghurt. In some of the smaller, picturesque shops, often decorated with Breton furnishings, you may see them being made. *Crêpes* are served plain or with jam, cheese, eggs, ham, etc. The buckwheat pancake *(crêpe de sarrasin)* is salted and often served as a starter while the wheat pancake *(crêpe de froment)* is sweet and served at dessert.

Also worth tasting are the Quimper wafer biscuits *(crêpes-dentelles)*, Pont-Aven butter cookies *(galettes)*, Nantes biscuits, Quintin oatmeal porridge and the *far* and *kouign amann* cakes. Among the sweets are the pralines from Rennes and berlingots (sweet drops) from Nantes.

Cider and wine – The local drink is cider *(cidre)*, of special note are the ciders from Fouesnant, Beg-Meil, and Pleudihen-sur-Rance.

The only Breton wine is **Muscadet**, which in 1936, was granted the *appellation d'origine contrôlée* (A.O.C.), literally "controlled place of origin". The people of Nantes guard it jealously and have founded a brotherhood, the Ordre des Chevaliers Bretvins, after "la petite brette" (little rapier), the nickname given to Anne of Brittany.

The grape, the *Melon de Bretagne*, has been cultivated since the early 17C, and gives a dry and fruity white wine which complements fish and seafood particularly well. Muscadet is produced in three distinct geographical areas, each with its own *appellation:* Muscadet, produced in the Grand-Lieu region; Muscadet de Sèvre et Maine, produced south of Nantes; and Muscadet des Coteaux de la Loire, produced in the Ancenis region *(for more information on local wines see Michelin Green Guide Châteaux of the Loire)*.

Vines still grow on the Presqu'île de Rhuys, but the wine drawn from them is a subject of Breton humour. "To drink it", the Bretons say, "you need four men and a wall: one man to pour it out, one to drink, two to hold him up and the wall to stop him from falling backwards." Distilled, on the other hand, it produces an excellent brandy.

Other Breton drinks worth tasting are mead, also called hydromel *(chouchen)*, strawberry liqueur *(liqueur de fraises)*, an orange-flavoured apéritif, and even a Breton whiskey.

J.D. Sudres/SCOPE

Seafood extravaganza

SOME RECIPES

Galettes de sarrasin – This traditional recipe for savoury buckwheat pancakes allows for infinite variety depending on your choice of filling. You will need: 500g (1lb 2oz) buckwheat flour, 100g (3.5oz) salted butter, 2 eggs, 500ml (16fl oz) cider. Make a well in the flour, break the eggs into it, add the cider and a little water, then mix in the melted butter and beat until you get a smooth, but not runny, batter. Leave this at room temperature for a few hours, then cook the pancakes over a hot flame for a couple of minutes in a heavy frying pan lightly greased with lard. Flip them over, butter them and garnish with sausages, bacon, onions, cheese, etc.

Cotriade – Named after the Breton word "Koateriad" meaning the contents of a cauldron, this is a Breton variation of the Provençal fish dish, *bouillabaisse.* For six to eight people you will need: 500g (1lb 2oz) conger eel (head end, chopped into 2cm (1in) chunks), 500g sea pike (in 8cm (4in) chunks), 500g mackerel and 500g whiting (cut each fish into 3), 400g (14 oz) pollack (in chunks), half a dozen sardines, 200g (6oz) lard or butter, 5 or 6 large onions, 2 cloves, 2kg (4lb 8oz) potatoes, 20g (1 tsp) mustard, 5cl (1 tbsp) cider vinegar, bouquet garni, salt, pepper, *croutons* (cubes of bread fried in butter until golden). The secret of this dish lies in the order in which it is cooked: in a large casserole, fry the onions and cloves in the lard until soft; add salt, pepper, bouquet garni, potatoes and chunks of conger, cover with about 5cm (2in) water and boil vigorously for 15 min; add the sea pike, mackerel and pollack and cook for a further 5 min; finally, add the whiting and the sardines and cook for 5 min. Strain the stock and set aside over a gentle heat. Set aside and keep warm some potatoes, the sardines and some chunks of mackerel. Put the rest of the fish and vegetables in a blender for a couple of minutes (the traditional Breton method is to pound them in an enormous pestle and mortar), then stir them into the stock. Serve the reserved fish and potatoes on separate plates, with the fish broth garnished with the *croutons* in bowls by the side.

Kig-ha-farz – This is a Breton version of the traditional French stew *(pot-au-feu)* and needs quite a lot of preparation time. For eight people you will need 500g (1lb 2oz) buckwheat flour, 750g (1lb 11oz) salt pork (soaked overnight), 500g blade bone of beef, 200g (6oz) salted butter, 2 dessert spoons of thick cream, 4 eggs (beaten), 200g raisins, 200g dried fruit, 500ml (16fl oz) milk, 4 onions, 2 cloves, 1 white cabbage, 6 turnips, 4 large carrots, the white of a leek, a stick of celery, bouquet garni, 2 dessert spoons of sugar, salt, an old linen tea towel folded in half and sewn into a bag and soaked for 10 min. In a very large casserole, bring to the boil 7l (just under 12pts) of water, adding the vegetables (except the cabbage) and the bouquet garni. Once the water is boiling, add the meat, season lightly and simmer for 2 hours. When 1 hour has passed make the *farz* by working together the flour, 200ml (7fl oz) of the stock, the milk, the eggs, 125g (4oz) of melted butter, salt, dried fruit and sugar to get a smooth dough. Leave to rest until the second hour is up; then pour into the tea-towel-bag, tie the neck firmly, plunge into the simmering pot and cook for a further 1 hour 30 min. Half an hour before cooking time is up, roughly chop the cabbage and blanch it in salted boiling water for 5 min. Empty out the water, add the rest of the butter and 200 ml of the stock and heat gently with a lid on until the stew is ready. Take out the bag of *farz* and leave to strain in a colander for 5 minutes. Arrange the meat on a warmed serving dish. Once the *farz* has cooled a little, roll the bag around on a pastry board until the contents have broken up into a granular consistency. Open the bag and arrange its contents around the meat. Decorate with the vegetables and cabbage and serve with the stock as a sauce on the side.

Kouign-amann – This Breton sweetmeat is made from 500g (1lb 2oz) flour, 250g (9 oz) butter, 200g (7oz) sugar, 10g (1tsp) baking powder, pinch of salt and an egg yolk. Work the flour, baking powder and salt into a dough with a little water and leave to rise for 30 min. Form the dough into a large flat pancake about 30cm (12in) in diameter, spread half the butter on this, taking care not to go right up the edge, and sprinkle on about a third of the sugar. Fold the pancake into four, pressing the outer edges firmly together, and leave for 10 min. Flatten the dough into a large pancake and cover with butter and sugar as before. Fold into four and leave for 10 min. Flatten out to form a pancake of 25-30cm (10-12in) about 1-2cm (just under 1in) thick. Paint with the egg yolk and sprinkle with the rest of the sugar. Cook in a very hot oven for 30 min. If the butter oozes out, use it to baste the kouign-amann until it has finished cooking.

Calvaire de Guimiliau

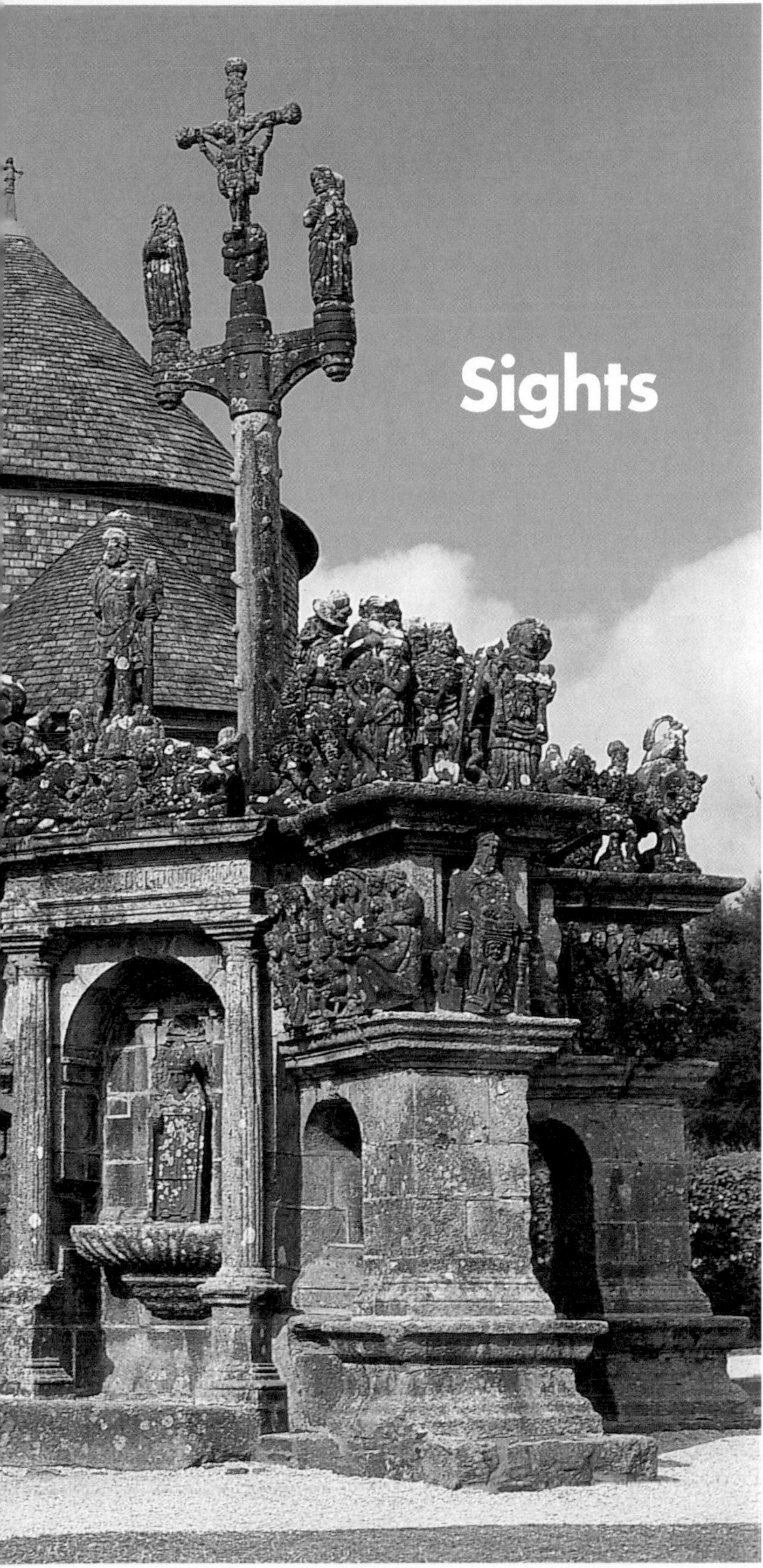

Sights

Cantin/CAMPAGNE CAMPAGNE

Les ABERS★

Michelin map 58 folds 3 and 4 or 20 folds 2 and 3

The northwest coast of Finistère, still known as the Coast of Legends, is broken up by estuaries called *abers* (Aber-Wrac'h, Aber-Benoît, Aber-Ildut), which create a fine sight at high tide.

The *abers* are different from the estuaries on the north coast (rivers of Morlaix, Jaudy and Trieux): their beds are not as deep nor their slopes as steep. Beyond the high tide mark the *aber* is prolonged upstream not by a small coastal river but by a tiny brook too small to dig a channel in the muddy estuary. There is no great port at the head of the estuary, as there is at Morlaix or Dinan.

The whole of this low and rocky coast, dotted with small islands, is particularly rich in different varieties of **seaweed**. Factories process most of it: the brown species in the manufacture of alginates and mannite, the fucus and floating weed as stock-feed; the remainder is sold as fertiliser *(see Introduction: Algae – qv)*.

ROUND TOUR STARTING FROM BREST

195km - 121 miles – allow one day

★**Brest** – *See BREST.*

Leave Brest by ② on the town plan, the road towards Roscoff.

Gouesnou – The 17C **church** ⓥ has a monumental north porch. The polygonal chevet (1615) surmounted by three pediments and the sacristy (1866) were restored following damage caused in the Second World War. Inside, note the

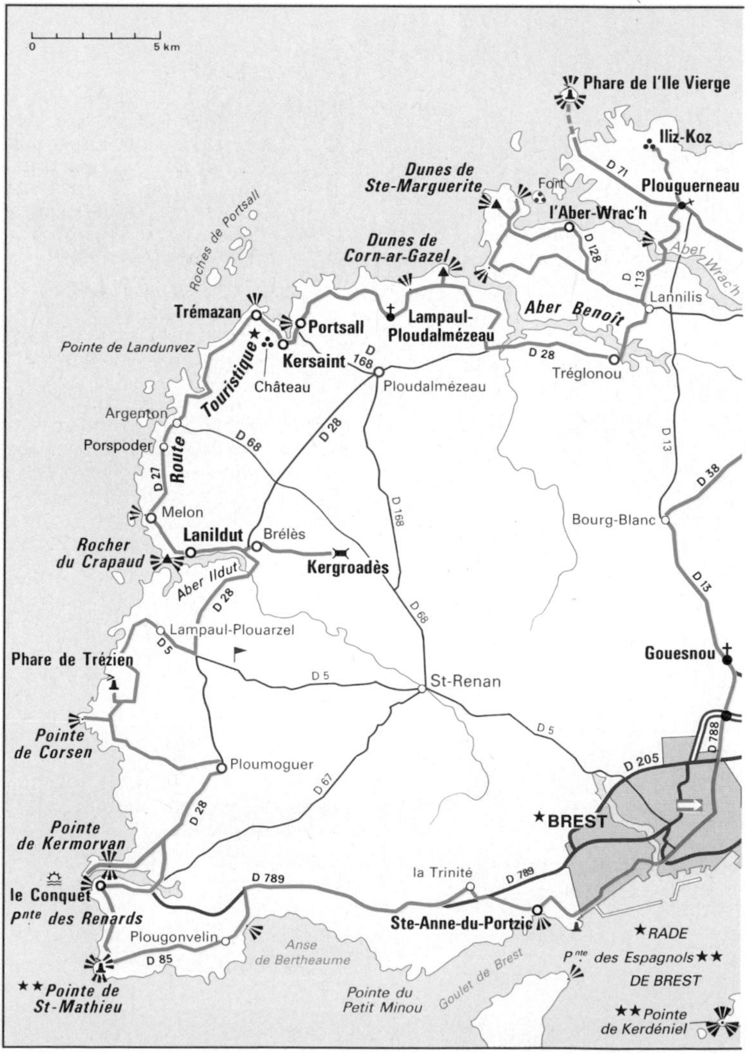

modern stained-glass windows by J. Le Chevalier (1970) and Renaissance niches on two tiers in the chancel. Under the trees below the church, to the west, is a fine Renaissance fountain with an altar adorned with a statue of St Gouesnou.

Take the road towards Lannilis and at Bourg-Blanc, turn right.

Chapelle St-Jaoua ⓥ – Standing in the centre of a shady parish close is a charming early 16C chapel which contains the tomb and effigy of St Jaoua. By the roadside, note the great 17C fountain built of large stones; curious semicircular shapes flanked by massive pinnacles crown the monument and pilasters.

Plouvien – In the **parish church** is a tomb in Kersanton granite dating from 1555. The recumbent figure rests on sixteen little monks depicted at prayer, reading or meditating.

Leave Plouvien to the east by the Lesneven road.

St-Jean-Balanant – The 15C **chapel** ⓥ was founded by the Order of St John of Jerusalem and was a dependant of the La Feuillée Commandery in the Monts d'Arrée. At the tympanum, note the low relief relating the Baptism of Christ. There is a fountain to the south of the chapel.

Continue towards Lesneven and at the fourth junction turn right towards Locmaria.

Chapelle de Locmaria – In front of the 16-17C chapel with its square belfry-porch, there is a fine **cross**★ with two cross-bars adorned with figures.

Go to Le Drennec and take the road on the left to Le Folgoët.

★★**Le Folgoët** – *See Le FOLGOËT.*

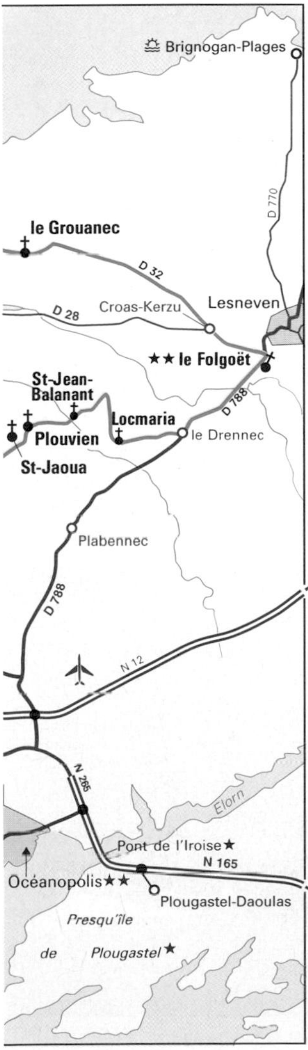

Take the direction of Lannilis and at Croas-Kerzu, bear right towards Plouguerneau.

At the entrance of Le Grouanec, note on the right an eight-sided Gallo-Roman cross embedded in the wall of a farm.

Le Grouanec – Beyond the village, on the right, in the small parish close (16C) is the fountain of Notre-Dame-de-Grouanec. Inside the **church**, the stained-glass windows by Max Ingrand, sculpted purlin and beams in the south aisle are noteworthy; ceramic crosses mark the Stations of the Cross. The fountain, Notre-Dame-de-la-Clarté, may be seen 100m from the church.

Plouguerneau – The village **church** is said to have been built on a cairn. On the left on entering, near the baptistery, there is an interesting collection of 17C wooden statuettes called the little saints. These statuettes are the result of a wish made by the villagers, who had miraculously escaped the plague; they were carried in the processions. The altar is in the shape of a wooden chest with The Last Supper carved on several panels. *Pardons* are held every year *(see the Calendar of Events at the end of the guide).*

Take the D 32 towards St-Michel.

At the exit to the village, on the right, is a small museum of maritime traditions which explains the techniques of seaweed-gathering down the years.

Ruines d'Iliz Koz ⓥ – Recent excavations have brought to light the ruins of the church and the presbytery of the old parish of Tremenac'h which have been silted up since the early 18C. It is an excellent example of Breton funerary art at the end of the Middle Ages. A signposted route enables visitors to discover the parish close and the most important elements of the site: church, ossuary, cemetery and the various tombs with ornamental motifs recalling the function of the tomb's occupant (knight, clerk or commoner).

Make for the St-Michel beaches.

Good sheltered beaches of fine sand in a cove.

Phare de l'Île Vierge ⓥ – Built between 1897 and 1902 and supplied by aerogenerators, this is the tallest lighthouse in France (82.5m - 270ft) and its beam has an average range of

52km - 32 miles. From the top (397 steps) the **panorama★** extends over the Finistère coast, ranging from Ouessant to the île de Batz in fine weather.

Return to Plouguerneau and proceed towards Brest.

2km - 1 mile further on, the old road is now a lookout point (small Calvary) affording a good **view★** of L'Aber-Wrac'h which is especially fine at high tide. Cross the *aber.*

Turn right at Lannilis.

L'Aber-Wrac'h – This little port, yachting centre and seaside resort has a sailing school overlooking the village.
The *corniche* road runs along the Baie des Anges; on the left stand the ruins of the 16C convent of Notre-Dame-des-Anges.

Bear right towards Ste-Marguerite Dunes, then right again towards Cézon Fort.

From the platform by the roadside, there is an interesting **view** of L'Aber-Wrac'h estuary, the ruins of Cézon Fort on an island commanding the approach to the estuary, and the lighthouse on the île Vierge.

Turn back and after Poulloc, bear right for the dunes.

Dunes de Ste-Marguerite – The footpaths through the dunes afford good views: to the left is Aber-Benoît and in the distance the Roches de Portsall, to the right L'Aber-Wrac'h channel studded with islets.
Seaweed is left to dry on the dunes for two to three days and then is sent to the processing factories.

Make for the Chapelle de Brouënnou and turn left towards Passage St-Pabu.

Half-way down, from the platform on the left, there is a good view over Aber-Benoît and St-Pabu.

Go to Lannilis via Landéda and then take the Ploudalmézeau road.

Aber-Benoît – The road crosses the *aber* and runs along it for a while giving good views of the pretty setting.

After 5km - 3 miles, turn right for St-Pabu and after St-Pabu follow the signposts for the camp site to reach the Corn-ar-Gazel Dunes.

Dunes de Corn-ar-Gazel – Beautiful **view** of Ste-Marguerite Peninsula, Aber-Benoît and its islets.

Turn round and follow the scenic road winding through the dunes and affording glimpses of the coast.

Lampaul-Ploudalmézeau – The **church** has a Renaissance north door, a magnificent **belfry-porch★** crowned by a dome with three lanterns, and a large chapel to the right of the chancel.
Roads through the dunes lead to vast sandy beaches.

Portsall – A small harbour is located in a sheltered bay. From a Calvary perched on a cliff a the far end of the harbour *(15 min on foot Rtn, access via Bar-an-Lan on the Kersaint road)*, a good **view** unfolds over the port, the coast and the Roches de Portsall in the distance.
These rocks are where the oil tanker *Amoco Cadiz* ran aground in 1978, polluting 160km - 99 miles of the French coast. One of its two enormous anchors (20 tonnes) is fixed to the harbour breakwater in memory of the shipwreck, on which a legal settlement was not reached until 1992.

Kersaint – Beyond the village, towards Argenton, are the ruins of the 13C **Château de Trémazan**.

Trémazan – From the large car park past the village, the **view★** extends over the Île Verte, the Roches de Portsall and Corn Carhai Lighthouse.

★**Scenic road** (Route touristique) – The *corniche* road follows a wild coast studded with rocks; note the curious jagged **Pointe de Landunvez**. The road runs through several small resorts, Argenton, **Porspoder** – where St Budoc, Bishop of Dol-de-Bretagne *(qv)* is said to have landed in the 6C – and Melon.

Mingani/CAMPAGNE CAMPAGNE

Harvesting seaweed

Turn right at the entrance of Lanildut.

Rocher du Crapaud – Overlooking the narrow channel of **Aber-Ildut**, it offers good views of the harbour and the *aber*, a picturesque estuary accessible to boats regardless of the tides. The northern bank is wooded, the southern bank has dunes and beaches.
The *aber* marks the notional boundary between the Channel and the Atlantic. However, sailors consider this demarcation to be further to the south at Pointe de Corsen *(see below)* in view of the sea-bed level.

After Lanildut, the road follows the aber as far as Brélès; bear right towards Kergroadès.

Château de Kergroadès ⓥ – The castle built in 1613 has been restored. The main courtyard is closed by a crenellated gallery and is surrounded by an austere main building flanked by two round towers and two wings built at right angles. There is a pretty well.

Return to Brélès and take the direction of Plouarzel and turn right after Lampaul-Plouarzel. The road then runs along Porspol Bay with Ségal Island in the distance, and through Trézien.

Phare de Trézien – The lighthouse (37m - 121ft high) has an average range of 35km - 22 miles.

Continue towards Porsmoguer Beach (Grève de Porsmoguer) and after some houses turn right.

The road passes by the Corsen Maritime Station (Station de Corsen) and leads to a ruined house on the cliff.

Pointe de Corsen – This 50m - 160ft cliff is the most westerly point in France. There is a fine **view** of the coast and islands.

Go to Ploumoguer passing through Porsmoguer Beach, then turn towards Le Conquet. After 5km - 3 miles, bear right for the Pointe de Kermorvan.

Pointe de Kermorvan – Its central part is an isthmus which gives a pretty view on the right of Blancs Sablons Beach and on the left of the **site★** of Le Conquet. The Croaë footbridge gives pedestrians access to the point; at the very tip, to the left of the entrance to the lighthouse, the rocky chaos makes a marvellous lookout point.

The road goes round the great estuary, where the harbour is situated, to Le Conquet.

Le Conquet – From this pretty **site★**, there is a superb view of the Pointe de Kermorvan. This is a fishing port for crawfish, lobster and crab and the departure point for the islands of Ouessant and Molène. The harbour *corniche* road, the coastal footpaths and especially the Pointe de Kermorvan are pleasant walks offering good views of the port, the Four Channel, the Ouessant archipelago and its many lighthouses in the distance. The **church**, which was restored in the 19C, has a fine 16C stained-glass window depicting the Passion in the chancel and 15C sculptures under the porch.

The road from Le Conquet to Brest is described in the opposite direction under BREST: Excursions.

ANTRAIN

Population 1 489

Michelin map 59 fold 17 or 20 fold 27

Antrain overlooks rich farmlands bordered by hedges and trees and green valleys, lying as it does high on the promontory before the confluence of the Couesnon and Loisance Rivers. It is a market town with steep little streets and 16 and 17C houses. Of its Romanesque church, there still remains a fine portal with a semicircular arch and buttresses on either side.

Église St-André – The church's construction dates for the most part from the 12C. The façade has a fine semicircular arched doorway with double recessed arches supported by small columns whose capitals and abacus are decorated with ovolo and saw-tooth moulding. The imposing 17C bell tower is topped by a dome with lantern turrets.

EXCURSIONS

Château de Bonne-Fontaine ⓥ – *1.5km - 1 mile south. Leave Antrain by Rues Général-Lavigne and Bonne-Fontaine.*
Built in 1547 as a feudal manor-house and remodelled in the 19C, this castle rises in the centre of a beautifully maintained park. The elegant turrets adorning the massive main range, the tall windows and the carved dormer windows balance the severity of the squat, machicolated pepperpot towers.

Tremblay – *4km - 2 miles south by the D 155 and the N 175.* The **church** which was built in the 11 and 12C, modified in the 16C and restored after a fire in 1801, is an example of Romanesque architecture. The solid square tower that rises above the transept crossing is topped by a pierced bell-turret. Inside notice the elegance of the canopy and the glory radiating outwards from the top of the great cross on the high altar. The Cross bears three heads symbolising the Holy Trinity at its centre, and at its foot the symbols of the Evangelists. The beam is ornate, entwined by a vine and ears of corn being pecked by birds. The six old wooden statues and the Christ, behind the entrance porch, are interesting.

Château du Rocher-Portail – *14km - 9 miles east by the D 155 and the D 102 to the left. Not open to the public.*
A drive bordered with chestnut trees leads to the castle set in a beautiful spot. Gilles Ruellan, one-time pedlar who became a councillor of state, built the castle in 1608. A long façade and two wings at right angles to it enclose a big courtyard; along its fourth side runs a granite balustrade and beyond it is the moat. The left wing's ground floor forms a beautiful arcaded gallery whose outer side looks out over a pool. An arched passageway through the right wing leads to a second courtyard closed by the outbuildings.

Monts d'ARRÉE★★

Michelin map 58 folds 5,6 and 15 and 16 or 20 folds 18 and 19

The Arrée Mountains are the highest in Brittany, yet their topmost point is less than 400m - 1200ft. They were perhaps proud peaks in the Primary Era *(see Introduction: Description of the Country)*, but erosion has done its work. The sandstone or granite summits have been turned into rounded hills or menez (Menez-Bré, *qv* and Ménez-Hom, *qv*). The quartz formations, cleared by the action of water on the schist around them, have become sharp crests, fretted into saw-teeth and bristling with needles; these are the rocks or *roc'hs* (eg Roc Trévezel). The picturesqueness of these "mountains" is due to the grim and barren face of nature. The peaks often shrouded in mist afford fine views.
The mountain chain is wooded in parts, especially towards the east, but the summits are usually quite desolate. There is not a tree on them; the heath is pierced by rocky scarps; here and there are clumps of gorse with golden flowers in spring and purple heather in September. A few poor hamlets stand far apart. On the hillsides small streams have dug valleys which are sometimes wild, often full of freshness. The whole area of the Monts d'Arrée is now protected following the creation of the **Parc naturel régional d'Armorique** *(qv)* in the midst of which the **Écomusée des Monts d'Arrée** has been established; this open-air museum reveals the rural life of the past.

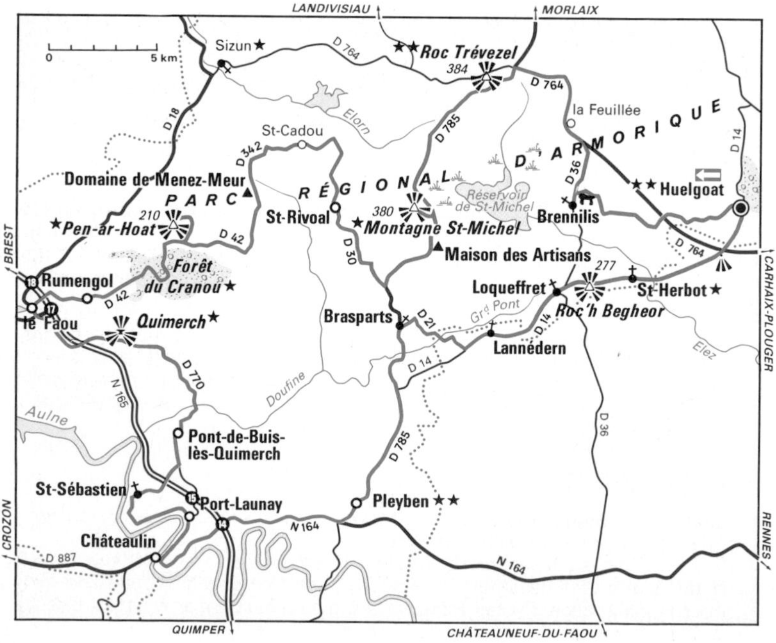

ROUND TOUR STARTING FROM HUELGOAT

122km - 76 miles – allow one day – local map previous page

★★**Huelgoat** – *Time: 30 min. See HUELGOAT.*

Leave Huelgoat south in the direction of Pleyben.

2km - 1 mile further on, the road offers an extensive view of Aulne Basin and the Montagne Noires.

★**St-Herbot** – The **church**★ ⓥ with its square tower, stands surrounded by trees. It is mainly in the Flamboyant Gothic style. A small Renaissance ossuary abuts on the south porch and on the north side a horseshoe staircase leads to the chapel. There is a fine Crucifix-Calvary in Kersanton granite (1571) in front of the building. Inside, the chancel is surrounded by a remarkable **screen**★★ in carved oak topped by a Crucifixion. Against this screen, on the nave side, are two stone tables for the tufts of hair from the tails of oxen and cows, which the peasants offer on the *pardon (qv)* to obtain the protection of St Herbot, the patron saint of horned cattle. Note also the richly decorated stalls (lift the seats) against the screen, the saint's tomb with a simple stone slab and recumbent figure on four small columns, the stained glass (1556) of the large chancel bay and the side windows depicting respectively the Passion, St Yves and St Lawrence.

Roc'h Begheor – *15 min on foot. Car park to the right of the road.* A path amid gorse leads to the summit at an altitude of 277m - 909ft, commanding a good **view**★ over the Monts d'Arrée and the Montagnes Noires.

Loqueffret – The 16C **church** ⓥ contains, in the south transept, a 17C gilded wood altarpiece; in the north arm, an impressive Trinity housed in a niche with carved shutters. At the end of the nave, in the gallery, are painted panels depicting Christ and the apostles. A fine cross adorned with figures stands on the south side of the church.

Lannédern – In the **parish close** *(qv)* is a Cross decorated with figures; note St Edern riding a stag. Inside the church ⓥ the saint's tomb (14C) and six polychrome low reliefs (17C) illustrating his life are of interest. Note also in the chancel, the 16C window depicting the Passion and 17C statues of the Virgin and St Edern.

Continue towards Pleyben and turn right after 1.5km - 1 mile.

Brasparts – The village has an interesting 16C **parish close** *(see Les ENCLOS PAROISSIAUX)*. On the Calvary, note St Michael killing the dragon and a simple *Pietà* with the Virgin surrounded by the Holy Women. The **church**, remodelled in the 18C, has a fine turreted porch. On entering, by the nave stands (on the right) a **Virgin of Pity**★ (16C), and on the left of the chancel, an altarpiece of the Rosary dating from 1668. In the chancel, left of the high altar, a fine 16C stained-glass window illustrating the Passion is noteworthy.

D'après photo Christiane Olivier

A house near Brasparts

Make for Pleyben.

★★**Pleyben** – *See PLEYBEN.*

Châteaulin – *See CHÂTEAULIN.*

Follow the south bank of the Aulne.

Port-Launay – This is the port of Châteaulin, on the Aulne. The long quay makes for pleasant walks.

Leave the Brest road on the right and continue along the Aulne, pass under the railway viaduct, bear right at the roundabout and 100m further on, turn left.

The road climbs up the hillside and affords a lovely view over the verdant valley.

Chapelle St-Sébastien ⓥ – The chapel stands near a farm. In the 16C **parish close** stand a triumphal arch surmounted by St Sebastian between two archers, and a fine Calvary with figures including the saint pierced by arrows. Inside the rather dilapidated chapel, 17C **altarpieces**★ in gilded wood are to be seen in the chancel and south transept; in the north transept are panels recounting the story of Loreto, a small Italian village in the Marches region to which, according to legend, the angels transported Mary's house from Nazareth in the 13C.

Follow the small road over the railway line and the Quimper-Brest motorway and turn left towards Brest.

Pont-de-Buis-lès-Quimerch – On leaving the village, below the road, on the left, can be seen a 300-year-old explosives factory. It produces ammunition for hunting, plastic materials and pyrotechnic devices.

★**Quimerch** – *Viewing table.* The **view** extends from Ménez-Hom to the Forêt du Cranou Forest taking in the Brest roadstead and the Presqu'île de Plougastel Peninsula.

Le Faou – *See Le FAOU.*

From Le Faou, take the D 42 to Rumengol.

Rumengol – *See RUMENGOL.*

★**Forêt du Cranou** – The road, hilly and winding, runs through the state forest of Cranou, which consists mostly of oaks and beeches. Picnic areas.

On leaving the Forêt du Cranou, bear right towards St-Rivoal; at the entrance to Kerancuru, turn left for Pen-ar-Hoat-ar-Gorré. In the hamlet (schist houses), turn left towards Hanvec and again left into an uphill road. Leave the car near the farm.

★**Pen-ar-Hoat** – Alt 217m - 712ft. *Time: 45 min on foot Rtn. Walk round the farm and bear left towards the line of heights; after passing between low walls, the climb ends among gorse bushes.* The **panorama** extends over the heath-clad hills: to the north are the hills bordering the left bank of the Elorn, to the east the nearer heights of the Arrée, to the south Cranou Forest and in the distance the Montagnes Noires and the Ménez-Hom, and lastly, to the west, the Brest roadstead.

Return to Kerancuru and bear left; 3.5km - 2 miles further on, left again.

Domaine de Menez-Meur ⌚ – The estate sprawls over 400ha - 988 acres in an undulating countryside. The tourist information centre (Maison du Parc) presents exhibitions devoted to the Parc naturel régional d'Armorique: audiovisual presentation, the Breton horse and local arts and crafts. A nature trail *(time: about 1 hour 30 min)*, accompanied by panels giving information on the region's flora, winds through the large enclosures where ponies, sheep, deer, wild boar, horses, etc roam.

Go to St-Rivoal, passing through St-Cadou.

St-Rivoal – After the village, below the Le Faou road, to the left, is the **Maison Cornec** ⌚, a small farm dating from 1702. It is one of the many exhibits dispersed throughout the park, which makes up the open-air museum devoted to the different styles of Breton architecture. The little house, built of schist and with a fine external covered stairway going up to the hayloft, comprises a large room with the living quarters for the farmer and his family round the great chimney and the domestic animals at the other end. Next to it is the barn with all the farming implements, and there are two bread ovens in the courtyard; the larger one (used collectively) is covered with turf.

Take the road in the direction of Brasparts.

The road winds through a countryside of hills, and of green and wooded valleys whose freshness contrasts with the bare rocky summits.

After 5.5km - 3 miles bear left towards Morlaix.

Maison des Artisans ⌚ – *North of Brasparts.* Part of the regional nature park, the centre is housed in St-Michel farmhouse; it displays Breton crafts: paintings, sculpture, pottery, weaving, gold and silverware, etc.

Continue towards Morlaix; take the road which branches off to the left.

★**Montagne St-Michel** – From the top of the rise (alt 380m - 1 246 ft) where there is a small chapel which reaches an altitude of 391m - 125ft at its summit, there is a **panorama** of the Monts d'Arrée and the Montagnes Noires. From the foot of the hill, a great peat bog called the Yeun Elez extends towards the east. In the winter mists, the place is so grim that Breton legend says it contains the Youdig, a gulf forming the entrance to Hell. Beyond it may be seen St-Michel reservoir which supplies the Monts d'Arrée thermal power station at Brennilis. Note the megalithic alignment on the rocky point to the right of the lake.
Fine views of the countryside, the mountains and Brennilis basin from the road passing by the Toussaines Signal Station (Signal de Toussaines, alt: 384m - 1 260ft).

★★**Roc Trévezel** – *See Les ENCLOS PAROISSIAUX.*

By the Roc-Tredudon pylon turn right towards Huelgoat and after 6km - 4 miles bear right to Brennilis.

Brennilis – This village has a 15C **church** ⏲ topped by a delicate pierced belfry. Inside, seven polychrome panels (17C) at the high altar and a stained-glass window (16C) in the chancel illustrate scenes from the life of the Virgin. In the south transept, there is a fine 16C altar adorned with low reliefs depicting the twelve sibyls.

Return to the entrance to Brennilis and turn right.

Dolmen – 100yds further to the right, a signposted path leads to a covered alleyway partly hidden by a tumulus.

Continue on the secondary road to Huelgoat.

ASSÉRAC

Population 1 239

Michelin map 6 fold 14 or 20 folds 51 and 52

Lying on the western periphery of the Parc naturel régional de Brière *(qv)*, this village has a shellfish breeding centre in the coastal waters. Nearby, the Trait de Mesquer salt marshes *(See Presqu'île de GUÉRANDE)* extend from Pont d'Armes.

EXCURSION

The west coast – *Round tour of 35km - 22 miles – about 1 hour 30 min. Take the D 33 west.*

Pen-Bé – This vantage point affords a **view** of the bay with its profusion of upstanding poles for mussel rearing, the Pointe de Merquel and Dumet Island in the distance.

Go to Kerséquin and bear left.

★**Pointe du Bile** – The **view** extends over two islets and the great ochre-coloured cliffs.
Continue via **Poudrantais**. The road offers glimpses of the cliff line.

Plage de la Mine d'Or – Two strange rocks, one in the shape of a menhir, interrupt this long stretch of beach at the foot of tall cliffs.

Cross **Le Haut-Pénestin**, a village with fine houses.

Pointe du Halguen – Heathland and pine trees cover this headland. Walk down to the rocky beaches which are backed by a short line of cliffs.
The road follows the Vilaine's lower bank.

Tréhiguier – This small fishing port is a mussel-breeding centre. Anchored in the estuary are pleasure craft mingling with the many motor and rowing boats used for mussel gathering. Walk to the **Pointe du Scal**★ to see the estuary widen between the Pointe du Halguen, to the left, and Pen-Lan headland.

Return to Assérac by the D 192 and the D 83.

AUDIERNE

Population 2 746

Michelin map 58 fold 13 or 20 fold 16 – Local map under Cornouaille: Cap Sizun – Facilities

This fishing port on the estuary of the Goyen, at the foot of a wooded hill and in a pretty **setting**★, is worth seeing. The large, sandy beach is 1.5km - 1 mile from the town, below Ste-Evette.
Its main activity is fishing for lobster and crab.

Grands Viviers ⏲ – *Access by Quai Pelletan and the scenic coast road.* This fish farm boasts some 30 pools full of crustaceans (lobster and crab).

La Chaumière ⏲ – *Opposite the fish farm.* The thatched cottage's fine interior contains 17 and 18C Breton furniture as well as objects used in everyday life of that period.

EXCURSION

Île de Sein – *From Audierne departures are from Ste-Evette landing stage. See Ile de SEIN.*

A Map of touring programmes is given at the beginning of the guide. To plan a special tour use the preceding Map of principal sights.

AURAY★

Population 10 323

Michelin map 6 fold 2 or 20 fold 36 – Local map under Golfe du MORBIHAN

This ancient town is built on the banks of the Loch or Auray River near the famous Sanctuaire de Ste-Anne-d'Auray *(qv)*. The attractive harbour, as seen from Promenade du Loch, and the town's old St-Goustan Quarter are both of interest to the tourist.

The Battle of Auray (14C) – The town is famous in Breton history for the battle that was fought under its walls in 1364 ending the War of Succession *(qv)*. The troops of Charles of Blois, backed by Du Guesclin *(qv)*, held a bad position on a marshy plain north of Auray. Jean de Montfort, Charles's cousin, Olivier de Clisson, and the English, commanded by Chandos, were in a dominating position.
Against Du Guesclin's advice, Charles attacked. It was a total defeat. His body was picked up on the battlefield. On seeing the corpse of his rival, whom the Bretons made into a saint, Montfort could not master his emotion. But Chandos roused him, saying: "You cannot have your cousin alive and the Duchy too. Thank God and your friends." Du Guesclin had fought like a desperate man: having broken all his weapons, he felled his opponents with his iron gauntlets. Amid the battle the English leader saw him, made his way to him and persuaded him to surrender by saying: "The day is not yours, Messire Bertrand, you will be luckier another time." As for Olivier de Clisson, he lost an eye in the fight.

Cadoudal, or the last Chouan – Cadoudal was a farmer's son. He was 22 years old when the **Chouannerie**, a Breton Royalist revolt, broke out in 1793. When the men of the Vendée were beaten, he carried on the struggle in Morbihan. He was captured, imprisoned at Brest but escaped, and took part in the action at Quiberon *(qv)*, came away unhurt, submitted to Hoche in 1796 and reopened the campaign in 1799. The troops that hunted him undertook huge engineering works; the banks and hedges of the country, which the Chouans used as defensive walls and hiding-places, were cleared away. Bonaparte offered the rebel a pardon and the rank of general, without success. The struggle ended only in 1804; Cadoudal had gone to Paris to try to kidnap Napoleon; he was arrested, sentenced to death and executed. The remains were buried in a tomb, built within sight of Cadoudal's house, on Kerléano Hill.

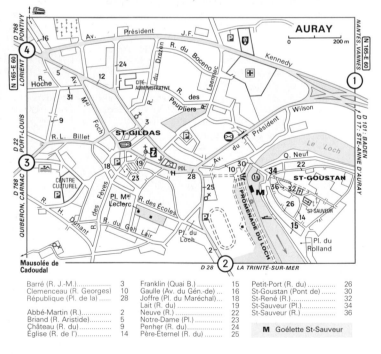

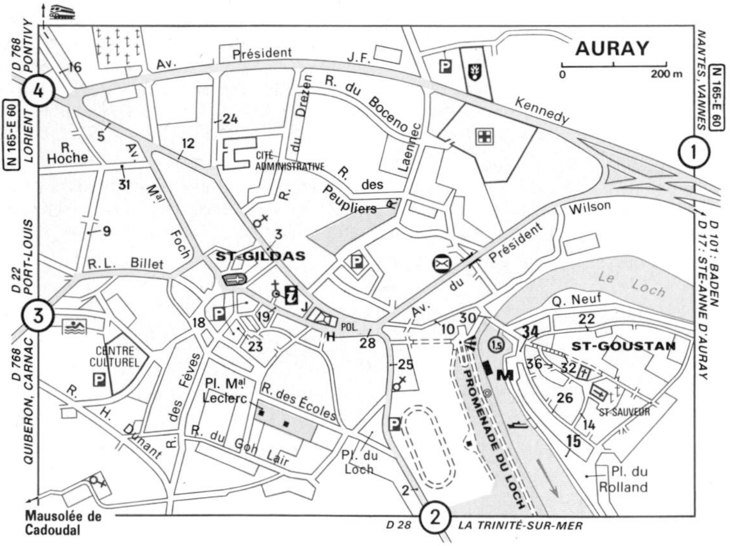

Barré (R. J.-M.) ... 3
Clemenceau (R. Georges) 10
République (Pl. de la) ... 28

Abbé-Martin (R.) ... 2
Briand (R. Aristide) ... 5
Château (R. du) ... 9
Église (R. de l') ... 14
Franklin (Quai B.) ... 15
Gaulle (Av. du Gén.-de) ... 16
Joffre (Pl. du Maréchal) ... 18
Lait (R. du) ... 19
Neuve (R.) ... 22
Notre-Dame (Pl.) ... 23
Penher (R. du) ... 24
Père-Éternel (R. du) ... 25
Petit-Port (R. du) ... 26
St-Goustan (Pont de) ... 30
St-René (R.) ... 32
St-Sauveur (Pl.) ... 34
St-Sauveur (R.) ... 36

M Goélette St-Sauveur

SIGHTS

★**Promenade du Loch** – There is a good **view** over the port, St-Goustan Quarter and Auray River, crossed by an attractive old stone bridge with cutwaters.
Moored in the loch is a schooner, the **Goélette St-Sauveur** (**M**) ⌚, which has been painstakingly reconstructed from an old hull. It contains information on the way of life in St-Goustan port during the last century, including slide shows with soundtracks complemented by numerous models of ships and filmshots of old views. A display of tools belonging to maritime carpenters evokes the construction techniques which were once used.

Near the old bridge note the En-Bas Pavilion, an attractive 16C house.

★**Quartier St-Goustan** – This little port, particularly lively in the evening, still has some beautiful 15C houses and other pretty dwellings in Place St-Sauveur (**34**) and up some of the steep, in places even stepped, little lanes leading off the square. The quay to the left of the square is named after Benjamin Franklin (**15**). In 1776, during the War of Independence, the famous American diplomat and statesman sailed from Philadelphia to negotiate a treaty with France and landed at Auray instead of Nantes due to the unfavourable weather conditions. The house (no 8) where he stayed bears a plaque.

★**St-Gildas** – This 17C church, with its Renaissance porch, contains a very fine stone and marble **altarpiece**★ (1664) attributed to Olivier Martinet at the high altar, and a baptismal font with a carved canopy. Note the 18C woodwork in the side chapels and elegant organ loft (1761) by the Auray organ-builder Waltrin.

Mausolée de Cadoudal – *Access via Rue du Père-Éternel, Place du Loch, Rue du Verger and towards Reclus.*
The small round building, topped with a dome, stands on Kerléano Hill, across from the hero's family home.

BOAT TRIP

★★★**Golfe du Morbihan** ⌚ – A pleasant excursion up the **Auray River**★ as far as Bono and round the gulf.

LE PAYS ALRÉEN

Round tour of 23km - 14 miles – time: about 3 hours. Leave Auray on the Avenue du Général-de-Gaulle.

Chartreuse d'Auray ⌚ – On the battlefield where he defeated Charles of Blois, Jean de Montfort (who became Duke Jean IV) built a chapel and a collegiate church, which was later transformed into a Carthusian monastery (from 1482-1790). In 1968 a fire ravaged the church and funeral chapel, since restored.
The funeral chapel was built in the early 19C to hold the bones of exiles and Chouans who were shot on the Champ des Martyrs in 1795, after the unsuccessful Quiberon landing *(see Presqu'île de QUIBERON)*; in the centre, the black and white marble mausoleum is decorated with remarkable high reliefs and bears the names of 953 exiles. The beautiful simple church is lit by modern grisaille windows. In the cloisters' galleries 18 panels depict the life of St Bruno. A fine 15C Virgin in boxwood and an 18C Christ are of interest.

Champ des Martyrs – The exiles and Chouans were shot in this enclosure during the Royalist insurrection (1793-1804). A chapel, in the style of a Greek temple, stands on the site where they were executed and buried before the remains were transferred to the Carthusian Monastery.

Follow the road to Ste-Anne-d'Auray.

The road skirts the Kerzo Bog (on the right) where the Battle of Auray was fought.

After 500m - about 1/3 mile bear left in the direction of St-Degan.

The road climbs the west slope of the deep valley of the Loch.

St-Degan – In the hamlet, turn left to see the **écomusée** (open-air museum) ⌚. Restored buildings, built of granite and roofed with thatch, surround the threshing area; you will see a house with furniture of the Bas-Vannetais, a building used both as living quarters and workplace with everyday objects, ploughing implements and craftsmen's tools.
An exhibit is devoted to Breton weddings.

Go to Brech and turn right.

At the entrance to Ste-Anne-d'Auray, in a bend on the right, is a monument erected in 1891 to the memory of the Count of Chambord, the Pretender who narrowly failed to oust the Third Regime at the beginning of the Third Republic and who used to participate in the pilgrimage to Ste-Anne.

★**Ste-Anne-d'Auray** – *See STE-ANNE-D'AURAY.*

Pluneret – In the cemetery, alongside the central alley, on the right, are the tombs of the Countess de Ségur, the author of children's books *(Les Malheurs de Sophie*, 1859) and of her son.

Proceed towards Bono and after 2km - 1 mile turn left for Ste-Avoye.

Ste-Avoye – Among picturesque cottages, near a fountain, stands a pretty Renaissance **chapel** ⌚ with a fine keel-shaped **roof**★. The lovely oak **rood screen**★ is carved and painted to represent the Apostles on the side facing the nave and the Virtues on the chancel side, surrounded by St Fiacre and St Lawrence on the left and St Yves on the right.

Turn back in the direction of Ste-Anne-d'Auray and bear left to Auray.

Cairn de BARNENEZ★

Michelin map 58 fold or 20 fold 5 – Local map under CORNICHE DE L'ARMORIQUE

This impressive **tumulus** ⓥ, a mound of dry stones – **cairn** *(qv)* in Brittany and Scotland, stands on the Kernéléhen Peninsula, dominating the Bay of Térénez and the Morlaix estuary. Discovered accidentally, it is now possible to see this ancient burial place in cross section. Excavations between 1955-68 revealed 11 burial chambers. The entrances all face south and were preceded by passages 7-12m – 23-39ft long. It would appear, from the colour of the stones, that there were two distinct periods of construction: the first tumulus in a local green stone dates from 4600BC while the second one, nearer the slope, is 200 years younger and is composed mainly of the light-coloured Stérec granite, of which the nearest deposit lies on an offshore island.

Île de BATZ

Population 746

Michelin map 58 fold 6 or 20 fold 5

Access: see the current Michelin Red Guide France

The island of **Batz** ⓥ (pronounced Ba), 4km - 2.5 miles long and 1km - half a mile wide, is separated from the mainland by a narrow channel, notorious for its treacherous currents. The ferry arrives in Kernoc'h Bay, which is fringed by the village and the modern buildings of the rescue station. This treeless – with the exception of the village – island has sandy beaches. To the north, the island is fringed by offshore skerries. The mild climate is particularly suitable for market gardening. On Batz the men are either sailors or farmers, and the women help in the market gardens or gather seaweed.

Boat trips ⓥ – These include tours of the bay of Morlaix and of the island.

SIGHTS

Church – The church in the centre of the village was built in 1873. Note in the choir the statues of the Virgin (14-15C) and St Paul the Aurelian (in wood, 17C), the Celtic saint of British origin who died on the island in 573. In the north transept, there is a piece of oriental material dating from the 8C, reputed to be 'the stole of St Paul' *(details at the Trou du Serpent)*.

Lighthouse (Phare) – *On the island's west side. 210 steps.* The 44m - 144ft tall lighthouse stands on the island's highest point (23m - 75ft). View of the island and reef-fringed coast.

Trou du Serpent – *Go beyond the lighthouse and after the ruined house on the dune, take the path to the right.*
The low-lying rock offshore is said to mark the spot where St Paul the Aurelian, with the help of his stole, cast out the dragon who was terrorising the island.

Chapelle Ste-Anne – *On the island's east side.*
A ruined Romanesque chapel stands on the site of the monastery founded by St Paul. *Pardon* on the Sunday nearest to 26 July.
From the nearby sand dunes there are fine views of the coast and offshore islets.

BATZ-SUR-MER

Population 2 734

Michelin map folds 13 and 14 or 20 fold 51 – Local map under Presqu'île de GUÉRANDE

Against a background of the ocean and the saltmarshes, Batz's tall church bell tower acts as a landmark for the town. The rocky coastline is broken by the sandy beaches of Valentin, La Govelle and St-Michel, the latter being protected by a breakwater, beside which stands the Pierre-Longue menhir.

SIGHTS

★**Église St-Guénolé** – The church belonged to a priory in the 13C and was rebuilt in the 15-16C. Its **bell tower**, 60 m - 190ft high, surmounted by a pinnacled turret, dates from 1677. In the **interior**, you will notice at once that the chancel is off-centre, that massive pillars support Gothic arches and that the wooden roof is shaped like the keel of a boat. The **keystones** in the north aisle are remarkably carved. One of the windows in the south aisle commemorates the consecration of the building in 1428.

Ascent to the bell tower ⓥ – *182 steps.* There is an extensive **panorama**★★ along the coast from the Pointe St-Gildas, south of the Loire, to the shores of the Presqu'île de Rhuys and, at sea, to Belle-Ile and Noirmoutier; you overlook the salt marshes *(see Presqu'île de GUÉRANDE)*.

★**Chapelle Notre-Dame-du-Mûrier** – The fine Gothic ruins of the chapel include a sculpted doorway which is flanked by a turreted staircase with its granite-covered roof. Legend has it that it was built in the 15C by Jean de Rieux de Ranrouët to keep a vow he made when in peril at sea. He was guided to safety by a burning mulberry bush (hence the name *mûrier*).

Sentier des Douaniers – Take the path in front of St-Michel Beach, turning to the left. It skirts the cliff edge and offers a view of the Grande Côte and, later, of Pierre-Longue menhir and impressive **rocks**★.

Return by Rue du Golf to La Govelle Beach.

Musée des Marais salants ⏱ – This museum of popular arts and traditions, indicated by **La Porteresse**, a monumental bronze sculpture by J. Fréour, contains, on the ground floor, a 19C Batz interior with its red-painted furniture and salt workers' clothes (for work or special occasions). The mezzanine is devoted to salt harvesting with the model of a salt marsh, wood tools used by the salt worker and the harvesting and handling of the salt (transportation, marketing, taxes). The tour ends with an audio-visual presentation on the salt marsh and its fauna.

BAUD

Population 4 658

Michelin map 63 fold 2 or 20 fold 36

The village is built on a hill surrounded by delightful countryside through which the rivers Blavet, Evel and Tarun flow.

SIGHTS

Chapelle de la Clarté – The 16C chapel with its venerated statue of Our Lady opens off the nave of the parish church (1927). *Pardon* on the first Sunday in July.

Fontaine Notre-Dame-de-la-Clarté – This fountain stands in the lower town, below the Locminé road, at the far end of the large car park.

Venus de Quinipily ⏱ – *2km - 1 mile southwest. Leave Baud by the road to Hennebont. At Coët Vin bear left; 500m - a third of a mile further leave your car (car park on right).*
From the other side of a wooden gate, a steep path leads up to the Venus, placed above a fountain, set in the park of the château de Quinipily (restored). The origins of the statue are uncertain. It has been taken for a Roman idol or an Egyptian Isis. As it was the object of almost pagan worship, it was thrown into the Blavet several times by order of the ecclesiastical authorities; it was placed here in the late 17C.

EXCURSIONS

Chapelle St-Adrien ⏱ – *7km - 4 miles northwest. Leave Baud on the D 3 towards Guéméné and after 3.2km - 2 miles turn right towards St-Barthélemy.*
The road follows the valley of the Blavet before reaching St-Adrien hamlet with its splendid 18C granite houses. The 15C chapel stands below the road, between two fountains; the one on the right is surmounted by a Calvary. Inside there is a simple rood screen, carved on the nave side and painted on the other. *Pardon* on third or fourth Sunday in August.

Chapelle St-Michel – *8km - 5 miles northeast, plus 15 min on foot Rtn. Leave Baud by the D 768 towards Pontivy and after 3km - 2 miles turn towards Guénin, then follow the signposts.*
Leave the car near the 16C chapelle de Manéguen, which is adorned with a carved band on the west façade; note the well (1878). *Take the uphill path to the left of the close.* At the summit (165m - 541ft) stands the Chapelle St-Michel. Wide **panorama**.

Étang de la Forêt – *13km - 8 miles southeast.*
A fine stretch of water (12ha - 30 acres) on the Loch with facilities for boat hire (pedal-boat) and fishing.

★**Poul Fetan, a typical Breton village of the past** ⏱ – *15km - 9 miles west by D 3. At Quistinec take the road to Hennebont.*
Overhanging the Blavet Valley, a quaint little 16C hamlet has been painstakingly reconstituted from ruins abandoned during the 1970s. A wash house (*poul* in Breton) and a spring (*fetan* in Breton) were the two reasons why man originally decided to settle in this locality. Among the charming thatched cottages, note the Maison du Minour (The Chef's House), the Inn (Auberge), where you may be served a typical Breton meal, the former bakery and the Museum of Man and the Environment (écomusée).

In summer, craftsmen attired in regional costume enlighten visitors on the trades of yesteryear (mid-19C): washerwomen rub the steaming linen, a baker kneads and bakes his dough, one farmer churns his butter while another mashes grains of millet to make a purée. A pottery workshop illustrates traditional sculpting and baking techniques. You can also see a few arpents of land sown with hemp, buckwheat and millet. The various farm animals include the "black magpie" (*pie noire*), a smallish cow typical of the Breton region.

La BAULE

Population 14 845
Michelin map 6 fold 14 or 20 folds 51 and 52 – Local map under Presqu'île de GUÉRANDE – Facilities
Town plan in the current Michelin Red Guide France.

La Baule is one of the best-known seaside resorts on the Atlantic coast and one of the most fashionable in Brittany. In 1879, the construction of La Baule was started near **Escoublac** *(qv)*, the old town which had been buried under the dunes. In 1840, measures were taken to fix the dunes by planting 400ha - 1 000 acres of maritime pines. The town is protected from the strong winds to the east and west by Chémoulin and Penchâteau Points and to the north by the forest.

★★**Sea Front** – Stretching for about 7km - 4 miles between Pornichet and Le Pouliguen, this elegant promenade, lined with luxurious hotels, modern buildings, the Casino and two thalassotherapy (salt-water cure) institutes, looks down upon a beautiful fine-sand beach and the bay of La Baule dotted with tiny islands.
Esplanade Benoît, reserved for pedestrians, ends at the west at the pleasure boat harbour *(port de plaisance)* which is in a well-sheltered channel *(étier)* linking the ocean to the salt marshes.

LA BAULE-LES-PINS

La Baule is extended eastwards by this resort, which was built in 1930, in an area forested with pine trees. The attractive Allée Cavalière leads to the Escoublac Forest.
Salt-water swimming pools in operation all year round are part of a thalassotherapy institute.

★**Parc des Dryades** – This lovely park, near the Place des Palmiers, is landscaped with trees of many varieties and colourful flower beds. On entering, on the left, is the bust of the founder of the resort, Louis Lajarrige.

EXCURSION

★**Presqu'île de Guérande** – *Round tour of 62km - 39 miles – about 5 hours 30 min. See Presqu'île de GUERANDE.*

Consult the **Index** *to find an individual town or sight.*

Château de BEAUMANOIR★

Michelin map 59 fold 12 or 20 fold 22

An avenue of beech trees leads for 1.5km - 1 mile to the main courtyard of the **château** ⓥ.
This residence was built in the 15C by Olive de Beaumanoir and modified in the 19C, using the most innovative technology and principles of hygiene of the age (running water, electricity, central heating). The château, outbuildings and park constitute a complete estate in the Victorian style – rare in France – as conceived by wealthy families, addicted to progress, at the end of the last century in Great Britain.
The rooms, open to the public, reconstitute the daily atmosphere of family life by means of 18 and 19C furniture and a collection of modern art.
Every year, the works of well-known contemporary artists are displayed and add extra interest to the visit.
The **outbuildings** bear a remarkable witness to the evolution of attitudes concerning the organisation of work in the late 19C and early 20C. Note in particular the **stables**, constructed of iron, glass, wood and bricks in an architectural style reflecting the taste of the time for combining these materials.
Beaumont was the setting for the films *Tess* (1979 by Roman Polanski) and *Je suis le Seigneur du château*, the French adaptation of Susan Hill's novel *I'm the King of the Castle* (1987 by Régis Wargnier).

Abbaye de BEAUPORT*

Michelin map 59 fold 2 or 20 fold 8

Beauport Abbey ⓥ, founded in the 13C by the Premonstratensians, was seen as an important spiritual and economic centre for the St-Brieuc diocese. Of the 13 and 14C church only the façade, open-air nave, north aisle and north arm of the transept remain. the long chapterhouse with its polygonal apse, lying to the east of the cloisters, is an excellent example of the Anglo-Norman Gothic style, in the pure Mont-St-Michel tradition.

In the northwest corner of the cloisters, to the right of the three fine depresed arches, which stood above the lavabo, is the elegant entrance to the large refectory which looks out over the sea. Pass into the lower court overlooked by the Duc building, a huge hostelry for receiving the pilgrims, and the cellar underneath the refectory, whose groined vaulting rests on eight massive granite columns.

The tour ends with the almonership, the room in which the monks collected the tax on salt and cereals, and the visitor's hostel, with its two naves, where you can see an unusual box bed open on two sides.

The "*Conservatoire du Littoral*", a national body in charge of preserving France's coastal heritage, has acquired the abbey estate and implemented a programme aimed at protecting the premises and organising guided tours for visitors.

The ***Practical Information*** *section at the end of the guide lists:*
– information on travel, motoring, accommodation, recreation,
– local or national organisations providing additional information,
– calendar of events,
– admission times and charges for the sights described in the guide.

BÉCHEREL

Population 599

Michelin map 59 fold 16 or 20 fold 25

Seigneurial lands from 1123 to 1790, Bécherel, perched on a hill (alt 176m - 577ft), was once a stronghold; only a few ruins still stand.

The streets, lined with old granite houses, with names such as Chanvrerie (*chanvre*- means hemp), Filanderie (*filandre* means fibre), etc. evoke former times when flax was cultivated and the purest linen thread was produced in the area.

From Thabor Gardens the view extends as far as Dol, Dinan and Combourg.

There is a book market on the first Sunday of the month.

Château de Caradeuc ⓥ – *1km - half a mile west.* This château, the former home of a famous attorney-general, Louis-René, Marquis de Caradeuc de la Chalotais (1701-85; *qv*), has a very fine **park*** dotted with statues and other monuments inspired by history and mythology. It has been nicknamed the "Breton Versailles" and is considered to be the largest park in Brittany. From the terrace north of the château there is an immense view towards Dinan and the Upper Valley of the Rance.

EXCURSIONS

Barrage de Rophémel – *Round tour of 40km - 25 miles – about 2 hours. Leave Bécherel on the road which passes in front of Château de Caradeuc. After 4km - 2.5 miles turn right.*

St-Pern – The head office of the Congregation of the Little Sisters of the Poor *(qv)* is established in the old château of the Tour St-Joseph.

After Plouasne the road continues to the lovely site of Néal Lake (Étang de Néal).

Guenroc – Its name comes from the white rocks which overlook it.

Barrage de Rophémel – Take the path to the small lookout point from where there is a view of the reservoir. This dam is part of the Rance tidal power scheme *(qv)*.

Go to St-Juvat via Tréfumel and the D 12.

St-Juvat – This pretty little village is made all the more attractive by its many flowers. Note, among other things, the 16 and 17C buildings, with chimneys carved out of *jauge*, a marine sediment dating from the tertiary era.

Retrace your steps along the D 12, then turn left into the D 39 towards Le Quiou.

Château de Hac ⓥ – This large manor-house, a 14C seigneurial residence, has survived without any major alterations. It once graced the assets of the Richemont, Hingant, Tournemine and Rieux families. It is built from Falun limestone (ancient marine deposits) in a style which exudes elegance and good taste.

The large rooms open to visitors house Gothic and Renaissance furniture; in particular an interesting collection of chests, for the most part Breton.

Return to Bécherel via Le Quiou or the D 26, right onto the D 2, then the D 68.

BEG-MEIL

Michelin map 58 fold 15 or 0 fold 32

Beg-Meil (meaning the Point of the Mill) is located at the mouth of Baie de La Forêt and opposite Concarneau. This resort has beaches both on its bay and oceanside. On the bay side there are small rocky wooded coves: Oiseaux Beach and La Cale Beach. On the ocean side there are dunes: the well-equipped Sémaphore Beach, while from the vast Dunes Beach (or Grande Plage), the Glénan archipelago is visible in the distance. From **Pointe de Beg-Meil** (Beg-Meil Point), there is a fine view of Concarneau and Baie de La Forêt.

Boat trips ⓥ – *During the season there is a regular service to Concarneau* (qv) *across the bay, St-Nicolas Island* (qv) *and Quimper* (qv) *via the Odet. (Description of trip in opposite direction under QUIMPER: Excursion* 3).

BELLE-ÎLE★★

Population 4 489

Michelin map 63 folds 11 and 12 or 230 folds 48 and 49

Access: see the current Michelin Red Guide France

This, the largest of the Breton islands, is a schist plateau measuring about 84sqkm - 32sq miles; 17km long and 5 to 10km wide – 11 miles by 3 to 6 miles. The mean altitude is 40m - 128ft (highest point: 63m - 200ft). It is crossed by numerous valleys, which cut deeply into the high rocks and finish up as beaches or harbours. The east side of the island, which is well protected, has many creeks with good bathing.

There is a marked contrast between the middle of the plateau, exposed to wind, sun and rain and covered with wheatfields alternating with patches of gorse, and the small sheltered valleys, with their lush fields, where whitewashed houses are clustered together.

Fouquet, Marquis of Belle-Ile – Belle-Ile belonged to the Abbey of Ste-Croix in Quimperlé *(qv)* and the Gondi family before it was bought in 1650 by the Superintendent Fouquet.

The latter, wishing to make the island a safe retreat in case of misfortune, completed the fortifications – he added 200 cannons. His immense wealth even enabled him to keep his own fleet, of which the flagship was the *Grand Écureuil* (Great Squirrel – the Fouquet coat of arms includes a squirrel with the motto: "Just how high shall I climb?"). This daring behaviour, added to the swindles and slights which he practised on Louis XIV, was his undoing. The final act was played out at Nantes, where the Court was visiting in 1661. D'Artagnan and the Musketeers seized Fouquet as he came out of the castle and put him in a coach which made all speed for Vincennes. He died in 1680.

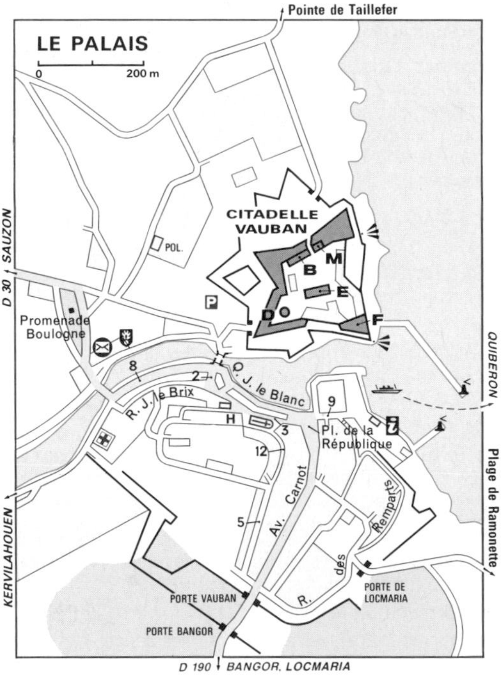

Citadelle (R. de la)	2	Gambetta (Quai)	8
Église (R. de l')	3	Simon (R. J.)	9
Ferry (Av. Jules)	5	Verdun (R. de)	12

B	Casemate	**F**	Bastion du Dauphin
D	Poudrière circulaire	**M**	Musée historique
E	Arsenal		

A fortified rock – As an outlying citadel of the French coast, Belle-Ile has been attacked many times by British and Dutch fleets. The British captured the island twice – in 1572 and 1761 – and occupied it until the *Treaty of Paris* (1763) returned it to the French.

The island has conserved its defensive system: in addition to Le Palais citadel, fortified by the military architect Vauban, there are several 18 and 19C isolated outworks (redoubts) around the coast.

Acadians and Bretons – In 1766, 78 Acadian families came to live on the island; they brought with them the potato many years before Parmentier introduced it to

France. These Acadians were descendants of the French who had lived in Canada since the beginning of the 17C and had refused to submit to the English who had held Nova Scotia from the time of the *Treaty of Utrecht*, 1713. The Acadian families were moved to New England and then, after the *Treaty of Paris*, to France and Belle-Ile.

A refuge for artists – Since the late 19C, numerous artists have been attracted by the beauty and calm of this isle: Claude Monet, Sarah Bernhardt and the composer Albert Roussel.

Barnacle picking – In December and January, visitors to the island will be astonished to see the extraordinary method by which the Breton fishermen gather the pedunculate barnacle *(pollicipes)*. As this barnacle lives at the bottom of the cliff, the fishermen are equipped as mountain climbers; they lower themselves down the sheer rock face and hack the barnacles off with hammer and chisel, constantly aware of the danger of a wave washing them away.
This crustacean, reserved exclusively for export, is sent mostly to Spain, where it is a delicacy; it is called *percebes* in Spanish, and is served with drinks.

LE PALAIS *time: 2 hours*

The island's main town (Population 2 435) is where most of the facilities are to be found. Boat services link it to Quiberon on the mainland. Arriving by boat or from the Rue des Remparts there is a good view of the port, with its fishing and pleasure craft, overlooked by the citadel.

★**Citadelle Vauban** ⓥ – *Cross the mobile footbridge over the lock, go through Bourg gate and follow the path along the* **huge moat**, *cut from the rock itself, as far as Donjon gate. A signposted tour takes visitors past all the sights of the citadel.*
Built in 1549 on the orders of Henri II, the citadel was enlarged by the Dukes Gondi de Retz and by Fouquet. Its double ramparts, powerful corner bastions and outward appearance show the influence of Vauban, who resided here in 1683, 1687 and 1689. Besieged at the end of the Seven Years' War, it fell into the hands of the English, who occupied it until the signing of the Treaty of Paris (1763). The citadel was also used as a prison for the twelve accomplices of the notorious woman poisoner Voisin and for the son of the Haitian politician Placide Toussaint-Louverture. It was subsequently abandoned by the army and sold in 1960.
The most remarkable buildings include: the **historical museum** (**M**), set up in the Louis-Philippe blockhouses featuring "maple leaf" vaulting and displaying a host of documents on the history of Belle-Ile and its illustrious visitors (Arletty, Claude Monet, Sarah Bernhardt); the **round powder magazine** (**D**) and its strange acoustics; the large **arsenal** (**E**) with superb oak timbering; the Lous XIII **storerooms**; the **blockhouse** (**B**) which contains the map room; finally the military prison and the cells.
The belvederes overlooking the sea and the **Bastion du Dauphin** (**F**) afford remarkable **views**★ of Le Palais, the north coast and its harbour, the île de Houat and the île d'Hœdic.

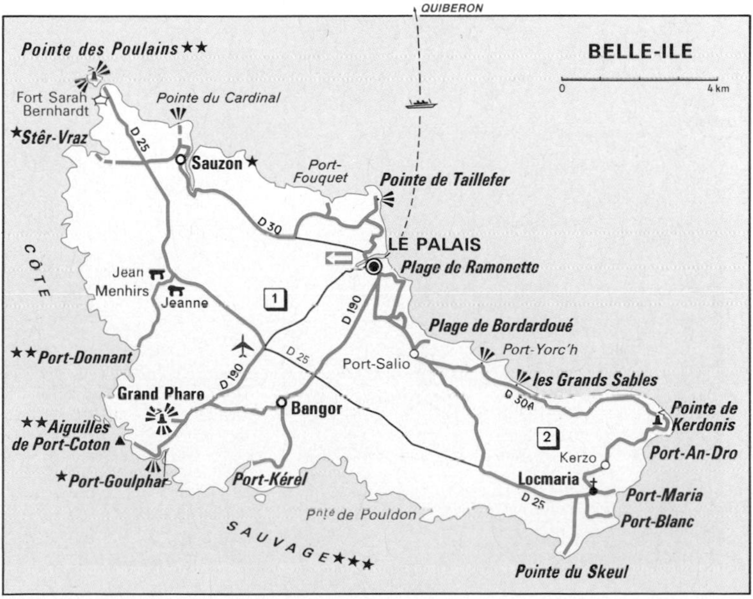

TOUR

★★★ 1 Côte sauvage *Round tour of 49km - 30 miles – about 3 hours 30 min – local map previous page.*

Leave Le Palais on Quai Gambetta and Promenade Boulogne and turn right towards the citadel. Near the coast, bear left and then right.

Pointe de Taillefer – Near the signal station there is a fine **view** over Le Palais roadstead, the Pointe de Kerdonis, Hœdic and Houat Islands and the Presqu'île de Quiberon.

Turn round and make for Sauzon.

Nearby is **Port-Fouquet**, a pretty, rocky creek.

★ **Sauzon** – This small port with its busy marina lies in a pretty **setting**★ on the east bank of the River Sauzon's estuary. A pleasant excursion *(1 hour 30 min on foot Rtn)* starting from the port, takes you round the **Pointe du Cardinal** and affords views over the approach to the port, the Pointe de Taillefer, the Presqu'île de Quiberon and the Pointe des Poulains.

★★ **Pointe des Poulains** – *30 min on foot Rtn.* From the car park, on the left overlooking a creek, is Fort Sarah Bernhardt, which is near the estate where the actress spent her summers. Make your way down the slip to the sandy isthmus which connects the island with the Pointe des Poulains on which stands a lighthouse and which is completely cut off at spring tide. From the point there is a **panorama**★ from left to right of the Pointe du Vieux-Château, the great rocks of the Côte Sauvage, the Île Groix, the peninsula and bay of Quiberon, Presque'île de Rhuys, the islands of Houat and Hœdic, Pointe de Taillefer and the Dog's Rock (Rocher du Chien).

★ **Stêr-Vraz and Stêr-Ouen** – These *abers* cutting deeply into the coastline are at the foot of the **birdlife reserve** on the Pointe du Vieux-Château.
On Kerlédan Moor, on either side of the road to Port-Donnant, stand the **menhirs Jean and Jeanne**, one of schist and the other of granite, said to be young fiancés punished because they wanted to meet before their wedding-day.

★★ **Port-Donnant** – *30 min on foot Rtn; car park.* The setting is superb: a fine sandy beach and a rolling sea enclosed between high cliffs. Bathing is dangerous.

Grand Phare ⏱ – The lighthouse opened near Goulphar in 1835 is 46m - 150ft high and has a beam which carries 44.5km - 26 miles. From the balcony there is a fine **view**★★ of Belle-Ile, the islands and the coast round Lorient and as far as the Presqu'île de Rhuys.

★ **Port-Goulphar** – Facilities. This is one of the most charming sites on the island. After Goulphar manor-house take a steep road downhill *(15 min on foot Rtn)* to the port, a long, narrow channel where the clear waters reveal richly-coloured algae, at the foot of picturesque cliffs. A group of islets marks its entrance. The best **view**★ of this curious mass of rocks can be enjoyed from the cliff facing the Grand Large Hotel.

Paterson/CAMPAGNE CAMPAGNE

Aiguilles de Port-Coton

★**Aiguilles de Port-Coton** – Port-Coton is called so because the sea there seems to boil and builds up a great mass of foam like cotton wool. At the end of the road loom the Needles *(photograph previous page)*. Follow the cliff edge to the right for a good view over Port-Coton Bay.

Bangor – This village takes its name from the religious settlement or *bangor* founded by the first Celtic monks who settled on the island.

Port-Kérel – This sheltered beach, in a rocky setting, is the most popular on the island.

Return to Le Palais by Bangor and Vauban Gates.

★2 Pointe de Kerdonis *Round tour of 33km - 20 miles – about 2 hours*

Leave Le Palais by Avenue Carnot and Rue Villaumez on the left.

Plage de Ramonette – Backing onto the point, this is Le Palais's beach.

At the entrance to Port-Salio, turn left.

Plage de Bordardoué – Go through the door in the former fortifications to discover a fine sheltered, sandy beach.

Turn round and bear left twice.

The road descends towards **Port-Yorck** with the Pointe du Bugul to the right and the Pointe du Gros Rocher to the left, which is extended by an islet on which stands an old fort. The road from Port-Yorck to the Pointe de Kerdonis commands superb **views**★★ over Houat and Hœdic and the neighbouring islands, the Morbihan coast and Le Palais roadstead.

Les Grands Sables – This, the largest beach on Belle-Ile, has traces of fortifications erected in 1747, as in the 17 and 18C British and Dutch forces made several attempts to land on the island.

Pointe de Kerdonis – At the southern tip of the island stands a lighthouse which commands the sea lane between Hœdic and Belle-Île.

Port-Andro – A sandy beach off a small valley where the English forces landed in 1761.

Locmaria – The village is reputed among the islanders as a place where sorcery occurs. In the shaded square stands the church of Notre-Dame-de-Boistord (1714) to commemorate, according to legend, a splendid elm cut down by the Dutch to replace a broken mast. The trunk cracked as it fell, terrifying the crew.

Port-Maria – A downhill road to the right of the church leads to this deep cleft in the rocks which offers a fine sandy beach at low tide.

Turn left on leaving Locmaria.

Port-Blanc – Facilities. Small cove overlooked by the cliffs of Arzic Point.

Pointe de l'Échelle – *Unsurfaced road after Skeul hamlet.* A semicircle of jagged rocks in a wild setting.

Turn back, bear left and after 2km - 1 mile, make a right turn to return to Le Palais by the Bangor and Vauban Gates.

BELLE-ISLE-EN-TERRE

Population 1 067

Michelin map 58 folds 7 and 8 or 20 south of fold 7

This old township stands in a picturesque area at the confluence of two rivers, the Léguer and the Guic.

Chapelle de Locmaria – *1km - half a mile north towards Trégrom and an uphill road to the right.*
The chapel, which stands in the cemetery, contains a fine 16C **rood screen** adorned with coloured wooden statues of the Apostles on one side.

EXCURSIONS

★**Menez-Bré** – *9km - 5.5 miles northeast. Take the D 116, the Guingamp road. 2.5km - 1.5 miles after Louargat, turn left into the steep uphill road (maximum gradient 18%.*
The Menez-Bré, a lonely hill with an altitude of 302m - 991ft, rises out of the Trégorrois Plateau to a height of 150m - 492ft. The chapelle of St-Hervé at the summit commands a wide **panorama**★: to the north where the plateau slopes gently towards the sea, cut by the deep valleys of the Trieux, of the Jaudy, the Guindy and

M. Cambazard/EXPLORER

Loc-Envel – Hanging keystones in the church

the Léguer; to the south over the maze of hills and valleys of Cornouaille; and to the southwest towards the Monts d'Arrée.

Loc-Envel – *4km - 2.5 miles south. Leave on the Callac road, the D 33, and turn right fairly soon into a winding and picturesque road.*
The Flamboyant Gothic style **church** of Loc-Envel rises from the top of a mound and dominates the village. To the left of the belfry-porch, note three small semi-circular openings through which the lepers followed the services. Particularly striking features, on entering, are the Flamboyant **rood screen★** and the rich decoration of the wood-panelled **vaulting★**: carved purlins and tie-beams, polychrome hammerbeams with the Evangelists and the two hanging keystones. Note as well a Christ in benediction above the high altar and a Holy Trinity with angels at the transept crossing. The 16C furnishings are in keeping with the statuary and carvings: the screens near the font, the ancient statues, the main window in the chancel and the later 17C altarpiece at the high altar.

Gurunhuel – *9km - 5.5 miles southeast on the D 22.*
Near the 16C church stands a Calvary of the same period. From the base rise three columns: the central one bears a Crucifixion with Christ between the Virgin Mary and St John on one side and a Virgin of Pity on the other. The other two crosses show the robbers; their souls are depicted in the form of little figures leaving their bodies and being received by an angel in the case of the good robber, and a demon in the case of the bad robber. Standing on the base are a Roman soldier, St Peter, St Michael and St Paul.

BÉNODET

Population 2 436
Michelin map 58 fold 15 or 230 fold 32
Local map under QUIMPER: Excursion – Facilities

This charming seaside resort lies in a pretty, verdant setting at the mouth of the Odet estuary.
Bénodet has a fine beach (facing south), a small harbour often used by yachts *(port de plaisance)* and also a casino.

Daily boat service for pedestrians and cyclists to Ste-Marine on the opposite bank of the Odet.

View over the Odet (E) – *Access by Avenue de Kercréven.* This viewpoint affords a fine view of the river, the pleasure boat harbour between wooded shores and the Pont de Cornouaille.

Pointe St-Gilles – *Take Corniche de la Plage, then follow the shore along Corniche de la Mer to Lichaven Dune.*

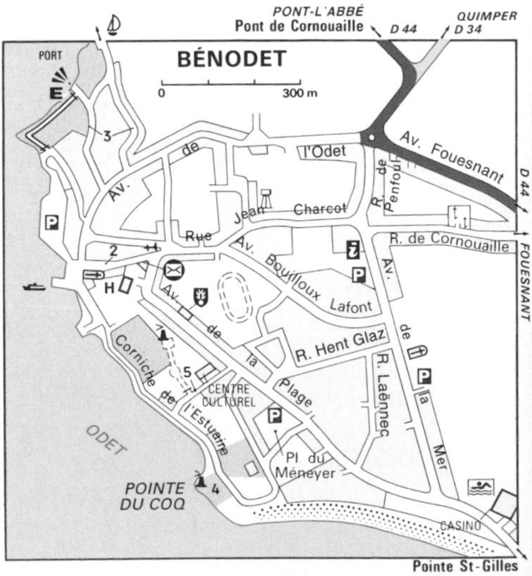

Église (R. de l')	2	Marteville (Square)	4
Kercréven (Av.de)	3	Phare (R. du)	5

E Point de vue sur l'Odet

C. Chevallier

Low-tide at Ste-Marine

Viewing table. The view extends to the left as far as Mousterlin Point and to the right as far as Loctudy.

Pont de Cornouaille – *1km - half a mile northwest on the D 44.*
This elegant modern bridge carries the D 44 across the Odet. The total length is 610m - 2 001ft and it rises to a height of 30m - 98ft above the water. There is a good **view★** of the port Ste-Marine, the estuary and the Odet, up-river.

EXCURSIONS

Botforn-en-Combrit – *4km - 2.5 miles west by the D 44, the road to Pont-l'Abbé.*
The **Musée de la musique mécanique** ⏲ contains musical instruments of exceptional quality (all in working order) dating from the late 19C to the mid-20C; they were played in cafés, fairs or on the street.
Accompanied by nostalgic melodies, the visitor discovers the pedal-operated player piano (1880), an early juke box, dance organ and so on.

From Bénodet to Concarneau on the coast road – *40km - 25 miles – about 3 hours.*
Leave Bénodet east by the D 44 towards Fouesnant and after 2km - 1 mile turn right.

Le Letty – A small hamlet by the Mer Blanche, a large lake sheltered by a dune and linked to the ocean by a narrow channel. Sailing school.

Return to the road to Fouesnant.

Le Perguet – Note on the right of the Chapelle of Ste-Brigitte, built in the 12C and remodelled in the 16C, an unusual stone staircase on the roof leading to the pierced bell tower crowning the transept crossing. There is a ceramic workshop *(atelier de céramiques)* 50m from the chapel.

After 2.5km - 1 mile, a fork to the right goes to the Pointe de Mousterlin.

Pointe de Mousterlin – From the end of the point, there is an extensive view of the coast from the Pointe de Lesconil to the Pointe de Trévignon, with in the distance the île aux Moutons and the îles de Glénan. The Eckmühl Lighthouse can be seen on the right after dark.

Turn round. After 2km - 1 mile bear right and 4.5km - 2.75 miles further on turn right.

⛱ **Beg-Meil** – *See BEG-MEIL.*

Turn back and after 3km - 2 miles bear right.

⛱ **Cap-Coz** – This small resort is built on a sandy spit, between the cliffs of Beg-Meil and the channel to Port-la-Forêt. The view extends on one side over La Forêt Bay, Beg-Meil and Concarneau and on the other side over Port-la-Forêt and La Forêt-Fouesnant. A pleasant excursion can be enjoyed by taking the **coastal path** *(1 hour on foot Rtn – access through a door after the pine grove at the far end of the great wall along the road leading to the beach).* This path runs along La Forêt Bay as far as La Roche-Percée, overlooking or crossing small coves and affording fine views of the coastline from Kerleven to the Pointe de Trévignon.

Fouesnant – *See FOUESNANT.*
The road runs along Kerleven Beach at the bottom of La Forêt Bay, then after a steep descent (15% – 1 in 7), along St-Laurent Cove and crosses Saint-Jean Bay to Concarneau *(qv)*. Beautiful **sites★** especially at high tide.

BOAT TRIPS

★★ **Up the Odet River** ⏲ – *Time: 1 hour 30 min; departure from Bénodet. Description of the trip down the Odet under QUIMPER: Excursions* 3.

Loctudy – *Crossing time: 30 min. See LOCTUDY.*

Îles de Glénan – *Crossing time: 1 hour 30 min. See Iles de GLENAN.*

BERVEN

Michelin map 58 fold 5 or 20 fold 4

The triumphal arch through which you enter the parish close *(qv)* is a fine specimen of Renaissance art with its three semicircular arches and its pilasters with capitals.

★ **Church** ⏲ – The 16C church has a façade surmounted by a square tower crowned with a dome with small lanterns and ornamented by balustrades; it was the first of its kind in Brittany (1573) and served as a model for many others.
A wooden rood screen stands before the very fine chancel **enclosure★**, ornamented on the front with small fluted granite columns and at the sides with wooden ones. In the chancel are 17C stalls with arm-rests in the form of winged caryatids. In the chapel to the left of the chancel is a 16C niche with shutters whose panels depict, in low relief, scenes from the life of the Virgin; in the centre is a statue showing the Virgin on a crescent moon. There is another niche at the far end of the nave, on the left, and on the shutters are illustrated six episodes in the life of Christ: His childhood on the left and the Passion on the right.

Ferme-musée du Léon ⏲ – *200m - 220yds after leaving Berven on the D 788 towards Lesneven, take the little road towards Quéran.* The buildings of an old family farmhouse, in which the original furniture has been kept on display, house this small museum of agricultural tools and equipment and horsedrawn carts, which evokes the evolution over the course of a century of country life in Léon.

BINIC

Population 2 798
Michelin map 59 fold 3 or 20 fold 8

Binic is a delightful resort whose port, in the past, sheltered fishing schooners in winter. It is now used by pleasure craft and a few coastal fishing boats.

Museum ⏲ – This little museum of "Brittany in days gone by", in a completely restored setting, evokes daily life in Binic a century ago with a display of head-dresses, Breton costumes and various objects related to marine life and deep-sea fishing. The visit is completed by several reconstructed scenes (classroom, forge, carpenter's workshop).

Jetée Penthièvre – The pier, closing off the outer harbour, is reached by Quais Jean-Bart and Surcouf. From a belvedere on the jetty there is a pleasant view of the beach with its raised huts dominated by a pine-topped knoll and the port.

EXCURSION

Round tour of 18km - 11 miles – *Time: about 2 hours 30 min. In Binic take the road towards Paimpol, and immediately turn left to Lantic. After 3km - 2 miles bear left in the direction of Trégomeur and 5km - 3 miles further on, right into an uphill road.*

Jardin zoologique de Bretagne ⏲ – At **Trégomeur**. The zoo consists of an undulating park of 12ha - 30 acres which contains animals such as lions, tigers, lynxes, African and Asian antelopes and kangaroos roaming in vast enclosures. Islands recreate a natural habitat for chimpanzees. Madagascar lemurs and numerous birds complete the collection. Several of these animals are part of a European breeding and conservation programme directed towards species in danger of extinction. A small train takes people for rides round the zoo in afternoons during the tourist season.

Go round the zoo and at the first junction turn right, follow the road which runs down into a verdant valley, bear left once and then keep turning right to reach the Chapelle Notre-Dame-de-la-Cour.

Chapelle Notre-Dame-de-la-Cour ⓥ – At **Lantic**. The chapel is a fine 15C building with stone vaulting. A beautiful **stained glass window**★ (15C) at the back of the high altar illustrates the life of the Virgin in eighteen panels; in the south transept, the window depicting St Nicholas is also 15C. The chancel contains the 17C tomb of Guillaume de Rosmadec in Kersanton granite as well as 14 and 16C statues. A 17C Calvary stands in the small square. *Pardon on* 15 August.

Return to Binic via Prido and the Ic Valley.

BLAIN

Population 7 434

Michelin map 6 fold 16 or 20 fold 54

An old Roman crossroads, Blain plays an important commercial role between Nantes, Redon and the Anjou.
The Nantes-Brest Canal separates the town from its castle (whose first construction dates from 1104).

Musée des Arts et Traditions populaires ⓥ – This museum devoted to folk art, located in the old presidial of the Dukes of Rohan, revives the past of the Blain area. On the second floor, around a village square, various shops have been reconstructed: the grocer's, the tobacconist's, the butcher's and the baker's, under the vigilant eye of the local policeman. The mezzanine houses the reconstructions of the chemist's, the clog-maker's and a hairdresser's.
On the first floor, two rooms are devoted to popular Christmas traditions. One displays thousands of bean kings (lucky trinkets hidden in Twelfth Night cakes), the other about a hundred Nativity cribs from all over the world. Last but not least, the museum has a room full of items unearthed during the excavation of Gallo-Roman sites in the Blain area.

Château de la Groulais ⓥ – This fortress, which originally belonged to Olivier de Clisson, became Rohan family property from 1407 to 1802. Despite the fact that in 1628 Richelieu razed the ramparts, impressive **ruins** still stand. The 14C **Drawbridge Tower** (Tour du Pont-Levis) with its pepperpot roof, overlooks the now dry moats. Beyond the outbuildings stand the 15C **King's Apartments** (Logis du Roi). The main façade with its tall pinnacled dormer windows, gargoyles and brick-patterned chimney stacks, reveals all the charm of the Renaissance. The rather severe looking **High Constable's Tower** (Tour du Connétable, 1386) is to the right.

★FORÊT DU GÂVRE

Round tour of 13km - 8 miles northwest on the D 15, the road to Guéméné-Penfao.

The road crosses the stands of oak interspersed with beeches and pines, which cover 4 400ha – 10 900 acres, to reach the Belle Étoile crossroads, the meeting point of ten converging avenues.

Turn right towards Le Gâvre and at La Maillardais turn left.

Chapelle de la Magdeleine – Formerly part of a leper hospital, this modest 12C chapel with a timber roof in its chancel has a charming 15C polychrome Virgin.

Return to La Maillardais and continue straight on to Le Gâvre.

Le Gâvre – The 13-15C church (restored) has a strange 17C lateral bell tower. Inside there is a timber barrel vault. The stained glass windows (1930) evoke the First World War.

Maison Benoist ⓥ is a 17C home with a corner turret. The ground floor exhibit is concerned with the Forêt du Gâvre: its flora, forestry, fauna (stuffed animals). The first floor displays Mme Benoist's interior as it was when she gave her home to the locality: local furnishings, headdresses, 18C porcelain Virgins.
In the attic, with its fine chestnut timbered ceiling, old trades are evoked: coopering, pit-sawing, knife sharpening, etc.
Not far from the school *(école)*, the **wooden shoe maker's home** shows the life of the shoe maker who lived and worked in his workshop.
Return to Blain.

To plan a special itinerary :
– consult the Map of touring programmes *which indicates the recommended routes, the tourist regions, the principal towns and main sights.*
– read the descriptions in the **Sights** *section which include Excursions from the main tourist centres.*
Michelin map no 230 indicates scenic routes, interesting sights, viewpoints, rivers, forests...

Château de la BOURBANSAIS*

Michelin map 59 fold 16 or 20 fold 25 – 14km - 9 miles southeast of Dinan

This impressive late 16C building, enlarged in the 18C, stands in an immense park. Three generations of the Huart family, counsellors to the Breton parliament, have contributed to the embellishment of the French-style garden.

Parc zoologique et jardin ⓥ – Situated in a lovely verdant setting (3ha - 7 acres), the zoo contains more than 500 animal species from the five continents: deer, wild animals, monkeys, birds, etc.
After the zoo go to the château. The main building is flanked by pinnacled turrets and saddleback-roofed pavilions characteristic of the 18C. One of the façades looks onto the garden. There are 18C urns perched on small columns in the middle of the lawn.

Château interior ⓥ – On the ground floor the rooms are decorated and furnished in the 18C style and contain 17C Aubusson tapestries and a fine collection of porcelain from the Dutch India Company. In the peristyle, added in the 19C, there is a display of documents, archives and personal objects belonging to the past owners, evoking the château's history. The kennels house a large hunting pack (over 80 hounds).

Île de BRÉHAT**

Population 461
Michelin map 59 fold 2 or 20 fold 8
Access: see the current Michelin Red Guide France

Bréhat is a much-frequented holiday resort. Its pink rocks stand out against the sea. Cars are not allowed; however tractors are used for transportation.

GEOGRAPHICAL AND HISTORICAL NOTES

A mild climate – Bréhat, which is about 3.5km - 2 miles long and 1.5km - 1 mile wide, consists of two islands joined in the 18C by a bridge built by Vauban. The coast, very broken and indented, is surrounded by 86 islets and reefs. Thanks to its mild climate (winter average 6°C - 43°F), mimosa, eucalyptus and fig trees grow out in the open and the façades are bedecked with geraniums. There is little rain, the clouds generally passing over the flat island to condense over the mainland. The island's interior is a labyrinth of paths lined with honeysuckle or flower-bedecked dry stone walls, low houses with masses of hydrangea bushes, villas with vast gardens, a couple of cows in a tiny field or sheep on the heath. Its southern part is more welcoming than the rugged north. This colourful island has attracted such personalities as Prosper Mérimée, Ernest Renan and Louis Pasteur.

A varied history – Bréhat owes its name (Breiz Coat: Brittany of the Woods) to an Irish monk, St Budoc, who landed on Lavrec Island in 470AD. A medieval fortress facing this island was destroyed by the English in 1409 and local people were hanged on the sails on Crec'h ar Pot mill (moulin) on North Island. La Corderie Bay, on the west coast, was used as anchorage. According to local tradition, it was a sea captain from Morlaix, Coatanlem, living in Lisbon, who revealed the existence of the New World to Christopher Columbus in 1484 – eight years before its official discovery – and showed him the course taken by the island's fishermen already familiar with Newfoundland waters. During the Wars of Religion, in 1591, Crec'h Tarek mill on South Island served as a place of execution. In 1598, Henri IV ordered the castle to be razed. In the 19C the island was frequented by privateers and during the last war, it was occupied by German troops until 4 August 1944.

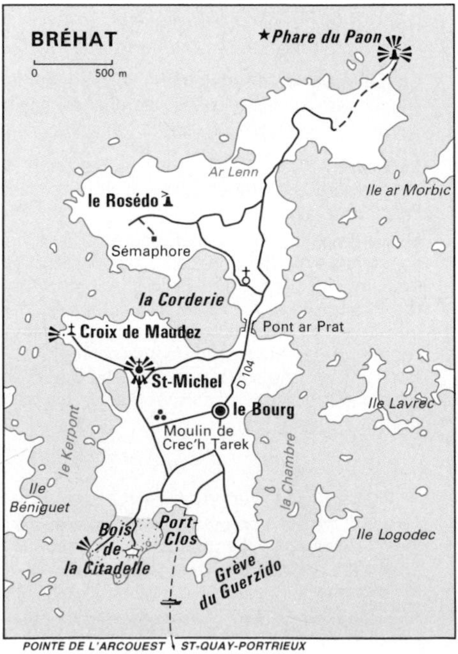

TOUR ⏱ *allow half a day*

The island is criss-crossed by paths with arrows at ground level showing the way.

Le Bourg – The houses of the island's capital are grouped around a small square lined with plane trees.
In the 12 and 18C church, which has an unusual bell tower, the high altar and the font grille are 17C and the lectern is 18C.

Bois de la Citadelle – Planted with conifers, the woods overlook the cliff. From the life-boat shelter below, there is a good **view**★ of Kerpont Channel, which is impressive at low tide when the mass of rocks is visible, and of the île Béniguet.

La Corderie – Bounded by Ar Prat Bridge (Pont Vauban) this vast bay between the two islands is the main harbour. Beautiful villas.

Grève du Guerzido – Petit and Grand Guerzido are beaches of pink shingle.

Croix de Maudez – Erected in 1788 amid the heather and facing the ocean, the cross evokes the memory of a monk named Maudez who founded a monastery in 570AD, on a neighbouring island. There is a fine **view**★ of the islands of Béniguet to the left and Maudez to the right and the reefs.

★**Phare du Paon** – *On the tip of North Island.* The paved platform at the foot of the lighthouse affords a remarkable **view** of the rugged coastline, the chasm, the pink rocks and the shingles. This is the wildest part of the island.

Port-Clos – This is a landing point for the boat service.

Phare du Rosédo – Dating from 1862, it stands inland.

Chapelle St-Michel – High on a mound (26m - 85ft; *39 steps*), this chapel serves as a landmark for ships.
There is an extensive **view**★ over the île Sud the Kerpont channel and the île Béniguet, Birlot Pool overlooked by the ruins of a once tide-operated mill *(see Usine marémotrice de la RANCE)*, La Corderie Bay and the île Nord and, in the distance, Talbert Spit (Sillon de Talbert).

BOAT TRIPS ⏱

★★**Tour of the island** – *Time: about 1 hour.* The tour allows the visitor to admire the changing aspects of the coast: the beauty of the northern rocks and cliffs, the Mediterranean charm of the eastern shore and the ever-changing colour of the sea, which is often a deep blue.

★**Estuaire de Trieux** ⏱ – This pleasant excursion along the Trieux Estuary, whose banks are in turn sheer, rocky and wooded and at times low-lying and under cultivation, offers views of the pretty site of Lézardrieux with its suspension bridge. The river flows at the foot of Château de la Roche-Jagu *(qv)*, which can be reached by a fairly steep path through woodlands.

Celtic Exodus from the British Isles

Celtic monks and hermits who played a part in evangelising Brittany in the 5-7C include:
St Budoc, who is thought to have been born in a cask in which his mother had been cast into the sea off Brest and which eventually landed both of them safe and sound in Ireland, from where the saint returned to Bréhat Island; St Goustan, a Cornish hermit who lived for a while on Hœdic Island, where there is now a church named after him; St Harvey (Hervé to the French), a wandering minstrel hermit (thought to be the son of a bard) who became Abbot of Plouvier before settling in Lanhourneau, and who is widely revered throughout Brittany; St Hernin, who gave his name to the place where he settled; St Mewan (St Méen to the French), who followed St Samson from Wales to Brittany, where he evangelised the Brocéliande region and founded the abbey of St-Méen-le-Grand; St Quay, who gave his name to St-Quay-Portrieux; St-Ronan, who gave his name to Locronan; St Winwaloe (Guénolé to the French), who founded the great monastery at Landévennec in the Cornouaille region.

BREST★

Conurbation: 201 480

Michelin map 58 fold 4 or 20 fold 17 – Local map under ABERS

Plan of conurbation in Michelin Red Guide France

After the full-scale destruction of the town during the Second World War, the centre of Brest was rebuilt on a geometrical (grid) layout. The main artery linking the naval base to the enormous Place de la Liberté is the wide **Rue de Siam**, once a tiny street. Running at right angles to this artery are roads leading to the River Penfeld or the Cours Dajot, from which there are good views of the magnificent roadstead, which, nowhere less than 10m - 33ft deep, is almost an inland sea in itself.

For several years now, Brest has ranked as Brittany's second university town. The Arts Centre and Congress Hall (Palais des Arts et Congrès, or Quartz) are witness to this cultural expansion. On the shore of Ste-Anne-du-Portzic *(qv)*, the Centre Océanographique de Bretagne and the Océanopolis offer opportunities for scientific research.

Pambour/CAMPAGNE CAMPAGNE

Poop of the schooner *La Recouvrance*

HISTORICAL NOTES

The English set foot in Brest (14C) – During the War of Succession which began in 1341, Montfort, ally of the English, was rash enough to let them guard the town. When he became Duke of Brittany, he tried in vain to drive out the intruders. The King of France had just as little success in his turn. At last, in 1397, Charles VI persuaded the King of England, Richard II, who had married Charles's eldest daughter, Isabella, to restore Brest to the Duke.

The "Belle Cordelière" – On 10 August 1513, St Laurence's Day, the English fleet of Henry VIII set out to attack Brest. The Breton fleet hurriedly set sail to meet it; however, under its panic-stricken commander it fled back to the Brest channel. The *Belle Cordelière*, the gift of Anne of Brittany to her Duchy and on which 300 guests were dancing when the order came to weigh anchor, covered the commander's retreat and bore the brunt of the attack. Fire broke out on board the *Cordelière* as she was fighting gun to gun with an English ship. The commander, Hervé de Portzmoguer, or as he was known in France, Primauguet, knowing that his ship was lost, exhorted his crew and his guests to die bravely with the words: "We will now celebrate the Feast of St Laurence who died by fire!" The two ships blew up together.

The work of Colbert (17C) – Colbert, the greatest Minister the French Navy ever had, completed the task begun by Richelieu, making Brest the maritime capital of the kingdom. To obtain good crews he set up the *Inscription Maritime* (marine record and administrative office), which still exists today. After completing their military service, fishermen between the ages of eighteen and forty-eight are placed on the French Naval reserve; the *Inscription Maritime* looks after them and their families throughout their lives.

Colbert also founded at Brest a school of gunnery, a college of marine guards, a school of hydrography and a school for marine engineers. From this enormous effort a magnificent fleet developed. Ships reached a tonnage of 5 000 and carried up to 120 cannons; their prows and sterns were carved by such artists as Coysevox.

Duquesne improved the naval dockyard, built ramparts round the town and organised the defence of the channel (Le Goulet). Vauban, the military architect, completed the projects. Tourville improved mooring facilities in the roadstead laying down buoys to which ships could moor instead of dropping anchor.

The "Belle Poule" – In 1778, during the American War of Independence, the frigate *La Belle Poule* encountered the British *Arethusa* and forced her to retreat. This victory was very popular at court and all the ladies wore a new hairstyle *La Belle Poule*, which included, perched on their tresses, a model ship in full sail.

The "Surveillante" – In 1779 a British captain, George Farmer, wagered that no French frigate could destroy his *Québec*. Du Couëdic, who commanded the frigate *Surveillante*, challenged the wager – a furious sea duel ensued.

After a spirited battle, north of Ushant, both ships were dismasted. The sails of the *Québec* fell across its guns, setting the ship on fire. Du Couëdic ordered rescue action. Later the *Québec* blew up with the wounded Farmer. Du Couëdic also died from his wounds. The *Surveillante* was brought back to Brest in triumph, and Du Couëdic was laid to rest in the Church of St Louis (destroyed in 1944).

Brest during the war In June 1940, when the impending arrival of the German forces was announced, the French naval and commercial authorities hastily cleared the port, destroying the installations and putting several bridges and buildings and four submarines undergoing repair work out of operation. Nonetheless, the port was immediately put to use by the German navy, which built a concrete shelter for submarines at **Laninon**. The port thus occupied a highly advantageous strategic position and represented a considerable threat to Allied forces sailing between the USA and Great Britain. As a consequence, the town was heavily bombarded for four years. When the Americans finally managed to enter the town in September 1944, after a siege of 43 days, they were greeted by nothing but ruins.

NAVAL TOWN *time: half a day*

Cours Dajot (**EZ**) – This fine promenade was laid out on the ramparts in 1769 by convicts from the naval prison.

** **View of the roadstead** – From the viewing table at the east end of the promenade, you see the Brest roadstead from the mouth of the Élorn, and past the Ménez-Hom and the Pointe de Roscanvel right over to Pointe de Portzic. The anchorage

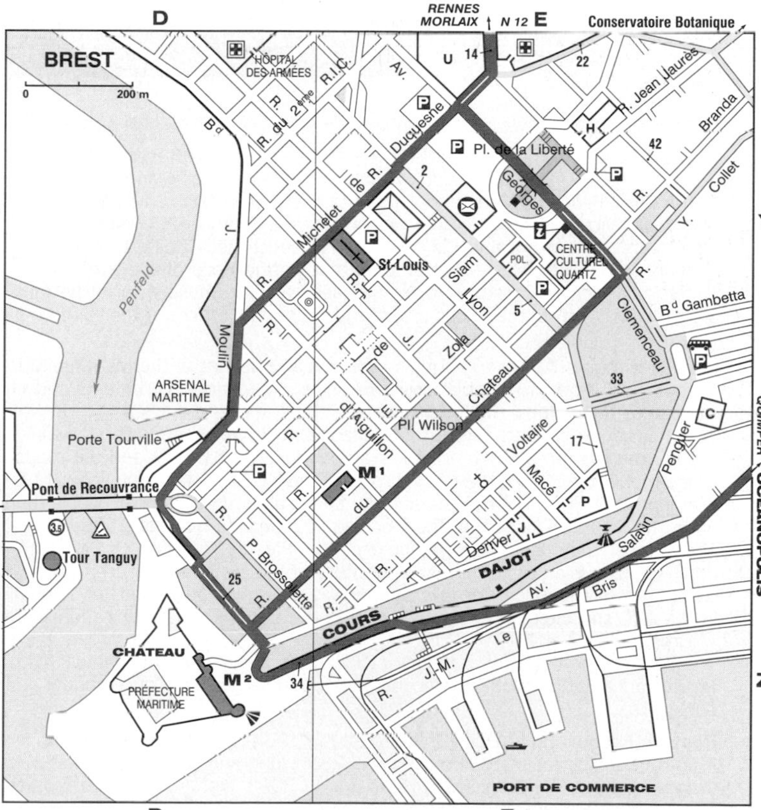

Clemenceau (Av. G.) EY
Jaurès (R. Jean) EY
Liberté (Pl. de la) EY
Lyon (R. de) DEY
Siam (R. de) EY

Algésiras (R.) EY 2
Colbert (R.) EY 5
Foch (Av. Mar.) EY 14
Frégate-la-Belle-Poule (R.) EZ 17
Kérabécam (R. de) EY 22
Marine (Bd de la) DZ 25
Reveillère (R. Amiral) EY 33
Roosevelt (Av. F.) DZ 34
11-Martyrs (R. des) EY 42

M¹ Musée des Beaux-Arts
M² Musée de la Marine

is vast (150km² - 58sq miles) and deep (12-20 m - 6-10 fathoms – over large areas), framed between heights and connected with many big estuaries. It communicates with the Atlantic through a channel with steep banks, 5km - 3 miles long and about 1 800m - 1 mile wide. This configuration explains why Brest has had such great military importance for more than 2 000 years.

To the left the Élorn estuary, spanned by Albert-Louppe Bridge (Pont Albert-Louppe), makes a safe anchorage for yachts. In the foreground is the commercial port. Beyond lies the île de Plougastel, hiding the southeast of the roadstead. On the south side of the roadstead, at Lanvéoc, is the Naval School; nearby the nuclear submarine base is situated on the Île Longue. On the horizon to the right you see the Presqu'île de Crozon and the opening of the channel between Portzic Fort and the Pointe des Espagnols. In front of the castle, the inner harbour, protected by its breakwater, serves as anchorage for the fleet.

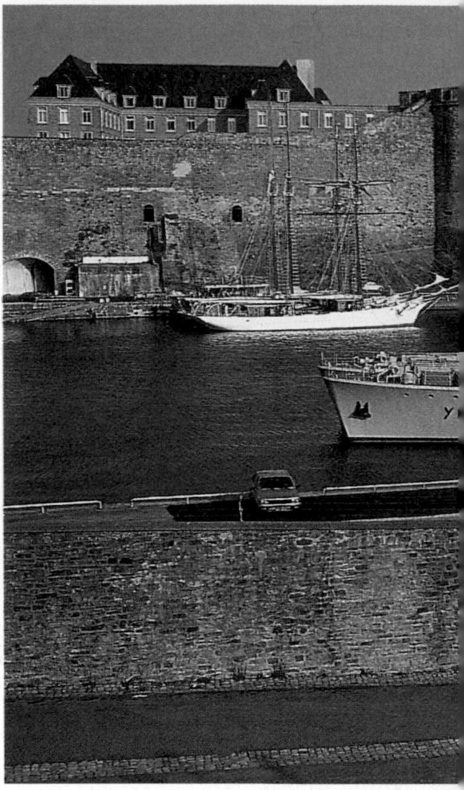
Brest – Training ships with the castle of Brest in the background

The building overlooking the roadstead between Brest and Ste-Anne-du-Portzic houses the naval base and school.

Castle (Château) (DZ) – The castle is the sole reminder of Brest's history.
It was in the 11C that Brest's stronghold first put in an appearance at the mouth of the River Penfeld on a site which had already been fortified by the Romans. It was to fall victim to innumerable sieges over the centuries. Towers and fortifications were built from the 12C to the 17C. Richelieu, Colbert, Duquesne and Vauban, from 1683, were to strengthen the fortifications of the site.
The curtain wall was restored after the last war. The museum and the ramparts are all that is open to the public; the castle houses the offices of the Harbour Police (Préfecture Maritime).

★ **Musée de la Marine (DZ M²)** ⓥ – This museum is an offshoot of the Maritime Museum in Paris and displays valuable **models** of ships, navigation instruments and charts illustrating the feats of the navy of sailing ships during the 18C.
The museum is entered through the Madeleine Tower (Tour Madeleine – 3C to 15C), from the top of which there is a good view of the port and the roadstead. At the foot of the terrace there is a display of the 5 622 pocket submarine, 11.87m - 39ft long by 1.68m - 5.5ft wide, and the taking aboard of the boat-people rounded up in the South China Sea by the teaching ship *Jeanne d'Arc* in 1988.
The tour continues along the watchpath of the Paradis Tower (Tour Paradis) (15C) in which there is an exhibition on the history of the castle. In the keep (14 to 17C) there are models of the *Cordelière*, a display of the various stages of shipbuilding in the 18C and interesting exhibits of ship decorations. There is a representation of Brest prison.
The Azénor Tower (Tour Azénor) (13C) gives a view of the Penfeld with the Recouvrance Bridge (Pont de Recouvrance), Tanguy Tower (Tour Tanguy) and the dockyard.

Pont de Recouvrance (DZ) – Inaugurated in 1954, this drawbridge is the largest in Europe. The steel span, about 87 m - 285ft long and weighing some 530 tons, swings between four concrete pylons 64m - 209ft high. The bridge crosses the Penfeld River just above the oldest section of the dockyard. Operated by a system of pulleys, the drawbridge can be fully raised within 150 seconds. Under the bridge you can see a 380mm cannon which came from the *Richelieu*, a 35 000-tonne battleship. Further upstream, the **Pont de l'Harteloire** (634m - 2 080ft long) spans the dockyard at a height of 40m - 128ft; note the series of storerooms, workshops, lifting appliances, slipways and dry docks.

G. Thouvenin/EXPLORER

★**Brest Naval Base (Base Navale) and Dockyard (Arsenal)** – It was in 1631 that **Cardinal Richelieu** decided to turn the city of Brest into a harbour. In 1666, **Colbert** developed the infrastructure that already existed along the banks of the Penfeld: the meandering, enclosed estuary of this river was a perfect site, able to protect the boats from heavy storms. From 1740 to 1790, **Choquet de Lindu** undertook to build a huge dockyard and, as early as 1742, the first three dry docks of Pontaniou were built. In the late 19C a pier was erected, defining the boundaries of a vast roadstead; in 1970 two jetties able to accommodate large-tonnage vessels (aircraft-carriers, cruisers, frigates) were added onto the pier. Docks no 8 (for careening only) and no 9 (construction work) were built in 1918 and extended in 1953. Their huge size (300m - 985ft long by 49m - 160ft wide) enables them to receive the largest ships belonging to the French fleet, over 250m - 820ft long and weighing more than 35 000 tonnes. At the same time, two other quays were built: Quai de l'Armement (555m - 1 821ft long), designed to equip and repair ships, and Quai des Flotilles (752m - 2 468ft long), which brings together most of the war vessels that make up the Atlantic fleet.
During the German Occupation in the Second World War, an underwater naval base was set up in Brest within 500 days. Its purpose was to protect the German submarines stationed in the Atlantic Ocean. As soon as the base became operational, it could accommodate up to 30 submarines. With a total area of 65 859m^2- 79 030 yd^2 covered by a 4m - 13ft thick slab, it was practically invulnerable; during the bombing of August 5, 1944, the impacts made by ten 6-tonne bombs caused only minor damage. This base is still in service today.

Visite de l'Arsenal (Tour of the Dockyard) ⏲ *(Access by Porte de la Grande Rivière west of the plan by Pont de Recouvrance – Open to French nationals only)* – A tour of the naval base will provide a good introduction to the French Atlantic fleet: the frigates and despatch boats *(avisos)* of the Groupe d'Action Sous-Marine, the mine sweepers, the helicopter-carrier *Jeanne d'Arc* and the aircraft-carrier *Charles-de-Gaulle*, with its huge steel hull moored along Quai de l'Armement (scheduled to be operational by July 1999). Visitors may also be shown round a warship, depending on the number of boats available.

Port de Commerce (**EZ**) – *As seen from the Cours Dajot.*
This was established in 1860, once the Penfeld became inadequate for accommodating both military and commercial shipping, for the use of the Brest Chamber of Commerce and Industry.

Traditional traffic is closely linked with the agricultural activities of west Brittany, and amounts to almost two million tonnes a year.
The commercial port imports oilseed and other products destined for livestock, as well as hydrocarbons and fertilisers; it exports mainly frozen poultry (for which it ranks as the world's number one port), potatoes and oils.
The port is also an important centre for naval repair work and encompasses three types of dry dock. The most recent of these, built in 1980, has the capacity to accommodate the largest commercial ships yet made (tonnage of over 500 000 tonnes). These installations, which include wet repair docks and a gas extraction station, make Brest the foremost French naval repair complex.

TOWN CENTRE *time: 2 hours*

★**Musée des Beaux-Arts** (**EZ M**[1]) ⏲ – The room on the first floor contains 17 and 18C paintings from the Italian (Crespi: *Martyrdom of St Sebastian*; Dolci: *St Philip Benizi*; Giordano; Canaletto), French (Bourdon; Van Loo; J-B Regnault) and Dutch Schools (Schlacken: *Mary Magdalene at Prayer*). Note the painting of Brest Port (1774) by L. van Blarenberghe.
On the ground floor, to the left, there is a display of ships by local artists (Gilbert; Noël: *Sailing Ships in Brest Roadstead*), works by Orientalists such as Guillaumet, Fromentin and Leroy (*Portrait of a Young Guide*), as well as *Two Parrots* by Manet. Perhaps the most interesting section for the visitor is the large collection of canvases by artists of the Symbolist movement (pastels by Lévy-Dhurmer, Henri le Sidaner and R. Ménard) and more particularly the Pont-Aven School. Note *By the Sea in Brittany* by Emile Bernard, *Green Corn at Pouldu* and *The Water-Carriers* by Paul Sérusier and *Day in September* by Maurice Denis.
The visit ends in a small room containing sculptures and drawings by Anne Quinquaud, which reflect a strong African influence.

Église St-Louis (**EY**) – This large modern church (1957) is in keeping with the vast Place St-Louis, which it overlooks. The impression of height is increased by the vertical lines of the adjoining bell tower.
The interior, which is very plain, emphasises the vertical theme. There are stained-glass windows by Léon Zack and Paul Boni (St-Louis), a *Crucifixion* by Kaeppelin and a modern tapestry by Olin.

Tour Tanguy (**DZ**) ⏲ – The tower stands opposite the castle, on the far bank of the Penfeld, overlooking the dockyard. This 14C construction, once the Quilbignon stronghold, houses the **Musée du vieux Brest**. Dioramas by Brest painter Jim-E-Sévellec depict the most significant periods of history in Brest: pre-Revolution *(first floor)*; from the Revolution to the present *(second floor)*.

★★OCÉANOPOLIS ⏲ *time: 2 hours*

The enormous crab-shaped complex of Océanopolis is located east of the commercial port *(port de commerce)* alongside the Moulin Blanc marina *(port de plaisance)*. This scientific and technical centre on marine life provides a window on all the activities linked with oceanology. Océanopolis also aims to be a "living place" where researchers, professional people, industrialists and the general public can be brought into contact with each other. In view of the tremendous variety of subject matter linked with the sea, Océanopolis is constantly improving and updating its exhibitions.

The visit begins on level 1.

Level 1 (Niveau 1) – This is mainly given over to temporary exhibitions on oceanographic research. Permanent features include a satellite image receiver enabling visitors to admire the view of earth seen from space. One room is entirely given over to a display on the "Brest roadstead". The bridge of a ship has been reconstructed and equipped with remote controls above an indoor pool with various model boats floating in it, giving visitors a chance to familiarise themselves with navigation and the problems associated with safety at sea.
Behind the ship's bridge, a door leads out to the outdoor section of the seals' pool. Inside once more, there is a model of a cliff with birds representing the main species to be found nesting on the Breton coast. A question-and-answer computer game in which visitors pretend to be a particular species of bird evaluates the reliability of their own nesting instincts!

Level 0 (Niveau 0) – Several giant aquariums illustrate the variety of submarine life along the Breton coastline. All the tanks are interesting and well-presented; some particularly memorable ones are described below:

Aquarium 16 – This simulates life on the continental shelf, the submerged, almost flat part of the continents, covered in sand and continental mud. This is the home of the pollack, the grey gurnard and the snub-nosed gurnard.

Aquarium 17 – The large mudflat that hugs the south coast of Brittany is between 50 and 100m - 164 and 328ft deep and maintains a relatively constant temperature of 10 to 12°C – 50 to 53.6°F. This is the ideal environment for large shellfish like the lobster.

Aquarium 22 – Here, the submerged section of a cliff is alive with the dainty wrass, small spotted dogfish, brill and dab.

Aquarium 19 – The Molène-Ouessant archipelago, a protected area which is part of the Parc naturel régional d'Armorique, houses colonies of grey seals. Sild and Ida, the seals which live in this aquarium, are sea calves which can be found in this area from time to time. They were born in captivity in Denmark in 1988.

Aquarium 21 – The Ocean Column, 3m - 10ft high, enables tiny fish to form shoals, thanks to a system of constant rotation of the water in the column. The water level is controlled with a suction pump activated by an ultra sonic monitor.

Aquarium 24 – The bed of zostera, elongated plants which make up a sort of submarine meadowland, reconstitutes this fragile coastline environment, which is particularly susceptible to pollution. Closer examination reveals the presence of the seahorse, the only fish in the world which swims in an upright position.
A model of a whale (rorqual) with some dolphins forms an eye-catching centrepiece to level 0.
Océanopolis is also a scientific research centre focusing on the study of marine mammals which live off the coasts of France, and a rescue centre for seals stranded on the shore. A reference library enables vistors to either consult or borrow (under certain conditions) books, magazines and videotapes on the subject of the sea. The Auditorium screens films produced by Océanopolis.
A souvenir shop offers a large selection of books on the subject of the sea.
The marina can be reached via the restaurant (not connected with Océanopolis).

★**Conservatoire botanique national de Brest** ⓥ *(east of the town by Rue Jean-Jaurès, then by the road to Quimper)* – This site was always a popular place for picnics and weekend strolls among the residents of Brest. However, over the years, the setting deteriorated to such an extent that the idea of a botanical park aimed to preserve "endangered plant species" saw the light of day. Today, the Vallon du Stang-Alar houses one of the most prestigious botanical gardens in the world. As well as a beautiful public garden boasting a wide variety of both common and rare exotic ornamental plants, the greenhouses and other conservatories contain many species threatened with extinction. The role of this park is not only to preserve endangered varieties, but also to study them and to try to revive them in their natural environment. Thus attempts have been made to resuscitate the *Hibiscus fragilis*, the *Lobelia parva*, the *Narcissus triandrus ssp capax*, which almost disappeared from the îles de Glénan a few years ago, or the *Limonium dendroides*, of which only four specimens remained in the wild. Playing areas for children and sports activities will delight nature lovers of all ages.

BOAT TRIPS ⓥ

★★**Île d'Ouessant** – *See Île d'OUESSANT.*

★**On the roadstead** – The tour includes a visit of the naval port, the commercial port and the fortified channel (Goulet de Brest). *Time: 1 1/2 hours.*

★**Across the roadstead** – The crossing links Brest to Le Fret on the Crozon Peninsula. *Time: 3/4 hour.*

EXCURSIONS

★**Presqu'île de Plougastel** – *Round tour of 56km - 35 miles – about half a day. Leave Brest by ⑤ on the town plan.*
You pass on the left the road leading to **Kerhuon**, a resort nicely situated on the west bank of the Élorn.

Pont Albert-Louppe – Inaugurated by President Gaston Doumergue in 1930, this bridge crosses the Élorn estuary. It is 880m - 2 887ft long and has three 186 m - 610ft spans. Four statues by the sculptor Quillivic stand at each end: a man and a woman from the Léon region on the Brest shore and a man and a woman from Plougastel on the opposite shore.
The bridge rises over 42m - 137ft high above the river and offers a very fine **view**★ over Élorn Valley and the Brest roadstead.

1km - half a mile after the bridge bear right towards Plougastel-Daoulas.

Plougastel-Daoulas – *See PLOUGASTEL-DAOULAS.*

★**Presqu'île de Plougastel** – *See PLOUGASTEL-DAOULAS for details of the rest of the drive.*

Fort Montbarey – Mémorial du Finistère ⓥ – *Leave Brest to the west over the Pont de Recouvrance towards Le Conquet; the fort is on the right as soon as you join the D 789.*

This fort was built in 1784 on the orders of Louis XVI. It bears the name of one of the king's ministers (1732-96). Several years ago it was converted into a major memorial site for Finistère. An organisation, AME, undertakes the maintenance of a list, by *commune*, of all the natives of Finistère who "died during and because of the war" between 3 September 1939 and 19 December 1946 (the date when the volunteers returned from fighting Japan). Visitors can see photographs, literature, objects and military equipment recalling the siege of Brest in 1944. Several vaulted rooms have been reconstructed as the various garrisons of the fort (butcher's, baker's, chemist's etc.).

★**Abers** – *Round tour of 197km - 122 miles – allow 1 day. See ABERS.*

Coastal tour to Le Conquet – *Round tour of 61km - 38 miles – about 2 hours 30 min. Leave Brest west by Pont de Recouvrance* (**DZ**) *and turn left into Rue St-Exupéry to reach Route de la Corniche.* This road overlooks the naval dockyard.

At 4-Pompes drive straight on; turn left at the entrance to Cosquer.

Ste-Anne-du-Portzic – It is located along the beach in Ste-Anne Bay; walk a short distance along the coastal path to enjoy fine views.
An uphill road leads to the **Centre Océanographique de Bretagne** at the Pointe du Diable on the sound (Goulet de Brest). The centre is the headquarters, on terra firma, of IFREMER (French Institute of Research for the Exploitation of the Sea). Since 1968 a campus has been built to accommodate the centre, with a port, fish farm and marine research facilities.

Take the D 789.

The road runs parallel to Trez-Hir beach, giving a good view of Bertheaume bay, then goes through Plougonvelin.

Fort de Bertheaume ⓥ – A pleasant walk along a coastal foot path leads to one of Vauban's fortified creations, at the entrance to the Brest Channel.

Carry on along the D 85.

Before you reach the Pointe de St-Mathieu, note on the right, near a house, two Gallic steles *(stèles)* topped by a cross, which are known as the Monk's Gallows.

★★**Pointe de St-Mathieu** – *See Pointe de ST-MATHIEU.*
From the Pointe de St-Mathieu to the Pointe des Renards, the *corniche* road runs along Porsliogan shore and affords a view of Ushant archipelago with Le Four Channel and Béniguet Island to the fore.

Pointe des Renards – This headland, to the left of Le Conquet Beach, offers lovely views of the Pointe de St-Mathieu, the île d'Ouessant and Molène.

Return to Le Conquet by Corniche du Port and the Pointe de Ste-Barbe (view of the port and the Pointe de Kermorvan).

Le Conquet – *See ABERS: Round Tour.*

Return to Brest by the direct road, the D 789, and by ⑥ on the town plan.

BRIGNOGAN-PLAGES

Population 836

Michelin map 58 folds 4 and 5 or 20 folds 3 and 4 – Local map under ABERS – Facilities

A seaside resort lying at the end of Pontusval Bay and possessing a magnificent sandy beach. On either side of Brignogan rock piles, sometimes curiously shaped, divide small beaches.

Pointe de Pontusval – This walk crosses a countryside dotted with blocks of granite. The Men Marz, at mid-distance, is a fine example of a menhir, 8m - 25ft high, surmounted by a Cross.

Chapelle Pol – The 19C chapel, Calvary and small watch tower, built on two rocks, are worth seeing.

EXCURSION

Goulven – *7.5km - 5 miles southeast. Take the road to Lividic Beach, then the coast road along Goulven Bay. At Plounéour-Trez, turn left just after the church.*
This little village has a restored 15-16C **church**. The **belfry**★, which dates from the Renaissance, is one of the finest in Brittany. To the right of the porch, which opens under the bell tower, is a fine Gothic doorway with twin doors and a carved stoup on the pier between them.
Inside the church are a monumental Renaissance stoup, a high altar in Kersanton granite and an altar decorated with six carved and painted panels illustrating St Goulven's miracles. The 16C organ loft has been built on to a former rood screen. Two fine 17C embroidered banners are displayed in the chancel in summer.

BULAT-PESTIVIEN

Population 446

Michelin map 59 folds 1 and 11 or 20 fold 21 – 17km - 11 miles southwest of Bourbriac

Bulat-Pestivien is a former pilgrimage centre. A *pardon* takes place on the Sunday after 8 September.

★**Church**- This fine building was put up in the 15 and 16C. The Renaissance tower, had a spire added in the 19C. There are remarkable porches.
Inside is a monumental sacristy – adorned with a frieze of macabre design – with a loggia which projects into the church. There is a curious lectern representing a peasant in the local Vannes costume; and a table, 5m - 16ft long and dating back to 1583, decorated with geometric designs, on which were placed offerings made at *pardons*.
Bulat possesses three sacred fountains: the fountain to the Virgin (1718) in the cemetery and, on either side of the Callac road out of town, the fountain of the Seven Saints (1683) and the Cock fountain (16C).
There is a fine Calvary (1550) with a striking Entombment at **Pestivien** *(1km - half a mile north of Bulat)*. Unfortunately it has been defaced.

CAMARET-SUR-MER

Population 2 933

Michelin map 58 fold 3 or 20 folds 16 and 17 –
Local map under Presqu'île de CROZON – Facilities

An important spiny lobster port, Camaret is also a quiet, simple seaside resort.
On the shore, to the left of the *Sillon*, a natural dike which protects the port, is Corréjou Beach.

The landing of 1694 – The Presqu'île de Crozon, which forms an advanced bastion for Brest, has been attacked many times by the British, Spanish and Dutch. Vauban, the military architect, fortified it in 1689. Five years later, during the reign of William III, an Anglo-Dutch fleet tried to make a landing, but the fort and hidden batteries covering the port were very effective; several ships were put out of action, and the landing troops were decimated. A charge by dragoons scattered the attackers, and the coastguard militiamen, with their pitchforks and scythes, completed the rout.

Submarine experiment – It was in Camaret Bay in 1801 that the American engineer **Fulton**, who had settled in France in 1797, carried out an underwater experiment. He had built a small vessel which, with a crew of five, could be propelled under water with jointed oars at a speed of two knots. It could stay under water for six hours. This rudimentary submarine was intended to affix to the hull of an enemy ship a bomb or "torpedo" containing 100lb of powder, which was to be exploded by a time mechanism. A British frigate, at anchor in the bay, was to serve as the target. Fulton attacked but, unfortunately for him, the ship, though unaware of his approach, weighed anchor and sailed away. This failure spoilt the inventor's chances and he returned to America. It was not until the end of the 19C that this ingenious idea was realised.

SIGHTS

Chapelle Notre-Dame-de-Rocamadour – This chapel stands at the end of the dike. It was built between 1610 and 1683 and restored after a fire in 1910. It was originally a pilgrimage chapel on the pilgrims' route to Rocamadour in Quercy; from the 11C the pilgrims from the north, who came by sea, used to disembark at Camaret to continue the journey by land. A *pardon* is held on the first Sunday in September.

Château Vauban – A massive tower surrounded by walls was built by the military architect Vauban at the end of the 17C on Sillon Point. It now houses temporary exhibitions from time to time. There are fine views of the Brest Channel, Pointe des Espagnols and the port and town of Camaret.

EXCURSIONS

★★★**Pointe de Penhir** – *3.5km - 2 miles southwest by the D 8. See Pointe de PENHIR.*

★★**Pointe des Espagnols** – *Round tour of 36km - 23 miles north – about 30 min. Leave Camaret towards Crozon: turn left at the top of a hill after passing the last houses. The rest of the drive is described under Presqu'île de CROZON.*

BOAT TRIP ⓥ

Les Tas de Pois – *See Pointe de PENHIR.*

Travel with Michelin Maps (scale 1 : 200 000) which are revised regularly.

CANCALE★

Population 4 910

Michelin map 59 fold 6 or 230 fold 12 – Local map under CÔTE D'ÉMERAUDE – Facilities

The **setting**★ of this fishing port and seaside resort is picturesque. To get a good view take the tourist road (route touristique – *one-way*) which branches off the D 76 to the right 2.5km - 1.5 miles after the Portes Rouges crossroad. As you drive into Cancale the **views**★ of the resort and Mont-St-Michel Bay are splendid.

The town has derived its gastronomic reputation for centuries from the **oysters** which flourish in the beds in the bay *(parc à huîtres)* and which oyster lovers come to eat in the hotels and bars around the port. Sales reached their highest level in the First Empire with 48 million oysters in one season.

Now only young oysters brought from Auray are cultivated in the bay, for a mysterious disease around 1920 decimated the native spat. Since then spat has begun to flourish in the immense beds in the open sea, and an oyster with a particular flavour is developing due to the richness of the plankton of Mont-St-Michel Bay.

CANCALE

Leclerc (R. Gén.)	**YZ**	20
Port (R. du)	**Z**	
Bricourt (Pl.)	**Y**	3
Calvaire (Pl. du)	**Z**	4
Du Guesclin (R.)	**Y**	8
Duguay-Trouin (Quai)	**Z**	9
Duquesne (R.)	**Y**	10
Fenêtre (Jetée de la)	**Z**	12
Gallais (Rue)	**Y**	13
Gambetta (Quai)	**Z**	14
Hock (R. du)	**Z**	16
Jacques-Cartier (Quai)	**Z**	17
Juin (R. du Mar.)	**Z**	18
Kennedy (Quai)	**Z**	19
Mennais (R. de la)	**Y**	22
République (Pl.de la)	**Z**	23
Roulette (R. de la)	**Z**	24
Rimains (R. des)	**Y**	25
Stade (R. du)	**Y**	27
Surcouf (R.)	**Y**	28
Thomas (Quai)	**Z**	30

D Monument aux Morts
E Maison de Jeanne Jugan
M¹ Musée des Bois sculptés
M² Musée des Arts et Traditions populaires
M³ La Ferme Marine Musée de l'Huître

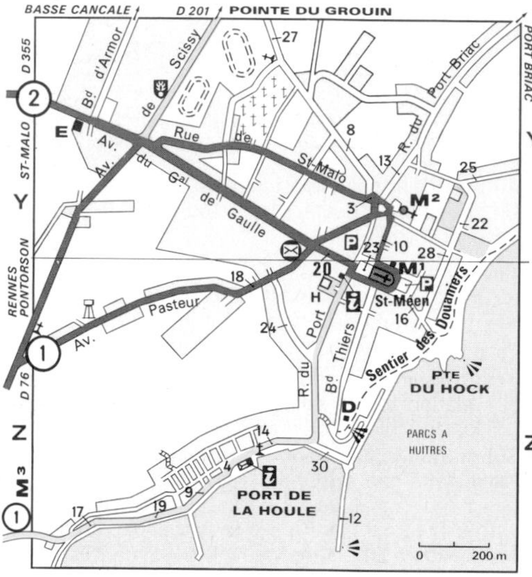

SIGHTS

★**Port de la Houle** (**Z**) – A bustling, animated area, the quays along the port teem with people unloading oysters, repairing nets, cleaning boats, or just waiting for the arrival of the fishing fleet at high tide.

Go to the Fenêtre jetty for a view of the bay and, at low tide, of the oyster beds. The port is surrounded by a picturesque district where sailors and fishermen lived. A street, the Vaubaudet or Val du Baudet, was the only link with the town of Cancale, the upper district, where the landsmen and traders lived.

★**Pointe du Hock and Sentier des Douaniers** (**Z**) – Sentier des Douaniers (Customs Officers Path), a watchpath, runs into Rue du Port (after some steps); it continues on 7km - 4 miles to the Pointe du Grouin From the Pointe du Hock you get a **view**★ over Cancale Rock (Rocher de Cancale), Mont-St-Michel Bay and the mount itself; below on the right, at the foot of the cliff, are the oyster beds. On either side of Pointe du Hock you may take Sentier des Douaniers and enjoy a walk overlooking the shore. If you follow the coastline as far as Port-Mer, you will get a splendid view of Pointe de la Chaîne opposite Cancale Rock.

Église St-Méen (**Z**) ⓥ – From the church tower's upper platform (189 steps), where there is a viewing table, you can enjoy a wide **panorama**★ of Mont-St-Michel Bay, Granville and some forty belfries. In clear weather you can see the îles Chausey.

Musée des Bois sculptés (**Z M¹**) ⓥ – An amazing collection of wood carvings by Abbot Quémerais (born in Cancale 1879, d1955) are exhibited here. More than 300 figures are sculpted in high relief on oak panels with such minute detail that each scene (*Ode to the Apple, Apotheosis of Sport*, etc) appears to be animated.

La Ferme Marine Musée de l'Huître (**Z M³** – *via* ①) ⓥ – This museum is located in St-Kerber, at the heart of an oyster-breeding farm, and has displays on the evolution of oyster-breeding techniques as well as the activities of oyster farmers across the centuries. A lovely collection of shellfish (more than 2 000 from all over

O. Franken/EXPLORER

Fines de Claire

the world), films and dioramas illustrate the way of life of this "gardener of the sea". There is a guided tour of the workshops, pools and shellfish tanks, as well as an explanation of tides, some of which here are the strongest in Europe.

Musée des Arts et Traditions populaires (**Y M**[2]) ⏱ – Housed in the old Eglise St-Méen (1714, now deconsecrated), the museum is devoted to the popular arts and traditions of the Cancale region (fishing, oyster breeding, farming, costumes, furnishings...) and to the life of Jeanne Jugan *(qv)*. There is also a presentation relating to the sailing school (École de Navigation des Rimains), which has been located in the town for over a hundred years.

Monument aux Morts (**Z D**) – This war memorial affords an extensive view of Mont-St-Michel Bay, Mont-Dol and the port and the oyster beds below.

Maison de Jeanne Jugan (**Y E**) ⏱ – The house is the birthplace of Jeanne Jugan *(qv)* (1792-1879), founder of the order known as the Little Sisters of the Poor.

EXCURSION

★★ **Pointe du Grouin** – *4.5km - 2.5 miles north by the D 201 – about 30 min – local map under CÔTE D'ÉMERAUDE. Leave Cancale by Rue du Stade* (**Y 27**)*, then turn right into the road which leads straight to the Pointe du Grouin. At the end of the road, after the Hôtel de la Pointe du Grouin, leave your car in a vast parking area and take a path, to the right of the signal station, which leads directly to the point.*
In a fine setting, this wild, rocky headland overlooks the sea from a height of 40m - 131ft and affords a **panorama** which stretches from Cap Fréhel to Granville and Mont-St-Michel Bay with, in the distance, the îles Chausey. At low tide one can take a path to a cave in the cliffside (height 10m - 32ft, depth 30m - 98ft).
The île des Landes, opposite, is an island with a bird sanctuary and nature reserve. Housed in the blockhouse is an exhibition on sea birds.

CARANTEC

Population 2 609

Michelin map 58 fold 6 or 230 fold 5 – Facilities

Carantec, which lies on a peninsula between the estuary of the Penzé and the Morlaix River, is a family seaside resort. There are several beaches suitable for bathing; the most important are Grève Blanche and Grève du Kélenn, the larger of the two.
A number of *pardons* are held at Carantec (*see the Calendar of Events at the end of the guide*).

SIGHTS

Church – The apse of this modern church contains a fine silver **processional cross**★ (1652) and a less ornate one in front of the altar.

Musée maritime ⏱ – The exhibits in this small maritime museum show the region's link with the sea (oyster breeding, privateering, Morlaix Bay's flora and fauna and seaweed collecting).

La Chaise du Curé – From this rocky platform, the **view★** extends from left to right over the Porspol and Blanche Beaches with St-Pol-de-Léon and Roscoff in the background, as far as the Pointe de Pen-al-Lann.

Pointe de Pen-al-Lann – *1.5km - 1 mile east, plus 15 min on foot Rtn. Take Rue de Pen-al-Lann and leave your car at a roundabout. Take the downhill path through pine trees to a rocky height.*
The **view★** extends along the coast from the Pointe de Bloscon crowned by the Chapelle Ste-Barbe, near Roscoff, to the Pointe de Primel; opposite you can see the castle on Taureau Island, which guarded the mouth of River Morlaix *(qv)*.

Île Callot – *From Grève Blanche port you can reach the island by car* (car park) *at mid-tide.*
The **Chapelle Notre-Dame** ⓥ on the island was founded in the 16C and rebuilt in the 17 and 19C. Inside is a 16C statue of the Virgin. *Pardon* on the Sunday after 15 August. The island is excellent for fishing.

CARHAIX-PLOUGUER

Population 8 198

Michelin map 58 fold 17 or 230 fold 20 – Local map under MONTAGNES NOIRES – Facilities

In the Roman era Carhaix was an important town commanding seven main roads; even today it is still the hub of a roadway network. In the centre of a cattle-rearing district, the town is a milk production centre.

La Tour d'Auvergne (1743-1800) – Carhaix's famous son is **Théophile-Malo Corret**, known as La Tour d'Auvergne. When still very young, he became keenly interested in the Breton language but he was a soldier at heart. During the Revolution his exploits were such that he, a junior captain at 46, was offered the most exalted rank; but he refused – he wanted to remain with his troops.
When there was a pause in his campaigns, he would bring his faithful Celtic grammar out. He finally retired and spent all his time studying his favourite subject.
When the son of his Celtic master was called up for the army, La Tour, moved by the old teacher's grief, took the young man's place and enlisted, at 54 years of age, as a private soldier in the 46th half-brigade. New exploits followed. Bonaparte offered La Tour a seat on the Legislative Council, but failed to overcome his modesty. He was awarded a sword of honour and the title of "First Grenadier of the Republic". He was killed in 1800, during the Rhine campaign. All the army mourned him.
Every year, on the Saturday preceding 27 June, Carhaix celebrates the name-day of La Tour d'Auvergne.

Église St-Trémeur – Rebuilt in the 19C, the church's porch opens onto the bell tower (16C); the tympanum over the doorway is adorned with the statue of St Trémeur, whose legend dates from the 6C.

Maison du Sénéchal – *No 6 Rue Brizeux.* This building has a 16C façade. The ground floor is of granite decorated with carvings and the corbelled upper storeys are faced with slate and adorned with statuettes. The tourist office *(syndicat d'initiative)* has its premises here (temporary exhibitions), and a small **Musée d'Ethnographie locale** (Museum of local Ethnography) ⓥ is open to the public on the first floor.

PLATEAU DU HUELGOAT

Round tour of 80km - 50 miles – Time: about 4 hours. Leave Carhaix by Rue Oberhausen and Rue des Abattoirs in the direction of Plounevézel. Turn right at Croissant Marie-Joffré. 3km - 2 miles further on, past the Lesquern hamlet on the left, take a bend on the right into an unsurfaced road.

Chapelle St-Gildas – The road leads through woodlands to the 16C chapel which has a square bell tower crowned by a stone spire and grotesques at the east end. The St-Gildas beacon (238m - 781ft) stands to the right.

Return to the main road and turn right.

After the junction for Carnoët, there is a view of the Monts d'Arrée.

Bear left towards Plourac'h.

Plourac'h – The Renaissance church in the form of a T was built largely in the 15 and 16C. The south face is the most ornate. The porch, which is Gothic in character, contains statues of the Apostles surmounted by canopies. A beautiful Renaissance doorway with windows on either side is crowned by three gables adorned with coats of arms. Near the font is an 18C altarpiece depicting the mysteries of the rosary and statues of St Adrian and St Margaret. Among the many statues ornamenting the church should be noted those of St Guénolé and St Nicodemus, dressed as a doctor of law, and a Descent from the Cross in which the Virgin wears a Breton cloak of mourning.

Continue towards Callac.

Fine views of this undulating countryside.

Callac – This town is dominated by the ruins of Botmel Church. In front of the stud farm stands a bronze statue of the stallion Naous, by Guyot. The town is also the home of the Breton spaniel, a pointer.

Take the road towards Guingamp and after 4km - 2.5 miles turn right.

Bulat-Pestivien – *See BULAT-PESTIVIEN.*

You arrive at Burthulet by the Rostrenen road.

Burthulet – The simple 16C chapel, with wall belfry, stands in melancholy surroundings; one does not question the legend that says: "The devil died of cold here".

M. Cambazard/EXPLORER

Plourac'h – Apostles on the south doorway

Make for Ty-Bourg and bear right.

St-Servais – The writer Anatole Le Braz *(qv)* was born here. 16C church.

Take the road opposite the church towards St-Nicodème. After 2km - 1 mile turn right.

★**Gorges du Corong** – *1 hour on foot Rtn. From the roundabout at the end of the road follow the path leading to the gorges.* The path runs along the river and into the Duault Forest. The river disappears beneath a mass of rocks to reappear as a series of cascades.

Turn round and bear right and right again in the direction of Locarn.

Locarn – Its **church** ⓥ contains 17C furnishings (altarpiece, pulpit, statues), a remarkable 16C stained-glass window, a carillon-wheel and the panels of a Flemish altarpiece, also of that period. Displayed in the presbytery is the **treasury**★. Note the following objects made of silver-gilt: St Henrin's bust and reliquary (in the form of an arm) both 15C, a processional cross (late 16C) and a 17C chalice.

Return to Carhaix-Plouguer via Trebrivan.

CARNAC★

Population 4 243

Michelin map 63 fold 12 or 230 folds 35 and 49 – Facilities

See the town plan in current Michelin Red Guide France

Carnac was already known as a prehistoric capital. The name of Carnac is often associated with megalithic monuments *(See Introduction: Breton Art).*

★★**Musée de Préhistoire J.-Miln – Z.-Le-Rouzic (M)** ⓥ – This Museum of Prehistory was founded in 1881 by the Scotsman James Miln (1819-81), who had excavated in Carnac and Kermario, and enriched by Zacharie Le Rouzic, native of Carnac.
In its new surroundings, these exceptional, beautifully displayed collections, cover prehistory from the Lower Palaeolithic (450 000BC) to the early Middle Ages.
The tour starts on the ground floor with an audiovisual presentation positioning the region's prehistory and archaeology in world prehistory; the stratigraphic column presents, via the different strata, the different civilizations.
Proceeding chronologically, the visitor is presented: Lower Palaeolithic (chipped stone, scrapers, points); Middle and Upper Palaeolithic (panels and documents); Mesolithic (primitive tools in wood or bone, shell ornaments, a reconstructed burial chamber); Neolithic Period, when man lived in settled communities and turned to

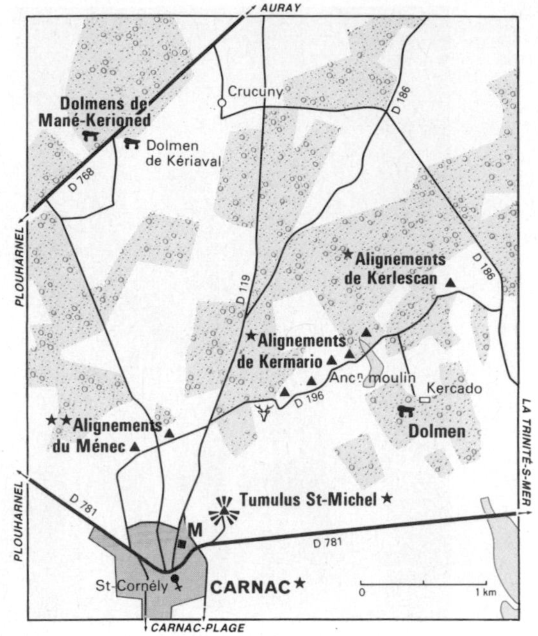

crop-growing and stock-raising, marked by the realisation of megalithic tombs: dolmens or collective burial tombs (placed with the dead were pottery, polished axes, jewellery); menhirs and alignments. Also exhibited here are necklaces made of variscite (a green semiprecious stone), fine polished axes in jadeite or fibrolite, beads and pendants, pottery, engraved stones, dolmens and objects related to daily life. The first floor covers the Bronze Age (socketed axes, gold jewellery), Iron Age (reconstructed burial tomb, salt oven, Celtic gold coins), to the Roman Era (model of a villa, statuettes of Venus, coins, objects related to daily life).

★**Church** – Pardon*: see the Calendar of events at the end of the guide.* This 17C church is dedicated to **St Cornely**, the patron saint of horned cattle; his statue stands on the façade between two oxen. A massive bell tower topped by an octagonal spire dominates the building. The porch on the north side is surmounted by a canopy in the form of a crown. Inside, the wooden vaults are covered with curious 18C **paintings** depicting the lives of the saint, Christ and St John the Baptist, and the Virgin. The communion table, pulpit and chancel screen are of the 18C and in wrought iron. In the chancel entrance, on the left, is a reliquary bust of St Cornely (18C gilt wood). The church's treasury is exhibited in the south aisle: chasuble, cross, chalices, monstrance, etc. The organ was built in 1775.

CARNAC-PLAGE

Carnac-Plage, with its gently shelving beach, has been developed in the shelter of the Presqu'île de Quiberon. View of the coast, Houat, Belle-Ile and the Presqu'île de Quiberon.

★★MEGALITHIC MONUMENTS (MÉGALITHES) *time: 2 hours 30 min.*

A tour of the numerous megalithic monuments (alignments, dolmens, tumuli) to the north of Carnac makes a fascinating excursion.
Since the footsteps of innumerable visitors pose a serious threat to the soil (which is essential for the study of the mysterious origins of the megaliths) the public authorities have had to take action to protect the Ménec, Kermario and Kerlascan Alignments. If plant life is allowed to grow again, this will prevent any further erosion of the soil, which will in turn prevent the foundations of the menhirs from becoming exposed. At Kermario, if conditions are favourable, a temporary footbridge enables visitors to observe the alignment in its entirety, while reflecting that it is an example of western Europe's first ever architecture.

★★**Alignements du Ménec** – The Ménec Alignments, over 1km - 0.8 mile long and 100m - 330ft wide, include 1 170 menhirs arranged in 11 rows. The tallest is 4m - 12ft high.
They begin with a semicircle of 70 menhirs partly surrounding the hamlet of Ménec.

★**Alignements de Kerlescan** – In this field (880 x 139m – 962 x 153yds), 540 menhirs are arranged in 13 rows and the whole is preceded by a semicircle of 39 menhirs.

★**Alignements de Kermario** ⌚ – 990 menhirs in 10 rows occupy an area similar to the Ménec Alignments.

★**Tumulus St-Michel** – The tumulus *(see illustration below)*, which is 120m long and 12m high - 395 x 38ft, is a mound of earth and stones covering two burial chambers and some twenty stone chests. Most of the artefacts found there are now in Carnac's Musée de Préhistoire and the Musée archéologique du Morbihan in

Alignements de Kerlescan

Vannes *(qv)*. On the top of the mound stands a chapel to St Michael, a small Calvary and the Touring Club de France viewing table; from here there is a **view*** of this megalithic region, the coast and the islands.

Dolmens de Mané-Kerioned – A group of three dolmens; the first has eight uprights with stylised engravings: axes, spirals, coats of arms, etc.

Tumulus de Kercado ⏱ – *Leave the car at the entrance to Kercado Castle.* This tumulus (3800BC) is 30m - 98ft across and 3.50m - 11ft high and covers a fine example of a dolmen. A menhir stands on the summit. Note the carvings on the table and four uprights.

EXCURSIONS

***Other Megaliths** – *8km - 5 miles northwest. Leave Carnac on the road to Lorient.*

Dolmens de Rondossec – *To the left on leaving Plouharnel.* Three underground chambers.

Menhirs du Vieux-Moulin – *After the level crossing.* These stand in a field to the right of the road.

Alignements de Ste-Barbe – *Near the road on the left in the direction of Kersily camp site.* Four menhirs on the edge of a field.

Dolmen de Crucuno – *Take a road to the right.* It rises against a farm in the centre of the hamlet of Crucuno. Only one chamber remains with the great table supported by eleven uprights.

Dolmen de Mané-Croch – *500m - 1/3 mile beyond Crucono, on the left.* A typical dolmen with side chambers.

Alignements de Kerzerho – *To the right of the road at the entrance to Erdeven.* 10 rows include 1 129 menhirs.

Abbaye St-Michel-de-Kergonan – *4km - 2.5 miles by the D 781 towards Plouharnel.* This Benedictine Abbey, founded in 1898, is part of the Abbaye St-Pierre in Solesmes *(see Michelin Green Guide to Chateaux of the Loire)*. An imposing granite building includes a plain church with wooden vaulting held up by granite pillars.

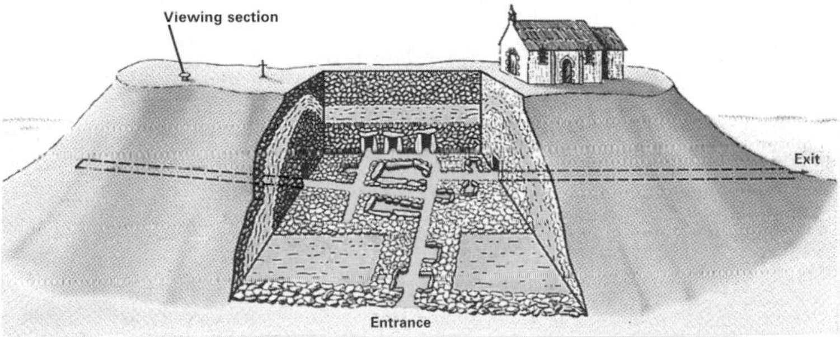

Tumulus St-Michel – Section of internal chambers and galleries

Beyond the abbey shop (books, produce and objects made by the nuns), a gallery houses an exhibit on the Benedictine Order: its origin, Cistercian Law, expansion, the height of its power with Cluny, etc. Gregorian chants.

Abbaye Ste-Anne-de-Kergonan – *5km - 3 miles. At Plouharnel, the road to Auray, the N 168, then the road to the right.*
This abbey, also belonging to the Benedictine Order, was founded by the Abbaye St-Pierre in Solesmes in 1897. Its west and south sides are supported by powerful buttresses. Gregorian chants.

CHAMPEAUX★

Population 390

Michelin map 59 fold 18 or 230 folds 27 and 28 – 9km – 6 miles northwest of Vitré

The **village square★** composes a harmonious scene with its collegiate church, its small town hall with a large hipped roof, and the few houses, former canons' residences, standing around an old well.

Collégiale – This 14 and 15C collegiate church, with a single nave, has some fine Renaissance canopied **stalls★** and an elegant door, of the same period, which opens onto the sacristy, the former chapter-house. To the left of the high altar and in a chapel to the left of the chancel are two stone and marble mausolea (1551-4) belonging to the d'Espinay family, who founded the church.
The two handsome Renaissance stained-glass windows★, made in Rennes *(qv)*, are noteworthy: depicted in the apse is the Passion of Christ and in the sacristy the sacrifice of Abraham. In the nave, the south chapel contains a 17C altarpiece recounting scenes of the Passion and the north chapel is adorned with a 14C Virgin – both of these works are in polychrome wood.
South of Champeaux, in a pleasant verdant setting, stands the **Château d'Espinay**, an elegant 15 and 16C building *(not open to the public)*.

CHÂTEAUBRIANT

Population 12 782

Michelin map 63 folds 7 and 8 or 230 fold 41

On the border of Brittany and Anjou, surrounded by woods dotted with pools, stands this old fortified town with its imposing castle.
At the town gates, on the road to Pouancé, at Carrière des Fusillés, there is a memorial to the 27 hostages executed by the Nazis on 22 October 1941. The recesses at the base contain soil from the place of execution.

Françoise de Foix and François I (16C) – Among the ladies of Châteaubriant were two whose memory has survived the centuries. One, Sibylle, gave a rare example of conjugal love; when her husband returned from a Crusade in 1250, she died of joy whilst embracing him.

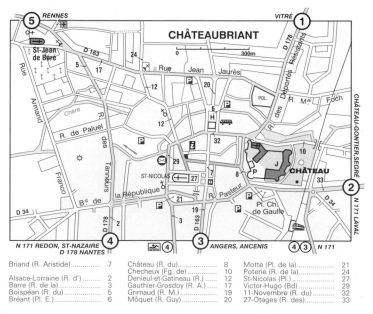

Briand (R. Aristide)	7	Château (R. du)	8	Motte (Pl. de la)	21
		Checheux (Fg. de)	10	Poterie (R. de la)	24
Alsace-Lorraine (R. d')	2	Denieul-et-Gatineau (R.)	12	St-Nicolas (Pl.)	27
Barre (R. de la)	3	Gauthier-Grosdoy (R. A.)	17	Victor-Hugo (Bd)	29
Boispéan (R. du)	5	Grimaud (R. M.)	19	11-Novembre (R. du)	32
Bréant (Pl. E.)	6	Môquet (R. Guy)	20	27-Otages (R. des)	33

The story of the second, Françoise de Foix, is less edifying. At the age of 11 she was married to Jean de Laval, Count of Châteaubriant. He was terribly jealous; he tried to keep his child-wife away from the dangers of the outside world and sulked in his castle. Nonetheless, Françoise grew in beauty, wit and culture and aroused great curiosity. François I sent word to the Count that he would like to meet her. Laval took no notice. When the king insisted, Laval went to Court, but unaccompanied; his wife, he said, liked to be alone, and moreover she was weak minded. The Count had arranged with his wife that she should join him only at a certain signal. A servant came upon the secret and sold it to the king. One fine day Laval saw Françoise alighting from her coach and being received with great honours. Mad with rage, he left the Court, leaving his wife unprotected. Dazzled by this brilliant new life, she yielded and became the King's favourite. However, royal loves are not eternal and she was superseded by the Duchess of Étampes. Laval returned, took his wife back to Châteaubriant and shut her up, with her daughter, aged seven, in a room hung with black. The child sickened and died. The mother held out for ten years, whereupon, it has been said her husband hastened her end in 1537 with a thrust of his sword.

SIGHTS

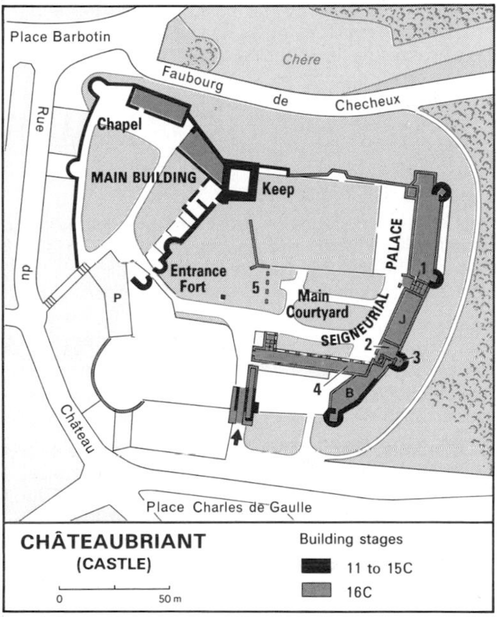

★**Castle (Château)** – A part of the castle, which has been remodelled several times, is feudal while another part, dating from the Renaissance, was built by Jean de Laval. You can stroll round it along the esplanade and the gardens which go right down to the Chère.

Enter through Place Charles de Gaulle.

All that remains of the feudal castle is a large keep on a height, connected with the entrance fort and the chapel by walls against which the two wings of the main building stand. The three wings of the Seigneurial Palace (Palais Seigneurial), opposite, are connected by elegant Renaissance pavilions. The roof is ornamented with dormer windows, which are emblazoned with the coats of arms of Châteaubriant, Laval and Montmorency.

The tour takes you up the central staircase (**1**) to a balcony from where there is a lovely view onto the Main Courtyard, embellished with gardens and a huge chestnut tree, the keep, and the city's roof-tops. Continue on to the room (**2**) of Françoise de Foix with its coffered ceiling and monumental early 17C carved wood chimney. Next to it is the oratory (**3**) with the tombstone of Françoise de Foix on which is carved an epitaph by Clément Marot (French Renaissance poet).

The Magistrate's Court (Tribunal d'Instance – **J**) occupies a part of the palace while the public library (**B**) is housed in the south wing.

There are only two sections left of the colonnade which surrounded the Main Courtyard: the covered gallery (**4**) which ends at a charming staircase-pavilion and the other section (**5**) enclosing the Main Courtyard.

Église de St-Jean-de-Béré – The church's oldest parts comprising the chancel and the transept crossing, which are built of fine red sandstone, date from the end of the 11C; the nave is 12C.

Outside, near the picturesque south porch (16C), is a rustic altar from which services were held at the time of the plague.

Inside you will see the ornately decorated altarpiece at the high altar (1665), in the north transept the altarpiece of the Virgin (1658) and left of the nave the altarpiece of St Blaise (1693).

A 17C panel representing the Eternal Father is placed in the nave across from the entrance; a Virgin and a statue of St Julian (15C) and other 17C statues including a St Elizabeth represented by Maria Theresa, Louis XIV's wife and St Augustine are also noteworthy. On the end wall are two low reliefs representing the Annunciation (13C) and the Visitation (15C).

CHÂTEAUGIRON

Population 4 166

Michelin map 6 fold 7 or 20 fold 41

This old town, which was famous for its hemp sailcloth used for rated ships in the 17C, has preserved an impressive fortified castle and picturesque half-timbered houses (mainly in Rue de la Madeleine). In the church a fine 16C wooden Crucifix hangs above the altar.

Castle (Château) – The moat, 13C keep, which in the 14C was capped by a pepperpot roof, and 15C clock tower next to the chapel are all that remain of the often-besieged castle. The living quarters, rebuilt in the 18C, house administrative offices. From Boulevard du Château there is a full view of the castle and its site.

EXCURSIONS

Manoir de Bois-Orcan – *North of town 2.5km - 1.5 miles and left on another road.* Reflecting in the moat beside a solitary weeping willow, the 16C manor-house, its main range flanked by two turrets and its chapel, makes a lovely picture.

Nouvoitou – *3.5km - 2 miles west on the D 34.*
The 15C **church** contains, in the nave and to the right, 15C polychrome and gilt alabaster panels. Outside note the 17C cemetery cross and a 16C tombstone.

CHÂTEAULIN

Population 4 965

Michelin map 58 fold 15 or 20 fold 18 – Local map under Monts d'ARRÉE

This little town stands on a bend of the Aulne, in the green and deep valley through which the canalised river flows. Two lines of shady quays are its most decorative feature. The tide does not reach Châteaulin but dies out a little way downstream, at Port-Launay, where small seagoing ships are tied up to the quay.

Salmon fishing – Châteaulin is the salmon fishing centre in the Aulne Valley; the salmon has always appeared on the town's coat of arms. Less often than in the past, the salmon come up the river to spawn, trying to leap the small waterfalls formed by the overflows from the locks. Angling (bait casting, spin casting) is done below the locks over a distance of some 100m especially in March and April.

Chapelle Notre-Dame ⏲ – *Access via Rue Graveran and a road to the left.*
The castle's former chapel (remodelled in the 17 and 18C) stands in an enclosure near some old 17C houses. Pass though the triumphal arch, there is a 15C Calvary cross presenting a rather unusual Last Judgment. The chapel was modified in the 17 and 18C, and was the object of extensive restoration work in 1991. In the nave there are some 13C vestiges (columns, capitals), and some 17C altarpieces.
From the small square there is a very good view of the Aulne Valley and the town.

EXCURSIONS

Cast – *7km - 4 miles southwest of Châteaulin on the D 7.* Standing in front of the church is an attractive sculpture, known locally as St Hubert hunting. The saint, accompanied by his squire and two basset hounds, is kneeling beside a minute horse and in front of a stag bearing a cross. Behind the town hall, in the presbytery's courtyard is a statue of St Tugen.

★★★MÉNEZ-HOM

Round tour of 54km - 34 miles – about 3 hours 30 min. Leave Châteaulin on the D 887 towards Crozon and after 3.5km - 2 miles, turn right; the road goes through Dinéault. You pass the massif of the Ménez-Hom on your left and come in sight of the Aulne before you reach the road to Trégarvan.

Musée de l'École rurale en Bretagne ⏲ – To the left of the crossroads is a museum created by the Parc naturel régional d'Armorique *(qv)*. A traditional school yard, shaded by lime trees, precedes the school building with a large classroom dating from the early 20C on the ground floor. On the first floor are the teacher's quarters and a room devoted to the history and development of Brittany.

Trégarvan – Beautiful **site★** by the Aulne. Fine **views** of the river.

Return to the Châteaulin road and turn right.

Argol – Go into the **parish close** by a monumental doorway built in the classical style in 1659. The equestrian statue of King Gradlon is part of an old Calvary and is similar in style to the horsemen of Ste-Marie-du-Ménez-Hom *(qv)* and the chapel of St-Sébastien *(see Monts d'ARRÉE)* and that on the entrance arch at Guimiliau. The church dates from 1573, and the charnel house from 1665.

Rejoin the road to Crozon and turn left. After 1.5km - 1 mile bear right.
Glimpses of Douarnenez Bay.

St-Nic – 16C **church** with a pierced belfry. Note a Descent from the Cross in the north chapel and an altarpiece of the Rosary in the south chapel.

Continue towards Plomodiern and after 1km - half a mile turn right.

Chapelle St-Côme ⏲ – This little chapel, built in homogeneous style and typically Breton in character, possesses a rare harmony of style. An elegantly decorated façade is surmounted by a well-proportioned bell tower. Inside, the mid-17C **woodwork**★, in the nave, testifies the skill of Breton craftsmen. The framework rests on purlins that are carved with flora and fauna-inspired motifs and many inscriptions. The corbels in the aisles depict strange figures; also worthy of note are a fine wooden Christ and the elegant group formed by the altarpiece and the front of the high altar.

Return to the Plomodiern road and take a restricted road, opposite, then turn right.

An overall view of Douarnenez Bay unfolds; on the way up, note a dolmen in a field 30m to the left.

Turn right towards Châteaulin and left immediately afterwards.

★★★ **Ménez-Hom** – *See MÉNEZ-HOM.*

Ste-Marie-du-Ménez-Hom – *See STE-MARIE-DU-MÉNEZ-HOM.*

Return to Châteaulin.

CHÂTELAUDREN

Population 947

Michelin map 59 fold 2 or 20 fold 8

The town, an important commercial centre, stands in the valley of the Leff, a river known for its trout. South of the town is a lake with bathing facilities.

★ **Chapelle Notre-Dame-du-Tertre** – Perched on a small mound, the chapel can be reached on foot, by the alley called *Venelle Notre-Dame*, or by car, leaving from *Place des Sapeurs-Pompiers*, by *Rue Aribart* and *Rue Notre-Dame*. The chapel, built in a variety of architectural styles, dates back to the early 14C and was subsequently enlarged in the 16 and 17C. The ninety-six 15C **panels**★ on the chancel vaulting, forming a group of unusual size in France, depict scenes from the Old and New Testaments; those in the chapel to the south of the chancel illustrate the lives of Saint Marguerite, Saint Fiacre and Mary Magdalene. There is a very fine gilded wooden **altarpiece**★ (1650) at the high altar; the chapel to the north of the chancel houses a white marble statue of Our Lady (15C). An alabaster *Virgin with Child* displayed in the central niche is characteristic of the works of art produced in Britain in the early 16C.

COMBOURG★

Population 4 843

Michelin map 59 folds 16 and 17 or 20 fold 26

This picturesque old town stands at the edge of a great pool and is dominated by an imposing feudal castle. The tourist information office is on Place Albert-Parent, inside the restored 16C Maison de la Lanterne. Tourists who only want to take a quick look at the castle from the outside should walk along the local road which branches off the Rennes road and runs beside the pool, facing the castle and the village.

Chateaubriand at Combourg – The castle, which was built in the 11C, was enlarged in the 14 and 15C and restored in the 19C. It belonged first to the Du Guesclin family, and then in the 18C to the Count of Chateaubriand, father of François-René, the great Romantic writer.

In his *Memoirs*, Chateaubriand *(qv)* recalled the two years he spent at Combourg in his youth, adding still more to their romantic nature. The Count, a sombre and moody man, lived very much in retirement; when the family met he would walk up and down for hours in the drawing room, in silence, while no one dared to speak. The Countess, who was unwell, kept only a distant eye on the children. Months passed without a visitor. Left to themselves, the young Chateaubriand and his sister Lucile grew close, sharing their boredom, their dreams and their tears.

The old castle, almost deserted, was gloomy; the pool, the woods and the surrounding heath exuded melancholy. The Cat Tower (Tour du Chat), in which François-René had his lonely room, was haunted; a former Lord of Combourg was said to return there at night in the form of a black cat, which the boy watched for anxiously. The owls fluttering against the window and the wind rattling the door and howling in the corridors made him shiver.

It was there that the dreamy and melancholy soul of one of the great Romantic writers, was formed, or perhaps confirmed.

★**Castle (Château)** ⓥ – The exterior of the castle appears like a powerful fortress: its four massive towers, with pepperpot roofs, its crenellated parapet walk, and its thick walls slit by narrow openings. The interior was rearranged in 1876. The tour takes you to the chapel, the drawing room (now divided in two), the Archives, where souvenirs of the author are displayed: autographs, awards, furniture, etc, and to François-René's austere bedroom in Cat Tower.
From the parapet walk there are views of the locality, the lake and the pretty, sweet-smelling **park** ⓥ.

EXCURSIONS

Château de Lanrigan ⓥ – *5km - 3 miles east. Leave Combourg on the road to Rennes and after the lake bear left onto the road that runs along the lake's south bank to the château.*
The small Château de Lanrigan with its well-balanced proportions would recall the smaller châteaux of the Loire if it were not built of granite. The château has a charming Renaissance façade; in the angle formed by the main building and its flanking tower, a gracefully constructed gallery adds an original note.

Cobac Parc ⓥ – *10km - 6 miles northwest on the D 73. At Lanhélin, follow the signs for the* Parc de Loisirs.
This country park, covering 10ha-25 acres, is one in which animals roam free (ponies, kids, donkeys) against a background of greenery. Amusements offered for young and old include a small train, merry-go-rounds, rope walk, boat rides... as well as a museum (200 of the region's animals, stuffed). There is a picnic area and a restaurant.

CONCARNEAU★★

Population 18 630
Michelin map 58 fold 15 or 20 folds 32 and 33 – Facilities

Concarneau offers a fascinating picture of a bustling fishing port, the charm of a walled town, enclosed in granite ramparts, and the facilities of a popular resort. It is France's first fishing port and the leading market for tunny caught in African waters and in the Indian Ocean *(details of fishing and maritime life pp 19-20)*, possesses three fish canneries and holds a colourful **fresh fish auction** *(criée)* ⓥ.
There is an attractive **general view★** of Concarneau, its fishing port and the bay from Moros Bridge (Pont du Moros) on entering the town by ② on the town plan.
The **Fêtes des Filets Bleus★** (Blue Nets Festival; *see the Calendar of Events at the end of the guide*) includes various folk events (dances and processions in local costumes). First held in 1905, it was originally organised to aid sardine fishermen and their families.
Annually on 14 July, in celebration of Bastille Day, about 100 old sailing ships gather in the bay.

★★WALLED TOWN (VILLE CLOSE) *time: 2 hours*

Narrow alleys cover the islet of irregular shape (350 x 100m - 1 150 x 330ft) linked to the mainland by two small bridges between which stands a fortified building. Massive ramparts, built in the 14C and completed in the 17C, surround the town. Cross the two small bridges and pass under a gateway leading to a fortified inner courtyard. There is a fine well.

★**Musée de la Pêche** (**M**[1]) ⓥ – This fishing museum is located in what used to be the arsenal which also served as barracks and a fishing school. In the courtyard *Commandant Garreau*, a lifeboat built in 1894, is exhibited. Accompanying notices, models, photographs, dioramas, and some 10 boats explain the history of Concarneau, its evolution as a port, traditional and modern fishing techniques (whale, cod, sardine, tuna, herring), boats, canning industry, shipbuilding, navigational equipment and rescue operations.
A large hall is devoted to exhibits relating to fishing in distant waters: an Azores whaleboat among other boats, a harpoon gun, a giant Japanese crab, a coelacanth (a fish whose origins date back 300 million years). The aquariums hold fish and other forms of marine life.
Outside (via Major's Tower – Tour du Major) a fishing boat is moored; climb aboard *Hémérica*, a trawler put out of commission in 1981, and relive the hard life of the fishermen.

Walk round the ramparts ⓥ – *Follow the signs. For the first part of the tour, go up a few steps on the left and follow the wall walk.*
Glimpses of the inner harbour and the fishing fleet can be caught through the loopholes. You also get an overall impression of the New Tower (Tour Neuve).
For the second part of the tour, return by the same path to the starting-point and

Concarneau

descend the steps. After skirting Esplanade du Petit Château, giving onto the marina, you overlook the channel between the two harbours. *When you reach a big tower turn a sharp left and go down a ramp to a walkway beneath the ramparts. Return to the town by Porte du Passage. By the corner of the Hospice take Rue St-Guénolé, which bears left towards Place St-Guénolé.*
From Place St-Guénolé a short alley to the right leads to **Porte aux Vins** (Wine Gateway) through the ramparts. As you go through the gate (porte) you will get a typical view of the trawlers moored in the harbour. Rue Vauban brings you back out of the walled town.

ADDITIONAL SIGHTS

The harbours – By way of Avenue Pierre Guéguin and Quai Carnot, take a quick look at the fishing port (port de pêche), where the main fishing fleet (trawlers and cargo boats) is moored; you may see the day's catch being unloaded. Then follow Avenue du Docteur-P.-Nicolas and walk round the pleasure boat harbour. The embarkation point for excursions is at the end of this quay, on the left.
On the left of Quai de la Croix is the marine laboratory (Laboratoire Maritime) of the Collège de France. Inside visit the **Marinarium** (**B M**[2]) ⓥ, an exhibition devoted to the sea world: aquariums, dioramas and audiovisual displays.
After passing the picturesque old fish market where fish used to be sold by auction, the 15C Chapelle N.-D.-de-Bon-Secours and a small lighthouse, you may skirt Port

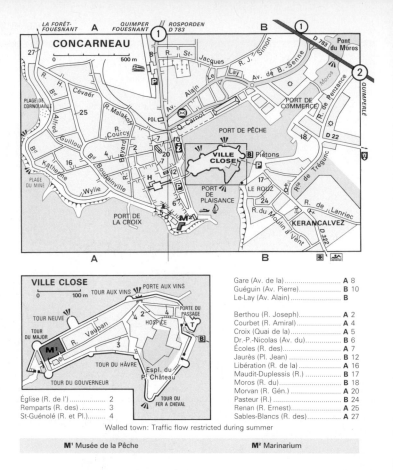

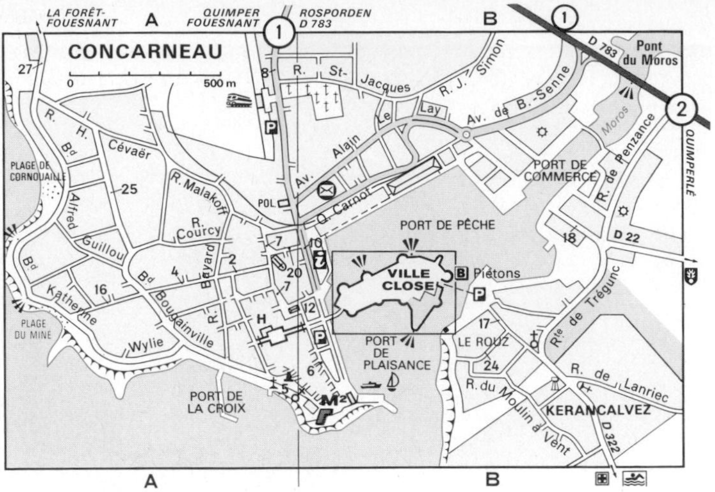

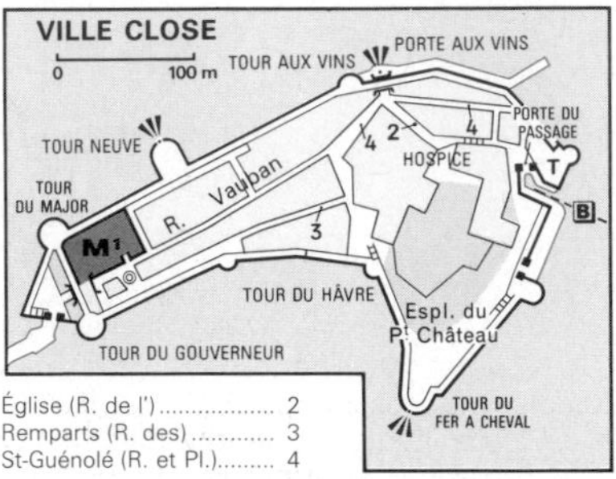

Église (R. de l') 2
Remparts (R. des) 3
St-Guénolé (R. et Pl.)......... 4

Gare (Av. de la) .... **A** 8
Guéguin (Av. Pierre) .... **B** 10
Le-Lay (Av. Alain) .... **B**

Berthou (R. Joseph) .... **A** 2
Courbet (R. Amiral) .... **A** 4
Croix (Quai de la) .... **A** 5
Dr.-P.-Nicolas (Av. du) .... **B** 6
Écoles (R. des) .... **A** 7
Jaurès (Pl. Jean) .... **B** 12
Libération (R. de la) .... **A** 16
Maudit-Duplessis (R.) .... **B** 17
Moros (R. du) .... **B** 18
Morvan (R. Gén.) .... **A** 20
Pasteur (R.) .... **B** 24
Renan (R. Ernest) .... **A** 25
Sables-Blancs (R. des) .... **A** 27

Walled town: Traffic flow restricted during summer

M¹ Musée de la Pêche **M²** Marinarium

de la Croix (follow Boulevard Bougainville), which is sheltered by a jetty. Looking back, there is a good view of the Pointe du Cabellou and, further on, of the Pointe de Beg-Meil. Out at sea are the îles Glénan.

The beaches (Les Plages) (**A**) – Go along Boulevard Katherine-Wylie, which runs beside Mine Beach and affords good views of La Forêt Bay and the Pointe de Beg-Meil, then take Boulevard Alfred-Guillou which leads to Cornouaille Beach.

EXCURSIONS

From Concarneau to Pont-Aven by the coast road – *45km - 28 miles – about 2 hours. Leave Concarneau by ② on the town plan towards Quimperlé and after 2.5km - 1.25 miles bear right.*

★**Pointe du Cabellou** – *Go round the point starting from the right.* The car park affords a fine **view**★ of the site of Concarneau and the walled town. The road skirts the rocky coastline amid the villas and pine trees and offers pretty views of Baie de la Forêt and the îles de Glénan.

Return to the main road and make for Quimperlé. Turn right at Pont-Minaouët and right again at Kermao.

The road goes through **Pouldohan** (fine beach and large sailing school) and Pendruc.

Pointe de la Jument – *15 min on foot Rtn.* Fine rocky site and view of Cabellou, the bay and Beg-Meil, and the coast of Loctudy in the distance.

Make for the Pointe de Trévignon going via Lambell where you turn right, Lanénos and Ruat.

On the way, note the vertical granite panels forming the walls of the farm buildings.

Pointe de Trévignon – An old fort stands at the tip of the headland; fishing boats and the lifeboat are berthed in the tiny port to the west. Fine **view**★ to the right of La Forêt Bay and Beg-Meil, Bénodet Bay, and on the left of the îles de Glénan and near the coast of Verte and Raguenès Islands.

Follow the road along Kersidan Beach. Bear right into the Glénan coast road, a good viewing platform; continue along Rue de Beg-Foz and turn right.

Raguenès-Plage – Sheltered by Raguenès Island which can be reached at half tide.
Continue in the direction of Port-Manech. At Trémorvézen, turn right after the chapel.
Kerascoët – A quiet hamlet with typical thatched farms.
The road then descends to the **Anse de Rospico** (Rospico Bay), a small cove with a beach.

At Kerangall, turn right towards Port-Manech. The remainder of the excursion is described in the opposite direction under PONT-AVEN: Excursions.

From Concarneau to Bénodet by the coast road – *40km - 25 miles – about 3 hours. The excursion is described in the opposite direction under BÉNODET: Excursions.*

BOAT TRIPS

There is a boat service between Concarneau and the îles de Glénan which also offers tours on the Odet.
In season there is a boat service between Concarneau and Beg-Meil.

CORNICHE BRETONNE★★

Michelin map 59 fold 1 or 20 folds 6 and 7

The scenic Breton coast road which joins Perros-Guirec and Trébeurden, following the Pink Granite coast which starts at the Pointe de l'Arcouest, is quite probably one of the most interesting runs in north Brittany.
The strange forms of the enormous rocks, which are the attraction of the Corniche Bretonne, are due to erosion. Granite is composed of quartz, mica and feldspar. The feldspar turns into kaolin (china clay), which is washed away by water, and the residue of quartz grains makes sand, which is carried away by rain and waves. Little by little, the stone changes shape and takes on surprising forms: almost perfect spheres, chiselled and fretted masses, boldly balanced piles and swaying stones. Erosion here has been very severe because the rocks are coarse grained and, therefore, easily broken up. Local imagination has given names to some of the rocks: Napoleon's Hat, St Yves, the Gnome, the Witch, the Death's Head, the Elephant, the Whale, the Ram, the Rabbit, the Tortoise, the Horse, the Thimble, the Torpedo, the Armchair, the Umbrella, the Sentinel, the Corkscrew, etc.

FROM PERROS-GUIREC TO TRÉBEURDEN

27km - 17 miles – about 6 hours – local map below

Perros-Guirec – *See PERROS-GUIREC.*
After the town of Perros-Guirec, the road skirts the small hill on which the signal station stands and a **view★** opens up straight ahead onto the rocks of Ploumanach, seaward of Sept-Îles, looking back of the beaches of Perros-Guirec and, in the distance, of the Port-Blanc coast.

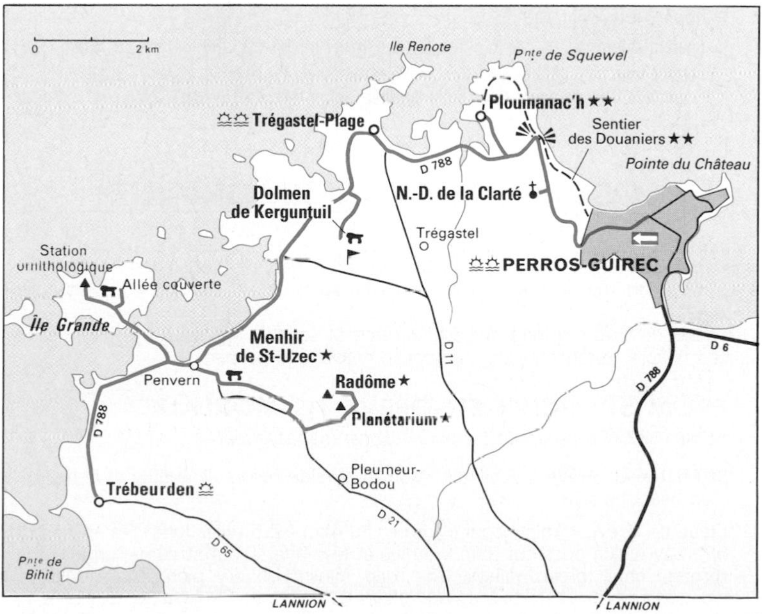

Chapelle Notre-Dame-de-la-Clarté – *See PERROS-GUIREC.*

★★ Ploumanach – *See PLOUMANACH.*

Trégastel-Plage – *See TRÉGASTEL-PLAGE.*
As you leave the village, on the right, at the end of a short rise, you get a view looking backwards, of Sept-Îles.

After 1.2km - 0.8 mile, turn left and then right.

Dolmen and Allée couverte de Kerguntuil – From the dolmen, by the roadside to the left, the passage grave can be seen at the end of a field; it is reached by walking in front of the farm buildings.
Then the road runs close to the sea, at high tide the shore can become wild and picturesque. It is a strange coast, dotted with islands and reefs.
Soon after a discotheque, right off the road, a dolmen looks down onto Kerivon shore.

Turn left towards Pleumeur-Bodou. At Penvern, bear left after the Café du Menhir.

★ Menhir de St-Uzec – A giant menhir is surmounted by a Crucifixion with instruments of the Passion surrounding the figure of a praying woman.

Take the road below the menhir to rejoin the Pleumeur-Bodou road, then turn left and 400m - 1/3 mile further on, left again.

★ Radôme and Planétarium – *See PLEUMEUR-BODOU.*

Île Grande – *Cross the bridge.* The island offers a landscape of heaths bordered by blue granite shores. There are megalithic remains, in particular a passage grave *(allée couverte)* northeast of the village.
A sort of hospital for sea birds, this **station ornithologique** ⓥ presents different bird species (guillemot, herring gull, black-headed gull, puffin, northern gannet and razorbill) on Sept-Îles *(qv)*. An audio-visual system provides a glimpse of the northern gannet in its natural habitat.

Return to the coast road and turn left towards Trébeurden.

Trébeurden – *See TRÉBEURDEN.*

Here are the names of a few French navigators who have won recent boat races (almost all of them Bretons!)

Gérard d'Abouville (b 1945) – Pacific Crossing in a rowing boat (1991)

Florence Arthaud (b 1957) – Route du Rhum (1990)

Alain Gautier (b 1963) – Solo Round-the-World Tour (1993)

Olivier de Kersauson (b 1944) – Solo Round-the-World Tour (1989)

Titouan Lamazou (b 1955) – Vendée Globe-Challenge (1990)

Serge Madec (b 1956) – Atlantic Crossing Record (1990)

Bruno Peyron (b 1955) – Round-the-World Race (Jules Verne Trophy) in 79 days 6 hours (1993)

Laurent Bourgnon (b 1966) Route du Rhum in 14 days 6 hours 28 min (1994)

Loïc Peyron (b 1959) Solo Cross-Atlantic Race Europe 1-Star (1992)
... as well as **Caradec**, **Colas** and **Gahinet**, who left us far too soon.

CORNICHE DE L'ARMORIQUE★

Michelin map 58 folds 6 and 7 or 20 fold 6

This short section of the Channel coast, which is part of the Golden Belt *(qv)* and is also known as the heather coast, should be seen by all tourists who visit northern Brittany.
The Lieue de Grève, a long, majestic stretch of sand, is followed by steep headlands skirted from a distance by the Armorican coast road proper.

FROM ST-MICHEL-EN-GRÈVE TO MORLAIX

59km - 37 miles – about 5 hours – Local map overleaf

St-Michel-en-Grève – Facilities. A small seaside resort. The church is nicely situated near the sea.

★ Lieue de Grève – This magnificent beach, 4km - 2.5 miles long, lies at the bottom of a bay which goes out 2km - 1 mile at low tide. Trout streams run into the sea through small green valleys. The road, which is very picturesque, follows the wooded coast and skirts the rocky mass of the Grand Rocher.

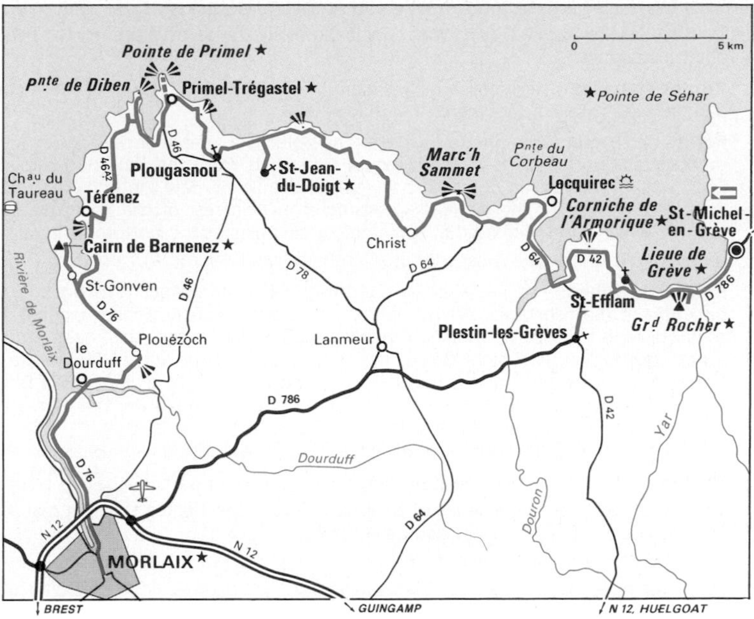

★**Climbing the Grand Rocher** – *45 min on foot Rtn.* A road to the left, just before the Grand Rocher, leads to a car park nearby from which a path runs to this 80m - 261ft vantage point. There is a very fine **view**★ of the Lieue de Grève. At high tide and especially with a northwesterly blowing in winter, the sight of the endless foaming rollers breaking on the beach and dashing against the seawall that protects the D 786 gives an excellent idea of the undertow.

St-Efflam – Next to the Chapelle St-Efflam, half hidden by lush vegetation, there is a fountain, which is surmounted by a massive dome. Efflam, a hermit who came from Ireland, landed with seven companions in 470 on the beach of the same name.

Bear left towards Plestin.

Plestin-les-Grèves – Facilities. It was here that Efflam lived, founded a monastery and died in 512. The 16C **church**, which burned down in 1944, has been restored; it contains the tomb of St Efflam adorned with his recumbent figure (1576). In the south aisle, to the left of the altar, a statue shows him vanquishing a dragon, the symbol of paganism. Modern stained-glass windows.
Near the port of Toul-an-Hery, the Hogolo Roman baths have recently been unearthed and are gradually being restored.

Return to the coast road.

★**Corniche de l'Armorique** – Between St-Efflam and Locquirec the road picturesquely follows the heavily indented coast. After the Pointe de Plestin there is a fine view of the cove of Locquirec and its headland at high tide. Before reaching the village you will see, on the right and in the distance, the Corniche Bretonne *(qv)* as far as Trébeurden; and on crossing the bridge, to the left is the attractive Tour d'Argent Manor-House.

Locquirec – *See LOCQUIREC.*

Beyond the mill, Moulin de la Rive, take the coast road overhanging the sea.

Marc'h Sammet Viewing Table – Built on a rocky headland, it commands splendid **views**★: to the east the beaches of Moulin de la Rive and the Sables Blancs and the rocky Point du Corbeau; to the north the Île de Losquet; to the west the Poul Rodou Beach (access 800m - 2 265ft below).

Go to the village of Christ and turn right. Follow the signposts to the scenic road (route touristique).

From the coast road there is a good view of the coast from the Pointe de Trégastel to the Pointe de Primel.

At St-Jean-du-Doigt Beach, bear left.

★**St-Jean-du-Doigt** – *See ST-JEAN-DU-DOIGT.*

Plougasnou – At the centre of this small town, the church, which is mostly 16C, has a Renaissance porch opening on to the square. In the chancel are fine 17C altarpieces. In the south aisle, the chapelle de Kéricuff closed off by an elegant Gothic arcade in oak contains a 16C wooden Trinity. A road from the church's east end leads (300m - 328yds from town) to the **Oratoire Notre-Dame-de-Lorette**, a granite oratory with a stone roof and two telamones framing the entrance.

Take the road past the tourist office and at the third junction turn right.

Go through Ste-Barbe. On the way down, the **view** extends over Primel, the beach, point and rocks.

★**Primel-Trégastel** – This beach of fine sand lies in a good setting near rocks comparable with those of Ploumanach and Trégastel.

★**Pointe de Primel** – *30 min on foot Rtn.* The point is a jumble of pink rocks. From the central spur, there is a fine **panorama** extending from the Baie de St-Pol-de-Léon to the Trébeurden coast. Out at sea are the île de Batz Lighthouse and the Sept Iles. The tip of the point is separated from the rest of the peninsula by a fissure (which can be crossed at low tide); a cave lies at the bottom of it.

After 1km - half a mile turn right. The road passes near the fish ponds.

Pointe de Diben – At Le Diben, a picturesque fishing village, turn right in the direction of the fish farms (Viviers-le-Port) and port; 100 m further on take the road opposite towards the port which leads a dike. Just before this, bear left into a path leading to the Pointe Diben: fine view over the bay and of the Pointe de Primel. Return to the D 46A 2 and follow a road to the right towards Port-Blanc, which gives access to a car park from which a track *(15 min on foot Rtn)* leads to a rock jutting out over the sea: lovely view of Port-Blanc Islet.
The road passes on the right the attractive Guerzit and St-Samson Beaches.

Térénez – This small, very pleasant and typically Breton port is a sailing centre.

The coast road offers **glimpses**★ of Morlaix estuary, the Château du Taureau and the peninsula topped by the Cairn de Barnenez.

At the entrance to St-Gonven, turn right.

★**Cairn de Barnenez** – *See Cairn de BARNENEZ*

Continue in the direction of Morlaix (qv).

Beyond Plouézoch, a fine tree-lined road descends into the picturesque valley of Le Dourduff where the fleet of spruce fishing boats belonging to the small oyster port of **Le Dourduff** is moored. After the bridge, the coast road runs along the River Morlaix and gives views of the sand dredging port, the yachting port with its lock, and the charming setting of the town, river and viaduct.

CORNOUAILLE★★

Michelin map 58 folds 13, 14 and 15 or 20 folds 16, 17, 18, 31 and 32

Historic Cornouaille, the Kingdom and then the Duchy of medieval Brittany, extended far to the north and east of its capital, Quimper, reaching Landerneau, the neighbourhood of Morlaix and Quimperlé.
The area included in our tour is much smaller and is limited to the coastal districts of Cornouaille, west of Quimper. This very extensive coastline is marked by two rocky peninsulas, Cap Sizun, "Le Cap", and the Presqu'île de Penmarch, which are its main tourist attractions. This is a maritime country in which fishing plays an important role; the ports of Guilvinec, Audierne and Douarnenez specialise in sardines and spiny lobster. The interior is densely cultivated (potatoes and early vegetables), and the countryside with its tranquil horizons is covered with small hamlets of whitewashed houses.

CAP

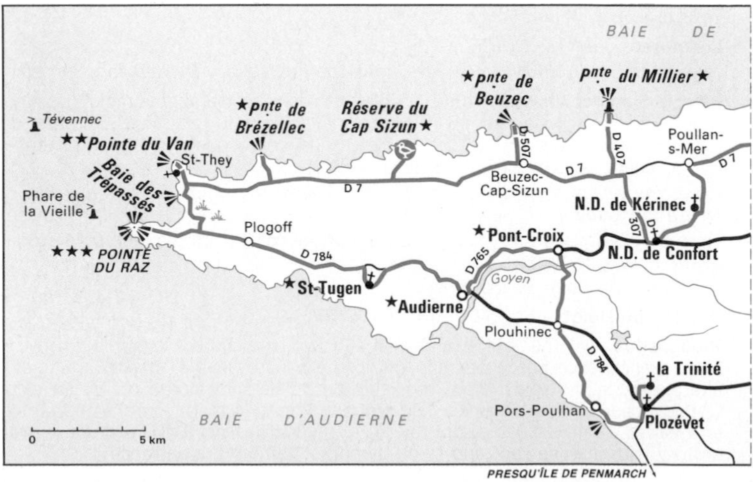

★★ CAP SIZUN

From Quimper to Plozévet

158km - 98 miles – allow 1 day – local map below

★★**Quimper** – *See QUIMPER.*

Leave Quimper northwest by Rues de Locronan and de la Providence.

The road goes up the rural valley of the Steïr with its wooded slopes and then through undulating countryside.

Plogonnec – The 16C **church**, remodelled in the 18C, has a fine Renaissance bell tower; it also has 16C stained-glass windows; in the chancel to the left of the high altar the windows recount the Transfiguration, above the altar the Passion and to the right the Last Judgment. At the entrance to the *placitre (qv)* at the east end of the church, there is a Gothic triumphal arch.

★★**Locronan** – *See LOCRONAN.*

The Douarnenez road with Forest of Nevet on its left, leads to the sea.

Kerlaz – 16 and 17C church with a pierced bell tower.
There is a good view of Douarnenez, which is reached after skirting the fine Ris Beach.

★**Douarnenez** – *See DOUARNENEZ.*

Leave Douarnenez, go through Tréboul and make for Poullan-sur-Mer where you turn left and then right and right again.

Chapelle Notre-Dame-de-Kérinec – The chapel, surrounded by trees, dates from the 13 and 15C; the elegant bell tower was struck by lightning in 1958 but an exact replica, as it appeared in the 17C, has been rebuilt. Note the flat east end and to the left the rounded pulpit dominated by a Calvary. Inside, look at the massive pillars of the transept crossing which suggest that a central bell tower was to be built but the project was most likely abandoned and in its place, a belfry porch was erected.

Église Notre-Dame-de-Confort – The 16C church with its galleried bell tower dating from 1736, has 16C **stained-glass windows** in the chancel, one of which is a Tree of Jesse. Over the last arch in the nave, on the north side, hangs a carillon wheel with twelve little bells. The chimes are rung to beg the Virgin for the gift of speech for children who have difficulties in speaking.
Alongside the chapel is a Calvary with a triangular base dating from the 16C; the 13 statues of the Apostles were redone in 1870.

Leave Confort in the direction of Pont-Croix and turn right, then left towards Beuzec-Cap-Sizun and again right after 2km - 1 mile.

★**Pointe du Millier** – A small lighthouse stands on this arid site. From the point *(15 min on foot Rtn)* there is a **view**★ of Douarnenez Bay and Cap de la Chèvre.

On leaving Beuzec-Cap-Sizun bear right.

★**Pointe de Beuzec** – From the car park there is a **view**★ of the approach to Douarnenez Bay, the Presqu'île de Crozon and in fine weather, of the Pointe de St-Mathieu.

SIZUN

D'après photo J.-L. Lemcrque/AZIMUT

A cormorant from the Réserve du Cap Sizun

★**Réserve du Cap Sizun** ⓥ – The most interesting time for a visit is at nesting time in the spring. Starting in March, most birds finish nesting by mid-July. The adults and chicks then leave the sanctuary progressively through the month of August. In the magnificent and wild setting of the Castel-ar-Roc'h, more than 70m - 230 ft above sea level, such sea birds as guillemots, cormorants *(illustration previous page)*, common herring gulls, lesser black-backed gulls, great black-backed gulls, which are the rarest of all, and black-legged kittiwakes can be seen, sitting on their nests and feeding their young.

J.-L. Le Moigne/JACANA

Lapwing

★**Pointe de Brézellec** – *Park the car by the lighthouse enclosure.* Go to the rock platforms nearby. There is a magnificent **view**★ along an exceptionally long stretch of coast of saw-tooth rocks and sheer cliffs: Presqu'île de Crozon, Pointe de St-Mathieu, Pointe du Van and Pointe de Tévennec can be seen. A narrow road (surfaced) descends steeply to a small fishing port.

Turn back and turn right towards Pointe du Van.

★★**Pointe du Van** – *1 hour on foot Rtn.* The 15C **Chapelle St-They** stands on the left of the path. On the point itself follow the half-hidden path, bearing always to the left, which goes right round the headland. The Pointe du Van, which is too big to be seen all in one glance, is, nevertheless, less spectacular than the Pointe du Raz, but it has the advantage of being off the tourists' beaten track. There is a **view**★★ of the Pointe de Castelmeur, the Pointe de Brézellec, the Cap de la Chèvre, the Pointe de Penhir, the Pointe de St-Mathieu and the Tas de Pois rocks on the right; the île de Sein, the Vieille Lighthouse and the Pointe du Raz on the left. It is recommended that you do not climb down the cliffs.

The landscape becomes ever harsher: no trees grow; stone walls and barren moss cover the final headland.

Turn round and take, immediately on the right, a small road which hugs the coast leading to the Baie des Trépassés and affording fine views of the jagged coastline from the Pointe du Raz to the île de Sein.

Baie des Trépassés – It was once thought that the drowned bodies of those who had been shipwrecked, and which the currents brought to the bay, gave the bay its name of Bay of the Dead. Another, less macabre explanation, based on the existence of a stream that flowed in the marshes, was that the original Breton name for the bay was *"boe an aon"* (bay of the stream), which became *"boe anaon"* (bay of the troubled souls). Now it is believed that the bay was the embarkation point from the mainland for Druids' remains which were taken over to île de Sein for burial. According to local legend, the town of Is *(qv)* once stood in the little valley which is now covered in marshes.

The swell runs unimpeded into the bay, where it breaks with an impressive display of force.

★★★**Pointe du Raz** –*See Pointe du RAZ.*

Take the road in the direction of Audierne and after 10km - 6 miles, turn right towards St-Tugen.

★**St-Tugen** – The nave and the tower of the **chapel** are in the 16C Flamboyant Gothic style, the transept and the east end in the 17C Renaissance style. There is a fine south porch surmounted by an elegant pierced tympanum, containing six statues of Apostles in Kersanton granite and three 16C statues of Christ, the Virgin and St Anne. Inside may be seen interesting 17C furnishings, including several altarpieces and a curious catafalque flanked at each end by statues of Adam and Eve. The baptismal chapel, surrounded with balustrades and painted panels, contains a chimney with granite firedogs. In the chancel the 17C statue of St Tugen stands. There is a 16C fountain below the chapel. A *pardon* is held *(see the Calendar of events at the end of the guide)*.

★**Audierne** – *See AUDIERNE.*
The road follows the verdant valley of the River Goyen or Audierne.

★**Pont-Croix** – *See PONT-CROIX.*
Go to Plouhinec, the native town of the sculptor Quillivic, and after the church turn right towards **Pors-Poulhan**, a tiny port sheltered by a pier. Before Plozévet, there are fine views of Audierne Bay and the Phare d'Eckmühl.

Plozévet – There is a 15C porch to the Gothic church. Five arches in the wooden vaulted nave are Romanesque and date from the 12C. To the right of the building flows a sacred fountain *(qv)*. A menhir has been placed here as a 1914-18 war memorial.

Follow the route 1km - half a mile further north.

Chapelle de la Trinité – The chapel is T-shaped; the nave was built in the 14C and the remainder added in the 16C. Outside note the charming Louis XII decoration (transitional style between Gothic and Renaissance with Italian influence) of two walls on the south transept side. Inside, the nave arches come down on to groups of columns with florally decorated capitals.

★PRESQU'ÎLE DE PENMARCH

From Plozévet to Quimper

100km - 62 miles – allow half a day – local map overleaf

The journey is made through *bigouden* country, which has become known through the women's local costume, in particular their unique headdress in the shape of a little lace menhir *(photograph p 31)*.
From Plozévet *(see above)* to the tip of Penmarch Peninsula the sea breaks against a great sweep of shingle, continually rolling and knocking the stones of the some 20km - 12 mile arc. The even coastline is altogether inhospitable and desolate. The little villages with their white houses, which lie back from the coast, turn to the hinterland for their livelihood.
The **Presqu'île de Penmarch** was one of the richest regions in Brittany up to the end of the 16C: cod-fishing (the "lenten meat") brought wealth to the 15 500 inhabitants. But then the cod deserted the coastal waters, and a tidal wave brought devastation. Final disaster came with the brigand **La Fontenelle** *(qv)* who took the locality by surprise in spite of its defences. He killed 5 000 peasants, burned down their houses and loaded 300 boats with booty which he then took back to his stronghold on the île Tristan.

Plozévet – *Description above.*

Leave Plozévet south towards Penhors; the road then follows the coastline.

Penhors – *For access to the chapel, make for the beach.* On the first Sunday in September the great *pardon* of Notre-Dame-de-Penhors, one of the largest of Cornouaille *(see the Calendar of Events at the end of the guide)* takes place. The night before (Saturday) there is a procession with torches. On Sunday afternoon the procession walks through the countryside until it comes to the shore line and back to the chapel where the benediction of the sea takes place.
Proceed to Plovan.

Plovan – A small 16C **church** with beautifully coloured modern (1944) stained-glass windows and a fine turreted belfry. Nearby is a 16C Calvary.

Chapelle de Languidou – The ruined 13-15C chapel still has some interesting elements, particularly the fine rose window.

Ch. Braud/DIAF

Ruined chapel at Languidou

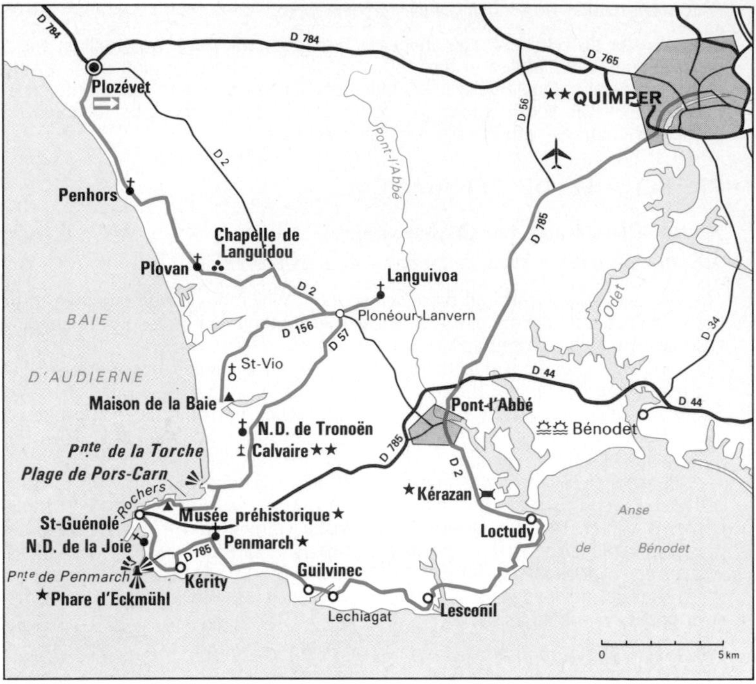

Make for Plonéour-Lanvern via Tréogat.

At the southwest exit of the village, take the D 156 towards Tréguennec, then the route indicated "Maison de la Baie d'Audierne" for about 3km - 2 miles, which takes you past the charming little chapel of St-Vio.

Maison de la Baie d'Audierne ⓥ – Tucked at the heart of a vast area of lakes, marshland and heaths, the Audierne Bay Visitor Centre is in fact a restored hamlet. Exhibitions, a thematic library and the opportunity to visit selected sites all introduce the public to the flora (grassy stretches of the dunes, reed beds, etc.) and the bird life of this part of *bigouden* country. A bird ringing centre is open to the public. To give an idea of the variety of bird life, 285 species of bird have been surveyed in Audierne Bay (in the open countryside: black-tailed godwits, plovers, dotterels, lapwings; on the beaches: oyster-catchers, sanderlings, gulls; in the reed beds: reed-buntings, purple herons, bitterns, ducks, etc.). When visiting the marshland, it is advisable to wear boots; visitors will also find binoculars useful *(these can be hired on site)*.

Chapelle de Languivoa ⓥ – *1.5km - 1 mile to the east of Plonéour-Lanvern.* This 14 and 17C chapel (restored) forms an imposing ensemble adorned by rose windows and Gothic arcading. The dismantled belfry porch still dominates the devastated nave and classical style entrance with its engaged Doric columns. The chapel contains the Virgin of Notre-Dame-de-Languivoa suckling her child. A *pardon* is held on 15 August.

At Plonéour-Lanvern take the road to Plomeur and after 2km - 1 mile turn right.

★★**Calvaire and Chapelle Notre-Dame-de-Tronoën** – *See Calvaire NOTRE-DAME-DE-TRONOËN.*

Continue along the road bearing right and right again.

Pointe de la Torche – The name is a corruption of the Breton "Beg an Dorchenn": flat stone point. Fine **view**★ of the St-Guénolé rocks and Audierne Bay. There is a tumulus with a large dolmen.

Plage de Pors-Carn – This great sandy beach along La Torche Bay is the terminal point of the telephone cable linking France and the USA.

★**Musée préhistorique finistérien** ⓥ – *At the entrance to St-Guénolé.* A series of megaliths and Gallic steles or obelisks called lec'hs stand around the museum. Start the visit from the left to see the exhibits in chronological order, from the Stone Age to the Gallo-Roman period. On display are, in the first gallery, a reconstruction of an Iron Age necropolis, Gallic pottery with Celtic decorations and a Gallic stele with spiral carving; in the south gallery, polished axes of rare stone, flint arrowheads, bronze weapons and chests with grooves.

The museum contains all the prehistorical antiquities discovered in Finistère except for the rich collection displayed in the Musée des Antiquités nationales at St-Germain-en-Laye *(see the Michelin Green Guide to Flanders, Picardy and the Paris Region).*

St-Guénolé – Facilities. The modern church is charming although a little dark; it stands near the old square tower, all that remains of the 15C church. Behind the fishing port (coastal fishing) are the famous **rocks** against which the sea breaks furiously.

Chapelle Notre-Dame-de-la-Joie – This 15C chapel with its pierced bell tower is flanked by turrets. The 16C Calvary is adorned with a *Pietà*. A *pardon* is held on 15 August.

★**Phare d'Eckmühl** ⏱ – Eckmühl Lighthouse stands at the very end of the Pointe de Penmarch. The lighthouse is 65m - 213ft tall and its light of 2 million candle-power has a range of 54km - 33.5 miles. From the gallery at the top of the tower (307 steps) there is a **view**★★ of Audierne Bay, the Pointe du Raz, the lighthouse on île de Sein, the coast of Concarneau and Beg-Meil and the îles de Glénan. Passing to the left of the lighthouse, you will reach the very tip of the point on which the old lighthouse – it now serves as a marker for ships at sea – a small fortified chapel and a signal station stand. The sea is studded with reefs covered in seaweed. Further east, as at Penmarch, the coast is a succession of rocky points and dunes.

Kérity – Small fishing port leaning more and more towards pleasure boating. The église Ste-Thumette (1675) has an elegant gabled front flanked by a turret.

★**Penmarch** – The parish includes several villages: St-Guénolé, Kérity, Tréoultré and St-Pierre. **St-Nonna**★ ⏱ was built in the 16C in the Flamboyant Gothic style.
At the east end and on the buttresses on either side of the doorway, ships and caravels are carved into high or low reliefs, recalling that the church was built with donations from shipowners. A gabled bell tower crowns the roof. Inside there are several old statues: in the south chapel, St Michael and St Anne carrying the Virgin and Child; in the south aisle hangs the *Vow of Louis XIII*.

Proceed to Guilvinec by the coast road.

Guilvinec – Facilities. This very active trawler and tunny fishing port has three fish canneries, which handle fish as it is unloaded. With **Lechiagat**, where numerous pleasure boats anchor, it forms a well-sheltered harbour. Beaches unfold behind the dunes as far as Lesconil.

Lesconil – Facilities. Small but bustling trawler fishing port. A picturesque scene occurs when the boats come in around 5.30pm.

Make for Loctudy via Palue-du-Cosquer and Lodonnec.

Loctudy – *See LOCTUDY.*

★**Manoir de Kérazan** – *See Manoir de KÉRAZAN.*

Pont-l'Abbé – *See PONT-L'ABBÉ.*

Leave Pont-l'Abbé by ① on the town plan and return to Quimper.

★★**Quimper** – *See QUIMPER.*

CÔTE D'ÉMERAUDE★★★

EMERALD COAST – Michelin map 59 folds 4, 5 and 6 or 230 folds 9, 10 and 11

This name is given to the part of the coast between the Pointe du Grouin and Le Val-André, which includes some famous beaches: Dinard, St-Lunaire, Paramé, etc. and the city of the privateers: St-Malo. The Côte d'Émeraude, which means Emerald Coast, is rocky, heavily indented and very picturesque. A series of points, from which fine panoramas can be seen, project into the sea. The coast is bisected by the Rance estuary. An enjoyable boat excursion between Dinan and St-Malo can be made on the estuary. The scenic road along the Emerald Coast is among the major tourist attractions of Brittany's north coast. Although it does not hug the coastline all the way, it offers many excursions to the points, enabling the visitor to enjoy spectacular sites with views and panoramas typical of this jagged coastline.

1 FROM CANCALE TO ST-MALO

23km – 14 miles – about 5 hours – local map below

★**Cancale** – *See CANCALE.*

Leave Cancale by ② on the town plan, turn right towards Pointe du Grouin 300m – about a quarter of a mile further on.

★★**Pointe du Grouin** – *See CANCALE: Excursion.*
The coast road follows the line of the cliffs as far as Le Verger, offering lovely views.

Chapelle Notre-Dame-du-Verger – *Bear right towards the beach.* This small chapel, rebuilt in the 19C, is venerated by the sailors of Cancale (pilgrimage 15 August). Inside there are models of different kinds of sailing vessels: sloops, three-masted ships, schooners, etc.
After Le Verger, there is a good view of the Du Guesclin Cove and Island. A small fort stands on it.

La Guimorais – A quiet seaside resort. Chevrets Beach stretches between Pointe du Meinga and the Presqu'île Bénard which encloses the harbour of Rothéneuf on the east.

The road skirts the harbour of Rothéneuf. This stretch of water almost completely empties itself at low tide; the flow of the tides was once used to work a mill.
On the right, the elegant 17C **Château du Lupin**, a *malouinière (qv)* built by a wealthy St-Malo shipowner, is of interest.

Rothéneuf and Le Minihic – *See ST-MALO: Rothéneuf.*
The road offers fine glimpses of the Bay of St-Malo.

Paramé – *See ST-MALO: Paramé.*

★★★**St-Malo** – *See ST-MALO.*
St-Malo extends southwards to St-Servan-sur-Mer *(qv)*.

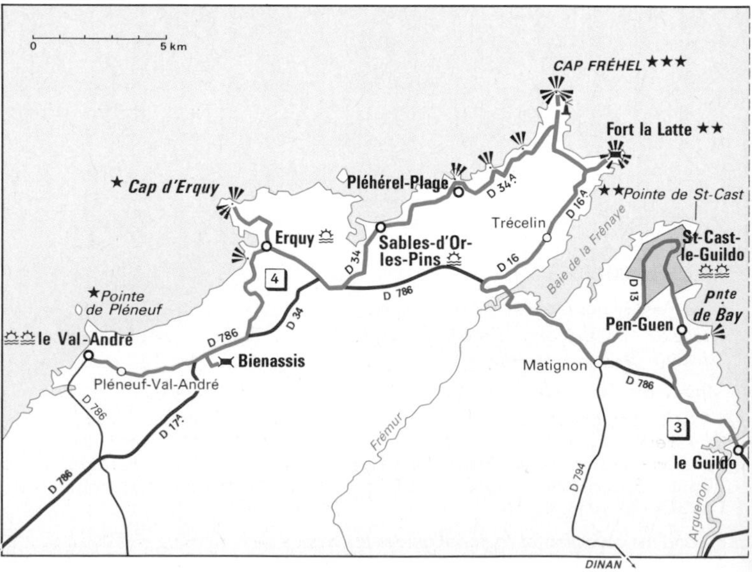

2 FROM ST-MALO TO DINARD

Here the tourist has a choice of two excursions *(see Vallée de la RANCE):*
The **crossing of the Rance estuary**, which goes over the crown of the Rance tidal power scheme *(usine marémotrice)* and affords fine glimpses of the estuary.
A **round tour**★ of the **Vallée de la Rance**★★ *(allow one day)*, a picturesque excursion; the visit to Dinan is worth the detour.

3 FROM DINARD TO CAP FRÉHEL

67km – 42 miles – about 4 hours – local map below

The coastal road is dotted with pleasant resorts, offering fine sandy beaches.

Dinard – *See DINARD.*
Unfortunately, the road does not follow all the indentations of the coast between Dinard and Cap Fréhel. However, it has interesting overhanging sections and opens up fine panoramas and remarkable scenery. Many fashionable and family resorts lie along the coast.

St-Lunaire – *See ST-LUNAIRE.*

★**Pointe de la Garde Guérin** – *15 min on foot Rtn.* After crossing the point at its base, turn right into a road as it descends to the foot of the hill, which is honeycombed with casemates *(car park)*. Climb on foot to the top of the promontory, from which a fine **panorama**★★ extends from Cap Fréhel to Pointe de la Varde.
The road traverses the Dinard golf course (60ha - 148 acres).

St-Briac-sur-Mer – This pleasant resort with its picturesque and varied sites, has a fishing harbour and a marina, and many good beaches. There are good views of the coast from the Emerald Balcony (Balcon d'Émeraude) and the Sailors' Cross (Croix des Marins – *access: from the Emerald Balcony by a path on the left, just before a bridge*).

As you come out of St-Briac cross Frémur River on a bridge 330m - 984ft long.

Fine views on the right of the resort and an islet with its castle.

Lancieux – This village has a very extensive beach of fine sand, from which there is a lovely view of Ebihens Island and the advanced points of the coast, St-Jacut-de-la-Mer, St-Cast and Cap Fréhel. In the centre of the village stands the old bell tower of the former church. The square tower is capped by a dome and its lantern turret.

In Ploubalay take the road towards Dinard and 800m – half a mile further turn left.

Château d'eau de Ploubalay ⏲ – The water tower has a circular terrace 104m-341ft high which offers an excellent **wide view**★★ of Ploubalay, the Dinan countryside, the Frémur River, St-Jacut, Pointe de St-Cast, Cap Fréhel, St-Malo and in clear weather the îles Chausey and Mont-St-Michel.

St-Jacut-de-la-Mer and Pointe du Chevet – Facilities. The road follows a long peninsula and goes through St-Jacut-de-la-Mer, a small fishing port and seaside resort. After skirting the beach of Le Rougeret, you will reach the high and picturesque cliff of

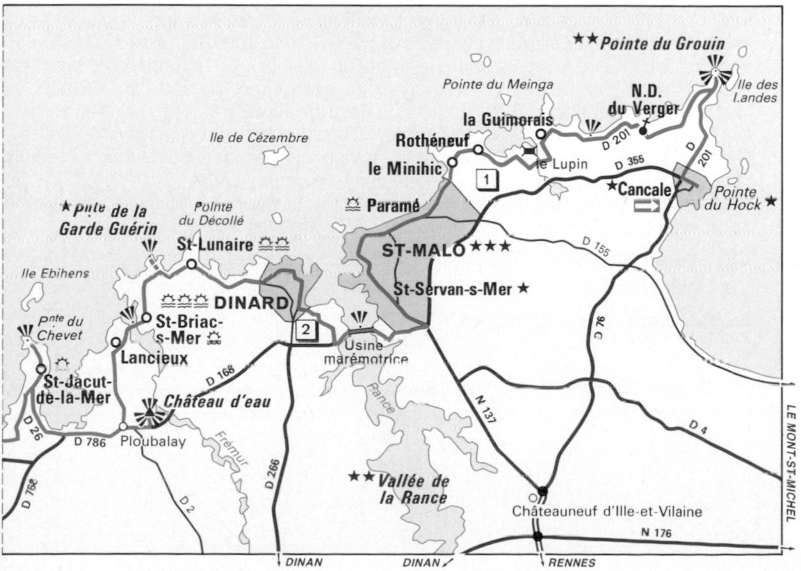

the **Pointe du Chevet**; there is a fine **view★** of the île Ebihens, opposite, and its tower; also, to the left, of the Bay of Arguenon (note the upstanding poles – *bouchots* – where mussels mature) and St-Cast, and to the right of the Bay of Lancieux.

Le Guildo – *See Le GUILDO.*

Go towards St-Cast by the coastal road.

Pointe de Bay – A good road on the right leads to a large car park. The **view★** includes the Arguenon estuary with its lines of mussel poles and the Presqu'île de St-Jacut and the île Ebihens.

Pen-Guen – Fashionable fine sandy beach.

★★ **St-Cast-le-Guildo** – *See ST-CAST-LE-GUILDO.*
Leaving St-Cast the road makes a big loop round the head of the Bay of La Frênaye.

After Trécelin, take the D 16^A which leads to the fort (car park).

★★ **Fort la Latte** – *See Fort la LATTE.*

★★★ **Cap Fréhel** – *See Cap FRÉHEL.*

4 FROM CAP FRÉHEL TO LE VAL-ANDRÉ

34km – 21 miles – about 2 hours 30 min – local map above

★★★ **Cap Fréhel** – *See Cap FRÉHEL.*
The tourist road, which twists and turns in the moor, affords striking **views★★** of the sea, cliffs and golden beaches. It goes through pine forest.

Pléhérel-Plage – The beach is on the right after a forest of conifers. A scenic view of Cap Fréhel and, in the foreground, a succession of tiny coves carved into the dunes may be enjoyed.

Sables-d'Or-les-Pins – Facilities. The Channel can be seen through the pine forest. From the fine sandy beach a group of small islands can be distinguished, especially that of St-Michel and its chapel.
After the Plurien intersection, the St-Quay coastline comes into view across St-Brieuc Bay.

As you enter Erquy go towards the cape.

★ **Cap d'Erquy** – *30 min on foot Rtn.* From the point where the road ends, there is an extensive view of grey-pink shingle beaches lapped by clear waters, opposite Caroual Beach, Vallées seashore, the Pointe de Pléneuf and Verdelet Islet and beyond St-Brieuc Bay, the Pointe de l'Arcouest and the île de Bréhat.
Pleasant footpaths bordered by bracken cross the heath dotted with patches of yellow and mauve and afford glimpses of the reefs: guided tours of this area are organised in July and August.

Erquy – In the 19C, a number of historians believed that Erquy was located on the alleged site of Reginea, a former Gallo-Roman settlement. It now appears they may have been mistaken. However, due to this misunderstanding, the inhabitants of Erquy have retained the charming name of "*Régineens*".
Set against a backdrop of rugged cliffs, this busy fishing port (2 000 tonnes of scallops in 1993) is gradually extending its influence. Its fishing fleet is made up of around 80 boats specialised in coastal fishing: fish (sole, turbot, gurnard, John Dory) and shellfish (scallops but also clams and queen scallops). Among the many beaches, that of Caroual stands out on account of its **view** of the bay and Cap d'Erquy, as well as its naturel topography, which ensures safe bathing for all children.
On the edge of the road leading to Cap d'Erquy stand two small guard rooms – the vestiges of Vauban's fortifications – along with a curious-looking, extremely rare cannonball foundry (a similar one may be found under Fort la LATTE); its purpose was to manufacture cannonballs for the batteries of artillery to fire at the approaching English, sailing forth in their 17C wooden ships.

Château de Bienassis – *See Le VAL-ANDRÉ: Excursion.*

Via Pléneuf-Val-André return to Le Val-André.

Le Val-André – *See Le VAL-ANDRÉ.*

Le CROISIC★

Population 4 428

Michelin map 6 fold 14 or 20 fold 51 – Local map under Presqu'île de GUÉRANDE – Facilities

An animated port where fishing boats and pleasure craft intermingle and an important centre for the cultivation of shellfish, Le Croisic overlooks the Grand Traict lagoon and is an agreeable small seaside town which has many summer holiday visitors. The **Plage Port-Lin**, facing the Atlantic, is 800m - half a mile from the centre of the town on the far side of the peninsula; the **Plage St-Goustan**, on the roadstead, is 1km - just over half a mile away.

Sea trips ⓥ – Two companies offer boat trips to Belle-Ile. A ferry service crosses the roadstead to La Turballe.

SIGHTS

★**Océarium** ⓥ – The Océarium (marine information centre) contains a didactic display on the techniques of commercial fish-breeding (presentations, videos, microscopes) and houses a collection of wonders of the deep from both temperate and tropical waters. A unique view of the fish occupying a pool containing 300 000l - 66 000 gal seawater is offered by a marvellous 11m - 36ft long tunnel through the pool.

Port – The port is well protected by the Tréhic jetty and is divided into several basins by three islets. It is a picturesque and busy scene in winter with the arrival of prawn boats. The quays are flanked by 17C houses often ornamented by wrought-iron balconies.
The new fish market *(criée)*, built on one of the islets commanding the access to the port, is a pleasant modern building.

Hôtel d'Aiguillon – The 17C building includes the town hall and a naval museum.

Église Notre-Dame-de-Pitié – This 15 and 16C church, with its 17C 56m - 84ft **lantern tower**, overlooks the port. Inside it has a short nave, with a flat east end illuminated by a window with Flamboyant tracery and 3 side aisles. A Virgin, Our Lady of the Wind, decorates the central pier of the Renaissance portal, which opens on to Rue de l'Église.

Old houses – To admire the beautiful corbelled and half-timbered houses, walk through the little streets near the church. Note nos 25, 20 and 28 in Rue de l'Église, no 4 Place du Pilori and nos 33 and 35 in Rue St-Christophe.

Mont-Esprit – This is a drive laid out on an artificial mound (30m - 98ft high) built (1814-6), coming to load salt from ships' ballast. From the top the salt-marshes and Batz can be seen to the east, to the west the town and in the distance the Atlantic.

Mont-Lénigo – Ships at one time unloaded their ballast here and in 1761 trees were planted. The **view**★ goes over the roadstead, the Tréhic jetty (850 m - 2 789ft long), and its lighthouse (1872) at the entrance to the port; the Pen Bron dike (1724) is across the way as is its marine centre. A shaded walk goes down to the esplanade where there is the memorial (1919) by René Paris, erected to Hervé Rielle, the coxswain, who saved 22 ships of the French fleet from disaster in 1692, by directing them to St-Malo.

★CÔTE SAUVAGE

Round tour of 26km - 16 miles – about 2 hours – local map under Presqu'île de GUÉRANDE. Leave Le Croisic by the D 45, the coast road.

After the cure centre (St-Jean-de-Dieu), the road follows the coast passing St-Goustan and its salt marsh where eels are raised. The Côte Sauvage (meaning wild coastline) with oddly shaped rocks (appropriately named the Bear, the Altar) ends at the **Pointe du Croisic**, passing the beaches of Port-Lin, Valentin and its sailing school and Batz-sur-Mer. Further on the view opens out over Pornichet, the Loire estuary and the coast as far as the Pointe St-Gildas.

Le Pouliguen – *See Le POULIGUEN.*

Kervalet – *See Presqu'île de GUÉRANDE.*

Batz-sur-Mer – *See BATZ-SUR-MER.*

Take the D 45 back to Le Croisic.

Presqu'île de CROZON★★★

Michelin map 58 folds 3, 4, 13 and 14 or 20 folds 16 and 17

The Crozon Peninsula affords many excursions typical of the Breton coast. Nowhere else, except perhaps at Raz Point, do the sea and coast reach such heights of grim beauty, with the giddy steepness of the cliffs, the colouring of the rocks and the fury of the sea breaking on the reefs. Another attraction is the variety of views over the indentations and estuaries of the Brest roadstead, the Goulet, the broken coast of Toulinguet, Penhir, Dinan Castle, Cap de la Chèvre and Douarnenez Bay. From the summit of the Ménez-Hom all these features can be seen arrayed in an immense panorama.

★★★ 1 FROM POINTE DE PENHIR TO POINTE DES ESPAGNOLS

Round tour starting from Crozon – 45 km – 28 miles – about 2 hours 30 min

Crozon – The town stands in the middle of the peninsula of the same name. The **church** is modern. The altar to the right of the chancel is ornamented with a large 17C **altarpiece★** depicting the martyrdom of the Theban Legion. Below are two 17C panels: the Flagellation, on the left, and the Bearing of the Cross, on the right. Note the pulpit after which that at Locronan was modelled.

Leave Crozon by the D 8, west of town and make for Camaret.

To the left, by Kerloch, there is a fine view of Dinan Bay and Point, the vast beaches of Kerloch and Goulien and, on a fine day, of the Pointe du Raz.

Camaret-sur-Mer – *See CAMARET-SUR-MER.*

Pointe du Toulinguet – An isthmus bounded by Pen-Hat Beach leads to the point on which a French Navy signal station stands. There is a view of Toulinguet rocks and of the Pointe de Penhir.

Return to the entrance to Camaret and bear right.

Alignements de Lagatjar – They include 143 menhirs discovered since the early 20C *(details on prehistoric monuments in the Introduction).*

★★★ **Pointe de Penhir** – *See Pointe de PENHIR.*

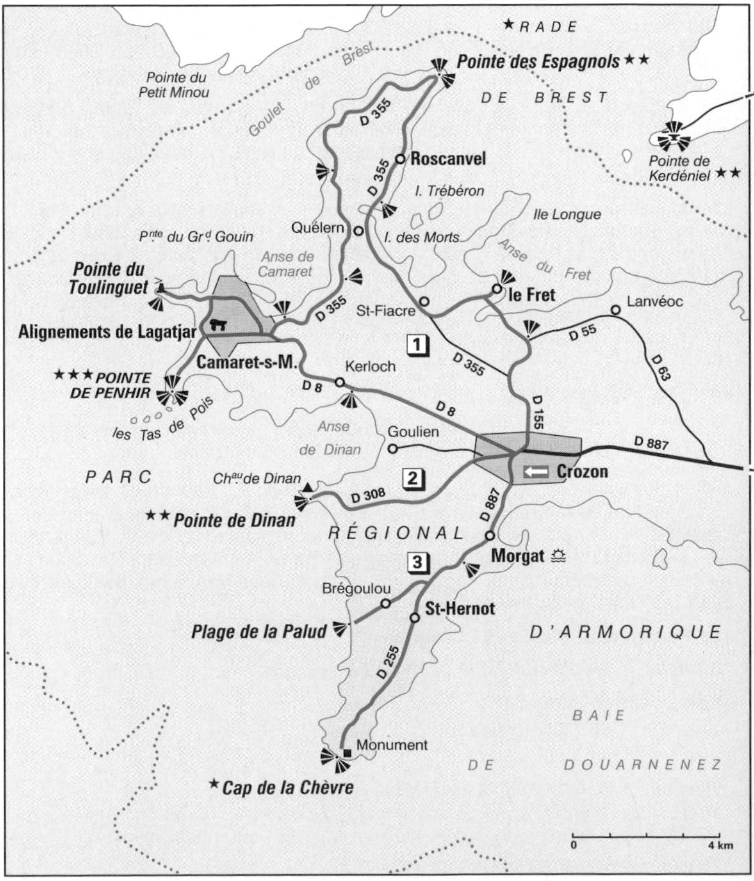

Return to the car and take the Camaret road again. Turn right after 1.5 km – 1 mile towards Crozon, to avoid the town; then take the road to Roscanvel, once a strategic road.

The view opens out to show Camaret Bay on the left and, on the right, the Brest roadstead. The road enters the walls which enclose the Presqu'île de Roscanvel before Quélern. These fortifications date from the time of Vauban and the Second Empire. This road running west is picturesque. The curious contrast between the slopes on either side of the peninsula is striking: the western slope, facing the west wind and the sea, is moorland and lacks vegetation; the eastern slope is covered with trees and meadows.
The road affords views of the Atlantic, Pointe du Toulinguet, Pointe du Grand Gouin, Camaret Bay, the Brest Sound and in the far distance, Pointe de St-Mathieu.

****Pointe des Espagnols** – From here one can see a remarkable **panorama** which includes the Brest Sound, overlooked by CNEXO (Centre National d'Exploitation des Océans), town and harbour of Brest, the Elorn estuary, the Pont Albert-Louppe, the Presqu'île de Plougastel, and the end of the roadstead.
Then the road skirts the eastern coast of the peninsula affording a good view on the left of the Brest roadstead, the Presqu'île de Plougastel and Longue, Morts and Trébéron Islands.

Roscanvel – The church was rebuilt after a fire in 1956 and now possesses fine dark stained-glass windows by Labouret, and a coloured terracotta Stations of the Cross by Claude Gruher.
Note the hedges of fuschia between the gardens.
The road, which to the south of Roscanvel goes round the end of the roadstead, affords fine views of île Longue (nuclear submarine base – *no entry*), and in the foreground, of the two smaller islands, Trébéron and Morts. You leave the peninsular territory once more by the ruined fortifications.

About 500 m – a third of a mile beyond St-Fiacre, turn left.

Le Fret – A small port with regular boat service to and from Brest *(qv)*. View of the Presqu'île de Plougastel from the jetty.
The road runs along the jetty bordering Le Fret Bay.

When you come to a fork, leave the Lanvéoc road on your left and turn right to Crozon.

Enjoy a last look back at the roadstead.

**2 FROM CROZON TO POINTE DE DINAN

6 km – 4 miles – about 2 hours – local map opposite

Crozon – *See Presqu'île de CROZON.*

Leave Crozon west by the D 308.

Windswept heathland follows after the pine groves.

****Pointe de Dinan** – *Time: 1 hour. Leave your car at the car park; continue on foot, by the path on the left for about 500 m – 1/3 mile.* A fine **panorama** can be seen from the edge of the cliff; on the left are Cap de la Chèvre, the coast of Cornouaille and Pointe du Raz; on the right, Pointe du Penhir and the Tas de Pois. Skirting the cliff to the right you will see the enormous rocky mass of **Dinan Castle** ("Château" de Dinan), where the point ends; a natural arch joins this rock, which looks like a fortified castle in ruins, to the mainland *(30 min on foot Rtn, over rocky ground; wear non-slip soles)*. Take the path over the natural arch.

*3 FROM CROZON TO CAP DE LA CHÈVRE

11km – 7 miles – about 2 hours – local map opposite

Crozon – *See section 1 of tour described above.*

Leave Crozon by the D 887 southwest.

Morgat – *See MORGAT.*
From Morgat to Cap de la Chèvre the road runs through an austere landscape of rocks and stunted heath, open to the ocean winds, with little hamlets of houses huddled together which seem to hide in the folds of the ground. To the left, the view gradually opens out over Douarnenez Bay, with the massive outline of the Ménez-Hom in the distance.
500m – a third of a mile past Brégoulou, leave the car in the car park from which you can enjoy a good view of the Tas de Pois and Pointe du Raz.

Plage de la Palud – *It is not advisable to bathe here: the waves are very strong.* Beautiful view of the rocky coastline.

St-Hernot – The **mineral collection** ⏲ housed in the old school, contains more than 500 specimens taken from the Presqu'île de Crozon. The collection shows the peninsula's geological wealth and history.

★**Cap de la Chèvre** – *Time: 30 min.* There is a French Navy signal station on the site. *Go round the signal station to the right to reach the point. Telescope.* From the former German observation point there is a fine **view** over the Atlantic and the advanced points of Finistère: (left to right) Pointe de Penhir and the Tas de Pois, the île de Sein, Cap Sizun and its headlands, Pointe du Van and Pointe du Raz to the south of Douarnenez Bay.
A **monument**, representing the wing of an aircraft stuck into the ground, is dedicated to the aircrew personnel of Aéronautique Navale killed or missing in active service in the Atlantic and Scandinavian regions. The names of the people concerned are engraved on the sides of a circular trench.

DAOULAS★

Population 1 640
Michelin map 58 folds 4 and 5 or 20 fold 18

This small town is located on the banks of the river which shares its name. The river's estuary forms one of the many inlets in the Brest roadstead.
The town owes its development largely to the presence of the abbey built here; the fates of both have been closely linked over the centuries.
Daoulas has inherited many artistic features which bear witness to its past. There are still some 15 and 17C houses along Rue de l'Église.

★**Parish Close (Enclos paroissial)** – The old abbey buildings are to the left. Opposite, and slightly to the right, a 16C **porch**★ takes the place of a bell tower and leads into the cemetery; it is surmounted by a slate roof, which was added last century, and reflects both Gothic and Renaissance styles in its architecture and decoration: numerous statues and a remarkable carved vine in which little figures and animals abound.
The old **abbey church** *(currently under restoration)* still has the original 12C west door, nave and north side aisle. In the east end the ossuary has been converted into a sacristy.
Follow the main alleyway through the cemetery to find the Chapelle of Ste-Anne, set down outside the parish close, which has a 17C doorway surmounted by a crocketed gable in which there is a niche housing the statues of St Anne and the Virgin.

Abbey (Abbaye) – This was founded around the year 500 and, until the 10C, played a major part in the history of Daoulas. It was razed by the Vikings, then rebuilt in the 12C by Augustinian canons, under whose care it flourished until the Revolution. The abbey now belongs to the Conseil Général of Finistère, which has converted it into a cultural centre, more particularly a venue for international archaeological exhibitions.

★**Cloisters** ⓥ – The garden in front of the cloisters contains several statues of saints (Augustine, Sebastian, Andrew).
The Romanesque cloisters, built in 1167 to 1173 (only three walls are still standing), is the only surviving example of this style of architecture in Brittany. The decoration consists of geometric designs and leaf motifs. A large basin decorated with ten masks in between panels with geometric patterns occupies the centre of the cloisters' central open space. Important excavations currently being carried out have revealed the remains of a building dating back prior to the 12C on this site.

Fountain and Oratoire Notre-Dame-des-Fontaines – A path leads to a garden of medicinal plants and a cool dell in which there is a fountain dating from 1550, with Catherine of Siena depicted in bas-relief work on it. A small oratory built in the 16C stands set back; it was embellished in the 19C with some remaining elements from the abbey: door, gallery surrounding the monks' choir, stalls and purlins. There are also two 13C statues, one depicting the Virgin and Child, the other St Thélo riding a stag.

EXCURSION

Dirinon – *5.5km - 3.5 miles north. Leave Daoulas on the N 165 to Brest.*
The church is crowned by a remarkable Renaissance bell tower: above the square tower, two sets of bells and two storeys of balustraded balconies are surmounted by a slender stone spire. Above the doorway, with its Gothic ogee arch, stands a statue of St Nonna, patroness of the parish, in a pilastered niche. Inside, the beam, purlins and hammerbeams are of interest. The vaulting is adorned with 18C paintings; the chancel is covered with 18C woodwork.
To the right of the church, a 16C chapel houses the tomb of St Nonna. The base of the 15C tomb, in Kersanton granite, is carved with the twelve Apostles.

DINAN★★

Population 11 591

Michelin map 59 folds 15 and 16 or 20 fold 25 – Local map under Vallée de la RANCE

Facilities

Dinan is located in a unique site: trees and gardens enhance the old town; its old houses and streets are girt by ramparts and guarded by an imposing castle, and it stands on a plateau overlooking the Rance 75m - 279ft below. The port begins at the foot of a viaduct which bestrides the valley and is used by the St-Malo and Dinard boat services and pleasure craft.

HISTORICAL NOTES

Du Guesclin against Canterbury – In 1357 the Duke of Lancaster besieged Dinan, which was defended by Bertrand Du Guesclin *(qv)* and his brother Olivier. After several encounters with the superior English forces, Bertrand asked for a forty days' truce, after which, he promised, the town would surrender if it were not relieved. In violation of the truce, Olivier, who had gone out of the town unarmed, was made prisoner by an English knight, Canterbury, who demanded a ransom of 1 000 florins. Bertrand challenged the Englishman to single combat. The encounter took place at a spot now called Place du Champ; a stele marks the spot. Lancaster presided. Canterbury lost and had to pay Olivier the 1 000 florins he had demanded and surrender his arms to Bertrand. He was also discharged from the English army. This success won Du Guesclin the admiration of a pretty girl of Dinan, Tiphaine Raguenel. The union of this cultivated woman with the rough warrior, later to be Constable, proved to be a happy one.

Du Guesclin's tombs – After more than twenty years' campaigning for the King of France, Bertrand du Guesclin died on 13 July 1380, at the gates of Châteauneuf-de-Randon, to which he had laid siege. He had asked to be buried at Dinan. The funeral convoy, therefore, set out for that town. At Le Puy the body was embalmed and the entrails buried in the Jacobins' church (now the Église St-Laurent). As the embalming was inadequate, the remains were boiled at Montferrand and the flesh was removed from the skeleton and buried in the Franciscans' church (destroyed in 1793). At Le Mans an officer of the King brought an order to bring the body to St-Denis; the skeleton was then handed over to him. Only the heart arrived at Dinan, where it was deposited in the Jacobins' church. It has since been transferred to the Église St-Sauveur.

So it was that, while the kings of France had only three tombs (for the heart, entrails and body), Du Guesclin had four.

★★OLD TOWN (VIEILLE VILLE) *time: 1 hour 30 min*

A medieval atmosphere can be felt as you walk through Dinan's old streets with their beautifully restored, picturesque half-timbered houses.

Place Du-Guesclin (**BZ**) In this square, bordered with 18 and 19C town houses, stands the equestrian statue of Du Guesclin; the square, with Place du Champ, served as a fairground during the Middle Ages.

Bear right on Rue Ste-Claire, then left on Rue de l'Horloge.

Hôtel Kératry (**BZ B**) – This attractive 16C mansion with three granite pillars, houses the tourist information office.

S. and N. Geary/FOTOGRAMM STONE

Dinan – Rue de l'Horloge

Maison du Gisant (**BZ D**) – During the restoration of this 17C house, the 14C recumbent figure (exhibited outside) was found.

Tour de l'Horloge (**BZ E**) ⌚ – Exhibited in the belfry are the clock, bought by the town in 1498, and the great bell, known as Anne, offered in 1507 by Duchess Anne. From the top of the Clock Tower (158 steps), there is a vast **panorama★★** of the town and its principle monuments and the surrounding countryside. Exhibition on Anne of Brittany.

★**Place des Merciers** (**BYZ 33**) – The old well and lovely old triangular-gabled houses with wooden porches paint a pleasant scene. Glance into nearby Rue de la Cordonnerie and Rue du Petit-Pain lined with corbelled houses; in the latter street stands the old market-place. At no 10 Rue de la Mittrie, Théodore Botrel (1868-1925), the songwriter, was born.

Take the pretty Rue de l'Apport.

Different types of half-timbered houses, characteristic of 15 to 17C Dinan architecture, can seen in Rue de l'Apport: houses with the upper floor resting on thick wooden pillars under which the merchants and tradesmen exposed their wares, houses with overhanging upper storeys and houses with large projecting display windows.

Cross Place des Cordeliers and take the Grande-Rue on the left to reach St-Malo church.

Église St-Malo (**AY**) – This Flamboyant Gothic church was begun in 1490 and finished in the 19C. The late 15C transept, chancel and chevet make a striking impression. Despite the severe disapproval of the inhabitants of Dinan, the perpetrators of the Revolution decimated the church, which was not restored to its congregation until 1803. During the Second Empire, the nave and aisles were, surprisingly enough, rebuilt according to the original design. The **stained-glass windows** date from the 20C and depict life in the various districts of Dinan during major religious festivals: Jerzual Gate, the old bridge and the Place des Cordeliers are all easily recognisable. The large polychrome organ dates from the 19C.
Retrace your steps, cross Place des Cordeliers and go down Rue de la Lainerie, in which there is a **well**. Take Rue de l'École until **Porte St-Malo** (St-Malo Gate). Just before this gate, to the right, a gateway marks the beginning of a pretty walk along the watchpath of the ramparts, with a bird's-eye view of the town. The walk leads past Tour du Gouverneur (**view★★**) and over Porte du Jerzual, before going down Rue Haute-Voie.

Rue du Rempart leads to the English Garden (Jardin Anglais).

Jardin Anglais (**BYZ**) – The terraced garden on the site of the old St-Sauveur cemetery offers a good overall **view★★**, especially from Tour Ste-Catherine, of the River Rance, the port, the enormous viaduct, 250m - 820ft long and 40m - 128ft high, and the ramparts. In the garden stands a statue of Auguste Pavie, diplomat and explorer of Indochina, who was born in Dinan.

Basilique St-Sauveur (**BZ**) – This basilica features a Romanesque porch surmounted by a Flamboyant Gothic gable opening off the façade. The wall to the right is 12C, except for the outside chapel added in the 15C. This is decorated with partially blind, bracketed twin arcades and beautifully sculpted capitals. The rest of the basilica is 15 and 16C. The original dome of the tower, which was destroyed by lightning, was replaced in the 18C by a timber steeple covered with slate.
Inside, the building's lack of symmetry is striking; the south side is Romanesque, while the north side, the transept and the chancel are Flamboyant Gothic. In the north transept, the heart of Du Guesclin is preserved behind a 14C tomb stone incorporated in a 19C tomb. Note the 18C high altar, the 12C granite font in the first chapel of the side aisle, and a 15C stained-glass window depicting the Evangelists in the fourth chapel of the side aisle. In the first chapel of the ambulatory on the south side is a carved polychrome figure of Our Lady of Virtue (13C). The modern stained-glass windows were made in the Barillet workshop.
As you leave the basilica, on Place St-Sauveur, there is a house with pillars on the left, in which Auguste Pavie *(see above)* was born in 1847.

Take the Rue de la Poissonnerie at the top of the square, and then go down Rue du Jerzual on the right.

Hôtel Beaumanoir (**BY N**) – A beautiful Renaissance porch, called the Pelican, adorns the entrance of this old mansion. In the courtyard, note the decoration of the windows and a 16C turret, which houses a lovely staircase.

Take Rue de la Poissonnerie, and then go down Rue du Jerzual to the right.

★**Rue du Jerzual** (**BY**) – This lovely cobbled street slopes steeply downhill. The 15 and 16C **shops** lining the street are now occupied by artists: glass-blowers, sculptors, weavers, etc. This was once the main street leading down to the port; imagine the constant comings and goings of the bourgeois, the hawkers with their overflowing carts and the tradesmen and apprentices running about.

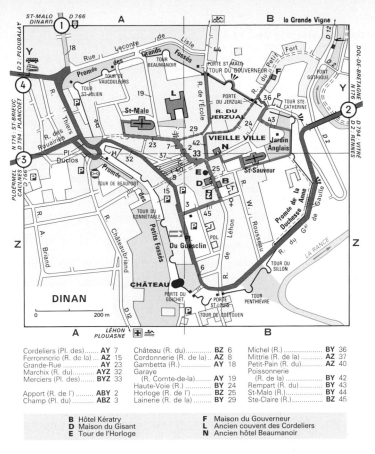

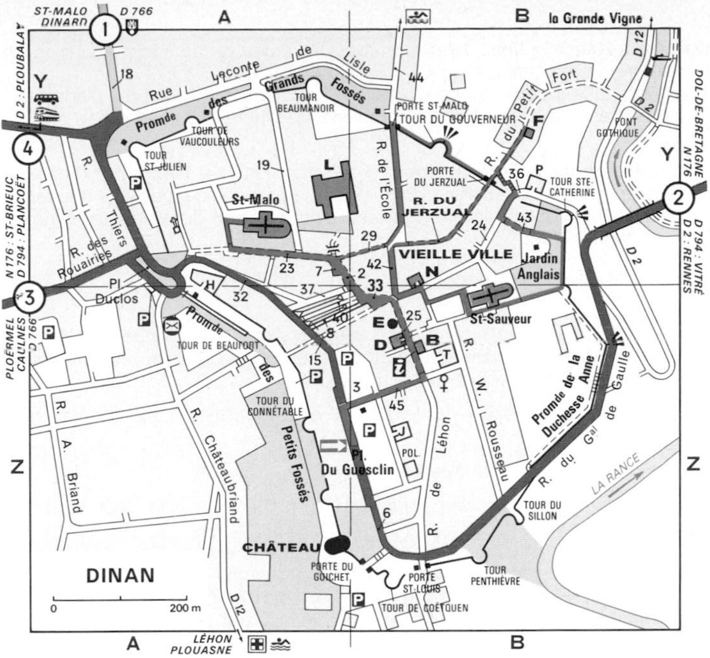

Cordeliers (Pl. des) .... AY 7	Château (R. du) .... BZ 6	Michel (R.) .... BY 36
Ferronnerie (R. de la) ... AZ 15	Cordonnerie (R. de la) .. AZ 8	Mittrie (R. de la) .... AZ 37
Grande-Rue .... AY 23	Gambetta (R.) .... AY 18	Petit-Pain (R. du) .... AZ 40
Marchix (R. du) .... AYZ 32	Garaye (R. Comte-de-la) .... AY 19	Poissonnerie (R. de la) .... BY 42
Merciers (Pl. des) .... BYZ 33	Haute-Voie (R.) .... BY 24	Rempart (R. du) .... BY 43
Apport (R. de l') .... ABY 2	Horloge (R. de l') .... BZ 25	St-Malo (R.) .... BY 44
Champ (Pl. du) .... ABZ 3	Lainerie (R. de la) .... BY 29	Ste-Claire (R.) .... BZ 45

B Hôtel Kératry
D Maison du Gisant
E Tour de l'Horloge
F Maison du Gouverneur
L Ancien couvent des Cordeliers
N Ancien hôtel Beaumanoir

Go through the 14C Jerzual Gate and follow Rue du Petit-Fort, which resembles Rue du Jerzual quite closely.

Maison du Gouverneur (**BY F**) – *At no 24.* This is a fine 15C mansion in which a weaving and high-warp tapestry workshop has been installed.

Carry on to get to the walk along the Banks of the Rance (described below).

ADDITIONAL SIGHTS

★**Castle (Château)** (**AZ**) ⓥ – The castle was built in different stages: the 13C Port du Guichet Gate, the 14C keep and the 15C Coëtquen Tower.
The Porte du Guichet is framed by towers pierced with arrow slits.
The keep, with its bold machicolations, houses a **museum** of the history of Dinan from prehistoric times to the early 20C. It also contains exhibits of local crafts: furnishings, costumes, lovely collection of headdresses, a weaver's workshop and so on. The top room displays works by painters who have drawn inspiration from the town and surrounding area, and by late 19C sculptors who worked in Dinan. From the terrace overlooking the watch path there is a lovely **panorama**★ of the region.
The Tour de Coëtquen, the old artillery tower, exhibits tombstones in a ground floor room. The spiral staircase is enhanced by old statues set in niches.

Promenade de la Duchesse-Anne (**BZ**) – From this promenade along the ramparts, there is a lovely **view**★ of the Rance, the viaduct and the port.

Ancien Couvent des Cordeliers (**AY L**) ⓥ – The former monastery is now a school. A handsome doorway, decorated by a frieze of eight small niches (which once contained statues), opens onto the path, which leads to the school. The 15C Gothic cloisters and the 13C turreted (pepperpot roofs) main courtyard are all that remain of the monastery. Good view of the east end of the Eglise St-Malo.

Promenade des Grands-Fossés (**ABY**) – This magnificent avenue is bordered on one side by Rue Leconte-de-Lisle and on the other by the northern ramparts. Admire the St-Julien, Vaucouleurs and Beaumanoir Towers and the Porte St-Malo.

Promenade des Petits-Fossés (**AZ**) – This promenade skirts the outside of the 13-15C ramparts. Looming above are the castle, and the Connétable and Beaufort Towers.

Banks of the Rance – *Time: 1 hour on foot. Go down to the Rance and cross the Gothic bridge (Pont Gothique).*
On the right, take a path *(no cars allowed)* which passes under the viaduct and follows the river in a green and sheltered **setting**, where it is pleasant to stroll as far as Léhon.

Maison d'Artiste de la Grande Vigne ⓥ – Overlooking the harbour of Dinan, the former house of **Yvonne Jean-Haffen** (1895-1993), a friend and student of the painter Mathurin Méheut, displays several hundred paintings and drawings depicting the Brittany of bygone days.

EXCURSIONS

★**Rance Estuary** ⓥ – *87km – 54 miles – allow 1 day. See Vallée de la RANCE.*
In season you can go down the Rance by boat, but if you wish to return the same day you will have to take a bus or train back.

★**Château de la Bourbansais** – *14km – 8.5 miles southeast. See Château de la BOURBANSAIS.*

Léhon – *2km – 1 mile south. See LÉHON.*

Corseul – *11km – 7 miles. Leave Dinan by ③ on the town plan, bear right onto the road to Plancoët.*
Already known to the Celts, Corseul was conquered and extensively modified by the Romans, as was most of the Armor area. A large quantity of artefacts dating back to those various periods are gathered in and around the town hall. Nearby in the Garden of Antiquities (Jardin des Antiques), columns and capitals can be seen; on the town hall's second floor is **the Musée de la Société archéologique de Corseul** ⓥ containing fossils from the Falun Sea (a marine deposit), polished and dressed stones, funerary urns, coins, Roman murals, everyday implements from Gallo–Roman times and pottery.
In the church, on the pillar to the right of the baptismal chapel, is the funerary stele of Silicia Namgidde (originally a Punic name), a Roman officer's mother, who died in Corseul.
The most remarkable vestige is the **Temple du Haut-Bécherel**, said to be the Temple of Mars *(1.5km – 1 mile on the road to Dinan and right on an uphill road)*. It is a polygonal tower with masonry in small courses, dating from Emperor Augustus's reign.

DINARD⛱⛱⛱

Population 9 918

Michelin map 59 fold 5 or 20 fold 11 – Local maps under CÔTE D'ÉMERAUDE and Vallée de la RANCE – Facilities

This smart resort, which lies in a magnificent setting on the estuary of the Rance, opposite St-Malo, is frequented by the international set and in particular by the British and Americans. The place was "launched" about 1850 by an American named Coppinger and developed by the British. Before that it was a small fishing village and an offshoot of St-Énogat.
The tourist will be interested by the extraordinary contrast between Dinard and St-Malo: the former, a luxurious resort with modern installations, intense social activity, princely villas and splendid gardens and parks; the latter, an old city surrounded by ramparts, possessing a family beach and a commercial port.

SIGHTS

★★**Pointe du Moulinet** (**BY**) – *Start from Grande Plage.*
A walk round this point offers a series of magnificent **views** of the coast from Cap Fréhel, on the left, to St-Malo on the right and, a little further on, of the Rance estuary.

★**Grande Plage or Plage de l'Écluse** (**BY**) – This beach of fine sand, bordered by luxurious hotels, the casino and convention centre (Palais des Congrès), extends to the end of the cove formed by Moulinet and Malouine Points.
Following the promenade along the beach to the left you will reach a terrace from which you can see St-Malo.

★**Promenade du Clair de Lune** ⓥ **and Plage du Prieuré** (**BYZ**) – This walk *(pedestrians only)* lies along a sea wall which follows the water's edge and offers pretty views over the Rance estuary. Lovely multicoloured flower beds and remarkable Mediterranean vegetation embellish the Promenade.
The **Plage du Prieuré** is at the end of the Promenade. It owes its name to a priory founded here in 1324.

DINARD

Féart (Bd) .... BYZ
Leclerc (R. Mar.) .... BYZ 28

Abbé Langevin (R.) .... AY 2
Albert-1er (Bd) .... AB 3
Anciens Combattants (Rue des) .... AZ 5
Barbine (R. des) .... AZ 7
Boutin (Pl. J.) .... BY 9
Clemenceau (R. G.) ...... BY 10
Coppinger (R.) .... BY 12
Corbinais (R. de la) .... AZ 13
Croix-Guillaume (R. de la) .... AZ 15
Douet-Fourchet (R. du) .... AZ 17
Dunant (R. H.) .... AY 19
Français-Libres (R.) .... BZ 22
Gaulle (Pl. du Gén.-de) . BZ 25
Giraud (Av. du Gén.) ..... BZ 26
Levavasseur (R.) .... BY 20
Lhotellier (Bd) .... AY 31
Libération (Bd de la) ..... AZ 32
Malouine (R. de la) .... BY 34
Mettrie (R. de la) .... BZ 35
Pionnière (R. de la) .... ABY 38
Prés.-Wilson (Bd) .... BY 40
Renan (R. E.) .... AY 43
République (Pl. de la) ... BY 44
St-Lunaire (R. de) .... AY 48
Vallée (R. de la) .... BYZ 50
Verney (R. Y.) .... BY 52

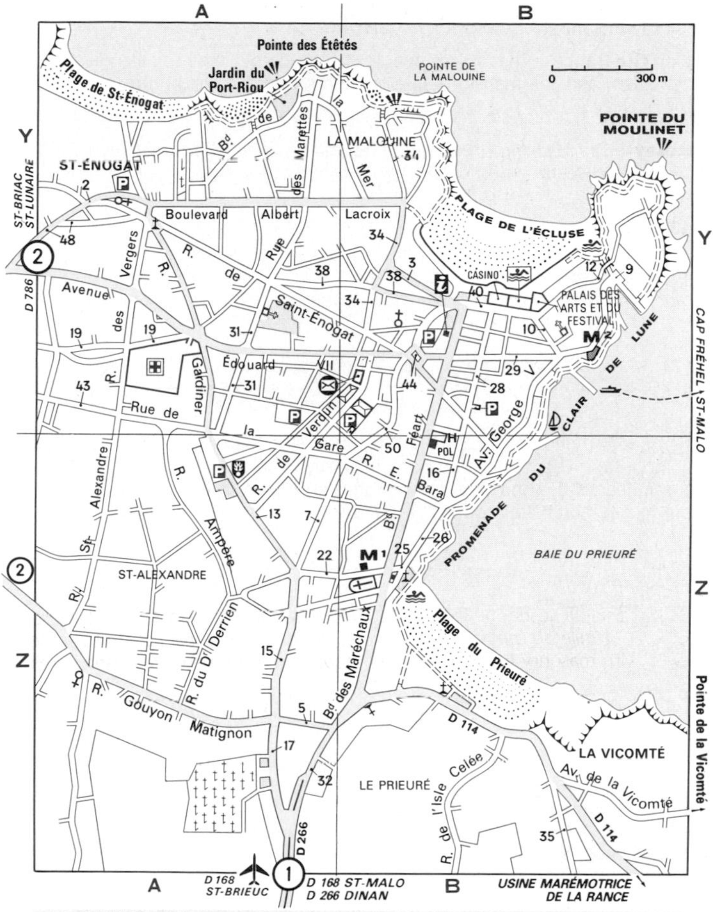

M[1] Musée du Site Balnéaire   M[2] Aquarium et Musée de la Mer

Musée du Site Balnéaire (**BZ M[1]**) ⓥ – The regional museum is housed in Villa Eugénie, built in honour of Napoleon III's wife, who was to have inaugurated the season in 1868. An exhibit traces the history of the six *communes* – Dinard, Pleurtuit, La Richardais, St-Briac, St-Lunaire, Le Minihic – which form the *canton.* A large section displays late 19 and early 20C resort life, an era of opulence, when magnificent villas and great hotels (Grand Hôtel, Grand Hôtel des Terrasses, Crystal Hôtel, to name a few) were built and excellent food was served.

Aquarium et Musée de la Mer (**BY M[2]**) ⓥ – The **Museum d'Histoire naturelle** (Natural History Museum) comprises an **aquarium** with 24 pools filled with fish and crustaceans from Breton waters.
Next is the **Musée de la Mer** (Marine Museum), which presents mementoes of Commandant Charcot's polar expeditions.

Pointe des Étêtes (**AY**) – View of the islands and the coast beyond St-Malo.

Jardin du Port-Riou (**AY**) – This terraced garden, below Pointe des Étêtes, offers a fine **view** as far as Cap Fréhel.

Plage de St-Énogat (**AY**) – The beach lies in a picturesque setting under steep cliffs.

★★ **Pointe de la Vicomté** (**BZ**) – *2 km – 1 mile – plus 1 hour on foot Rtn.* The Vicomté, a fine estate divided into lots, is becoming one of Dinard's most fashionable quarters. Walk along the circular road *(chemin de ronde)*, which starts at Avenue Bruzzo and offers splendid **vistas** towards the roadstead, the Rance estuary and the Usine marémotrice de la Rance.

BOAT TRIPS ⏱

★★★ **St-Malo** – *Crossing: 10 min. See ST-MALO.*

★★★ **Cruise to Cap Fréhel** – *From St-Malo with stop-over at Dinard. Description of Cap Fréhel under Cap FRÉHEL.* On the way out the boat skirts the coast as far as Cap Fréhel, and goes round Cap Cézembre lîle de on the way back.

★★ **Dinan, via the Rance** – *See Vallée de la RANCE.*

Cruises on the Rance – The cruises enable you to discover the small creeks nestled along the coast, and the mansions, *malouinières (qv)*, perched atop the cliffs.

Île de Cézembre – A fine sea trip. The island has a popular beach of fine sand.

★ **Îles Chausey** – *See Michelin Green Guide Normandy.* A small archipelago of granite islands, islets and reefs.

AIR TRIPS ⏱

Regular daily flights leave for the Channel Islands of Jersey and Guernsey. The sights are described in the Michelin Green Guide Normandy and the hotels and restaurants are listed in the Michelin Red Guide Great Britain and Ireland.

Mont DOL★

Michelin map 59 fold 6 or 20 fold 12

This granite mound, though only 65m - 208ft high, overlooks a great plain and resembles a small mountain. The remains of many prehistoric animals – mammoth, elephant, rhinoceros, reindeer, etc – and flint implements have been unearthed on its slopes.
It is possible to go round the mound by car by way of the surface road *(chemin de ronde).*

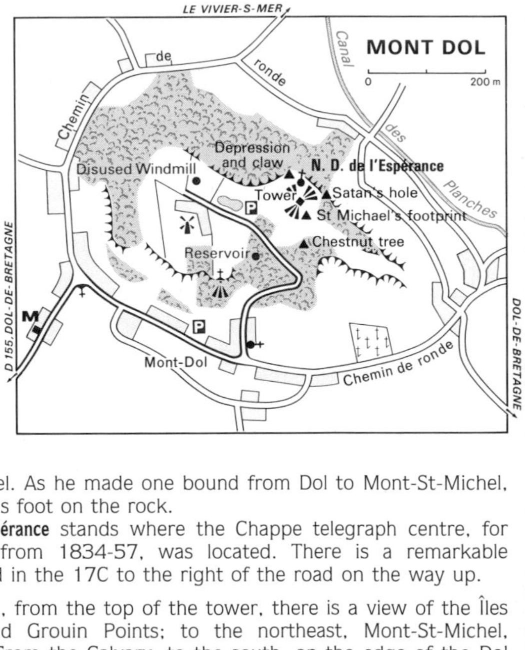

The summit is reached from the Église de Mont-Dol (opposite) on a road with a hairpin bend and an average gradient of 1 in 6.
With a little imagination and the help of the plan, you can reconstruct the legendary struggle which took place here between **St Michael** and Satan. Satan was thrown down so violently that he made a depression in the rock and scratched it with his claw. With one blow of his sword, the Archangel made a hole in the mountain into which he hurled his enemy. But the Devil reappeared on Mont-St-Michel and mocked St Michael. As he made one bound from Dol to Mont-St-Michel, the saint left the imprint of his foot on the rock.
The **Chapelle Notre-Dame-de-l'Espérance** stands where the Chappe telegraph centre, for Paris-Brest communications from 1834-57, was located. There is a remarkable gigantic chestnut tree planted in the 17C to the right of the road on the way up.

★ **Panorama** – To the north, from the top of the tower, there is a view of the Îles Chausey and Cancale and Grouin Points; to the northeast, Mont-St-Michel, Avranches and Granville. From the Calvary, to the south, on the edge of the Dol Marsh, Dol and its fine cathedral can be seen with the Hédé heights in the background; and below, the Dol Marsh.

Marais de Dol – This is the name given to land reclaimed from the marshes and the sea in Mont-St-Michel Bay. Seen from the mound the countryside looks strange and monotonous; it extends for about 15 000 ha - 40 000 acres from the mouth of the Couesnon River to near Cancale. The old shore-line ran through Cancale, Châteauneuf, Dol and St-Broladre and along the stretch of road between Pontorson and St-Malo. This former marshy area consists of two land-types: white marsh, made up of silt from a marine deposit and black marsh, made up of peat bogs.
Some 12 000 years ago, the sea covered the Marais de Dol, it then receded uncovering a large part of the bay. Bit by bit, forest and vegetation took possession of the land abandoned by the sea.

In the 8C banks of limestone shells and sand closed the marsh off from the sea. In the 11C, a dike was built on these sand banks and the land inland was slowly drained. In the 12C, Guyoult River was diverted to Le Vivier-sur-Mer.
Following the drainage of the Marais de Dol, accomplished by the inhabitants over the centuries, 12 000 ha - 29 650 acres have been reclaimed as arable farmland. Apple trees dot the fields and long lines of poplars and willows divide the land into a chequerboard pattern.
The establishment of large-scale mussel-beds in the area around Le Vivier-sur-Mer, in full expansion, has somewhat modified its appearance.

The polders – When the marshes had been reclaimed, work was started on areas that had always been part of the sea-bed; these lay beyond the marsh and to the west of the Couesnon Canal. They have been transformed into polders using the same methods as in the Netherlands. The areas now appear as an empty plain cut across by canals and dikes with new buildings and modern farms. The main roads branch off the Pontorson-St-Malo road and are built on dikes, expanding with the polders from Chapelle Ste-Anne to Mont-St-Michel, and crossing the lines of poplars that mark each new stretch of land reclaimed from the sea. Only exceptionally high tides reach the top of the banks along the bay. Grass grows on them, forming the famous salt pastures *(prés-salés)*; the sheep which graze there yield delicious meat.

Église de Mont-Dol – *In the village.* In this restored church, fine 12 to 14C frescoes recounting the life of Christ were found in the nave: on the north side is the Entrance into Jerusalem, the Kiss of Judas; and on the south side Hell, the Descent into Limbo and the Entombment.

Musée "Les Trésors du mariage ancien" ⌚ (**M**) – This unusual museum has a **collection★** of 350 glass domes containing bridal headdresses (it used to be customary to display the headdress in its glass dome on the mantelpiece of the couple's home), distaffs (one of the symbols of marriage in France) and bridal robes. The display evokes the history of marriage over more than a century (1835-1950) through a dozen life-size scenes presenting the unfolding of a wedding day in chronological order (curious or unusual objects such as lingerie, crockery and furniture).

DOL-DE-BRETAGNE★

Population 4 629
Michelin map 59 fold 6 or 20 fold 12

Dol, a former bishopric and proud of its fine cathedral, is now the small capital of the "Marais" (marsh) district. It stands on the edge of a cliff, about 20 m – 64ft high, which was washed by the sea until the 10C, when marine deposits began forming; the deposit enabled the construction of the sea dike, now a section of the Pontorson-St-Malo tourist road.

SIGHTS

★★ **Cathédrale St-Samson** – *Time: 30 min.*

The cathedral is a vast structure, built of granite in the 12 and 13C and completed during the next three centuries. It gives an idea of the importance that the bishopric of Dol then enjoyed.
On the outside, the most interesting part is the south wall, which includes two porches: the splendid **great porch★** (14C) and the little porch (13C) with its fine pointed arcade. Seen from the north, the cathedral looks like a fortress; its crenellated parapet was linked to the old fortifications of the town.
The interior, 100m - 328ft long, is impressive. Notice in the chancel: the medallion-glass **window★★** (13C restored), the eighty stalls (14C), the carved wood Bishop's throne (16C) and, above the high altar, the 14C wooden Statue of the Virgin, coloured in 1859. In the north arm of the transept, is the tomb of Thomas James, Bishop of Dol (16C); it is the work of two Florentine sculptors, Antoine and Jean Juste. In the north aisle note the Christ Reviled; in the axial chapel there are two 18C reliquary figures of St Samson and St Magloire.

★ **Promenade des Douves** – This public garden (also known as Promenade Jules Revert) has been traced along the north part of the old ramparts. One of the 12 defence towers, the large Tour des Carmes, can still be seen. Its offers a fine **view★** of the Mont Dol and the Marais de Dol.

Museum (Musée historique de Dol) ⌚ – The museum is installed in the 16C treasury and is devoted, for the most part, to the history of Dol: dioramas, wax figures, models and arms; there is, also, a section on the Revolution (dioramas). The treasury contains a fine collection of polychrome wooden statues (13-19C) of saints as well as 17-18C glazed earthenware from different Breton Schools (in particular rare statues of Virgins).

DOL-DE-BRETAGNE

Chateaubriand (Pl.) 7
Grande-Rue des Stuarts 10
Le-Jamptel (R.) 12

Briand (Av. Aristide) 2
Carmes (R. des) 3
Cathédrale (Pl. de la) 4
Çeinte (Rue) 6
Écoles (R. des) 8
Mairie (Pl. de la) 13
Normandie (Bd de) 14
Paris (R. de) 15
Saint-Malo (Rue de) 17
Touliers (Place) 19

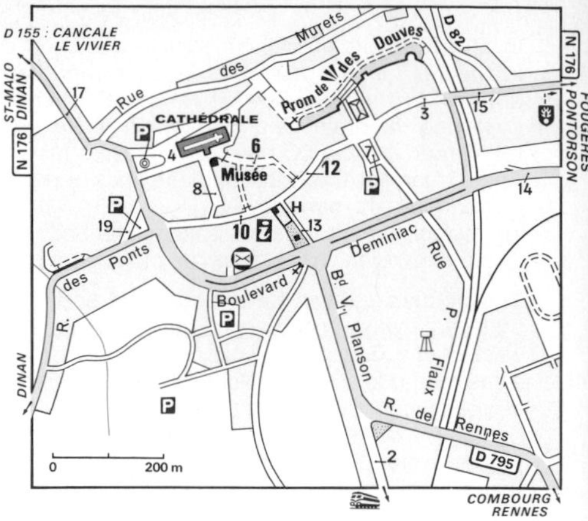

Old houses – The streets near the cathedral precincts have interesting old half-timbered houses, town houses, and shops.

Grande-Rue des Stuarts (**10**) – No 17 (florist) dates from the 11 and 12C and has Romanesque arcading; no 27 (antique-dealer) is 13C; no 33 is a 1617 dwelling with fine dormer windows; no 18, a former Templars' inn with a 12C vaulted cellar, is now transformed into a bar-*crêperie*; a charming 16C courtyard is at no 32.

Rue Le-Jamptel (**12**) – No 31 (hardware store) dates from the 12 or 13C; no 27 is a 15C house decorated with pillars.

Rue Ceinte (**6**) – This street where the chapter-house used to be located. No 1, an old shop with a granite counter, and no 4, now a *crêperie*, are both 15C; no 16 dates from 1668.

EXCURSIONS

Round tour of 30km - 18.5 miles – *Time: about 1 hour 45 min. Leave Dol south-east of the town plan on the D 795. Leave the road to Épiniac on your left, 600m – about a third of a mile further turn left then turn right into a tarmac road.*

Menhir de Champ-Dolent – The dolmen, one of the finest in Brittany, stands 9.50m - 30ft high (width: 8.70m - 31ft). The granite comes from Bonnemain located 5km - 3 miles south. The name Champ-Dolent (Field of Pain) refers to a legendary struggle which is supposed to have taken place here.

Return to the road to Combourg.

Musée de la Paysannerie ⓥ – At **Baguer-Morvan**. Made up of three large buildings, this museum retraces the past 100 years in the life of the peasant farmer: reconstructed furnished interiors, photographs and postcards, farming equipment (tractors, threshers, harvesters...) and tools (rakes, knives, hammers...). Cider tasting is offered at the end of the tour.

Continue on the D 795 and then left towards Épiniac.

Épiniac – In the north aisle of the **church**, on the altar, is a 16C polychrome high relief representing the Dormition of the Virgin; in the chancel is a finely carved 17C wood canopy.

Follow the D 85 then bear left.

Broualan – In the centre of the village near a small yet remarkable Calvary stands a 15C church, enlarged in the 16C. The east end is decorated with pinnacled buttresses and lovely Flamboyant windows. The small columned bell tower rests on the large arch which separates the nave from the chancel. Inside, several small granite altars and finely worked credences (side tables) can be seen. The tabernacle of the high altar is supported by angels. Note the 16C polychrome stone *Pietà*.

Via La Boussac return to Dol-de-Bretagne.

Abbaye N.-D.-du-Tronchet – *10km – 6 miles. Leave Dol southwest of the town plan on the N 176 and bear left towards Le Tronchet.* This former Benedictine abbey was built in the 17C. Large cloisters and a hostel (which houses the presbytery) stand amid the ruins. The church contains beautiful 17C woodwork.

The length of time given in this guide
– for **touring** *allows time to enjoy the views and the scenery*
– for **sightseeing** *is the average time required for a visit.*

DONGES

Population 6 377

Michelin map 6 fold 15 or 20 folds 52 and 53 – 17km – 11 miles east of St-Nazaire

The oil port of Donges, which is an annexe of the port of Nantes-St-Nazaire *(qv)*, has constructed three berths for large oil tankers. The town is also an important refining centre representing half of Elf Aquitaine's refining capacity in France.
The village, at some distance from the refinery complex, was rebuilt after the Second World War.

★**Church** ⓥ – This is built of concrete and granite. A huge Calvary set in a parabolic arc, with a stained glass window by Max Ingrand as background, dominates the west façade. Standing back and to the right is the square bell tower crowned by a slender, copper-covered steeple. Inside there is a feeling of simplicity and upwards sweep emphasised by the pure line of the nave's sharply pointed arches; stained glass windows in the side chapels are also by Ingrand.

DOUARNENEZ★

Population 16 457

Michelin map 58 fold 14 or 20 fold 17 – Local map under CORNOUAILLE – Facilities

The four localities of Douarnenez, Ploaré, Pouldavid and Tréboul have merged to form the *commune* of Douarnenez, which today is known as a city boasting three ports (museum-port, fishing port and sailing harbour), a European centre for fish canning, a seaside resort and a thalassotherapy spa. The town itself, nestling in a prettily-curved bay, presents colourful, picturesque façades that have seduced many an artist, namely Auguste Renoir, Eugène Boudin, Emmanuel Lansyer, etc. Although "the era of the sardine" now belongs to the past, visitors will appreciate the old-fashioned atmosphere which permeates the maze of narrow streets encircling the port.
According to local tradition, Douarnenez was the original site of the palace belonging to King Marc'h; the island located at the entrance to the estuary of Pouldavid bears the name of his nephew Tristan. Before being called Douarnenez in 1541 (*douar an enez* means the land of the island), the harbour was known as Hameau de St Michel (St-Michael's Hamlet) and then, in 1520, Bourg de l'Ile Tristan (Village of Tristan's Island).

La Fontenelle (16C) – According to local tradition, the palace of King Marc'h was at Douarnenez and the island at the mouth of the Pouldavid estuary was, therefore, given the name of his nephew, Tristan *(qv)*.
In the 16C this island was the lair of Sire Guy Eder La Fontenelle *(qv)*, the most dangerous of the robber barons who devastated the country during the conflicts of the League.
La Fontenelle seized the île Tristan. To obtain materials for fortifications he demolished those of Douarnenez. His cruelty was legendary. In 1598 he agreed to lay down his arms on condition that he be allowed to keep the island; this was granted by Henri IV. But in 1602 the King took his revenge: involved in a plot, La Fontenelle was sentenced to be broken on the wheel in Paris.

DOUARNENEZ

Anatole-France (R.) .... **Y** 2
Duguay-Trouin (R.) .... **Y** 15
Jaurès (R. Jean) .... **YZ**
Jean-Bart (R.) .... **Y** 24
Voltaire (R.) .... **Y** 62

Baigneurs (R. des) .... **Y** 5
Barré (R. J.) .... **YZ** 7
Berthelot (R.) .... **Z** 8
Centre (R. du) .... **Y** 10
Croas-Talud (R.) .... **Z** 14
Enfer (Pl. de l') .... **YZ** 16
Grand-Port (Quai du) .... **Y** 19
Grand-Port (R. du) .... **Y** 20
Kerivel (R. E.) .... **YZ** 21
Laënnec (R.) .... **Z** 25
Lamennais (R.) .... **Z** 27
Marine (R. de la) .... **Y** 32
Michel (R. L.) .... **Y** 36
Monte-au-Ciel (R.) .... **Z** 37
Péri (Pl. Gabriel) .... **Y** 42
Petit-Port (Quai du) .... **Y** 43
Plomarc'h (R. des) .... **YZ** 44
Stalingrad (Pl.) .... **Z** 56
Vaillant (Pl. Édouard) .... **Y** 59
Victor-Hugo (R.) .... **Z** 60

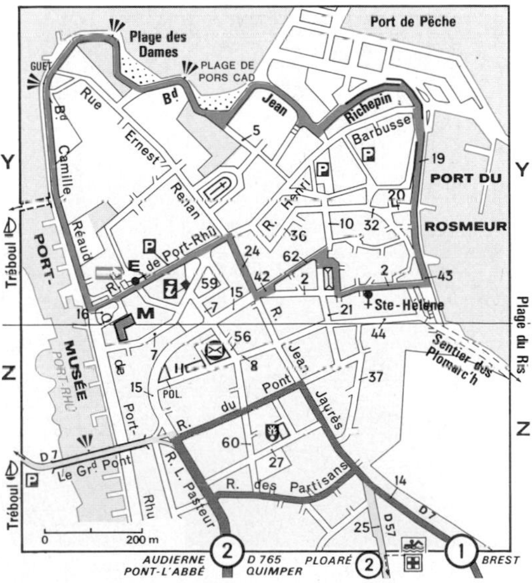

E Chapelle St-Michel
M Musée du Bateau

SIGHTS *time: 3 hours*

Start from Place de l'Enfer.

★★ **Port-Musée** ⌚ – This Port Museum is both a centre of conservation of boats and a permanent workshop where expertise in this field is passed on. It offers a good opportunity to rediscover the recent maritime past. The various elements of the Port Museum, established on the wonderful site of Port-Rhu, once the commercial harbour of Douarnenez, contain displays on all aspects of maritime and harbour life, from ships afloat, to construction sites and an onshore museum containing 230 boats.

Musée du bateau (**YZ M**) – This Boat Museum is located in an old canning factory and contains an **outstanding collection**★ of fishing, transport and pleasure boats from France and abroad. The Irish curragh can be found beside the Welsh coracle or the Norwegian oselvar; clinker-built ships are next to carvel-built ships. Most of the exhibits are of wood; however, there are some boats made from the skins of horses, deer, seals or even whales. Many of the craft are displayed in full sailing rig.

Musée à flot – This comprises about forty boats, twenty-six of which are open to visitors, moored in three harbour docks. In the first basin, **fishing boats** include: trawlers, lobster boats, shellfish boats, sardine boats and tunny boats. Visitors can go aboard one of the lobster boats, the *Notre-Dame-de-Rocamadour*. In another basin are larger **coastal vessels** such as the *Saint-Denys*, the *Anna Rosa* or the *Northdown*. The variety of boats displayed encompasses a British steam tug, a Norwegian coaster and a Breton *sablier* (used for transporting sand). **Pleasure craft** include the *Ariane*, built in 1927, the *Viviane*, dating from 1859, as well as cruising vessels and modern racing boats moored on the premises.

Chantier naval – A 53m - 174ft 19C three-master clipper on which construction work is expected to last several years is currently on Place de l'Enfer, at the centre of the shipyard. Along the quays, a wooden breakwater has been reconstructed in the old-fashioned style with repair workshops and presentations which enlighten visitors on the trades of marine ropemakers, sail-makers and carpenters.
At the centre of the wet dock, the *Scarweather*, a British lightship can be visited from the bridge down in the hold, going through the radio room.
Trips out to sea, by the hour or half-day, organised by the associations in charge of conventional boats, round the visit off nicely.

Take Boulevard Camille-Réaud.

This route brings the visitor to the viewpoint of the "Guet", where the Port-Rhu River runs into the bay.

Port-Rhu River and Plage des Dames (**Y**) – A *corniche* road runs along the shore and affords picturesque views of Tristan Island, a superb view of the bay, the Tréboul district, the narrow streets clustering round the port, and the estuary, which is spanned by a viaduct 24m - 78ft high. There lies Port-Rhu, the former commercial port of Douarnenez. The path skirts Plage Porscad, then Plage des Dames.

★ **Boulevard Jean-Richepin and Nouveau Port** (**Y**) – Follow this boulevard, which offers superb **views**★ of Douarnenez Bay. You will see the new fishing port, which is developing in the shelter of a jetty some 741m - 800yds long. The view from the new jetty is worth admiring as you get a wider view of the bay.

F. Molveck/Le Port-Musée, Douarnenez

Port-Rhu

★**Port du Rosmeur** (**Y**) – This fishing port, the pulse of the local economy, is ranked 6th in France in terms of tonnage. Here you may witness typical scenes of a coastal fishing town: the return of the boats loaded with the day's catch at eleven o'clock at night, the open-air fish market at 6.30 in the morning (*for guided tours, apply to the Tourist Information Office*). The most common types of fish caught off Douarnenez include mackerel, cod, whiting, monkfish, coalfish, tunny fish, sardine and crayfish. A walk along Rosmeur pier also offers a good view of the harbour district.

Take Rue A.-France uphill to the left.

Chapelle Ste-Hélène (**Y**) – This chapel, in the Flamboyant Gothic style, was remodelled in the 17 and 18C. Over the side altars are 18C pictures and at the end of the nave, two 16C stained glass windows.
Return to Place Gabriel-Péri by way of the covered market. Every morning there is a charming, bustling open-air market.

Continue along Rue Jean-Bart and turn left into Rue de Port-Rhu.

Chapelle St-Michel (**Y E**) ⓥ – This was built in 1663 and has a semicircular chancel and transept, and a small domed belfry. 17C paintings on the vaulting.

Return to Place de l'Enfer.

Tréboul – Tréboul is linked to Douarnenez by a pedestrian passageway running along the estuary of Port-Rhu and the outer walls of the Port-Musée (offering visitors a charming stroll in a pleasant setting) as well as by Grand Pont, a large metal bridge for cars spanning the Port-Rhu estuary and affording a splendid **view** of the Port-Musée site.

Port de Plaisance (**Yachting Harbour**) – Set up in the Bay of Tréboul, it can accommodate up to 700 boats. The bay serves as a fantastic natural venue for nautical events and a great many competitions are staged here every year.

Boat Rides ⓥ – Boats can be hired for fishing expeditions, to visit sea caves or for cruises to Morgat.

PLOARÉ

Church ⓥ – *Rue Laënnec. Access by ② on the town plan, the D 57.* The church dates from the 16 and 17C. It is crowned by a fine Flamboyant and Renaissance **tower**★, 55m - 180ft high, with a crocketed steeple with four pinnacles at the corners (two Gothic, two Renaissance).
The façade is flanked with Gothic buttresses surmounted by pinnacles, while the buttresses of the apse and transept are crowned with small Renaissance lanterns. Inside note the high altar's carved altarpiece and a 17C painted wooden group representing the Holy Trinity.
Laënnec (1781-1826), the inventor of the stethoscope, is buried in the cemetery. Kerlouarnec, the country house where this eminent physician died, can be seen at the end of a fine avenue leading to the Chapelle de Ste-Croix (1701).

POULDAVID

By ② of the town plan, the D 765 towards Audierne, and take the first road on the left.

Church ⓥ – *32 steps.* Built on the hillside, the church has a 15C porch, a 14C arcaded nave and a 16C chancel. The chancel vaulting is adorned with sixteen 16C painted panels illustrating scenes from the Passion. Housed inside are several old statues; note the late 16C *Pietà* on the stone altar.

EXCURSIONS

★**Sentier des Plomarc'h and Plage du Ris** (**Z**) – *Time: 2 hours 30 min on foot Rtn. Access via Rue des Plomarc'h east of the town plan.*
The path begins at Port du Rosmeur and runs along the side of a slope affording some very picturesque **views**★ of Douarnenez. It leads to Plage du Ris. Return by the Locronan road.

★**Pointe de Leydé** – *Round tour of 6km – 4 miles to the west. At Sables-Blancs Beach (Tréboul district), turn left into the road to Roches Blanches and leave the car on the parking area just after the Village de Vacances. Follow the Roches Blanches coastal path (signposted in orange) which runs along the sea and leads to the Pointe de Leydé.* The point affords a lovely **view**★ of the Bay of Douarnenez.

From there, you can either return by the road leading back to Tréboul, or continue by the path leading to the localities of Poullan-sur-Mer and Beuzec.

Le Juch – *8km – 5 miles. Leave Douarnenez by ② on the town plan, the D 765. 6km – 4 miles further on, turn left for Le Juch.*

Fine **view** of Douarnenez Bay, the Presqu'île de Crozon and Ménez-Hom. Inside the 16-17C **church** ⏲, the old 16C stained glass window at the east end shows scenes from the Passion; to the left and right of the chancel are statues depicting the Annunciation, placed in niches with 16C painted shutters. To the right of the sacristy door, in the north aisle is St Michael overcoming a dragon known as the Devil of Le Juch. *Pardon* on 15 August.

Guengat – *14km – 9 miles by ② on the town plan, the D 765. 11km – 7 miles further on, turn left, for Guengat.*
In the Gothic **church** ⏲ at the entrance to the choir is, on the left column, a Flemish statue of St Barbara and, on the right column, a 16C *Virgin and Child.* In the choir itself are 16C **stained-glass windows★** depicting the Passion (centre), the Last Judgment (right) and the Virgin between St John the Baptist and St Michael (right), and a carved frieze with animals (hare, fox, wild boar), people and floral decoration. It is worth going into the cemetery to see the fine Calvary.

EMERALD COAST★★★

See CÔTE D'ÉMERAUDE

Les ENCLOS PAROISSIAUX★★

Michelin map 58 folds 5 and 6 or 230 folds 4, 5, 18 and 19

Parish closes *(qv)*, which are a special feature of Breton art, are to be found mostly in Lower Brittany. The route runs through the picturesque Élorn Valley and the foothills of the Monts d'Arrée *(qv)* and includes only a few of the more interesting ones. There are many others, especially that of Pleyben *(qv)*, further to the south.

ROUND TOUR STARTING FROM MORLAIX

130km – 81 miles – allow 1day

★**Morlaix** – *See MORLAIX. Leave Morlaix by ③ on the town plan.*

★★**St-Thégonnec** – *See ST-THÉGONNEC.*

Go round the east end of the church and bear left.

★★**Guimiliau** – *See GUIMILIAU.*
On the outskirts of Guimiliau, before the bridge under the railway, note lower down on your left a fountain decorated with three figures.

★**Lampaul-Guimiliau** – *See LAMPAUL-GUIMILIAU.*

Landivisiau – *See LANDIVISIAU.*

Head towards Landerneau, then turn right via the intersection at La-Croix-des-Maltotiers.

Bodilis – *Time: 15min.* The **church★** (16C) is preceded by a Flamboyant bell tower pierced with three openings at the base. The large 17C sacristy, jutting out from the north aisle, is very handsome, with a roof in the shape of an inverted hull, a richly decorated cornice and buttresses ornamented with niches. A porch opens on the south side. The interior has remarkable **decorations★**: purlins, tie-beams, hammerbeams, statues and gilded altarpieces. The font canopy is carved from Kersanton granite. There is also a colourful Entombment in high relief on the porch wall.

Rejoin the D 712 Landerneau and bear right.

Moulin de Brézal – The mill, which has an interesting façade with a Flamboyant doorway, stands in a pleasant setting below a pool. On the opposite side of the road is the ruined Chapelle de Pont-Christ (1533).

★**La Roche-Maurice** – *See La ROCHE-MAURICE.*

Landerneau – *See LANDERNEAU.*

Leave Landerneau by ② on the town plan, towards Sizun.

The road follows a pleasant wooded valley studded with fine rocks.

★**La Martyre** – *Left after 7km – 4 miles. Time: 15min.* This **parish close★**, the oldest in the Léon region, opens onto a triumphal arch with a Flamboyant balustrade and a small Calvary. The ossuary (1619) is adorned with a curious caryatid and macabre motifs. The 14-16C church has a fine historiated **porch★** (*c*1450) on its south side. Inside, note the carved purlins, tie-beams, altarpieces and 15C chancel screen. The chancel is lit by 16C **stained-glass windows★**. A *pardon* is held on the second Sunday in May and the second Sunday in July.

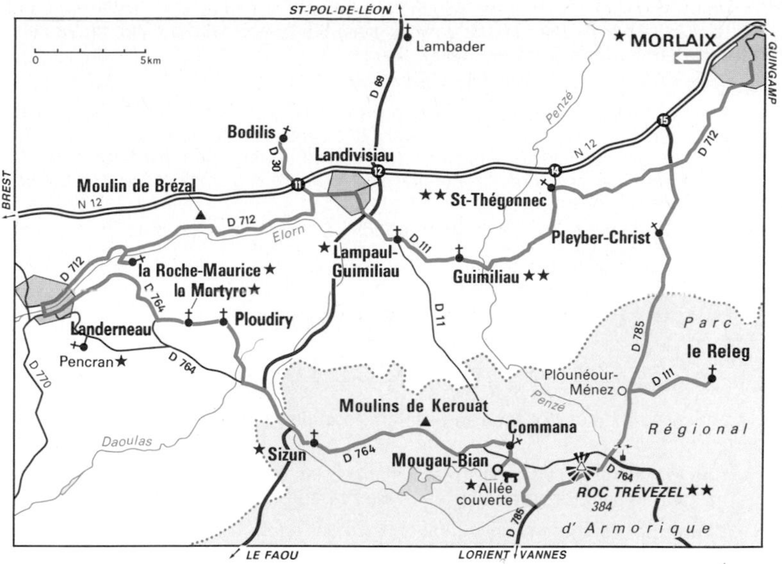

Ploudiry – The village, formerly the largest parish of the Léon region, has an interesting close. On the façade of the ossuary (1635), Death is depicted striking down men of all social classes. The church, rebuilt in the 19C, retains a fine south **porch★** dating from 1665. The high altar, adorned with polychrome high relief carvings and the side altars are good specimens of 17C Breton art. In the chancel is a 17C window depicting the Passion.

Pass through Le Traon and turn left towards Sizun.

★**Sizun** – *See SIZUN.*

Proceed to Carhaix.

Moulins de Kerouat ⌚ – Under the auspices of the Parc naturel régional d'Armorique *(qv)*, the 19C village of Kerouat has been revived. You will see its mills, dwelling house, outbuildings (stable, barn) and bread oven; learn how a water mill functioned with its scoop wheel and mechanism (gears on the ground floor, millstone on the upper floor), and how the miller lived.
The overseer's house is characteristic of the region with its projecting wing perpendicular to the main part of the building; it is where meals were served.

Continue onto Carhaix and at Ty Douar bear left.

Commana – The village stands on an isolated foothill of the Monts d'Arrée. Within the close is a 16-17C **church★** with a fine south porch. Inside, there are three interesting altarpieces. Note the **altar★** to St Anne (1682) in the north aisle and an *Ecce Homo* in wood on a pillar in the transept, to the right. The canopied font is ornamented with five statues: Faith, Hope, Charity, Justice and Temperance.
In the summer there is an exhibit of sacred art in the charnel-house.

Mougau-Bian – Beyond the hamlet, to the right, is a **covered alleyway★**, 14m - 46ft long; some of the uprights are carved on the inside with lances and daggers.

Return to the road to Carhaix and bear right; 1km – half a mile further on, take an uphill road to the right to join the Morlaix road, and turn left.

★★**Roc Trévezel** – This rocky escarpment, which juts up on the skyline (384m - 1 260ft), is in a remarkably picturesque spot in a truly mountainous setting. *Take the path (30min on foot Rtn) near a signpost. Go towards the left, cross a small heath, bearing to the right, and make for the most distant rocky point.* From here the **panorama★★** is immense. To the north, the Léon Plateau appears, bristling with spires; in clear weather you can see the Kreisker spire at St-Pol-de-Léon and to the east Lannion Bay; to the west, the end of the Brest roadstead; to the south, the St-Michel Mountain and, beyond it, the dark line of trees on the Montagnes Noires.

Proceed in the direction of Morlaix.

The road passes near the Roc-Trédudon relay tower and offers lovely **views** of the Léon region as it descends.

Near Plounéour-Ménez, turn right.

Le Releg – Nestling in the valley, a 12-13C church and the ruins of the monastery buildings, are all that remain of the former Cistercian abbey. It is a simple, austere building, although the façade was restored in the 18C; note the staircase leading up to the monk's dormitory. Around the chancel are statues of St Benedict and St Bernard. Two *pardons* are held every year: Ste-Anne's with a Celtic music concert and that of Notre-Dame-du-Releg.

Turn back and bear right towards Morlaix.

Pleyber-Christ ⏱ – It has a small parish close. The Gothic-Renaissance **church** is preceded by a triumphal arch (1921) dedicated to the dead of the First World War. Inside the building, which has fine carved purlins and remarkable beams, are some old pews and three lovely altarpieces. There is a small ossuary to the left of the church.

Continue towards Ste-Sève; after 3.5km - 2 miles, take the road on the right to return to Morlaix.

Le FAOU

Population 1 522

Michelin map 58 fold 5 or 20 fold 18 – Local map under Monts d'ARRÉE

The town, at the head of the Faou estuary, occupies a **site**★ which is full of character at high tide.

Rue Principale – The main street is flanked, on one side, by old houses with overhanging upper storeys and slate-covered façades.

Church – The 16C church stands on the river bank. It has an elegant 17C domed bell tower, a double transept, a canted east end and an ornately sculpted south porch.

CORNICHE DE TÉRÉNEZ

Round tour of 25km - 16 miles – about 1 hour. Leave Le Faou west by the D 791 in the direction of Crozon.

At first the road affords views over the estuary of the Le Faou River and, in the distance, of the Presqu'île de Plougastel *(qv)*. Further on, as you skirt the Aulne estuary, you will see Landévennec *(qv)* ahead, on the right and, soon afterwards, the whole of Landévennec Peninsula and the course of the Aulne. At the end of a short rise you will overlook the narrow part of the Aulne Valley, crossed by the Pont de Térénez.

Pont de Térénez – This elegant structure has a central span of 272m - 893ft; from the bridge there is a fine view of the valley.

Turn around, and about half-way up the hill turn right into a road which leaves the river and reaches a plateau.

Belvédère – From the viewpoint on the right of the road, there is a scenic **view** of a bend of the Aulne Valley, Trégarvan hamlet and the north face of Ménez-Hom.

Go to Ty-Jopic via Rosnoën passing by the Quimerch radio station and bear left.

Quimerch – *See Monts d'ARRÉE.*

Return to Le Faou on the road running downhill.

Le FAOUËT

Population 2 869

Michelin map 58 fold 17 or 230 fold 20

This village is the centre of a very picturesque district extending between the Stêr Laër and the Ellé, two rivers flowing from the Montagnes Noires.

Halles – The covered market with its great slate roof supported at the sides on short granite columns and at the ends by massive porches, was built in 16C. Inside, three aisles lie under the fine timberwork. A domed pinnacle crowns the building.

Grand-Place – In this shady square in front of the market, stands a monument to **Corentin Carré**, the youngest soldier of France. In 1915 he enlisted at the age of fifteen, and died in aerial combat in 1918. He was then a sergeant-major.

EXCURSIONS

★**Chapelle St-Fiacre** – *2.5km - 1.5 miles southeast on the D 790. See Chapelle ST-FIACRE.*

Round tour of 30km - 19 miles – *About 3 hours. Go north towards Gourin, on leaving Le Faouët turn right and make for the chapel bearing right all the way.*

Chapelle Ste-Barbe – *See Chapelle STE-BARBE.*

Return to the Gourin road and turn right and 500m - 547yds further on turn right towards Rostrenen. Take the D 121 on the left to Langonnet.

The road goes up the **Ellé Valley**.

To the left, in a bend, two pillars mark the entrance to Langonnet Abbey.

Abbaye de Langonnet – Rebuilt in the 17-18C, the abbey, now a home for retired priests, has kept its 13C chapterhouse which has been converted into a chapel. Its graceful palm-leaf vaulting is noteworthy.

Take the road to Priziac opposite the abbey entrance and after 3km - 2 miles, turn right.

The road skirts **Étang du Bel-Air** (Bel-Air Lake) which has facilities for water sports (fishing, pedalos at Priziac).

Turn right towards Le Faouët and after 1km – half a mile bear left.

Chapelle St-Nicolas ⏲ – *Temporarily closed to the public.* The little chapel stands alone in a beautiful setting of pines and fine trees. The style of the building is Gothic strongly influenced by Renaissance design. The Renaissance **rood screen★** *(being restored)*, which is interesting to compare with the Gothic one to be found at St-Fiacre, is a fine piece of Breton sculpture on wood. Above an attractive screen, the legend of St Nicholas is shown in nine panels, while on the other side, caryatids separate niches containing figures of the Apostles. There are also polychrome 16C statues in stone. *Pardon* on second Sunday in July.

Return towards Le Faouët.

By the bridge spanning the Ellé, a pleasant walk may be enjoyed along the river to the Chapelle Ste-Barbe.

Le FOLGOËT★★

Population 3 094

Michelin map 58 fold 4 or 230 folds 3 and 4 – Local map under ABERS

You should see this little village and its magnificent Basilica of Our Lady (Notre-Dame) during the great *pardon (See the Calendar of events at the end of the guide)*. It is the best known in the Léon region and one of the largest in Brittany. The ceremonies begin at 6pm the day before and continue the next day. The *pardon* of St Christopher with the blessing of cars is on the fourth Sunday in July.

Legend – The name Folgoët (Fool's Wood) recalls the legend attached to the foundation of the shrine. In the middle of the 14C, a poor half-wit named Salaün lived in a hollow oak in a wood, near a spring not far from Lesneven. He knew only a few words, and he constantly repeated them: "Itron Gwerc'hez Vari" (Lady Virgin Mary). After his death a lily grew on his grave; the pistil made the words "Ave Maria" in gold letters. Men dug up the earth and found that the lily sprang from Salaün's mouth. News of the miracle spread in Brittany. The War of Succession was raging at the time. The Pretender Montfort vowed that if he won he would build a sumptuous chapel to the Virgin. After his victory at Auray *(qv)*, he gave orders for the building to begin. The altar was to stand over the spring where the simpleton used to drink. The work was completed by Montfort's son in 1423.
The chapel was pillaged during the Revolution. To save it from being demolished, twelve farmers joined together to buy it. It was returned to the parish at the Restoration, and has been gradually repaired since.

★★ **Basilique** – *Time: 30min.* A great esplanade with inns on each side leads up to the basilica, but is not even wide enough to hold the crowd on *pardon* days. The **north tower★** of the façade supports one of the finest bell towers in Brittany.
The basilica is square in shape, which is unusual; the Chapel of the Cross, whose east wall is an extension of the flat east end, branches off the chancel. This chapel has a fine **porch★**. Salaün's fountain, where pilgrims come to drink, stands outside, against the east wall. The water comes from the spring under the altar.
Inside is a masterpiece of Breton art of the 15C, the admirably carved granite **rood screen★★**. Five 15C Kersanton granite altars stand in the east end. The Chapel of the Cross and the apse are adorned by fine rose windows. There is a 15C statue of Our Lady of Folgoët.
Left of the basilica the little 15C manor-house of **Le Doyenné**, though much restored, forms an attractive group with the pilgrim's inn and the church.
In the inn, a small **museum** ⏲ contains a collection of 15, 16 and 17C stone statues, archives and 15C furnishings.

Respect the life of the countryside
Drive carefully on country roads
Protect wildlife, plants and trees

FOUESNANT★

Population 6 524

Michelin map 58 fold 15 or 230 fold 32 – Facilities

This town is in the middle of one of the most fertile areas in Brittany; the villages stand among cherry and apple orchards. This is also where the best Breton cider is produced. The costumes and headdresses of Fouesnant are a very pretty sight at the feast of the apple trees and at the *pardon* of St Anne *(See the Calendar of events at the end of the guide)*.
Its beaches and small ports make it a popular seaside resort.

Church (Église) – Built in the 12C, the church, remodelled in the 18C, was restored. On the square stands a small 17C Calvary; the monument to the dead, left of the porch, the work of the Breton sculptor Quillivic, is remarkable for the stately yet serious expression of the peasant woman wearing a local headdress.
Inside the church, the tall granite pillars are adorned with fine Romanesque capitals. An unusual stoup is built into an engaged pillar. A triumphal arch, with pointed arch and four recessed orders, separates the nave from the transept where the altar stands. Naive statues are located in the chancel and entrance.

EXCURSION

La Forêt-Fouesnant – *3.5km - 2.25 miles east*. Facilities. This village possesses a **parish close** and a 16C Calvary with four corner pilasters. The church porch, dating from 1538, is adorned with two old, rough-hewn statues of St Roch and St Mélar. Inside, at the high altar are an altarpiece and, on either side, two 17C statues. The chapels at the far end of the church contain, to the right, a wooden statue of St Alan and to the left, a font (1628) with a piscina and a basin hewn from the same block. In the chapel on the south side of the chancel stands a *Pietà*. Breton and Celtic music is played in the background all day.

Port-la-Forêt – This port for pleasure craft has been built near La Forêt-Fouesnant; it can hold 800 boats.
There are boat services to the îles de Glénan *(qv)* and up the Odet *(See QUIMPER: Excursions* 3).

FOUGÈRES★★

Population 22 239

Michelin map 59 fold 18 or 230 fold 28.

This former stronghold is built in a picturesque setting on a promontory overlooking the winding valley of the Nançon. Below it, on a rocky height almost entirely encircled by the river, stands a magnificent feudal castle whose walls, with their thirteen big towers, are among the most massive in Europe.
The town centre (Place Aristide-Briand, Place du Théâtre, Rue Nationale and the neighbouring streets) has been transformed into a pedestrian precinct. The classical buildings in this area are the works of Gabriel.

HISTORICAL NOTES

A frontier post – Standing on the border of Brittany and France, Fougères acquired great military importance in the early Middle Ages, when its barons were very powerful. The most famous was Raoul II. He lived in the middle of the 12C under Conan IV, known as "the Little", Duke of Brittany. This weak duke submitted to Henry II Plantagenet, King of England and Duke of Normandy, but the proud Raoul revolted against the English yoke. He formed a league with some of the Breton nobles and rebelled against Henry II. In 1166 Henry II surrounded Fougères, which capitulated after three months' siege. The castle was completely demolished, but Raoul immediately began to rebuild it, and part of his work still stands.
In the 13C the fief passed to some Poitou noblemen, the Lusignans. They claimed to be descendants of the fairy Mélusine and gave her name to the finest of the towers that they added to the walls.
Fougères is an example of a formidable fortress which was often taken. Among those who fought their way into it were St Louis, Du Guesclin, Surienne, a leader from Aragon in the service of the English (at night without striking a blow), La Trémoille, the Duke of Mercœur and the men of the Vendée.
After the union of Brittany and France, there were a succession of governors at Fougères; ten of its towers bear their names. The castle was then mainly used as a prison. In the 18C it became private property. The town bought it in 1892.

Chouan country – Victor Hugo, in *Quatre-vingt-treize* (Ninety-three), and Balzac, in *Les Chouans*, introduced Fougères and its region into their stories of the royalist rebellion. They gleaned their information on the spot. In 1836 Hugo, accompanied by

Juliette Drouet (who was born at Fougères), gave a glowing account of the town and castle. "I should like to ask everyone," he wrote, "have you seen Fougères?" Balzac stayed with friends at Fougères, explored the neighbourhood with survivors of the rebellion and wrote his novel there in 1828.

The Breton and Vendéen revolt continued, with a few pauses, from 1793 to 1804. Its supporters were named after their call imitating the hoot of an owl *(chat-huant)*. The instigator of the movement was the Marquis of La Rouërie (1756-93), who was born at Fougères. His life was a real adventure story. A turbulent youth resulted in a warrant for his arrest; to avoid the Bastille prison, he fled to Switzerland. Thinking he had a religious vocation, La Rouërie shut himself in a Trappist monastery. But he then felt the call to arms. Discarding the habit, he went to America, where the War of Independence was being fought, and became a general in the American Army. He returned to France on the eve of the Revolution. When it broke out the Marquis refused to emigrate and prepared for resistance by ambuscade, well suited to the Breton countryside.

He organised stores of hidden arms and provisions and recruited a secret army which would rise at a sign. But the plotter was betrayed and obliged to flee. He went into hiding and died, worn out, in January 1793. The following month the Convention decreed the mass levy: Brittany rebelled, and the war foreseen by La Rouërie broke out.

The town of the shoe – In the 13C and for 300 years, Fougères capitalised on the manufacture of cloth: wool followed by hemp. Fougères sail cloth supplied the French fleet until the arrival of steam.

In 1832 the making of woollen slippers began; leather shoes followed in 1852, the workers sewing them by hand and at home. 1870 saw the introduction of sewing-machines, and mechanical techniques gained ground daily. In 1890 about thirty factories were mass-producing cheap shoes, chiefly for women. After the First World War the eighty factories in the town felt the effects of foreign competition and the world crisis. The remaining ones now manufacture shoes, mostly for women.

H. Marcou/PIX

Fougères

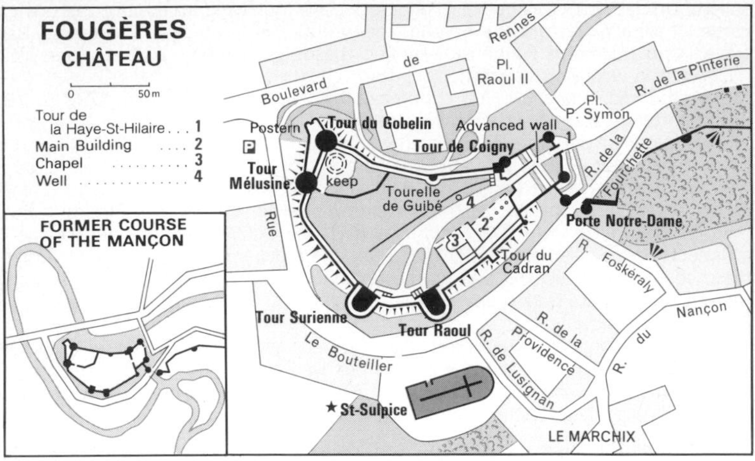

★★THE CASTLE *time: 1 hour 30 min*

The castle is a fine example of military architecture of the Middle Ages. There is an interesting general view from the public garden *(see Additional Sights below)*. The site is curious. A loop in the river, washing a rocky eminence, shaped like a very narrow peninsula, formed an excellent defensive position. Military architects took advantage of this site to build ramparts and towers and turn the peninsula into an island by a short diversion of the Nançon at the base of the loop. As the castle was connected with the upper town by the city ramparts, the garrison could take part in its defence; they also had the advantage of being able to retire into the fortress and hold it as a frontier post for the Duchy of Brittany should the town fall. The fortress, as we see it, has suffered greatly over the centuries. The wall is complete, with its curtains closely following the lie of the land and its thirteen towers. Unfortunately, we can no longer see the high keep that commanded all the defences; it was razed in 1166 by King Henry II of England and there are now only traces which can be seen when visiting the castle's interior. The main buildings which occupied part of the inner court were also demolished down to their foundations, in the beginning of the 19C. History tells us that the defenders often succumbed and that attackers were able to seize these high walls, either by surprise attack or after long sieges. An outer tour of the castle shows the attackers' point of view; an inner tour, that of the defenders.

★**Outer tour** – *Park your car in Place Raoul II, skirt the fortifications and then, left, along Rue Le Bouteiller.*

As you circle the walls you will see the splendid towers in all their variety of appearance and structure. At the start you will also see, in the middle of the north rampart, the 14C Guibé Turret, a corbelled sentry-post built onto the wall.

Going round the spur formed by the ramparts towards the west, you will see how massively the defences are concentrated at this point. The whole forms a triangle with two towers at the base and a postern at the apex. The 15C postern today looks out on empty space, but it was once connected with a double arcade that crossed the moat to communicate with an outwork. The 13 and 14C Gobelin Tower, to the left of the postern, and the 14C Mélusine Tower, to the right, are round and overlook the walls from a height. Stripped of their machicolations and with their upper parts probably rebuilt, they have lost much of their proud aspect. The Mélusine Tower is regarded as a masterpiece of military architecture of the period; it is over 13m - 41.5ft in diameter, with walls 3.50m - 11ft thick and rising 31m - 99ft above the rock.

Further on are two squat, horseshoe-shaped towers, the Surienne and the Raoul, which mark the last stage in the building of the castle (15C). Built to serve as platforms for artillery, they contain several storeys of very strong and well-preserved gun platforms. To resist enemy artillery fire, their walls are 7m - 22ft thick. At the end of the 15C, artillery had been in use for nearly a century and a half, and siege warfare often took the form of an artillery duel at short range.

Opposite the two towers stands the Eglise St-Sulpice. On the right is the Marchix District (see Additional Sights below).

Still following the walls, you will see the 13C Cadran Tower, two centuries older than the others. It is small, square and badly damaged, not nearly as strong as its neighbours and recalling the time when fire-arms had not yet taken the place of bows and arrows. Further on, Our Lady's Gate is the only one left of the four rampart gateways preceding the four gates in the walls which encircled the town. The left-hand tower, which is higher and is pierced with narrow loopholes, dates from the 14C; that on the right, with very ornamental machicolations, dates from the 15C, as do the Surienne and Raoul Towers.

Go under the gate and follow Rue de la Fourchette, then turn a sharp right into Rue de la Pinterie.

50m further on cross the gardens laid out along the former parapet-walk. From there you get a good view of the Nançon Valley and the castle.

To leave the garden, go under the ruins of a beautiful chapel doorway and go once more into Rue de la Pinterie on the left. This leads to the castle entrance.

★★ **Inner tour** ⏲ – The entrance *(see plan previous page)*, preceded by a moat filled from a diversion of the Nançon, is through the square tower of La Haye-St-Hilaire. To reach it, you first had to go through a town gate and the wall before it. The castle has three successive walls. The *Avancée* (advanced wall) was guarded by three 13C towers pierced with loopholes. When this line of resistance had been crossed, attackers would enter a small courtyard on the island formed by a second diversion of the river, and would come under the converging fire of defenders posted on the four sides. Thus exposed, the attackers had to cross a second moat before reaching the main ring of fortifications, guarded by four towers dating from the 12 and 15C.

When both lines had been stormed, they would burst into the main inside courtyard; but the defenders still had a chance to rally. A third position, the redoubt, girt with a wall and two towers, and the keep (demolished after the 12C), made a long resistance possible, and from these positions the garrison could still seek safety in flight through the postern.

Entering the main inside courtyard, go round the walls on the wall walk. This enables one to appreciate the might of such a fortress and also to enjoy some good views of Fougères.

At the end of the highest wall of the castle is Mélusine Tower, which from the top *(75 steps)* commands a fine view of the castle and the town. Further on are the remains of the keep and north wall, and beyond, the Guibé Turret and the Coigny Tower (13 and 14C), whose second and third storeys were turned into a chapel in the 17C. The summit was disfigured by the addition of a loggia during its first restoration in the 19C.

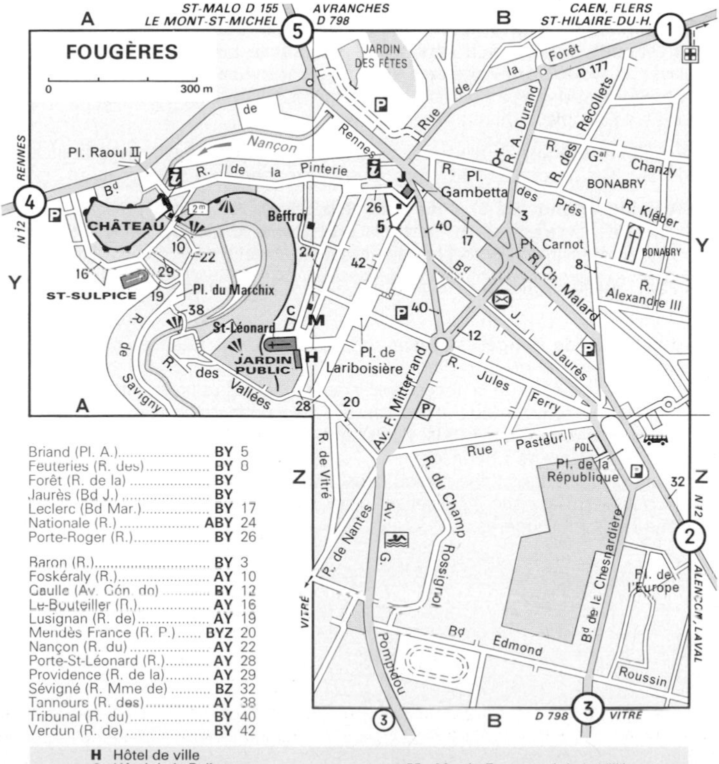

Briand (Pl. A.)	BY	5
Feuteries (R. des)	BY	8
Forêt (R. de la)	BY	
Jaurès (Bd J.)	BY	
Leclerc (Bd Mar.)	BY	17
Nationale (R.)	ABY	24
Porte-Roger (R.)	BY	26
Baron (R.)	BY	3
Foskéraly (R.)	AY	10
Gaulle (Av. Gén. de)	BY	12
Le-Bouteiller (R.)	AY	16
Lusignan (R. de)	AY	19
Mendès France (R. P.)	BYZ	20
Nançon (R. du)	AY	22
Porte-St-Léonard (R.)	AY	28
Providence (R. de la)	AY	29
Sévigné (R. Mme de)	BZ	32
Tanneurs (R. des)	AY	38
Tribunal (R. du)	BY	40
Verdun (R. de)	BY	42

H Hôtel de ville
J Hôtel de la Bellnaye (Tribunal d'instance)
M Musée Emmanuel-de-la-Villéon

ADDITIONAL SIGHTS

★**Église St-Sulpice** (**AY**) – A Gothic building in the Flamboyant style; although erected between the 15 and the 18C, it has great homogeneity. It has a slim 15C slate-covered steeple. The inside is enriched with 18C woodwork; nonetheless the 15C granite **altarpieces**★ in the chapels retain our attention. The Lady Chapel (on the left) contains the altarpiece dedicated to Anne of Brittany, the church's donor. In the niche, underneath Brittany's coat of arms, is the miraculous 12C statue of the Nursing Virgin (Notre-Dame des Marais). Off the south aisle, in the Chapelle des Tanneurs, there is an imposing altarpiece adorned with vine leaves, crockets, small animals and the instruments of the Passion.

★**Jardin Public** (**AY**) – This lovely garden, at the foot of St-Léonard and the town hall, is laid out partly in terraces on the site of the former town walls and partly on the slopes down into the Nançon river valley. Follow the low wall prolonging the balustrade to the entrance for an extensive view of the woodlands typical of the Fougères region. From the terrace closed off by the balustrade, there is an interesting general **view**★ of the castle.

Quartier du Marchix – This area around Place du Marchix (the site of the former market at the heart of the old town) (**AY**), with its picturesque old houses, has always been of interest to painters.

Take Rue Foskeraly.

From Rue Foskeraly, which skirts the Nançon, there are good views of the old ramparts now converted into a public garden. Take a walk along Rue du Nançon with its 16C houses. There are other interesting houses at the corner of Rue de la Providence and Rue de Lusignan as well as in Rue de Lusignan.
On Place du Marchix are two fine 16C houses, nos 13 and 15. Take Rue des Tanneurs to cross the bridge over the Nançon; looking back, you will see a picturesque group formed by the backs of the houses of Place du Marchix.

Église St-Léonard (**AY**) – The 15-16C church has a richly decorated 16C north façade and a 17C tower. It is lit through modern stained-glass windows by Lorin; however, in the Chapel of the Cross, on the left as you go in, are two 12C scenes of St Benedict's life, and in the baptismal chapel pieces of 16C **stained-glass windows**★.

Town Hall (**Hôtel de Ville**) (**AY H**) – A 16C building with a Renaissance doorway (partly walled up).

Musée Emmanuel de la Villéon (**ABY M**) ⓥ – The museum is located in a 16C house (restored) with a porch with wood and granite pillars.
It displays the works (drawings and watercolours) by **Emmanuel de la Villéon** (1858-1944), an Impressionist painter, born in Fougères. His works were inspired by the landscape and people of his native Brittany.

Beffroi – Rising proudly above the ramparts, this octagonal belfry was built in the 14 and 15C. It is decorated with gargoyles and topped by a slate-covered steeple.

Place Aristide-Briand (**BY 5**) – **The Hôtel de la Belinaye** (**J**), which presently houses the Magistrates' Court, was the birthplace of **Charles Armand Turpin de la Rouërie**. A statue was erected in 1993 to commemorate the bicentenary of his death.

Cattle Fair (**Marché aux Bovins de l'Aumaillerie**) – *2km - 1 mile to the southeast. Leave Fougères by* ②.

Forêt domaniale de Fougères – *3km - 2 miles northeast. Leave Fougères on* ① *on the town plan, the road to Flers.*
Those who like walking in a forest will spend hours strolling in the fine beech woods, along the forest roads. They can see two dolmens in ruins and a line of megalithic stones called the Druids' Cord (Cordon des Druides) near the Chennedet crossroads (carrefour de Chennedet).
At Landéan, on the edge of the forest, near the Recouvrance crossroads (carrefour de la Recouvrance) are the 12C cellars (now closed) once used as a secret hide-out by the lords of Fougères.

Cap FRÉHEL★★★

Michelin map 59 fold 5 or 230 fold 10 – Local map under CÔTE D'ÉMERAUDE

The **site** ⓥ of this cape is one of the grandest on the Breton coast. Its red, grey and black cliffs rise vertically to a height of 70m - 229ft and are fringed with reefs on which the swell breaks heavily. The coastal **panorama**★★★ is vast in clear weather: from the Pointe du Grouin, on the right, with the Cotentin in the background, to the île de Bréhat, on the left. The famous outline of Fort la Latte *(qv)* is visible on the right.

The **lighthouse** ⓥ *(145 steps)*, built between 1946 and 1950, is lit by a xenon flash lamp; the light carries only 200m - 656ft in foggy weather but it can be seen 120km - 74.5 miles away when it is clear. From the gallery at the top of the tower, there is an immense view of the horizon: you may see Bréhat to the west, Jersey to the north, Granville, a part of the Cotentin Peninsula and the îles Chausey to the northeast. At a point 400m - 437yds from the lighthouse a siren mounted in a shelter gives two blasts every minute in foggy weather.

Walk round the cape *(tour: 30min)*, beginning left of the lighthouse. After passing the extreme point where the siren stands, you can look down on the Fauconnière rocks, crowded with seagulls and cormorants; the contrast between the mauvish-red of the rocks and the blue or green of the sea is striking. Near the Restaurant de la Fauconnière take a steep path on the right; halfway down, it reaches a platform from where there is another fine view of the Fauconnière rocks and the deep blue sea.

Boat trips ⓥ, to view Cap Fréhel from the sea, leave from **St-Malo** and call in at Dinard.

Pambour/CAMPAGNE CAMPAGNE

Cap Fréhel

Cairn de GAVRINIS★★

Michelin map 63 fold 12 or 2340 fold 50 – Local map under Golfe du MORBIHAN

The Gavrinis Tumulus is the most interesting megalithic monument in Brittany *(details on prehistoric monuments p 40)*. It is situated on the Island of Gavrinis, at the mouth of the Golfe du Morbihan, south of Larmor-Baden, from which it can be reached.

Crossing and tour ⓥ – 6m high and 50m round (20ft and 164ft), the tumulus is made of stones piled on a hillock. It was discovered in 1832 and contains: (1) a covered gallery 14m - 46ft long with twenty-three supports, on which lie nine tables – the supports are covered with carvings; (2) the funeral chamber, probably a royal tomb (2.50m - 8ft on one side), with a ceiling made of a single granite slab, resting on supports also covered with carvings.

From the top of the tumulus there is a wide view of the Golfe du Morbihan.

On the tiny island of **Er Lanic**, a little south of Gavrinis, are two tangent circles of menhirs *(cromlechs)* in the form of a figure eight, half of which is submerged. This gives evidence of the subsidence of the soil which created the gulf in prehistoric times. At low tide the menhirs reappear.

Piquer/CAMPAGNE CAMPAGNE

Cairn de Gavrinis (detail)

Îles de GLÉNAN

Michelin map 58 fold 15 or 230 fold 32 – Access: Boat services ⓥ

The archipelago consists of nine islets surrounded by reefs and lies off Concarneau.

Tour – Boats go to the **île St-Nicolas** which has a few houses, a skin diving school (Centre International de Plongée) and a breeding pool for crustaceans. A footpath goes round the island affording good views of the coast from Penmarch to Le Pouldu. To the north lies the **île Brunec** and to the south the **île du Loch**, which can easily be distinguished by the chimney from a former seaweed factory. Both are privately owned. **Penfret** with its lighthouse, **Cigogne** (The Stork) identified by its 18C fort and the annexe of the marine laboratory of Concarneau *(qv)*, **Bananec**, which is linked to St-Nicolas at low tide, and **Drénec** are islands from which the internationally famous sailing school, the Centre Nautique de Glénan, operates.

The **île Giautec** and other uninhabited islands are kept as bird sanctuaries; gulls, terns, oyster catchers and cormorants nest there.

Château de GOULAINE

Michelin map 67 fold 4 or 232 fold 28

The **château** ⓥ, surrounded by vineyards, was built between 1480 and 1495 by Christophe de Goulaine, Groom of the Bedchamber to Louis XII and François I. He built it on the foundations of an old medieval fortress which, with those at Clisson and Nantes, had been used to defend the Duchy of Brittany against France.

Remains from this military past include a machicolated tower and a small castle in front of a bridge spanning a moat. This handsome residence consists of a Gothic 15C main building of calcareous tufa from the Saumur region, and two wings added in the early 17C.

Interior – A spiral staircase leads to the first floor, which opens into the **Great Hall**, in which the most striking feature is the richly sculpted, monumental Renaissance chimney-piece. A beautiful 16C Flemish tapestry depicting the Fall of Phaethon adorns the wall. The **Blue Room** still has its early 17C décor intact: blue and gold coffered ceiling, chimney-piece with Corinthian columns and caryatids, panelling decorated with pastel landscapes, and a large majestic Gobelins tapestry. The **Grey Room** has interesting panelling and mythological scenes on its piers.

Volière à papillons – An enormous greenhouse next to the castle's curtain wall contains tropical flowers and shrubs and is an aviary for butterflies.

La GRANDE BRIÈRE★★

Michelin map 63 folds 14 and 15 or 230 fold 52

Also known by the name of **Grande Brière Mottière**, this region covers 7 000ha - 17 297 acres of the total 40 000ha - 98 840 acres belonging to the **Parc naturel régional de Brière**. (*See the chapter Practical information*). Lying to the north of St-Nazaire, the area is renowned for its wildfowling and fishing. The world at large was to discover this region in 1923, through the pages of Alphonse de Chateaubriant's novel, *La Brière*.

Brière in the past – In early geological times the area was a forested, undulating basin which reached the hills of Sillon de Bretagne. Neolithic man (7500BC) was expelled from the area, when there was a momentary maritime incursion. Marshes formed behind the alluvial banks deposited by the Loire. The trees died and were submerged and vegetable matter decomposed to form **peat bogs**, often entrapping fossilized tree trunks, known as "**mortas**", over 5 000 years old.

Brière from the 15 to the 20C – This swampy area was subdivided, water pumped and the drainage improved. In 1461, the Duke of Brittany, François II, decreed the area the common property of all Briérons, an act which was to be confirmed by several royal edicts. For centuries the Briérons (17 parishes divided into 21 *communes*) have cut the peat, gathered the reeds and rushes for thatching, woven baskets with the buckthorn, tended their gardens and kept poultry. They have trapped leeches, harpooned eels, placed eel-pots in the open stretches of water and wickerwork traps to catch pike, tench and roach; and hunted with their dogs in a boat hidden by a clump of willow trees. For ages the Briéron has propelled with a pole his **blin**, a flat-bottomed boat, loaded with cows or sheep going to pasture. In spite of these activities, the Briéron women also had to work to make ends meet. In the 19 and early 20C, two workshops in St-Joachim employed approximately 140 women to make wax orange blossoms. These flowers were used to make splendid brides' headdresses exported throughout Europe *(see Bride's House below)*.

The Briéron of the 20C has remained closely attached to the land but, by force of circumstance, he is turning more to local industries: metallurgy in Trignac and dockyards and aeronautics at St-Nazaire. Nevertheless, he continues to fish, shoot, graze animals or cut reeds and pay his annual fee. Change is inevitable, roads now link the islets, locks have been built, marsh has become pastureland but despite it all, La Grande Brière has retained its charm and when the Briéron returns home he fishes and shoots for his own pleasure. Many of those who have boats will take visitors on trips along the canals and smaller channels beautiful with yellow irises *(mid-May to mid-June)* and pearl-white water lilies *(mid-June to late July)*.

★★ **Boat trips** – Larger canals are linked by smaller bulrush-bordered channels, great pools open up vast horizons broken only by the steeples of the surrounding villages. In winter the flooded marshes, with reeds the colour of ripe grain, are bathed in colours reflecting an ever-changing sky. The Brière has its charm in all seasons: the mass of flowers in spring; the summer cloak of green slashed by the black banks and the russet tints of autumn with the cries of wildfowl overhead.

PARC NATUREL RÉGIONAL DE BRIÈRE

Created in 1970, the Brière Regional Nature Park covers 21 *communes* spread over 40 000ha - 98 840 acres of which 15 000ha - 37 000 acres are marshland. Its duties include the creation of traditional types of housing (the Lock Keeper's House, Brière thatched cottage...), the restoration of a typical Brière village (Kerhinet), exhibits, and cultural (folklore events) and recreational (rambling, cycling, canoe, kayak) activities.

The park also offers excellent opportunities for the study and observation of the local bird population.

Maison du Parc: 177 Île de Fédrun – 44720 Saint-Joachim ☎ 02 40 91 68 60.

Round tour starting from St-Nazaire

83km - 52 miles – about half a day

St-Nazaire – *Time: 3 hours. See ST-NAZAIRE.*

Leave St-Nazaire by the N 171, the road to Nantes.

Trignac – This rural community has seen the implantation of new industries. A road to the left leads to the **Pont de Paille** which affords a **view** of Trignac Canal. At **Montoir-de-Bretagne** turn left onto the D 50.

St-Malo-de-Guersac – This, the largest of the islets (13m - 43ft high), offers a **view** from Guérande in the west to the hilly region, Sillon de Bretagne, to the east. The road passes near new slate-roofed houses.

Rosé – A boat-building centre, this small port, was the former departure point for the boats plying upstream to Nantes and Vannes.

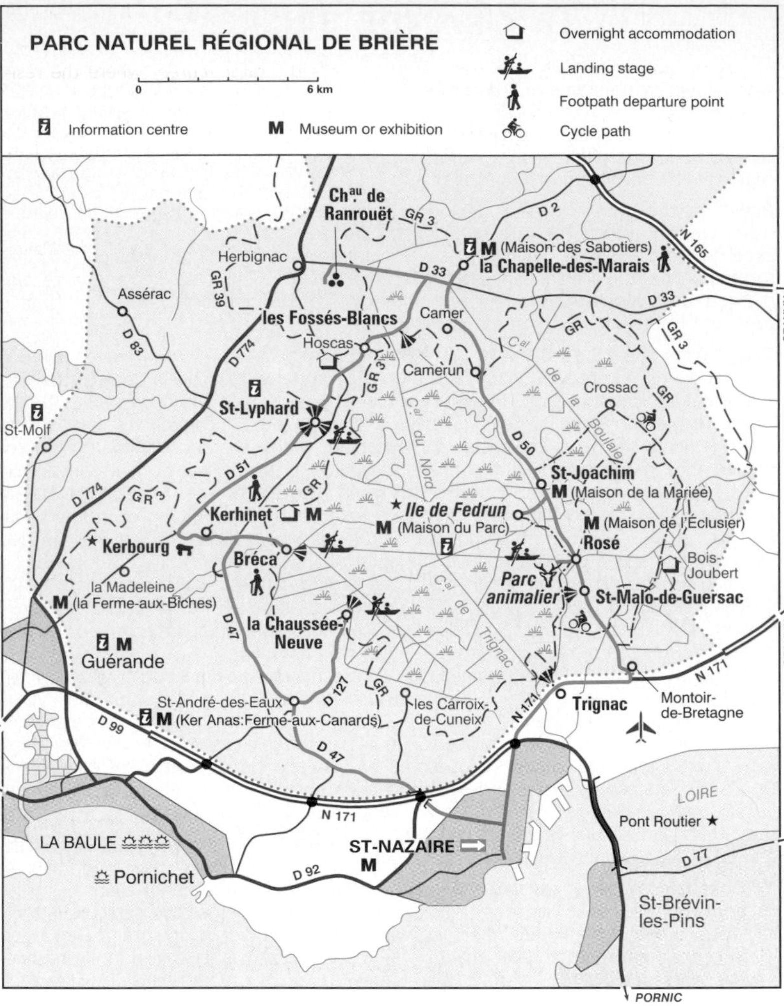

Maison de l'Éclusier ⏱ – The house is located on Rosé Canal. The lock keeper operated the two locks which regulated the water level of the marsh. There is an exhibit devoted to the fauna (stuffed animals) and flora to be found in the marshland. An aquarium contains the main species of Brière fish. Slides and various documents illustrate the formation and evolution of the marsh. Docked alongside the canal is a reconstruction of the *Théotiste*, which was used to transport peat.

Parc animalier ⏱ – *Field-glasses can be hired. Cross the bridge over the canal and take the path to the right to the reception building* (pavillon d'accueil) *800m - 875yds further on. It can also be reached by boat (landing stage to the right of the bridge).* A path *(about 1.8km - a mile)* cuts through this nature reserve (26ha - 64 acres), with observation posts where silence and patience will be rewarded. There are descriptive panels to help you identify the flora and fauna. In a wood and reed building Brière activities are displayed.

Bear left before St-Joachim.

★**Île de Fédrun** – Linked to the St-Joachim road by two bridges, this, the most attractive of the islets, is entirely surrounded by marshland. The islet has two roads: one which divides it in two and the other which runs around it. At no 130 of the circular road is the **Maison de la Mariée** (Bride's House) ⏱. The interior of the house, arranged in typical Brière style, displays a collection of bridal headdresses decorated with wax orange blossoms and an explanation of how they are made. At no 180 are the administrative services of the Regional Nature Park (Maison du Parc). No 308, the **Chaumière Briéronne** (Brière Thatched Cottage) ⏱, shows a typical Brière cottage interior with costume exhibits, farming tools and equipment, an 1862 cadastral plan (has not been revised since), and a display of ducks' webbed feet: each webbed foot has been marked to identify its owner.
An audiovisual presentation illustrates marsh life, peat harvesting and a Brière wedding. The low, flower-bedecked houses retain the traditional thatched roof.

The cottages on the islet's outer shores are backed by a **dike**, often planted with vegetables and fruit trees, which, itself borders the **canal** *(curée)* where the residents tie up their boats.

St-Joachim – The village, once a wax orange blossom manufacturing centre, extends along the two islets of **Brécun** (alt 8m - 26ft) and **Pendille**, dominated by the tall white spire of its 19C **church** with very low aisles. The altar is adorned by a stone Calvary and the ambulatory has fine Romanesque arcading.
The road crosses the sparsely populated islets of **Camerun** and **Camer**.

La Chapelle-des-Marais – At the entrance to the village, on the right, is the **Maison du Sabotier** (Sabot-Maker's House), where the last Briéron craftsman lived. In the **church**, the granite pillars stand out against the white stone; in the chapel to the right of the chancel, there is a polychrome statue of St Corneille, protector of the flocks.

Take the road in the direction of Herbignac and after 4km - 2.5 miles turn left.

Château de Ranrouët ⓥ – *Leave the car in the car park (grassy) and go behind the old farm buildings.* This 12-13C fortress, dismantled in 1618 by Louis XIII and burnt during the Revolution, is spectacular with its six round towers and moat (dried-up). Note in particular the 16C modifications designed to counter improved artillery (barbican, fortified curtain wall). Cannon balls embedded in the right tower wall recall that the castle once belonged to the Rieux family, whose coat of arms included ten gold cannon balls.

Turn around and bear right towards Pontchâteau; at Mayun, turn right.

Les Fossés-Blancs – From a landing stage on the canal to the north, there is a fine view of the Brière. A tour of the marsh provides an opportunity to study the flora and, occasionally, the fauna.

St-Lyphard – In the **church's belfry** ⓥ *(135 steps)* a lookout point has been set up. A **panorama**★★ extends onto the Brière and from the Loire estuary to the mouth of the Vilaine encompassing Guérande and its salt marshes.

Follow the road towards Guérande and turn left.

★ **Dolmen de Kerbourg** – This covered alleyway stands on a mound near a windmill.

Continue in the direction of Le Brunet.

Kerhinet – A group of thatched cottages (restored) make up this charming hamlet *(visited on foot only)*. One of the cottages presents a modest **Brière interior** ⓥ (dirt floor, meagre furnishings and kitchen utensils). In the shed are tools used for peat harvesting, farming and fishing.
In season, the arts and crafts centre (maison des artisans) displays works by artists from Guérande Peninsula.

Go on to Le Brunet and from there the road continues to Bréca.

Bréca – Good view over the Brière and Bréca Canal.

Return to Le Brunet; continue to La Chaussée-Neuve via St-André-des-Eaux.

La Chaussée-Neuve – It was from this former port that the boats loaded with peat used to leave. From here there is a wide **view**★ over the Brière.

Return to St-André-des-Eaux, and bear left to return to St-Nazaire.

D. Casteur/PIX

Thatched roofs in the Grande Brière region

GRAND-FOUGERAY

Population 1 996
Michelin map 63 fold 6 or 230 fold 40

This small town includes a partly Romanesque church; on its south side stands a 13C cemetery cross. On Place de l'Église is a 15C house, the former law courts of the lords of Fougeray.

Keep (Donjon) – *Follow the directions for Sion and 50m after the crossroads bear right into a pine-bordered lane.*
All that remains of the old castle is the keep. During the War of Succession, in 1354, Du Guesclin *(qv)* captured the castle by cunning. Having learnt that firewood was to be delivered to the castle, he and his men disguised themselves as woodcutters. Once inside the castle, they brought out their weapons and slaughtered the garrison.

EXCURSION

Langon –*12km - 7.5 miles. Leave Grand-Fougeray west on the D 54 and at Port-de-Roche left on the D 56.*
From Port-de-Roche Bridge, which crosses the Vilaine River, there are pleasant views.
On the village square stand the parish church and the Chapelle Ste-Agathe.
The chapel is a small Gallo-Roman building with a single nave and lovely brick-and-stonework. Most likely devoted to Venus, as evidenced by the remains of frescoes discovered in the apse, the chapel was, in the Middle Ages, consecrated to St Agatha. The parish church was rearranged from the 13 to the 17C. Inside are 17C wood altarpieces and a 15C canopied stone baptismal font. On the wall of the north apsidal chapel is a 14C fresco representing God the Father.
Overlooking the town, on Moulin moor (lande du Moulin), stand the Young Women of Langon (Demoiselles de Langon); about 30 menhirs which, legend has it, represent some young women who one day preferred dancing on the moor to going to vespers.

Île de GROIX★

Michelin map 58 fold 12 or 230 fold 34 – Facilities
Access: see the current Michelin Red Guide France

Groix Island is smaller (15km^2 - 6sq miles; 8km - 5 miles long; 2 to 3km - 1 to 2 miles wide; up to 49m - 161ft in height) than its neighbour, Belle-Ile *(qv)*, but has the same geological form – a mass of schist rock. The coast to the north and west is wild and deeply indented: there you will see cliffs and giant rocks, valleys and creeks; while the east and south sides are flatter and along the coast there are many sheltered sandy creeks. Small villages dot some of the still cultivated fields and the vast expanses on which gorse and heather grow.

TOUR ⏱ *allow 1 day*

Groix – This is the island's capital with its low slate-roofed houses grouped round the church. The bell tower is crowned by a tunny fish weather vane, recalling the island's great tunny fishing days of the early 1900s.

Locmaria – Facing the open sea, this village, with its winding streets, has a small harbour, where fishing and pleasure boats seek shelter behind a jetty.

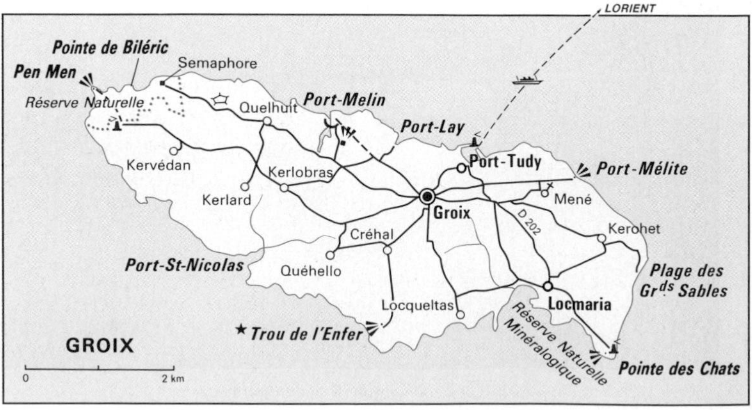

Pen-Men – The western tip of the island, to the right of Pen-Men Lighthouse, is a rocky headland, offering splendid views of the Morbihan coast extending from Talut Point to Port-Manech. This, the **Réserve naturelle François Le Bail**, is home to thousands of birds.

Plages des Grands Sables – This is the island's largest beach; garnets can sometimes be found in the sand.

Pointe de Bileric – Near the Beg-Melen signal station *(not open to the public)*, many black-legged kittiwakes can be seen nesting in this bird sanctuary.

Pointe des Chats – On this point, the lowest part of the island, stands a small lighthouse; fine view of the south coast. There is a mineralogy reserve where visitors can see garnets, needles of blue glaucophane and green lepidolite, but of course the taking of samples is strictly forbidden.

Port-Lay – This safe anchorage, where trawlers used to shelter, lies in a beautiful **setting★**.

Port-Melin – The little creek can only be reached on foot down a steep slope. From the platform, there is a good **view** of the approach to Port-Tudy and of the Lorient coast in the distance.
The statue is of the Breton poet, J.-P. Calloc'h, native of the island (1888-1917), who wrote in Celtic, under the pseudonym of Bleimor.

Port-Mélite – A rocky cove with a beach. The view extends from the Étel Bar to the Pointe du Talut.

Port-St-Nicolas – A large bay with deep, clear waters hemmed in by cliffs.

Port-Tudy – Sheltered by two piers, this port offers a direct link with Lorient, on the mainland. Former tunny fishing port, it is now a safe harbour for trawlers and pleasure boats.
Housed in an early 20C canning factory, the **Ecomusée de l'île de Groix** ⏱ presents interesting exhibits (explanatory panels, photographs...) on the island's geography, history and ethnography. The displays include the island's soil, its people and their different occupations: farming (the women worked the land, while the men were at sea), fishing (from 1870-1940 the île de Groix possessed France's most important tunny fishing fleet; note the ship model of a 2-masted tunny fishing boat) and family life. Utensils, costumes and household items complete the exhibit. The *Kenavo*, the last coastal fishing cutter built on the île de Groix, can be hired for a boat trip round the island; contact the tourist office *(syndicat d'intiative)*, for details.

★**Trou de l'Enfer** – This deep opening (*trou* means hole, *enfer* means hell*)* in the cliff face into which the sea surges with great force, is a wild barren site with a beautiful **view** of the Pointe St-Nicolas and the rocky coast.

GUÉHENNO★

Population 836

Michelin map 63 fold 3 or 230 fold 37 – 11km – 7 miles southwest of Josselin

The **Calvary★** *(qv)* stands in the cemetery near the church. It dates from 1550, was destroyed in 1794 and restored in the last century. All its beauty lies in its perfect composition. Carved in the shaft of the central cross is Jesse, father of David. In front of it stands a column, with the instruments of the Passion, on which a cock is perched, in allusion to the denial of St Peter. Behind this monument is a small ossuary, whose entrance is protected by the figures of two guards on duty. A low relief framed in the left gable depicts the Passion.

GUÉRANDE★

Population 11 665

Michelin map 63 fold 14 or 230 fold 51 – Local map under Presqu'île de GUÉRANDE

The town surrounded by ramparts, standing on a plateau overlooking the salt marshes, has kept the appearance of the Middle Ages.
Every year in August there is a three day Interceltic Festival at the foot of the fortifications.

★**Walk round the ramparts (Remparts)** – The ramparts, in which there is still no breach, were built in the 14 and 15C. They are flanked by six towers and pierced by four fortified gateways. In the 18C the Duke of Aiguillon, Governor of Brittany, had the moats filled in (although the north and west sections still contain water) and arranged the present circular promenade, which the tourist can follow by car or on foot *(the watch path is not open to the public)*.

GUÉRANDE

St-Aubin (Pl.) 17
St-Michel (R.)

Bizienne (Fg) 2
Bouton d'Or (R. du) 3
Brière (R. de la) 4
Capucins (R. des) 5
Marché-aux-Bois (Pl.) 8
Peupliers (R. des) 12
Pourieux (Bd Émile) 13
Psalette (Pl. de la) 14
St-Armel (Fg) 16
St-Michel (Fg) 19
Ste-Anne (Fg) 21
Saulniers (R. des) 24
Sœurs-Grises (R. des) 25
Tricot (R. du) 27
Vannetaise (R.) 29
Vieux-Marché (Pl. du) 31

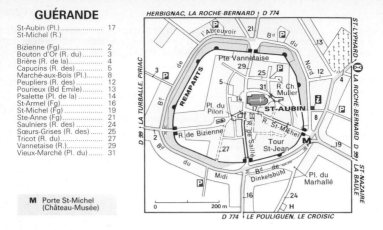

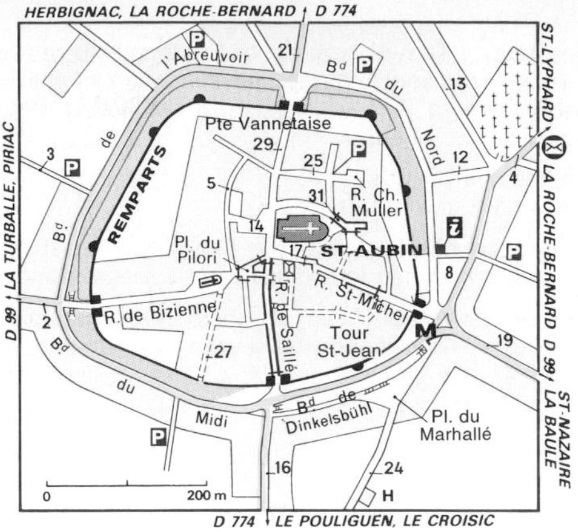

M Porte St-Michel (Château-Musée)

★**Collégiale St-Aubin** – This collegiate church, built from the 12 to the 16C on the site of a baptistery, features a granite west façade decorated with bell turrets and crocketed pinnacles. To the right a 15C outside pulpit is embedded into a buttress. The **interior** is imposing with large 15C pillars in the transept. The Romanesque columns of the nave support Gothic arches with **capitals** portraying grotesque and floral decoration. The 15C chancel, with aisles opening onto four 16C chapels, is lit by a magnificent 18C **stained-glass window** showing the Coronation of the Virgin and the Assumption. On the left, the small 14C lancet window shows the life of St Peter. The chapel to the right, oddly enough called the **crypt**, contains a Merovingian sarcophagus (6C) discovered under the chancel, a recumbent figure and a tombstone, both 16C. In the nave is a 16C carved wooden Christ.

Porte St-Michel (Château-Musée) (M) ⌚ – The gatehouse was once the governor's house (15C) and is now a local museum; a spiral staircase goes up to the different floors. On the first floor, once the soldiers' living quarters, two interiors have been reconstructed: that of the Briéron inhabitant with its waxed furniture and that of the saltmarsh worker with its furniture painted a deep plum-red colour. The second floor, where the governor resided, is embellished with paintings, porcelain from Le Croisic, pottery and other everyday objects typical of the area, as well as part of the collegiate church's rood screen. On the third floor (note the beautiful timber-work) a weaving loom (1832), and old bourgeois, saltmarsh worker and farm tenant costumes, on life-size figures, are exhibited.
The relief plan of a salt pan shows how it is equipped and how it works.

Presqu'île de GUÉRANDE★

Michelin map 63 folds 13 and 14 or 230 folds 51 and 52

This is a very interesting district in which you may see, besides the curious landscape of salt marshes, several beaches, of which La Baule is the finest, the picturesque Côte Sauvage, busy fishing ports, Guérande and its ramparts, and Batz and its church.

The former gulf – In the Roman era, a great sea gulf stretched between the rocky île de Batz and the Guérande ridge. A change of level of approximately 15m - 50ft turned the gulf into marshland.
Sand brought down by the currents linked the île de Batz with the mainland through the strip on which La Baule and Le Pouliguen stand. To the west the sandy Pen Bron Point has not quite reached the island; a channel remains open opposite Le Croisic through which the sea flows at high tide into the Grand and Petit Trait, vestiges of the former gulf. At low tide it retreats, exposing mud flats on which the coast dwellers raise oysters and mussels, clams and periwinkles. The rest of the marsh is used for salt pans.

Salt marshes – The salt marshes cover 1 800ha - 4 448 acres divided into two basins: Mesquer and Guérande, forming a huge quadrilateral delimited by clay embankments. The sea, brought in by the tides through canals *(étier)*, irrigates the salt marsh. Every 15 days, during the salt harvest, the salt pan worker allows the seawater to flow through a gate into a type of settling pond *(vasière)* used for removing the impurities (sand, clay, etc). Then with the drop in water level the water flows through a series of evaporating ponds where the wind and sun cause the water to evaporate, producing brine. In the 70m^2 - 853sq ft pools called *œillets* the brine finally rests and crystallises.
From June to September the salt-pan worker harvests two kinds of salt: table or white salt collected (3-5kg – 7-11lb per day per *œillet*) with a flat spade *(lousse)* and coarse or grey salt collected (40-70kg – 88-154lb per day per *œillet*) at the bottom of the

pond with a large flat rake *(lasse)* onto a tray. The salt is put to dry on little platforms *(trenet)* built on the banks, then piled in large heaps *(mulons)* at the edge of the salt-pans before being stored in sheds in September.
When not harvesting salt, the salt pan worker looks after the salt marsh: repairing the dikes, raking the settling pond (October-March), cleaning and preparing the salt pans (April-May) and removing the salt before the next harvest.

Hugh/EXPLORER

A salt marsh worker

A hard struggle – The salt pans of Guérande were very prosperous until the Revolution, for, thanks to a relic of the former rights of the province, the salt could be sent all over Brittany without paying the *gabelle* or salt tax. Dealers or salt makers could exchange it in neighbouring provinces for cereals. Trafficking by "false salt makers" or smugglers often occurred.
Today about 8 000 *œillets* are harvested, they produce an average of 10 000 metric tons of coarse salt a year. Guérande salt is rich in sodium chloride and weak in magnesium, potassium and other trace elements.

Cliffs and dunes – The cliffs and rocks of the Côte Sauvage, between the Pointe de Penchâteau and Le Croisic, offer a striking contrast to the immense sandy beach at La Baule.
In 1527 a violent wind spread the sand accumulated in the Loire estuary over the village of **Escoublac** *(qv)*. After this gale, which lasted for several days, sand continued to accumulate, and in the 18C the last inhabitants finally left. The village was rebuilt several miles further back. The pines planted to fix the dunes form the Bois d'Amour of La Baule. The coast, which became very popular in the 19C, took the name of **Côte d'Amour**.

TOUR

Round tour of 62km - 39 miles – about half a day

La Baule – *See La BAULE.*

Leave La Baule to the south. On reaching Le Pouliguen turn left immediately after the bridge.

Le Pouliguen – *See Le POULIGUEN.*

The road hugs the coast and there is soon a fine view of the shore south of the Loire as far as the Pointe de St Gildas and Banche Lighthouse.

★**Côte Sauvage** – *See Le CROISIC: Excursion (opposite direction).*

★**Le Croisic** – *See Le CROISIC.*

Batz-sur-Mer – *See BATZ-SUR-MER.*

Kervalet – A small village of salt marsh workers with a chapel dedicated to St Mark.

Saillé – Built on an island amidst the salt marshes, this town is the salt capital. A former chapel contains the **Maison des Paludiers** ⌚. Engravings, tools, furnishings and costumes illustrate the life of the salt marsh worker.

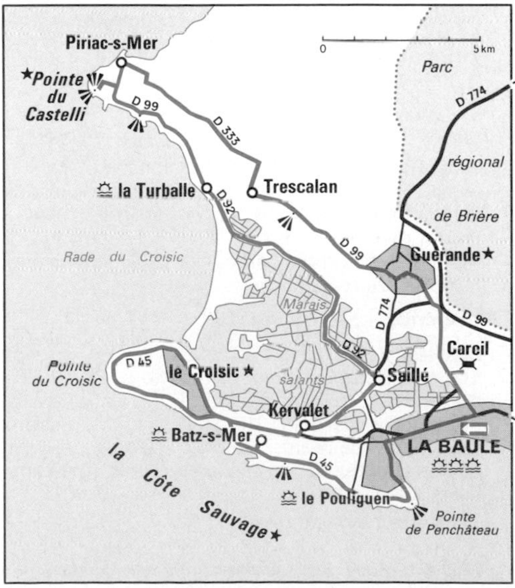

Guérande salt marshes

Turn left into the road to Turballe through the salt flats.

La Turballe – The town stretches along the seafront. The fish auction (La Criée) stands in the middle of the busy artificial port which receives both pleasure craft and sardine boats. The modern granite église St-Anne has a low bell tower adjoining the apse. The chancel is lit by small stained-glass windows (1937).
The **view** is beautiful along the coast after Lerat.

After Penhareng, turn left twice.

★**Pointe du Castelli** - *From the car park a path along the cliff ridge takes you to the point.* There is a nice view of the rocky creeks. On the right île Dumet and the low shore of Presqu'île de Rhuys are visible. On the left are the roadstead and peninsula of Le Croisic with the church towers of Batz and Le Croisic.

Piriac-sur-Mer – A small resort and fishing village. In the square, in front of the church, there is a fine group of 17C houses.

To leave Piriac take the road that runs beside the harbour towards Mesquer, turn right towards Guérande. Go through St-Sébastien.

Trescalan – The main square is dominated by a small Calvary topped with a pediment. The **church** ⓥ with buttresses has fine columns with capitals and inside, in the south aisle, is a statue of St Bridget.
From the D 99, as it runs along the Guérande ridge, there is a fine view of the salt marshes and the harbour of Le Croisic. In the evening the light effects on the marshes are remarkable.

★**Guérande** – *See GUÉRANDE.*

Château de Careil ⓥ – This former 14C stronghold was altered in the 15 and 16C and is still inhabited. Of the two wings, one is Renaissance with gracious shell-shaped dormer windows; the second is plainer, its dormer windows have armorial decorated pediments. The stone flagged guardroom and the adjoining drawing room have fine beams. Take a spiral staircase which goes up to the soldiers' living quarters; note the fine timbered ceiling. The captain's room has a chimney which bears a Maltese cross.

Return to La Baule by the D 92.

La GUERCHE-DE-BRETAGNE

Population 4 123

Michelin map 63 fold 8 or 230 folds 41 and 42

This small town, once a manorial estate with Du Guesclin as its overlord, still retains some old houses and an interesting church.
Every Tuesday, since 1121, an important fair and market is held around the town hall and the squares in the town centre.

Church (Église) – Only the chancel, with its triple-sided apse, and the Romanesque tower, with its massive buttresses, remain from the original building erected in 1206. The nave and south aisle were rebuilt in the 16C; the north aisle and the bell tower, with openings at the top, date from the end of the 19C. The splendour of this church lies in its 16C stalls with their amusing Gothic misericords – the carved decoration of the woodwork is clearly of the time of Henri II (1547-59) a more advanced period – and the remains of the 15 and 16C stained-glass windows in the south aisle. Note the purlins embellishing the nave's wooden vaulting and at the rear of the apse a stained-glass window depicting the Assumption.

Old houses – About 15 porched and half-timbered houses dating from the 16 and 17C can be found on Place du Général-de-Gaulle, near the church, and in the neighbouring streets of Rue du Cheval-Blanc and Rue de Nantes.

EXCURSIONS

★ **La Roche-aux-Fées** - *Round tour of 43km - 27 miles – about 2 hours 30 min. Leave La Guerche west on the Rennes road, D 463. At Visseiche turn left.*
You soon reach an arm of Marcillé Lake (Étang de Marcillé) formed by the junction of the Seiche and Ardenne Valleys; hence its curved shape.

On leaving Marcillé-Robert, cross the Seiche and bear left towards Retiers which follows the bank of the other arm of the lake. Turn right after 800m – half a mile to Theil and then right again 3km - 2 miles further on. On the right, 800m – half a mile from the road, stands La Roche-aux-Fées (Fairies' Rock).

★ **La Roche-aux-Fées** – *Photograph below.* This is one of the finest megalithic monuments in Brittany. Built in purple schist, it consists of 42 stones, of which half a dozen weigh between 40 and 45 tons each. There is a massive portico entrance and then a low ceilinged corridor leading to a large, very high compartmented room.

Turn round and go to Le Theil then turn left towards Ste-Colombe.

Lac des Mottes ⓥ – Charming artifical lake amidst magnificent trees.

When within sight of Ste-Colombe, turn left.

Retiers – Pretty small town where the church contains five paintings and three 17 and 18C altarpieces in carved wood.
Cross Arbrissel, the birthplace of Robert d'Arbrissel who founded the famous abbey of Fontevraud where he is buried.

From Rannée (see Michelin Guide Châteaux of the Loire) return to La Guerche.

J.S.R./PIX

La Roche-aux-Fées

Château de Monbouan – *Round tour of 36km - 22 miles – about 2 hours 30 min. Leave La Guerche west on the D 463, the road to Châteaugiron and after 1km - half a mile bear right.*

After Carcraon, which is at the end of a lake – with its shaded shores arranged for fishermen (shelters, landing-stages) – you come to Bais.

Bais – The town is built on the side of a hill and overlooks the small valley of the Quincampoix. The porch of the Gothic church, which was called the lepers' porch, stands over a fine Renaissance doorway consisting of twin doors beneath a triangular pediment. The rich and fantastic decoration of the doorway juxtaposes skulls, salamanders, the bust of François I and Aphrodite triumphant.

Louvigné-de-Bais – The chapel with barrel vaulting north of the chancel is the only remnant of an earlier **church** (11C). The 16C building has Gothic arcades with short pillars. The altarpiece of the high altar is 17C. There are superb **stained-glass windows★**: in the south aisle windows of the Resurrection and the Transfiguration designed by a painter from Vitré in 1542 and 1544; in the north aisle Christ's descent to Hell made in 1567 and very nicely repaired in 1607; a window of 1578 of the life of St John and, the nearest to the chancel, a window (16C) of the life of the Virgin.

Château de Monbouan ⓥ – In a lovely verdant setting stands the Château de Monbouan (1771). It is surrounded by a moat and vast outbuildings set a right angles. Inside, several rooms can be visited: the old kitchen, the drawing room, and the entrance hall with its great staircase and graceful wrought-iron balustrade, which is decorated with paintings after cartoons by Boucher.

Drive to Moulins and from there bear left to La Guerche-de-Bretagne.

Lac de GUERLÉDAN★★

Michelin map 59 fold 12 or 230 folds 21 and 22

At the heart of the Argoat, the waters of the River Blavet form a winding reservoir known as Guerlédan Lake, a magnificent stretch of water surrounded by trees. It is one of the finest sights of inland Brittany and a lovely place for water sports.

★★**Boat trips** ⓥ – Boats, leaving from Beau Rivage and Sordan Bay, offer tours of this beautiful lake.

TOUR OF THE LAKE

Round tour of 44km - 27 miles starting from Mur-de-Bretagne – about 3 hours 30 min.

Mur-de-Bretagne – *See MUR-DE-BRETAGNE.*

Take the D 35 southwest and after crossing two bridges over the canal and the Blavet, turn right.

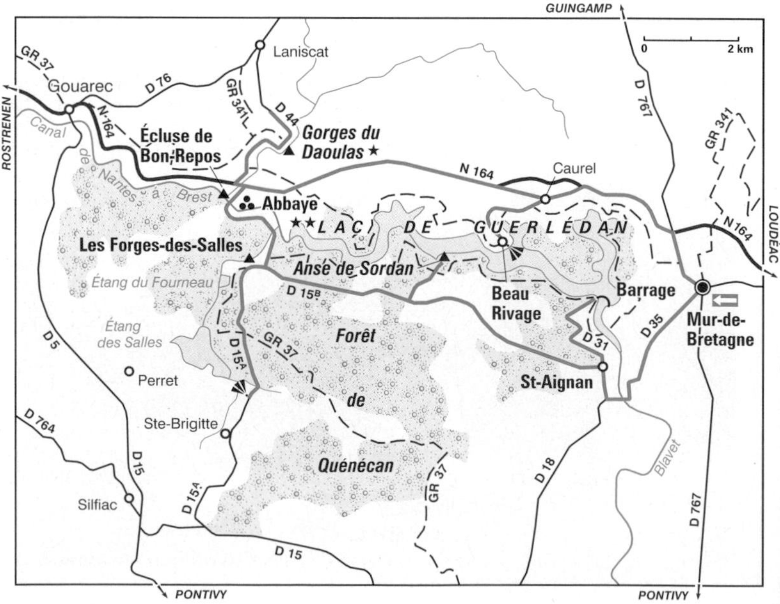

St-Aignan – In the charming 12C **church** note in particular a beautiful carved wooden image of the Tree of Jesse to the north of the chancel and a depiction of the Trinity surrounded by Evangelists, in the same medium, to the south. There is also a statue of St Mark and a *Pietà*.
On leaving the village, to the left, an **électrothèque** ⏲ has been set up in the Regional Centre (Maison du pays) and contains a display on the construction of the barrage de Guerlédan, as well as collections of exhibits evoking the history of electricity: measuring instruments, electric household appliances or electrical equipment used by the railway services. Visitors can operate some of these exhibits themselves.

Barrage de Guerlédan – A viewpoint overlooks this dead-weight dam (45m - 147ft high, 206m - 240yds long along the top and 33.50m - 109ft thick at the base) with a capacity of 55 million m^3 - 15 565 000ft^3 and extending over 12km - 7 miles in the Blavet Gorges. The power station at the foot of the dam generates an average of 23 million kWh per year. Below the dam is the former port of the Nantes-Brest Canal, now fallen into disuse between Guerlédan and Pontivy.

Come back by the same road and bear right.

The road runs through a countryside of fields and pastureland.

Before entering the Forêt de Quénécan bear right.

Anse de Sordan – Pleasant site on the edge of the Lac de Guerlédan.

Forêt de Quénécan – The forest of 2 500ha – 6 175 acres stands on an uneven plateau overlooking the Blavet Valley. Apart from beech and spruce around Lake Fourneau (Étang du Fourneau) and Les Forges des Salles, the forest, abounding in game (deer, wild boar), consists of pine, scrubland and heath.

Les Forges des Salles – Les Forges **Hamlet** ⏲, tucked at the bottom of a wooded valley, was the site of an iron and steel industry in the 18 and 19C. Quite apart from the site's remarkable testimony to a complete period of industrial history, the setting itself is charming. Since the mining and processing of iron ore was stopped, in 1880, this collection of well-designed buildings has not been altered. The buildings of schist, which are arranged around the ironmaster's house, include some which are open to visitors; these are the former homes of blacksmiths (arranged as exhibition rooms). Some have been furnished according to their original style and function: the school, the accounts office, the canteen, the chapel, the joiner's workshop and a small smithy.
East of the castle, at the top of the terraced pleasure garden (the **Thabor**), there is a lovely view over the valley and the various stretches of water in it.

Continue in the direction of Ste-Brigitte.

There are fine views on the right of Lake Fourneau.

Via Les Forges des Salles return to the main crossroads, then bear left.

The road runs down the valley of the Forges stream, then enters the Blavet Valley.

Leave the car in the car park before the bridge to the left.

Écluse de Bon-Repos – The lock on the Blavet River, the old corbelled bridge, the former lock keeper's house and the overflow form a pretty picture.

Go over the bridge and take the towpath to the right.

Abbaye de Bon-Repos ⏲ – This 12C Cistercian abbey, a dependent of the Abbaye de Boquen *(qv)*, rebuilt in the 14C and embellished in the early 18C, was sacked and destroyed during the Revolution. The fine façade of the abbot's lodging, the sober architecture of the conventual buildings and the vast size of the church may still be admired.

Make for the N 164 and turn left towards Gouarec; immediately after the bridge bear right to Daoulas Gorges.

★**Gorges du Daoulas** – Go up the gorges. The fast flowing waters of the Daoulas run in a narrow, winding valley with steep sides covered with gorse, broom and heather. To join the Blavet, which has become the canal between Nantes and Brest, the river has made a deep cut through a belt of schist and quartzite. The slabs of rock rise almost vertically; some end in curious needles, with sharp edges.

2km - 1 mile further on reverse into a lane before two houses at the place known as Toulrodez and turn back.

The road towards Loudéac, which you take to the left, crosses undulating country and provides views of the lake. After 5km - 3 miles turn right into the road towards the water, after dropping down into a small pine wood it provides a beautiful **view**★ of the Lac de Guerlédan.

Beau-Rivage – Leisure and sailing centre.

Proceed to Caurel and turn right towards Loudéac. After 3.5km - 2 miles turn right to return to Mur-de-Bretagne.

Le GUILDO

Michelin map 59 fold 5 or 230 folds 10 and 11 – 10km – 6 miles south of St-Cast - Local map under CÔTE D'ÉMERAUDE

This village lies in a picturesque setting on the shore of the Arguenon estuary. From the bridge across it you will see, on the east bank, the ruins of Le Guildo Castle. In the 15C this was the seat of Gilles de Bretagne, a carefree and gallant poet, who led a happy life at Le Guildo. However, Gilles was suspected of plotting by his brother, the reigning duke, and thrown into prison. As he did not die fast enough, he was smothered. Before Gilles died he summoned his brother to the judgment of God. A short time later the Duke, prostrate with remorse, expired.

Les Pierres Sonnantes – *3km – 2 miles west on the D 786, the road to Erquy. After the bridge, bear right on the road which goes to the harbour, leave your car on the quay (car park) and take a lane along the Arguenon (15 min Rtn).*
Opposite the ruins of the castle *(to the right, on the far bank)*, you will find a pile of rocks known as "the ringing stones" which emit a metallic note when you strike them with a stone of the same type. This resonance is due to the perfectly even grain of the rocks.

GUIMILIAU**

Population 791
Michelin map 58 folds 5 and 6 or 230 folds 4 and 5
Local map under Les ENCLOS PAROISSIAUX

The fame of the small village of Guimiliau is due to its remarkable parish close *(qv)* and to the magnificently ornamented furniture of its church.

**PARISH CLOSE *time: 45 min*

****Calvary** (**Calvaire**) – The Calvary, the most curious and one of the largest in the region, dates from 1581-8 and includes over 200 figures. On the upper part stands a large cross with a thorny shaft bearing four statues: the Virgin and St John, St Peter and St Yves. On the platform are 17 scenes from the Passion and a composition representing the story of Catell-Gollet *(qv)* above the Last Supper. The figures on the frieze are numerous and depict, in no chronological order, 15 scenes from the life of Jesus. The four Evangelists stand at the corners of the buttresses.

***Church** (**Église**) – This 16C building was rebuilt in the Flamboyant Renaissance style at the beginning of the 17C.
Go round the south side of the church to see the charming triple-panelled apse. Continue round the building, to the façade where the bell tower (1530) stands, all that remains of the original church.

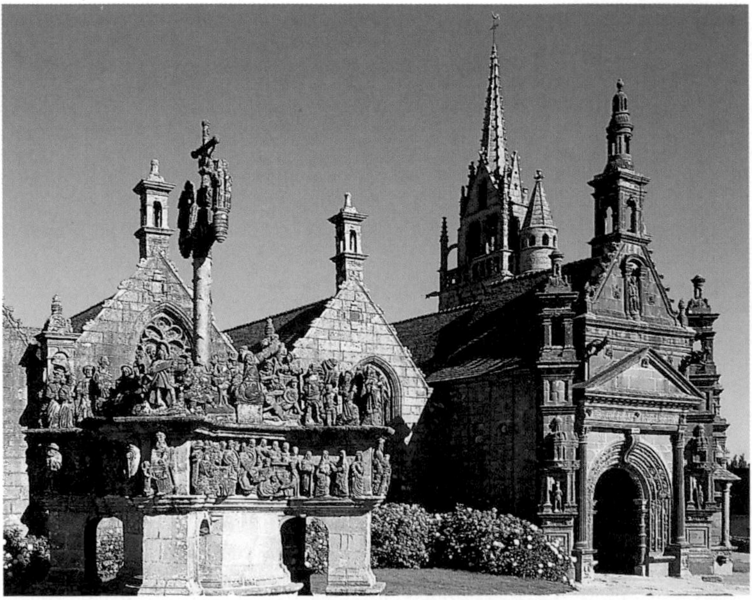

G. Boutin/EXPLORER

Guimiliau parish close

The **south porch★★** is remarkable. The recessed arches adorned with statuettes give an interesting picture of the Bible and the Gospels. Above the triangular pediment over the porch is the statue of St Miliau, King of Cornouaille and patron saint of the area. To the left of the porch is a small ossuary with low reliefs depicting scenes from the life of Christ. The inside of the porch is a fine example of a form of decoration frequent in Brittany *(see Introduction: Breton Art)*. Under the usual statues of the Apostles is a frieze ornamented with rose medallions, strapwork and scenes from the Old Testament. Note on the left side, near the date 1606, the Creation of Woman. In the end wall two round arched doorways, surmounted by a statue of Christ, frame a Kersanton granite stoup.
Inside, the nave and side aisles are roofed with panelled vaulting. At the end of the north aisle is a fine carved oak **baptistery★★** dating from 1675. Eight spiral columns support an elaborately carved canopy, crowned by a dome which shelters a group representing the baptism of Our Lord. To the right of the organ are two beautiful embroidered banners (1658).
In the **organ loft** are three 17C **low reliefs★**; on the nave side, David playing the harp, and St Cecilia at the organ; opposite the baptistery, the Triumph of Alexander.
The **pulpit★**, dating from 1677, is ornamented at the corners with statues of the four Sibyls. The panels carry medallions representing the Four Evangelists surrounded by the Cardinal Virtues.
The chancel with its central stained glass window (1599) is closed by a 17C altar rail. Note from right to left: the colourful **altarpiece of St Joseph**, on which can be seen St Yves, the patron saint of barristers between a rich man and a poor one, and the blind St Hervé with his wolf; the **altarpiece of St Miliau**, representing scenes from the Saint's life; the **altarpiece of the Rosary**, with 15 mysteries in medallions, is surmounted by a Trinity.

Chapelle funéraire – The funerary chapel in the Renaissance style, dating from 1648, has an outdoor pulpit set in one of the windows.

Sacristie – Built in 1683, the sacristy carries a statue of St Miliau on its conical roof.

GUINGAMP

Population 7 905

Michelin map 59 fold 2 or 230 folds 7 and 8

Located on the edge of Armor *(qv)* and Argoat *(qv)*, Guingamp is a commercial and industrial (electronic construction, food processing) town, which has greatly developed in the past 20 years.

SIGHTS

★**Basilique N.-D.-de-Bon-Secours** (**B**) – This church was built in the Gothic style in the 14C (a Romanesque part remains at the transept crossing); but two centuries later the south tower collapsed, demolishing the nave's south side. The town asked several architects to plan its reconstruction. One old master presented a purely traditional Gothic design; but a young man named Le Moal submitted plans in which the Renaissance style, almost unknown in Brittany at that time, appeared. Quite unexpectedly the people of Guingamp awarded the prize to the innovator. Since then the church has had the unusual feature of being Gothic on the left and Renaissance on the right.
At the west end, two tall towers, the 13C Clock Tower to the left and the Renaissance Tower to the right, frame a very fine round arched doorway with delicate decorations, half sacred and half profane.

Enter by the Notre-Dame-de-Bon Secours doorway which opens into Rue Notre-Dame.

Transformed into an oratory, the chapel houses a Black Virgin, the church's patroness. A great *pardon (qv)* draws thousands of pilgrims. After the torch-lit procession, three bonfires are lit on Place du Centre in the company of the bishop, who also presides over the ceremony.
Inside, the church is unusual with its numerous pillars and graceful flying buttresses in the chancel. The triforium is adorned with trilobed arches with a quadrilobed balustrade while lower down the nave has striking Renaissance decoration.

Place du Centre (**AB**) – On the square are a few old houses (nos 31, 33, 35, 39, 48) at the corner of Rues St-Yves and du Cosquet; the fountain called **"la Plomée"**, with three lead and stone basins dating from the Renaissance.

Hôtel de Ville (**B H**) ⏲ – The town hall (1699) housed in the old hospital (Hôtel-Dieu), was formerly an Augustinian monastery. The cloisters, great staircase and fine Italian-style chapel (1709) may be visited. In the chapel, in season, temporary exhibitions are held.

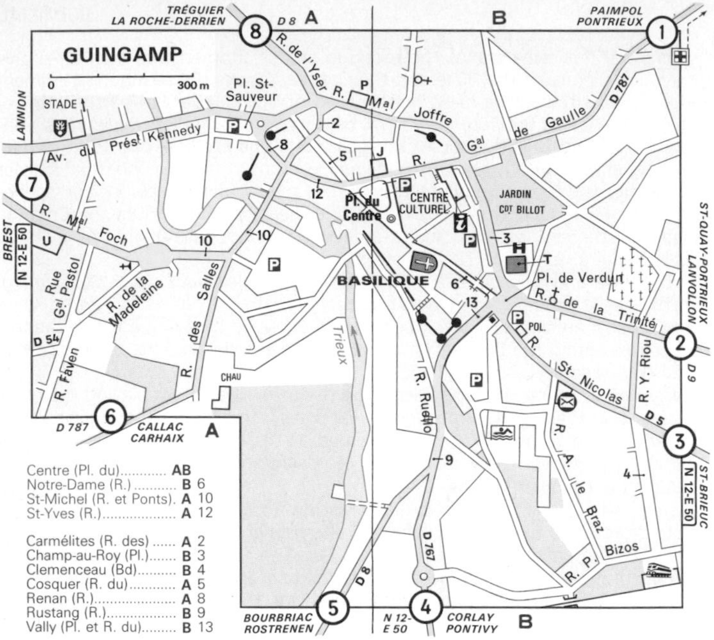

Among the permanent collection are paintings by Sérusier (in the great hall) and the Pont-Aven School.

Ramparts – Standing on Place du Vally (**B 13**) are all that remains of the castle (1438-42) – the ramparts.
Ruins of the fortifications which once surrounded the town can be seen not far from Rue du Maréchal Joffre (**AB**) and Place St-Sauveur (**A**).

EXCURSIONS

★**Menez-Bré** – *13km - 8 miles west – about 1 hour 15 min. Leave Guingamp on ⑦, the road to Brest. 11.5km - 7miles from Guingamp, after a house on the right, turn right (signposted) into a steep uphill road (max. gradient 1 in 5.5) which leads to the summit of the Menez-Bré. See BELLE-ISLE-EN-TERRE: Excursions.*

Grâces – *3.5km - 2 miles. Leave Guingamp on the D 54, west on the town plan. Turn right after 2km - 1 mile; in the village centre stands the large church.*
Originally the **Église Notre-Dame** (Church of Our Lady) would appear to have been a pilgrims' chapel, probably founded by Queen Anne. Built in the 16C, it was slightly altered in the 17C and restored in the 19C. The four gables of the single aisle give it a saw-tooth silhouette from the south.
Inside, note the nave's tie-beams and the superb carved purlins. A satirical picture of drunkenness is the main theme; but there are also hunting scenes, monsters, and a poignant Holy Face surrounded by little angels. A wooden shrine contains the relics of Charles of Blois, killed at the Battle of Auray *(qv)*.

VALLEÉ DU TRIEUX

Round tour of 39km - 24 miles – time: about 2 hours. Leave Guingamp on ⑤ on the town plan.

The road follows the Trieux Valley and then, for a short while, goes into Kerauffret Wood which lies over on the left. The almost flat countryside is pleasant.

Bourbriac – Rising in the centre of the town and surrounded by gardens, is the church with its soaring bell tower 64m - 210ft high. There have been several buildings erected on the site: of the first there remains a crypt probably of the 10 or 11C; of the Romanesque church which followed, there is the very high transept crossing – the tower above it was burnt down in the fire of 1765 and has been replaced by a pinnacle. In 1535 building on the west tower began; it is a remarkable example of the style that was to come: while the big pointed arched porch and all the lower floor are in the Flamboyant style, the remainder of the tower is definitely Renaissance. The spire was added in 1869. Inside, the sarcophagus of St Briac, dating from Merovingian times, is invoked as a cure for epilepsy.
Go towards Plésidy and then in the direction of St-Péver.

After 2km - 1 mile, note on the left below the road the small **Manoir de Toul-an-Gollet**, a pleasant 15C granite with a pepperpot turret and mullioned windows.

Turn left at the crossroads and before the bridge over the Trieux, take a small road to the right.

Chapelle N.-D.-de-Restudo ⓥ – This 14-15C chapel retains traces of 14C frescoes depicting the Last Supper and chivalric scenes in the nave and chancel which are separated by a great pointed arch. *Pardon* on 30 June in honour of St Eligius.

Turn back and take the road back to Guingamp.

The Trieux Valley offers varied scenery.

After 2km - 1 mile bear right to Avaugour.

Chapelle d'Avaugour ⓥ – The chapel stands in an attractive setting and contains a finely carved wood sacrarium (shrine) of the 16C and interesting statues of the Apostles.

Make your way up the Trieux Valley back to Guingamp on ④ of the town plan.

HÉDÉ

Population 1 500

Michelin map 59 fold 16 or 230 fold 26

The village stands on a hill between the Ille-et-Rance Canal and a pond. Houses, hanging gardens and the ruins of a feudal castle, on a rocky promontory, create a picturesque scene. The Romanesque **church** ⓥ contains an alabaster Virgin and a high altar in wood; both date from the 17C.

Les Onze écluses – *1.5km - 3/4 mile northeast by the road to Combourg at the tiny village of La Madeleine. After the bridge over the canal, bear left to the car park by the lock keeper's house.*
There are eleven locks, three before and eight after the bridge, to negotiate a drop of 27m - 89ft on the Ille-et-Rance Canal. Pleasant walk in a pretty setting along the towpath.

EXCURSION

Round tour of 17km - 10 miles. *Time: about 2 hours 30 min. Leave Hédé west on the D 221.*

★**Église des Iffs** ⓥ – The church is an attractive Gothic building with an entrance porch and bell tower, as well as fine Flamboyant style windows in the south wall. Inside are nine lovely 16C **stained-glass windows**★ inspired by the Dutch and Italian Schools (16C): scenes of the Passion (in the chancel), Christ's childhood (in the north chapel), the Story of Susannah and the Two Elders (in the south chapel). Found in the nave are two low reliefs representing the Apostles and a font carved with a hare playing a musical instrument (1458), a double 15C baptismal font, a Stations of the Cross, carved in wood by Colette Rodenfuser (1965), and an odd-looking triangular high altar.

★**Château de Montmuran** ⓥ – *800m – half a mile north of Les Iffs.*
The 17C main building, the façade of which was remodelled in the 18C, is ensconced between 12C towers and a 14C entrance fort. A drawbridge across the moat leads to the narrow portcullised gateway framed by two massive round machicolated towers. One of these towers houses the guardroom and a small museum evoking the castle's history. Behind the entrance fort an external staircase goes to the chapel where Du Guesclin *(qv)* was knighted in 1354 after a skirmish with the English in the neighbourhood. He later married, as his second wife, Jeanne de Laval.
From the towers *(84 steps)*, there is a vast panorama of the Hédé and Dinan countryside.

Turn around and bear right.

Tinténiac – *See TINTÉNIAC.*

Return to Hédé on the road to Rennes.

HENNEBONT

Population 13 624

Michelin map 63 fold 1 or 230 fold 35

Hennebont is a former fortified town on the steep banks of the Blavet (good fishing). A *pardon* takes place at Hennebont on the last Sunday in September *(see the Calendar of Events at the end of the guide)*.

The siege of 1342 – During the War of Succession *(qv)* one of the Pretenders, Jean de Montfort, was held prisoner in the Louvre. In 1342 his wife, Jeanne of Flanders, was besieged in Hennebont by Charles of Blois and the French. The countess fought like a true knight, but the assailants opened a breach in the walls. The garrison, demoralized, compelled her to negotiate. She obtained permission to march out with the honours of war if her reinforcements did not arrive within three days. Before the set date, the English fleet sailed up the Blavet and saved the town.

SIGHTS

Basilique N.-D.-de-Paradis – On Place Maréchal-Foch stands the 16C basilica. Its very big **bell tower★** is surmounted by a steeple 65m - 213ft high. At the base of the tower a fine Flamboyant porch ornamented with niches leads into the nave, which is lit by stained-glass windows by Max Ingrand. A Renaissance gallery houses the organ (1652).

Puits ferré – Old iron well (1623), with fine wrought-iron work.

Porte Broërec'h and ramparts – This gateway (restored), a vestige of the 13C fortifications, was once used as a prison. *Go through the gate and take a stairway on the left up to the wall walk.* The 15C ramparts of the old fortified town afford a lovely view of the Blavet Valley spanned by the railway viaduct. Gardens are laid out along the walls.
The **Tours Broërec'h** (Broërec'h Towers) ⏲ house exhibitions.

Haras (Stud) ⏲ – Set up in a former abbey, the Hennebont Stud supplies around 70 breeding animals (draught horses, Breton post-horses, Anglo-Arabs, French saddle horses, ponies) to stations in South Finistère, Morbihan and Ile-et-Vilaine. The tour includes a visit to the stables, saddle room, riding ring and carriage hall. You may visit the ruins of the abbey within the grounds (note the 17C gateway).

Parc de Kerbihan – *Access by Rue Nationale and Rue Léo-Lagrange (the latter reserved for pedestrians)*. The park, bordered by the St-Gilles stream, is planted with species (all labelled) from the five continents.

Écomusée industriel de Inzinzac-Lochrist ⏲ – The open-air museum occupies the site of the Hennebont Ironworks, one of Brittany's most important companies, which operated from 1860-1966.

Musée des Métallurgistes des Forges d'Hennebont – Located on the Blavet River's north bank in the old research laboratory, the museum concentrates on the heart of the iron and steel industry of Brittany – the technology used by workshops, social conditions and family life, the rise of trade unions and the strikes that resulted, the effect of the wars – with exhibits of machines, tools, documents, etc. There are short films on metal work at Hennebont foundries.

Maison de l'Eau et de l'Hydraulique – Near the dam, in the Hennebont Ironworks caretaker's house, is an exhibit devoted to the Blavet River: its canalisation, its traffic, fish, windmills...

RIVIERE D'ÉTEL

Round tour of 70km - 43 miles – time: about 3 hours 30 min. Leave Hennebont southeast on the D 9.

Kervignac – The new houses stand on the left of the road. Skilfully reconstructed after a fire in 1944, the small city encircles a charming modern church.
The plan of the Church of Our Lady of Pity (Notre-Dame-de-Pitié) is that of a Greek cross. The four sides consist of a lower part in granite, which supports the clerestory containing stained glass windows, the work of the master glassworker Gabriel Loire; above rises a triangular gable. In one of the re-entrant angles is a square tower surmounted by a small belfry with a pierced spire. Inside, the lovely polished pinewood panelling goes well with the glowing stained-glass windows depicting the life of the Virgin Mary and with the sober wooden Stations of the Cross outlined in charcoal and chalk.

★**Merlevenez** – This little town's **church★** is one of the few Romanesque churches in Brittany which has kept intact its elegant doorways with chevron and saw-tooth archivolts, its depressed arches in the nave, its historiated capitals and dome on squinches rising above the transept crossing. Modern stained-glass windows by Grüber illustrate scenes from the Life of the Virgin.

Via the road to Carnac and a small road on the left go to Ste-Hélène.

Ste-Hélène – In this village stands a fountain to which sailors from Étel came in pilgrimage before embarking on the fishing boats. If breadcrumbs thrown in the fountain floated to the surface the sailor would return safely from the fishing expedition.

Take the road to the right of the town hall (mairie) *and make for the Pointe de Mané Hellec .*

The route gives access to the pretty **River Étel★**, a small bay dotted with islands that specialise in oyster farming.

Pointe de Mané-Hellec – *By a small transformer station, turn left into a surfaced road.* Lovely view of St-Cado and its chapel, Pont-Lorois, the River Étel and the Forêt de Locoal-Mendon.

Return to Ste-Hélène and take the road to Plouhinec; after 2km - 1 mile bear left. At the entrance to Pont-Lorois, turn right to Barre d'Étel.

Barre d'Étel – The ocean breaks, before the River Étel, known for its bank of quicksand *(barre)*, which offers a spectacular scene in bad weather. Navigation is difficult and requires constant surveillance. The view extends over the île de Groix Island, Belle-Ile and the Presqu'île de Quiberon. The small fishing port of **Étel** lies on the river's south bank. It is home to a fleet of about 10 fishing boats, which sail to the Azores, and a small fleet of trawlers, which fish along the coast.
River Étel, which abounds in fish, flows 30km - 18.5 miles inland to the *commune* of Nostang.

Turn back.

Pont-Lorois – This short and pretty run gives a glimpse of the wide estuary, which on the left opens out into a bay and on the right narrows into a deep channel which winds down to the sea.

After the bridge, bear left in the direction of Belz and left again.

Chapelle St-Cado – *15 min on foot Rtn.* This chapel, like the church at Merlevenez, is one of the few Romanesque buildings in the Morbihan. Its general simplicity, with unornamented rounded arches, capitals with very plain decoration and dim lighting, contrasts with the fine Flamboyant style gallery running on the inside of the 16C façade. It is in this chapel that the deaf sought help from St Cado whose stone bed and pillow can still be seen. The chapel, the Calvary and the little fishermen's houses make a charming Breton **scene★** especially at high tide. The St-Cado fountain stands below the east end.

H. Connezan/EXPLORER

In St-Cado, bear left after the transformer station.

The road runs along the River Étel passing the Kerhuen dolmen.

Make for Belz bearing right; at Belz turn left and take the road towards Pluvigner. After Locoal-Mendon, turn left towards the Pointe du Verdon.

Pointe du Verdon – As with all the points of the bay, the far end of the Pointe du Verdon is devoted to oyster farming; after crossing the isthmus and before taking the uphill road through the pines, bear right to reach a platform from which there is a fine view over the oyster beds. At low tide it is possible to walk round the point.

Take the direction of Langombrac'h, which you pass on the left and make for Landévant. At the town entrance, turn left towards Merlevenez.

This road passes the extreme point of the River Étel which is best seen at high tide.

At Nostang, the D 164 leads straight back to Hennebont.

Île de HŒDIC

Population 140
Michelin map 63 fold 12 or 230 fold 50
Access: boat service from Quiberon and Vannes ⓥ

Separated from the île d'Houat by the Sœurs Channel, the smaller (2.5km by 1km - 1.5 miles by 0.5 mile) Hœdic Island has the same granite formation with beaches and rocky headlands. Two lagoons extend east of the town while the island is covered in sparse heathland where wild carnations, a few cypresses, fine fig trees and tamarisks grow. Fresh water is supplied by an underground water bearing bed.
The boats dock at Argol Harbour. There are two other harbours – Port de la Croix and Port Neuf – which attract pleasure craft to the island. Tourism and fishing are the two main sources of income of the island. A gently sloping road leads to the town with a small chapel on the right and a menhir on the left.

Town – The south-facing houses stand in groups of three or four. Near the former beacon is the **Église St-Goustan** named after a Cornish hermit, who came to the island for a few years. It has fine 19C **furnishings**; note the two angels in white marble by the high altar.

Ancien fort – The old fort, built in 1859 and partly hidden by the dunes, can be seen on the road to Port de la Croix. There is also a ruined 17C English fort at Beg-Lagatte.
Footpaths by the sea take you round the island to discover the beaches and admire the lovely **view** of the mainland, Houat Island, Belle-Ile and of the reefs.

Île d'HOUAT

Population 390
Michelin map 63 fold 12 or 230 folds 49 and 50
Access: see the current Michelin Red Guide France

This island (Île d'Houat: 5km - 3 miles long and 1.3km - 3/4 mile wide) of the Ponant archipelago, situated 15km - 9 miles off the Morbihan coast, is a granite ridge fringed by cliffs. Because of its location commanding the access to Quiberon Bay, it was occupied three times by the English in the 17 and 18C. The boats dock in the new harbour on the north coast. A road leads uphill to the town.

Town – Pretty houses, whitewashed and flower-bedecked, line the winding streets and alleyways leading to a square in the centre of the town in which stands the communal well, and to another square next to the church.
The church, built in the 19C, commemorates St Gildas, an English monk and patron of the island, who visited Houat prior to founding the monastery of St-Gildas-de-Rhuys *(qv)*.

Go round the church and follow the path skirting the cemetery.

From the lookout point, there is a fine **view★** of the harbour and of the Presqu'île de Rhuys.

Beaches (Plages) – There are numerous beaches nestling in small creeks but the loveliest extends to the west, facing the île de Hœdic, near the old harbour which was damaged in a violent storm in 1951.

HUELGOAT★★

Population 1 742
Michelin map 58 fold 6 or 230 fold 19 – Local map under Monts d'ARRÉE

The forest, lake, running water and rocks make Huelgoat one of the finest **sites★★** in inner Brittany which come under the aegis of the Parc natural régional d'Armorique *(qv)*.
Huelgoat is not only a good excursion centre but a favourite place for anglers (especially for carp and perch in the lake and trout in the river).

★★THE ROCKS *time: 1 hour 30min on foot*

Access – *In Rue de Berrien past the lake and follow the signposted path.*

Chaos du Moulin – The path cuts through the rocks dominating the course of the River Argent. This pile of rounded granite rocks, surrounded by greenery, is very picturesque.

Grotte du Diable – *To reach this, climb down an iron ladder.* A brook babbles under the rocks.

Théâtre de Verdure – Beautiful setting.

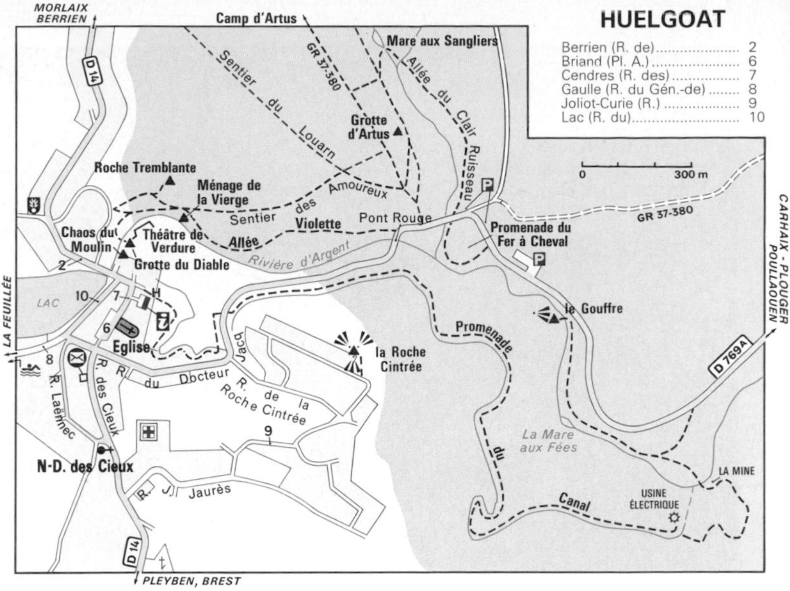

Roche Tremblante – *Left bank.* By leaning against this 100-ton block at a precise point, you can make it rock on its base.

Ménage de la Vierge – An enormous pile of rocks shaped rather like kitchen utensils.

An uphill path, known as Lovers' Walk (Sentier des Amoureux), leads directly through the woods to Artus's Cave and to Boars' Pool (see The Forest below).

Allée Violette – A pleasant path in the woods along the left bank of the River Argent.

To return to the centre of Huelgoat, at Pont-Rouge, turn right into the road from Carhaix and then take Rue du Docteur-Jacq.

★THE FOREST

Extending over 1 000ha - 2 471 acres, the Forest of Huelgoat lies at the foot of the southern slope of the Monts d'Arrée mountain range. Its tortured topography consists of a series of hills divided by deep valleys. The forest features a great many different landscapes and colours; it also contains strange, picturesque sites which have inspired many traditional tales and legends. *(Visitors can discover these sites with the help of signposts and car parks; see below).*

Promenade du Fer à Cheval and Le Gouffre – *30 min on foot. After Pont-Rouge, take the Horseshoe Walk on the right.*
A pleasant walk through the woods along the River Argent. *Then return to the Carhaix road for 300 – about 328yds.* A stairway *(39 steps)* leads down to the chasm. The River Argent flowing from the lac d'Huelgoat, falls into a deep cavity to reappear 150m further on. A path leads to a lookout point *(15 min Rtn – difficult and no security ramp)* commanding a view of the chasm. You can continue this walk through the woods by the river passing near the Mare aux Fées (Fairies Pool) and combining it with the the Promenade du Canal.

Follow the signposts to the mine (La Mine), turn right at the bridge into an unsurfaced road and at the former mine, continue along an uphill path to the right to the power station (usine électrique). A footbridge spans the canal and leads to the opposite bank.

Promenade du Canal – *2 hours on foot Rtn on Rue du Docteur-Jacq.* This walk follows the bank of the upper canal. A reservoir and two canals were dug in the 19C to work the silver-bearing lead mines, already known to the Romans. The waters were used to wash the ore and drive a crusher. From the far end of the canal walk you may continue on to the chasm; *this walk is described in the opposite direction see below.*

Walk – *1 hour 30 min on foot Rtn. From the car park after Pont-Rouge, take Allée du Clair-Ruisseau.*
This path half-way up the slope affords fine views of the rock-strewn stream bed. A stairway *(25 steps)* on the left leads down to the **Mare aux Sangliers** (Boars' Pool) in a pretty setting of rocks shaped rather like boars' heads, hence the name. Cross over the rustic bridge to Allée de la Mare on the left.

J.-P. Lescourret/EXPLORER

Rocks at Huelgoat

After the great stairway *(218 steps)* which provides the quickest access to **Camp d'Artus** (Artus's Camp) you can see up above, on the right, the entrance to **Grotte d'Artus** (Artus's Cave).

Continue up the path which after 800m - half a mile takes you to the camp. Boulders mark the entrance which was dominated by an artificial mound.

It is an important example of a Gallic fortified site, bordered by two enclosures. In spite of the encroaching vegetation, it is possible to go round the camp by a path *(1km - half a mile)* following the remaining second elliptical enclosure which is fairly well preserved.

ADDITIONAL SIGHTS

Church – A 16C church with a modern belfry stands near the main square in the town centre. Inside there are sculpted purlins and to the left of the chancel is a statue of St Yves, the patron saint of the parish, between a rich man and a pauper.

Chapelle N.-D.-des-Cieux – Overlooking Huelgoat, this Renaissance chapel with its 18C bell tower, has curious painted low reliefs depicting scenes from the life of the Virgin and the Passion around the chancel and the side altars. A *pardon* takes place on the first Sunday in August.

La Roche Cintrée - *Take the road to Carhaix and follow the signposts. After 110yds take the uphill road on the left.*
From the top of the rock *(time: 15 min on foot Rtn)*, there is a view of Huelgoat (somewhat limited), north onto the Monts d'Arrée and south onto the Montagnes Noires.

Château de la HUNAUDAYE*

Michelin map 59 north of folds 14 and 15 or 230 north of fold 24

The **castle ruins** ⏲ of La Hunaudaye Castle rise in a lonely, wooded spot. Still impressive and severe, they reflect the power of the great barons, equals of the Rohans, who built the castle.
The castle, built in 1220 by Olivier de Tournemine, was partly destroyed during the War of Succession *(qv)*. Rebuilt and enlarged by Pierre de Tournemine in the 14C, enriched in the early 17C by Sébastien de Rosmadec, husband of one of the Tournemine heiresses, it was dismantled and then burnt by the Republicans at the time of the Revolution. The pillage of the castle stones was only stopped when the property was bought by the French government in 1930.
The shape is that of an irregular pentagon with a tower at each corner. The two smallest derive from the first building, the other three were built in the 14-15C. The moat was once fed by two lakes. A bridge, replacing the original drawbridge, gives access to a large rounded doorway surmounted by a coat of arms. This leads to the courtyard.

Pass along the 14-15C keep on the left, the 13-15C Tour Noire at the foot of which traces of the kitchens (**1**) can still be seen, to reach Glacière Tower.

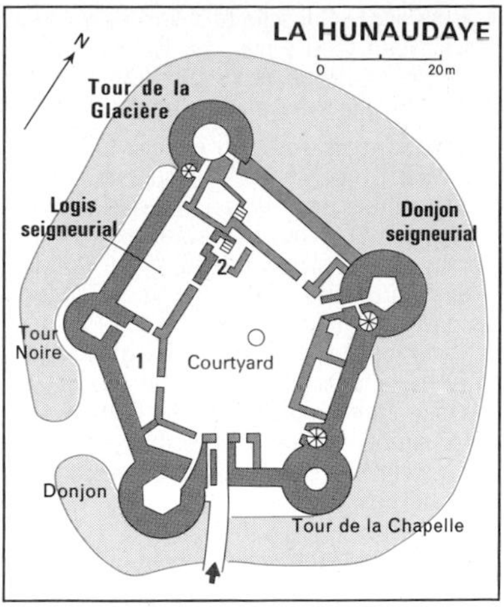

Tour de la Glacière – This 15C tower is north facing, hence its name *(glacière* = ice-house). Go up the spiral staircase to admire the elegant structure and chimneys, and the view of the moat.

Logis seigneurial – 15-16C. The walls and the splendid Renaissance stairway (**2**) give some idea of the lay-out of this great manor-house.

Donjon seigneurial – This 15C tower of this manorial keep with its spiral staircase (73 steps) is the best preserved. The monumental chimney-pieces and loopholes in the walls are note worthy. View of the courtyard and moat.

The fifth tower closing off the pentagon is the 13-14C Chapel Tower.

This site is the setting for a performance, in period costume, of various aspects of life in a medieval castellany. The actors belong to the Compagnie Médiévale "Mac'htiern".

JOSSELIN★★

Population 2 338

Michelin map 63 fold 4 or 230 fold 37 – Facilities

This small town stands in a picturesque setting. Its river, the Oust, reflects the famous castle of the Rohan family. Behind the fortress-castle, on the sides and the summit of a steep ridge, old houses with slate roofs are scattered around the basilica of Our Lady of the Brambles (Basilique Notre-Dame-du-Roncier).

The prosperity of the region depends on tourism and local industries such as meat canning and cardboard manufacturing.

HISTORICAL NOTES

The Battle of the Thirty (14C) – By the middle of the 14C Josselin Castle had already been razed and rebuilt. It belonged to the Royal House of France; Beaumanoir was its Captain; the War of Succession *(qv)* was raging. Josselin supported the cause of Blois; the Montfort party held Ploërmel, where an Englishman, Bemborough, was in command. At first the two garrisons had frequent encounters as they ravaged the countryside; then the two leaders arranged a fight between thirty knights from each camp: they would fight on foot, using sword, dagger, battle-axe and pike.

After taking Communion and praying all night at Our Lady of the Brambles, Beaumanoir's men repaired, on 27 March 1351, to the rendez-vous on the heath at Mi-Voie, between Josselin and Ploërmel (5km - 3 miles from Josselin at a place called Pyramide; a stone column marks the spot today). In the opposite camp were twenty Englishmen, six Germans and four Bretons. The day was spent in fierce hand-to-hand fighting until the combatants were completely exhausted. Josselin won; the English captain was killed with eight of his men, and the rest were taken prisoner. During the struggle, which has remained famous as the Battle of the Thirty, the Breton leader, wounded, asked for a drink. "Drink your blood, Beaumanoir, your thirst will pass!" replied one of his rough companions.

Constable de Clisson (14C) – Among the owners of Josselin the greatest figure was Olivier de Clisson, who married Marguerite de Rohan, Beaumanoir's widow. He acquired the castle in 1370. He had a tragic childhood; for when he was only seven his father was accused of betraying the French party in the War of Succession and beheaded in Paris. His widow, Jeanne de Belleville, who had been quiet and inconspicuous hitherto, became a fury. She hurried to Nantes with her children and, on the bloody head of their father nailed to the ramparts, made them swear to avenge him. Then she took the field with 400 men and put to the sword the garrisons of six castles which favoured the French cause. When the royal troops forced her to flee, she put to sea and sank every enemy ship that she met.

With this training Olivier became a hardened warrior and his career, first with the English and then in the army of Charles V, was particularly brilliant. He was a comrade in arms of Du Guesclin and succeeded him as Constable. All-powerful under Charles VI, he was banished when the King went mad, and he died in 1407 at Josselin. At this time the castle, entirely rebuilt and guarded by nine towers, was a very important stronghold. It then passed to the Rohan family, who still own it.

The Rohans at Josselin (15 and 17C) – In 1488, to punish Jean II de Rohan for having sided with the King of France, the Duke of Brittany, François II, seized Josselin and had it dismantled. When his daughter Anne became Queen of France she compensated Jean II, who was able in the rebuilding of the castle to create a masterpiece worthy of the proud motto of his family: "Roi ne puis, Prince ne daigne, Rohan suis" (I cannot be king, I scorn to be a prince, I am a Rohan). The owner of Josselin showed his gratitude to the Queen in the decoration of the palace; in many places, the letter A is carved in the stone, crowned and surmonted by the girdle which was Anne's emblem, and accompanied by the royal *fleur-de-lys*. In 1629, Henri de Rohan, the leader of the Huguenots, Richelieu's sworn enemies, met the Cardinal in the King's antechamber where the cleric, who had just had the keep and five of the nine towers of Josselin razed, announced with cruel irony: "I have just thrown a fine ball among your skittles, Monsieur."

★★ CASTLE (CHÂTEAU) *time: 45 min*

To get a good **view★** of the castle stand on Ste-Croix Bridge, which spans the River Oust. From this point the building has the appearance of a fortress, with high towers, curtain walls and battlements. The windows and dormer windows appearing above the walls belong to the palace built by Jean II in the 16C.
The castle is built on a terrace of irregular shape, surrounded by walls of which only the bases remain, except on the side which is seen from the bridge. The isolated "prison tower" marked the northeast corner of the enclosure.
The delightful **façade★★** of the main building which looks out onto the old courtyard, now the park, makes a striking contrast with the fortifications of the outer façade. Nowhere else in Brittany has the art of the sculptor in that hard material, granite, been pushed to such limits: brackets, florets, pinnacles, gables, crowns and curled leaves adorn the dormer windows and balustrades.
Only the ground floor, restored in the 19C, is open. to the public. In the panelled dining room stands an equestrian statue of Olivier de Clisson by Frémiet. After the antechamber, in which are hung portraits of the Rohan family, is the richly furnished drawing room with its delicately carved chimney which bears the current Rohan motto, "A plus" (To more). There are over 3 000 books and some portraits in the library.

Musée des Poupées (**B M**) – In the castle's old stables, 500 dolls from the Rohan collection are exhibited. These come from many different countries (France, Netherlands, Austria, North America, etc) and date from the 17 to the 20C. The dolls (in wood, wax, celluloid, porcelain...) are dressed in religious or traditional costumes. Miscellaneous doll accessories are also exhibited. There are temporary exhibitions here in summer.

Morcime/CAMPAGNE CAMPAGNE

Josselin

JOSSELIN

Beaumanoir (R.) A 2
Le-Berd (R. Georges) B 12
Trente (R. des) B 30

Briend (R. Lucien) B 2
Chapelle (R. de la) A 3
Clisson (R. O. de) B 4
Coteaux (R. des) A 5
Devins (R. des) A 6
Douves-du-Lion-d'Or (Rue) A 7
Duchesse-Anne (Pl.) B 8
Fontaine (R. de la) B 9
Gaulle (R. Gén.-de) A 10
Libération (Pl. de) B 13
Notre-Dame (Pl.) B 14
Rohan (Pl. A.-de) B 16
Rohan (Cours J. de) B 17
St-Jacques (R.) B 18
St-Martin (Pl.) A 20
St-Martin (R.) A 22
St-Michel (R.) B 23
St-Nicolas (R. et Pl.) B 24
Ste-Croix (Pont) A 27
Ste-Croix (R.) A 28
Texier (R. Alphonse) A 29
Vierges (R. des) B 32

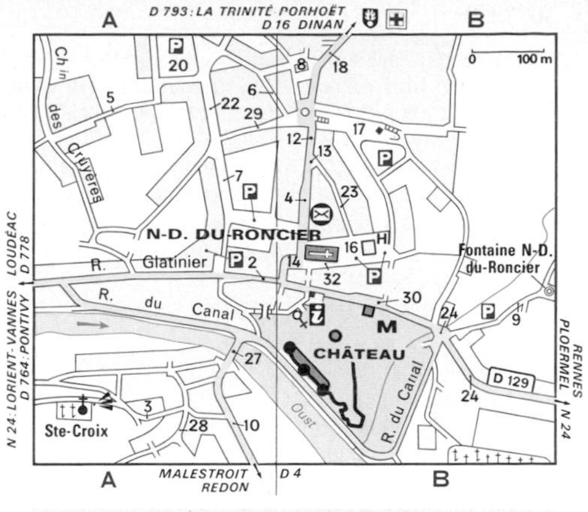

M Musée de Poupées

ADDITIONAL SIGHTS

★**Basilique N.-D.-du-Roncier** (**B**) – Founded in the 12C and several times remodelled (east end's spire built in 1949), the basilica is, generally speaking, Flamboyant in style; note the wonderful gargoyles which adorn its three sides and the stone statue of the Virgin at the entrance door. It is famous for its great *pardon (see the Calendar of Events at the end of the guide)*. This has been called the "barkers' pardon" since 1728, when three children were cured of epilepsy at the festival.
The name, Our Lady of the Brambles, is based on a very old legend. Around the year 800 a peasant, cutting brambles in his field, discovered a statue of the Virgin, hence its name. An oratory made of branches, followed by a chapel in wood, then, in *c*1000, by a Romanesque chapel (rebuilt in the late 12C) were built on this spot.
Inside, in the south chapel, is the **mausoleum**★ of Olivier de Clisson and his wife Marguerite de Rohan (15C). The chapel of the Virgin of the Brambles is left of the chancel (modern statue; the former statue was burned in 1793). In the nave is a fine wrought-iron pulpit of the 18C. The organ case is 16C. The modern stained-glass window in the north transept was designed by Grüber.

Ascent to the tower ⓥ – *Access from Place A.-de-Rohan.* The tower commands a view of the northeast façade, the castle's inner courtyard and the country-side beyond.

Chapelle Ste-Croix (**A**) ⓥ – Built on the side of the hill is this chapel with its 11C nave. From the surrounding cemetery, which is ornamented with a Calvary (16C), there is a pretty view of the Oust and the castle.
After a visit to the chapel, stroll in the picturesque Ste-Croix district with its narrow streets and old houses some of which are corbelled.

Fontaine N.-D.-du-Roncier (**B**) – Built in 1675, the fountain is still a place of pilgrimage.

Old houses – The old houses are found in the basilica's precinct especially on Rue des Vierges and Place Notre-Dame. Nevertheless, the most picturesque are in Rue des Trente; there is the picturesque house at no 7, dating from 1624 and beside it a house built in 1663.

JUGON-LES-LACS

Population 1 283

Michelin map 59 folds 14 and 15 or 230 fold 24

The town of Jugon adjoins the dike which holds back the Rivers Rosette and Rieule to form the great lac de Jugon (67ha – 166 acres), popular for boating and fishing. The church, which was partly rebuilt in the 19C, retains its 13C porch, a saddle-back roofed belfry (15C) and the south transept doorway adorned with stylised carvings. In Rue du Château stands the former Sevoy mansion (1634) built on the rock.

EXCURSIONS

★**Château de la Hunaudaye** – *9km - 5 miles north. Leave Jugon west on the N 176 towards St-Brieuc and after 2km - 1 mile bear right. At St-Igneuc turn right after the church in the direction of Pléven, and by Le Clos du Puits Café, turn left.*

Ferme d'antan de St-Esprit-des-Bois en Plédéliac ⓥ – Go into the courtyard surrounded by the traditional buildings on a small holding with their usual implements: out-

buildings, cart and wood sheds, stables, cellar, bread oven, 1873 forge, recently restored and enhanced by the addition of a collection of tools of days gone by. The communal living room, with its great chimney-piece, is furnished in typical Breton style.
The tour ends with a film projection illustrating the everyday life of a peasant family in this very farm at the beginning of the century.

Go round the farm and bear right; once on the road to Pléven turn left at the village of Chêne au Loup and 600m - 656yds further on turn right towards Château de la Hunaudaye.

★**Château de la Hunaudaye** – *See Château de la HUNAUDAYE.*

Abbaye de Boquen – *15km - 9 miles southwest on the D 792, in the direction of Collinée. At Plénée-Jugon take the signposted road which runs through the Arguenon Valley.*
The abbey was founded by the Cistercian Order in 1137 and grew considerably. However, it began to decline under the *commendam* system and during the Revolution and the building was later sacked; in 1936 the first monk returned. The abbey is now occupied by nuns.

Leave the car in the car park opposite the reception area.

On the left, where silence is observed, are the conventual buildings. The church in the sober Cistercian style has a 12C nave and transept, a 15C chancel with a flat chevet lit through fine grisaille windows. Note the statue of Our Lady of Boquen (15C) and a statue of Christ in simple style. A stairway in the north transept leads to the monks' dormitory.

Manoir de KÉRAZAN★

Michelin map no 58 fold 15 or 230 fold 32 – 4km – 2.5 miles north west of Loctudy

The **manor-house** ⏱ is situated in a large park full of tall trees and consists of a main building with large windows, which was rebuilt in the 18C, and a wing set at right-angles, dating from the 16C. The estate was bequeathed to the Institut de France by Joseph Astor in 1928. The rooms, richly decorated and furnished, bear witness to the luxurious setting the Astors aimed to create.
Louis XV woodwork, both authentic and reconstructed, adorns the great hall, the billiards room, the corner room and the green hall. The dining room, decorated with painted panelling, contains a display of a number of works by **Alfred Beau** (1829-1907). This ceramic painter, who was associated with the Porquier de Quimper faïence works (hence the well-known PB insignia), created many works of art from plates and trays, as well as by painting works on enamel which was then framed in either plain or carved wood, giving the impression that they were real paintings. The true masterpiece has to be the life-size cello made from polychrome faïence, for which the manufacture process involved fifteen different firings. The library is as it was arranged by Joseph Astor's father, mayor of Quimper and a great admirer of Beau; the furniture and the layout of the shelves have not been changed. As a whole, the rooms contain a collection of paintings and drawings in which Brittany and the Breton way of life in days gone by play an important role. Various Schools are represented, from the 16C to the 20C (Frans Francken, Charles Cotter, Lucien Simon, Maurice Denis).The tour ends in the blue hall, once a chapel, which houses the Astor family's memorabilia and a collection of 19C weapons.

Domaine de KERGUÉHENNEC

Michelin map 69 fold 3 or 230 folds 36 and 37

The Kerguéhennec **estate**, in a pleasant, verdant setting, includes a classical-style château, wooded park and lake. It was acquired by the Morbihan *département* in the 1970s and transformed into a **contemporary art centre** ⏱.

Park and Sculptures ⏱ – An arboretum with fine trees is located in the 170ha - 442 acre park. Dotted throughout the park are modern sculptures including Giuseppe Penone's bronze *Charm's Way* (1986), Étienne Hajdu's *7 Columns to Stéphane Mallarmé* (1969-71), and Ulrich Ruckrien's blue granite *Bild Stock* (1985). On the lake float red polyester sculptures (1986) by Marta Pan.

Château – The château, built in the early 18C by local architect Olivier Delourme, consists of a main building, with two projecting wings and symmetrically opposed outbuildings, the whole enclosing a vast court of honour, closed by a fine grille.
The inside, restored in the late 19C, can be visited: dining room, drawing room with its fine chandeliers and candelabra, billiard room, and library.
Temporary exhibitions and seminars are held in the old stables.
The greenhouse contains bright red flower pots, the work of Jean-Pierre Raynaud, called *1 000 Cement Pots Painted for an Old Greenhouse* (1986).

Château de KERJEAN★

Michelin map 58 fold 5 or 230 fold 4 – 5km – 3 miles southwest of Plouzévédé

Kerjean Castle ⓥ, half-fortress, half-Renaissance mansion, stands in the midst of a huge park. Towards the middle of the 16C Louis Barbier inherited a fortune from his uncle, a rich abbot of St-Mathieu, and decided to build a castle which would be the finest residence in Léon. In 1710 part of the building burned down, later the castle was sacked. However, the castle, which has belonged to the State since 1911, has since been restored except for the right wing. The buildings are guarded by a moat and ramparts; enter the main courtyard via the old drawbridge.

Tour – *Time: 1 hour.* A main building with two wings and a large portico enclose the main courtyard, which is adorned with a fine Corinthian-columned Renaissance *well.* The dwelling house contains a museum of Breton art with fine 17 and 18C **furnishings:** box beds, chests, grain chests.

The kitchen, a vast room with a ceiling 6m - 20ft high, has two monumental chimneys facing each other, one of which was used as the bread oven, and a large copperware collection. The stairs lead down to the food stores.

On the courtyard's other side is the chapel. Inside it is decorated with a wooden vault in the shape of a ship's keel and carved beams and purlins. The coachhouse wing, which once housed the stores, a forge and the servants' quarters, has been restored. There is a slide show on the history of Kerjean. A door leads to an alley supported on a gallery with eight arches, which give a good overall view of the main courtyard and the buildings around it.

A. Pennec

Château de Kerjean – A box bed

The park contains a charming Renaissance fountain, consisting of a niche surrounded by four colonnettes, set into a little stone wall. The noise of the spring, mingled with the warbling of the birds, makes a pleasant background in which to meditate. On leaving, to the left of the central avenue, note the dovecot, a stone tower 9m - 29.5ft in diameter.

Every year, there are temporary exhibitions held, devoted to contemporary art in spring, and the history of Brittany in summer. During July and August, evening theatre performances are on offer.

KERMARIA★

Michelin map 59 folds 2 and 3 or 230 fold 8 – 3.5km – 2 miles northwest of Plouha

The **Chapelle de Kermaria-an-Iskuit★** (House of Mary who preserves and restores health) ⓥ is a popular scene of pilgrimage (third Sunday in September). This former baronial chapel, in which a few of the bays of the nave are 13C, was enlarged in the 15 and 18C. Above the south porch, in the archives, is the former 16C courtroom, with a small balcony. The inside of the porch is adorned with statues of the Apostles.

The walls over the arcades are decorated with 15C **frescoes★**. The best preserved, in the nave, depict a striking dance of death: Death, in the shape of jumping and dancing skeletons and corpses, drags the living into a dance; those depicted include pope, emperor, cardinal, king, constable, bourgeois, usurer, lover, lord, ploughman, monk, etc. Above the high altar is a great 14C Christ. In the south transept are five alabaster **low reliefs★** of scenes from the life of the Virgin. There are numerous wooden statues, including, in the transept, a curious 16C figure of the Virgin suckling her unwilling Child and a Virgin in Majesty (13C).

EXCURSION

★**Lanleff** – *5.5km - 3 miles. Leave Kermaria west on the D 21 to the left and after Pléhédel, bear left..*

In the village, away from the road, stands the **temple★**, a circular building, a former chapel or baptistery built by the Templars in the 11C on the model of the Holy Sepulchre in Jerusalem. Twelve round-arched arcades connect the rotunda with an aisle set at an angle with three oven-vaulted apsidal chapels to the east. Note the simple decoration of the capitals: small figures, animals, geometrical figures, foliage.

KERNASCLÉDEN★★

Population 382

Michelin map 58 fold 18 or 230 folds 21 and 35

This small village possesses a beautiful church built by the Rohan family.

★★**Church** – *Time: 30min.* Though the church at Kernascléden was consecrated in 1453, thirty years before the Chapelle de St-Fiacre (*qv*), there is a legend that they were built at the same time and by the same workmen. Every day, angels carried the men and their tools from one site to the other.

A characteristic feature of this church is the striving for perfection that appears in every detail. The very slender tower, the foliated pinnacles, rose carvings and delicate tracery help to adorn the church without overloading it. Two porches open on the south side. The left **porch★**, which is the larger, is ornamented with statues (restored) of the twelve Apostles (*details of porches p 42*).

Inside, the church has pointed stone vaulting. The vaults and walls surmounting the main arches are decorated with 15C **frescoes★★** representing episodes in the lives of the Virgin and Christ. The finest are the Virgin's Marriage, Annunciation (left of chancel) and Burial (right of chancel). In the north transept are eight angel-musicians; over the triumphal arch (on the chancel side), the Resurrection of Christ. On the walls of the south arm are fragments of a dance of death and a picture of Hell (facing the altar), which is remarkable for the variety of tortures it depicts. There are many 15C statues in wood and stone: Our Lady of Kernascléden to the left of the high altar, St Sebastian and a *Pietà* in the nave.

EXCURSIONS

Château et Forêt de Pont-Calleck ⏲ – *4km - 2miles south. Take the D 782 in the direction of Le Faouët and at Kerchopine, turn left.*

The road skirts the site of Notre-Dame-de-Joie, a children's home housed in **Château de Pont-Calleck** (Pont-Calleck Castle) which was rebuilt in 1880 (*only the park is open to visitors*). The tiny Chapelle Notre-Dame-des-Bois stands at the entrance to the park.

Continue towards Plouay.

The road runs through the **Forêt de Pont-Calleck** (Forest of Pont-Calleck). A small road to the left runs down steeply and leads to a lake which affords a lovely view of the castle's site. Return to the Plouay road for a pleasant drive through the narrow Valley of the Scorff.

Local maps and town plans in Michelin Guides *are oriented with north at the top.*

LAMBADER

Michelin map 58 fold 5 or 230 fold 4 – 8km – 5 miles northeast of Landivisiau

The 15C **Chapelle Notre-Dame**, ruined after the Revolution and restored at the end of the 19C, is crowned by a belfry-porch 58m - 190ft high.

Inside is a very fine carved wood **rood screen★** in the Flamboyant style (1481), bearing statues of the Virgin and the Apostles, and an ornate staircase leads to the gallery. The altars on either side of the rood screen and at the end of the nave are adorned with granite statues from a former 16C Calvary.

A sacred fountain with a *Pietà* stands below on the south side of the chapel.

LAMBALLE

Population 9 874

Michelin map 59 folds 4 and 14 or 230 folds 23 and 24

Lamballe is a picturesque commercial town built on the slope of a hill crowned by the church of Notre-Dame-de-Grande-Puissance. It is an important market centre.

Bras-de-Fer before Lamballe (1591) – The town, which was the capital of the County of Penthièvre from 1134 to 1420, suffered a great deal in the War of Succession (*qv*). During the League it was one of the strongholds of Mercœur, Duke of Penthièvre (Charles IX made the county a duchy). In 1591 Lamballe was besieged by the famous Calvinist captain La Nouë, nicknamed Bras-de-Fer (Iron-Arm), because he wore a metal hook in place of the arm he had lost; he was seriously wounded during the siege and transported to Moncontour (*qv*) where he died. Henri IV felt his loss keenly. "How terrible", he exclaimed, "that such a little fortress destroyed so great a man; he alone was worth an army!" In 1626 César of Vendôme, Lord of Penthièvre, the son of Henri IV and Gabrielle d'Estrées, conspired against Richelieu and the castle was razed by order of the Cardinal. Only the chapel remains.

LAMBALLE

Bario (R.) 3
Cartel (R. Ch.) 8
Dr-A.-Calmette (R. du) 15
Leclerc (R. Gén.) 29
Martray (Pl. du)
Val (R. du)
Villedeneu (R.) 45
Augustins (R. des) 2
Blois (R. Ch. de) 5
Boucouets (R. des) 7
Charpentier (R. Y.) 14
Dr-Lavergne (R. du) 16
Foch (R. Mar.) 19
Gesle (Ch. de la) 23
Grand-Boulevard (R. du) 24
Hurel (R. du Bg) 25
Jeu-de-Paume (R. du) 26
Marché (Pl. du) 30
N-Dame (R.) 33
Poincaré (R.) 34
Préville (R.) 35
St-Jean (R.) 37
St-Lazare (R.) 38
Tery (R. G.) 39
Tour-aux-Chouettes (R.) 42

M Maison du Bourreau (Musées)

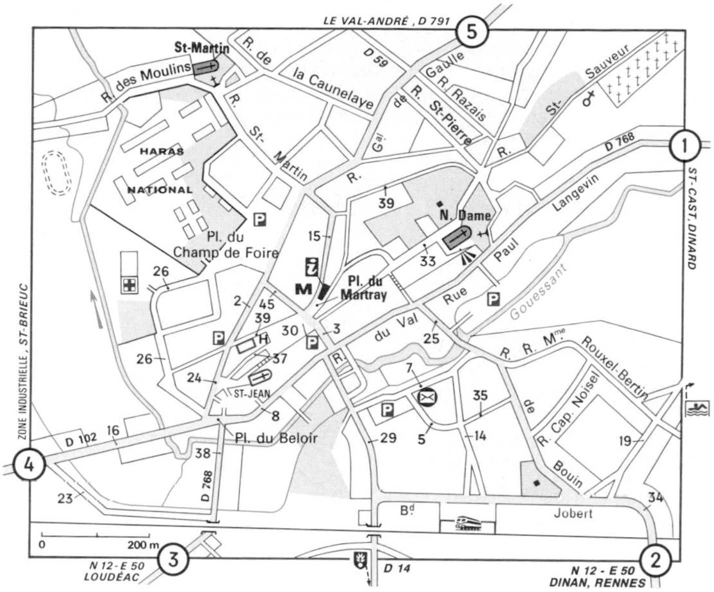

The Princess of Lamballe (Revolution) – In 1767, at the age of twenty, the Prince of Lamballe (the heir to the Duchy of Penthièvre) led such a dissolute life that his father, the Duke, in an effort to reform him, married him to a Piedmontese princess; but the heir did not mend his ways, and he died, worn out with debauchery, three months later.

In 1770, when Marie-Antoinette married the future Louis XVI, she made friends with the young widow, who remained faithfully attached to her for twenty years. When the tragedy of the Revolution took place, the Princess of Lamballe bravely stood by the Queen. She died a year before her: in the massacres of September 1792, the rioters cut off her head and paraded it on a pike.

SIGHTS

★ **Haras national (Stud Farm)** ⏲ – Founded in 1825, the stud contains 70 stallions (draught horses). From the beginning of March to mid-July, all the stallions are sent out to breeding stands in the Côtes d'Armor and the north of Finistère. The stud houses a school of dressage (40 horses) and a riding centre (20 horses). The visit includes the stables, blacksmith's shop, carriage house, harness room, riding school and main court.

Place du Martray – Old half-timbered houses. The most remarkable is the 15C **Maison du Bourreau** (Executioner's House) (**M**) which now contains the tourist information office and two museums.

Musée du Pays de Lamballe ⏲ – *Ground floor.* Devoted to popular arts and traditions, displays of pottery from Lamballe, etchings of the old town, headdresses and costumes of the region are shown.

Musée Mathurin-Méheut ⏲ – *First floor.* Works by the local painter M. Méheut (1882-1958) as well as Breton costumes, *pardons* and traditional trades.

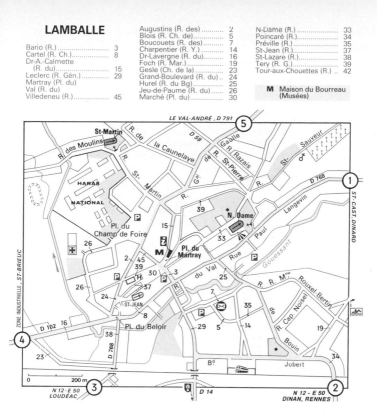

Groom by Mathurin Méheut

Collégiale Notre-Dame ⊙ – The Gothic collegiate church has Romanesque features, in particular the remarkable north doorway with slender columns and carved capitals supporting the recessed arches, a bay in the nave and the north transept. At the entrance to the south aisle in the chancel is a fine carved wood rood screen in the Flamboyant style. On the south side of the church with its buttressed gables, there is a terrace, built in the 19C, which affords a fine view of the town and the Gouessant Valley. A shady esplanade is located left of the church.

Eglise St-Martin – The old priory of Marmoutier Abbey was remodelled many times in the 15-18C. In front of the church is a small, shady square. On the right is an unusual little porch (11-12C) with a wooden canopy (1519). The handsome bell tower has an 18C steeple.

LAMPAUL-GUIMILIAU*

Population 2 037

Michelin map 58 fold 5 or 230 fold 4 – 4km – 2 miles southeast of Landivisiau –
Local map under Les ENCLOS PAROISSIAUX

This village has a complete parish close (*qv*). The church is especially noteworthy for its rich decoration and furnishings.

*PARISH CLOSE *time: 30min*

Triumphal arch (Porte triomphale) – The round arched gateway to the cemetery is surmounted by three crosses (1669).

Funerary chapel (Chapelle funéraire) – The former ossuary (1667) abuts on the arch and has buttresses crowned with small lantern turrets. Inside is the altar of the Trinity, with statues of St Rock, St Sebastian and St Pol and his dragon.

Calvary (Calvaire) – Very plain (early 16C) and, sadly, damaged.

***Church (Eglise)** – The church is dominated by a 16C bell tower, whose steeple was struck by lightning in the early 1800s. The apse, with a sacristy added in 1679, forms a harmonious whole in which the Gothic and classical styles are blended. The porch on the south side dates from 1533 (*details of porches p 42*). Under it are statues of the twelve Apostles and, between the two doors, a statue of the Virgin and Child and a graceful Kersanton stoup.

****Interior** – A 16C **rood beam** (*illustration p 39*) spans the nave, bearing a Crucifix between statues of the Virgin and St John. Both its faces are adorned with sculptures representing, on the nave side, scenes from the Passion and, on the chancel side, the twelve Sibyls separated by a group of the Annunciation. The pulpit dates from 1759. At the end of the south aisle is a **font** surmounted by a fine canopy dating from 1651. Higher up, on the right of the St Lawrence altarpiece, is a curious stoup (17C) representing two devils writhing in holy water; above, the Baptism of Christ.

In the chancel are 17C stalls, and on each side of the high altar, carved woodwork: on the left, St Paul on the road to Damascus and his escape; on the right, St Peter's martyrdom and the divine virtues. The side altars have 17C altarpieces. The altar of St John the Baptist, on the right of the chancel, is adorned with low reliefs of which the most interesting (left) represents the Fall of the Angels after Rubens. The altar of the Passion, on the left of the chancel, has an **altarpiece** in eight sections in high relief with lifelike figures and, on the top, the Resurrection. On either side are two panels showing the Birth of the Virgin (left), a rare theme in Brittany, and the Martyrdom of St Miliau (right), King of Cornouaille beheaded by his jealous brother. In the north side aisle is a 16C *Pietà* with six figures carved out of a single piece of wood and also a 17C banner, embroidered in silver on a velvet ground (in an open cupboard). The impressive 1676 **Entombment** in polychrome tufa was carved by the naval sculptor Anthoine. Note the expression of the Christ figure in particular. The organ case is 17C. The sacristy contains a 17C chest.

G. Biollay/DIAF

The Last Supper (detail)

LANDERNEAU

Population 14 269

Michelin map 58 fold 5 or 230 fold 4 – Local map under Les ENCLOS PAROISSIAUX

Located between Léon and Cornouaille, Landerneau, once the capital of Léon, is a small port and active market town, on the Élorn estuary.

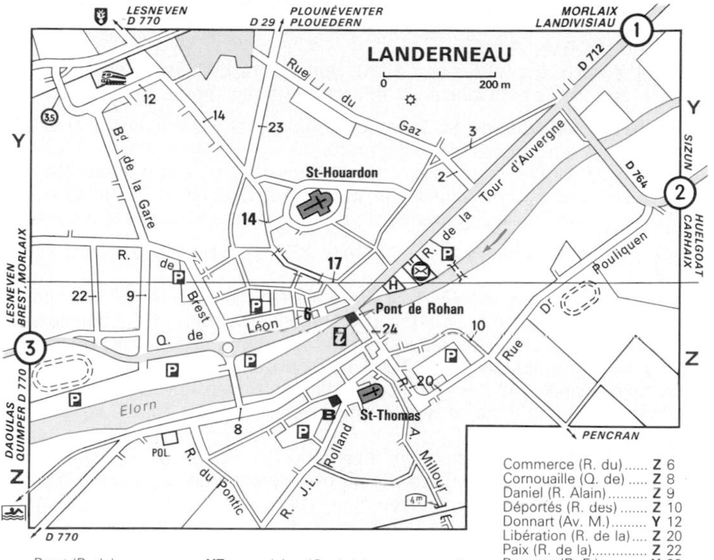

Brest (R. de) ... YZ
Fontaine-Blanche (R. de la) ... Y 14
Gaulle (Pl. Gén.-de) ... Y 17
Léon (Quai de) ... Z
Pont (R. du) ... Z 24
Audibert (R. Gén.) ... Y 2
Cartier (R. Jacques) ... Y 3
Commerce (R. du) ... Z 6
Cornouaille (Q. de) ... Z 8
Daniel (R. Alain) ... Z 9
Déportés (R. des) ... Z 10
Donnart (Av. M.) ... Y 12
Libération (R. de la) ... Z 20
Paix (R. de la) ... Z 22
Pengam (R. F.) ... Y 23

B Ancien ossuaire

SIGHTS

Pont de Rohan (**Z**) – Built in the 16C, this picturesque bridge, lined with houses with overhanging upper storeys, is one of the last inhabited European bridges. Walk to the front of the town hall and enjoy the scene of the bridge, with its slate-covered houses and overfall.

Église St-Houardon (**Y**) – The Renaissance domed tower and the porch (1604) on the south side of this church remain.

Église St-Thomas-de-Cantorbéry (**Z**) ⓥ – This 16C church has a belfry-porch (1607) with three superimposed balconies. Inside, note the amusing decoration of the purlins in the north aisle and the great 18C altarpiece at the high altar.

Ancien Ossuaire (**Z B**) – This former ossuary was erected as an annexe to the church of St Thomas in 1635.

Old houses – These are to be found mainly on the right bank of the River Élorn: no 9 Place du Général-de-Gaulle (**Y 17**), the turretted house (1664) known as the house of Duchess Anne; the façade at no 4 Rue de la Fontaine-Blanche (**Y 14**); at no 5 Rue du Commerce (**Z 6**), house with decorated turret and dormer windows (1667) and at the corner of the Pont de Rohan and Quai du Cornouaille is the so-called Maison des Rohan (Rohan House) (1639) with its sundial.

EXCURSIONS

★★**Les Enclos Paroissiaux** – *Round tour of 130km - 81 miles. See Les ENCLOS PAROISSIAUX.*

★**Pencran** – *See PENCRAN.*

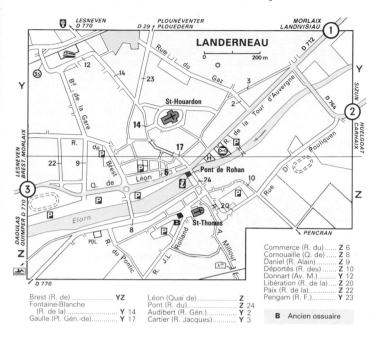

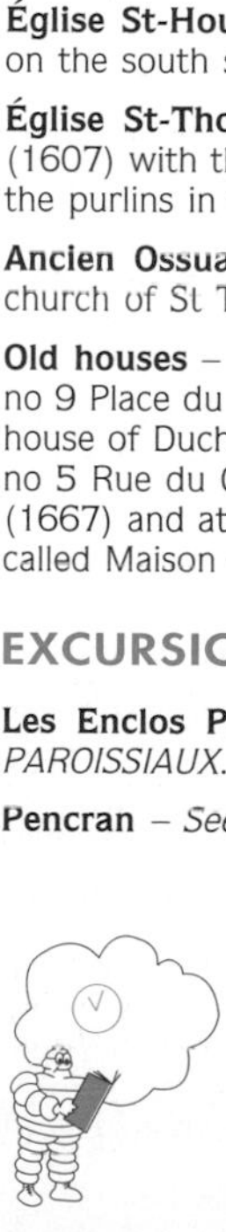

Admission times and charges for the sights described are listed at the end of the guide. Every sight for which there are times and charges is identified by the symbol ⓥ in the Sights *section of the guide.*

LANDÉVENNEC★

Population 374

Michelin map 58 folds 4 and 5 or 230 fold 18

Situated on the Presqu'île de Landévennec, which is part of the Parc naturel régional de l'Armorique (*qv*), the village of Landévennec stands in a pretty **site★** at the mouth of the River Aulne, which is best seen by taking the steep downhill road to the right from Gorréquer. A lookout point to the right offers a fine **view★** of Landévennec. Below is the course of the River Aulne, with the île de Térénez; beyond, the Presqu'île de Landévennec and the River Faou.

A steep descent leads to the settlement, a little summer resort surrounded by woods and water and, due to the mild climate, Mediterranean vegetation.

Nouvelle abbaye bénédictine St-Guénolé - *Halfway bear right into a tree-lined alley and follow the signposts.*

An audiovisual show offers a glimpse of the abbey's life past and present. The very plain church contains a polychrome wood statue of St Guénolé (15C), in sacerdotal vestments and a monolithic pink granite altar. Services are held and there is a shop.

Ruines de l'ancienne abbaye ⓥ – *Entrance 220yds below to the right of the village centre.*

The monastery founded by the Welsh St Guénolé (Winwaloe) in the 5C and remodelled several times ceased to exist in the 18C and only the ruins of the Romanesque church remain. The plan can be deduced from the column bases, wall remains and doorway: a nave and aisles with six bays, transept, chancel and ambulatory with three radiating chapels. At the entrance to the south transept, there is a monument thought to be the tomb of King Gradlon (*qv*). Near the church lie the ruins of a 17C conventual building.

In 1990, an **abbey museum** (musée) ⓥ of a very modern design was inaugurated on this site. It houses objects unearthed during excavations, including a wooden sarcophagus predating the 10C, discovered in 1985, and models illustrating the different stages of construction of the abbey (a number of panels on the history of the monastic movement in Brittany during the Middle Ages). An audiovisual display retraces the history of the abbey and its occupants to the present.

The tour of the site is completed with a visit to a room given over to "archaeological techniques", where excavation work is carried out in season.

LANDIVISIAU

Population 8 264

Michelin map 58 fold 5 or 230 fold 4 – Local map under Les ENCLOS PAROISSIAUX

Landivisiau is a busy town. Its cattle fairs are among the largest in France.

SIGHTS

Église St-Thivisiau – A modern church in the Gothic style, St-Thivisiau still has the bell tower and the fine granite **porch★** of a former 16C church. Note the elegant canopies above the statues of the Apostles and the delicate ornamentation round the doors.

Fontaine de St-Thivisiau - *Take the narrow Rue St-Thivisiau.*

This 15C fountain is decorated with eight granite low reliefs.

Chapelle Ste-Anne – The chapel in the middle of the churchyard was an ossuary in the 17C. The façade is adorned with six caryatids. Death is represented to the left of the west doorway.

LANMEUR

Population 2 084

Michelin map 58 fold 6 or 230 folds 5 and 6

Local map under CORNICHE DE L'ARMORIQUE

The small town of Lanmeur is situated in a market garden area on the Trégorrois Plateau.

Church (**Eglise**) – Only the crypt and the bell tower of the original church have been retained in the edifice rebuilt in 1904. Note the curious statue of St Mélar. The pre-Romanesque **crypt★** (*access to the left of the main altar, light switch at the foot of the stairway*) is ascribed to the 8C and is one of the oldest religious buildings in Brittany. The vaulting rests on eight massive pillars, two of which are decorated. A fountain stands to the right of the west door.

Excavations have brought to light two rare and very old (6C?) carved gold figurines.

Chapelle de Kernitron – *In the cemetery close.*

This large building has a 12C nave and transept and 15C chancel. Look at the outside of the Romanesque doorway of the south transept: the tympanum depicts Christ in Majesty surrounded by the symbols of the Evangelists.
Inside, at the entrance to the south aisle, there is a fine carved wooden screen; in the nave, a rood beam carries Christ on the Cross between the Virgin and St John; to the right of the high altar stands a statue of Christ in Fetters and in the chapel facing the entrance a statue of Our Lady of Kernitron (*pardon* on 15 August) with, to the right in a small chapel, a charming statue of St Anne and the Virgin.

LANNION*

Population 16 958
Michelin map 59 fold 1 or 230 fold 6

Lannion, a port spread out on both banks of the River Léguer, will attract the tourist with its typical "Old Brittany" character and with its proximity to the main beach resorts of the Côte de Granit rose (Pink Granite Coast) (*qv*). It is the birthplace of the novelist **Charles Le Goffic** (*qv*) (1863-1932), whose statue by Jean Boucher stands at the corner of Avenue Ernest-Renan and Rue de la Mairie.
The Centre de Recherches de Lannion and the Centre National d'Études des Télécommunications, where research is undertaken in telecommunications and electronics, have been built 3km - 2 miles north of Lannion at the crossroads of the road to Perros-Guirec and that of Trégastel-Plage.

LANNION

Augustins (R. des) .... Z 3
Leclerc (Pl. Gén.) .... Y 17
Pont-Blanc
(R. Geoffroy-de) .... Z 25

Aiguillon (R. d') .... Z 2
Buzulzo (R. de)................ Z 4
Chapeliers (R. des)......... Y 6
Cie-Roger-de-Barbé (R.)... Y 7
Coudraie (R. de la) .... Y 8
Du Guesclin (R.).............. Z 9
Frères-Lagadec (R. des) .. Z 12
Keriavily (R. de)............... Z 14
Kermaria (R. et Pont)....... Z 16
Le-Dantec (R. F.) .... Y 18
Letaillandier (R. E.) .... Z 20
Mairie (R. de la).............. Y 21
Palais-de-Justice
(Allée du).................... Z 24
Pors-an-Prat (R. de) .... Y 26
Roud-Ar-Roc'h (R. de)...... Z 28
St-Malo (R. de)................ Z 29
St-Nicolas (R.)................. Z 30
Trinité (R. de la).............. Y 32

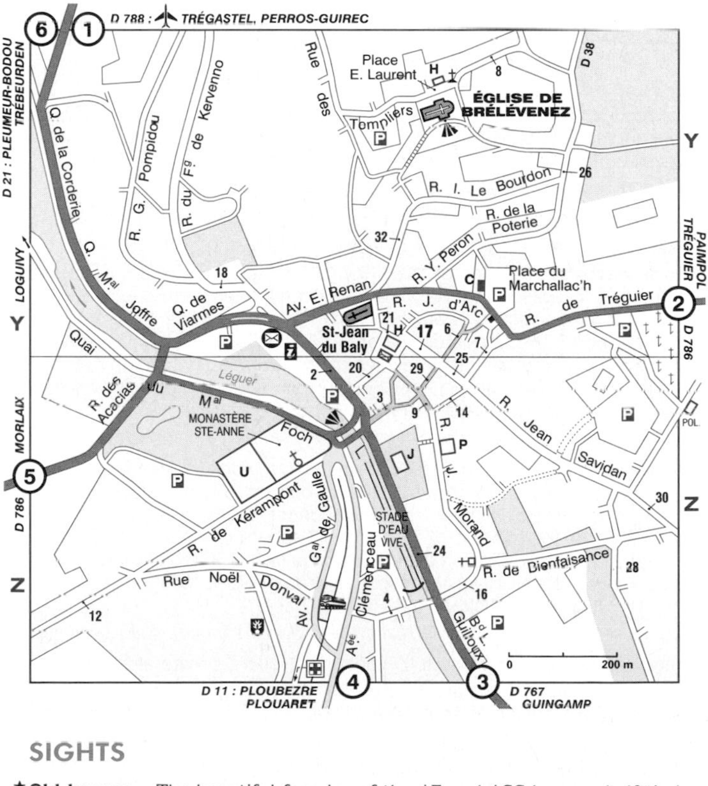

SIGHTS

★**Old houses** – The beautiful façades of the 15 and 16C houses, half-timbered, corbelled and with slate roofs, may be admired especially at Place du Général Leclerc (nos 23, 29, 31, 33), Rue des Chapeliers (nos 1-9), Rue Geoffroy-de-Pont-Blanc (nos 1 and 3) and Rue Cie-Roger-de-Barbé (nos 1 and 7). At the corner of the latter, on the left, a granite cross has been sealed in the wall at the spot where the Chevalier de Pont-Blanc distinguished himself in the heroic defence of the town during the War of Succession (*qv*).

★**Église de Brélévenez** (**Y**) – The church was built on a hill by the Templars in the 12C and remodelled in the Gothic period. The bell tower is crowned by a granite spire and dates from the 15C.

Access – *The church is reached on foot up a staircase (142 steps) which tends to be a meeting point for artists; by car, via Rues Le-Dantec, du Faubourg-de-Kervenno and des Templiers to the right.*
When you reach the terrace, there is an attractive view of Lannion and Léguer Valley. Before entering look at the curious Romanesque apse which is decorated with engaged round pillars, carved capitals and modillions.
Inside, on the left, is a stoup, which was used to measure tithe wheat. In the chapels to the right and left of the chancel are 17C altarpieces. Under the chancel and ambulatory, the Romanesque crypt, which was remodelled in the 18C, contains a marvellous 18C **Entombment**★, in which the subjects, carved in polychrome stone, are depicted life-size.

Église de St-Jean-du-Baly (**Y**) – 16-17C. Over the door of the sacristy to the left of the high altar is a fine 18C portrait of St John the Evangelist.

Bridge (Pont) (**Z**) – From the bridge, there is a good view of the port and of the vast Monastère Ste-Anne.

EXCURSIONS *local map opposite*

1 Castles and chapels

Round tour of 50km - 31 miles – time: about 3 hours.

Leave Lannion on ④ on the town plan, the road to Plouaret. 1.5km - 1 mile after Ploubezre, bear left at a fork where five granite crosses stand and 1.2km - 3/4 mile further on, turn left.

★**Chapelle de Kerfons** ⓥ – In a lovely setting, the chapel in front of which is an old Calvary, is surrounded by chestnut trees. Built in the 15 and 16C, it has a flat east end, a modillioned cornice along the south wall and a pinnacle turret decorated with telamones crowning the gabled south transept. It contains a late-15C carved **rood screen**★ and fragments of old stained glass remain in the windows of the chancel and north transept.

Turn back and take the road on the left.

Soon the road starts to wind downhill providing good views over the ruins of Tonquédec in the Léguer Valley. After crossing the swiftly flowing river you will see the castle on the left (*car park*).

★**Château de Tonquédec** – *See Château de TONQUÉDEC.*

Turn back and at the first crossroads bear left to join the road to Plouaret, then turn left again; and after 1km - half a mile turn left.

Château de Kergrist ⓥ – One of the principal attractions of the château lies in the variety of its façades. The north façade is Gothic with dormer windows set in tall Flamboyant gables; the main building, which belongs to the 14 and 15C, nevertheless features an 18C façade on the opposite side, while the wings running at right angles, which were built at an earlier date, have classical fronts overlooking the gardens. The formal French gardens extend as far as the terrace which overlooks a landscaped English garden and the woods.

Return to the Plouaret road and bear left; after 2.2km - 1.5 miles, turn left.

Chapelle des Sept-Saints ⓥ – This 18C chapel, surrounded by greenery, is unusual in that it is built in part on top of an imposing dolmen. From the outside, a small door in the south arm of the transept leads under the dolmen which has been turned into a crypt for the cult of the Seven Sleepers of Ephesus. According to legend, seven young Christians walled up in a cave in the 3C woke up two hundred years later. Every year, an Islamic-Christian pilgrimage (*see the Calendar of events at the end of the guide*) is held in this Breton chapel.

Via Pluzunet and Bardérou you will reach the road to Lannion, then bear left.

Caouënnec-Lanvézéac – The **church** ⓥ contains a lovely, ornate altarpiece.

Proceed towards Lannion and at Buhulien bear left in the direction of Ploubezre and 100m - 109yds after a farm at Pont-Keriel, turn left into an unsurfaced path through the woods.

Château de Coatfrec – There are fine ruins of this large 16C mansion.

Make for Ploubezre and turn right to Lannion.

Book well in advance
as vacant hotel rooms are often scarce in high season.

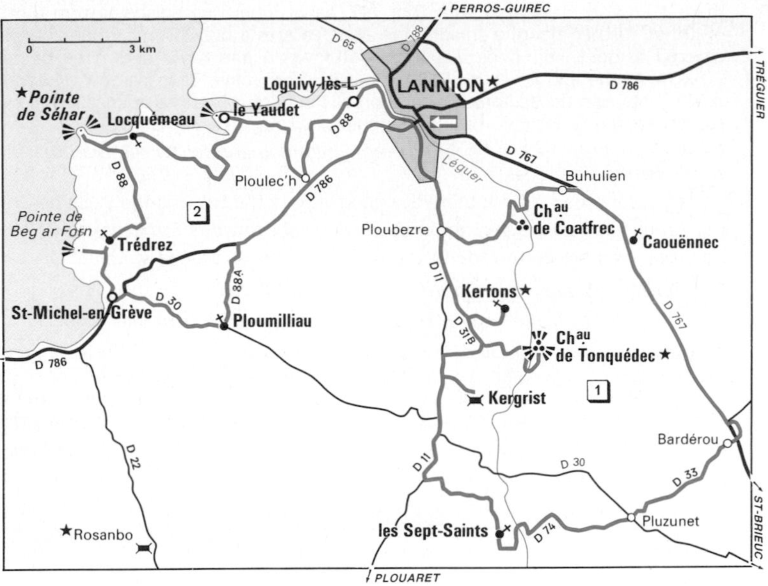

2 Tour of towns in the Léguer Estuary

Round tour of 32km - 20 miles – about 2 hours.

Leave Lannion by Quai du Maréchal-Foch.

The south bank of the River Léguer is very picturesque, especially at high tide.

Loguivy-lès-Lannion – This town on the outskirts of Lannion clings to the hillside in a pleasant setting. The **church**, nestled in a verdant landscape along the banks of the Léguer, is 15C. A curious outdoor stairway leads to the wall-belfry (1570). Inside the church, in the chapel to the right of the chancel, there is a 17C wooden **altarpiece** depicting the Adoration of the Three Wise Men with shepherds in Breton costume playing the bagpipes and the bombardon. The fine wooden balustrade in the chancel dates from the same period.
At the back of the chancel there is a beautiful polychrome statue of St Ivy, patron saint of the parish.
Against the wall of the parish close, to the right of the triumphal doorway, stands a 15C fountain which contains a statue of St Ivy in bishop's robes. In the cemetery, a second **fountain**, made in granite and dating from 1577, plays beneath yew trees which are several centuries old.

Le Yaudet – This hamlet, in its beautiful setting, was the episcopal seat in the early centuries of our era and was destroyed by the Danes (*c*848); it has remains of Roman walls and an interesting **chapel** overlooking the bay. Inside, above the altar, is a curious sculpted panel depicting the Trinity: a recumbent figure of the Virgin with the Infant Jesus at her side; God the Father is sitting in an alcove at the foot of the bed over which hovers a dove symbolising the Holy Spirit. A *pardon* is held on the third Sunday in May and on 15 August.
From the car park, the Corps de Garde footpath leads to a viewpoint, which affords a lovely **view** of the Léguer.

Return to the centre of Le Yaudet and turn right.

The road descends to Pont-Roux and climbs up again to reveal a fine **view** of the Léguer estuary and of the coast as far as Trébeurden.

At Christ, bear right towards Locquémeau.

Locquémeau – The town overlooks the beach and the fishing harbour which are reached by a *corniche* road to the left at the entrance to the town. The 15C **church** ⓥ, which has a wall-belfry flanked by a turret, contains interesting 18C altarpieces and fine sculpted tie beams, purlins and hammerbeams.

★**Pointe de Séhar** – Leave your car near the port of Locquémeau and make for the point, from which the **view**★ extends westwards as far as the Pointe de Primel and eastwards to the resort of Trébeurden.

Trédrez – St Yves (*qv*) was Rector of Trédrez from 1284-92. The **church** was completed in 1500 by Philippe Beaumanoir to whom we owe many of the region's churches, with their characteristic wall belfries. Note inside the 14C granite font crowned with a beautifully carved wood canopy (1540). In the south side aisle, there is an altar decorated with four 17C panels depicting episodes from the Life of Christ; further along, a small stone altar features a polychrome wood altarpiece covered in gold leaf, depicting a beautiful Virgin and Child in a Tree of Jesse (1520). At the end of every hammerbeam angels have been carved (*illustration p 39*). Note also the sculpted decoration of the purlins and the animals swallowing the end of the tie beams. Facing the pulpit is a fine 16C Christ.

Leave Trédrez by the road going towards Kerbiriou and follow the road that leads to the Beg-ar-Forn headland.

Shortly before the car park there is a good view of the bay and the Lieue de Grève.

Turn round and at the second junction turn right towards St-Michel-en-Grève.

The road runs beside the sea to the town and affords a good view.

St-Michel-en-Grève - *See CORNICHE DE L'ARMORIQUE.*

Take the road to Lannion on leaving St-Michel-en-Grève, then bear right.

Ploumilliau – The 17C **church** ⌚ contains, in the south transept, thirteen wooden **panels**, carved and polychrome, which illustrate scenes from the Life of Christ (Last Supper, the Passion, the Resurrection). There is also, on the wall opposite the sacristy, a curious portrayal of Ankou (Death), so often mentioned in Breton legend.

Return to the Morlaix-Lannion road to the north; turn right towards Lannion.

LANRIVAIN

Population 510

Map 58 fold 8 or 230 fold 21 – 7km – 4 miles northwest of St-Nicolas-du-Pélem

In the cemetery stands a 15C ossuary with trefoil arches. To the right of the church is a 16C Calvary adorned with huge granite figures.

Chapelle N.-D.-du-Guiaudet ⌚ – *1.5km - 1 mile north by the road towards Bourbriac. At the entrance to the hamlet of Guiaudet take an alleyway marked by two granite pillars on the right.*
The chapel, which dates from the late 17C, has over the high altar a sculpted scene representing a recumbent Virgin holding the Infant Jesus in her arms. The bell tower contains a carillon of 16 bells which plays two hymns dedicated to Our Lady.

Forteresse de LARGOËT★

Michelin map 63 fold 3 or 230 fold 37 – 15km – 9 miles northeast of Vannes

These imposing feudal ruins, also known as **Tours d'Elven** (Elven Towers) ⌚, stand in the middle of a park. The road (Vannes to Ploërmel road) to the towers branches off left between two pillars.
The Forteresse de Largoët belonged to Marshal de Rieux, who was first a councillor of Duke François II and then tutor to his daughter, Anne of Brittany. When the troops of the King of France, Charles VIII, invaded Brittany in 1488, all the Marshal's strongholds, including Largoët, were burnt down or razed to the ground.
Pass through the 15C entrance fort built against the first entrance gate (13C). Of the castle there remains an impressive 14C keep, 44m - 144 ft high, with walls 6 to 9m - 19 to 29 ft thick. Near the keep is a smaller tower flanked by a lantern tower.

LARMOR-PLAGE

Population 8 078

Michelin map 63 fold 1 or 230 fold 34

Looking out over the ocean, across from Port-Louis, Larmor-Plage has lovely, fine, sandy beaches much appreciated by the people of Lorient.

Church (Église) – The parish church, built in the 12C, was remodelled until the 17C. The 15C porch, uncommonly situated on the north façade because of the prevailing winds, contains statues of the Apostles and above the door a 16C painted wood Christ in Fetters.
The inside contains interesting furnishings: a 17C altarpiece at the high altar and in the north aisle, at the Jews' altar, a Flemish-style 16C altarpiece, which portrays forty small figures on the slopes of the Calvary; to the right is a 16C polychrome statue of Our Lady of the Angels and in the south aisle a 16C *Pietà* in stone; from the same period are statues of St Efflam and St Barbara, in the chancel.
Every year, on the Sunday before or after 24 June, there is a blessing of the Coureaux (the channel between the île de Groix and the coast). By tradition, warships leaving Lorient salute the Church of Our Lady of Larmor with three guns, while the priest blesses the ship, has the church bells rung and hoists the flag.

Fort la LATTE★★

Michelin map 59 fold 5 or 230 fold 10 – Southeast of Cap Fréhel – Local map under CÔTE D'ÉMERAUDE

A gate marks the entrance to the park. Follow the lane to **Fort la Latte** ⓥ; you will pass a menhir known as Gargantua's Finger.
This stronghold, built by the Goyon-Matignons in the 14C, remodelled in the 17 and restored in the early 20C, has kept its feudal appearance. It stands on a picturesque **site**★★, separated from the mainland by two gullies, which are crossed by drawbridges. You will visit in succession: the two fortified enclosures, the inner courtyard, around which are located the guard room, the Governor's living quarters, the cistern and the

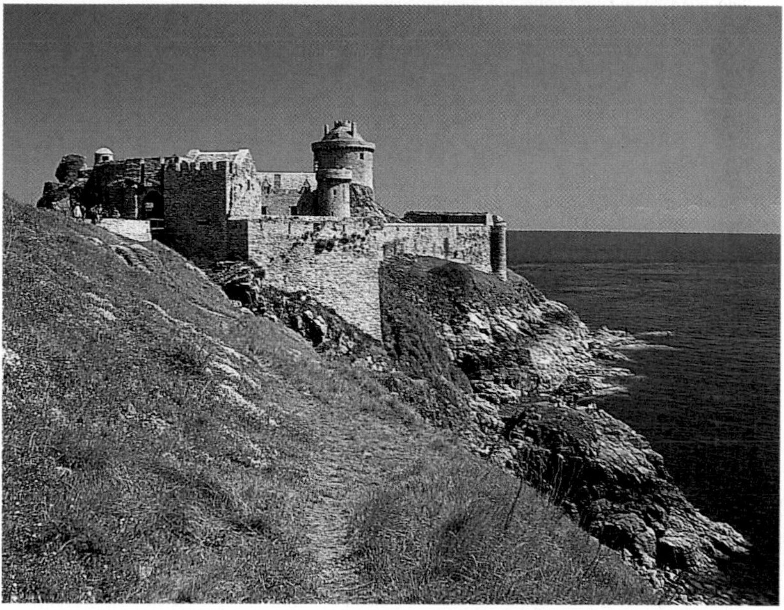

Picard/CAMPAGNE CAMPAGNE

Fort la Latte

chapel. Cross the thick walls made to shield the defender from cannon balls and go to the Échauguette Tower (Tour de l'Échaugette) and the cannon ball foundry. A look-out post takes you to the keep. From the parapet walk, there is a **panorama**★★ of Sévignés Cove, Cap Fréhel, the Bay of La Frênaye, Pointe de St-Cast, the Hébihens archipelago, the resorts of St-Briac and St-Lunaire, Pointe du Décollé, St-Malo, Paramé and Rothéneuf, the île de Cézembre, the Pointe du Meinga and the walls of the fort. It is possible to walk up to the top of the tower (*difficult steps*).

LÉHON

Population 3 219

Michelin map 59 folds 15 and 16 or 230 fold 25

In Léhon stands the Prieuré St-Magloire, a priory built in the 12C on the site of an abbey founded by Nominoë in the 9C and ransacked by the Norsemen in 975.

PRIEURÉ DE ST-MAGLOIRE *time: 45 min*

Church – The church, rebuilt in the 13C and restored in the late 19C, has a rounded doorway adorned with small columns and surmounted by a horizontal string-course decorated with heads. The Angevin-style pointed vaulted nave contains the tombs of the Beaumanoir family and a 13C stoup.

Cloisters ⓥ – The 17C cloisters, now in ruins, open off the church's north side; they have square pillars decorated with moulding at the base.

Conventual Buildings – A small **museum** ⓥ exhibits capitals of the old Romanesque cloisters and pottery fragments from the monastery kitchens. The beautifully restored **refectory** is illuminated on the garden side by a Gothic façade decorated with trilobed arcaded tracery; note the old kitchen with its granite hot plate.
The **dormitory** houses several treasures including the reliquary of St-Magloire.
In the attic admire the fine vaulting in the form of an inverted ship's hull.

Gardens ⓥ – Excavations have uncovered an underground passage which was, in fact, a covered canal linking the abbey to the Rance running down below.

LESNEVEN

Population 6 250

Michelin map 58 fold 4 or 230 folds 3 and 4 – Local map under ABERS

Now an important commercial centre and the hub of a road network, Lesneven was founded in the 5C by a Breton chief; it was once under Léon's seneschalship.
The town has preserved several 17 and 18C granite houses, including one with a corner turret, at the intersection of Rue de Jérusalem and Rue du Comte Even.
The statue of one of the town's sons, Adolphe Le Flô (b 1804), general, War Minister in 1871 and Ambassador to Russia, adorns the square of the same name.

Musée de Léon ⌚ – Located in the Ursuline convent's chapel, this museum is devoted to the history of the Léon region.
Note the authentic decree signed by Louis XIV authorising the creation of an Ursuline convent in Lesneven; a section pertains to General Le Flô. Displayed in the popular arts and traditions section are fine furnishings and 19C costumes.

LOCMARIAQUER★★

Population 1 309

Michelin map 63 fold 12 or 230 fold 50 – Local map under Golfe du MORBIHAN

The village commands the channel into Morbihan Bay.

SIGHTS

Up by the cemetery, take the signposted path to the car park.

★★ **Ensemble mégalithique de Locmariaquer** ⌚ – This group of three megaliths is an important part of a programme of conservation and restoration of megalithic sites.

Grand Menhir brisé – This menhir was probably broken on purpose as long ago as the Neolithic period, when it measured 20m - 64ft and weighed almost 350 tons. It is set on the axis of the Er-Grah tumulus, but its relation with this monument has not yet been clearly explained. It is the largest menhir known to us.

Table des Marchands – The origin of the name of this dolmen has provoked considerable dispute, and experts are not sure whether the dolmen in fact bears the name of the family to which it belonged. It has been restored recently, and its tumulus has been rediscovered. A 7m - 23ft corridor leads to a funerary chamber in which the base stele is decorated with crooks arranged symmetrically. The slab which forms the ceiling is in fact part of a large menhir, the two other parts of which can be found at the Tumulus d'Er-Grah, not far from here, and in the Cavin de Gavrinis (*qv*), 4km - 2.5 miles from here. This slab features axe and crook motifs and part of a bovine figure.

Tumulus d'Er-Grah – This very elongated monument is situated north of the other megaliths. It is thought that its original length was more than 170m - 558ft. The tumulus is currently the object of examination.
The excavations carried out in the area immediately surrounding the dolmen have revealed not only traces of dwellings – fireplaces, fragments of earthenware, mills for grinding grain – but also an alignment of 16 ditches, suggesting that this was once the site of ancient dressed stones.

★ **Dolmen de Mané-Lud** – It stands surrounded by houses on the right at the entrance to the village. The stones which remain standing inside the chamber are carved.

★ **Dolmen de Mané-Rethual** - *In the centre of the village and to the right of the former town hall, take a path which passes by a group of houses and gardens.* A long covered alleyway leading to a vast chamber, the supports of which are carved.

Church (Église) – It retains its 11C oven vaulted chancel and transept. The nave and aisles were rebuilt in the 18C. There are remarkable **capitals** adorned with geometrical designs or foliage at the transept crossing and in the chancel, and a fine stoup.

BOAT TRIP

★★★ **Golf du Morbihan** - *See Golfe du MORBIHAN.*

EXCURSION

Megalithic Monuments - *Round tour of 5km - 3 miles. From Place Évariste-Frick, take Rue Wilson.*
On leaving the village take the road on the right leading to **Kerlud** village, a remarkable group of small farms built in granite. Opposite the last house is the partly hidden **Dolmen de Kerlud**.

Return to the main road and bear right; beside the beach turn right again.

★**Dolmen des Pierres-Plates** – A menhir indicates the entrance to this dolmen. Two chambers are linked by a long alleyway. Remarkable engravings decorate the supports. A terrace affords a fine view of the Pointe de Port-Navalo and the Pointe du Grand-Mont, the île d'Houat with Belle-Île in the distance, and the Presqu'île de Crozon.

Turn round and follow the shoreline as far as the Pointe de Kerpenhir.

★**Pointe de Kerpenhir** – *Continue past the blockhouse.* The point where a granite statue of Our Lady of Kerdro stands protecting sailors (*kerdro* is Breton for safe return), affords a **view**★ onto the Morbihan channel.
The road to the left offers a fine glimpse of the bay.

★**Tumulus de Mané-er-Hroech** – *At Kerpenhir take a path to the left of the road which climbs up to the tumulus.* A stairway *(23 steps)* gives access to the funerary chamber and to the dry-stone structure forming the tumulus.

Return to Locmariaquer.

LOCMINÉ

Population 3 346
Michelin map 63 fold 3 or 230 fold 36

Lacminé (*lieu des moines* = place where the monks are), which owes its name to an abbey founded here in the 6C, had two churches identical in plan: Eglise St-Sauveur (16C) and Chapelle of St-Colomban. Only their façades remain; behind is a modern church (1975) built on the site of the nave and aisles.
In the square are two corbelled houses; one is adorned with two wooden statues.

Chapelle N.-D.-du-Plasker – *To the left of the east end of the modern church.* This 16C rectangular chapel *(currently under restoration)* is decorated in the Flamboyant style. Note inside a 16C altarpiece with a *Virgin and Child* and a 17C altar.

EXCURSION

Domaine de Kerguéhennec – *8km - 5 miles east on the D 1 and D 123. See Domaine de KERGUÉHENNEC .*

LOCQUIREC

Population 1 226
Michelin map 58 fold 7 or 230 fold 6 – Facilities

Built on a rocky peninsula of the "*Ceinture dorée*" *(qv)*, Locquirec is a small fishing port and marina as well as a seaside resort.

★**Church** – Once the property of the Knights of Malta, this charming church has a Renaissance turreted bell tower. The *placître (qv)* is covered with early 19C tombstones, remains of the churchyard. The central alley is paved with memorial plaques made of Locquirec stone.
Inside, the panelled vaults of the chancel and transept are covered with 18C paintings. At the high altar is a 16C **altarpiece**★ illustrating scenes of the Passion in high relief in a simple style. On the left of the chancel is a niche containing the statue of Our Lady of Succour, flanked by a Tree of Jesse and six low reliefs depicting the life of the Virgin. In the south transept there is a 15C Trinity. In the nave, spanned by a handsome rood beam, and to the left against the pillar nearest to the chancel, is a 16C alabaster *Pietà*.

★**Pointe de Locquirec** – *30 min on foot Rtn.* A walk starting near the church's east end round the Pointe de Locquirec offers fine views of Lannion Bay and coastline.

LOCRONAN★★

Population 796

Michelin map 58 folds 14 and 15 or 230 fold 18 – Local map under CORNOUAILLE – Facilities

The little town once prospered from the manufacturing of sailcloth. Traces of its golden age are to be found in its fine **square**★★, with its granite houses built during the Renaissance, old well, large church and pretty chapel. There are fine houses in the side streets (Rues Lann, Moal, St-Maurice).

The Troménies – The hill or mountain of Locronan, which overlooks the town, presents a very original spectacle on days devoted to *pardons*, which are known here as *Troménies*. There are the **Petites Troménies** (*see the Calendar of events at the end of the guide*), when the procession makes its way to the top of the hill, repeating the walk that St Ronan, a 5C Irish saint, according to tradition, took every day, fasting and barefooted.

The **Grande Troménie**★★ takes place every sixth year on the second and third Sundays in July *(the last one took place in 1995)*. Carrying banners, the pilgrims go round the hill (12km - 7.5 miles), stopping at twelve stations. At the different stations each parish exhibits its saints and reliquaries. The circuit follows the boundary of the former Benedictine priory – built on the site of the sacred forest, the "Nemeton", which served as a natural shrine –, founded in the 11C, which was a place of retreat. Hence the name of the *pardon* Tro Minihy or Tour of the Retreat, gallicised as Troménie.

SIGHTS

★★**Église St-Ronan and Chapelle du Penity** ⓥ – The accoladed and inter-communicating church and chapel form a harmonious ensemble. The 15C church is remarkable for its unity of style and stone vaulting. The decoration of the **pulpit**★ (1707) relates the life of St Ronan, and the 15C **stained-glass window**★ in the apse depicts scenes of the Passion. Among the old statues note that of St Roch (1509). The 16C chapel houses the tomb of St Ronan (the recumbent figure dates from the early 16C and is one of the earliest works in Kersanton granite). Note too a 16C Descent from the Cross in polychrome stone with six figures. The base is decorated with two beautiful **bas-reliefs**★, depicting the apparition of the resurrected Jesus to Mary Magdalene and the disciples of Emmaus, and two 15C statues (Christ in Fetters and St Michael weighing souls).

From the cemetery behind the church there is a good view of the church's flat east end.

Chapelle N.-D.-de-Bonne-Nouvelle ⓥ – *300m - 328yds by Rue Moal, which starts from the square and leads down the slope of the ridge.*

With the Calvary and the fountain (1698), this 14C chapel forms a typically Breton scene. Inside is an Entombment; note also the diaphragm arch between the nave and chancel and the stained glass windows by Alfred Manessier.

Museum ⓥ – *On the Châteaulin road.*

The ground floor is devoted to the 19C: Quimper faience, sandstone objects, local costumes and recreation of a typical interior. On the first floor the exhibits relate to the *Troménies (see above)* and to ancient crafts. There are also pictures and engravings by contemporary artists of Locronan and the surrounding area.

Skritelleoueg Breizh, Conservatoire de l'affiche en Bretagne ⓥ – This museum, located in the old manor-house of the Daniélou family, is devoted to collecting, conserving and restoring posters of all types (political, cultural, advertising, etc.). Temporary exhibitions focus on various selections from this collection in more detail.

EXCURSIONS

★**Montagne de Locronan** – *2km - 1 mile east. Leave Locronan on the Châteaulin road.*

After 700m – about half a mile go straight along an uphill road (max. gradient 1 in 9). This goes along the side of the hill providing views of the bay, Ménez-Hom and the Porzay hollow.

From the top (289m - 948ft), crowned by a **chapel** ⓥ (note the stained-glass windows by Bazaine), you will see a fine **panorama**★ of Douarnenez Bay. On the left are Douarnenez and the Pointe du Leydé; on the right Cap de la Chèvre, the Presqu'île de Crozon, Ménez-Hom and the Monts d'Arrée. To the right of the entrance is a granite pulpit.

Chapelle de Kergoat – *3.5km - 2 miles on the Châteaulin road.* The Gothic chapel is dominated by its domed belfry; it has a fine 17C east end. The **stained-glass windows**★ are old and one shows the Last Judgment (1555). Pilgrimage Sunday following 15 August.

Ste-Anne-la-Palud ⏲ – *8km - 4 miles northwest. Leave Locronan by the D 63 to Crozon. After Plonévez-Porzay, turn left.*
The 19C chapel contains a much-venerated painted granite statue of St Anne *(qv)* dating from 1548. The *pardon (qv)* on the last Sunday in August, one of the finest and most picturesque in Brittany (*photograph p 28*), attracts thousands.
On the Saturday at 9pm the torchlit procession progresses along the dune above the chapel. Afterwards, high Mass is celebrated outside. The following Sunday and Tuesday a high Mass and vespers are pronounced followed by a procession with people dressed in Breton costumes bearing crosses, statues and banners.

LOCTUDY

Population 3 622

Michelin map 58 fold 15 or 230 fold 32 – Local map under CORNOUAILLE

Loctudy is a quiet little seaport and resort at the mouth of the River Pont-l'Abbé.

Port – An animated fishing port on weekday evenings, when the fishing fleet (prawns, burbot, sole and sea bass) comes sailing in.
A pretty view of the île Chevalier, in Pont-l'Abbé estuary and Île-Tudy and its beach can be had from the quays.

Church – Dating from the beginning of the 12C and remodelled several times: the porch added in the 15C, its façade and belfry built in the 18C. In spite of the additions, the **interior**★ is elegant and well proportioned with its nave, chancel, ambulatory and radiating chapels in pure Romanesque style. Admire the capitals and column bases carved with small figures, animals, scrolls, foliage and crosses.
In the cemetery to the left of the church, near the road, is the 15C Chapel of Pors-Bihan. Left of the lane leading to the church is a Gallic stele 2m - 6ft high surmounted by a cross.

BOAT TRIPS

★★**Quimper along the River Odet** ⏲ – *Description of the tour under QUIMPER: Boat trips.*

Île-Tudy ⏲ – *12km - 8 miles from Pont-L'Abbé along the CD 144. A* pretty fishing port accessible from Loctudy by boat (*passengers and two-wheeled vehicles only*).

Îles de Glénan – *See Îles de GLÉNAN.*

Manoir de l'Automobile à LOHÉAC★★

Michelin map 63 fold 6 or 230 fold 39

This **Motor Museum** ⏲, set up in La Courneuve manor-house (*from Lohéac, take the D 50 towards Lieuron*), contains a collection of over 160 cars of all types, ages and nationalities, specialising particularly in private and sports cars.
The tour begins in the old manor-house, taking in a collection of "golden oldies" from the turn of the century, before moving on to an impressive line-up of Alpines (A 210 Le Mans, Coach A 106, Berlinette Tour de France A 108, A 110 GT4, A 310 1600 VE). Further on, there are examples of essentially the whole Lamborghini production (from the 350 GT to the Diablo). Dozens of Maseratis, Ferraris, Porsches and Rolls-Royces rub fenders with Dauphine Renaults, R8s or R12s, Citroëns, Peugeots (convertibles 301-403, from the Sixties and Seventies) and Volkswagens.
The next stop on the tour is the **Chapelle des Moteurs** (Engine Chapel), an original display of several vintage engines in an old chapel. Other features of the museum include the reconstructions of a forge, a garage and an old-fashioned filling station fully equipped with tools, materials and authentic equipment connected with vehicle repair and maintenance.
The spacious first floor houses an exhibition of lavish foreign cars known as the "*belles étrangères*" and at the end of it is a wall of illuminated signs bearing the names of leading manufacturers associated with the motor industry.
The area devoted to miniature models relates the glorious history of the steam engine, illustrated by over 3 000 exhibits. Finally, the museum has a projection room, in which good films of cars are shown.

The **Michelin Maps** *for this region are shown in the diagram on page 3.*
The text refers to the maps which, owing to their scale or coverage, are the clearest and most appropriate in each case.

LORIENT

Conurbation 107 088

Michelin map 63 fold 1 or 230 folds 34 and 35

The modern city of Lorient boasts proudly of being the site of 5 ports: the fishing port of Keroman (*see Sights below*), a military port, with dockyard and submarine base (capacity: 30 submarines), a passenger port, with ships crossing the roadstead and sailing to the île de Groix, the Kergroise commercial port, which specialises in the importing of animal foodstuffs, and the Kernevel pleasure boat harbour, with a wet dock located in the centre of the city; it is the starting point for transatlantic competition. An annual Interceltic Festival (Festival Interceltique, *see the Calendar of Events at the end of the guide*) is held in Lorient.

Parc à bois – On your way into Lorient, coming from Lanester, after taking the Pont St-Christophe, skirt the River Scorff and you will see black posts sticking out, particularly striking at low tide. They are probably the remains of the mast pond started in 1826. The wood, used for naval construction, was plunged into the muddy sand to protect it from rotting and from ship worms.

HISTORICAL NOTES

The India Company – After the first India Company, founded by Richelieu at Port-Louis, failed, Colbert revived the project in 1664 at Le Havre. But as the Company's ships were too easily captured in the Channel by the British, it was decided to move its headquarters to the Atlantic coast. The choice fell on "vague and vain" plots of land located on the right bank of the Scorff. Soon afterwards, what was to be known as the "Compound of the India Company" was born. Since all maritime activities were focused on India and China, the installations built on that site bore the name "*l'Orient*" (French for the East). In those days, the arrogant motto of the India Company – *Florebo quocumque ferar* (I shall prosper wherever I go) – was fully justified by the flourishing trade which it exercised. But a new naval war loomed ahead. So Seignelay turned the "Compound" into a royal dockyard patronized by the most famous privateers (Beauchêne, Duguay-Trouin, etc.).

In the 18C, under the stimulus of the well-known Scots financier Law, business grew rapidly; sixty years after its foundation, the town already had 18 000 inhabitants. The loss of India brought the Company to ruin, and in 1770 the State took over the port and its equipment. Under the Empire it became a naval base.

Despite the loss of monopoly, the company resumed trading in 1785 as the New India Company but ceased its activities in 1794.

The war years – Lorient was occupied by the Germans on 25 June 1940. From 27 September 1940 the city was subject to bombardments, which intensified as the war raged on, and was destroyed in August 1944. The fighting between the entrenched German garrison and the Americans and locally-based Free French Forces which encircled the Lorient "pocket" devastated the surrounding area so that when the townspeople returned on 8 May 1945, all that greeted them was a scene of desolation.

SIGHTS

The Ingénieur-Général Stosskopf Submarine Base (Base des sous-marins) ⊙ *and the Dockyard (Arsenal) are not open to foreigners.*

Port de pêche de Keroman (**Z**) – *Best seen in the morning when the fishermen return with the day's catch (depending on the tide).* Partly reclaimed from the sea, the port of Keroman is the only French harbour designed and equipped for commercial fishing; it is the leading port in France for the value and variety of fish unloaded. It has two basins set at right angles: the Grand Bassin and the Bassin Long (totalling 1 850m - 6 070ft of docks). The Grand Bassin is sheltered by a jetty 250m - 265yds long which is used as a loading and unloading quay for cargo steamers and trawlers. The basin has two other quays, one with a refrigerating and cold-storage plant for the trawlers and fish dealers; and the other, as well as the quay at the east end of the Bassin Long, where the trawlers unload their catch. In front of the quays is the 600m - 650yds long market hall (*criée*) where auctions are held, and, close behind it, the fish dealers' ware-houses which open onto the car park, where lorries destined for the rest of France are loaded.

In six bays of the slipway, trawlers can be dry-docked or repaired. A large area round the basins, available for the industries and commerce connected with fishing, completes the zone.

The port of Keroman sends out ships for all kinds of fishing all the year round. The largest vessels go to sea for a fortnight, especially to the Irish Sea for coalfish and carry their own ice-making equipment (which can make up to 400 metric tons a day) to the fishing grounds.

Église Notre-Dame-de-Victoire (**YZ B**) – Better known to the locals as the church of St-Louis, it stands in Place Alsace-Lorraine which is, itself, a successful example of modern town planning. The church is built in reinforced concrete and has very plain lines. It is square with a flattened cupola roof and a square tower flanking the façade. The beauty of the church lies in its **interior★**. Little panes of glass, yellow and clear, reflect the outside light into the building from the top of the rotunda and the bays in the lower section consist of brightly-coloured splintered glass. Covering the wall at the back of the high altar is a mural in pastel tones, while in the nave a striking monochrome Entombment faces an Annunciation. The Stations of the Cross drawn in outline only, show each at its most dramatic moment.

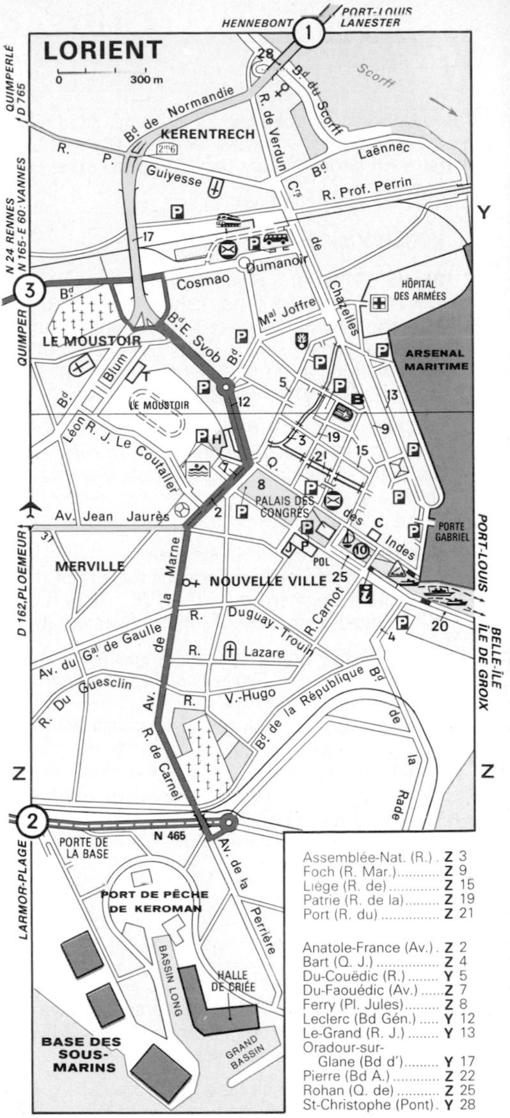

B Église N. D. de-Victoire

THE COAST BETWEEN SCORFF AND LAÏTA

Round tour of 47km - 29 miles – about 2 hours 30 min. Leave Lorient by ② on the town plan passing the Kernével road on the left.

Larmor-Plage – *See LARMOR-PLAGE.*

The old road from Larmor follows the coast fairly closely, passing many small seaside resorts. Note the kaolin quarries on the right. After Kerpape the drive affords extensive views of the coast of Finistère, beyond the cove of Le Pouldu and over to the île de Groix.

In the foreground are the coastal inlets in which lie the little ports of Lomener, Perello Kerroch and Le Courégant and the large beach of **Fort-Bloqué** dominated by a fort. Go through Guidel-Plages on the Laïta estuary. From Guidel make for the Pont de St-Maurice (*6km - 4 miles Rtn*) over the Laïta. The **view★** up the enclosed valley is magnificent.

From Guidel continue on via Coatermalo and Gostel to Pont-Scorff. At Pont-Scorff take the road towards Quéven.

Zoo de Pont-Scorff ⏲ – In a woodland setting on the steep banks of the Scarve, the zoo, which specialises in breeding big cats, contains thirteen species from the cat family: lions, tigers, leopards, ocelots, snow leopards, lynxes, pumas etc., as well as many other types of animal from all over the world: bears, wolves, llamas, bison, hippopotamuses, webfooted animals, birds and monkeys.

Return to Lorient passing through Quéven.

BOAT TRIPS ⏲

★★ **Belle-Île** – *See BELLE-ILE.*

★ **Port-Louis** – *Crossing time: 30 min. See PORT-LOUIS.*

★ **Île de Groix** – *See Île de GROIX.*

LOUDÉAC

Population 9 820

Michelin map 59 fold 13 or 230 folds 22 and 23

This little town, at the heart of Brittany, still holds some large fairs and markets. The region specialises in intensive farming, mainly chicken and pigs, and the countryside is dotted with large hangars flanked by tall silos. Loudéac is also well known for its **race meetings** ⓥ.

EXCURSIONS

Rigole d'Hilvern – *8km - 5 miles west.*
This channel, which winds its way along a ridge, was dug during the Empire to regulate the flow of the Brest-Nantes Canal. Its role has been taken over by the Blavet pumping station, so it is no longer filled with water; however, a conservation society is working to get it restored. A footpath follows the course of the Hilvern Channel along the ridge for 62km - 38.5 miles.

La Chèze – *10km - 6 miles southeast on the D 776.*
In this village, which has preserved the vestiges of a 13C castle, is the **Musée régional des Métiers de Bretagne** (Breton Crafts Regional Museum) ⓥ. The centre evokes the crafts and trades of yesteryear with reconstituted workshops of the slate roofer, harness-saddle maker, cartwright, wooden shoe maker and blacksmith.

Querrien – *11km - 7 miles east.*
The little village of Querrien was the site of the miraculous apparition of the Virgin to a young shepherdess in the 17C. There is an annual pilgrimage in the sanctuary in honour of Our Lady of Infinite Succour (Notre-Dame-de-Toute-Aide).

La Ferrière – *16km - 10 miles southeast. Leave Loudéac on the road to Rennes and after 12km - 7 miles bear right towards La Trinité-Porhoët and right again 2km - 1 mile further on.*
In the village stands a vast 14C **church** with a belfry-porch. Inside, in the chancel is a stained-glass window depicting the Virgin (1551); in the north transept a window of the Tree of Jesse of the same date, a Romanesque Virgin in lime wood, the so-called Our Lady of La Ferrière and a granite late 15C Annunciation; in the nave a 16C Crucifixion (on the right).
The square opposite the church is adorned with a 15C Calvary-cross.

MALESTROIT

Population 2 367

Michelin map 63 fold 4 or 230 fold 38

Near the Lanvaux Moors, this picturesque town, built along the Oust Canal, contains interesting Gothic and Renaissance houses. Malestroit was, during the Middle Ages, one of Brittany's nine baronies.

Old houses – Half-timbered or in stone, these houses are located mostly in the St Gilles precincts. On Place du Bouffay one of the residences has humorous carvings on its façade, another has a pelican in wood. Stroll along Rue au Froment, Rue aux Anglais, Rue des Ponts and the Rue du Général-de-Gaulle.

St-Gilles – This 12 and 16C church is curious for the juxtaposition of styles and the double nave. Notice the south doorway, with its two doors with 17C carved panels, flanked by massive buttresses adorned with the symbolic attributes of the four Evangelists. The lion of St Mark is mounted by a youth symbolising St Matthew, and St Luke's ox rests on a pedestal adorned with the eagle of St John. About 3pm the shadows of the ox and the eagle between them suggest the well-known profile of Voltaire. Left of the high altar is a 16C stained-glass window dedicated to St Gilles and in the south chapel a 16C *Pietà*.

Morcime/CAMPAGNE CAMPAGNE

Carved figure on a house in Malestroit

EXCURSION

St-Marcel. *3km - 2 miles west on the D 321.*

Spread over a forested park is the **Musée de la Résistance bretonne** (Museum of Breton Resistance) ⓥ, which vividly retraces this very important part of local Breton history. The visit starts with a film which summarises the important events in the Second World War: German war effort, invasion of Europe, Allied preparation of the landing and the landing itself, and the Liberation.

Then follow exhibits, organised chronologically, with explanatory panels, slides and films, models, arms, uniforms, etc, evoking the war and its effect on Brittany. To illustrate wartime rationing, a street has been reconstituted, with its local grocery, petrol pump and restaurant; the black market and the collaboration are also explained. In the park part of the Atlantic Wall has been rebuilt; further on there is a garage, during the Occupation, with its gas-run cars, an American Army camp and finally a collection of military vehicles and weapons belonging to both the German and Allied armies.

Bear left on leaving, after 1km – half a mile, a monument stands commemorating the battle which occurred between members of the Maquis (French Resistance Movement) and the Germans on 18 June, 1944.

La MEILLERAYE-DE-BRETAGNE

Population 1 097

Michelin map 63 fold 17 or 230 fold 55

The presence of a nearby abbey did much to stimulate the growth of this town which stands on an eminence near the **Forêt de Vioreau** (800ha - 1 977 acres).

Abbaye de Melleray ⓥ – *2.5km - 2 miles on the road to Riaillé.*

Founded in 1142 near a lovely lake, this Cistercian abbey has buildings which date from the 18C. The **Église Notre-Dame-de-Melleray**, completed in 1183, has been restored to its Cistercian severity, including a series of grisaille windows. Note the pointed white stone arches resting on square pink granite pillars. In the flat chevet, admire the gracious 17C wood polychrome **statue of the Virgin**.

Opposite the entrance avenue there is a curious 15C granite Calvary.

Grand Réservoir de Vioreau – *5km - 3 miles south.*

This vast reservoir with its leafy banks and sandy beaches attracts sailing enthusiasts. It is linked with several pools and feeds the Nantes-Brest canal.

MÉNEZ-HOM★★★

Michelin map 58 fold 15 or 230 fold 18

Ménez-Hom (alt 330m - 1 082ft), a detached peak at the west end of the Montagnes Noires, is one of the great Breton viewpoints and a key position commanding the approach to the Presqu'île de Crozon. On 15 August a folklore festival is held at the summit.

It is reached by taking the road, 2km - 1 mile, which branches off the road between Châteaulin and Crozon, 1.5km - 0.75 mile after the Ste-Marie-du-Ménez-Hom (qv).

Panorama – *Viewing table.* In clear weather there is a vast panorama. You will see Douarnenez Bay, bounded on the left by the Cornouaille coast as far as the Pointe du Van, and on the right by the coast of the Presqu'île de Crozon as far as Cap de la Chèvre. To the right the view extends to the Pointe de St-Mathieu, Tas de Pois Rocks, the Pointe de Penhir, Brest and its roadstead, in front of which you will see the île Longue on the left, the île Ronde and the Pointe de l'Armorique on the right, with the estuary common to the Rivers Faou and Aulne, which nonetheless separate as they flow inland. The nearer valley – that of the Aulne – follows a fine, winding course, spanned by the suspension bridge at Térénez. In the distance are the Monts d'Arrée, the montagne St-Michel crowned by its little chapel, the Châteaulin Basin, the montagne de Noires Montagnes, Locronan, Douarnenez and Tréboul.

Go as far as the mark of the Geographical Institute (Institut géographique) to get a view of the horizon from all sides. You will then see, in the Doufine Valley, the village of Pont-de-Buis.

Gourmets...

The introductory chapter of this guide describes the region's gastronomic specialities and best local wines.

The annual Michelin Red Guide France offers an up-to-date selection of good restaurants.

MONCONTOUR

Population 901

Michelin map 59 fold 13 or 230 fold 23

Moncontour, an old city built on an outcrop in the 11C, is located at the junction of two valleys. The town was taken by the supporters of the Catholic League under the reign of Henri IV, but was recaptured by the royal army in 1590. It was in this town, won back to the King's cause, that François de la Nouë, known as Bras-de-Fer, died 4 August 1591, having been mortally wounded during the siege of Lamballe *(qv)*. The ramparts, partially demolished in 1626 on Richelieu's orders, are still rather attractive; pretty little streets and flights of steps lead to gateways used in the races. Château des Granges, rebuilt in the 18C, stands on a hill to the north of the town.

Eglise St-Mathurin – The church, built in the 16C and extensively remodelled in the 18C, has remarkable 16C **stained-glass windows★**: those in the north aisle relate in succession scenes from the life of St Yves, St Barbara and St John the Baptist, and in the south aisle, the Tree of Jesse and St Mathurin. Behind the marble high altar (1768), the restored window depicts scenes from the Childhood of Christ.

EXCURSIONS

Chapelle N.-D.-du-Haut – *3km - 2 miles southeast. Leave Moncontour on the road towards Lamballe. At the crossroads, after the filtering plant, turn right towards Collinée, then after about 800m - 875yds turn right again, cross Trédaniel and continue straight ahead (Calvary on the left) until you reach the chapel at 600m - 656yds.* You will see the wooden statues of seven healer-saints: St Mamertus, who is invoked against colic, St Livertin and St Eugenia for headaches, St Leobinus for eye ailments, St Méen for madness, St Hubert for sores and dog bites and St Houarniaule for fear. A *pardon* is held on 15 August.

Château de la Touche-Trébry ⌚ – *6km - 4 miles east on the road to Collinée; then the second road on the left, the D 25.*

Although built at the end of the 16C, La Touche-Trébry looks like a medieval castle. It stands, facing a pond, protected by its defensive walls forming a homogeneous whole, unaltered in character by the restorations that have taken place. Two pavilions, resting against two huge towers (the one on the right has crumbled), watch over the entrance which consists of two gates, one of which is smaller than the other, and is topped by a wall walk.

The courtyard is regular in shape with the main building, with its symmetrical façade, at the far end. On either side, at right angles, are the two wings with pointed roofs; next to them are the outbuildings, not as tall, extending all the way to the two entrance pavilions. In the corners between the main building and the side wings stand four turrets. The towers and turrets all have domed roofs.

Inside the castle there are some fine chimney-pieces.

MONTAGNES NOIRES★★

Michelin map 58 folds 16 and 17 or 230 folds 19 and 20

With the Monts d'Arrée *(qv)*, the Montagnes Noires form what Bretons call the spine of the peninsula. These two little mountain chains, mainly of hard sandstone and quartzite, are not quite alike. The Montagnes Noires are lower (326m - 1 043ft as against 384m - 1 229ft); their crest is narrower; their slopes are less steep and their heaths are less extensive.

The chain's name (*noire* means black) suggests that it was once covered with forest. As in all inland Brittany, the ground became bare with time. Since the end of the last century reafforestation has been going on, and the fir woods, now numerous, once more justify the name of Black Mountains.

Quarrying of Breton slate carried out on a large scale in the past, is now concentrated on the eastern end of the chain, in the district of Motreff and Maël-Carhaix.

ROUND TOUR STARTING FROM CARHAIX-PLOUGUER

585km – 53 miles – allow half a day – local map below

Carhaix-Plouguer – *See CARHAIX-PLOUGUER.*

Leave Carhaix-Plouguer west towards Pleyben and after 2.5km – 1.5 miles turn left.

The road then enters the picturesque Valley of the Hyère.

At Port-de-Carhaix, after crossing the Nantes-Brest Canal, bear right.

1.5km - 1 mile further on, note the **Calvaire de Kerbreudeur** on the left, parts of which are thought to date from the 15C.

St-Hernin – In this place, where the Irish St Hernin is said to have settled, is a 16C parish close. The church and charnel house were remodelled in the 17C. On the beautiful slender Calvary note St Michael slaying the Dragon.

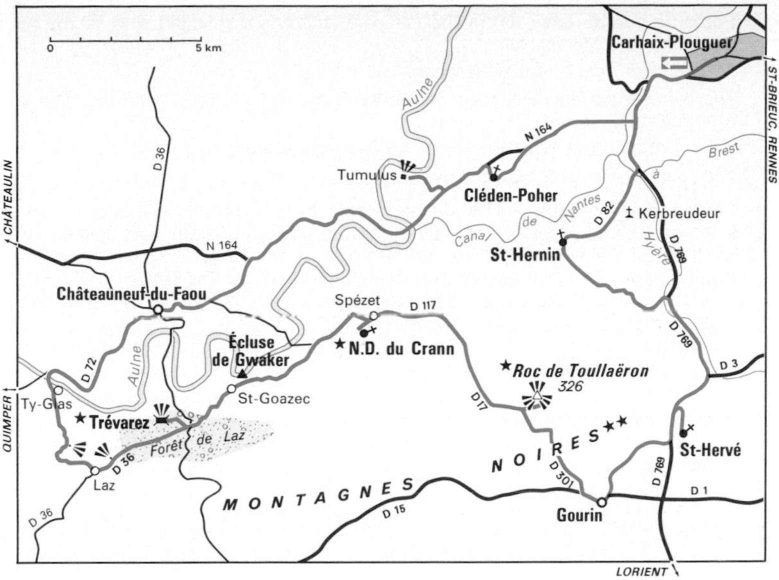

Take the road to Moulin-Neuf and bear right on the road Carhaix-Plouguer to Gourin. Old slate quarries can be seen to the right and left.

Chapelle St-Hervé – *Access is via a road to the left.* This small 16C building with a pierced pinnacle is decorated in the Flamboyant Gothic style. A *pardon* is held on the last Sunday in September.

After crossing the crest of the Montagnes Noires, the road runs down to Gourin.

Gourin – Once a centre of slate production, Gourin also has white stone quarries and raises horses, cattle and poultry. The 16C church, topped by a domed bell tower with lantern turrets, contains in the south aisle, to the left of the entrance, a 16C *Pietà* in polychrome wood.

At Gourin, take the Quimper road, and at the bottom bear right towards Châteauneuf-du-Faou.

The road climbs towards the crest of the Montagnes Noires.

★**Roc de Toullaëron** – *30 min on foot Rtn; 5km – 3 miles from Gourin, leave your car and take a stony lane bordered with oak trees (private property, no picnicking) to the right. At the end of the lane, climb up the rocks.*
From the top, which is the highest point in the Montagnes Noires (326m - 1 043ft), a wide **panorama**★ may be enjoyed in clear weather: to the west is the densely wooded Valley of Châteaulin; to the north, the Monts d'Arrée; to the south, in the distance, the Breton plateau slopes gently down to the Atlantic.

Make for Spézet; on leaving Spézet take the Châteauneuf-du-Faou road, bear left.

★**Chapelle Notre-Dame-du-Crann** - *See Chapelle NOTRE-DAME-DU-CRANN.*

Return to Spézet and before entering bear left and after 2km – 1 mile, left again. At the entrance to St-Goazec, turn right.

Écluse de Gwaker – This is one of the many locks on the Nantes-Brest Canal. There is a pretty waterfall at the end of the large pool, forming a pleasant setting.

After St-Goazec, bear right towards Laz.

The road climbs into the lovely forest of Laz, which is mostly coniferous.

★**Park and Château de Trévarez** ⓥ – This 85ha - 210 acre forest park is laid out around an imposing neo-Gothic château built in the "Belle Epoque" style and currently undergoing restoration. The signposted paths wind their way through the woods, making for a pleasant stroll whatever the season: admire the camellias (April), the azaleas and hydrangeas (July), fuchsias and rhododendrons. A pond, a water garden and several fountains add a refreshing touch. The château terrace offers a **splendid view** of the Châteauneuf-du-Faou region. The former stables, whose original design was extremely modern for their time, have kept their stalls and loose-boxes; these have been converted into a small museum and are used for exhibitions and other educational activities organised throughout the year. This charming outing can be complemented by a train ride and a "Breton tea" (with traditional Breton cakes).

★**Point de vue de Laz** – From the car park, there is a splendid view of the Aulne Valley and the Ménez-Hom.

At Laz, turn right towards Kerohan.

The picturesque downhill road, hemmed in by rocky ridges, affords a fine view over the Aulne Valley.

After Ty-Glas, bear right towards Châteauneuf-du-Faou.

The road crosses and then follows the Aulne.

Châteauneuf-du-Faou – This village is built in very pretty surroundings on the slope of a hill overlooking the Aulne. It is an angler's delight with salmon swimming up the Aulne from the sea and also pike. In the church, the baptismal chapel decorated in 1919 with scenes from the life of Christ by **Paul Sérusier** (1865-1927), a painter of the Nabis group, is of interest. A *pardon* is held on the third Sunday in August at the Chapelle Notre-Dame-des-Portes.
The road from Châteauneuf to Carhaix-Plouguer is charming for the short distance that it follows the Aulne.

After 1.5km - 1 mile beyond the confluence with the Nantes-Brest Canal, bear left towards La Roche and then right after some 500m - 547yds.
The road runs past farmyards to a hillock. From the top of the tumulus, there is a fine **view** of a loop of the Aulne.

Return to the road to Carhaix-Plouguer.

Cléden-Poher – The village has a fine **parish close★** (*qv*) dating mainly from the 16C. The 15-16C church contains interesting altarpieces: three Flemish-style 16C panels at the high altar; the altarpiece of the Rosary (1694) in the south aisle; the altarpiece of the Pentecost (17C) in the north aisle. Much of the vaulting has preserved its panelling painted in 1750. In the cemetery are an ossuary turned into a chapel with a fine timber roof, a Calvary (1575) and two curious sacristies with keel vaulting.

Return to Carhaix-Plouguer.

J.-L. Barde/SCOPE

Fountain in Trévarez park

MONTFORT-SUR-MEU

Population 4 675
Michelin map 59 fold 16 or 230 fold 25

This charming small town, built of local red stone, is located at the confluence of the Rivers Meu and Garun.
It was founded by Raoul I who, in 1091 had a castle built on a hill, which he called Montfort.

Écomusée du pays de Montfort ⓥ – The regional museum is housed in the 14C **Tour de Pagegaut** (Papegaut Tower), all that remains of the medieval construction. It is named after a game of skill.
A spiral staircase takes you up to the temporary and permanent exhibits held on the different floors, which present Montfort and its region (landscapes, folklore: collection of dolls in traditional costumes and headdresses).

Maison natale de saint Louis-Marie Grignion de Montfort ⓥ – *15 Rue de la Saulnerie.*
The missionary Louis-Marie Grignion de Montfort was born in this house in 1673 (d1716; canonised in 1947). Several rooms (restored) with fine stonework are open to the public. The garden overlooks the Meu Valley.

EXCURSION

La Chapelle-Thouarault – *7km - 4 miles east on the D 30, then right on the D 68 to Cintré.*
At the place called "Basse-Vallée" the **Musée et Atelier d'art animalier** (animal art museum and workshop) ⓥ displays, in about forty dioramas, 250 stuffed animals placed in a minutely detailed reconstruction of their natural habitat. Many examples of local fauna are on display, enabling visitors to observe at their leisure scenes of animals going about their daily way of life – underground as well as under water – which they would rarely so much as glimpse in the wild.

Omelette de la Mère Poulard

Visitors to the Mont-St-Michel will no doubt come across this speciality, the invention of local innkeeper Annette Poulard (1851-1931). Her excellent omelettes won their reputation in the late 19C, when they featured on the menu of her hotel as a stop-gap for hungry travellers while they waited for more substantial dishes. After the death of La Mère Poulard, there was much speculation over possible secret recipes or special culinary techniques which might explain why her omelettes had been more than usually light and tasty. Annette Poulard had herself claimed in a letter dated 1922 that the process was quite simple, "I break the eggs in a bowl, I beat them up well, I put a nice knob of butter in the frying pan, I throw the eggs in and stir continuously."
The great French gourmet Curnonsky (1872-1956), however, insisted that one need look no further for the great explanation than Balzac's hero Dr Rouget *(La Rabouilleuse)*, who beat up the eggs yolks and whites separately before mixing them in the frying pan.

MONT-ST-MICHEL***

Population 72
Michelin map 59 fold 7 or 231 fold 38

The Mont-St-Michel has been called "the Marvel of the Western World" owing to its island setting, its rich history and the beauty of its architecture; at any season of the year it leaves an indelible impression.
When the crowds have gone its more elusive charm is evident, particularly at dawn and dusk.
The Feast of the Archangel Michael (*see the Calendar of events at the end of the guide*) early in the autumn is celebrated as a religious and popular festival and attracts large crowds.
Like its counterpart, St Michael's Mount off the south coast of Cornwall (*see the Michelin Green Guide England – The West Country*), Mont-St-Michel is a granite island about 900m - 984yds round and 80m - 262ft high; it is joined to the mainland by a dike.
As the bay is already partially silted up (*see Marais de Dol under Mont DOL*), the Mount is usually to be seen surrounded by huge sand banks which shift with the tides and often reshape the mouths of the neighbouring rivers.
The course of the Cousenon, which used to threaten the dikes and polders with its wandering, has been canalised and the river now flows straight out to sea to the west of the Mount. Its former course, northwest from Pontorson, used to mark the frontier between the Duchies of Normandy and Brittany.
The movement of the tides in the bay is very great and the difference in sea level between high and low water can be over 40ft, the highest in France. As the sea bed is flat, the sea retreats a long way exposing 15km - 9 miles of sand. The tide comes in very rapidly, not quite at the speed of a galloping horse, as has been said, but of a person walking at a brisk pace. This phenomenon, which is aggravated by numerous currents, can spell danger to the unwary.
The Mont-St-Michel has been silting up for several decades. Indeed, every year the sea deposits around 1 000 000m^3 - 35 315 000ft^3 of sediment in the bay. In part, this can be blamed on mankind since between the mid-19C and 1969 a number of regional initiatives were taken, resulting in constructions that accelerated the formation of polders (canalization of the Couesnan River, building of a dike then a dam). In 1995 a joint project was commissioned by the state and by local municipalities, intended to return the Mont to the sea. Ideally, this would make it possible to replace the dike by a footbridge under which cross-currents would once again flow between the mainland and the island. It would also help restore the scouring action of the Couesnan and the two other coastal streams. The implementation of this project is hoped to be completed by the year 2000.

HISTORICAL NOTES

An amazing achievement – The abbey's origin goes back to the early 8C, when the Archangel Michael appeared to Aubert, Bishop of Avranches, who founded an oratory on the island, then known as Mont Tombe. In the Carolingian era, the oratory was replaced by an abbey and from then until the 16C a series of increasingly splendid buildings, in the Romanesque and then the Gothic styles, succeeded one another on the Mount which was subsequently dedicated to the Archangel.
The well fortified abbey was never captured.
The construction is an amazing achievement. The blocks of granite were transported from the îles Chausey or from Brittany and hoisted up to the foot of the building. As the crest of the hill was very narrow, the foundations had to be built up from the lower slopes.

Pilgrimages – Even during the Hundred Years War pilgrims came flocking to the Mount; the English, who had possession of the area, granted safe conduct to the faithful in return for payment. People of all sorts made the journey: nobles, rich citizens and beggars, who lived on alms and were given free lodging by the monks. In times of great calamity, the pilgrimage to Mont-St-Michel prompted such excessive displays of religious fervour that the ecclesiastical authorities were obliged to intervene. Hotels and souvenir shops flourished. The pilgrims bought medals bearing the effigy of St Michael and lead amulets which they filled with sand from the beach.
Of the many thousands of people crossing the bay some were drowned, others were lost in the quicksands; this gave rise to the longer dedication of St Michael in Peril from the Sea.

Decline – The abbey came to be held *in commendam* (by lay abbots who received the revenue without exercising the duties), and discipline among the monks grew lax. In the 17C the Maurists, monks from St Maur, were made responsible for reforming the monastery but they only made some deceptive architectural changes, tinkering with the stonework. More dilapidation ensued when the abbey became a prison. From being the local Bastille, before the Revolution, it was converted in 1811 into a national prison where political prisoners such as Barbès and Blanqui were detained. In 1874,

Y. Arthus-Bertrand/ALTITUDE

Mont-St-Michel

the abbey and the ramparts passed into the care of the Historic Monuments Department (Service des Monuments Historiques). Since 1969 a few monks have again been in residence, conducting services in the abbey church.

Stages in the Abbey's Construction – The buildings date from the 11 to 16C.

Romanesque Abbey – 11-12C. Between 1017 and 1144 a church was built on the top of the Mount. The previous Carolingian building was incorporated as a crypt – Our Lady Underground (Notre-Dame-sous-Terre) – to support the platform on which the last three bays of the Romanesque nave were built. Other crypts were constructed to support the transepts and the chancel which projected beyond the natural rock.
The conventual buildings were constructed on the west face and on either side of the nave. The entrance to the abbey faced west.

Gothic Abbey – 13-16C. This period saw the construction of:
– the magnificent Merveille buildings (1211-28) on the north side of the church, used by the monks and pilgrims and for the reception of important guests;
– the abbatial buildings (13-15C) on the south side comprising the administrative offices, the Abbot's lodging and the garrison's quarters;
– the Fort and the outer defences (14C) on the east side, which protected the entrance, moved to this side of the Mount.
The chancel of the Romanesque church had collapsed and was rebuilt more magnificently in the Flamboyant Gothic style (1446-1521) above a new crypt.

Alterations – 18-19C. In 1780 the last three bays of the nave and the Romanesque façade were demolished.
The present bell tower (1897) is surmounted by a beautiful spire which rises to 157m - 515ft and culminates in a statue of St Michael (1879) by Emmanuel Frémiet.

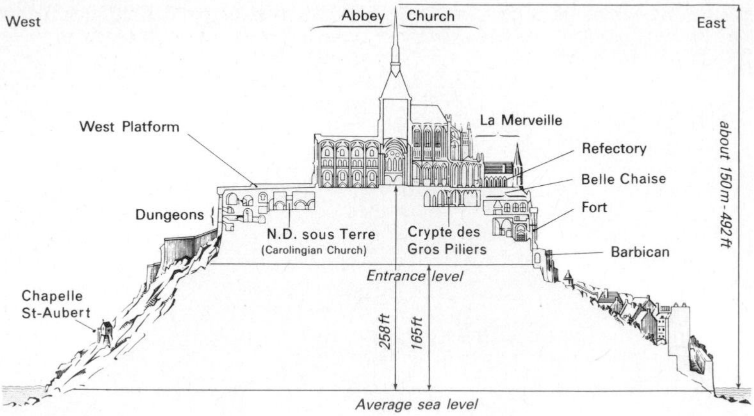

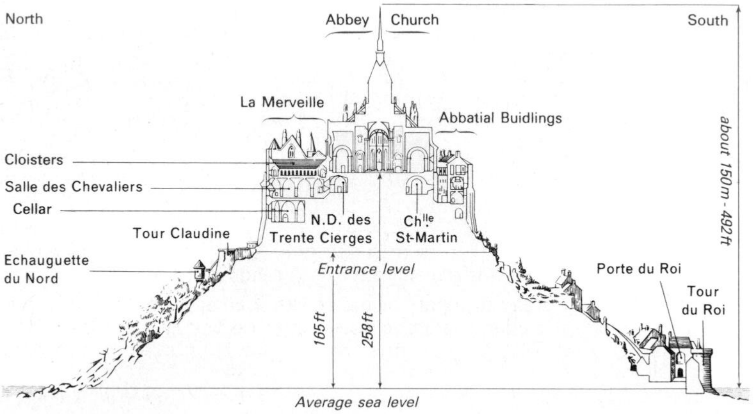

★★★ THE ABBEY *Leave the car in the car park* ⓥ

The **tour of the abbey** ⓥ does not go from building to building nor from period to period but from floor to floor through a maze of corridors and stairs.

Outer Defences of the Abbey – A flight of steps, the Grand Degré, once cut off by a swing door, leads up to the Abbey. At the top on the right is the entrance to the gardens; more steps lead up to the ramparts.
Through the arch of an old door is a fortified courtyard overlooked by the Fort, which consists of two tall towers shaped like mortars standing on their breeches and linked by machicolations. Even this military structure shows the builder's artistic sense: the wall is attractively constructed of alternate courses of pink and grey granite. Beneath a pointed barrel vault, a steep and ill-lit staircase, known as the Pit Steps (Escalier du Gouffre), leads down to the beautiful door which opens into the Guard Room, also called the Gatehouse (Porterie).

Guard room or Gatehouse (**B**) – This hall was the focal point of the Abbey. Poor pilgrims passed through on their way from the Merveille Court to the Almonry. The Abbot's visitors and the faithful making for the church used the Abbey Steps.

Abbey Steps – An impressive flight of 90 steps rises between the abbatial buildings (left) and the abbey church (right); it is spanned by a fortified bridge (15C). The stairs stop outside the south door of the church on a terrace called the Gautier Leap (Saut Gautier – **E**) after a prisoner who is supposed to have hurled himself over the edge. The tour starts here.

West Platform – This spacious terrace, which was created by the demolition of the last three bays of the church, provides an extensive **view★** of the Bay of Mont-St-Michel.

★★ **Church** – The exterior of the church, particularly the east end with its buttresses, flying buttresses, bell turrets and balustrades, is a masterpiece of light and graceful architecture. The interior reveals the marked contrast between the severe and sombre Romanesque nave and the elegant and luminous Gothic chancel.
The church is built on three crypts which are visited during the tour.

★★★ **La Merveille** – The name, which means the Marvel, applies to the superb Gothic buildings on the north face of the Mount. The eastern block, the first to be built between 1211 and 1218, comprises from top to bottom, the Refectory, the Guests' Hall and the Almonry; the western block, built between 1218 and 1228, consists of the cloisters, the Knights' Hall and the cellar.
From the outside the buildings look like a fortress although their religious vocation is suggested by the dignity and purity of their line. The interior is a perfect example of the evolution of the Gothic style, from a simplicity which is almost Romanesque, in the lower halls, through the elegance of the Guests' Hall, the majesty of the Knights' Hall and the mysterious luminosity of the Refectory, to the cloisters which are a masterpiece of delicacy and refinement. The top floor comprises the cloisters and the Refectory.

★★★ **Cloisters** – The cloisters seem to be suspended between the sea and the sky. The gallery arcades display heavily undercut sculpture of foliage ornamented with the occasional animal or human figure (particularly human heads); there are also a few religious symbols. The double row of arches rests on delightful slim single columns arranged in quincunx to enhance the impression of lightness. The different colours of the various materials add to the overall charm. The lavatorium (lavabo), on the right of the entrance, recalls the ceremonial "washing of the feet" which took place every Thursday.

★★ **Refectory** – The effect is mysterious; the chamber is full of light although it appears to have only two windows in the end wall. To admit so much light without weakening the solid side walls which support the wooden roof and are lined with a row of slim niches, the architect introduced a very narrow aperture high up in each recess. The vaulted ceiling is panelled with wood and the acoustics are excellent.

Old Romanesque Abbey – The ribbed vaulting of this former abbey marks the transition between Romanesque and Gothic. The tour includes the Monk's Walk (Promenoir des Moines) and part of the old dormitory.

"Grande Roue" – This huge wheel brings back the days in which the abbey served as a prison. Operated by five to six prisoners who would tread inside it, the wheel was used for hoisting provisions and pieces of equipment.

Crypts – The chancel and transepts of the church are supported by three undercrofts or crypts; the most impressive is the **Crypte des Gros Piliers**★ (Great Pillared Crypt) with its ten pillars 5m - 16ft round, sculpted in granite coming from the îles Chausey.
The second floor consists of the Guest's Hall (Salle des Hôtes) and the Knights' Hall (Salle des Chevaliers).

★ **Guests' Hall** – Here the Abbot received royalty (Louis IX, Louis XI, François I) and other important visitors. The hall, which is 35m - 115ft long, has a Gothic ceiling supported on a central row of slim columns; the effect is graceful and elegant.
At one time it was divided down the middle by a huge curtain of tapestries; on one side were the kitchen quarters (two chimneys) and on the other the great dining hall (one chimney). One can easily imagine the opulence of the banquets held in the Guests' Hall.

★ **Knights' Hall** – The name of this hall may refer to the military order of St Michael which was founded in 1469 by Louis XI with the abbey as its seat.
The hall is vast and majestic (26 x 18m - 85 x 58ft) and divided into four sections by three rows of stout columns.
It was the monks' workroom, where they illuminated manuscripts, and was heated by two great chimneys. The rooms on the lower floor are the Almonry and the Cellar.

Cellar – This was the storeroom; it was divided in three by two rows of square pillars supporting the groined vaulting.

Almonry – This is a Gothic room with a Romanesque vault supported on a row of columns.

Abbatial buildings – Only the Guard Room is open.

★★ THE TOWN

Outer Defences – The Outer Gate is the only breach in the ramparts and opens into the first fortified courtyard. On the left stands the Citizens' Guard Room (16C) which presently houses the Tourist Information Office; on the right are the "Michelettes", English mortars captured in a sortie during the Hundred Years War. A second gate leads into a second courtyard. The third gate (15C), complete with machicolations and portcullis, is called the King's Gate because it was the lodging of the token contingent maintained on the Mount by the King in assertion of his rights; it opens into the Grande-Rue where the Abbot's soldiers lodged in the fine arcaded house (right).

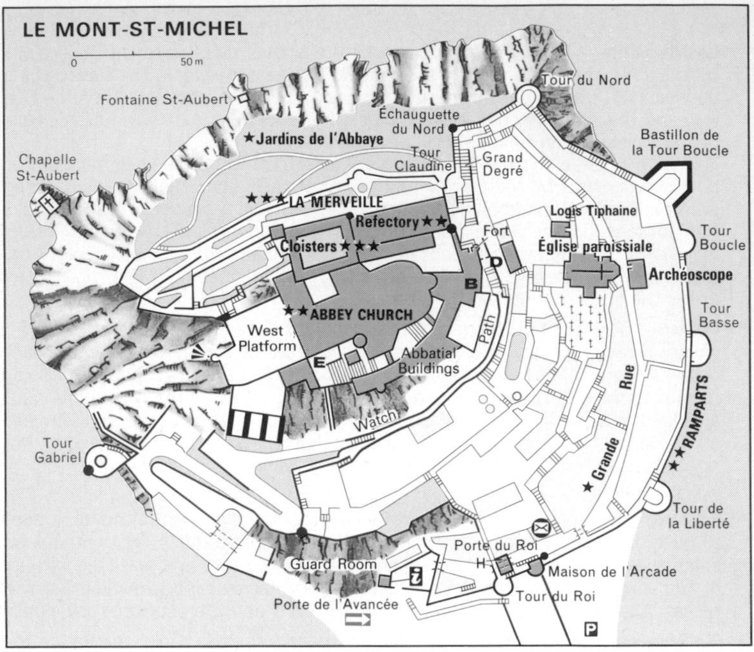

B Salle des Gardes ou Porterie
D Maison ancienne "la Truie-qui-file"
E Terrasse "le Saut Gautier"

★**Grande-Rue** – This picturesque narrow street climbs steeply between old (15-16C) houses, several of which have retained their original name – le **logis Saint-Etienne**, le **Vieux logis**, la **Sirène**, la **Truie qui file** (**D**) – and ends in a flight of steps. In summer it is lively and crowded with restaurants and the stalls of souvenir merchants, as it was in the Middle Ages at the height of the most fervent pilgrimages.

★★**Ramparts** – These are 13-15C. The sentry walk offers fine views of the bay; from the North Tower the Tombelaine Rock, which Philippe Auguste had fortified, is clearly visible.

★**Abbey Gardens** ⓥ – A pleasant place for a stroll with a view of the west side of the Mount and the Chapelle St Aubert.

Archéoscope ⓥ – This magical mystery tour takes you back in time to the Mount's origins. The seismic phenomenon of Scissy Forest, the Archangel Michael's appearance before Bishop Aubert, the different stages of the Mount's construction and its architectural splendour, are all explained by sophisticated special effects coordinated by a computer: models emerge out of water, slides flash on screens, the whole show is accompanied by light and sound effects.

Église paroissiale St-Pierre – The building which dates from the 11C has been much altered. The apse spans a narrow street. The parish church contains a Crucifix and other furnishings from the Abbey; the chapel in the south aisle contains a statue of St Michael covered in silver; in the chapel to the right of the altar there is a 15C statue of the Virgin and from the gallery hang numerous pilgrim banners.

Logis Tiphaine ⓥ – When Du Guesclin was captain of the Mount, he had this house built (1365) for his wife, Tiphaine Raguenel, an attractive and educated woman from Dinan, while he went off to the wars in Spain: the Constable's room (tester bed, chest), dining room (six-doored sideboard, chimney bearing the arms of Du Guesclin, 17C copperware) and Tiphaine's room (cupboard, tester bed, wax figure).

BOAT TRIPS

Baie du Mont-St-Michel – Starting at Vivier-sur-Mer, the *Sirène de la Baie*, an amphibious vehicle, takes you to Cancale; views of its oyster beds and mussel breeding poles.

With this guide,
use the appropriate Michelin Maps *(scale 1 : 200 000)*
shown below the contents table on page 3.
The common symbols will make planning easier.

Golfe du MORBIHAN★★

Michelin map 63 folds 2, 3, 12 and 13 or 230 folds 36, 37, 50 and 51

The Morhiban Gulf, an inland sea dotted with islands, offers some of the most unusual scenery in Brittany. It has the most delicate light effects, and its sunsets are unforgettable. A visit, especially by boat, is essential.

HISTORICAL NOTES

In 1C BC the Veneti – after whom Vannes is named – lived around the Golfe du Morbihan. They were the most powerful tribe in Armor and when Caesar decided to conquer the peninsula he aimed his main effort at them. It was a stiff task, for the Veneti were fine sailors and had a fleet which made it useless to attack them by land. The decisive struggle, therefore, had to be waged afloat. The Roman leader had a large number of galleys, built and assembled at the mouth of the Loire which were under the command of his lieutenant, Brutus.

The encounter, which took place before Port-Navalo, is said to have been watched by Caesar from the top of the Tumulus de Tumiac *(qv)*. On the other hand, geologists declare that the gulf did not exist at the time of the Gallic War. In all events, it is certain that the battle took place off the southeast coast of Brittany.

The Gauls put to sea with 220 large sailing ships, with high, strong hulls. The Romans opposed them with their large flat barges, propelled by oarsmen. The total and unexpected victory of Brutus was due to several causes: the sea was smooth and this favoured the galleys, which could not face bad weather; moreover, the wind dropped completely during the battle, becalming the Veneti in their sailing ships. Finally the Romans had sickles tied to long poles. When a galley drew alongside an enemy sailing ship, an agile sailor heaved the sickle into its rigging. The galley rowed on at full speed, the rope drew taut and the blade cut the rigging; mast and sails came tumbling down. Two or three galleys then attacked the ship and boarded it.

After this victory Caesar occupied the country of the Veneti and made them pay dearly for their resistance. All the members of their Senate were put to death, and the people were sold into slavery.

GEOGRAPHICAL NOTES

Mor-bihan means "little sea", while *Mor-braz* means "great sea" or ocean. This gulf, which is about 20km - 12 miles wide and 15km - 9 miles deep from the sea to the inner shore, was made by a comparatively recent settling of the land. The sea spread widely over land already despoiled by river erosion leaving inlets and estuaries which run far into the interior, and innumerable islands which give the Morbihan its special character. The rivers of Vannes and Auray form the two largest estuaries. About forty islands are privately owned and inhabited; the largest are the île d'Arz and the île aux Moines, both *communes*. The gulf is tidal; at high tide the sea sparkles everywhere around the low, flat and often wooded islands; at low tide, great mud-banks lie between the remaining channels. A narrow channel, before Port-Navalo permits passage both at high and low tide.

Morbihan is thronged with boats fishing between the islands, as well as with pleasure boats and oyster barges using Auray and the port of Vannes. There are many oyster beds in the rivers and along the islands.

★★★THE GULF BY BOAT

The best way to see the gulf is by boat. There are excursions starting from Vannes, Locmariaquer, Port-Navalo or Auray.

Île d'Arz – The island, 3.5km - 2 miles long, has several megalithic monuments.

★**Île aux Moines** ⓥ – This former monastic fief is the largest of the Morbihan Islands (7km - 4 miles long) and the most populous. It is a particularly quiet and restful seaside resort where mimosas and camellias grow among palm trees, lemon and orange trees. Its woods have poetic names: Bois des Soupirs (Wood of Sighs), Bois d'Amour (Wood of Love), Bois des Regrets (Wood of Regrets). The beauty of the island women, often sung by Breton poets, is no doubt responsible for these gallantries.

There are several sights worth visiting: the town with its picturesque alleyways; from Pointe du Trech, north of the island, there is a good view of Pointe d'Arradon and the gulf – note the odd-looking Calvary, its base composed of different levels and with stairs on its right side; southwards are the Boglieux and Penhap dolmens; and Pointe de Brouël, east of the island, affords a view of the île d'Arz.

★THE SHORES OF THE GULF

1 From Vannes to Locmariaquer

49km - 30 miles – about 3 hours 30 min – local map overleaf

★★**Vannes** - *Time: 2 hours 30 min. See VANNES.*

Leave Vannes on the D 101. After 5km - 3 miles bear left towards Pointe d'Arradon. The road skirts Arradon (Facilities).

Port-Navalo and the Golfe du Morbihan

★**Pointe d'Arradon** – *Turn left towards Cale de la Carrière.* From here there is a very typical **view**★ of the Golfe du Morbihan in which you can distinguish, from left to right: the îles de Logoden; in the distance, the île d'Arz; then the île d'Holavre, which is rocky and the île aux Moines. To reach the point take the path bordering the rocks, behind the hotel.

Turn round and go to Le Moustoir and bear left.

At the place called Moulin de Pomper note on the left the old tidal power mill *(see Usine marémotrice de la RANCE).*

Turn left towards Port-Blanc where you will embark for the île aux Moines.

★**Île aux Moines** - *2.5km -1.5 miles – plus 15 min by boat Rtn. Bicycle rental. Description above.*
The road next skirts Kerdelan Creek (on the left there is a good view of the gulf and, in the distance, of the île aux Moines), then passes by Pen-en-Toul marshes (marais) on its right.

Larmor-Baden – A little fishing port and large oyster-farming centre. From the port there is a fine view of the other islands and the entrance to the gulf.

★★**Cairn de Gavrinis** – *See Cairn de GAVRINIS.*
On the left are lovely vistas of the River Auray.

Bono – From the new bridge is a picturesque **view**★ of Bono, its river and harbour and the old suspension bridge. You will notice piles of whitewashed tiles used to collect oyster spat *(see CANCALE).* The **church** contains modern **stained-glass windows**★.

Before taking the new bridge towards Auray, bear left onto a downhill road.

As you leave Kernours, on the right in a small pine forest is a right-angled dolmen. On this same road continue to **Mané-Verh** which offers glimpses of the River Auray.

★**Auray** – *See AURAY.*

Leave Auray by ② on the town plan, then after 8km - 5 miles bear left.

The road skirts megalithic monuments.

★★**Locmariaquer** – *See LOCMARIAQUER.*

2 From Vannes to Port-Navalo and Back

79km - 49 miles – about 4 hours – local map right

★★**Vannes** – *Time: 2 hours 30 min. See VANNES.*

Leave Vannes on the Nantes road on the town plan. After St-Léonard, turn right.

The road runs along the east bank of the bay; there are several viewpoints.

★**Presqu'île de Rhuys** – At St-Colombier you enter the peninsula, which encloses the Golfe du Morbihan to the south. Its flora is reminiscent of that of the south of France.

J. Kaken/CAMPAGNE CAMPAGNE

Sarzeau – Facilities. Birthplace of **Lesage** (1668-1747), satirical dramatist and author of *Turcaret* and *Gil Blas*. On the small square, to the right of the church, stand two lovely Renaissance houses.

From Sarzeau go towards Brillac, the road follows the coast for some distance.

Le Logeo – A pretty little port sheltered by the Gouihan and Stibiden Islands.

Go as far as Le Net and bear right.

★**Tumulus de Tumiac or Butte de Cézar** - *15 min on foot. Leave your car in the car park and take a dirt track to the right.* From the top of the tumulus there is an extensive **view**★ of the gulf, Quiberon Bay and the islands. This was the observatory from which Caesar is supposed to have watched the naval battle agains the Veneti.

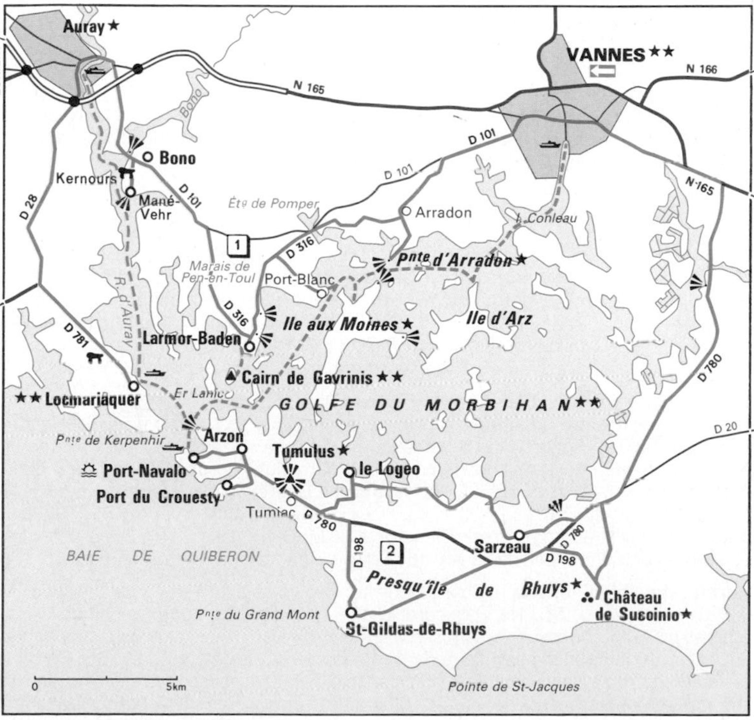

Arzon – In obedience to a vow made to St Anne *(qv)* in 1673, during the war with Holland, the sailors of Arzon march in the procession of Ste-Anne-d'Auray every year on Whit Monday. Two stained glass windows (1884) in the chancel of the church recount the story of this vow.

Port-Navalo – A small port and seaside resort. The roadstead is enclosed to the south by a promontory on which stands a lighthouse (benches and telescope), and to the north by Bilgroix Point which offers a good **view**★ of the Golfe du Morbihan. The beach faces the open sea.

Port du Crouesty – Located on the bay of the same name and southeast of Port-Navalois lies this pleasure boat harbour. Alongside it is a large residential complex. The 4 docks are well sheltered and can hold over 1 100 boats. From the tourist car park there is a good view of the site. Fine walk along the quayside.

St-Gildas-de-Rhuys – *See ST-GILDAS-DE-RHUYS.*

★**Château de Suscinio** – *See Château de SUSCINIO.*

From St-Colombier return to Vannes on the road on which you came.

MORGAT

Michelin map 58 fold 14 or 230 fold 17 – Facilities

Morgat is a well-sheltered seaside resort. The great sandy beach is enclosed to the south by a point covered with pine woods, Beg-ar-Gador. On the north side, a rocky spur separates Morgat Beach from that of Le Portzic.

The harbour – Fishing boats go out from the harbour, sheltering behind a jetty where 400 pleasure craft can also anchor. Morgat offers all types of fishing to the keen sportsman. From the new jetty, there is a good **view** over the cliff, the natural arch or Gador Gate, Douarnenez Bay and Ménez-Hom.

★**Les grandes grottes** – The first group of big caves, situated beyond Beg-ar-Gador, includes Ste-Marine and the Devil's Chamber (Chambre du Diable). The second group is at the other end of the bay. The finest grotto is that of the Altar (l'Autel), 80m - 262ft deep and 15m - 49ft high. One of its attractions is the colouring of the roofs and walls.

Les petites grottes – Small caves at the foot of the spur between Morgat and Le Portzic beaches can be reached at low tide.

MORLAIX★

Population 16 701

Michelin map 58 fold 6 or 230 fold 5 – Local map under Les ENCLOS PAROISSIAUX

The first thing the tourist will notice at Morlaix is its colossal viaduct. This structure bestrides the deep valley in which lies the estuary of the Dossen, commonly called the River Morlaix. The town is busy but the port, though it is used mostly by yachts, has only limited commercial activity (sand, wood, fertilisers).

HISTORICAL NOTES

Queen Anne's Visit – In 1505, on King Louis XII's recovery from a serious illness, Queen Anne of Brittany decided to make a pilgrimage to the saints of her duchy. She stayed at Morlaix; a wealthy city, which received the Queen sumptuously. She was presented with a little golden ship studded with jewels and a tame ermine wearing a diamond-studded collar (the ermine is Anne of Brittany's emblem). The showpiece of the festival was a live Tree of Jesse representing all the sovereign's ancestors.

If they bite you, bite them! – In 1522 an English fleet of sixty ships came up the river on the tide. The dignitaries of Morlaix were away that day. Pillage followed. But the English troops lingered in the wine cellars and the citizens had time to come back. They fell on the intoxicated intruders and a hard fight ensued. It was then that the town added to its coat of arms a lion facing the English leopard with the motto: "S'ils te mordent, mords-les!"
To guard against another attack the people of Morlaix built, in 1542, the Bull's Castle at the harbour entrance. Louis XIV took it over and made it a state prison in 1660.

Cornic, the "blue" officer – Charles Cornic, known as Duchesne, was the great Morlaix seaman of the 18C. He was born in 1731, and at the age of eight he was sent against his will to work as a ship's boy on a privateer. His exploits were nonetheless such that the King made him lieutenant of a vessel in his Grand Corps. But Cornic was never to be more than an "upstart", a "blue" officer (those officers who had risen through the ranks wore a completely blue uniform), forever subjected to the taunts of

the "red" officers (those who had been through the Marine Guard school, almost all of whom were of aristocratic birth, wore a red and blue uniform). He served for a while with the Merchant Navy, but finally left active service in 1778, retiring never having risen above the rank of captain.
After the Revolution, he was promoted to the rank of Colonel General of the Artillery of Bordeaux in 1790, then deputy minister of the Dalbarade Navy. He later returned to Morlaix, where he studied the setting of buoys in the bay and the defence of the coast. He died in Morlaix in 1809.

The tobacco farm (18C) – There was a tobacco factory founded by the India Company and also a "farm" which had a monopoly of sales. Prices were exorbitant and smuggling thrived. Ships loaded in England with smoking and chewing tobacco and snuff landed on the coast at night. Battles were fought between the smugglers and the farm men.
Morlaix is still a tobacco market. It has a large factory where cigars, cigarillos and snuff are made. Annually it produces approximately 300 million cigars and cigarillos, 30 tons of chewing tobacco and 5 tons of snuff.

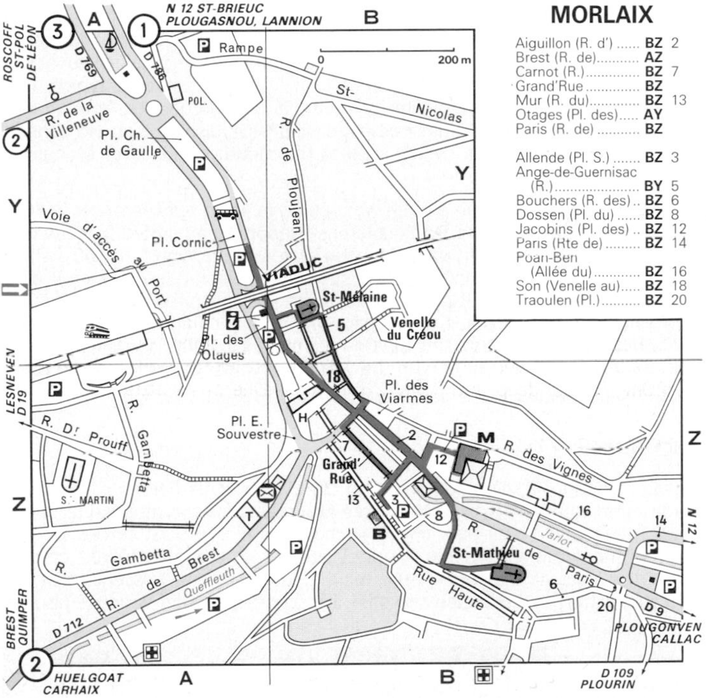

B Maison "de la Reine Anne" **M** Musée des Jacobins

OLD MORLAIX *time: 2 hours*

Leave your car in Place Cornic.

★**Viaduc** (**ABY**) – From Place des Otages there is a good view of the viaduct, an imposing two-storeyed structure, 58m - 190ft high and 285m - 935ft long.

Go up the stairs to the right of the viaduct.

On the left is the 16C Hôtel du Parc, an impressive horseshoe-shaped building.

Église St-Mélaine (**BY**) – The present church, which dates from 1489, is in the Flamboyant Gothic style with an interesting porch on the south side.
Inside, note the modern stained-glass windows designed by Labouret and the vaulting adorned with purlins and tie-beams. A coloured wood panel in the south aisle depicts the Annunciation, the Nativity and the Flight into Egypt; in the north aisle are a font crowned with a carved wood canopy and a Descent from the Cross.

Rue Ange-de-Guernisac (**BY 5**) – This street is lined with fine corbelled and half-timbered houses: the Hôtel du Relais de France at no 13, and the houses at nos 9, 6 and 5 are of interest. Take a look in the picturesque alleyways, Venelle du Créou (**BY**) and Venelle au Son (**BZ 18**).

*Bear right into Rue Carnot (**BZ 7**).*

★**Grand'Rue** (**BZ**) – *Pedestrian precinct.* Here you will see picturesque 15C houses adorned with statues of saints and grotesques, and low-fronted shops with wide windows, especially at nos 8 and 10. Originally these old houses, called **skylight houses**, comprised a large central area with skylights on to which opened the other rooms, linked by a spiral staircase supported by a lovely carved newel post. Queen Anne's House *(see below)* has a fine collection and many illustrations of newel posts.

Walk round Place S.-Allende and up a ramp leading to Rue du Mur.

Maison de la Reine Anne (**BZ B**) ⌚ – This 16C corbelled mansion, three storeys high, has a façade adorned with statues of saints and grotesques. With its courtyard lit by a skylight, the **interior**★ is a perfect example of the skylight house. In one of the courtyard's corners, there is a magnificent spiral staircase, 11m - 36ft high, carved from one piece of wood. The newel post is adorned with saints carved in the round: St Roch, St Nicholas, St Christopher and St Michael. Between the first and second floors, note the fine sculpture of an acrobat with his barrel. There is a monumental stone chimney-piece opposite the staircase.

★**Musée des Jacobins** (**BZ M**) ⌚ – The museum is housed in the former Church of the Jacobins, which has a fine early 15C **rose window**★ at the east end. The exhibits include the finds from archaeological digs in the region, mementoes of Morlaix's famous citizens and of Old Morlaix with its skylight houses: 16C carved newel posts. Also on display are a large collection of 13-17C religious statues, typical 17C furniture of the Léon region (chests, tester beds), household objects, farming and craft implements, and a collection of **modern paintings**★. On display is an old cannon from the privateer's ship *Alcida*, which sank at the mouth of the River Morlaix in 1747 (found in 1879).

Église St-Mathieu (**BZ**) ⌚ – The church was rebuilt in 1824 but the tower is 16C. Inside, it has a basilical plan and Doric columns supporting a pointed barrel vault. To the left of the high altar is an unusual wood statue of the **Virgin**★ (*c* 14C) which opens. When closed it represents the Virgin suckling the Infant Jesus; open it contains a group of the Holy Trinity. On the shutters are illustrated six scenes from the life of Christ: the Annunciation, the Nativity, the Presentation at the Temple, the Flagellation, the Resurrection and the Descent into Hell. In the north aisle stands a fine 16C wooden statue of Christ with the Virgin Mary and St John the Evangelist.

Via Rue de l'Aiguillon and Place des Otages, return to Place Cornic.

EXCURSIONS

★**Plougonven** – *12km - 7 miles southeast on the D 9 towards Callac.*
This village, nestling at the foot of the Arrée Mountains, has an interesting parish close *(qv)*. The **Calvary**★★ was built in 1554; the cross in two tiers, carries, above, the statues of the Virgin and St John, and, below, two guards; the thieves' crosses stand on either side. At the foot of the main cross there is a Descent from the Cross. On the platform and around the base are scenes depicting various episodes

D. Thaulin-Hommell

Morlaix

in the life of Christ: the Temptation in the Desert, His Arrest, etc. The charnel house presents a trefoil arcade and a basket-handle arched doorway.
The **church**, built in 1523 and badly damaged by fire in the early 20C, is dominated by a graceful belfry with a balcony, a turreted staircase and striking gargoyles.

Ploujean - *3km - 2 miles north via ① on the town plan.*
This town, situated in the suburbs of Morlaix, is famous as the birthplace of the poet Tristan Corbière (1845-75), and of the first French astronaut, J.-L. Chrétien. In the 11C church, remodelled in the 15C, note a fine 15C statue of the Virgin on a pillar in the Romanesque nave. In the chapel to the right of the chancel, stands Marshal Foch's pew which he used whenever he stayed at his nearby estate (north-east of Ploujean). There is a monument dedicated to him at the church's east end.

Guerlesquin – *23km - 14 miles by the D 712 east and the D 42 south.*
This small town, with its atmosphere of yesteryear, is a good example of a type of urban plan where the central area is subdivided, by the location of the different public buildings (prison, market, church...), into "squares" lined with houses similar in style: all built in granite with regular stonework; some date from the 15C. On Place Prosper-Proux stands the old prison, the Présidial (1650), flanked by four battlemented turrets; the prison was on the ground floor and the guards lived above.

MUR-DE-BRETAGNE

Population 2 049
Michelin map 59 fold 12 or 230 fold 22

This is one of the liveliest towns in the interior of Brittany.

Chapelle Ste-Suzanne – The chapel stands to the north of the town in a very pretty wooded setting. The splendid oak trees which surround it are several centuries old and inspired the painter Corot (1796-1875) on several occasions. The chapel's elegant **belfry-porch** dates from 1760. Inside, the remarkable 18C **painted ceiling★**, recently restored, is dedicated to Ste Suzanne.

Rond-Point du Lac – In the village, a road to the right leads to a roundabout, which affords a lovely **view★** of Guerlédan Lake and dam *(qv)*.

EXCURSION

Vallée du Poulancre – *6.5km - 4 miles north to St-Gilles-Vieux-Marché.* The valley is deeply sunk between rocky and wooded slopes and forms narrow and very picturesque gorges. It leads to the pretty flower-bedecked village of St-Gilles-Vieux-Marché.

NANTES★★★

Conurbation 492 255

Michelin map 67 fold 3 or 230 folds 54 and 55 or 232 fold 28

Plan of the conurbation in the current Michelin Red Guide France.

Nantes is many cities combined: a city of the arts, a great industrial city, and the seat of a big university.
Located at the confluence of the rivers Loire, Sèvre and Erdre, Nantes is the historic capital of the Dukes of Brittany and has now become the capital of the region called Pays de la Loire. The three ports of Donges, Nantes and St-Nazaire have merged and follow the estuary from Nantes up to the Atlantic Ocean.
At the heart of the city, opposite the southern station, the new **Cité des Congrès** (**HZ**) is equipped with high technology facilities which place it at the forefront of the conference centres on the Atlantic coast.

HISTORICAL NOTES

Nantes, capital of Brittany – Nantes, first Gallic and then Roman, was involved in the bloody struggle between the Frankish kings and the Breton noblemen. But it was the Vikings who did the most damage. In 843 the pirates landed, rushed into the cathedral, where the Bishop was saying Mass, and put the prelate, the clergy and the congregation to death. In 939, young Alain Barbe-Torte (Crookbeard), a descendant of the great Breton chiefs, who had taken refuge in England, returned to the country and drove the invaders out of Brittany. Having become duke, he chose Nantes as his capital and rebuilt it. Nantes was the capital of the Duchy of Brittany several times during the Middle Ages, in rivalry with Rennes. The dukes of the House of Montfort *(qv)*, especially **François II**, governed as undisputed sovereigns and restored the prestige of the town and its title of capital.

Edict of Nantes (13 August 1598) – In 1597, Brittany, tired of disorder and suffering caused by the League and also of the separatist ambitions of its Governor, Philip of Lorraine, sent a pressing appeal to Henri IV, asking him to come and restore order. Before the castle he whistled with admiration. "God's teeth", he exclaimed, "the Dukes of Brittany were no small beer!" The royal visit was marked by a great historic event: on 13 August 1598, Henri IV signed the *Edict of Nantes*, which, in ninety-two articles, settled the religious question – or so he thought.

Sugar and "ebony" – From the 16 to the 18C, Nantes had two main sources of revenue: sugar and the slave trade, known discreetly as the "ebony trade". In the Antilles, the slaver would sell the slaves bought on the Guinea coast and buy cane sugar, to be refined at Nantes and sent up the Loire. The "ebony" made an average profit of 200%.
Philosophers inveighed against this inhuman traffic, but Voltaire, whose business acumen is well known, had a 5 000 *livres* share in a slave ship from Nantes. At the end of the 18C the prosperity of Nantes was at its height: it had become the first port of France; its fleet included 2 500 ships and barques. The big ship-owners and traders founded dynasties and built the fine mansions on Quai de la Fosse and the former Feydeau Islet.
It was said of the Nantais **Cassard** (1672-1740) that he was France's "greatest seaman". The daring, skill and luck with which he passed convoys of supplies through the strictest blockade have remained legendary.

All drowned – In June 1793, Nantes numbered many royalists. The Convention sent **Carrier**, the Deputy of the Cantal, there as its representative in early October. Carrier had already spent some time at Rennes *(qv)*. His mission was "to purge the body politic of all the rotten matter it contained".
The revolutionary tribunal had filled the prisons with Vendéens, priests and suspects, and a problem arose: how to make room for new arrivals. Carrier chose drowning. Condemned people were put into barges which were scuttled in the Loire, opposite Chantenay. When informed, the Convention immediately recalled its delegate. He was put on trial and was sent before the Nantes Revolutionary court, sentenced to death and guillotined in December.
In 1832 tragedy gave way to farce. The **Duchess of Berry**, a mortal enemy of Louis-Philippe, was convinced that Brittany was still legitimist and scoured the Nantes countryside. Her failure was complete. She took refuge at Nantes but was betrayed. The police invaded the house (**HY B**) and found it empty, but kept it under surveillance. Feeling cold, they lit a fire in one room. Their surprise was great when the chimney-shutter fell open and out on all fours came the duchess and three of her followers, black as sweeps and half suffocated. They had spent sixteen hours in the thickness of the wall.

Development – The abolition of the slave trade by the Revolution, the substitution of French beet for Antilles sugar cane under the Empire, and finally the increase in tonnage and draught of ships, making them unable to reach Nantes, were great blows to the town. Nantes abandoned its maritime ambitions and turned to metallurgy and

the making of foodstuffs. A manufacturer named Collin developed a method of preserving food (1824) which had been patented by Appert in 1809.
In 1856 Nantes, again with an eye to the sea, founded an outer port at St-Nazaire; the city then dug a lateral canal in 1892. As of 1911, when dredging techniques had improved, the canal was abandoned and shipping returned to the estuary. Merchant ships of 8.25m - 27ft draught can now come up to Nantes when tides are high.

Nantes today – Over the years, Nantes has been reconstructed and transformed, a process which is still going on. An effort was made to preserve the 18C character of its old districts and the many new buildings have been nicely incorporated into the town as exemplified by Le Corbusier's living unit (*unité d'habitation*, 1955) at **Rezé** or the media centre at Quai de la Fosse. The east of **île Beaulieu**, with its regional centre identifiable by its metallic blue dome, forms a striking contrast with the western section of the harbour, bristling with cranes and warehouses and popular districts. Located on the former **île Gloriette** (**GZ**) are the Faculties of Medicine and Pharmacy. While on the former **île Feydeau** (named after the intendant of Brittany Feydau de Brou) (**GZ**) Nantes has retained one of the most splendid examples of 18C civilian architecture in France, only a few steps away from this "temple of good taste" stands the highly modern **Cité des Congrès** *(see above)*, combining efficiency and comfort.

Place de Bretagne (**GY 27**) in the centre of town, is witness to this change: the 24-storey Tour de Bretagne, rises opposite the 1954 Social Security and 1961 Post-Office buildings. North of Nantes, on the south bank of the Erdre, is the university campus. A pedestrian zone, in the Change district, includes Place du Change, Rue des Halles, Rue des Carmes, Rue du Moulin, Rue Ste-Croix and Rue de la Juiverie.

A city of flowers – Nantes the city profited from Nantes the port in innumerable ways. In the 17C the arrival of exotic plants produced an interest in botany and gardens. This phenomenon has not only enhanced the city but has also remained important to it ever since, as can be seen today, with the 570ha - 1 408 acres of greenery scattered throughout the city.
The parks, gardens and squares planted with magnolias, rhododendrons, camellias, exotic trees etc. are a delight to all. Note the Jardin des Plantes, the Parc de Procé, the Parc de la Beaujoire and the landscaped cemetery *(cimetière paysager)* to name but a few. Nantes is famous worldwide on account of its horticultural production, consisting principally of lily-of-the-valley, camellias and magnolias.

The port – The port installations in Nantes are managed by the Autonomous Port Authority of Nantes-St-Nazaire. The port with the Cheviré industrial zone, located on the river's north bank, offers 5km – 3 miles of public quays and equipment, which include cranes, grain silos, cold store plants etc. Basse-Indre and Couëron are annexes of the port.
Port traffic, concentrating mainly on the Quays Wilson, Roche-Maurice and Cheviré, is made up mainly of timber, fruit, early vegetables, sugar, fertilisers, wine, petroleum products, grain and tin plate. Nantes is the leading port of France for the import of timber. Thanks to the recent acquisition of container ships, Nantes is now ranked 3rd port in France.

Industrial activity – From an economic viewpoint, this region is traditionally known for its naval construction (Chantiers de l'Atlantique, ACB, Leroux et Lotz) and its food industry (Biscuits Nantais, LU, Saupiquet, la Cana, Val Nantais). But the local industry has become firmly established in a number of other areas – aeronautics, mechanics, computer technology, electronics and plastics processes – a fact confirmed by the presence of leaders such as Aérospatiale, Famat and Matra MHS.
This industrial dynamism also relies on a healthy tertiary sector (banking, engineering, communications, advertising) and a strong intellectual tradition thanks to its twelve prestigious graduate schools, its university campus and, more recently, its research centre featuring 1 500 scientists and 120 scientific laboratories.

★★ CHÂTEAU DES DUCS DE BRETAGNE (HY) ⏱ *time: 2 hours*

The golden age of the castle was the age of Duke François II, when court life was truly regal: five ministers, seventeen chamberlains and a host of retainers attended the Duke. Life was sumptuous and morals liberal.
The present building was begun by Duke François II in 1466 and continued by his daughter, Anne of Brittany. Defence works were added during the League by the Duke of Mercœur. From the 18C onwards the military took possession, destroyed some buildings and erected others lacking in style. The Spaniards' Tower (**1**), which had been used as a magazine, blew up in 1800 (*the north part of the castle was destroyed – the sites of the destroyed buildings are indicated by a broken line on the plan overleaf*). From Charles VII to Louis XIV, nearly all the Kings of France spent some time at the castle: Louis XII married Anne of Brittany in its chapel (1499); it was here that Henri IV signed the *Edict of Nantes* in 1598. Chalais, Cardinal de Retz, Gilles de Rais (Bluebeard) and the Duchess of Berry were imprisoned in its towers.

A. Le Bot/DIAF

Nantes – Château des Ducs de Bretagne

An arm of the Loire washed the south, east and northeast walls until the building of a quay in the 19C and the filling up in the 20C of a branch of the Loire.

The fortress – The moat has now been reestablished; the ditches which guarded the north and west sides have been turned into gardens and the old ditches have been restored on the other sides. An 18C bridge leads to the former drawbridge which is flanked by two massive round towers dating from the time of Duke François.

The palace – Behind the massive defensive walls, the court was used for jousting and tournaments, also for the performance of mystery plays and farces.
The 15C **Bakery Tower** (*not open to the public*), also called Tower of Hell, was used as a prison, a theory confirmed by the graffiti one could see on the walls.
The elegant **Golden Crown Tower**★ (Tour de la Couronne d'Or), whose name may be explained by the presence of a nearby well, presents fine Italian-style loggias and connects two pavilions pierced by rows of windows The 15C **Jacobins Tower** was also used as a prison (carved graffiti).
The **main building**, built by François II and extended two storeys by Anne of Brittany, was the ducal palace. It is decorated by five tall Gothic dormer windows with ornate pinnacles.

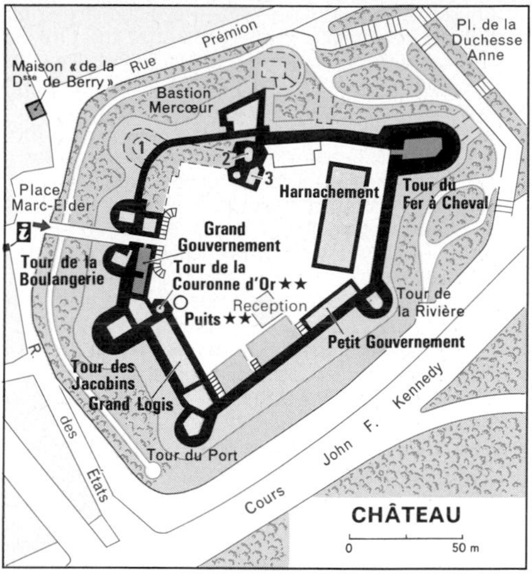

This part of the castle took the name **Governor's Major Palace** after the 1670 fire, which destroyed a whole wing of the castle. It then became the home of the governor of Brittany. During the reign of the dukes, it had been their palace and had been used for meetings concerning the Duchy.
Over the **well★★**, which probably dates back to the days of François II, there is a wrought-iron framework, which represents the ducal crown. The seven-sided curb of the well has seven pulleys and seven gargoyles for the overflow.
The Renaissance **Governor's Lesser Palace** was built under François I; the military **Saddlery**, dating back to 1784 was the armoury.
The old keep (**2**) is, in fact, one of the four polygonal towers, which enclosed the original castle built in the 13C and enlarged in the 14C; it is part of an 18C mansion, which houses the porter's lodge (**3**).
The **Horseshoe Tower** is 16C. In the restored rooms, special lighting enhances the vaulting with armorial-decorated keystones. Temporary exhibitions are held alternately, presenting the works formerly displayed in the Musée des Salorges.

Nantes derives its name from the *Namnètes*, a Gallic tribe who made the town their capital. The Romans developed it as a trading centre; the Vikings pillaged then occupied Nantes. In the early 20C, a plan for urban renewal greatly altered the face of the town, as did the massive destruction of the Second World War. The cathedral, striking for its Gothic unity despite the long building period, was bombed during the war, and had been nearly completely restored in 1972 when fire largely destroyed the roof. The medieval castle is remarkable for its contrasts: outside, a fortress with its crenellated towers; inside, a typical Renaissance palace. These rare historic buildings are the architectural pride of Nantes.

CATHÉDRALE ST-PIERRE ET ST-PAUL (HY) ⌚ *time: 30 min*

This imposing building, begun in 1434, completed in 1893 and restored after serious fire damage in 1972, is remarkable for its austere façade restored in 1930: two plain towers frame a Flamboyant window; note the 15C canopied niches which decorate the pillars supporting the towers. The three portals reveal finely sculpted recessed arches and on the central portal stands a statue of St Peter. From the north side one can see the chevet with its ring of fine apsidal chapels crowned by graceful pinnacles.

★★ **Interior** – Here, at Nantes, white stone replaces the granite used in purely Breton cathedrals. Being less heavy, this stone made it possible to build vaults 37.50m - 123ft high (the vaulting of Westminster Abbey is 30.50m - 100ft high).
As you enter you will be struck by the nave's pure, soaring lines, a fine example of Flamboyant work. Stand under the organ loft to appreciate the effect; you will see a double row of vertical lines springing from the ground and shooting without a break up to the delicately carved keystones of the vaults, where they cross.
Everything is based on elevation and the dimension of 37.50m - 123ft loses significance. Seen from this angle, the slender ribs of the pillars mask not only the flat wall surfaces that separate them but all the lines, curved or horizontal, of the arcades, the triforium or the upper windows which could break the harmony of this vista, composed entirely of parallel vertical elements.
Go round the building to the right.
In the south transept is the decorative masterpiece of the cathedral and a very great Renaissance work: the **tomb of François II★★**. It was carved between 1502 and 1507 by Michel Colombe, a sculptor who was born in Brittany but settled in the Touraine. It was commissioned by Anne of Brittany to receive the remains of her father, François II, and her mother, Marguerite of Foix, and it was placed in the

Church of the Carmelites. The Revolutionary Tribunal ordered it to be demolished, but the courageous town architect of the time, instead of obeying the order, hid various pieces of the tomb in his friends' homes. It was reconstructed after the Revolution and transferred to the cathedral in 1817.
The Duke and Duchess recline on a black marble slab placed on a rectangular one in white marble. The statues grouped round them are symbolic: the angels supporting their heads represent their welcome to Heaven; the lion crouching at the feet of François stands for power, and Marguerite's greyhound for fidelity. The four large corner statues personify the four Cardinal Virtues: for the Duke, Justice (crowned and holding a sword) and Strength (helmeted and armed and expelling a dragon from a tower); Prudence and Temperance guard the Duchess. Prudence has two faces: in front, a young girl with a looking glass, symbolising the future, and behind, an old man representing the past. Temperance holds a bridle to signify control over passions, and a clock representing steadiness.
Below the recumbent figures are sixteen niches containing the statues of saints interceding for the deceased, notably St Francis of Assisi and St Margaret, their patrons. Below the saints, sixteen mourners, partly damaged, represent their people's sorrow.
This magnificent group is lit by a superb modern **stained-glass window**, 25m - 80ft high and 5.30m - 14ft wide devoted to Breton and Nantes saints, the work of Chapuis. You should pause at the transept crossing, where the impression of height is astonishing.
In the north arm of the transept is the **Cenotaph of Lamoricière★**, the work of the sculptor Paul Dubois (1879). The General is shown reclining under a shroud. Four bronze statues represent Meditation and Charity (at his head) and Military Courage and Faith (at his feet). Lamoricière (1806-65), a great African campaigner who came from Nantes, captured the Arabian Emir Abd-el-Kaderin 1847 during the wars in Algeria. He later fell into disgrace and when exiled by Napoleon III commanded Papal troops against the Italians. It is the Catholic paladin who is honoured here.
The apsidal chapel contains lovely abstract stained-glass windows by Jean Le Moal.

GOING OUT IN NANTES

To learn about all the various forms of entertainment (festivals, plays, concerts, films) organised in and around Nantes, consult the monthly bulletin issued by the Tourist Information Office: "*Des Jours et des Nuits*".

Main Venues:

Opéra/Théâtre Graslin, 1, Rue Molière.
Auditorium du Conservatoire, Rue Gaëtan-Rondeau, île Beaulieu.
Espace 44, Rue du Général-Buat.
Théâtre de Poche Graslin, 5, Rue Lekain.
Palais des Sports Beaulieu, Rue André-Tardieu, île Beaulieu.
Cité des Congrès, 1, Rue de Valmy.

Public Transport (Semitan)

The 2 tramway routes (27km - 17 miles), the longest in France, and the 57 bus routes make for quick and convenient travelling in the city of Nantes (operational all year, except on 1 May).
Transport tickets, used for both buses and tramways, can be purchased from automatic vending machines, from TAN establishments and TAN kiosks (the main one is at the stop known as Commerce).
The best way to visit the town is to buy a daily pass, called *"ticket journalier"* (18F), which permits unlimited travelling for the whole of the day.

TOWN CENTRE

★★ **Musée des Beaux Arts** (**HY M[1]**) ⓥ – The museum is housed in an imposing late 19C building, the main part of which is flanked by projecting wings. The collections, enriched by exhibits from the depository, cover the 13C to the present. A central patio is surrounded by large galleries with works exhibited in chronological order.
Among the Italian Primitives note Perugino's *Saint Sebastian* portrayed as an elegant page holding an arrow; the 17C is represented by such masters as Rubens *(The Triumph of Judas the Maccabee)* and Georges de La Tour *(Saint Peter's Denial, The Angel Appearing to Joseph in His Dream, The Hurdy-Gurdy Player)*.

Representing the 18C French School are Greuze *(The Guitarist)* and Watteau (*Harlequin, Emperor of the Moon*). Classicism and Romanticism are represented by Ingres's fine portrait *Madame Senonnes*, Delacroix's *Kaïd, The Moroccan Chief* and Courbet's The *Winnowers*.

The 20C collections are displayed in seven large galleries. In the first, works illustrating the period from Impressionism to the Fauves include Monet's *Nymphéas*, Emile Bernard's *Apple Tree Beating*, representing the Pont-Aven school, Sonia Delaunay's *Yellow Nude*, a Fauve work, and *Château de Clisson* by Nantes artist Metzinger.

The second gallery contains a collection, which must be unique in a provincial museum, of paintings by Vasili Kandinsky executed during the years he taught at the Bauhaus (1922-1933). The homogeneity of this collection, which features in particular *Black Frame* and the bright *Évènement doux*, revolves around the idea of a "microcosm".

The third gallery exhibits different artistic movements from the period 1913-1945, notably two works by the Constructivist Gorin, *Two Women Standing* by a Magnelli at the intersection of Futurism and Cubism, as well as two paintings by Chagall executed at a particularly testing time in his life, *Red Horse* and *Obsession*.

The fourth gallery plunges the viewer into the cultural context of the period 1940-60, with figurative works by Lapicque *(Sunset on the Salute)*, Hélion *(Still Life with Pumpkin)* and abstract works by Poliakoff, Hartung, Bissière and the Nantes artist Camille Bryen.

The fifth gallery covers the period from 1960-75. It focuses principally on the Nantes artist Martin Barré, but also exhibits the interesting work of François Morellet, representing Kinetic art.

The sixth gallery is largely given over to the Seventies and Eighties. Note in particular *Promenade of the Blue Cavalier*, a charming abstract work by Thiéval, large "canvases" by Viallat and above all two Picassos, among the master's last works, **Couple★** and **Man Seated with Walking Stick.** Finally, there are three works by Dubuffet, including *Setting with two Figures F 106*.

The final gallery devotes a large area to contemporary European artistic expression. Rebecca Horn's *Hydrapiano*, with the bizarre behaviour of its long column of mercury, is particularly eye-catching.

Place Maréchal-Foch (**HY**) – Two fine 18C hotels, built from the plans by Ceineray, flank the Louis XVI Column which was erected in 1790. From the square, commonly called Place Louis XVI, which is prolonged by Cours St-André and St-Pierre, you can readily appreciate the dimensions of the cathedral, in particular its soaring height.

Porte St-Pierre (**HY**) – This 15C gateway stands on the remains of a 3C Gallo-Roman wall. The gateway is built into an elegant turreted building, which was once part of the episcopal residence.

Skirt the cathedral façade; go through the portal on the left.

La Psalette (**HY D**) – This 15C building with a polygonal turret formerly contained the chapter-house but is now part of the sacristy.

Take the vaulted passageway on the right.

From the small square you can see the other side of La Psalette.

Bear right on Impasse St-Laurent then left into Rue Mathelin-Rodier (the name of the architect of the cathedral and part of the castle).

It was in the house at no 3 (**HY B**) that the Duchess of Berry *(qv)* was arrested.

Pass the Château des Ducs de Bretagne on the left.

Plateau Ste-Croix – It is an area where 15 and 16C half-timbered houses still stand: no 7 Rue de la Juiverie, no 7 Rue Ste-Croix, nos 8 and 10 Rue de la Boucherie, no 5 Rue Bossuet and Place du Change.

Église Ste-Croix (**GY**) – This 17C church is surmounted by the former town belfry crowned with trumpeting angels. The palm tree decoration of the chancel vaulting contrasts with the round vaulting of the nave. Large Flamboyant windows open onto the aisles. The furnishings are 18C.

★**The 19C town** – It was the financier **Graslin**, Receiver General for Farmlands at Nantes, who was responsible for the creation of this area. By way of Place du Pilori, surrounded by 18C houses, make for **Place Royale** (**GZ**), which was built by Crucy, the architect of the Stock Exchange (Bourse). This is adorned by a fountain representing Nantes (1865).

Rue Crébillon (**GZ 60**) is narrow, commercial and very busy.

Opening onto Rue Santeuil on the left, is a curious stepped shopping arcade, the **Passage Pommeraye★** (**GZ 150**), built in 1843, which goes down to the Stock Exchange. Great fluted columns support galleries lined with elegant shops, and statue-adorned pedestals serve as bases for lamps.

Return to Rue Crébillon, the fine **Place Graslin** (**FZ**) dominated by the Corinthian-style Grand Théâtre (1783). The café on the corner, La Cigale, still has a turn-of-the-century air and fine mosaics. Leading off from the same corner is **Cours Cambronne★** (**FZ**) lined with late-18C and early-19C pilastered houses.

Barillerie (R. de la)	**GY**	9
Boileau (R.)	**GZ**	15
Budapest (R. de)	**GY**	31
Calvaire (R. du)	**FY**	33
Crébillon (R.)	**FGZ**	60
Feltre (R. de)	**GY**	79
Fosse (R. de la)	**GZ**	81
J.-J.-Rousseau (R.)	**FGZ**	99
Juiverie (R. de la)	**GY**	105
Marne (R. de la)	**GY**	120
Orléans (R. d')	**GZ**	135
Paix (R. de la)	**GZ**	138
Racine (R.)	**FZ**	
Royale (Pl.)	**GZ**	
Santeuil (R.)	**GZ**	183
Scribe (R.)	**FZ**	187
Verdun (R. de)	**GY**	199
Albert (R. du Roi)	**GY**	3
Anne-de-Bretagne (Pont)	**FZ**	6
Audibert (Pont Gén.)	**HZ**	7
Belleville (R. de)	**EZ**	13
Bossuet (R.)	**GY**	16
Boucherie (R. de la)	**GY**	18
Bouhier (Pl. R.)	**EZ**	19
Bouille (R. de)	**GY**	21
Bourse (Pl. de la)	**GZ**	24
Brasserie (R. de la)	**EZ**	25
Bretagne (Pl. de)	**GY**	27
Briand (Pont A.)	**HZ**	28
Brunellière (R. Ch.)	**FZ**	30
Ceineray (Quai)	**GY**	36
Change (Pl. du)	**GY**	37
Château (R. du)	**GY**	40
Clemenceau (R. G.)	**HY**	46
Clisson (Cours Olivier de)	**GZ**	48
Commerce (Pl. du)	**GZ**	49
Constant (Bd Clovis)	**EY**	51
Contrescarpe (R. de la)	**GY**	52
Copernic (R.)	**FZ**	54
Coulmiers (R. de)	**HY**	57
Delorme (Pl.)	**FY**	63
Desgrées-du-Lou (R. du Col.)	**EY**	64
Distillerie (R. de la)	**GY**	66
Douet-Garnier (R. du)	**EY**	69
Duchesse-Anne (Pl.)	**HY**	72
Duguay-Trouin (Allée)	**GZ**	73
Estienne-d'Orves (Crs d')	**HZ**	76
Favre (Quai F.)	**HYZ**	78
Frachon (Bd B.)	**EZ**	82
Haudaudine (Pont)	**GZ**	90
Hélie (R. F.)	**FY**	91
Henri-IV (R.)	**HY**	93
Hermitage (R. de)	**EZ**	94
Hôtel-de-Ville (R. de l')	**GY**	96
Kennedy (Crs J.-F.)	**HY**	106

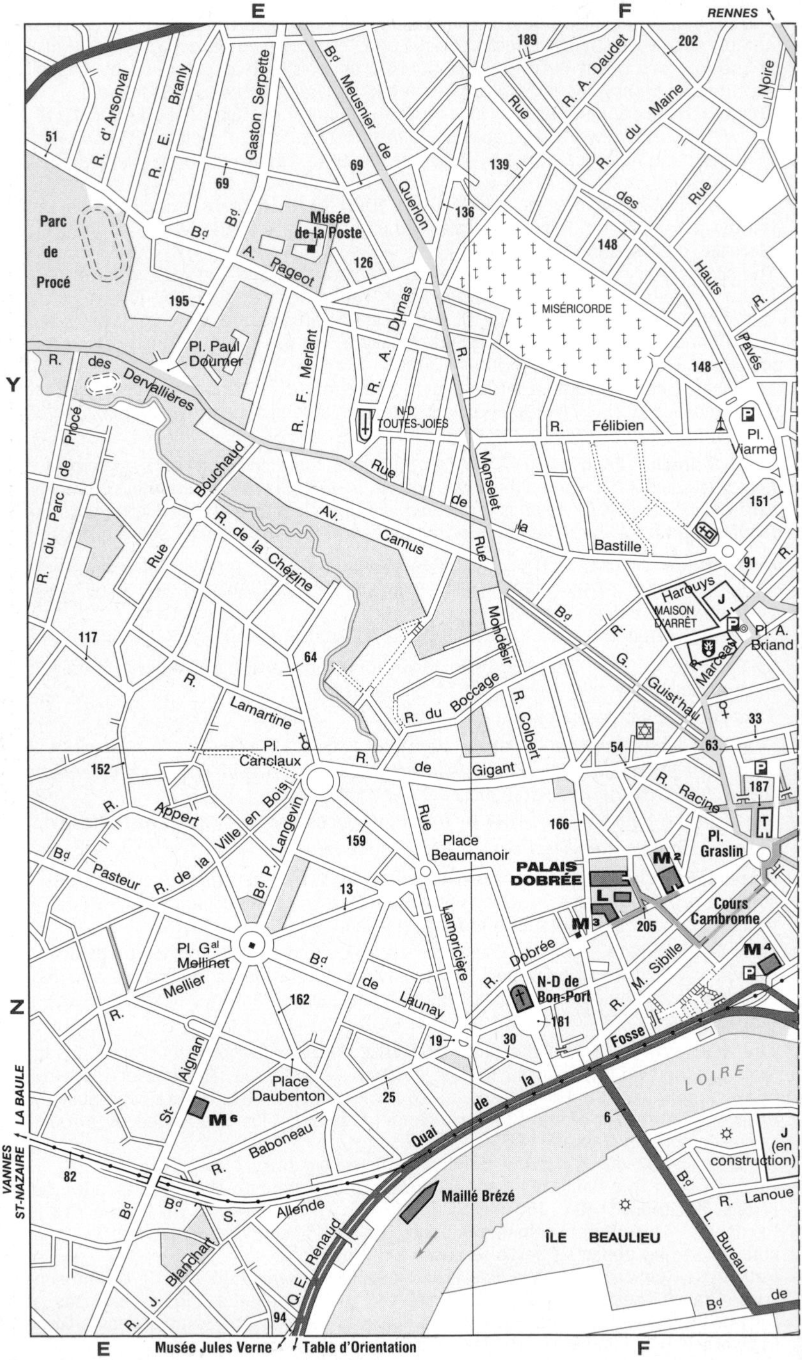

Korvégan (R.) .... GZ 107
Lattre-de-Tassigny
(R. Mar. de) .... FGZ 109
Leclerc (R. Mar.) .... GY 114
Littré (R.) .... EY 117
Martyrs-Nantais-
de-la-Résist. (Bd) .... HZ 121
Mathelin-Rodier (R.) .... HY 123
Mercœur (R.) .... FGY 124
Merson (Bd L.-O.) .... EY 126
Nations-Unies (Bd des) ..... GZ 132
Painlevé (R. Paul) .... EY 136
Pelleterie (R. de la) .... EFY 139
Petite-Hollande (Pl.) .... GZ 142
Pilori (Pl. du) .... GY 144
Poitou (R. du) .... FY 148
Pommeraye (Pas.) .... GZ 150
Porte-Neuve (R.) .... FGY 151
Raspail (R.) .... EYZ 152
Refoulais (R. L. de la) .... HY 153
République (Pl. de la) .... GZ 156
Ricordeau (Pl. A.) .... GZ 157
Riom (R. Alfred) .... EZ 159
Rollin (R.) .... EZ 162
Roosevelt (Crs F.) .... GZ 165
Rosière d'Artois
(R. de la) .... FZ 166
St-André (Cours) .... HY 168
St-Mihiel (Pont) .... GY 172
St-Pierre (Crs) .... HY 174
St-Pierre (Pl.) .... GY 175
St-Rogatien (R.) .... HY 177
Salengro (Pl. R.) .... GY 180
Sanitat (Pl.) .... FZ 181
Simon (R. Jules) .... EY 189
Talensac (R.) .... GY 192
Thomas (Bd A.) .... EY 195
Turenne (Allée de) .... GZ 198
Villebois-Mareuil (R.) .... FY 202
Voltaire (R.) .... FZ 205
Waldeck-Rousseau (Pl.) .. GHY 207
50-Otages (Crs des) .... GYZ 208

B Maison « de la duchesse de Berry »
D La Psalette
F Église St-Nicolas
L Manoir de la Touche
M[1] Musée des Beaux-Arts
M[2] Muséum d'Histoire naturelle
M[3] Musée archéologique
M[4] Musée de l'Imprimerie
M[6] Musée de la Poupée et des Jouets anciens
M[7] Maison de l'Erdre

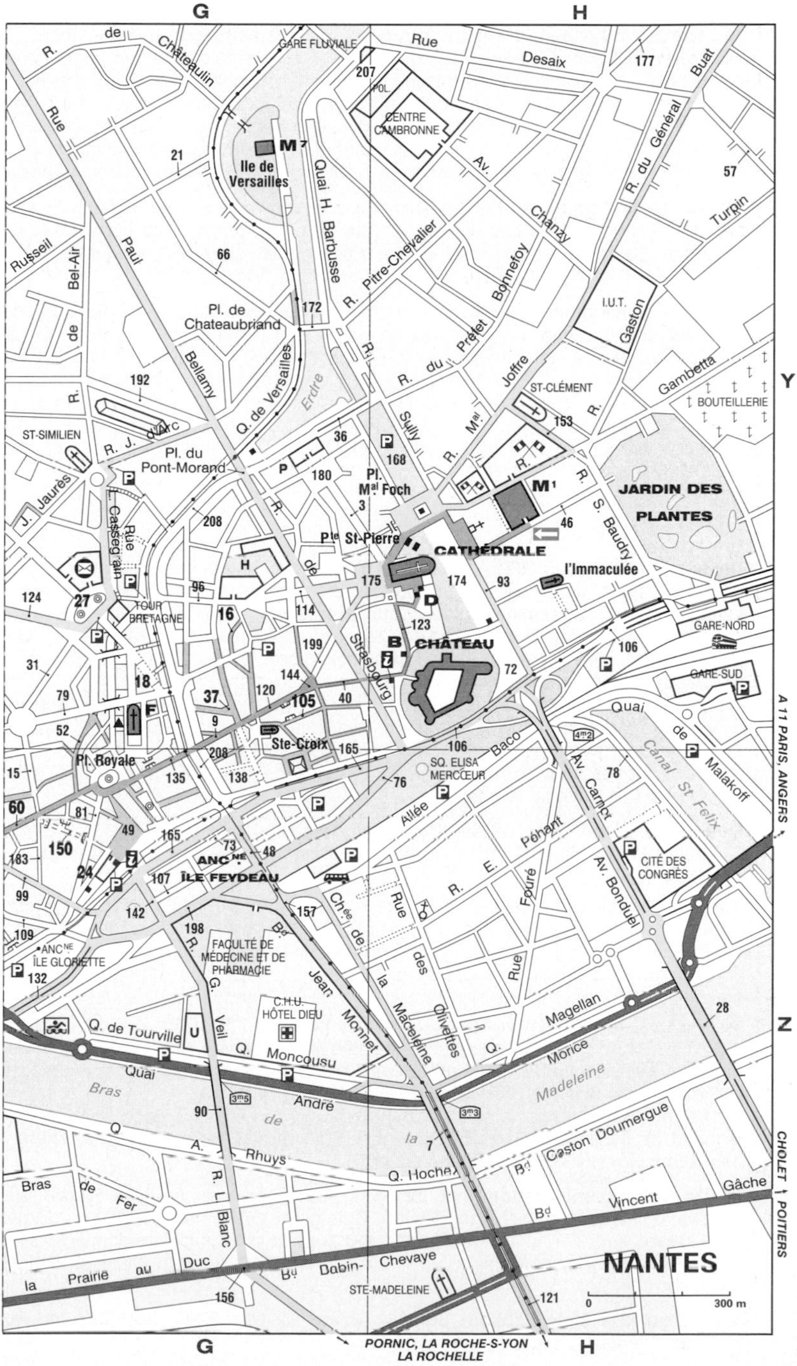

★★ **Muséum d'Histoire naturelle** ⓥ (**FZ M²**) – Originally set up in the Cabinet Dubuisson in 1799, this natural history museum was later moved to the former Mint (Hôtel de la Monnaie) and inaugurated in 1875. It houses several important collections in such varied areas as zoology, regional fauna, osteology, palaeontology, prehistory, sciences of the earth, mineralogy and ethnography. The section devoted to shells is remarkable on account of the sheer beauty and variety of the exhibits. A vivarium presents reptiles and batrachians from all over the world.
The museum features an auditorium (conferences and educational activities), a public library with scientific books, as well as a "Science and Nature" area specially designed for groups of pupils.

★ **Palais Dobrée** (**FZ**) ⓥ – This Romanesque-style mansion was built in the 19C by the Nantes ship-owner and collector **Thomas Dobrée** (1810-95).
On the ground floor Romanesque and Gothic sculptures from Nantes and the Val de Loire are presented in a modern setting: 4 large statues from the cathedral's bell tower, decorated purlins and corner posts; the armoury exhibits items from the Bronze Age to the 19C. Displayed around the reliquary containing the heart of Anne of Brittany (1516) are medieval ivories and alabasters, champlevé enamels (12-14C) from the Limousin, Rhine and Moselle regions, paintings and jewellery. On the first floor are 16-19C furnishings, paintings, tapestries, painted enamels, gold and silversmith work, ceramics, portraits, jewellery and Dobrée family memorabilia.

Manoir de la Touche (**FZ L**) ⓥ – This house is known as Jean V's Manor-House, because Jean V, a duke and member of the Montfort family, died here in 1442. Exhibited inside are collections (arms, documents, paintings, costumes, etc.) evoking the French Revolution and the Wars of the Vendée (1793-5).

★ **Musée archéologique** (**FZ M³**) ⓥ – *Entrance Rue Voltaire.* The first floor of this archaeological museum concentrates on Greek and Etruscan pottery and all that is Egyptian (sarcophagi, canopic vases – funerary urns, the covers of which are in the form of an animal or human head – bronze and painted statuettes).
The second floor concentrates on local civilizations covering prehistory to the invasion of the Norsemen, with displays of arms, tools, terracotta and bronze vases, jewellery, items from St-Nazaire dating from the neolithic to the Bronze Age, and Gallo-Roman objects excavated at Rezé (Loire-Atlantique).

ADDITIONAL SIGHTS

★ **Ancienne île Feydeau** (**GZ**) – Between 1926 and 1938 the islet was linked to the mainland and a second island, the île Gloriette, by filling in several arms of the Loire. The islet has retained its 18C appearance, especially between Place de la Petite Hollande and Cours Olivier-de-Clisson (no 4 was the birthplace of Jules Verne, *qv*). It was here that rich ship-owners used to build their vast mansions which stretch from the central street, Rue Kervégan, right back to one of the outer avenues, Allées Turenne or Duguay-Trouin. Curved wrought-iron balconies and grotesque masks, probably the work of seafaring craftsmen, adorn the façades. The inner courtyards have staircases with remarkable vaulting.
Opposite, on the northern bank, there are also some fine 18C houses (nos 7 and 11) on **Place de la Bourse** (**GZ 24**).

Quai de la Fosse (**EFZ**) – Several 18C mansions line this quay (nos 17, 54, 70), including no 86, Hôtel Durbé, whose outbuildings served as a warehouse for the India Company *(qv)*.

Musée de l'Imprimerie (**AZ M⁴**) ⓥ – Before entering the workshop, visit the gallery with its lithographs, illuminated manuscripts and engraved wood. In the workshop, composition and printing techniques are illustrated with machines – lithographic and typographic presses, copper-plate engraving press, type-setting and casting machines – all in perfect working order.

Maillé-Brézé ⓥ – Docked on the Loire, this escort ship (132.65m - 434ft long and 12.70m - 40ft wide) was launched in 1957 and served until 1988. The visit includes anti-submarine and anti-aircraft weapons and detection systems, the command post and the officers' and sailors' living quarters.
In the officers' quarters, a small museum evokes the life of French Admiral Jean Armand de Maillé (1619-1646) through literature and various exhibits. There is an interesting tour of the machine room.

Église Notre-Dame-de-Bon-Port (**FZ**) ⓥ – Also known as the **Église St-Louis**, this unusual building overlooks Place Sanitat. This great cubic mass (1846) is adorned by a fresco and a triangular pediment and topped by a majestic dome. Massive hexagonal pillars support the dome decorated alternatively with panels of stained glass and frescoes.

★ **View from Ste-Anne Lookout point** – *Access via Quai E.-Renaud* (**EZ**) *and Rue de l'Hermitage.*

From the terraced lookout point there is a good view of the port installations with cranes in the foreground and shipyards and Beaulieu Islet in the distance. A viewing table *(table d'orientation)* helps the visitor pinpoint Nantes' main sights and its new buildings.

★**Musée Jules-Verne** ⓥ – *No 3 Rue de l'Hermitage* (**EZ 94**). A 19C mansion houses the museum devoted to Jules Verne (1828-1905), one of the first to write science fiction novels such as *Five Weeks in a Balloon, A Journey to the Centre of the Earth* and *Around the World in Eighty Days.*

His life is retraced with the help of memorabilia: autographs, furniture, personal objects, portraits, busts, a planisphere showing his extraordinary journeys, and a collection of his works. Near the Jules Verne museum stands the statue of St Anne, blessing the port. Cross the shaded Place des Garennes which is overlooked by the west front of the Eglise Ste-Anne and take Rue des Garennes to reach Square Maurice-Schwob.

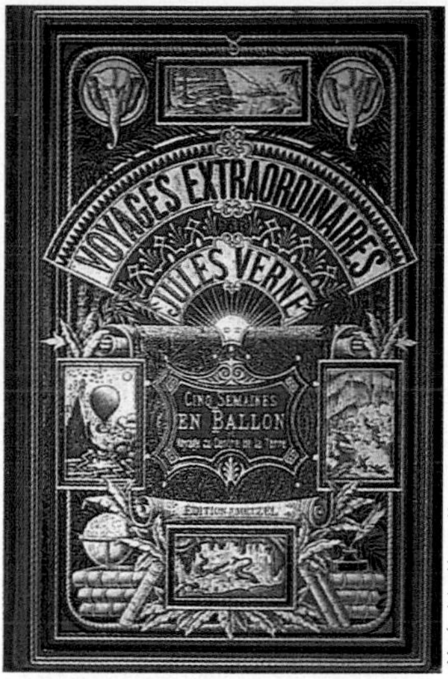

Musée Jules Verne, Nantes

Book cover of an original Hetzel edition

The twenty years that Jules Verne spent in Nantes from his birth on Feydeau Island in 1828 until he set up house in Paris in 1848, undoubtedly helped to strengthen his vocation as a writer of fiction, whose exceptional talent and boundless imagination successfully combined dream, scientific fact and adventure. The sight of the great port crowded with ships, their holds giving off all kinds of smells, or the equally fascinating scene of the steam-driven machines at the Indret factory, the tales of voyages he listened to from his uncle Prudent, once a privateer, lessons in reading and writing with Madame Sambin, the widow of the captain of an ocean-going vessel, or imaginary shipwrecks conjured up while playing among the little islands of the Loire; all these things played a part inspiring the author's imaginative genius when he came to write *Voyages extraordinaires*, which earned him the acclaim of more than 25 million teenagers even before he was universally acknowledged to be a great writer.

Square Maurice-Schwob – *Access by Boulevard Saint-Aignan* (**EZ**). Overlooking the Loire, this garden is dominated by an expressive statue of a Breton woman cursing the sea. One can make out part of the port, the tip of Beaulieu Islet and Rezé.

Planétarium ⓥ – *Access by Quai E.-Renaud* (**EZ**) *and Rue de l'Hermitage* (**EZ 94**). *No 8 Rue des Acadiens.*

In the planetarium, the visitor discovers the mysteries of the universe: the sun, moon, stars and planets are projected onto the dome. Each show takes a different theme.

Musée de la Poupée et des Jouets anciens (**EZ** M^6) ⓥ – *No 39 Boulevard St-Aignan.*

Tableaux with dolls, their furnishings, knick-knacks and accessories have been set up in display cabinets illustrating daily life (the first ball, grandmother's house, wedding celebration) and trades (laundress, seamstress, chimneysweep). One display case shows the evolution of the doll between 1830 and 1930; the different costumes reflect the changes in fashion of the times.

On the second floor old toys are exhibited: toy cars, soldiers, magic lantern, and also children's clothes.

Parc de Procé (**EY**) – It is a pleasure to stroll through this undulating park (16ha - 40 acres) landscaped with perspectives and rhododendrons, azaleas, oaks, etc.

Musée de la Poste (**EY**) ⓥ – *No 2 bis rue du Président Herriot.*

Located in the post office's regional headquarters, the museum recounts the history of the postal system from the mounted couriers to the post office box to private messenger services. Displays include the model of a 19C relay post, uniforms worn by the postilion and postman, scales, stamp-making machines, telephones, calendars, etc. An audiovisual show ends the visit.

★**Jardin des Plantes** (**HY**) – Opposite the station, decorated with brightly coloured mosaics, is this very fine garden which was created in 1805. It is beautifully landscaped and contains, in addition to the masses of white, pink, purple and yellow camellias, magnolias, rhododendrons and splendid trees, several fine ponds and wooden sculpture. A statue of Jules Verne *(qv)* is a reminder that Nantes was the writer's native town.

Chapelle de l'Immaculée (**HY**) ⏲ – The former Chapelle des Minimes is in an older area of Nantes where 17C porches adorn the houses, and streets narrow to alleys. It was built in the 15C Flamboyant style by Duke François II. The façade and aisles are 17C and the 19C pulpit has small columns intertwined with a vine and snake. Modern stained-glass windows light the interior.

Église St-Nicolas (**GY F**) – The basilica was built in 1854 in the Gothic style. There are fine views of the building and its tall spire (85m – 279ft) from Place Royale and of the east end from Rue Cacault.

Île de Versailles (**GY**) – Once covered with marshland, the islet was landfilled during the building of the Nantes-Brest Canal. A charming Japanese garden has been landscaped with rock gardens, waterfalls, and lanterns.
The **Maison de l'Erdre** (House of the River Erdre) (**M**[7]) ⏲ displays the river's flora and fauna; the river, until the 19C, flowed into the canal.

★BOAT TRIP ON THE ERDRE ⏲

Landing stage: Quai de la Motte Rouge (Gare fluviale – **GY***).*

This is a favourite trip for the Nantais in a pleasantly green countryside dotted with manor-houses; the 16C Château de la Gascherie with its ornate windows is notable. The Erdre widens beyond Sucé to form Lake Mazerolles.

EXCURSION

Château de Goulaine – *13km – 8 miles southeast on the N 149, then the D 119 towards Haute-Goulaine. See Château de GOULAINE.*

Calvaire NOTRE-DAME-DE-TRONOËN★★

Michelin map 58 fold 14 or 230 fold 31 – Local map under CORNOUAILLE

The Calvary (Calvaire) and Chapelle of Notre-Dame-de-Tronoën stand beside Audierne Bay, in the bare and wild landscape of the dunes.

★★**Calvary** – The calvary (1450-60) is the oldest in Brittany. The childhood and Passion of Christ are recounted on two friezes. The intensity and originality of the 100 figures are remarkable. Details of the sculpted figures, although worn by exposure, can be fully appreciated. The scenes are depicted in the round or in high relief in a coarse granite from Scaer, which is friable and tends to attract lichen (the Last Supper and the Last Judgment on the south face are greatly damaged). Three scenes on the north face are in Kersanton granite: the Visitation, an unusual Nativity with a sleeping Joseph and the Magi in 15C vestment. Christ and the thieves are also carved in hard granite.

Chapel (Chapelle) ⏲ – The 15C chapel has a pierced belfry, flanked by turrets. Beneath the vaulted roof are old statues. The ornate south door opens on to the Calvary. A *pardon* takes place annually (*see the Calendar of Events at the end of the guide*).

Chapelle NOTRE-DAME-DU-CRANN★

Michelin map 58 fold 16 or 230 fold 19 – 8.5km – 5 miles east of Châteauneuf-du-Faou – Local map see MONTAGNES NOIRES

The **Chapel of Our Lady of Crann** ⏲, built in 1532, stands on the side of the road in a verdant setting. It contains some remarkable 16C **stained glass windows**★★ and has a flat east end.

In the south aisle you will see the window illustrating the legend of St Eligius, who is the patron of farriers. In the south transept are the Death and Coronation of the Virgin. Above the south aisle, is the stained-glass window of St James the Greater, in three bays. The window in the chancel depicts scenes of the Passion in twelve bays. Above are the Last Judgment and the Triumph of Christ. The upper part of a window in the north transept shows the Adoration of the Shepherds, and the lower part, the Adoration of the Magi; another, on the right, shows the Martyrdom

of St Lawrence in three panels. The window in the north aisle represents the Baptism of Jesus Christ.
The high altar is framed between two niches with **shutters★** decorated with carvings; that on the left contains a statue of the Virgin Mother; the niche on the right contains a group of the Trinity. A *pardon is* held on Trinity Sunday *(see the Calendar of Events at the end of the guide)*

Y. Caoudal/AZIMUT

Notre-Dame-du-Crann – Stained-glass window

Île d'OUESSANT★★

USHANT – Population 1 062

Michelin map 58 fold 2 or 230 fold 1

An excursion to the île d'Ouessant ⓥ by sea is of the greatest interest, since it enables you to see Brest Channel, Pointe de St-Mathieu, Four Channel, the famous Black Stones (Pierres Noires) reef and the Green Stones (Pierres Vertes) reef, the Islands of Béniguet and Molène, and Fromveur Channel. The island itself is extremely curious. On the way to Ouessant the boat usually anchors off and sometimes calls at **Molène**. There the pastures on the rare patches of earth in this archipelago are so small that, according to a local jest, a Molène cow which has all four feet in one field grazes from another and manures a third.

Nature – Ouessant is 7km - 4 miles long and 4km - 2.5 miles wide and its highest point is 60m - 197ft above sea level. It is famous in marine history for the danger of its waters due to frequent fog, strong currents (the Fromrust to the northwest and the Fromveur to the southeast) and countless reefs.
In winter the wind is master and hurls the waves against the broken and rocky shores with the utmost fury for as much as ten days on end. The scene is often sinister when the fog comes down and the mournful howl of the foghorns mingles with the roar of the storm.
Few tourists know the island in this inhospitable guise, for the summer season brings calm and a quieter atmosphere, similar to that of the coasts of Brittany. The climate is mild. In January and February, Ushant has the highest mean temperature in France. The colonies of sea birds that nest on the island's cliff and on the neighbouring islets are particularly numerous in the autumn when the migrants from northern Europe fly in, attracted by the beams of the two lighthouses.
The **Parc naturel régional d'Armorique** *(qv)* to which Ouessant has been attached since 1969, helps maintain its traditional character.

The men and their work – The majority of the island's population is made up of women and men who have retired from the Navy or the merchant marine. Their principle occupations are stock raising and food crops.
Vegetables and potatoes grow in beautifully maintained lots. The grain cultivated on larger parcels of land is used as feed for poultry and also as a supplementary fodder crop for the cattle's diet. The livestock (sheep, dairy cows, horses) consists mainly of sheep with brown wool, which graze on meagre tufts of salt grass; the result is meat with a splendid flavour, comparable to the famous *prés salés* of Mont-St-Michel Bay. They live in the open and take shelter from northwesterly or southwesterly gales behind low dry-stone walls built in a star formation or wood shelters. Though from early February (first Wednesday: a great cattle fair) before lambing to late September they are tethered in twos to a stake; they wander freely the rest of the year, their owner's mark being nicked on their ears.
A few dairy cows are raised and two riding centres have reintroduced horsebreeding. The cultivation of algae and the raising of mussels have developed into very promising enterprises.
The men of Ouessant work on the continent (Brest region), at sea (the Navy or merchant marine), fishing (coastal or in deeper oceans) or on oil platforms.

Tradition – The important part played by the women of Ouessant in family life was recognised by an old custom by which it was the girls who proposed marriage. Women's traditional dress is severe and not often worn; it is made of black cloth and consists of a short skirt and a small *coiffe*; the hair is combed back and falls on the shoulders. The character of the people is reflected in the customs, which were observed until 1962, for when a member of a family was lost at sea. The friends and relatives would meet at the man's home to pray and watch over a little wax cross that stood for him; the sad vigil would last all night. The next day at the funeral service, the cross would be deposited in a reliquary in the church. Later, at some major ceremony, it would be put in a mausoleum in the cemetery where the crosses of all the missing were assembled. These little wax crosses are called *Proëlla* crosses. The word means "the homecoming of souls".

Coast of Ushant

TOUR *time: allow 1 day*

Roads from Lampaul lead to the best sites but many paths and tracks enable the visitor to criss-cross the island, to reach the fine cliffs, the pretty little creeks and to discover the flora as well as the marine fauna: herring gulls, cormorants, oyster catchers, puffins, terns, etc.

Lampaul – This is the island's capital. Note the old houses kept in excellent repair; the shutters are painted in green or blue, the island's traditional colours. A small monument containing the *Proëlla* crosses *(see above)* stands in the cemetery.
The tiny port, west facing, is picturesque, while the sandy beach of Le Corz nearby extends to the south.

★★★**La Côte Sauvage** – *Leave Lampaul west by an uphill road; after 500m - 547yds, bear right.*

Écomusée de l'île d'Ouessant ⓥ – At the hamlet of **Niou Uhella**, two traditional houses have been restored and rearranged by the Parc naturel régional d'Armorique *(qv)*. Visitors will see in one of them furniture typical of the island built of wood from wrecked vessels, painted in blue, symbol of the Virgin's protection, and in the second a display of farm and domestic implements and costumes, etc, which depicts aspects of life on Ouessant; an exhibit on the island's geology and population is upstairs.

Carry on towards the coast.

Moulin de Karaes – This is the island's last mill (restored) with its round stone base. It was used to mill barley from which bread was still made at the beginning of the 20C.

Phare de Créac'h – This lighthouse, with that at Land's End, marks the entrance to the English Channel; it has two tiers of revolving beams. The light is cast by four lamps giving a total of 20 million candlepower and an average range of more than 60km - 37 miles.
In the old machine room, there is a small **Centre d'Interprétation des Phares et Balises** (Lighthouse Museum) ⓥ retracing their history from Antiquity to the present. It shows how the original lighthouse was a tower, with, at its summit, a light fuelled by burning coal, wood or oil. The exhibit includes turbines, lens, lamps, beams and recounts the life of the lighthouse keeper. An audiovisual show completes the tour.

Go round the lighthouse to the right to view the coast.

Its extraordinarily jagged **rocks**★★★ (rochers) pounded by the sea are very impressive. A gangway in front of the lighthouse gives access to Pointe du Créac'h where the fog-horn stands. Cargo boats and oil tankers can be seen on the horizon; some 300 ships pass daily in the area which is patrolled day and night by the French Navy.

Turn back and bear right towards Pointe de Pern.

Chapelle N.-D.-de-Bon-Voyage – Also known as the Chapelle St-Gildas after the English saint who came here in the 5C, it was built at the end of the 19C. The people of Ouessant come to the chapel every year for the island's *pardon* on the first or second Sunday in September.

Lherpinière/CAMPAGNE CAMPAGNE

★**Pointe de Pern** – This, the western-most point of the island, extends into the sea in a series of rocks and reefs lashed by the rollers. In the distance is the unmanned Nividic Lighthouse (Phare de Nividic).

Presqu'île de Feunteun Velen – *At Lampaul, take the road skirting the cemetery.* Pass near the small port of Lampaul, where the boat from Brest sometimes drops anchor. The jetty gives shelter to the fishing boats.

The road goes round the deep Lampaul Bay bounded by the Corz and Le Prat Beaches, with the Le Grand Truk and Youc'h Corz rocks in the centre, then descends gently towards Pointe de Porz Doun Note on the left the white pyramid of Le Runiou (Pyramide du Runiou), a landmark for shipping; on the right is the great cove of Porz Coret.

Pointe de Porz Doun – The cliff-lined point at the southern tip of the island affords a fine **view** over Lampaul, Pointe de Pern and Jument Lighthouse (built from 1904-12; unmanned) which reaches a height of 42m - 138ft and houses a fog-horn.

Phare du Stiff – *Leave Lampaul by the road running along the north side of the church.*

The road rises gently to the island's highest point (alt 60m - 197ft), Pointe de Bac'haol. The lighthouse, built by the military architect Vauban in 1695, comprises two adjoining towers, one containing a spiral staircase *(126 steps)* and the other three small superposed rooms. The light has a range of 50km - 31 miles thanks to a lamp of 1 000 W giving a total of 600 000 candlepower. From the top a vast **panorama**★★ unfolds over the islands and the mainland from Vierge Lighthouse to Pointe du Raz.

Nearby stands the new radar-tower (height 140m - 459ft) which controls the sea lane off the island.

Paths lead to the tip of the **Presqu'île de Cadoran** (Cadoran Peninsula) from which may be enjoyed a pretty view of Beninou Bay, sometimes frequented by a seal colony, and Keller Island, favoured by nesting birds.

Crique de Porz Yusin – *Leave Lampaul north by a road running past the island's electricity generating plant.*

The road passes several hamlets with white houses adorned with brightly coloured shutters and surrounded by small gardens, on the way to Porz Yusin, one of the few sheltered spots on the north coast.

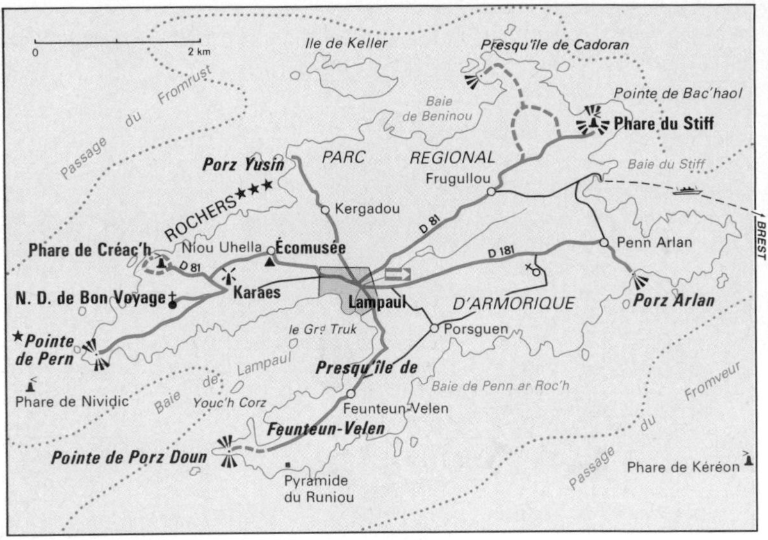

This pretty rocky setting is ideal for birdwatching. There are also very fine varieties of seaweed.

Crique de Porz Arlan – *Leave Lampaul by the road skirting the cemetery, then turn left.*

The road runs across the plateau, leaving on the right the 1863 Chapelle N.-D.-d'Espérance and on the left the airfield, before bearing right towards picturesque Porz Arlan.

In this creek nestle a tiny sandy beach and a small port sheltered by a jetty. From this charming site the beautiful **view** extends over the rocky coastline, Fromveur and Kéréon Lighthouse, and the île de Bannec.

PAIMPOL

Population 7 856

Michelin map 59 fold 2 or 230 fold 8 – Facilities

Town plan in the current Michelin Red Guide France

Pierre Loti's novel *Pêcheur d'Islande* (Fisherman of Iceland, 1886) and Botrel's *(qv)* song *The Paimpolaise* (the cliff mentioned in the song is located near the town, towards Pointe de Guilben) brought both literary fame and popularity to Paimpol. Life has changed a great deal, however, since those days when deep-sea fishing was done off the banks of Iceland. The fishermen now tend to fish along the coast; the port, large and impersonal, contains mostly pleasure boats. The town retains a certain prosperity as a market for early vegetables. Oyster farming has brought wealth to the region.

Place du Martray – In the centre of the town, the square retains fine 16C houses; note at the corner of Rue de l'Église the house with a square corner turret where Loti used to stay and where Gaud, the heroine of *Pêcheur d'Islande*, lived.

Square Théodore-Botrel – In the square stand an isolated 18C bell tower, all that remains of a former church, and a monument to the popular singer Théodore Botrel, who died in Pont-Aven *(qv)* in 1925.

Musée de la Mer ⓥ – *Rue de la Benne.* Paimpol's seafaring activity, from the time of the Icelandic fishing expeditions to the present day, is recalled by models, photographs and navigational instruments.

★★POINTE DE L'ARCOUEST

9km – 5 miles. Leave Paimpol north on the D 789 and after 2km – 1 mile bear right on a dirt track.

Tour de Kerroc'h – This tower stands in a pretty wooded setting. From the first platform there is a fine **view★** of Paimpol Bay.

Return to the road to Pointe de l'Arcouest.

Ploubazlanec – In the cemetery is a wall on which the names of men lost at sea are recorded.

At Ploubazlanec, take the road east to Pors-Even.

Perros-Hamon – Note the small chapel dating from 1770; the west façade is adorned with statues from the former Chapelle de la Trinité and under the south porch a list of those lost at sea.

Continue in the direction of Pors-Even and bear left at the first junction.

Croix des Veuves – From this spot, where sailor's wives awaited the return of boats from fishing expeditions, there is a good **view** of the approach to Paimpol Bay and Bréhat.

Turn back and bear left twice to go down to the harbour.

Pors-Even – In this small fishing village facing Paimpol lived the fisherman who was Loti's model for Yann in *Pêcheur d'Islande.*

Return to Ploubazlanec and turn right.

★★ **Pointe de l'Arcouest** – On the way down to the creek of Arcouest there are remarkable **views** of the bay and of the île de Bréhat at high tide. Each summer the place is invaded by a colony of artists and men of science and letters. A monument – two identical pink blocks of granite set side by side – has been erected to the memory of Frédéric and Irène Joliot-Curie, who were frequent visitors to Arcouest (below the car park, before the point's larger car park).

Loguivy-de-la-Mer – *5km – 3 miles north. Leave Paimpol towards Pointe de l'Arcouest, then take the D 15.*
This fishing port, the second in the Côtes d'Armor *département*, is simply a creek in which boats are grounded at low tide.
Climb the promontory that encloses the creek on the left to get a view of the mouth of the River Trieux, Bréhat and the many islands.

★★ **Île de Bréhat** – *From Pointe de l'Arcouest allow 2 to 4 hours to cross and visit Bréhat. See Île de BRÉHAT.*

★LA CÔTE DU GOËLO

Round tour of 47km – 24 miles – about 4 hours

Take the D 786 south towards St-Quay-Portrieux and on leaving Paimpol, turn left.

Pointe de Guilben – This is the cliff mentioned in the song by Botrel *(qv)*. From the point which ends in a long spur cutting the cove of Paimpol in two, there is a lovely view of the coast.

After Kérity, a road to the left leads to the Abbaye de Beauport.

★ **Abbaye de Beauport** – *See Abbaye de BEAUPORT.*

Return to the St-Quay road, turn left and past the pool, turn left again into an uphill road.

Ste-Barbe – The sea can be seen from the small square *(placître – qv)* of the chapel, the porch of which is decorated with a statue of St Barbara. A path *(car park)*, 250m - 274yds further on takes you to a viewing table from where one can see beyond the meadow, Paimpol Bay and its nearby islands, the oyster-beds, Port-Lazo and Mez du Goëlo Lighthouse.

At Plouézec, turn left and at St-Riom left again to Port-Lazo.

Port-Lazo – At the end of the road there is a view of Paimpol Bay.

Return to St-Riom; bear left.

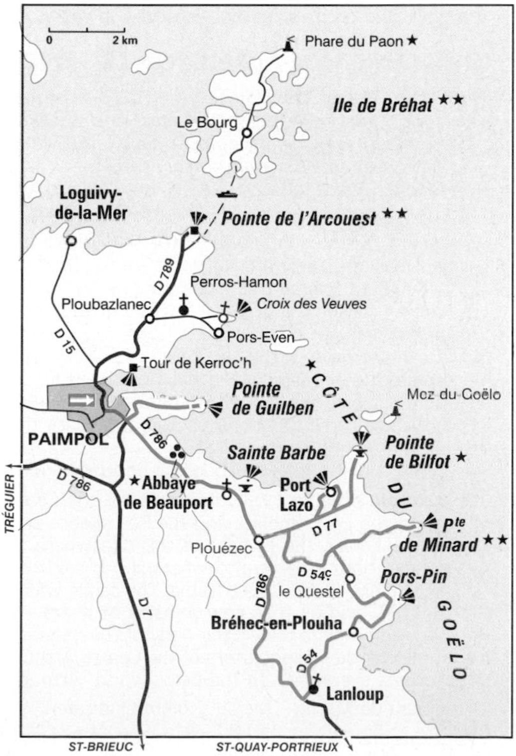

★**Pointe de Bilfot** – From the viewing table, the **view** extends westwards to the île de Bréhat and eastwards to Cap Fréhel. Between the small lighthouse at Mez du Goëlo nearby and Paon Lighthouse at Bréhat in the distance, the bay is studded with rocks.

Turn back and at the entrance to Plouézec, bear left.

★★**Pointe de Minard** – Make for this rocky platform which affords a wide **view** over St-Brieuc Bay and cap d'Erquy, the Paimpol Cove and the île de Bréhat.

After a picturesque run along the coast to Le Questel, bear left twice after the hamlet.

Pors Pin – A small creek with rocks curiously shaped by erosion.

Return to the first junction and make a left turn.

The road runs along the edge of the bare cliff offering glimpses of St-Brieuc Bay and leads to a **viewpoint** *(car park)*. The **view**★ extends over the site of Bréhec-en-Plouha, Pointe de la Tour, St-Quay rocks and the coast from Erquy to Le Val-André.

Bréhec-en-Plouha – A small harbour sheltered by a dike and a modest seaside resort at the bottom of a cove bounded by Pointe de la Tour on the right and Pointe de Berjule on the left. St Brieuc and the first emigrants from Britain landed at Bréhec in the 5C *(see Introduction: Historical Table and Notes)*.

Go up the green valley of the Kergolo stream.

Lanloup – The 15-16C church has an interesting south porch *(see Introduction: Breton Art)* flanked by buttresses with niches and with St Lupus and St Giles standing on the pediment. The twelve Apostles, carved in granite, on ornate corbels precede the doorway topped by a 14C Virgin. In the cemetery are a cross (1758) and the tomb of the composer Guy Ropartz (1864-1955) in an alcove to the right of the porch.

Return to Paimpol via Plouézec.

Forêt de PAIMPONT★

Michelin map 59 fold 15 and 63 fold 5 or 230 folds 38 and 39

The Forest of Paimpont – the ancient "Brocéliande" where, according to the songs of the Middle Ages, the sorcerer Merlin and the fairy Viviane lived *(see Introduction: Tradition and Folklore)* – is all that remains in the east of the great forest which, in the early centuries of our era, still covered a large part of inner Brittany extending almost 140km - 85 miles distant. The cutting and clearing that went on for centuries have reduced the forest so that it now covers an area of only 7 067ha - 27 sq miles where 500ha - 2 sq miles belong to the state. Recently great areas have been replanted with conifers which will increase the industry of the massif.
A few charming corners remain, especially in the vicinity of the many pools.

BROCÉLIANDE, LAND OF LEGEND

This route leaves from St Léry and follows a round tour through the forest of Paimpont, past the best-known sites. In the wake of the great fire of September 1990, nature is gaining the upper hand, and, although some trees many centuries old have been lost for ever, gorse, heather, broom and ferns are composing a new landscape, which clearly has its own charm. The reforestation of the areas destroyed by the fire will be completed this year.

St-Léry – On the south side of the 14C **church** is a Renaissance porch with two elegant basket-handle arched doors surmounted by delicately carved ogee mouldings. Sculpted figures frame the door on the right: the Virgin, the Angel Gabriel, St Michael slaying the dragon, and one of the damned. The leaves of the door are beautifully carved.
Inside, in the nave, is the 16C tomb of St Léry, and opposite it is a little bas-relief in sculpted wood depicting the life of the saint. The lovely Flamboyant chapel in the south side aisle is illuminated through a stained glass window dating from 1493 which is dedicated to the Virgin Mary. Beneath the gallery, the clock can be seen through a glass door.
Near the church, note a 17C house decorated with three lovely dormer windows.

Château de Comper ⓥ – The Montforts, the Charettes, the Rieux, the Lavals, the Colignys, the La Trémoilles and the Rosmadecs are the great families who have at some point been the owners of this site where the fairy Viviane is supposed to have been born. This is also where she is said to have brought up Lancelot, the gallant Knight of the Round Table. The castle was destroyed twice, in the 14C and in the 18C, and all that now remains of it are two sections of curtain wall, the postern and a huge tower; the body of the main building was restored in the 19C. The castle is the headquarters of the Centre Arthurien, which organises exhibitions and events every year on the Celtic world, Arthurian legend or the Middle Ages.

Tombeau de Merlin – Merlin's tomb is indicated by two schist slabs and some holly.

Fontaine de Jouvence – Ordinary-looking fountain said to have magic powers.

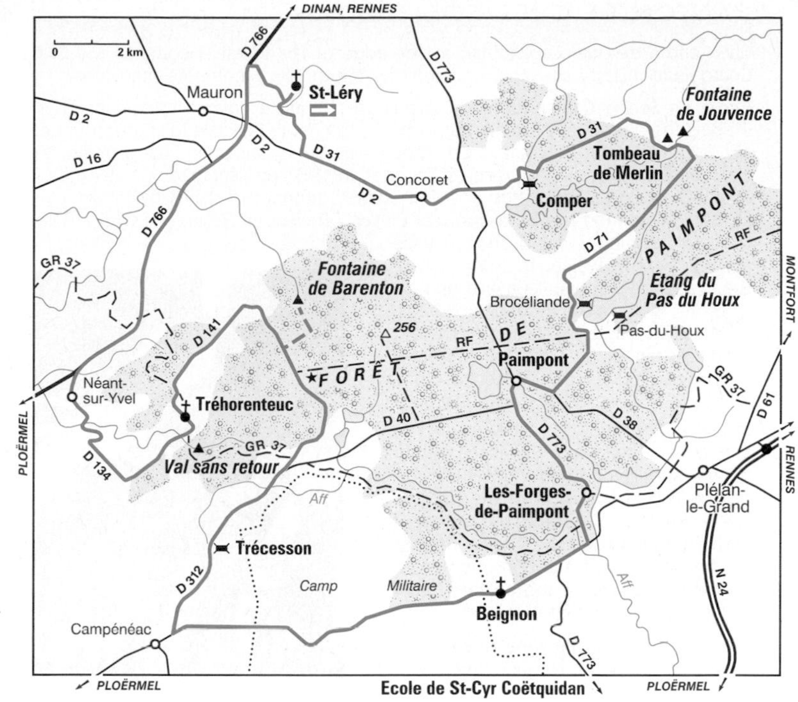

Étang du Pas-du-Houx – This lake, which is in a very pretty setting, is the largest in the forest (86ha - 212 acres). Two châteaux were built on its shores in 1912: Brocéliande, in the Norman style, and Pas-du-Houx.

Paimpont – This market town, deep in the forest near a pool amidst tall trees, dates back to the Revolution. It owes its origins to the founding of a monastery in the 7C which, raised to the status of abbey in the late 12C, survived until the Revolution. The 17C north wing houses the town hall and the presbytery.
The 13C abbey church was decorated in the 17C with richly ornate **woodwork**. Busts, carved medallions and festoons of fruit and flowers have been executed with remarkable skill. Note in particular the 15 and 16C statues, including one of St Judicaël, in stone, and a St Méen, in wood, the 16C high altar and some beautiful 17C woodwork. The **treasury** ⌚, in the sacristy, displays a statue of St Anne carrying the Virgin and Child (15C), an interesting arm reliquary of St Judicaël (15C) and, most importantly, a magnificent ivory Christ (18C).

Les Forges de Paimpont – This pretty hamlet, next to a lake, owes its name to the forges which were here between the 16 and late 19C. They were fuelled by iron ore and local wood and produced a highly valued metal.

Beignon – The church contains some beautiful 16C stained glass windows. In the chancel, behind the altar, there is a representation of the Crucifixion of St Peter, and, in the north transept, is one of the Tree of Jesse.

Château de Trécesson ⌚ – This castle, surrounded by a pool, was built at the end of the 14C in reddish schist and still has its original medieval appearance. A striking gatehouse flanked with corbelled turrets commands the entrance.

Tréhorenteuc – In the **church** ⌚ and sacristy, mosaics and pictures illustrate the Legend of the Val sans retour and the Barenton fountain. In the chancel: stained glass window of the Holy Grail; painting of the Knights of the Round Table.

Val sans Retour – Known as the "Valley of No Return", this is one of the places most heavily steeped in legend in the Forêt de Paimpont. It can be found by taking the unsurfaced track, for pedestrians only, after the second car park. This leads to the Fairies' Mirror and False Lovers' Rock (Miroir des Fées et Rocher des Faux Amants). Legend has it that Morgana the witch, jealous of a knight who had been unfaithful to her, cast a spell over the valley preventing anyone who had done wrong from leaving it. Only Lancelot, who remained faithful to Guinevere, was able to break the spell. At the Fairies' Mirror, note the splendid **Golden Tree** (Arbre d'Or), the work of François Davin, which marks the furthest spot reached by the fire of 1990.

Fontaine de Barenton – Water from the fountain spilling over "Merlin's Step" (Perron de Merlin – a stone near the fountain) was said to unleash wild storms.

CANTON DE GUER-COËTQUIDAN

The Canton de Guer-Coëtquidan at the edge of the forest is home to the St-Cyr-Coëtquidan military academy and, further south, the Monteneuf megaliths.

École de St-Cyr-Coëtquidan – Coëtquidan military academy houses the training schools for élite officers of the land forces: the École Spéciale Militaire, founded in 1802 by Napoleon Bonaparte, commonly known as St-Cyr or Coët in military circles; the École Militaire Interarmes, founded in 1961 by Général de Gaulle; the École Militaire du Corps Technique et Administratif, founded in 1977 by President Giscard d'Estaing and the Bataillion des Élèves-Officiers en Réserve (EORs – Reserve Officers' Training Cadet Corps). A wide avenue, next to which, to the south of the N 29, are statues of Bayard and Du Guesclin, leads to the modern buildings. On the lawns there are statues of the last four field marshals of France: Maréchal de Lattre de Tassigny, Maréchal Juin, Maréchal Koenig and Maréchal Leclerc.

★**Musée du Souvenir** ⓥ – This museum, famed for its memorial ("France" by Antoine Bourdelle) in honour of 17 000 officers killed in action, is to the right of the Cours Rivoli. It retraces the history of officer training from the Ancien Régime to the present and contains numerous documents, uniforms and military decorations connected with this elite.

P. Wysocki/EXPLORER

St-Cyriens

Site mégalithique de Monteneuf ⓥ – Located on the moor lying between Guer and Monteneuf, this megalithic site is seen as one of the most important in central Brittany; it is currently being excavated and restored. More than twenty huge blocks of purple schist have been raised with the help of the Engineers from the nearby military college of Coëtquidan. A 9km - 5.6 mile long pedestrian itinerary takes you past the Loge Morinais (Morinais Hut – schist gallery graves), the Menhirs de Chomet, the Menhirs de Coëplan, the Bordoués (gallery grave) and Pierres Droites (Standing Stones – over 400 officially listed menhirs flanking the road D 776, thought to have been knocked down towards the end of the first millenium on the orders of the Church).

PARISH CLOSES★★

See Les ENCLOS PAROISSIAUX

PENCRAN★

Population 1 182

Michelin map 58 fold 5 or 230 fold 4 – 3.5km – 2 miles south of Landerneau

This small village has a fine 16C parish close.

★PARISH CLOSE *time: 30 min*

Triumphal Arch (**Porte Triomphale**) – The arch, which was added in the 17C, is crowned by three lantern-turrets.

★**Calvary** (**Calvaire**) – This great cross with two cross-bars framed by the thieves' crosses is set in the wall to the right.

Church (**Église**) – This rectangular church has an elegant belfry with a double balcony. On the south side of the church is an interesting though weather-beaten **porch**★ (1553) with covings adorned with angels and musicians; on the pillars statuettes illustrating scenes from the Old Testament – Noah's Ark is on the right; under the ornate carved canopies, statues of the Apostles.
Inside the church, old statues include a *Pietà* and an Annunciation against the pillars of the nave and St Apollonia (1555) in the south aisle. In the chancel, to the left of the high altar, is a fine **Descent from the Cross** (1517) in the Flemish style.

Ossuaire – The ossuary dates from 1594.

Pointe de PENHIR★★★

Michelin map 58 fold 3 or 230 fold 16

Penhir Point is the finest of the four headlands of the Presqu'île de Crozon *(qv)*. A memorial (150m - 164yds off the road) to the Bretons of the Free French Forces has been erected on the cliff.

Leave the car at the end of the surfaced road. Go on to the platform at the end of the promontory for a view of the sea 70m - 229ft down below. Telescopes. Time: 45 min.

The setting is magnificent as is the **panorama**: below are the great isolated rocks called the **Tas de Pois**; on the left is the Pointe de Dinan; on the right, Pointe de St-Mathieu and Pointe du Toulinguet, the second with its little lighthouse, and at the back the Ménez-Hom. In the distance, the Pointe du Raz and the île de Sein can be seen on clear days to the left, and Ouessant over to the right.
Tourists who enjoy scrambling over rocks should take a path going down to the left of the platform and monument. Halfway down the sheer drop of the cliff there is a view of a little cove. Here take the path on the left which climbs towards a cavity covered with a rock beyond which is the **Chambre Verte**, a grassy strip. From here there is an unusual view of the Tas de Pois Rocks and the Pointe de Penhir.

PERROS-GUIREC

Population 7 497

Michelin map 59 fold 1 or 230 folds 6 and 7

Local map under CORNICHE BRETONNE – Facilities

This much-frequented seaside resort (casino, seawater treatment centre), built in the form of an amphitheatre on the pink granite coast, overlooks the fishing and pleasure boat harbour, the anchorage and the two gently sloping, fine sand, sheltered beaches (*ideal for children*) of Trestraou and Trestignel.

Church (Église) ⓥ – A porch with delicate trefoil arches abuts onto the massive 14C belfry topped by a dome (1669) crowned by a spire. Go into the **Romanesque nave★**, all that remains of the first chapel built on the spot. Massive pillars, cylindrical on the left and with engaged columns on the right, support capitals which are either historiated or adorned with geometrical designs. It is separated by a diaphragm arch from the Gothic nave built in the 14C at the same time as the chancel. In this arch is a rood-beam on which Christ is surrounded by the Virgin and St John. The church has a 12C granite stoup decorated with small figures and several old statues: an *Ecce Homo* (15C), St Lawrence and St Catherine (16C), St James, patron of the parish (17C). The round-arched south porch is richly ornamented.

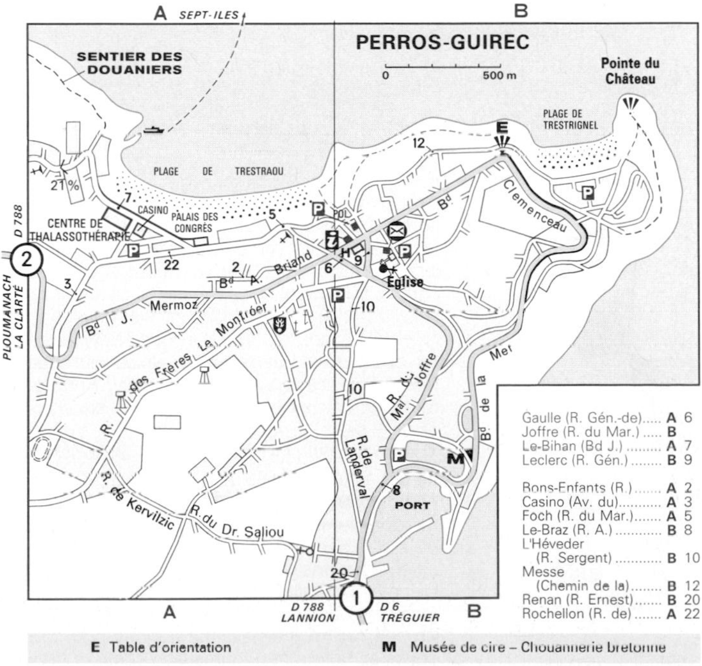

Musée de Cire Chouannerie Bretonne (**B M**) ⓥ – This wax museum has reconstituted historical scenes with figures dating from La Chalotais to Auguste Renan. Note the collection of regional head dresses from Lower Brittany.

Pointe du Château – From this steep little viewpoint, there is a lovely **view★** over the site of Perros-Guirec, Sept-Îles, the île Tomé and the coast as far as Port-L'Épine.

Viewing Table (Table d'orientation) (**B E**) – A splendid **view★** of Pointe du Château, Trestrignel Beach, Port-Blanc, Trélevern, Trévou, île de Tomé, Sept-Îles and of the rocks below.

EXCURSIONS

★★ **Ploumanach by Sentier des Douaniers** – *3 hours on foot Rtn. Go preferably in the morning at high tide.*
Follow the edge of the cliff as far as Pors-Rolland to reach the lighthouse via Pointe de Squewel. *Description of Ploumanach under PLOUMANACH.*

La Clarté – *3km – 2 miles by ② on the town plan.*
The pretty rose granite **Chapelle Notre-Dame-de-la-Clarté★** stands 200m - 219yds back from the road. In the 16C the lord of Barac'h, whose ship was in danger in fog off the coast, vowed to build a chapel to Our Lady at whatever spot on the coast that first emerged from the fog. The promised chapel was built on the height which enabled him to take his bearings; to commemorate the circumstances, it was called Our Lady of Light (Notre-Dame-de-la-Clarté). The south doorway is adorned with sculptures in low relief: on the lintel, an Annunciation and *Pietà*; two coats of arms and a *Virgin and Child* frame the mullioned window in the registry; under the porch are two 17C wood statues and 16C door panels. The tall nave includes three bays decorated with carved roses and foliage; the 15C stoup ornamented with three Moorish heads and the Stations of the Cross by Maurice Denis (1931) are noteworthy. A *pardon* is held every year (*see the Calendar of Events at the end of the guide*).
Take Rue du Tertre which starts on the north side of the chapel, leading to the top of a rocky knoll which affords a good **view★** over Pleumeur-Bodou and the Radôme and Planétarium, Ploumanach, Sept-Îles, Perros-Guirec and Pointe du Château.

★★ **Signal Station (Sémaphore)** – *3.5km – 2.5 miles west. Leave Perros-Guirec by ② on the town plan..*
From the roadside lookout point the **view★** extends to the rocks of Ploumanach, seawards to Sept-Îles and behind to the beaches of Perros-Guirec, and in the distance along the Port-Blanc coastline.

Louannec – *5km – 3 miles east on the D 6.*
In the church, where St Yves was once the parish priest, to the right of the altar, there is a 15C carved wood group of St Yves. In a glass cabinet is an ancient chasuble (13C) said to have belonged to St Yves.

BOAT TRIP

Sept-Îles ⓥ – *Boats tour the islands. The islands became a sea bird sanctuary in 1912.*

Rouzic – *Landing forbidden.* The boat goes near the island, also known as Bird Island, where a large **colony★** of northern gannets, some 12 000 pairs, settle from February to September; they can be observed from Grande Island's ornithological centre (closed-circuit remote control television). One can see guillemots, razorbills, lesser and great black-backed gulls, puffins, crested cormorants, black-legged kittiwakes, oyster catchers and petrels all of which reproduce in March and leave at the end of July. Another interesting feature is the presence of a small colony of grey seals (around a dozen).
The boat then skirts Malban and Bono Islands.

D'après photo Baranger/JACANA

Sept-Îles – A puffin

Île aux Moines – The boat stops at the island *(1 hour)* where you may visit the old gunpowder factory, the **lighthouse** (phare) ⓥ (83 steps; range 40km - 25 miles) which offers a fine panorama of the islands and the coast, the ruined fort erected by Vauban on the far tip and below the former monastery with its tiny chapel and well.
On the return journey, the curious pink granite rocks at Pointe de Ploumanach come into view.

PLEUMEUR-BODOU

Population 3 677

Michelin map 59 fold 1 or 230 fold 6 – Local map under CORNICHE BRETONNE

This village, situated between Lannion and Penvern, not far from the Corniche Bretonne(*qv*), has given its name to the radar dome, near which a telecommunications museum and planetarium have been set up.

★**Radôme and Musée des Télécommunications** ⓥ – The Pleumeur-Bodou telecommunications centre, inaugurated in 1962 and situated 1km - 0.6 mile from the sea between Lannion and the pink granite coast, is the historic site of the first transatlantic communication via the satellite **Telstar** between France and the United States (Andover) on 11 July 1962. Besides the radar dome and the museum, the Pleumeur-Bodou site is occupied by a dozen or so giant antennae which communicate with the five continents.

The **Telecommunications Museum**, situated in a building shaped like an immense Delta wing, retraces one and a half centuries of inventions, progress and continuously updated technology. Eight areas, each on a particular theme, illustrate this ever more rapidly developing industry:

– *whispering worlds* (a big-screen, audiovisual display on the urgent need for communication, using the pioneers of telecommunications themselves: Morse, Branly, Siemens, General Ferrié, Pender, Marconi etc.);

– *cables under the sea* (reproduction of the interior of a cable-ship, the submarine robot **Scarab**);

– *radio communications* (exhibition of long-wave or decametric transmitters);

– *satellites* (**Intelstat 5**, the white room);

– *networks* (manual telephone operation, old-fashioned telephone receivers);

– *state-of-the-art facilities* (Integrated Services Digital Networks (ISDN) – known as Réseau Numérique à Intégration de Services (RNIS/Numéris) in France, videophones, pocket telephones);

– *flights of fancy* (extracts from novels, cartoons and films on the subject of telecommunications);

– and finally, the visit ends with the enormous antenna horn protected by the **Radar Dome** (Radôme) – a huge white balloon 64m - 210ft in diameter – a pioneering achievement in space telecommunications. A **son et lumière show**★ inside the radar dome retraces the development of this antenna.

★**Planétarium du Trégor** ⓥ – Beneath a dome (20m - 65.5ft in diameter), the spectator travels through the universe.

An audiovisual slide show presents Brittany today: flora and fauna, natural resources and high-tech industries.

In the hall is an exhibit on astronomy and astrophysics.

Photo ARTUS

Musée des Télécommunications and Radôme

Walkers, campers, smokers...
please be careful!

Fire is the worst threat to woodland.

PLEYBEN★★

Population 3 446
Michelin map 58 folds 15 and 16 or 230 folds 18 and 19
Local map under Monts d'ARRÉE

The great feature of Pleyben is its magnificent parish close, built from the 15 to the 17C. *Pardon* on the first Sunday in August.

★★PARISH CLOSE *time: 30 min*

The monumental door was rebuilt in 1725.

★★**Calvary** (**Calvaire**) – Built in 1555 near the church's side entrance, it was displaced in 1738 and given its present form in 1743. Since then new motifs and scenes have been added to the monument: the Last Supper and Washing of the Disciples' Feet date from 1650. The huge pedestal with triumphal arches enhances the figures on the platform.
To follow the life of Christ start at the corner with the Annunciation and move in an anticlockwise direction to discover the Nativity, the Adoration of the Shepherds, etc.

★**Church** (**Église**) ⓥ – The church, dedicated to St Germanus of Auxerre, is dominated by two belfries, of which that on the right is the more remarkable. It is a Renaissance **tower**★★ crowned with a dome with small lantern turrets. The other tower has a Gothic spire linked to the corner turret at the balustrade level. Beyond the arm of the south transept is a curious quatrefoil sacristy, dating from 1719, with cupolas and lantern turrets.
Inside, the nave has 16C panelled **vaulting**★; the ribs and the remarkable **purlin** are carved and painted with mythological and religious scenes.
At the high altar is an altarpiece with turrets and a two storey tabernacle (17C). At the centre of the east end is a 16C **stained-glass window**★ depicting the Passion. Note the pulpit, the organ case (1688), the Baptism of Christ over the font and the many coloured statues including St Yves between the rich man and the pauper.

Chapelle funéraire ⓥ – A former 16C ossuary where exhibitions are held. The façade of this funerary chapel is adorned with basket-handled twin arches.

PLOËRDUT

Population 1 359
Michelin map 59 fold 11 or 230 fold 21 – 7km – 4 miles northwest of Guéméné-sur-Scorff

The **church** (13-17C) has a fine Romanesque nave and side aisles. The rounded arches rest on solid square **capitals**★ adorned with geometrical designs. Note the charnel-house abutting the south side of the church, which has a granite enclosure.

EXCURSION

Chapelle N.-D.-de-Crénenan ⓥ – *5km – 3 miles southeast via the D 132 and the D 1 towards Guéméné-sur-Scorff.*
It has 15-16C features and the tall square belfry dates from the 19C. Inside, the painted vaulting relates scenes from the life of the Virgin and the **purlins** especially show great originality. To the left of the altar is a Tree of Jesse with a statue of Notre-Dame-de-Crénenan, and to the right stand St Anne and the Virgin and Child.

PLOËRMEL

Population 7 258
Michelin map 63 fold 4 or 230 fold 38

This little town, in the centre of an agricultural area at the limit of Upper Brittany, was once the seat of the Dukes of Brittany and it was from Ploërmel that the Englishman, Bemborough, set out for the Battle of the Thirty *(qv)* (1351).

SIGHTS

★**Église St-Armel** (**Y**) – St Arthmael, who founded the town in the 6C, is shown taming a dragon which he leads away with his stole.
The church dates from the 16C. The Flamboyant Gothic and Renaissance north **portal**★ presents two finely carved doors. The scenes depicted take both religious (Christ's Childhood, Virtue Trampling on Vice) and comic themes. The Apostles have been sculpted on the door panels.
The magnificent 16 and 17C **stained-glass windows**★ have been restored: Tree of Jesse (in the side aisle), life of St Arthmael (in the north transept); there are also modern windows by Jacques Bony.

PLOËRMEL

Forges (R. des)	Z	16
Gare (R. de la)	Y	
Gaulle (R. Ch.-de)	Z	20
La Mennais (Pl. J.-M. de)	Y	29
Patarins (R. des)	Z	32
Armes (Pl. d')	Y	2
Beaumanoir (R.)	Y	3
Carmes (Bd des)	Y	7
Dr.-Louis-Guillois (Av. du)	YZ	10
Dubreton (R. du Général)	Z	12
Francs-Bourgeois (R. des)	Y	17
Giraud (R. du Général)	Z	23
Herses (R. des)	Y	25
Hôtel-de-Ville (Pl.)	Z	26
Leclerc (R. du Gén.)	Z	30
Porte Bergault (R. de la)	Z	34
Rohan (R. Alain de)	Z	36
Sénéchal-Thuault (R.)	Z	37

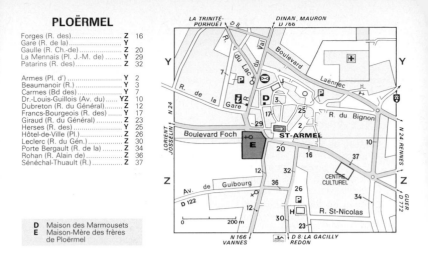

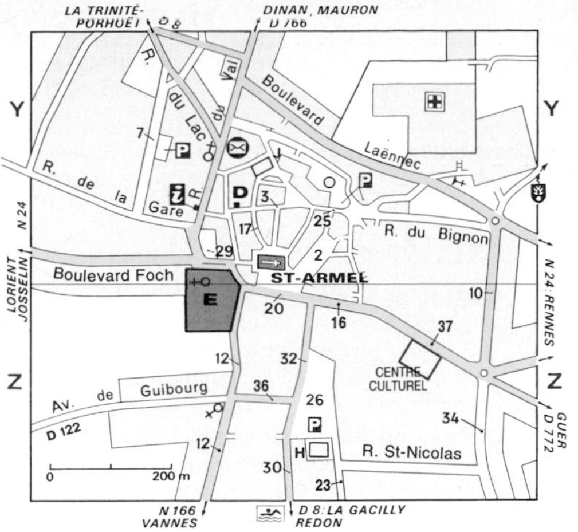

D Maison des Marmousets
E Maison-Mère des frères de Ploërmel

In the chapel to the north of the chancel are white marble statues of Dukes Jean II and Jean III of Brittany (14C). In the south transept, behind the Kersanton granite tomb of Philippe of Montauban and his wife, is a fine 14C recumbent figure in white marble. Below the wood vaulting the purlins are worth noticing (light switch).

Old houses – Rue Beaumanoir, so-called in memory of the hero of the Battle of the Thirty *(qv)*, contains (at no 7) the 16C **Maison des Marmousets★** (**Y D**) adorned with woodcarvings, and opposite the 16C former house of the Dukes of Brittany. Other old houses may be seen in Rue des Francs-Bourgeois.

Maison-Mère des Frères de Ploërmel (**YZ E**) – The order was founded in 1819 by the abbot Jean-Marie de La Mennais (1780-1860), brother of the famous author Lamennais *(qv)*.

Astronomical Clock (Horloge astronomique) – *Enter the abbey's courtyard via Place J.-M.-de-La-Mennais.*
The clock was created between 1850 and 1855 and was intended for the instruction of the future teachers of the coastal schools.

Musée du Père Jean-Marie de la Mennais ⌚ – It is housed in one of the community buildings, near the Astronomical Clock. There is an exhibition on the Ploërmel Order in front of it. The tomb of Father La Mennais is in the chapel.

Étang au Duc – *2.5km – 1.5 miles north. Leave Ploërmel by Boulevard du Maréchal-Foch west of the plan.*
Locally known as "the lake" it is a popular excursion (with an area of 250ha - 718 acres). There is an artificial beach and a water sports centre.

EXCURSION

Château du Crévy ⌚ – *8km – 5 miles south or the N 166 to La Chapelle-Caro.*
This castle dates back originally to the 3C, was rebuilt in the 14C, and has since been frequently remodelled.
The castle houses a **Musée du Costume★** (Costume Museum) with a remarkable collection of men's, women's, and children's fashion and dress from the 18C to the present. Tableaux with dressed models and furnishings of the period (Ancien Régime, Napoleonic period, Belle Époque...) illustrate the fashions and tastes of the time.

Lizio: Écomusée de la ferme et des métiers ⌚ – *17km - 10.5 miles south on the N 166 to Chapelle-Caro, then on the D 4 via Roc-St-André, then follow the signposting.* Amidst numerous tools and authentic items, old-fashioned shops and businesses have been reconstructed to form a display of about fifty trades which are no longer practised.

PLOUESCAT

Population 3 689
Michelin map 58 fold 5 or 230 fold 4

In the centre of this little town of the Léon region is a fine 17C **covered market** (halle) whose vast roof is supported on splendid beams held up on oak supports.
The indented coastline offers fine sandy beaches: Poulfoën, Frouden, Pors Meur and Pors Guen, and Kernic Bay.

EXCURSIONS

Château de Maillé ⓥ – *4km - 2.5 miles from Plouescat on the D 30 south towards Landivisiau.* An alley lined with chestnut and beech trees leads to this large 14 and 16C manor-house built in granite and flanked by a square Renaissance wing. The west front has an elegant mansard roof with pediments in the form of a pagoda or scroll.

Château de Kergomadeac'h – *7km – 5 miles from Plouescat by the D 10, the St-Pol-de-Léon road, then right towards Moulin-du-Chatel. Turn right by a Calvary.* Built in 1630, it is the last fortified castle to have been erected in France. Though it is now in ruins, the original square plan with the round machicolated towers at each corner is still evident. The tall chimneys are still standing. There is a small manor-house in a verdant setting to the right.

Manoir de Traonjoly ⓥ – *7.5km – 5 miles. Leave Plouescat east by the D 10 towards Roscoff and left at Cléder. Beyond the town, on the left, an alley marked by two granite pillars leads to the manor-house. Go round a farm and into the park.* This gracious manor-house was built in the 16 and 17C and was made even more attractive by the addition of the tall Renaissance dormer windows. A massive square tower stands in one corner of the main court which is enclosed by the living quarters and a terrace with a stone balustrade.

PLOUGASTEL-DAOULAS

Population 11 139
Michelin map 58 fold 4 or 230 fold 17

Plougastel is the centre of a strawberry-growing district; shallots, tomatoes, early fruit and vegetables and hothouse flowers are also cultivated.

★★ **Calvary** – *Illustration p 45.* Built in 1602-4 to commemorate the end of the Plague of 1598, the Calvary is made of dark Kersanton granite and ochre stone from Logonna. It is more harmonious then the Guimiliau Calvary but the attitude of the 180 figures seems more stiff. On either side of the Cross, the two thieves (do not appear at Guimiliau) are surmounted by an angel and a devil respectively. On the Calvary base an altar is carved under a portico; above is a large statue of Christ leaving the tomb.
The **church** ⓥ is built of granite and reinforced concrete; inside it is brilliant with blue, green, orange and violet all used in its decoration. The furnishings include altars and wooden altarpieces.

Musée du Patrimoine ⓥ – This museum of local history, traditions and ethnology contains various documents, objects, tools and items of furniture and clothing relating to everyday life from the 18C until the present. Displayed in more detail are the cultivation of linen and strawberries, and marine activites linked with exporting these two crops, as well as trawling for scallops in Brest bay. The ground floor features the reconstruction of the inside of a late-19C peasant dwelling.
The first floor houses, in a glazed gallery, a beautiful collection of costumes, the oldest of which dates from 1820, and an interesting display window of the *"Breuriez"*, a traditional ceremony which takes place every All Saints' Day, bringing together the members of a particular confraternity to honour their dead around an apple tree, the *"Gwezen an anaon"*.

EXCURSIONS

Chapelle St-Jean – *4.5km – 3 miles northeast on the D 29 towards Landerneau and after crossing the Brest-Quimper expressway bear left then right.*
The 15C chapel, remodelled in the 17C, stands in a verdant **site**★ on the banks of the Élorn.

★ PRESQU'ÎLE DE PLOUGASTEL

Round tour of 35km – 22 miles – about 2 hours

Lying away from main roads, Plougastel Peninsula is a corner of the Breton countryside, which may still be seen in its traditional guise.
Narrow, winding roads run between hedges through farming country, characteristically cut up into squares. There are few houses apart from occasional hamlets

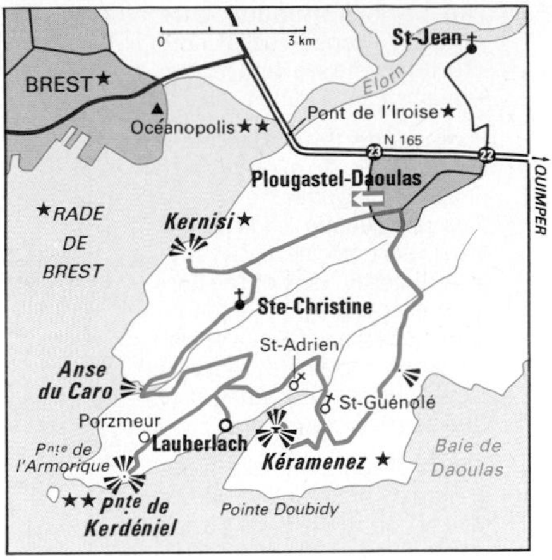

grouped round their little chapels. Here everything seems hidden away; you are deep in the strawberry country, but you will not see the strawberries, which grow in open fields, unless you get out of your car and look through the gaps in the hedges. Vast glassed-in areas shelter vegetables and flowers. In May and June, however, when the strawberries are picked, there is plenty of life on the roads; often you will come upon lorries fitted with open racks in which the little baskets of strawberries are carefully packed.

Leave Plougastel-Daoulas by a road to the right of the church; follow the signposts to Kernisi.

★**Panorama de Kernisi** – *At the entrance to the hamlet of Kernisi, leave the car and make for a knoll.* From here you will see a panorama of the Brest roadstead, the outer harbour and town of Brest, the Élorn estuary and the Pont Albert-Louppe.

Turn round and at the second main junction, bear right towards Langristin.

Chapelle Ste-Christine ⓥ – This 16C chapel possesses old statues in the north transept. There is a small Calvary dating from 1587.

Anse du Caro – From this pleasant setting, there is a view of Brest and Pointe des Espagnols, which forms the south shore of the Brest Sound.

Go back in the direction of Plougastel-Daoulas and after 3km - 2 miles, turn right.

★★**Pointe de Kerdéniel** – *15 min on foot Rtn. Leave the car at the bottom of Kerdéniel and after the houses turn right and take the lane on the left (signposts) to the block-house.* The view extends, from left to right, over Le Faou estuary, the mouth of the Aulne, Ménez-Hom, île Longue, Presqu'île de Crozon's east coast to Pointe des Espagnols and Brest Sound.
Continue by car towards Pointe de l'Armorique to Porzmeur, a tiny fishing port in a pleasant setting.

Turn back and after 3km – 2 miles, bear right.

Lauberlach – A small fishing port and sailing centre in a pretty cove.

Take the road on the right towards St-Adrien.

From the hillside, the road gives fine glimpses of Lauberlach cove and passes the Chapelle St-Adrien (1549) on the right.

Then turn right towards St-Guénolé.

At Pennaster, go round Lauberlach cove. The Chapelle St-Guénolé (1514) stands in a wooded setting on the left side of the road.

At the first junction beyond St-Guenolé, take an uphill road on the right; turn right, then left into a stony lane.

★**Panorama de Keramenez** – *Viewing-table.* An extensive panorama over the Presqu'île de Plougastel and the southern section of Brest roadstead.

Return to Plougastel-Daoulas by the fishing ports of Tinduff and Lestraouen and Lanriwaz.

PLOUMANACH★★

Michelin map 59 fold 1 or 230 fold 6 – Local map under CORNICHE BRETONNE – Facilities

This little fishing port on the pink granite coast, belonging to the municipality of Perros-Guirec and well situated at the mouths of the two picturesque Traouiéros Valleys, has become a well-known seaside resort, famous for its piles of **rocks**★★. You will get a good view of them by going to the lighthouse.

SIGHTS

★★**Parc municipal** – This park extends from Pors-Kamor, where the lifeboat is kept, to Pors-Rolland. It is a sort of reserve where the rocky site is kept in its original state. The most interesting feature is Pointe de Squewel, formed of innumerable rocks separated by coves. The Devil's Castle (Château du Diable) also makes a fine picture.

The park is studded with curiously-shaped rocks: note a turtle by the sea, and inland, a mushroom, a rabbit, etc.

Promenade de la Bastille – *Entrance opposite the Chapelle St-Guirec.*
This promenade leads to another part of the rocks and gives a better view of the harbour entrance. On a small island stands Costaeres' modern manor where Sienkiewicz, the author of *Quo Vadis*, used to live.

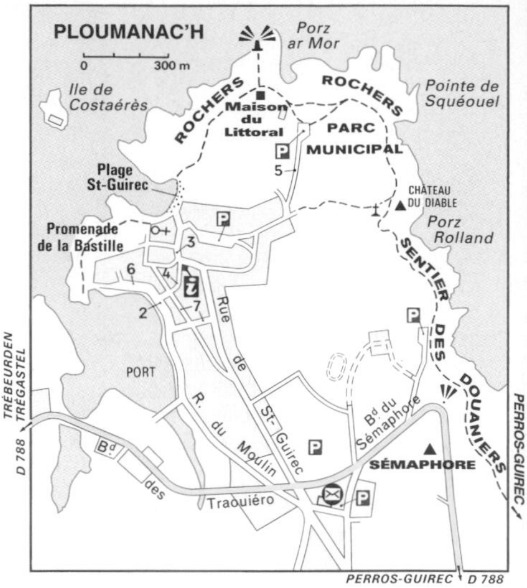

Bellevue (Q. de)	2	Fournier (R. A.)	5
Centre (Pl. du)	3	Pointe (R. de la)	6
Centre (R. du)	4	Port (R. du)	7

Beach (Plage) – The beach lies in the Bay of St-Guirec. At the far end on the left, on a rock washed by the sea at high tide, stands the oratory dedicated to St Guirec, who landed here in the 6C. A granite statue of the saint has taken the place of the original wooden effigy which had suffered from a disrespectful tradition: girls who wanted to get married stuck a pin into his nose.

Lighthouse (Phare) – Go down to the beach, pass in front of the Hôtel St-Guirec and follow the uphill path to the lighthouse, passing among splendid **rocks★★**. Note the unusual shapes: a skull, a clog turned upside down, a foot. From the platform the view extends from Trégastel to the beach at Trestel and beyond it to the coast towards Port-Blanc, taking in Sept-Îles and the Presqu'île de Perros-Guirec.

EXCURSION

★★ **Perros-Guirec by the Sentier des Douaniers** – *3 hours on foot Rtn. Go preferably in the afternoon at high tide.*
A path along the edge of the cliff leads from Pors-Rolland to Trestraou, the main beach of Perros-Guirec *(qv)*.

M. Fouorou/AZIMUT

Municipal Park, Ploumanach

The **Michelin Maps** *for this region are shown in the diagram below the table of contents on page 3. The text refers to the maps which, owing to their scale or coverage, are the clearest and most appropriate in each case.*

PONT-AVEN★

Population 3 031

Michelin map 58 fold 11 or 230 fold 33

The town lies in a very pleasant setting at the point where the River Aven, after flowing between rocks, opens out into a tidal estuary. The Aven used to drive numerous mills, hence the saying: "Pont-Aven, a famous town; fourteen mills, fifteen houses". Today only one mill remains in operation. Pont-Aven is also famous for *Galettes de Pont-Aven* (butter cookies).

The place has been a favourite resort of painters; the Pont-Aven School, headed by Gauguin, was formed in about 1888. The poet and songwriter Théodore Botrel *(qv)* spent a great part of his life in Pont-Aven and is buried here. Botrel started the Festival of the Golden Gorse (Fête des Fleurs d'Ajoncs – *see the Calendar of Events at the end of the guide*).

Pont-Aven School – Between 1886-96 more than 20 painters (Charles Laval, Paul Sérusier, Charles Filiger, Maurice Denis...) grouped around Paul Gauguin seeking to invent new forms of artistic expression. The meeting between Paul Gauguin and Émile Bernard in 1888 was the beginning of the Synthetist group. Rejecting the Impressionist and Pointillist movements, their work was characterised by painting from memory, two-dimensional patterns, bright vivid colours and spiritual subjects.

The Caisse Nationale des Monuments Historiques has set up **La Route des Peintres**, which includes five itineraries of a day or two each, described in a book of the same name (*available in English*). The tours start in an art gallery, concentrating on the works of local and visiting artists in Cornouaille 1850-1950, then take the visitor off to discover the landscapes which inspired the art.

Breton Women by Gauguin

SIGHTS

★**Bois d'Amour** – *Access via Promenade Xavier-Grall.*
A footpath follows the meanders of the Aven and climbs the hillside. With the aid of maps produced by the tourist office, this pleasant walk unfolds to visitors the places which inspired the painters of the Pont-Aven School.

Promenade Xavier-Grall – *Access via Rue Émile-Bernard.*
This promenade (named after the poet and reporter **Xavier Grall**, 1930-81), along the Aven, passes by the mill course and gates, which regulated the water to the mills, and old wash-houses scattered on either side of the river. Footbridges span the river, which winds between the Porche-Menu rocks.

The banks of the Aven – *30 min on foot Rtn. Walk to the right of the bridge towards the harbour.*
Follow the river bank lined with rocks and ruined water-mills. On the river's east bank, there is an enormous rock called Gargantua's shoe (soulier de Gargantua). In the square, beside the harbour, is a statue of Botrel and on the opposite bank, amid the greenery, stands the house where he lived. About 800m - 875yds further on, there is a view of the fine stretch of water formed by the Aven. The once prosperous port (oysters, wine, salt and grain) is now used by pleasure boats.

Chapelle de Trémalo – *Access via Rue Émile-Bernard and right onto the D 24, the Quimper road (signposted).*
This characteristic early 16C Breton country chapel is set amid fine trees. It has a lop-sided roof, with one of the eaves nearly touching the ground. Inside is a 17C wooden Christ, which was the model for Gauguin's *Yellow Christ* where, painted in the background, is the village of Pont-Aven and Ste-Marguerite Hill.

Museum (Musée) ⏱ – The modern wing is for temporary exhibits and the old wing recounts with photographs and documents the history of Pont-Aven: the town, port, Gorse-Bloom Festival, and the Pont-Aven painters and their lodgings (Pension Gloanec).
The first floor houses the permanent collection concentrating on the Pont-Aven School *(see above)*: Maurice Denis *(St John Bonfire at Loctudy)*, Émile Jourdan *(Trémalo Chapel)*, Rouillet *(The Port in Pont-Aven)*, Gustave Loiseau *(View of Pont-Aven)*, Henri Moret *(Seascape)*.

EXCURSIONS

Nizon – *3km – 2 miles northwest. Leave Pont-Aven by the D 24 towards Rosporden.*
The small **church** (restored) with its squat pillars dates from the 15 and 16C and contains many old statues. The colours of the stained-glass windows by the master glazier Guével are remarkable. The Romanesque Calvary was used as a model by Gauguin for his *Green Christ.*

From Pont-Aven to Concarneau on the coast road – *45km – 28 miles – about 1 hour 30 min. Leave Pont-Aven west on the D 783, the Concarneau road and after 2.5km – 1.5 miles, turn left.*

Névez – In the **Chapelle Ste-Barbe** ⏱ there are some old wooden statues, in particular the large statue of St Barbara and her tower.

Beyond Névez, in the direction of Port-Manech, take the road on the left leading to Kerdruc.

Kerdruc – In a pretty **setting★** overlooking the Aven, this small port still has some old thatched cottages.

Port-Manech – Facilities. A charming resort with a well-sited beach on the Aven-Belon estuary. A path cut in the hillside links the port to the beach and offers fine views of the coast and islands.

Make for Rospico Cove via Kerangall. The rest of the excursion is described in the opposite direction under CONCARNEAU: Excursions.

PONTCHÂTEAU

Population 7 549

Michelin map 63 fold 15 or 230 folds 52 and 53

The church of Pontchâteau, which is perched on a hill in a region of windmills, now no longer in use, overlooks the little town with its houses built in terraces on the banks of the River Brivet.

EXCURSIONS

Calvaire de la Madeleine – *4km – 2.5 miles west. Leave Pontchâteau on the D 33 towards Herbignac. Leave the car in the car park on the left side of the road.*
St Louis-Marie Grignion de Montfort (*qv*; 1673-1716), a famous preacher, had the Calvary built in 1709 on the heath of the same name. Destroyed under Louis XIV, it was rebuilt in 1821.
From the Temple of Jerusalem, a fortress-type oriental palace, an alley crosses the park and leads to Pilate's Court or Scala Sancta, the five high reliefs of which represent the Passion. It is the first station in the Stations of the Cross which, further on (on the left) are continued by large white statues derived from the local folklore. From above the Calvary the view extends to the Brière, St-Nazaire and Donges. The small chapel at the foot of the Calvary houses the original Christ (1707) in wood as well as frescoes recounting the life of the preacher, Montfort. *(Pilgrimages on Sundays in summer).*

Fuseau de la Madeleine – *800m - 875 yds. Take the road to the left of the statue of the Sacred Heart, cross the park and bear left at the first crossroads.*
This menhir, 7m - 23ft tall and 5m - 16ft in circumference, stands in the middle of a field.

St-Gildas-des-Bois – *10km – 6 miles northeast on the D 773.*
The church, formerly a Benedictine abbey, dates from the 12 and 13C and was remodelled in the 19C. Inside this reddish sandstone edifice are elegant 18C furnishings: choir stalls, 2 stone altarpieces, an interior porch in painted wood and a wrought-iron grille which was originally at the chancel. Modern stained glass windows are by Maurice Rocher.

PONT-CROIX★

Population 1 762

Michelin map 58 fold 14 or 230 fold 17 – Local map under CORNOUAILLE

A small town built up in terraces on the south bank of the Goyen, also known as the River Audierne. Its narrow streets, hemmed in between old houses, slope picturesquely down to the bridge. A great procession take place there on 15 August. Take Petite and Grande-Rue-Chère; the latter is a charming stepped street.

★**Église Notre-Dame-de-Roscudon** ⏲ – The church is interesting with its Romanesque nave dating from the early 13C. The chancel was enlarged in 1290 and the transept was built in 1450 and crowned by the very fine **belfry**★ with a steeple 67m - 223ft high which served as a model for those of Quimper Cathedral. The polygonal apse was rebuilt in 1540. There is an elegant south **porch** (late 14C) with three tall decorated gables.

Inside, the church contains fine furnishings: in the apsidal chapel is a **Last Supper** carved in high relief in wood (17C); on the right of the chancel, the Chapel of the Rosary (Chapelle du Rosaire) has fine **stained glass** (*c*1540); and in the adjacent Chapel of the Holy Family (Chapelle de la Sainte-Famille) and the Chapel of the Dead (Chapelle des Trépassés) in the north transept are stained-glass windows by Gruber (1977-8). The organ loft dates from the 16C.

Pont-Croix – Notre-Dame-de-Roscudon

PONTIVY

Population 13 140

Michelin map 59 fold 12 or 230 fold 220

This little town stands on the Blavet in a green, pleasant and picturesque area.
The old town, with its narrow, winding streets, contrasts with the geometrical town plan laid out by Napoleon.

Napoléonville – Pontivy was a prosperous town and in 1790 declared wholeheartedly for the Republic. Napoleon, who was Consul at the time had a barracks, town hall, court and school built and, to ensure communication with the sea, he had the Blavet canalised. During the wars of the First Empire, coastal navigation between Brest and Nantes was very dangerous because of British cruisers in the Channel. Napoleon, therefore, decided to build a canal linking the two ports. As Pontivy was about halfway between them, the Emperor also decided to develop it into a town that would be the military and strategic centre of Brittany.

From 1806 the straight roads of the new town could be seen as they were dug out of the ground. The grateful townspeople called the city "Napoléonville". By the fall of the Empire, Napoléonville became Pontivy once more. It changed again under the Second Empire to Napoléonville but in due course reverted again.

SIGHTS

★**Old houses** (**Y**) – To admire the old half-timbered and corbelled houses of the 16 and 17C, walk along **Rue du Fil**, Place du Martray, the centre of old Pontivy, Rue du Pont and Rue du Docteur-Guérin. At the corner of Rues Lorois and Général-de-Gaulle, note the turreted house (1578), which is presumed to be the hunting pavilion of the Rohan family, and at Place Anne-de-Bretagne, the elegant 18C buildings.

Castle (Château) (**Y**) ⏲ – The castle was built in the 15C by Jean II de Rohan *(qv)*. The façade is flanked by two large machicolated towers with pepperpot roofs, all that remains of the four towers of the perimeter wall. The ramparts with walls 20m - 64ft high, are surrounded by a moat, which has always remained dry. The main building, remodelled in the 18C, is adorned with cusped pediments and a spiral staircase. The visit includes the guardroom, rooms on the first floor giving onto the wall-walk, the Duke's room with its ornate ceiling and the chapel.

Église Notre-Dame-de-Joie (**Y**) – The 16C church, built in the Flamboyant style, has in the north chapel, a statue of Notre-Dame-de-Joie, venerated by the local people since 1696 when an epidemic decimated the town. There is a 17C altarpiece in the south chapel.

PONTIVY

Nationale (R.) .... YZ
Pont (R. du) .... Y 28

Anne-de-Bretagne (Pl.) .... Y 2
Caïnain (R.) .... Z 3
Couvent (Q. du) .... Y 4
Dr.-Guépin (R. du) .... Y 5
Fil (R. du) .... Y 6
Friedland (R.) .... Y 8
Gaulle (R. du Gén. de) .... Y 9
Jaurès (R. Jean) .... Z 10
La Mennais (R. J.-M.-de) .... Z 13
Le Goff (R.) .... Z 16
Lorois (R.) .... Y 17
Marengo (R.) .... Z 19
Martray (Pl. du) .... Y 20
Niémen (Q.) .... Y 27
Presbourg (Q.) .... Y 32
Recollets (Q. des) .... Y 33
Viollard (Bd) .... Z 38

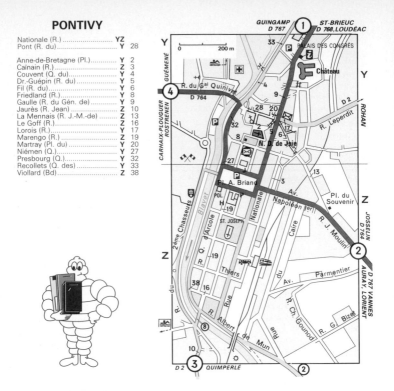

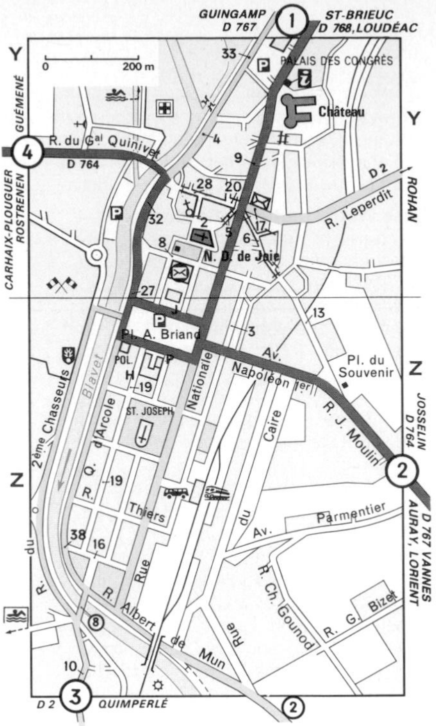

EXCURSIONS

★★**Lac de Guerlédan** – *67km – 42 miles – about 3 hours 30 min. Take the D 156 to Guerlédan by the church in Stival (see below).*
The road follows the Blavet Valley.

At Le Corboulo, turn right and 500m - 547yds further on, left towards St-Aignan. The rest of the excursion to the lac de Guerlédan is described under Lac de GUERLÉDAN.

Stival – *3.5km – 2 miles northwest. Leave Pontivy on ④ on the town plan, the road to Guéméné-sur-Scorff.*
The former Chapelle St Mériadoc, now the **parish church** ⊙, dates from the 16C. The fine **stained-glass windows**★ (1552) by Jehan Le Flamant depict a Tree of Jesse at the east end, scenes from the Passion in the south transept and Baptism of Christ near the font. Note also a 16C Virgin Nursing in the north transept and St Isidore in the south transept. An 18C ciborium crowns the high altar.

Blavet Valley – *Round tour of 40km – 25 miles – about 3 hours. Leave Pontivy on Rue Albert-de-Mun, in the direction of Auray and turn right at Talvern-Nenez.*

Chapelle St-Nicodème ⊙ – This 16C chapel is preceded by a massive tower with a granite steeple. A Renaissance doorway leading to a 16C staircase opens at the base of the tower. Inside, a frieze carved with angels and musicians runs round the base of the panelled vault.
To the left of the chapel, a Gothic fountain empties into three piscinas in front of three niches surmounted by richly carved gables. There is a less ornate fountain in front. The presbytery, at the chapel's east end, has dormer windows and chimneys decorated with carvings. *Pardon* on the first Sunday in August.

Turn right after the chapel.

St-Nicolas-des-Eaux – The little town is built on the side of a hill. With its chapel above the town, surrounded by thatch roofed houses, St-Nicolas-des-Eaux is certainly unusual.
The road crosses the Blavet, and following the tongue of land encircled by the river bends back on itself before crossing to the narrow isthmus which overlooks the inner banks of the loop.

★**Site de Castennec** – From the turret-belvedere to the left of the uphill road, there is a magnificent view downstream of the valley and from the car park of St-Nicolas-des-Eaux and of the valley upstream.

Turn left after Castennec.

Bieuzy – The **church** ⊙, with its high, modern tower, looks even taller since it stands on an islet. The 16C chevet, marred by a war memorial, has Renaissance Gothic

ornament. The stained-glass windows form an attractive series and the woodwork and beams are also worth looking at.
To the left of the church, note two Renaissance houses with bread oven and well. Below, to the right of the road, stands a gabled fountain.
Many farms in the area have graceful 17-18C wells which are of interest.

Go to Melrand passing through La Paule.

Melrand – Take the road towards Guémené in order to cross this typically Breton town, with its granite houses, and reach the Calvary. At the top is the Holy Trinity; the shaft is ornamented with the heads of the Apostles; the base depicts the Entombment and Christ bearing the Cross. The whole stands on another base which bears two more recent statues of the Virgin and St John.
The **Ferme archéologique** (Archaeological Farm) ⊙ consists of an excavated village, Lann Gouh (meaning old heath), dating back to *c*1000 and a reconstituted farm. The signposted (descriptive panels) visit ends at a medieval garden.

Return to Melrand and follow the road towards Pontivy for 6.5km – 4 miles then turn left.

Quelven – The imposing **chapel** ⊙ was built at the end of the 15C and stands surrounded by old granite houses. The exterior is richly decorated in the Flamboyant style. The stark interior features a gallery built of stone in the nave, a 16C alabaster low relief in the south transept, two stained-glass windows (16C), including a Tree of Jesse, in the chancel, to the left, and in the south transept.
To the left of the chancel is an opening statue of Our Lady of Quelven showing the Virgin Seated with the Infant Jesus in her lap; within it has twelve low reliefs relating the life of Christ. A very popular *pardon* is held every year *(see the Calendar of Events at the end of the guide)*. Below, 500m - 547yds to the left of the chapel stands the 16C fountain of Notre-Dame-de-Quelven surmounted by a gabled niche.

To return to Pontivy, take the direction of Gueltas and turn right and after 3km – 2 miles left.

Abbaye Notre-Dame-de-Timadeuc – *22km – 14 miles – about 1 hour 30 min. Leave Pontivy by Rues Lorois and Leperdit.*

Chapelle Ste-Noyale ⊙ – Standing in the midst of lawns and trees is an elegant 15C ensemble dedicated to St Noyale and a granite cross. The long and narrow chapel has a finely ornamented south porch and a belfry porch (finished in the 17C). The paintings on the panels inside depict the life of St Noyale.

Noyal-Pontivy – The large **church** was built in the 15C and has Flamboyant decoration. The massive square tower set on the south transept is surmounted by a tall polygonal stone spire.

Continue towards Rohan.

Rohan – Formerly a viscounty and later a duchy, the town retains hardly any trace of the rule of the Rohan family. The Nantes-Brest Canal, the wooded banks, the lock and the Chapelle Notre-Dame-de-Bonne-Encontre (1510) make a pretty picture.

2km – 1 mile beyond Rohan, bear right into the road leading to the abbey.

Abbaye N.-D.-de-Timadeuc ⊙ – A Cistercian abbey founded in 1841 in a wooded setting. Although the monastery is not open to the public, one is allowed to attend the religious services. Slides shown with commentary at the gatehouse. Bookstore and produce made by the monks: cheeses, crystallized fruit, vegetables. It is also possible to share the monks' life of praying and silent meditation at a number of centres, open to both groups and private individuals.

PONT-L'ABBÉ

Population 7 374

Michelin map 58 folds 14 and 15 or 230 folds 31 and 32 – Local map under CORNOUAILLE

This town, which stands at the head of an estuary, owes its name to the first bridge *(pont)* built by the monks *(abbés)* of Loctudy between the harbour and the lake *(étang)*. It is the capital of the Bigouden district which is bounded by the estuary of the Odet, the coast of Penmarc'h and Audierne Bay. *Bigouden (qv)* costume is most original and is still worn, for example, during the Embroidery Festival (*Fête des Brodeuses*), where it lends a picturesque note to the scene. Local specialities are embroidery and the making of dolls.
The shipyards (fishing and pleasure boats) also play a significant role in the town's activities.

The "Stamped Paper" Revolt (1675) – The glory that Louis XIV won for France cost a lot of money. In 1675 Colbert decreed that all legal acts must be recorded on stamped paper. He also reimposed taxes on tobacco and pewter vessels which Brittany had taken over, a few years before, at a cost of 2 million livres. Anger was great but repression, in the guise of the wheel and the hangman's noose, was powerful; the Parliament that protested was exiled to Vannes. Pont-l'Abbé, in particular, suffered at the suppression of the rebellion; its castle was pillaged.

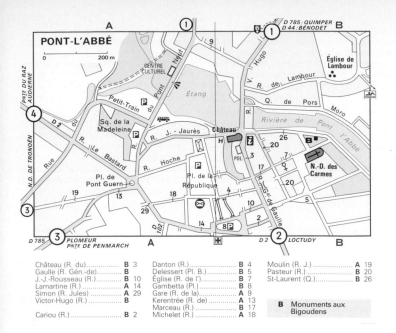

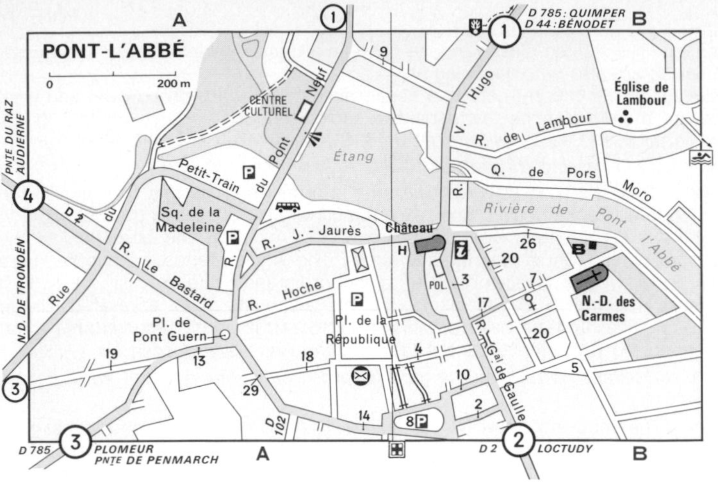

Château (R. du) ... B 3
Gaulle (R. Gén.-de) ... B
J.-J.-Rousseau (R.) ... B 10
Lamartine (R.) ... A 14
Simon (R. Jules) ... A 29
Victor-Hugo (R.) ... B

Cariou (R.) ... B 2
Danton (R.) ... B 4
Delessert (Pl. B.) ... B 5
Église (R. de l') ... B 7
Gambetta (Pl.) ... B 8
Gare (R. de la) ... A 9
Kerentrée (R. de) ... A 13
Marceau (R.) ... B 17
Michelet (R.) ... A 18
Moulin (R. J.) ... A 19
Pasteur (R.) ... B 20
St-Laurent (Q.) ... B 26

B Monuments aux Bigoudens

SIGHTS

Église Notre-Dame-des-Carmes (**B**) ⓥ – Former 14C chapel of the Carmelite monastery. On the right going in stands an 18C font; the canopy comes from the Église de Lambour *(qv)*. Above the high altar is a 15C stained-glass window with a rose 7.7m - 25ft in diameter. To the left, the Chapelle Ste-Anne is a modern processional banner; in the nave statues of the Virgin and St John, both of the 16C, flank Christ. As you come out, turn right to go round the church and look at the flat chevet crowned by an unusual domed belfry. *Pardon* on the Sunday after 15 July.

Castle (Château) (**B**) – This 14-18C fortress has a large oval tower or keep with a building attached. Go round the tower to see the turret overlooking Rue du Château. Inside the keep you may visit the **musée Bigouden** ⓥ (taped commentary on each floor) housed on three floors *(79 steps)*, which has collections of Bigouden costumes, beautifully embroidered headdresses and 19C furniture (box beds, dressers, chests), models of boats, sailing equipment... The tour ends with a visit to a **Maison du Pays bigouden** *(see below)*.

Monument aux Bigoudens (**B B**) – This monument by the sculptor F. Bazin stands in a verdant setting by the quayside.

Église de Lambour (**B**) – The ruined church retains a fine 16C façade and some bays of the 13C nave. The bell tower was razed during a peasant revolt *(see below)*.

EXCURSIONS

Chapelle N.-D.-de-Tréminou ⓥ *– 2km - 1 mile west on Rue Jean-Moulin* (**A 19**). Standing in a shaded close this 14 and 16C chapel (restored) has a belfry which is set above the nave.

Near this chapel, in 1675, the Cornouaille peasants in revolt adopted the "peasant code". Closely linked with the "stamped paper" revolt, this mass uprising was severely crushed and many bell towers in the vicinity were razed to the ground in reprisal. A *pardon* takes place on the fourth Sunday in September.

Maison du Pays bigouden ⓥ *– 2km - 1 mile on ② on the town plan, the road to Loctudy.*

A fine alley bordered by chestnut trees leads to the Ferme de Kervazégan. Built around the courtyard are the farmhouse and outbuildings (sheds, cowshed, pigsty, stable). The farmhouse is a solid squat building with dressed stone covered with lime; inside, the two rooms, which were lived in, are furnished with Bigouden furnishings (cupboards decorated with copper studs, box beds, longcase clock) and utensils (churn, creamer, salting tub).

In the outbuildings are the farm tools (apple crusher, press...).

Plomeur *– 5.5km – 3.5 miles southwest. Leave Pont-L'Abbé by ③ on the town plan.* The Église Ste-Thumette dates from 1760 and its massive façade is flanked by low turrets. Inside are several 15C statues in the chancel and transept, and an unusual pregnant Virgin in the south transept. At the far end of the nave is a Romanesque capital.

PORNICHET

Population 8 133
Michelin map 63 fold 14 or 230 fold 52 – Facilities

Originally a salt marsh workers' village, Pornichet became a much-frequented seaside resort in 1860. The town was known as a place of rendezvous for Parisian publishers. The beach is the continuation of the 8km - 5-mile-long stretch of fine sand which makes up Côte d'Amour *(qv)*. The town is composed of two distinct districts: Old Pornichet, to the southeast, which is a busy administrative centre all the year round, and Pornichet-les-Pins to the northwest, with its large villas surrounded by greenery.

Boulevard des Océanides – It runs along the beach, affording good **views** of La Baule, Le Pouliguen and Pointe de Penchâteau and leads to the small fishing port and to the pleasure boat harbour, shared also by La Baule, which can take over 1 000 boats. Pornichet also boasts a casino, a thermal treatment centre and the well-known racecourse of Côte d'Amour region created on reclaimed marshland.

PORT-LOUIS*

Population 2 986
Michelin map 63 fold 1 or 230 fold 34 – Facilities

Port-Louis is a small fishing port (tuna) and seaside resort where many of the inhabitants of Lorient may be found. It still has its 16C citadel, 17C ramparts, as well as several interesting old houses (Rue de la Poste, Rue des Dames, Petite Rue, Rue du Driasker).
Port-Louis was originally called Blavet. During the League, the Duke of Mercœur captured it with the help of the Spaniards. Forty young girls fled in a ship, but the Spaniards saw them and gave chase. Rather than be taken by the victorious enemy, all forty girls joined hands and jumped into the sea.
It was under Louis XIII that Blavet took the name of Port-Louis in honour of the King. Richelieu made it a fortified port and the headquarters of the first India Company *(qv)*, which failed. When Colbert founded the second India Company, Lorient was built to receive it. From that time on, Port-Louis declined. Under Louis-Philippe the town found new life in sardine fishing and canning in oil.
The town has two **fishing harbours**: Locmalo in Gâvres cove and, opposite Lorient, La Point, which has been equipped with 200 moorings for pleasure boats.

**CITADELLE *time: 1 hour 30 min*

The citadel is at the entrance to the Lorient roadstead. Its construction occurred in different stages: in 1591, during the Spanish occupation by Juan del Aguila; continued in 1616-22, by Marshal Brissac and completed in 1636 under Richelieu. Built on a rectangular plan, the citadel is bastioned at the corners and sides; 2 bridges and a demilune protect the entrance. The citadel has always been a prison – among its "occupants" was Louis Napoleon, the future Emperor Napoleon III.
A signposted path directs you to the parapet walk (note the cannons facing the île de Groix) which looks onto two courtyards and the different parts of the edifice of which some contain museums, the **Musées de la Citadelle** ⓥ.

Musée du Port-Louis – In the entrance pavilion or keep. Exhibits trace the town's maritime past and the citadel's history.

Musée de la Compagnie des Indes, Port-Louis

Porcelain bowl

★★ **Musée de la Compagnie des Indes** – Housed in the new wing of the Lourmel barracks, this India Company Museum traces the history of this prestigious company from the founding of Lorient, its expansion in the 18C, its crews, cargoes, trading posts (in India, Africa, China), maps, furnishings and engravings.
One gallery concentrates on the theme of the India Company's fleet: shipbuilding, cargoes, models of *Comte d'Artois* (with cargo and passengers) and *Comte de Provence* (both built in the Lorient shipyards).

★ **Salle de l'Arsenal** – Housed in the Arsenal, in a room which has fine woodwork, ship's models (corvettes, frigates, merchant ships, cruisers, etc), portraits of seamen, paintings and documents pertaining to navigation on the Atlantic are on display. Reduced model of the *Napoleon's* (launched in Cherbourg in 1850) engine room.

Poudrière – The former Powder Factory contains 17 to 20C arms (torpedoes, mines, mortars, munitions, etc) and documents on naval artillery.

Musée de Bateaux – The Boat Museum focuses on a lifeboat, *Commandant Philippes de Kerhallet*, manned by 12 oarsmen, built in Le Havre in 1857 and used between 1897-1939 at Roscoff. Also on display are old and modern lifesaving equipment and several fishing boats.

Ramparts – Built between 1649 and 1653 by Marshal Meilleraye, these ramparts envelop the town on two sides. On Promenade des Pâtis, a door in the wall leads to a fine sandy beach from where there is a pleasant view onto Pointe de Gâvres, île de Groix, Larmor-Plage and the citadel's Groix bastion, named as such because it is across from the île de Groix.

Le POULIGUEN

Population 4 912

Michelin map 63 fold 14 or 230 fold 51 – Local map under Presqu'île de GUÉRANDE

Lying to the west of La Baule, this former fishing village is separated from the latter by a channel *(étier)*, spanned by two bridges. The village with its narrow streets became a fashionable resort in 1854. The beach is sheltered by a pleasant 6ha - 15 acre wood; the pleasure boat harbour is upstream from that at La Baule.

★ **La Côte Sauvage** – This stretch of coast starts from the Pointe de Penchâteau. Skirted by boulevards and footpaths, the coastline alternates rocky parts with great sandy bays and has numerous caves which are accessible only at low tide.

Chapelle Ste-Anne-et-St-Julien ⓥ – *Place Mgr-Freppel.* Standing near a Calvary, this Gothic chapel has a 16C **statue of St Anne** with the Virgin and the Infant Jesus in the north aisle, and a stained-glass window representing St Julian (in the chancel). At the west end, on either side of the porch are two interesting **bas-reliefs** depicting the Coronation of the Virgin and the Adoration of the Magi.

QUESTEMBERT

Population 5 076

Michelin map 63 fold 4 or 230 folds 37 and 38

A small friendly town located in a verdant countryside. Around the marketplace stand elegant granite town houses (16-17C) with carved pediments. In Rue St-Michel, in a garden, is an odd-looking turret, the roof of which is held up by two carved busts of "Questembert and his wife".

Marketplace (Halles) – Built in 1552 and restored in 1675. The remarkable timberwork covers the three alleys.

Chapelle St-Michel – This small 16C chapel stands in the cemetery. On the north side is a Calvary. This monument, as well as the one built on Place du Monument, recalls the victory of Alain-le-Grand over the Norsemen in 888 at Coët-Bihan *(6.5km – 4 miles southeast of Questembert)*.

EXCURSION

Chapelle N.-D.-des-Vertus ⓥ – *6.5km – 4 miles southwest on the D 7.* This lovely 15-16C chapel dedicated to Our Lady of Virtue is located beside the road near a farm. Note the portal with double basket arched windows, on the south side corbels carved in the shape of animals or figures support the ogee-shaped mouldings of the door and windows. The Flamboyant bay is at the chevet. A *pardon* is held the Sunday after 15 August.

La Vraie-Croix – *8km – 5 miles west by D 1.* This charming village decked with flowers (awarded First Prize for the prettiest flowered village in 1994) still has its chapel resting on ribbed vaulting. In the old days, the road used to run underneath the vaulting. The lower part of the building appears to date back to the 13C. Two flights of steps carved in stone on the outside of the chapel lead to the upper section, which was rebuilt in 1611.
The building houses a gilded reliquary cross containing a fragment of the Cross of Our Lord.

Presqu'île de QUIBERON★

Michelin map 63 folds 11 and 12 or 230 folds 35 and 49

This former island is now attached to the mainland by a narrow isthmus. This natural jetty acts as a breakwater for a great bay which is often used by warships for exercises and firing practice (Polygone de Gâvres).
The landscape of the peninsula varies; the sand dunes of the isthmus are fixed by maritime pines. The ocean coast, known as the "Wild Coast" (Côte Sauvage), is an impressive jumble of cliffs, rocks, caves and reefs; to the east and south are wide beaches and two lively fishing ports.

Hoche repels the exiles (July 1795) – Quiberon saw the rout of the Royalists in 1795. The French exiles in England and Germany had made great plans; 100 000 men, led by the princes, were to land in Brittany, join hands with the Chouans and drive out the "Blues". In fact, the British fleet which anchored in the Quiberon roadstead carried only 10 000 men, commanded by Puisaye, Hervilly and Sombreuil. The princes did not come. The landing began on the beach at Carnac on 27 June and continued for several days. Cadoudal's Chouans *(qv)* joined them. But the effect of surprise was lost; long preparations and talk among the exiles had warned the Convention; **General Hoche** was ready, and he drove the invaders back into the peninsula. Driven to the beach at Port-Haliguen, the exiles tried to re-embark. Unfortunately, the British ships were prevented by a heavy swell from getting near enough to land and the Royalists were captured. The Convention refused to pardon them. Some were shot at Quiberon and others were taken to Auray and Vannes *(qv)* and shot there.

TOUR

Quiberon – *Town plan in the current Michelin Red Guide France.* Facilities. At the far end of the peninsula, Quiberon is a popular resort with its fine south-facing sandy beach and proximity to the Côte Sauvage. **Port-Maria**, which is the departure point for boat services to Belle-Île, Houat and Hœdic, is a busy harbour and a fishing port where a few sardine boats can still be seen. Some of the catch is marketed to be eaten fresh; the rest is canned in the local factories.

★★ 1 ROUND TOUR OF LA CÔTE SAUVAGE

18km – 11 miles – about 2 hours

Go to Port-Maria and bear right into the coast road (signposted "route côtière"*).*

Dumoulin/CAMPAGNE CAMPAGNE

Quiberon's Côte Sauvage

This wild coast is a succession of jagged cliffs where caves, crevasses and inlets alternate with little sandy beaches with crashing rolling waves *(bathing prohibited; ground-swell)*. Rocks of all shapes and sizes edge the coast, forming passages and labyrinths in which the sea boils and roars.

Small granite steles line the road on the left and mark the main sights: Port-Pilote, Trou du Souffleur, Pointe du Scouro, Grotte de Kerniscob, etc, which should be seen on foot.

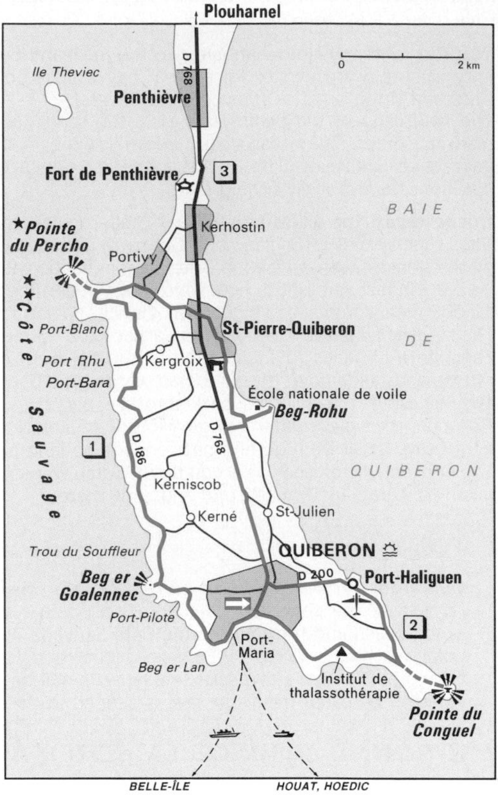

Beg er Goalennec – Go around the Café Le Vivier and over the rocks to reach the tip of the promontory from where there is a pretty view over the whole length of the Côte Sauvage.

After Kroh-Kollé, bear left.

The road runs downhill towards **Port-Bara**, a cove prickling with rocks, before going inland. Surfaced roads lead to Port-Rhu and Port-Blanc; the latter has a nice white sandy beach.

★**Pointe du Percho** – *Go on foot to the tip of the point.* A lovely **view**★ opens out, on the left, to the Côte Sauvage, on the right, to the Isthme de Penthièvre, its fort and beach, and beyond the islands of Belle-Île and Groix.
The last stele indicates Beg en Aud, the furthest point on this coastline.

Cross Portivy and drive to St-Pierre-Quiberon.

St-Pierre-Quiberon – Facilities. This resort has two beaches on either side of the small port of Orange. Take Rue des Menhirs to see the St-Pierre lines made up of 22 menhirs on the right.

Beg-Rohu – Rocky home of the **École nationale de Voile** (National Sailing School).

Return to the main road and turn left for Quiberon.

2 ROUND TOUR OF POINTE DU CONGUEL

6km – 4 miles – about 1 hour 30 min

Leave Quiberon to the east by Boulevard Chanard.

Drive round the **Institut de Thalassothérapie** – salt-water cures for arthrosis, rheumatism, over-exertion and the after-effects of injuries.

Pointe du Conguel – *Viewing table. 30 min on foot Rtn.* From the tip of the point there is a view of Belle-Ile, Houat and Hœdic Islands, the Morbihan coast and Quiberon Bay. Teignouse Lighthouse, near which the battleship *France*, which sank in 1922 after striking a reef, can also be seen.

Go to Port-Haliguen.

On the left there is an aerodrome with a runway for light aircraft. Beyond Fort-Neuf, note the bustle created on the beach by the various sailing clubs and schools. The view opens out over the bay and the Morbihan coastline. Pass on your right, an obelisk commemorating the surrender of the exiles in 1795.

Port-Haliguen – A small fishing and pleasure boat harbour (summer regattas).

Return to Quiberon by Rue de Port-Haliguen.

3 ISTHME DE PENTHIÈVRE

This provides road and rail links between the former island and the mainland.

Fort de Penthièvre – Rebuilt in the 19C, it commands the access to the peninsula. A monument and a crypt commemorate 59 members of the Resistance shot here in 1944.

Penthièvre – This small resort has two fine sandy beaches on either side of the isthmus.

Plouharnel – Located at the edge of Bego Cove, the **galion de Plouharnel** ⏲ a modern replica of an 18C galleon, displays a collection of shells and shell pictures including the Piazza San Marco in Venice, a Japanese pagoda, etc.
On the opposite side of the road, in an old blockhouse, is the **Musée de la Chouannerie** ⏲. The Chouannerie *(qv)* movement, a Breton Royalist revolt, is recounted with dioramas peopled with terracotta figures, depicting the movement's main antagonists and Chouan arms, costumes, guillotine etc.

BOAT TRIPS

★★ **Belle-Île** – *See BELLE-ÎLE.*

Île de Hoedic – *See Île de HŒDIC.*

Île d'Houat – *See Île d'HOUAT.*

QUIMPER★★

Conurbation 59 437
Michelin map 58 fold 15 or 230 fold 18 – Local maps under CORNOUAILLE and Excursions below

The town lies in a pretty little valley at the junction (*kemper* in Breton) of the Steir and Odet Rivers. This used to be the capital of Cornouaille, and it is here, perhaps, that the traditional atmosphere of the province can best be felt. The **Festival de Cornouaille★** *(see the Calendar of Events at the end of the guide)* is an important folk festival.

HISTORICAL NOTES

St Corentine's fish – For centuries the town was called Quimper-Corentin, after its first bishop. According to legend, Corentine lived on the flesh of a single, miraculous fish. Every morning he took half the fish to eat and threw the other half back into the river. When he came back the next day the fish was whole once more and offered itself to be eaten again. Corentine was the adviser and supporter of King Gradlon *(qv)*.

Four men of Quimper – The statue of **Laënnec** (1781-1826) commemorates the most illustrious son of Quimper – the man who invented the stethoscope (*see Ploaré under DOUARNENEZ*).
Streets are named after Kerguelen, Fréron and Madec, three other famous men of Quimper. **Yves de Kerguelen** (1734-97) was a South Seas explorer; a group of islands bears his name. **Élie Fréron** (1718-76) was a critic, bitterly opposed to Voltaire and other philosophers. **René Madec** (1738-84) was a hero of adventure. As a cabin boy in a ship of the India Company, he jumped overboard and landed at Pondichéry. He served a rajah and became a successful man. The British found a relentless enemy in him. When he returned to France, enormously rich, the King gave him a title and the Cross of St-Louis, with a colonel's commission.

QUIMPER FAÏENCE

Over the centuries, the evolution of Quimper faïence has been enriched by numerous contributions giving fresh impetus to its production and encouraging creativity, with the result that it impossible to talk of any one particular style when discussing this art form.

A dynasty of faïence makers – In 1690, a southerner, Jean Baptiste Bousquet, a faïence maker from St-Zacharie near Marseilles, settled on the site which was to become Locmaria, a suburb of Quimper on the banks of the Odet, where it has been revealed that potters were active as early as the Gallo-Roman era. Bousquet founded the first Quimper faïence works, where he adopted his favoured style from Moustiers faïence ware. His son Pierre succeeded him in 1708 and associated himself with a faïence maker from Nevers, Pierre Belleveaux, and later on with a faïence maker from Rouen, Pierre-Clément Caussy. Both these were to play an important role in the evolution of Quimper faïence, one by enriching it with new shapes, colours (yellow) and

Nevers decorative motifs, the other by introducing rich iron red to the Quimper palette and adding some 300 decorative designs (tracings). It is this blend of expertise and working methods handed down to Quimper "painters" over the centuries which has made Quimper, now a real guild centre for this craft, the seat of an artistic production distinguished by the diversity of style it encompasses. Two more faïence works were established in Quimper towards the end of the 18C, Porquier faïence works, founded by François Eloury *c*1772 and with which the name of **Alfred Beau** *(qv)* is linked, and Dumaine faïence works, over which Jules Henriot assumed directorship in 1884.
It was *c*1840 that faïence ware decorated with Breton motifs appeared (such as the "little Breton", a caricature character which was to usurp traditional motifs), and that production began to be industrialised. The series of "Breton Scenes" created by A. Beau was inspired by tales and engravings, and his later series of "Breton Legends" met with resounding success.
The techniques currently in use at Quimper are directed towards decoration entirely done by hand, which demands considerable manual dexterity.

The Age of Artists – The creativity of artists, both associated with and independent from the faïence works, allied itself with spirit of enterprise and the faïence makers' craft, giving rise to unique works of art. Under the encouragement of Jules Verlingue, one of the last great directors of the "Grande Maison" faïence works, production took a new direction, laying greater emphasis on inventiveness and attracting in this way a long succession of artists from 1920 onwards. One of the first, **René Quillivic** (1879-1969), sculptor and ceramic painter, produced some striking works with designs based on woodcuts.
The "*Ar Seiz Breur*" ("Seven Brothers" – a reference to seven Breton heros) movement was founded in 1923 by René-Yves Creston, Jeanne Malivel and Jorg Robin with the aim of modernising traditional Breton folk art by combining it with Art Deco and Cubism. Many of the works produced by the artists who were members of this movement can be seen in exhibitions on this period.
The Odetta trademark, registered in 1922, produced works in sandstone, in dark tones made iridescent with enamel. Artists whose signatures adorn such work include Georges Renaud, René Beauclair, one of the most prolific, Louis Garin, Paul Fouillen and Jacques Nam, whose passion for cats earned him the task of illustrating Colette's *Dialogue de bêtes* (conversations between Toby-chien the dog and Kiki-la-doucette the cat, 1904).

★★CATHÉDRALE ST-CORENTIN (BZ) *time: 1 hour 30 min*

This fine Gothic cathedral was built from the 13C (chancel) to the 15C (transept and nave). The two steeples were only erected in 1856, being modelled on the Breton steeple of Pont-Croix. To pay for their building the Bishop asked the diocese's 600 000 faithful to each subscribe one *sou* a year for five years. The sea air quickly toned down the new stone, and it is difficult to believe that the upper part of the façade was four centuries later than the lower part.
After seeing the north side of the building make for the façade. Between the spires stands the statue of a man on horseback: this is King Gradlon *(qv)*. Until the 18C, on 26 July each year, a great festival was held in his honour. A man would climb up behind him, tie a napkin round his neck and offer him a glass of wine. Then he drank up the wine himself, carefully wiped the King's mouth with the napkin and threw the empty glass down on the square.
Any spectator who could catch the glass as it fell received a prize of 100 gold *écus*, if the glass was not broken. It used to be said that to save money the Town Council had a few sawcuts made in the stem of the glass.

Enter through the main door.

During the League, in the 16C, the nave was used as a place of refuge by the local people. Mass was said there among palliasses, boxes and hanging linen. Plague broke out there, killing 1 500 people.
The first thing that strikes you on entering the church is the fact that the choir is quite out of line with the nave due to the presence of a previous building. One theory is that in the early 13C, the cathedral craftsmen incorporated a small sanctuary, separated from the old Romanesque chancel by an alley and set off to the left, as the apsidal chapel. The new chancel linked this "chapel" to the nave.
The cathedral has a remarkable set of 15C **stained glass**★★ in the upper windows, mainly in the nave and transept, depicting canons, lords and ladies surrounded by their patron saints.
The tourist, going round the fine 92m - 302ft long building, will see in the side chapels, tombs (15C), altars, frescoes, altarpieces, statues, old (St John the Baptist, 15C alabaster) and modern works of art, a 17C pulpit adorned with low reliefs relating the life of St Corentine, and in the chapel beneath the south tower an Entombment copied from that in Bourges Cathedral and dating from the 18C.

QUIMPER

Astor (R.) .... AYZ 2
Chapeau-Rouge (R. du) .... AY 9
Kéréon (R.) .... AY
Kerguélen (Bd de) ...... BZ 23
Parc (R. du) .... BZ 34
St-François (R.) .... BZ 45
St-Mathieu (R.) .... AZ 47

Bécharles (Av. de) ...... BV 3
Beurre (Pl. au) .... BY 4
Boucheries (R. des) ... BY 6
Concarneau (R. de) .... BX 10
Gare (Av. de la) .... BX 15
Guéodet (R. du) .... BY 16
Gutenberg (Bd) .... BX 17
Jacob (Pont Max) .... AZ 18
Le-Hars (R. Th.) .... BZ 24

Libération (Av. de la) .. BX 25
Locmaria (Allées) .... AZ 26
Luzel (R.) .... BY 28
Mairie (R. de la) .... BY 29
Moulin-Vert (R. du) ..... AV 30
Pont-L'Abbé (R. de) .... AX 35
Potiers (Ch. des) .... BX 37
Poulguinan (Bd de) ..... AX 38
Résistance-et-du-Gén.-de-Gaulle (Pl. de la) . AZ 40

Ronarc'h (R. Amiral) .... AZ 42
St-Corentin (Pl.) .... BZ 43
Ste-Catherine (R.) .... BZ 48
Ste-Thérèse (R.) .... BZ 50
Sallé (R. du) .... BY 52
Steir (Q. du) .... AZ 53
Terre-au-Duc (Pl.) .... AY 54
Tour-d'Auvergne (R. de la) .... BX 58
Ty-Nay (Rte de) .... BV 60

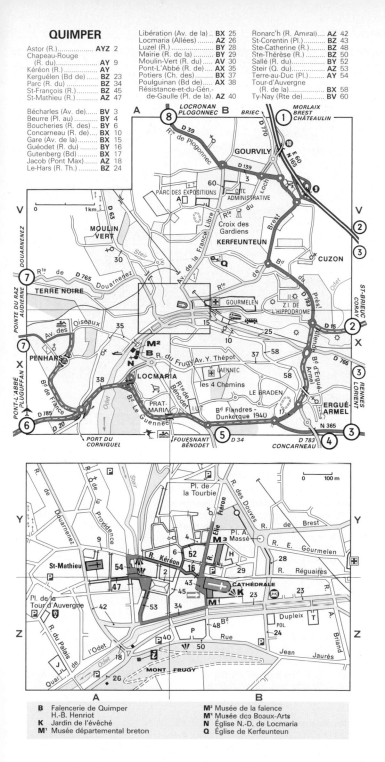

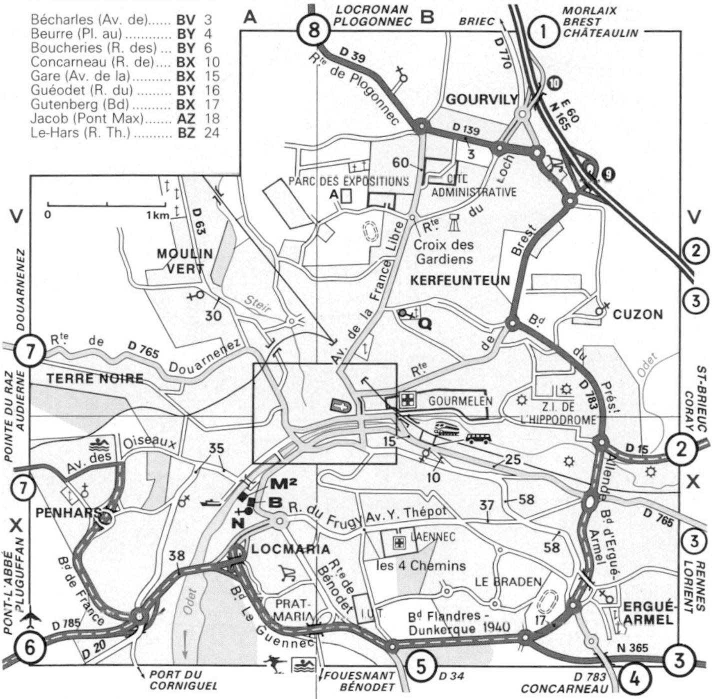

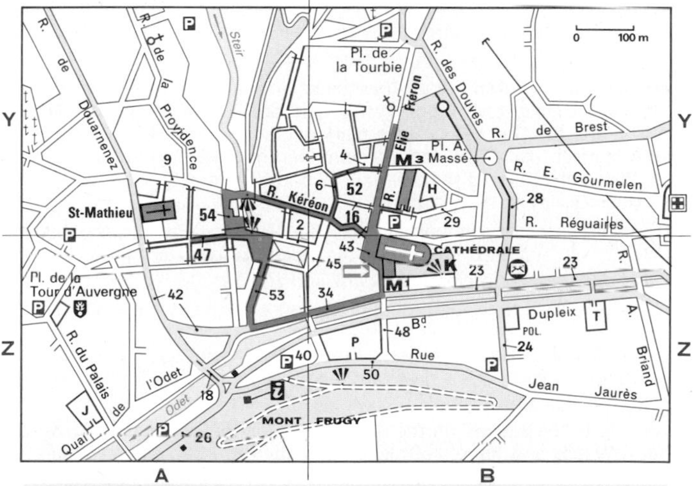

B Faïencerie de Quimper H.-B. Henriot
K Jardin de l'évêché
M¹ Musée départemental breton
M² Musée de la faïence
M³ Musée des Beaux-Arts
N Église N.-D. de Locmaria
Q Église de Kerfeunteun

★OLD QUIMPER *time: 2 hour 30 min*

The old district stretches in front of the cathedral between the Odet and the Steir. Rue du Parc along the Odet leads to Quai du Steir. This small tributary has now been canalised and covered before its confluence with the Odet, to form a vast pedestrian precinct. Note on the right, the elegant covered market, rebuilt in 1979 after a fire.

From the bridge, there is a lovely view upstream of the Steir lined with flower-bedecked houses.

J. Labbé/PIX

Quimper – Rue Kéréon

Place Terre-au-Duc (**AY 54**) – A picturesque square lined with old half-timbered houses. This was the lay town opposite the episcopal city and included the Law Courts, prison and the Duc de Bretagne market.
Take Rue St-Mathieu (**AZ 47**) which has some fine houses, then cross the square diagonally. Bear right to cross the Steir by the bridge from which there is a lovely view with Mount Frugy in the distance.

★ **Rue Kéréon** (**ABY**) – A busy shopping street. The cathedral and its spires between the two rows of old corbelled houses make a delightful picture.

Turn left into Rue des Boucheries then right into Rue du Sallé.

Rue du Sallé (**BY 52**) – Note the beautiful old house of the Mahault de Minuellou family.
Cross the tiny Place au Beurre to reach the **Rue Élie-Fréron**; walk up to no 22 to admire a corbelled house with a slate roof, and a Renaissance porch at no 20.

Go down to the cathedral.

At the entrance to the square, on the right, opens **Rue du Guéodet** (**BY 16**) where a house with caryatids and figures of men and women in 16C costume stands. On the left, in the square itself, stands the town hall, which houses the Musée des Beaux-Arts.

★★ **Musée des Beaux-Arts** (**BY M**[3]) ⏲ – This Fine Arts Museum, housed behind an undamaged 19C façade, has been entirely rebuilt following categorically modern architectural principles, based on the idea of transparency. It contains a collection of paintings representing European painting from the 14C to the present. The museum has its own unique atmosphere, largely due to the mixing of natural and artificial lighting, in which it is possible to view the works in – quite literally – a new light.
On the ground floor, two rooms are devoted to 19C Breton painting: *A Marriage in Brittany* by Leleux; *A Street in Morlaix* by Noël; *Potato Harvest* by Simon; *Widow on Sein Island* by Renouf; *Flight of King Gradlon* by Luminais and *Fouesnant Rebels* by Girardet. One room is devoted to **Max Jacob** (1876-1944), who was born and grew up in Quimper. His life and work are evoked through literature, memorabilia, drawings, gouaches, and in particular a series of portraits signed by his friends Picasso, Cocteau and others.

At the centre of the first floor, the architect **J.-P. Philippon** designed an area fitted in pale beech wood to set 23 paintings from the dining room of the Hôtel de l'Épée, executed by the painter **Lemordant** (1878-1968). The area around the edges displays the work of different European Schools up to the contemporary period: Flemish (**Rubens, Van Schriek**); Italian (**Bartolo di Fredi**); Spanish; and French. Note in particular works by **Boucher, Fragonard, Van Loo**, *View of the Château de Pierrefonds* by **Corot** and *View of Quimper Harbour* by **Boudin**.

★**Musée départemental breton** (**BZ M'**) – This museum, devoted to regional history (archaeology, ethnology, economy), occupies what used to be the episcopal palace, a large edifice built from the 16 to 19C adjoining the cathedral.
The rooms have been wonderfully restored and are now galleries arranged both chronologically and thematically.
After a brief display on prehistory, the visitor enters the first rooms devoted to the environment and way of life in one of the Gallo-Roman cities of the Osismes: coins, monumental mosaics, vases and funerary urns, silverware, figurines of Venus and mother-goddesses, etc.
The medieval section displays, among other things, a stone likeness of King Marc'h, Romanesque capitals, and tomb stones, including the magnificently sculpted tombstone of Grallon of Kervaster.
The galleries of medieval and modern statues bring to mind the various religious cults which inspired this art form. The display includes two large 16C stained glass windows.
Devoted to an exhibition on the theme "Ils ont des chapeaux ronds... Vêtements et costumes en Basse-Bretagne" (They have round hats... Clothing and costumes of Lower Brittany), the following galleries contain traditional folk dress worn every day and during festivals.
The galleries which contain furniture retrace the history (17C to 20C) of the domestic space occupied by folk furniture and the use to which it was put, from the grain and linen chests of Léon to the "petits meubles" mementoes by Plovézet. It is particularly interesting to see the role played by the cupboard in both the marriage ritual and in the attempt to create a "modern Breton piece" between the World Wars.
The final section is devoted to Quimper faïence and displays a rich collection of exhibits dating from the 18C to the present, illustrating the evolution of this decorative art form which reflects at once everyday life, creative spirit and perhaps even the dreams of an entire region.
The museum regularly houses temporary exhibitions.
The Rohan tower houses a remarkable large **spiral staircase**★ ending under a magnificent carved oak canopy.

Jardin de l'évêché (**BZ K**) – Situated between the cathedral and ramparts, the garden offers a good **view**★ of the cathedral chevet and spires, the Odet lined by the Préfecture with its ornate dormer windows, the former Ste-Catherine hospital and Mont Frugy. Some vestiges of the old ramparts can be seen in Boulevard de Kerguélen (**BZ 23**) and Rue des Douves (**BY**).

Musée des Beaux-Arts, Quimper

Le Pardon de Kergoat by Jules Breton

ADDITIONAL SIGHTS

★**Musée de la faïence** (**AX M^2**) ⌚ – *Start your tour on the first floor.* This faïence museum, located on the banks of the Odet, is in the old Maison Porquier dating from 1797. It contains a rich collection of almost 2 500 items which it displays in rotation, retracing on two floors several centuries of the history of Quimper and its faïence. Passing the riot of shapes and colours as one room succeeds another enables the visitor to appreciate the diversity of style in the Quimper faïence production, as well as to follow its evolution. The tour also explains the craft itself, giving details of techniques, artists and anonymous craftsmen (throwers, kiln-chargers and painters), to whom the museum pays homage in the form of a tall, colourful bas-relief.

Jean-Yves Uguet

Dish decorated with Breton figures, HB faïence works (late 19C)

The first two rooms are given over to the sequence of stages in the manufacturing process and to the tools and materials used.
The marvellous works displayed in the following two rooms illustrate the blend of different styles: Rouen, with essentially floral motifs (floral basket is a particularly popular subject), vivid and varied colours (including the red unique to this area, which comes from a clay rich in iron oxide); Nevers, with biblical or mythological scenes, blue monochromes, two distinctive yellows (one from a lead antimony base, the other, stronger, from a uranium oxide base), the technique of decorating on fixed white (enamel), at a stroke (the paint brush produces both shape and colour in a single application).
The ground floor is reserved for 20C production concentrating on that from the period between the World Wars, which was particularly varied and prolific: from the shapes, colours and complex motifs by Quillivic or **Mathurin Méheut** (*qv*) to the highly refined ones of René Beauclair, or even the very original works by Giovanni Leonardi, to name but four artists.
The final gallery houses exhibitions on various themes.

Faïenceries de Quimper HB Henriot (**AX B**) ⌚ – Tour of the faïence workshops.

Église Notre-Dame-de-Locmaria (**AX N**) – This Romanesque church, rebuilt in the 15C and then later restored, is on the banks of the Odet. The plain interior contains, in the north side aisle, three tombstones dating from the 14, 15 and 17C, and, on the rood beam, a robed Christ. In the south side aisle, a door leads to the garden of the old Benedictine priory (16C-17C) which has a cloistral gallery dating from 1669 and two 12C arches.

Mont Frugy (**ABZ**) – From Place de la Résistance a path *(30 min on foot Rtn)* leads to the top of this wooded hill, 70m - 22ft high. From the lookout point there is a good **view**★ of the city.

Église St-Mathieu (**AY**) – This church, rebuilt in 1898, retains a fine 16C stained-glass window of the Passion halfway up the chancel.

EXCURSIONS

1 From the banks of the jet to the Odet

Round tour of 27km - 17 miles – about 2 hours 30 min

*Leave Quimper on Avenue de la Libération (***BX 25***), at the first major roundabout, turn left on the road to Brest and take the second road to the right to Coray. 700m - 766yds further on, take the road towards Elliant.*

The road runs beside the River Jet and offers views of the wooded countryside and pastureland.

Ergué-Gabéric – In the chancel of the early 16C church there is a stained-glass window depicting the Passion (1571) and a 17C group of the Trinity. The organ loft dates from 1680.

Bear right after the church towards the Chapelle de Kerdévot.

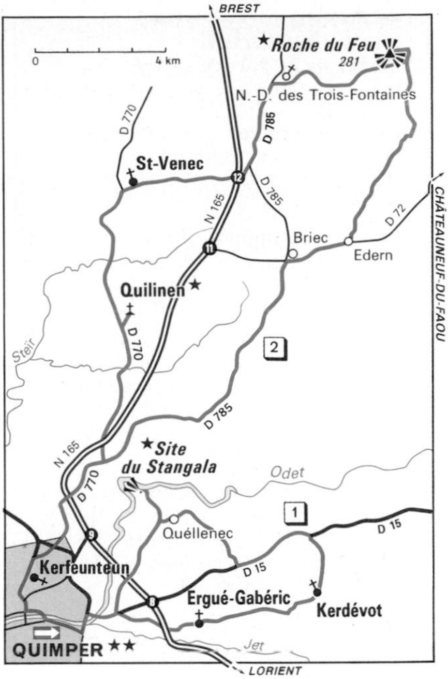

Chapelle de Kerdévot ⏱ – The 15C chapel stands in an attractive setting near a Calvary, which is of a later date and unfortunately somewhat damaged. Inside, a late 15C Flemish **altarpiece★** standing on the high altar depicts six scenes from the life of the Virgin. There is a 17C statue of Our Lady of Kerdévot in painted wood in the nave.

Leave Kerdévot by the road on the left of the chapel, then turn left towards Quimper. After 3km - 2 miles turn right towards the hamlet of Lestonan. Go through Quellénec, turn right into a partly surfaced road 600m - 656yds to the Griffonès car park.

★**Site du Stangala** – After crossing an arboretum (red oak, copper beech, etc.), bear left through woodland to reach two rocky platforms. The site is a remarkable one: the rocky ridge overlooks the Odet from a height of 70m - 230ft as the river winds between wooded slopes. Opposite and slightly to the right, the hamlet of Tréouzon clings to the slopes. Ahead, in the distance, to the left of the television tower, Locronan Mountain, with its characteristic outline and the chapel perched on its summit, can be picked out easily.

On the way back to the car park, a road to the left leads down to the bank of the Odet *(30 min Rtn).*

To return to Quimper, bear right as you leave the narrow road.

2 Chapels and calvaries

Round tour of 57km - 35 miles – about 3 hours

Leave Quimper on Rue des Douves (**BY**). *Shortly after a cemetery at the entrance of Kerfeunteun, turn right.*

Église de Kerfeunteun (**BV Q**) ⏱ – A small square belfry with a stone spire surmounts the west façade.

The church was built in the 16 and 17C but the transept and chancel were rebuilt in 1953. It has kept a beautiful stained glass window (16C) above the high altar, depicting a Tree of Jesse with a Crucifixion above.

800m - 875yds further on, turn right towards Brest, then left in the direction of Briec and at Ty-Sanquer, left again.

★**Calvaire de Quilinen** – Near the main road, hidden by the trees, stands the **Chapelle Notre-Dame-de-Quilinen** ⏱ with its unusual Calvary. Built *c*1550 on two superposed triangular bases with the points opposite one another, the Calvary reveals a rough and naïve style. As the Cross rises to the figure of Christ above the two thieves who are placed close together, the statues become more and more slender. The other side of the Cross represents Christ resurrected.

The south portal of the 15C chapel is decorated by a graceful Virgin between two angels.

Return to the main road and bear right; after 5km - 3 miles, turn right towards the nearby Chapelle de St-Venec.

Chapelle de St-Venec ⏱ – In front of this Gothic chapel is a Calvary (1556) on a triangular base similar to that of Quilinen and on the other side of the road stands a charming 16C fountain.

Take the chapel road, pass under the Quimper-Brest motorway and turn left towards the Chapelle Notre-Dame-des-Trois-Fontaines.

This large chapel was built in the 15-16C; the Calvary is badly damaged.

Proceed to the Gouézec road and turn right.

★**La Roche du Feu (Karreg an Tan)** – *30 min on foot Rtn.* From the car park, take a path to the summit (28m - 899ft) which affords an extensive **panorama★** over the Montagnes Noires, Ménez-Hom and the Aulne Valley.

Return to Quimper via Edern and Briec.

3 Along the banks of the Odet

Round tour of 48km - 30 miles – about 2 hours 30 min

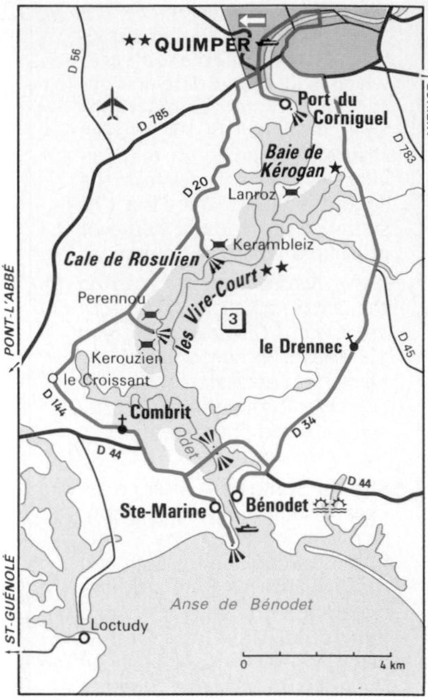

Leave Quimper on the Boulevard de Poulguinan to Pont-l'Abbé. After the roundabout, uphill, bear left.

Port du Corniguel – This is the port of Quimper from which wine, timber and sand are exported. Fine view of the Odet and the Baie de Kérogan.

Return to the Pont-l'Abbé road, and then turn left towards Plomelin. At the next junction, bear left towards the Cale de Rosulien.

Cale de Rosulien – *Road unsurfaced at the end.* A ruined mill stands on the right. From the dock, there is a good view of the **Vire-Court★★** *(see below).*

Return to the junction, turn left and after the entrance to Perennou Castle, bear left towards the Odet (signposts).

From the car park, take a path *(15 min on foot Rtn)* to the banks of the Odet with good views of the river.
Before the Croissant junction where you bear left for Combrit, the road crosses the deep Combrit Cove, which presents a fine sight at high tide.

Combrit – The 16C church has a square domed belfry flanked by two turrets. Inside, note the carved purlins and beams; in the chapel to the right of the chancel, there is a fine alabaster group of the Trinity in an alcove; to the left of the chancel is a 16C altarpiece from Catalonia. An ossuary (17C) stands next to the south porch.

Proceed in the direction of Bénodet, then bear right for Ste-Marine.

Ste-Marine – This small resort on the west bank of the Odet has a good sandy beach with a fine view over Loctudy and Pointe de Lesconil, the île aux Moutons and the îles Glénan, and a small pleasure boat harbour, from which you can enjoy a lovely view of Bénodet and the Odet. There is a ferry for pedestrians crossing between Ste-Marine and Bénodet.

Go over the Pont de Cornouaille (qv).

Bénodet – *See BÉNODET.*
The return road is further inland from the east bank of the Odet.

Le Drennec – Standing in front of the chapel, beside the road, is a charming 16C fountain. A trefoil niche beneath a crocketed gable contains a *Pietà.*

Pass through Moulin-du-Port to return to Quimper.

BOAT TRIPS

★★**Down the Odet** – The woods and castle parks, which lie along the river form a fine, green landscape. The **Port du Corniguel**, at the mouth of Kérogan Bay, adds a modern touch to the picture.

★**Baie de Kérogan** – The estuary at this point looks like a lake.

★★**Les Vire-Court** – The Odet here winds between high, wooded cliffs. This wild spot has its legends. Two rocks at the narrowest point of the gorge are called the Maiden's Leap (Saut de la Pucelle). Another rock is called the Bishop's Chair (Chaise de l'Evêque). Angels are said to have made it in the shape of a seat for the use of a saintly prelate of Quimper who liked to meditate in this lonely place. A little further on, the river bends so sharply that a Spanish fleet, coming up to attack Quimper, did not dare go through. Having taken on water at a fountain now called the Spaniards' Fountain, the ships turned back. On the west bank, before Le Perennou, ruins of Roman baths can be seen.

Bénodet – *See BÉNODET.*

QUIMPERLÉ★

Population 10 748

Michelin map 58 fold 12 or 230 fold 34

This little town is prettily situated at the confluence *(kemper)* of the Rivers Ellé and Isole, which join to form the Laïta. It consists of an upper town, dominated by the Église Notre-Dame-de-l'Assomption, and a lower town grouped about the former Abbaye of Ste-Croix and Rue Dom-Morice. Quimperlé was once a fairly important harbour but today it is chiefly used for small pleasure craft which sail along the Laïta to discover the Forêt de Carnoët and Le Pouldu.

SIGHTS

★★**Église Ste-Croix** ⓥ – The church, which is interesting archaeologically, was built in the 12C, but had to be rebuilt in 1862, except for the apse and the crypt, when its bell tower collapsed. The new bell tower stands alone.

The plan is copied from that of the Holy Sepulchre at Jerusalem. It includes a rotunda with three small apsidal chapels opening into it and a porch, the whole forming a Greek cross.

The **apse**★★, with its blind arcades, columns, capitals and windows, is the finest specimen of Romanesque art in Brittany. A Renaissance stone **altarpiece**★ (part of an old rood screen) stands against the façade.

The **crypt**★★ has remarkable capitals and two 15C tombs with recumbent statues. In the gallery dividing the church and sacristy, there is a 16C Entombment carved in stone.

On leaving the church, take Rue Ellé which skirts the north side and affords a good view of the east end and the bell tower.

★**Rue Dom-Morice** (**9**) – This narrow alley is lined with 16C half-timbered and corbelled houses; no 7, the **Maison des Archers** (1470) is noteworthy.

Museum (**M**) ⓥ – Located in the Maison des Archers, the museum traces the history of the house and of the archers who lived there. Two floors are devoted to Quimperlé, its activities, famous men and regional costumes.

Rue Brémond-d'Ars (**4**) – There are some half-timbered and old 17C houses at nos 8, 10, 11 and 12. At no 15 bis note the staircase of the Présidial, a former law court. Note, also, the ruins of the Église St Colomban.

Église Notre-Dame-de-l'Assomption ⓥ – This 13 and 15C church, surmounted by a large square tower, is also known as St Michel. Pass under the archway on the right, built into one of the buttresses, to get a glimpse of the fine carved porch (1450). Inside, look at the oak-panelled vault with a sculpted cornice, magnificent Flamboyant piscinas and, near the north door, a 15C font. Among the more interesting wooden statues note that of Our Lady of Good Tidings (Notre-Dame-de-Bonne-Nouvelle) (16C).

EXCURSIONS

★**Rochers du Diable** – *12km - 7 miles northeast, plus 30 min on foot Rtn. Leave Quimperlé on the D 790 towards Le Faouët and after 4.5km - 3 miles turn right and go through Locunolé.*

There is a pretty run as the road descends towards the Ellé. *Cross the bridge and turn left towards Meslan; after 400m - 437yds, leave the car in the car park to the left.* Paths lead up to the top of the Devil's Rocks drop vertically to the fast-flowing waters of the Ellé.

QUIMPERLÉ

Brémond-d'Ars (R.)	4
Carnot (Pl.)	
Écoles (Pl. des)	10
Genot (R.)	19
Mellac (R. de)	
St-Michel (Pl.)	
Savary (R.)	
Bourgneuf (R. du)	3
Couëdic (R. du)	8
Dom-Morice (R.)	9
Gaulle (Pl. Ch.-de)	18
Jaurès (Pl. Jean)	22
La-Tour-d'Auvergne (R. de)	23
Leuriou (R.)	24
Madame-Moreau (R.)	25
Moulin-de-la-Ville (Pont du)	29
Paix (R. de la)	32
Salé (Pont)	37

M Musée (Maison des Archers)

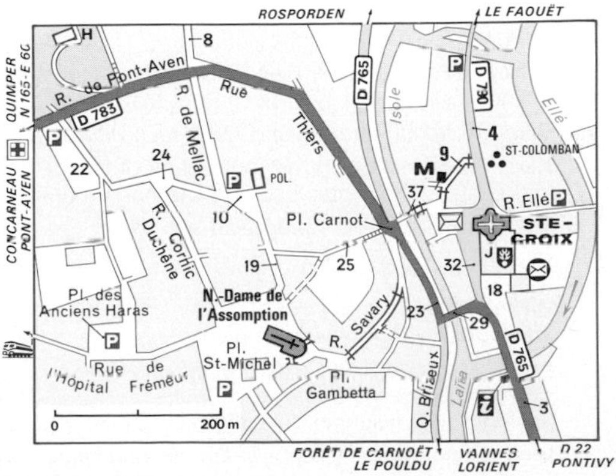

Round tour of 43km - 27 miles – *Time: about 2 hours 30 min. Leave Quimperlé via Quai Brizeux.*

Forêt de Carnoët – Sadly, the violent gales of October 1987 had particularly devastating effects on this forest, flattening almost 120ha - 297 acres of beech and oak trees out of the 750ha - 1 852 acres which constitute the State Forest of Carnoët. Repair work has begun, and will eventually restore the forest to its original glory. Nonetheless, bordered by the Laïta, the forest offers pretty sites and pleasant walks *(some paths are reserved for walking and riding)*. On the edge of the forest at Toulfoën, a *pardon* is held, which is still known as the Bird Festival *(Fête des Oiseaux) (see the Calendar of Events at the end of the guide).*

500m - 547yds beyond Toulfoën, turn left towards the Rocher Royal.

The road winds through the forest to the banks of the Laïta where the **Rocher Royal** can be seen, a rocky ridge towering above the river, and the ruins of the Château de Carnoët. This is the legendary dwelling of the Count of Commore, the Bluebeard of Cornouaille. After hearing a prediction that he would die by the hand of his son, he put his first four wives to death as soon as they conceived. The fifth wife, Triphine, before she died, was able to save her son, who became **St Trémeur**. Commore, on meeting the Saint, was struck by his resemblance to his mother and immediately had him beheaded. Then, according to the legend, Trémeur picked up his own head, walked towards his father's castle and threw a handful of earth against the building which collapsed, burying Commore alive.

Return to the Le Pouldu road, turn left and at a major junction, left again.

Pont de St-Maurice – The bridge over the Laïta gives a fine **view★** of the river and its steep banks.

Turn round and after 700m - 766yds, turn right.

St-Maurice – This stands in a green and pleasant **site★**: the Laïta is on the right with a lake on the left. Nearby are remains of the chapter-house of the former Abbaye St-Maurice, founded in the 12C.

Le Pouldu – Facilities. This small port lies at the mouth of the River Laïta.

The **Chapelle Notre-Dame-de-la-Paix** ⏲ near Grands Sables Beach, stands in a grassy close, the entrance of which is flanked by a monument to Gauguin *(qv)*. The chapel escaped ruin by being transported 26km - 16 miles and rebuilt here. The bays have flame and lily-shaped tracery with stained-glass by Manessier and Le Moal. Below the timber roof, the rood beam carries a Christ with a red loincloth and a second group depicting a *Pietà*.

Drive along Grands Sables Beach then turn left towards Doëlan.

View of the île de Groix and Pointe du Talut.

Doëlan – A small fishing port commanding the entrance to a deep, sheltered estuary.

Return to Quimperlé via Clohars-Carnoët.

Round tour of 37km - 23 miles – *Time: about 1 hour 30 min. Leave Quimperlé to the southwest on the D 16 and at Gare-de-la-Forêt, bear right.*

Moëlan-sur-Mer – Facilities. In the **church**, note the four 18C confessional boxes in the Italian style. Pass along the south side of the church and by the chevet, take the lane leading to the **Chapelle St-Philibert-et-St-Roch** ⏲ which is picturesquely placed near a 16C Calvary. Alongside is the St-Roch fountain. A *pardon* takes place on the second Sunday following 15 August.

Proceed to Brigneau.

A menhir stands on the left-hand side of the road. There is a fine view over Brigneau Bay.

Brigneau – A tiny fishing port where pleasure craft also find shelter.
The road follows the coastline. Thatched-roofed houses are found along the way.

At Kergroès, bear left.

Kerfany-les-Pins – On the Bélon River, this small seaside resort has a pretty site and a sandy beach. Fine view over Port-Manech and the Aven estuary.

Take the uphill road beyond the beach and at Lanriot, turn left.

Bélon – This locality, on the south bank of the Bélon, is famous as an oyster-farming *(qv)* centre. The oyster-beds on the north bank can be seen at low tide.

Return to Quimperlé via Moëlan-sur-Mer.

QUINTIN

Population 2 602

Michelin map 59 folds 12 and 13 or 230 fold 22

In the past, Quintin was well known for its fine linen which was used for headdresses and collars. In the 17 and 18C the industry expanded to the manufacture of Brittany cloth which was exported to America but decline set in at the Revolution when there were 300 weavers in the town. The old houses of Quintin rise in terraces on a hill; the River Gouët forms a fine stretch of water below.

SIGHTS

Basilica (Basilique) ⓥ – Built on the site of a collegiate church in 1887. The relics of St Thuriau and a piece of the Virgin's girdle, brought from Jerusalem in the 13C by a lord of Quintin (Geoffroy Botrel or Botherel), are kept in the basilica. There are also four stoups made of shells from Java and the old crowned statue of Notre-Dame-de-Délivrance (Our Lady of Safe Delivery), which is venerated by expectant mothers in particular; a 14C font in the north transept and two 14C recumbent figures in the chancel. At the east end of the basilica stands the 15C New Gate (Porte Neuve), all that remains of the ramparts which surrounded the town. In Rue Notre-Dame, beyond the parvis, is the 15C fountain of Notre-Dame-d'Entre-les-Portes with two former chapter-houses with decorated façades opposite, at nos 5 and 7.

Old houses – There are fine 16-17C corbelled houses lining the picturesque Place 1830, Rue au Lait (nos 12, 13) and Grande Rue (nos 37 and 43). In Place du Martray, the Hôtel du Martray, the town hall and the house at no 1 date from the 18C.

Château ⓥ – *Access via Place 1830.* The château is made up of an older 17C building and a grand 18C building, flanked by a low-lying wing at a right angle, visible once through the entrance gate.
The **museum**, housed in the 18C part of the château, recounts Quintin's history and that of the chateau's previous owners. Displayed inside are: 18-19C fans, hand-painted India Company *(qv)* plates, Meissen tableware, archives and Quintin linen. In the kitchens is an unusual piece: an 18C granite oven with 7 holes (used for heating platters).
A succession of vaulted rooms are visited in the old part of the château and its cellars, which overlook the lake.
Every summer a variety of exhibitions is organised.

Menhir de Roche-Longue – *800m - 875yds further on by the road beyond the Calvary which skirts the pool.*
At the top of the hill, a menhir 4.70m - 14ft high stands in a field to the left.

Château de Robien ⓥ – *2km -1 mile south on the road to Corlay (D 790).*
The 18C château stands on the site of two others, which were successively destroyed. Of the first, there remain only the ruins of a 14C chapel near the present building. The austerity of the granite façades is relieved by a central rotunda and projecting wings at either end. A pleasant walk may be enjoyed in the park which is planted with different species of trees and through which flows the Gouët.

Usine marémotrice de la RANCE

Michelin map 59 fold 6 or 230 fold 11 – Local map under Vallée de la RANCE

The use of tidal power is nothing new to the Vallée de la Rance. As early as the 12C, riverside dwellers had thought up the idea of building little reservoirs which, as they emptied with the ebb tide, drove **mill wheels**. To double the output of a modern industrial plant, it was tempting to try to work out a means of using the flow as well as the ebb tide. The French electricity authority (EDF), therefore, searched for new technical methods of producing electricity and successfully set up, between the headlands of La Briantais and La Brebis, a **usine hydro-électrique** (hydro-electric power station) ⓥ operated by both the flow and ebb of the tide.
The Rance estuary is closed by a dam 750m - 800yds long, making a reservoir of 22sqkm - 8 sq miles. The road which connects Dinard and St-Malo runs along it. The lock is 65m - 213ft long and enables boats to pass through the dam. The road crosses the lock by means of bascule bridges.
The **power station** is in a huge tunnel nearly 390m - 400yds long in the very centre of the dam. In this room, are the 24 AC generators of a combined capacity of 240 000kW which can produce 600 millionkWh per year (equal to the annual consumption of a city comparable to Rennes and its outskirts).

Walk along the dam to the platform.

From there the **view★** extends over the Rance estuary as far as Dinard and St-Malo. The dam lies between the power station and the right bank with its centre on the small island of Chalibert. There are six sluice-gates at the eastern end which regulate the emptying and filling of the reservoir, thus controlling the water supply to the power station.

Vallée de la RANCE★★

Michelin map 59 folds 5, 6, 15 and 16 or 230 folds 11 and 25

The Rance estuary, lying between St-Malo and Dinard, is among the places most frequented in Brittany. Upstream, Dinan is a typical old inland town.
The Rance is a perfect example of a Breton river. It forms a deep gulf between Dinan and the sea, flowing with many branches and inlets over a level plateau. This curious gulf is due to the flooding by the sea of an ordinary but steep-sided valley: the stream itself and the bottom of the valley have been "drowned" by a mass of tidal water. All that remains visible of the original valley is its steep sides, sloping into the sea. The Rance proper is a small river without much water, which winds along above Dinan.

★★BOAT TRIP ⏲

5 hours Rtn – not counting the stop and tour of Dinan

The boat follows the Noires breakwater (Môle des Noires) and crosses the Rance estuary for a brief stop at Dinard. It enters the Rance, leaving the Corniche d'Aleth on the left (St-Servan), passes in front of Pointe de la Vicomté and Rocher Bizeux and then enters the lock of the Rance dam. You will go up the river, between its great banks, through a series of narrow channels and wide pools. After Chatelier Lock (Écluse du Chatelier), the Rance gets narrower and narrower and becomes a mere canal just as you come within sight of Dinan, perched on its ridge.

★★**Dinan** – *See DINAN.* Your boat will stop for a longer or shorter time according to the tide – from 8 hours to only 15 min.
The scenes on your way back will be changed by the difference in the direction of the light and its intensity.

★ALONG THE BANKS OF THE RANCE

Round Tour Starting From St-Malo

87 km - 54 miles – allow one day

★★★**St-Malo** – *Time: 3 hours 30 min. See ST-MALO.*

Leave St-Malo by ③ on the town plan. Turn right by the aerodrome.

La Passagère – Fine view over the Rance.

Make for the Chapelle du Boscq and St-Jouan-des-Guérets to St-Suliac.

On the right notice the Boscher mill, once a tidal mill.

In St-Suliac, before the church, bear left in the direction of Mont Garrot. 1 km - 1/2 mile further on leave the car near an old crenellated watchtower.

From the foot of the tower, there is a wide **panorama**★ of St-Suliac Cove, St-Malo, the Dol countryside, the River Rance and Pont St-Hubert

Mont Garrot – *15 min on foot Rtn.* A path to the right leads to the point, passing behind a farm. Notice the views of the Vallée de la Rance on the way.

From La Ville-ès-Nonais continue onto the Pont St-Hubert .

Pont St-Hubert – From this suspension bridge, there is a pleasant view of the Rance, the Port St-Jean slipway and, on the rocky bank opposite, the St-Hubert slipway.

Return to La Ville-ès-Nonais, bear right.

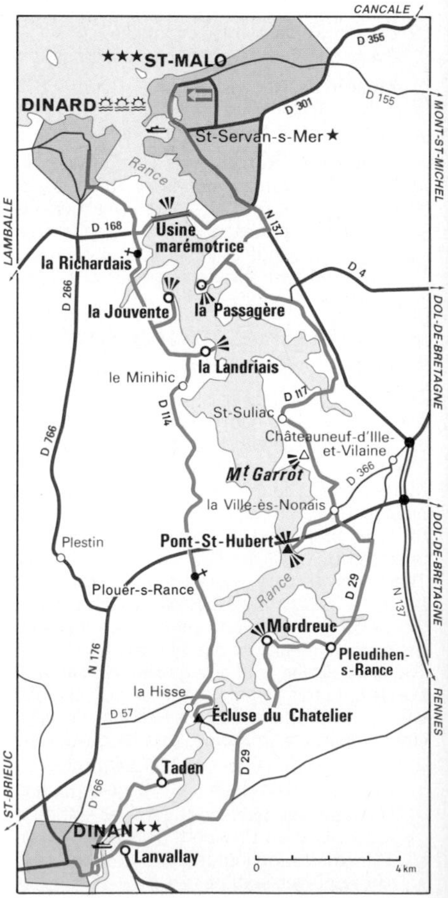

Pleudihen-sur-Rance – The farm's outbuildings house the **Musée de la Pomme et du Cidre** (Apple and Cider Museum) ⌚. Before visiting the museum stop by the orchard planted with different varieties of apple trees.
Inside the museum, the apple, its origin, the different varieties, diseases, cultivation and picking are explained. A film illustrating the different apple-related trades (eg. cooperage) and a tasting end the tour.

Cale de Mordreuc – From this lovely place there are good views of Pont St-Hubert downstream, the deepening valley upstream and just opposite a promontory on which lie the ruins of an old castle.

Lanvallay – A remarkable **view★** of the old town of Dinan, its ramparts and its belfries. Below flows the Rance, spanned by a long viaduct.

★★ **Dinan** – *See DINAN.*

Take the road which passes under the Dinan viaduct and skirts the harbour.

Taden – When you cross the village, on your way to the slipway, glance at the porch and keep which is flanked by a 14C turret. The towpath, which used to link Dinan to the écluse du Chatelier, is a favourite spot for fishermen and a pleasant place to stroll. Taden Plain is the home of a number of aquatic birds: black-headed gulls, herring gulls, coots, etc.

Return to the road towards Dinard. As you leave La Hisse turn right before the level crossing.

Écluse du Chatelier – This lock regulates the Dinan basin.
Continue onto **Plouër-sur-Rance**. Inside the 18C church are carved tombstones.

After Plouër-sur-Rance and Le Minihic bear right and then 250 m - 273 yds further on right again.

La Landriais – The port contains naval dockyards. The walk along Hures Promenade (on foot take Chemin de ronde des Douaniers) from the car park and as it skirts the Rance for 2 km - 1 mile affords fine views.

On your way back after 1.2km - 3/4 mile turn right after 1 km - 1/2 mile turn right again.

Cale de la Jouvente – Across from La Passagère. There is a nice view of the Rance and the île Chevret.

La Richardais – The church is dominated by its pierced tower and the Calvary surmounting it. On the walls of the nave runs a fresco (1955) depicting the Stations of the Cross by Xavier de Langlais. In the transept is a fresco illustrating the arrival of St Lunaire and St Malo on the Breton coast. From the fine wood vaulting resembling the upturned keel of a ship, 4 lamps in the form of wheels hang down. Five stained glass windows are by Max Ingrand.
On leaving La Richardais by the north, you get a viewpoint of the tidal power scheme and the Rance estuary.

Reach Dinard by ① on the town plan.

☆☆☆ **Dinard** – *See DINARD.*

Usine marémotrice de la Rance – *See Usine marémotrice de la RANCE.*

Return to St-Malo by the direct route along the crest of the dam.

Pointe du RAZ★★★

Michelin map 58 fold 13 or 230 fold 16 – Local map under CORNOUAILLE

Pointe du Raz ⓥ, at the tip of Cornouaille, is in a very attractive setting. Walk round the signal station in front of which stands a statue of Our Lady of the Shipwrecked (Notre-Dame-des-Naufragés) to enjoy a wide **panorama**★★ of the horizon: straight ahead is the île de Sein and beyond, in clear weather, the Ar Men Lighthouse. Between the île de Sein and the mainland is the fearful Raz du Sein or tide race which, so an old saying has it, "no one passes without fear or sorrow"; to the northwest can be seen Tévennec Lighthouse (Phare de Tévennec) standing on an islet.

Y. Arthus-Bertrand/ALTITUDE

Pointe du Raz

Recently, protective measures have been taken to preserve the site and its environment. A new visitors' centre has opened, the **Porte du Cap Sizun** *(information centre, exhibit area, restaurants and shops). To reach the end of the point, motorists must pay to leave their car in the parking area. It takes about 15min to follow the way-marked paths to the far end. A free shuttle provides transportation for those with difficulty walking.*

REDON

Population 9 260

Michelin map 63 fold 5 or 230 folds 38 and 39

Redon, the centre of an active region, is the meeting point of three départements (Ille-et-Vilaine, Loire-Atlantique and Morbihan) and two regions (Brittany and Pays de Loire). In Redon, the River Vilaine and the Nantes-Brest Canal converge at the pleasure boat harbour (tourism on inland waterways).

Traditions are still well implanted in the region around Redon; markets and fairs (the popular chestnut fair, Teillouse Fair, held the fourth Saturday in October) take place here. While the town's industrial activities include the production of computers, automobile seats and bodies, children's clothes and lighters.

Église St-Sauveur (**Y**) – This former abbey church, founded in 832, was a great pilgrimage centre throughout the Middle Ages and until the 17C. This accounts for the impressive size of the building. In 1622 Richelieu was the commendatory abbot. It was cut off from its 14C Gothic bell towers (**D**) by a fire in 1780. A remarkable Romanesque sandstone and granite **tower**★ stands at the transept crossing. From the neighbouring **cloisters** (17C), occupied by the College of St Saviour, the superimposition of its arcades can be seen. From the esplanade planted with chestnut trees and overlooking Rue Richelieu, one has a good view of the chevet with its buttresses.

The **interior** reveals a dimly-lit low nave (11C) with wood vaulting separated from the side aisles by flat pillars. The 12C vaulting at the transept reveals remains of frescoes; note the carved pillars in the transept crossing. A 17C altarpiece in stone and marble takes the form of the chancel which, with the ambulatory, is 13C.

REDON

Douves (R. des) YZ
États (R. des) Y 12
Grande-Rue Z 23
Notre-Dame (R.) Y 32
Victor-Hugo (R.) Y 50

Bonne-Nouvelle (Bd) Y 2
Bretagne (Pl. de) Y 3
Desmars (R. Joseph) Y 5
Douves (Pont des) Z 6
Duchesse-Anne (Pl.) Y 7
Duguay-Trouin (Quai) Z 8
Du Guesclin (R.) YZ 9
Enfer (R. d') Z 13
Foch (R. du Mar.) Y 16
Gare (Av. de la) Y 17
Gascon (Av. E.) Y 19
Jeanne-d'Arc (R.) Z 25
Jeu-de-Paume (R. du) Z 26
Liberté (Bd de la) Y 30
Parlement (Pl. du) Y 31
Plessis (R. du) Z 33
Port (R. du) Z 36
Richelieu (R.) Y 39
St-Nicolas (Pont) Z 43

D Clocher

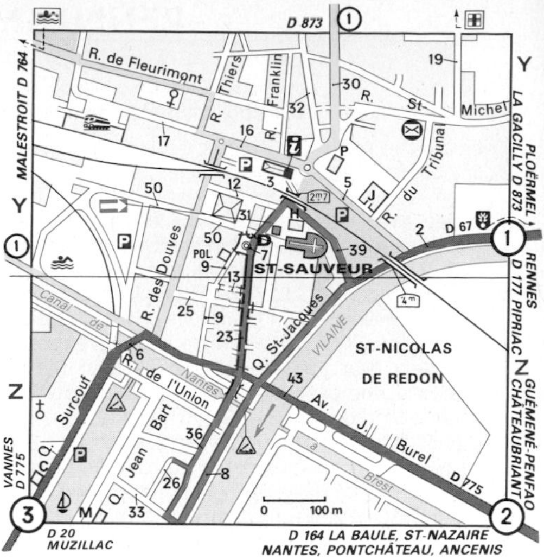

The old town – The old town contains elegant 15-18C town houses. Leave from the Eglise St-Sauveur and walk along Grande Rue, noting nos 22, 25, 38, 44, 52 and 54; look down Rue d'Enfer and Rue Jeanne-d'Arc. Cross the flower-decorated bridge which spans the Nantes-Brest Canal. In Rue du Port across from no 6, Hôtel Carmoy, are three corbelled houses. Go into Rue du Jeu-de-Paume which has, at no 10, the old customs barracks, a 4-storey building with a severe façade and a wall with a scene of swineherds and fishmongers dressed in costumes of the past. Return to Rue du Port where old salt houses (no 40) can be seen; occupying no 3 Rue du Plessis is the Hôtel Richelieu. Quai Duguay-Trouin is lined with stately ship-owners' homes of which nos 15, 7, 6 and 5 are particularly worth looking at. By way of Quai St-Jacques, where ramparts in ruins still stand, and Rue de Richelieu, you return to the church.

EXCURSIONS

Rieux – *7 km - 4 miles south on ③ on the town plan towards Vannes.* The **church** (1952) has a slim belfry built against the side of the main vessel. The groined brick vaulting springs from roughly-hewn capitals supported by short columns. The unfaced stonework of the walls is interrupted only by the vividly-coloured **stained-glass windows★** of unevenly cut glass by Job Guével.
On entering the village, in a bend, take the road to the left which leads you to a car park, from where there is a pleasant view of the Vilaine Valley and Redon; occupying the wooded promontory are castle ruins.

Ile aux Pies – *12 km - 7 miles northwest. Leave Redon by the D 65 and then the D 764 to Ploërmel* (**Y**), *at St-Vincent-sur-Oust, turn right.*
The road leads to the bank of the Oust, a peaceful river, partly canalised, flowing through verdant countryside. A path to the left gives a view of the île aux Pies. This is a good place for climbing, canoeing and kayaking.

St-Just – *19 km - 11.5 miles northeast. Leave Redon on ① on the town plan (D 177) towards Rennes and turn left, to St-Just.*
This small town lies at the centre of an area rich in **megaliths**, especially in the **Cojoux Moor** (Landes de Cojoux signposted path). Lovely viewpoint on the étang de Val (rock climbing).

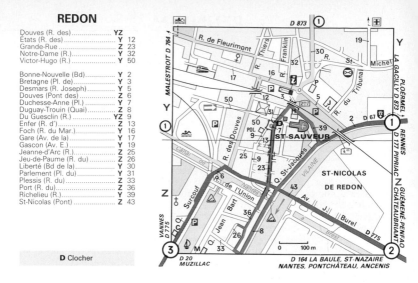

RENNES★★

Conurbation 245 065
Michelin map 59 fold 17 or 230 fold 26
Plan of conurbation in the current Michelin Red Guide France

Over the last few years Rennes, regional capital of Brittany, has been implementing a policy of restoration of its heritage; resurfacing of stonework, renovation work, introduction of pedestrian zones have all played a part in highlighting the essentially dignified air of this city, also emanating from the classical style buildings. Rennes, a city of artistic and historical interest, where good food is highly valued, exudes atmosphere from its narrow, winding medieval streets, lined with charming half-timbered houses with carved sills, which happily escaped the ravages of a huge fire in 1720. The public buildings and numerous private mansions on the two "royal" squares (Place du Palais and Place de l'Hôtel de Ville) give these an air of sober elegance. It is here, at the very heart of the city, delimited to the south by the lively quays along the Vilaine, that the people of Rennes come to do their shopping, watch a play or go for a drink with their friends.
South of the River Vilaine lie the residential suburbs and the industrial zone, which have been built to a modern urban plan (Le Colombier). West of Boulevard de La Tour d'Auvergne stand the glass Law Courts, a good example of contemporary architecture. Three industrial zones have attracted many plants manufacturing cars, railway equipment, the building industry and public works and transportation, etc.
Recently Rennes has become a centre of the electronics and communications industry (the French Telecom videotex service, MINITEL was conceived here). Rennes is also a university city: two universities, a medical school and several other specialised schools, with a total student enrolment of 38 000.

HISTORICAL NOTES

Du Guesclin's beginnings (**14C**) – Bertrand Du Guesclin *(qv)* was born in the Castle of La Motte-Broons (now disappeared), southwest of Dinan. He was the eldest of ten children and by no means handsome. On the other hand, he was bursting with energy and good sense. Bertrand spent his childhood among peasant boys whom he taught to fight. In this way he acquired strength, skill and cunning – and rough manners. His family was ashamed of him and kept him out of sight.
In 1337, when Du Guesclin was seventeen, all the local nobles met for a tournament at Rennes. Our hero went to it in peasant dress, mounted on a draught horse. He was kept out of the lists. His despair at this was such that one of his cousins from Rennes lent him his armour and charger. Without giving his name, Bertrand unseated several opponents. At last a lance thrust lifted his visor and his father recognised him. Delighted and proud, he exclaimed: "My fine son, I will no longer treat thee scurvily!"

The Duchess's marriage (1491) – In 1489, when François II died, his heiress, Anne of Brittany *(qv)*, was only twelve, but this did not prevent wooers from coming forward. Her choice fell on Maximilian of Austria, the future Emperor. The religious marriage was performed by proxy in 1490.
Charles VIII, who had an unconsummated marriage with Margaret of Austria, daughter of Maximilian, asked the Duchess's hand for himself; he was refused and laid siege to Rennes in August 1491. The starving people begged their sovereign to accept the marriage. She agreed and met Charles VIII. Anne was small and thin and slightly lame, but she had gaiety and charm; she knew Latin and Greek and took an interest in art and letters. Charles was short and ill-favoured, with large, pale eyes and thick lips always hanging open; he was slow-witted, too, but loved power and had a taste for pomp. Quite unexpectedly the two young people took a liking to each other, which grew into tender affection. Their engagement was celebrated at Rennes. There remained, however, the problem of freeing the fiancés. The Court of Rome agreed and the wedding took place in the royal Château de Langeais, in the Loire Valley, on 6 December 1491 *(see Michelin Green Guide Châteaux of the Loire)*. The marriage united Brittany to France.

The great fire of 1720 – At the beginning of the 18C the town still looked as it did in the Middle Ages, with narrow alleys and lath-and-plaster houses. There was no way of fighting fire, for there was no running water. In the evening of 22 December 1720, a drunken carpenter set fire to a heap of shavings with his lamp. The house burned like a torch and immediately others around it caught fire.
The ravaged areas were rebuilt to the plans of **Jacques Gabriel**, the descendant of a long line of architects and himself the father of the Gabriel who built the Place de la Concorde in Paris. A large part of the town owes its fine rectangular street pattern and the uniform and rather severely distinguished granite houses to this event. In order that they might be inhabited more quickly, new houses were divided into apartments or flats which were sold separately. This was the beginning of co-ownership.

The La Chalotais affair – In 1762, the Duke of Aiguillon, Governor of Brittany, clashed with Parliament over the Jesuits. The Jansenist lawyers **(robins)** opposed the Society of Jesus, whose colleges made it very powerful in Brittany – that of Rennes

had 2 800 pupils. La Chalotais, the Public Prosecutor, induced Parliament to vote for the dissolution of the Order. His report had a huge success: 12 000 copies were sold in a month. Voltaire wrote to the author: "This is the only work of philosophy that has ever come from the Bar."
Aiguillon, who defended the Jesuits, asked Parliament to reverse its vote. It refused. Louis XV summoned the Councillors to Versailles, scolded them and sent three into exile. On returning to Rennes the Members of Parliament resigned rather than submit. The King had La Chalotais arrested and sent him to Saintes; the other Councillors were scattered over various provinces, but the Paris Parliament took the side of the Rennes Parliament and Louis XV hesitated to go further. Aiguillon, lacking support, retired in 1768. The Assemblies had defeated the royal power. Revolution was on the march.

A Great Mayor: Leperdit – In 1793, before going to Nantes where he became notorious, **Carrier** *(qv)* was appointed to represent the Convention at Rennes. There he found a Mayor named Leperdit, who was a tailor and a simple fellow but a man of great character and coolness. The Convention man wanted to execute prisoners. Leperdit stood up to him bravely. "No mercy", said Carrier; "those people are outside the law." "Yes," answered the Mayor, "but not outside humanity." Fortunately for Rennes and its Mayor, Carrier did not stay long.
In 1794, when Leperdit was addressing a crowd who were demanding bread, stones were thrown and he was wounded on the forehead. Bleeding but still calm, he said to the ruffians: "I cannot, like Christ, change these stones into bread; as for my blood, I would give the last drop if it would feed you."

★★OLD TOWN (VIEUX RENNES) (ABY) *time: 1 hour 30 min*

This is the part of the old town which escaped the fire *(see above)*. It contains a maze of 15 and 16C houses with overhanging storeys and lordly mansions with sculpted façades which can be seen as you stroll in the cathedral district.

Basilique St-Sauveur (AY) – 17 and 18C. Inside this basilica are a fine gilded wooden **canopy** and an **organ loft** (17C). To the right is a chapel consecrated to Our Lady of Miracles who saved Rennes from the English during the siege of 1357. Note the numerous ex-votos which have been donated in gratitude to Our Lady.

Rue St-Sauveur (AY 75) – At no 6 stands a 16C canon's residence.

Rue St-Guillaume (AY 68) – At no 3, a beautiful medieval house, known as **Maison Du Guesclin**, contains the restaurant Ti Koz.

Rue de la Psalette (AY 60) – This street is lined with old houses.

Rue du Chapitre (AY 9) At no 22 is a Renaissance house; no 8 is the **Hôtel de Brie** (17C); at no 6 the 18C **Hôtel de Blossac** with a fine granite **staircase** (on left on entering) with marble columns and a wrought-iron handrail.

Rue St-Yves (AY 77) – At nos 6 and 8 are 16C houses.

Rue des Dames (AY 14) – No 10 is the Hôtel Freslon de la Freslonnière.

Cathédrale St-Pierre (AY) ⏲ – This, the third cathedral built on the site since the 6C, was finished in 1844 after fifty-seven years' work. The previous building collapsed in 1762 except for the two towers in the classical style flanking the façade. The **interior★** is very rich, its stucco facing covered with paintings and gilding. The cathedral contains a masterpiece: the gilded and carved wood **altarpiece★★** in the chapel before the south transept. Both in size and in execution, this 16C Flemish work is one of the most important of its kind. The scenes represent the life of the Virgin.

H. Weiller/EXPLORER

Cathédrale St-Pierre

Portes Mordelaises (**AY B**) – The city's main entrance, these gates are all that remain of the 15C ramparts. The Dukes of Brittany passed through it on their way to the cathedral for their coronation. In 1598 the silver-gilt keys of the city were presented there to Henri IV. At this kind of ceremony the Béarnais made a statement which always went down well: "These are beautiful keys," he would say, "but I would rather have the keys to the hearts of your citizens."

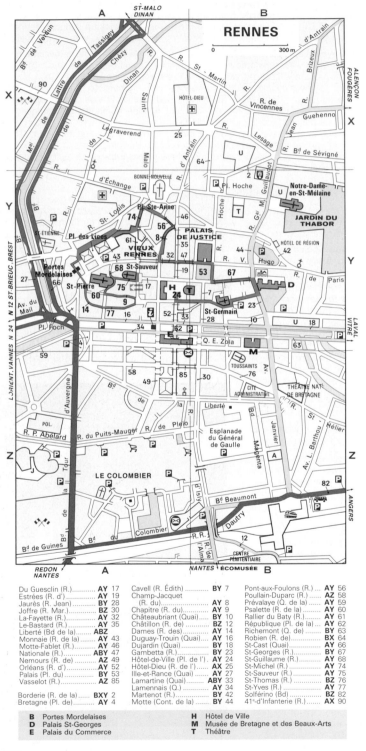

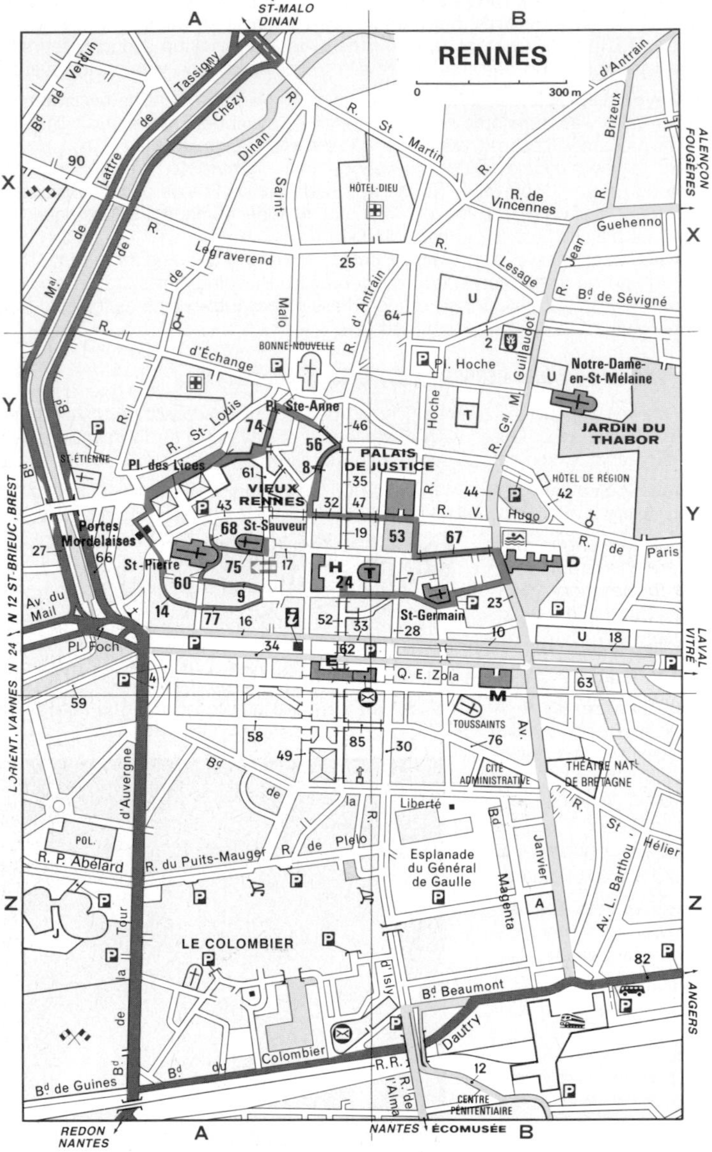

Du Guesclin (R.) .... AY 17
Estrées (R. d') .... AY 19
Jaurès (R. Jean) .... BY 28
Joffre (R. Mar.) .... BZ 30
La-Fayette (R.) .... AY 32
Le-Bastard (R.) .... AY 35
Liberté (Bd de la) .... ABZ
Monnaie (R. de la) .... AY 43
Motte-Fablet (R.) .... AY 46
Nationale (R.) .... ABY 47
Nemours (R. de) .... AZ 49
Orléans (R. d') .... AY 52
Palais (Pl. du) .... BY 53
Vasselot (R.) .... AZ 85

Borderie (R. de la) ...... BXY 2
Bretagne (Pl. de) .... AY 4
Cavell (R. Édith) .... BY 7
Champ-Jacquet (R. du) .... AY 8
Chapitre (R. du) .... AY 9
Châteaubriant (Quai) ..... BY 10
Châtillon (R. de) .... BZ 12
Dames (R. des) .... AY 14
Duguay-Trouin (Quai) .... AY 16
Dujardin (Quai) .... BY 18
Gambetta (R.) .... BY 23
Hôtel-de-Ville (Pl. de l') . AY 24
Hôtel-Dieu (R. de l') ...... AX 25
Ille-et-Rance (Quai) .... AY 27
Lamartine (Quai) .... ABY 33
Lamennais (Q.) .... AY 34
Martenot (R.) .... BY 42
Motte (Cont. de la) .... BY 44
Pont-aux-Foulons (R.) ... AY 56
Poullain-Duparc (R.) ...... AZ 58
Prévalaye (Q. de la) ...... AY 59
Psalette (R. de la) .... AY 60
Rallier du Baty (R.) .... AY 61
République (Pl. de la) ... AY 62
Richemont (Q. de) .... BY 63
Robien (R. de) .... BX 64
St-Cast (Quai) .... AY 66
St-Georges (R.) .... BY 67
St-Guillaume (R.) .... AY 68
St-Michel (R.) .... AY 74
St-Sauveur (R.) .... AY 75
St-Thomas (R.) .... BZ 76
St-Yves (R.) .... AY 77
Solférino (Bd) .... BZ 82
41e-d'Infanterie (R.) .... AX 90

B Portes Mordelaises
D Palais St-Georges
E Palais du Commerce
H Hôtel de Ville
M Musée de Bretagne et des Beaux-Arts
T Théâtre

Place des Lices (**AY**) – Jousts and tournaments were once held on this square. At no 34 stands a 17C stone mansion, the Hôtel de Molant, with a mansard roof; inside, there is a sumptuous oak staircase with *trompe-l'œil* paintings (a skyscape) and woodwork decorating the ceiling of its stairwell. At nos 26 and 28 the 17C *hôtels* have wide staircases with hull-shaped roofs.

Rue St-Michel (**AY 74**) – This street is lined with half-timbered houses and still has the inns and taverns dating from the time when it was part of the city's suburbs.

Place Ste-Anne (**AY**) – The coloured half-timbered houses, Gothic and Renaissance in style, surround a 19C neo-Gothic church. The house formerly occupied by Mayor Leperdit is at no 19. This square is next to Rue d'Échange, which contains the Jacobin Convent where Anne of Brittany was betrothed to the King of France.

Rue du Pont-aux-Foulons (**AY 56**) – This is a shopping street with 18C half-timbered houses.

Rue du Champ-Jacquet (**AY 8**) – This street leads to an oddly-shaped triangular square of the same name. It is lined to the north with tall half-timbered 17C houses and is overlooked by the stone and wood façade of Hôtel de Tizé (no 5).

The itinerary continues along Rue La Fayette and Rue Nationale into the classical part of the city with its majestic buildings.

★★ **Palais de Justice** (**BY**) ⏱ – *The Law Courts were badly damaged by fire in February 1994 and are currently under restoration. A history of this handsome monument is nonetheless given below, in the hope that it will not be too long before visitors are able to admire it in all its former glory.*

The Law Courts, home of the Breton Parliament, stand on the **Place du Palais**★, *which is surrounded by 17 and 18C buildings.*

J.-D. Sudres/EXPLORER

Place du Champ-Jacquet

The setting up of the Parliament of Brittany in Rennes in 1554 (the seat of Parliament was shared with Nantes until 1561) was the making of the town as regional capital and aristocratic city. On the construction site of the future Parliament house, built to house the political and judicial services of the parliamentary aristocrats, royal and Parisian art arrived on Breton soil.

The architecture and décor of the mansion, which was the first stone building in a town of wood, were to influence the whole of Haute-Bretagne. The design of local architect Germain Gaultier was reworked for the façade by the Court architect of Marie de' Medici, Salomon de Brosse. Building went on from 1618 to 1655. A tax of 1 *sou* per pitcher of wine and 3 deniers per pitcher of cider provided the necessary funds for the building work (a journeyman earned between 7 and 12 *sous* a day).

In June 1995, Jean-Loup Roubert's project on the interior redesigning of the Palais de Justice was ratified by the French authorities. This project will involve restoring the ground floor gallery to its former glory, as well as the Assizes Chamber on the first floor. By 1998 the Court of Appeal will once again be housed on its original and historical premises.

Rue St-Georges (**BY 67**) – This animated street, lined with cafés and restaurants, has many old houses: nos 8, 10 and 12 form a remarkable group of 17C half-timbered houses. No 3, the 16C Hôtel de Moussaye, has a lovely Renaissance façade with sculptured pilasters.

Members of Parliament

Brittany's Parliament, one of the thirteen provincial parliaments which made up the Kingdom of France, initially had its seat in Rennes for part of the year and Nantes for the other, before finally the decision was taken in 1561 to establish a single Parliament seat in Rennes. It was the Supreme Court of 2,300 Breton tribunals, as well as fulfilling a legislative and political function. It was not slow to restrict its recruitment catchment net; from 1678, only noblemen or those "with the lifestyle of a nobleman" were admitted as members. In the following century applicants had to prove that they had at least four generations of noble blood in the family. The 100-120 councillors and presidents bought their seats, usually for a very high sum (about 100 000 **livres** by the mid-17C), and because these were hereditary this meant that extremely young people were sometimes inheriting them, at younger even than 20 years of age. There was an entry examination, but the level of this was very low.
Salaries were very low, and the renowned "sweeteners" received from clients, known as **"épices"** (spices) because they consisted mainly of sweetmeats, preserves and other such comestibles, were only really adequate for magistrates of long-standing office. However, the members of Parliament enjoyed many considerable privileges, not the least of which was undoubtedly exemption from payment of debts, and were acknowledged as the ruling class of Rennes. They exercised power over thousands of lawyers. It was traditional that they should have large families; the thirty-three children borne to one president by his wife raised hardly the flicker of an eyelid.

Palais St-Georges (**BY D**) – Preceded by a beautiful garden, this former Benedictine abbey (1670) now houses administrative services.

Église St-Germain (**BY**) – This Flamboyant church (15-16C) with its 17C gable (on the south side) retains certain characteristics typical of a Breton cathedral: wood vaulting and its beams with sculpted ends. In the south transept the beautiful 16C **stained-glass window** recounts the life of the Virgin and the Passion. The nave contains modern stained-glass windows by Max Ingrand.

Place de l'Hôtel de Ville (**AY 24**) – This regal square is the centre of the classical district. On its west side stands the Town Hall (Hôtel de Ville) and on the east side, the theatre. To the south, beyond Rue d'Orléans, the view is blocked by the **Palais du Commerce** (Trade Hall) (**E**), an imposing building decorated with monumental sculpture.
The **Town Hall** (**H**) ⓥ was built to the plans of Jacques Gabriel in 1734-43, after the fire of 1720. A central tower, standing back from the façade, carries the great clock – "le gros", as the townspeople call it – and is joined by two curved buildings to two large annexes. Inside are the former chapel and a lovely 17C Brussels tapestry. The right wing contains the Pantheon of Rennes, a hall dedicated to the memory of men who have died for France. Provided no official reception is being held, the public is admitted to the left wing of the building and can see the monumental staircase, the 18C Brussels tapestries and the hall where a wedding's civil ceremony is performed.
The **theatre** (**T**), joined by arcaded buildings, was built in 1832.

★★MUSÉE DE BRETAGNE AND MUSÉE DES BEAUX-ARTS

(**BY M**) *time: 2 hours 30 min*

These two museums are housed, respectively, on the ground floor and first floor of the former university.

★★**Musée de Bretagne** ⓥ – This museum recalls the history of Brittany. Through the exhibits (objects, models, carved figures) different eras are evoked: prehistory, Gallo-Roman Armorica, medieval Brittany and Brittany under the *ancien régime.*
In the second-to-last gallery, concerned with modern Brittany (1789-1914), costumes, everyday objects, tools and furnishings, characteristic of Rennes, are displayed. An audiovisual programme presenting Brittany of today occurs in the last gallery.

★★**Musée des Beaux-Arts** ⓥ – The Museum of Fine Arts contains an important collection of works covering the 14C to the present. Among the 16C masters are Veronese *(Perseus Rescuing Andromeda)* and Maerten van Heemskerk *(St Luke Painting the Portrait of the Virgin)*. The 17C is well represented (Rubens, Jordaens, and Champaigne); **The Newborn** by Georges de La Tour is a masterpiece.
The 18C is exemplified by the works of Chardin *(The Basket of Plums; Peaches and Grapes)* and Greuze *(Portrait of a Young Girl)*.

Among the 19C canvases are Jongkind, Corot, Boudin and Sisley. Works of the members of the Pont-Aven School *(qv)* are also on display: Bernard *(Yellow Tree)*, Gauguin *(Oranges)* and Sérusier *(Solitude, Argoat Landscape)*.
The last gallery, concerned with the 20C, displays works by Laurent, Picasso, Utrillo, Vlaminck, Tanguy and contemporary artists such as De Staël, Poliakoff and Asse. Old drawings, porcelain and fine Egyptian, Greek and Etruscan archaeological artefacts are also on show.
A small room presents works by 19 and 20C Breton painters who painted Brittany, its landscapes and activities, such as Blin, Lemordant and Cottet.

★★ JARDIN DU THABOR (BY) *time: 1 hour*

In the 16C the Benedictine Abbey of St-Mélaine stood on an elevated site, beyond the city walls. The monks called the place Thabor in memory of the biblical Mount Tabor. The abbey's former orchards were transformed in the 19C to their present appearance by Bülher and Martenot and completed by the placing of Lenoir's statues. The beauty of the different flowers (roses, dahlias, chrysanthemums, camellias, rhododendrons...) and trees (oak, beech, sequoia, cedar...), spread over more than 10ha - 25 acres, composed of a French garden, botanical garden, rose garden, landscaped garden and an aviary, makes these gardens particularly pleasant whatever the season.

Église Notre-Dame-en-St-Mélaine (**BY**) – This church was rebuilt in the 14 and 17C. The tower and transept, both of the 11C, are all that remain of the former St-Mélaine Abbey's church.
In the south arm of the transept a 15C fresco represents the Baptism of Christ. The decoration inside the church is modern: stained-glass windows by Le Moal and a tapestry and a painting (1942) by Mériel-Bussy.
Go round the building, on the left, to see the 17C cloisters which have been restored, adjoining the north side of the church, with beautiful carvings and a well. To the left of the square is the former bishop's palace (17-18C).

GOING OUT IN RENNES

To learn all about the entertainments and cultural events staged in and around Rennes, consult *"Spectacle-Info"*, a magazine issued by the Tourist Information Office every three months.

Main Venues:

Théâtre de la Ville/Opéra, Place de la Mairie. ☎ 02 99 28 55 87.

Théâtre National de Bretagne, 1, Rue St-Hélier. ☎ 02 99 30 88 88.

Théâtre de l'ADEC, 45, Rue Papu. ☎ 02 99 33 20 01.

Le Triangle, 30, Boulevard de Yougoslavie. ☎ 02 99 53 01 92.

Espace Instrumental du Conservatoire, 26, Rue Hoche. ☎ 02 99 28 55 72.

Péniche Spectacle, "l'Arbre d'eau", Quai St-Cyr. ☎ 02 99 59 35 38.

Every year the first week in July is devoted to the summer festival, an event known as **"Les Tombées de la Nuit"**. This convivial celebration serves to perpetuate local customs and discover new artists, combining street performances with the more traditional arts: theatre, opera, sacred music, etc.

EXCURSIONS

★**Écomusée du pays de Rennes** ⊙ – *8km - 5 miles south of Rue Maréchal-Joffre (signposted).*
Located between city and country, the **Ferme de la Bintinais** (Bintinais Farm) was for a long time one of the largest properties around Rennes. The museum illustrates by means of a remarkable collection of tools and farming equipment, reconstituted interiors, costumes, etc. the evolution of rural life on a farm, near an urban area – the city of Rennes – as from the 16C. There is also a display on earlier construction methods. Take a walk across the 15ha - 37 acre estate and discover some of the many sights: gardens, beehives, orchards, and cultivated plots of land which illustrate the evolution of local farming techniques.
In November 1994, the botanical park was complemented by the presence of livestock: 14 country breeds of endangered farm animals. All these races are characteristic of Brittany and its surrounding region: horses (Breton draught post-horses), cows (Pie Noire, froment du Léon, Nantaise and Armoricaine), pigs (Blanc de l'Ouest and Bayeux), goats, sheep (from Ushant, Landes de Bretagne and the Avranchin) and poultry (La Flèche hens, the Coucou de Rennes and the famous Gauloise Dorée).

The commentaries on the notice boards provide scientific explanations, while at the same time recounting unusual tales and legends. This museum also organises demonstrations and other celebrations: lettuce competition, harnessing contest for Breton draughthorses, feast of the swine, etc... and many other festive events testifying to the vivacity of Rennes' long-standing traditions and customs.

Forêt de Rennes – *11km - 7 miles northeast.*
In this 3 000 ha - 7 410 acre State Forest, forest roads and a long-distance footpath (GR 39) wind throught the beautiful oak, beech, pine, birch and chestnut trees.

VALLÉE DE LA VILAINE

Round tour of 36km - 23 miles – about 1 hour

Leave Rennes on the D 177 towards Redon.

Cross the river at Pont-Réan in beautiful surroundings. As you leave the town, turn left.

Le Boël – You can enjoy a pleasant walk by the river, which runs between rocky hills in a verdant setting.

Return to Pont-Réan and after crossing the bridge over the Vilaine, turn right.

Bruz – This country town is an example of successful planning in rural surroundings with its tiny square on the north side of the church. The **church★** ⏲ (1950), which is built of pink veined schist, is beautiful. A pointed spire rises above the square tower that forms the porch at its base. The interior blends well; daylight enters on all sides through square panes of glass decorated with a picture of three fishes within a circle; in the apse through stained-glass windows depicting the Seven Sacraments and in the two arms of the transept through windows, to the south of the Crucifixion and to the north of the Virgin Mary. The organ is flanked on either side by the long, narrow stained-glass windows of unequal height that can be seen in the façade.

Parc ornithologique de Bretagne ⏲ – This small park contains an interesting collection of more than 1 000 birds from every continent.

From Bruz one can reach the old Boël mill (4km - 2.5 miles) by taking the D 77 south and 3km - 2 miles further on bear right and then turn left before the level crossing.

Return to Rennes by Chartres-de-Bretagne.

La ROCHE-BERNARD

Population 766

Michelin map 63 fold 14 or 230 fold 52

This little old town, picturesquely sited on the spur of La Garenne, overlooks the River Vilaine. Its naval dockyards were famous in the 17C.
The port stands on a tributary of the river. It was very prosperous in the past due to its trade of wood, wheat, wine, salt and spices. It has now become a pleasure boat harbour (capacity for 300 boats).

A real Republican – The town of La Roche-Bernard welcomed the Revolution and opposed the Chouans *(qv)*. In 1793, 6 000 "Whites" (Royalists) easily defeated the 150 "Blues" (peasants) who were defending the town. Mayor Sauveur refused to flee; he was imprisoned. He was ordered to shout, "Long live the King! " and he replied, "Long live the Republic! " He was shot down. He became a hero of the Republic by decree; the town was named La Roche-Sauveur until 1802.

SIGHTS

★**Bridge (Pont)** – The suspension bridge, built in 1960, stands more than 50m - 160ft above the river. Stop at either end or on the *corniche* roads upstream to see how it blends with the landscape.

★**Viewpoint** – From a bend in the road towards La Baule, a rocky viewpoint *(23 steps)* dominates the Vilaine Valley extending its views onto the wooded slopes, on the right the suspension bridge and on the left the pleasure boat harbour on the Rhodoir. On a rock, a commemorative plaque for the launching of *La Couronne* (1634), France's first battleship, has been placed.

Old district – Across from the viewpoint and on the other side of the road begins **Promenade du Ruicard**, which overlooks the port. It goes into Rue du Ruicard and leads through a maze of small streets, some of which are stepped. Houses of the

16 and 17C follow: nos 6 and 8 are well restored, no 11 has an interesting doorway, no 12 has a turret.
Passage de la Quenelle, with its dormer windows surmounted by sculpted pediments, leads to **Place Bouffay** where the guillotine stood in 1793. Situated on the square is the town hall, which is also known as the "House of the Cannon" (Maison du Canon) (1599) because of the cannon (from the *Inflexible* which sought refuge in the estuary after a sea battle) placed in the corner. On the left opens Rue de la Saulnerie with a 15C house.
In Rue Haute-Notre-Dame stands the small 11C Chapelle Notre-Dame, rebuilt in the 16 and 19C. The first church built in the city, it was converted into a Protestant church in 1561, and then during the Terror used to store fodder; it became Catholic once again in 1827.

Musée de la Vilaine maritime ⏲ – The 16 and 17C Château des Basses-Fosses, on a spur on the west bank of the Vilaine, houses this museum of rural and maritime life on and along the Vilaine.
The ground floor explains the intense maritime activity which the river once had. The diorama of the Vilaine recreates the atmosphere which reigned along it in the early 1900s. A reconstructed cabin shows how life was on board a coastal fishing vessel. Upstairs, rural life is shown with exhibits of houses and the different kinds of timberwork, roofing, and dormers; the old trades through tools belonging to the carpenter, mason and roofer; local costumes and headdresses.

Boat Trip on the River Vilaine ⏲ – Boats go down the Vilaine to the Barrage d'Arzal (Arzal Dam) or up to Redon.

EXCURSIONS

Missillac – *13km - 8 miles southeast by the N 165 – E 60 towards Pontchâteau.*
The 19C church, built in the Gothic style, contains in its north apsidal chapel a graceful 17C wood **altarpiece★** ornamented with angels and prophets.
Separated from the town by a small stretch of water beside the wood, the 15C **Château de la Bretesche** (Bretesche Castle), with its low crenellated ramparts and water-filled moat, stands in an outstanding **site★**.

Barrage d'Arzal – *Round tour of 19km - 12 miles. Take the road towards Vannes; after 2km - 1 mile bear left.*
This dam on the Vilaine forms a freshwater reservoir thus eliminating the effect of the tides and making the trip easier for the coasting vessels that ply upstream to Redon. It is also an attractive stretch for pleasure craft. A road follows the crest of the dam over the river.

Past the dam, turn left to return to La Roche-Bernard.

Parc zoologique de Branféré – *18km - 11 miles northwest on the N 165 – E 60, the N 165 in the direction of Muzillac, after 8km - 5 miles turn right: follow the new "Blue Route" signposted and arrowed, for the park and château.*

Le Guerno – The village, once a popular place of pilgrimage, has a 16C church built where a Templars' Chapel once stood. The church's exterior has on its south side a pulpit, stalls and bench (reserved for the clergy); the altar is backed against the Calvary (on the square). The round tower, on the west side, is capped by an 18C lantern turret.
The inside is decorated by 16C stained-glass windows and choir stalls; 22 carved panels, also 16C, ornament the loft. At the transept two cylindrical columns support the vaulting. The trunk of the column on the left is hollow to collect offerings.

Once outside Le Guerno bear right then left onto the avenue which goes to Château de Branféré.

On the way note two lovely 18C fountains dedicated to St Anne and St Mary.

Parc zoologique de Branféré ⏲ – The château stands in 50ha - 124 acres of parkland, where over 200 species of exotic animals and countless birds roam amidst the trees and a series of lakes.

Moulin de Pen-Mur ⏲ – *17km - 11 miles west on the N 165 – E 60; leave this road at Muzillac and follow the signs for "Site de Pen-Mur".*
The mill, prettily located near a lake, contains an exhibition on the production of paper by hand using traditional 18C methods, showing all the stages from cutting up rags to the drying process.

Château de Léhélec – *18km - 11 miles to the north by the D 774. At Péaule, take the D 20 in the direction of Redon and after 8km - 5 miles turn right.*

Foleux – The pleasure boat harbour is located in a lovely site at the confluence of the Rivers Vilaine and Trévelo.

After Foleux skirt the Vilaine – from here there is a good view of the wide valley.

Bear right then turn left three times before taking the road which leads to the château.

Château de Léhélec ⓥ – Surrounded by woodland, this manor-house, built of ferruginous schist, offers on its south front an attractive perspective of the three courtyards bordered by the 16 and 18C outbuildings. One of these buildings houses a small rural museum containing regional furniture and everyday objects. Visitors are also admitted to two rooms lit by tall windows – the drawing room and dining room on the ground floor. In the entrance hall note the staircase with its 18C wrought-iron hand-rail.

ROCHEFORT-EN-TERRE★

Population 645

Michelin map 63 fold 4 or 230 fold 38

This charming small, old town occupies a picturesque **site★** on a promontory between deep dells. This landscape of rocks, woods, ravines, orchards and old houses bright with geraniums attracts many painters.

★**Old houses** – In the heart of the town stand old 16 and 17C town houses which you can see as you stroll along Rue du Porche, Place des Halles and Place du Puits. At Place du Puits note the former law court, the entrance of which is surmounted by a set of scales.

Rochefort-en-Terre – Old houses

Castle (Château) ⓥ – The only features that remain of the castle, destroyed in 1793, are the imposing entrance fort, sections of the walls, the underground passages and the outbuildings. The latter were restored at the turn of the century by the American Alfred Klots with parts – most notably the dormer windows – from the 17C Kéralio Manor-house near Muzillac.

The four rooms open to visitors are a good example of the studied décor of enthusiastic collectors avid for knowledge, whose eclectic spirit is reflected in the variety of the furniture and objets d'art they have assembled. Note a beautiful collection of Madonnas in Quimper faïence. A small museum of folk art adjoining the old workshop of the owners evokes one or two aspects of the way of life in Rochefort in days gone by (lovely collection of headdresses). Another room contains the doors from the old dining room of a mansion, which were painted *c*1880.

From the terrace, behind the castle, there is a fine view of the Gueuzon valley and the Grées schist plateau.

Église Notre-Dame-de-la-Tronchaye – The 12, 15 and 16C church has a façade embellished with four gables pierced with Flamboyant bays. Inside, the chancel contains 16C stalls and, left of the high altar, a white stone Renaissance altarpiece. In the south arm of the transept, a 17C altarpiece behind a fine 18C wrought-iron grille bears the venerated statue of Our Lady of la Tronchaye, which was found in the 12C in a hollow tree where it was hidden at the time of the Norsemen invasions. The statue is the object of a pilgrimage on the Sunday after 15 August. In the north arm of the transept is a wrought-iron baptismal font and white stone Renaissance altarpieces; one of the altarpieces is decorated with 3 niches, each of which contains a painted wood statue. At the back of the nave the magnificent gallery in finely carved wood comes from the old rood screen as does the canopy over the high altar.

On the square stands a small 16C Calvary with three tiers of carved figures: the scenes of the Passion, the Crucifixion and the Deposition (both at the top) are represented.

EXCURSION

Malansac: Parc de Préhistoire ⓥ – *3km - 2 miles east on the D 21 towards Malansac then the D 134 to St-Gravé.*
Gwenfol site, with its lakes and old slate quarries, is now an outdoor museum of prehistory. Different tableaux composed of people and animals (life-size models) accompanied by explanatory panels illustrate the Palaeolithic to the Neolithic Ages with such scenes as the discovery of fire, flint knapping, hunting, family life and the erection of a menhir.

Château de la ROCHE-JAGU★

Michelin map 59 fold 2 or 230 fold 7

The **castle** ⓥ was built in the 15C at the top of the steep wooded slopes which form the west bank of the River Trieux. It was restored in 1968. Together with other fortresses, no longer extant, it commanded the river and thus retains its defensive aspect. On the west façade, note the corbels which supported the former wall-walk and its five doors. The tour includes several rooms with French-style ceilings and large chimneys, the small chapel and its two oratories. There is a magnificent view of the **setting**★ of the Trieux from the covered wall-walk in front of the east wall. The river forms a steep-sided loop at the foot of the castle which can be reached by a footpath to the right. Notice the ornate chimneys.
During the summer, exhibits and displays take place in the castle.

La ROCHE-MAURICE★

Population 1 603
Michelin map 58 fold 5 or 230 fold 4

The village, situated on a hillside and dominated by the ruins of a castle, has a fine parish close.

★PARISH CLOSE *time: 30 min*

Three crosses featuring Christ and the thieves mark the entrance.

Church (Église) – An elegant, twin-galleried belfry crowns the 16C building. The **south porch**★ is delicately carved with bunches of grapes and statuettes of saints.
Inside, note the Renaissance **rood screen**★ decorated on the side facing the nave with twelve statues carved in the round, including nine Apostles and three popes, and on the chancel side with low reliefs of saints. Behind the high altar, a large **stained-glass window**★ (1539) illustrates the Passion and the Resurrection of Christ. Also of interest is the panelled ceiling adorned with angels and coats of arms, carved purlins and beams.

★**Ossuaire** – This ossuary dates from 1640 and is one of the largest in Brittany. Above the outside font, Death (*Ankou – qv*) is shown armed with an arrow, threatening small figures framed in medallions representing all social classes: a peasant, a woman, a lawyer, a bishop, St-Yves, a pauper and a rich man; an inscription reads "*Je vous tue tous*" (Death comes to all).

D'après photo R. Le Thomas/AZIMUT

La Roche-Maurice, Ankou

*The **Practical Information** section at the end of the guide lists:*
– information on travel, motoring, accommodation, recreation,
– local or national organisations providing additional information,
– calendar of events,
– admission times and charges for the sights described in the guide.

Château des ROCHERS-SÉVIGNÉ

Michelin map 63 fold 8 or 230 north of fold 42

The Rochers-Sévigné Château, which was the home of the Marquise de Sévigné (1626-96), is a place of literary interest. Admirers of the famous *Letters* will enjoy visiting the castle and park.

The Marquise de Sévigné at Les Rochers – The Marquise used to stay frequently at the château, largely to save money as her husband and her son had spent three-quarters of her fortune, and after 1678 she lived there virtually until she died at Grignan (her daughter's home) in the Drôme.

Her letters give a picture of life as it was led at Les Rochers. Up at eight o'clock, Mass in the chapel at nine, a walk and then lunch. In the afternoon, needlework, another walk, talks and letter writing. Charles, the Marquise's son, used to read learned books aloud. Sometimes the readings would go on for five hours. The reader's stamina and the audience's staying-power seem worthy of admiration. Supper at eight. After dinner Charles would read again, this time from amusing books "to keep himself awake". The circle broke up at ten at night, but Mme de Sévigné went on reading or writing in her room until midnight.

The only variety in this country life was that created by the visits of local ladies and gentlemen or a little trip to Vitré when the legislative bodies of the district met there. The Marquise describes, sometimes with a touch of malice, the provincial nobility, their dress, their airs and graces and their faults. The official banquets, at which 400 bottles of wine were emptied, filled her with astonishment. "As much wine passes through the body of a Breton", she wrote, "as water under the bridges".

The noble lady took an interest in repairs to the building but felt dizzy when she saw carpenters perched on the roof: "One can only thank God", she wrote, "that some men will do for 12 *sous* what others would not do for 10 000 *écus*." That did not prevent her from keeping a sharp eye on the accounts and deploring the high cost of living.

Château ⓥ – The château was built in the 15C and remodelled in the 17C. It consists of two wings set at right angles. Besides the chapel built in 1671 for the "exemplary" Abbot of Coulanges, the marquise's maternal uncle, two rooms in the large north tower are open to visitors. That on the ground floor was the "Green Room" ("Cabinet Vert"). It still contains some of Mme de Sévigné's personal possessions, family pictures and her portrait; there is a collection of autographs and documents in a glass case. The 16C chimney-piece is adorned with the Marquise's initials (Marie de Rabutin-Chantal – MRC).

Garden – In the French-style garden, rearranged following designs by Le Nôtre, is the semicircular wall that Mme de Sévigné called "that little wall that repeats words right into your ear" because of its double echo (stones mark the places where the two conversationalists should stand).

Park – Beyond the garden lies the large, wooded park, which is crossed by avenues, the names of which recall the Marquise and her literary environment: the Mall, the Lone Wolf, Infinity, the Holy Horror, My Mother's Whim, My Daughter's Whim, Royal Avenue.

Château de ROSANBO★

Michelin map 58 fold 7 or 230 fold 6 – 8km - 5 miles west of Plouaret

The **château** ⓥ stands on the foundations of an old 14C castle, overlooking the Bô valley, hence its Breton name meaning "rock *(ros)* on the *(an)* Bô".

The different periods of construction can be seen as you enter the courtyard: the 15C manor-house to the west, which was enlarged in the 17C (with mansard roofs) and 18C, and finally restored in the 19C.

The rooms open to the public are furnished and decorated with good taste: seigneurial chapel, Breton room, kitchen, dining room and neo-Gothic drawing room. Archive documents have recently made it possible to reconstruct the most authentic rooms of the residence, the dining room and the 18C drawing room.

The **library** contains over 8 000 volumes dating mainly from the 17C. The vast room overlooks a terrace with an enormous ornamental pond.

The château is bordered to the northeast by a magnificent **French style garden**, which is the work of Achille Duchêne, the famous 19C landscape architect. Note in particular the **hedges**, almost 2 500m - 2 734yds long, and the green arbours (small clearings in shrubs) which once had specific functions, such as horse-riding ring, training area, tennis area, etc.

To choose a hotel, a restaurant or a campsite consult the current edition of the annual Michelin Red Guide France *and the annual Michelin Guide* Camping Caravaning France.

ROSCOFF★

Population 3 787

Michelin map 58 fold 6 or 230 fold 5 – Facilities

Roscoff is a much-frequented seaside resort and a medical centre using seawater treatment (thalassotherapy); it is also a fishing port for lobster and spiny lobster, a pleasure boat harbour and a great vegetable market and distribution centre to England. Fishing and pleasure boats dock behind two jetties near the town centre, beyond the old ramparts. A pier to the east of Pointe de Bloscon closes off the deep-water harbour from which car ferries sail to and from Plymouth and Cork.
The University of Paris and the scientific research body Centre National de la Recherche Scientifique (CNRS) have set up a laboratory in the town for oceanographic and biological research.

SIGHTS

★**Église Notre-Dame-de-Croac-Batz** (**Y**) – This Gothic church was completed in 1545, funded by the privateers and merchants of the town. For this reason the outside walls and tower feature sculpted ship's nails as ex-votos. The church has a remarkable Renaissance **belfry**★ with lantern turrets, one of the finest examples of its type in Brittany. Inside, on the retable of the altar to the Sacré-Cœur (south aisle), there are four 16C **alabaster bas-reliefs**★ from the Nottingham studio depicting the Flagellation, the Crucifixion, the Ascension and Pentecost. The **altarpiece** of the 17C high altar has six wreathed columns and is richly decorated with statues of the Evangelists, cherubs and pampres. The organ case dates from the 17C. The font (1701) was restored in 1991.
In the church close are two chapel-ossuaries: that in the southwest corner dates from the 16C and has been dedicated to St Brigitte; that in the northwest corner (early 17C) did not originally have a door at all, as it was used purely to store bones.

★**Aquarium Charles-Pérez** (**Y**) ⏱ – The aquarium has a central pool and several tanks in which most of the creatures to be found in the Channel are shown in their natural state. The first floor is devoted to the history of the biological centre and a maritime exhibition.

Old houses – The houses in Place Lacaze-Duthiers (**Y 13**) and Rue Amiral-Révellière (**Y 20**) date from the 16 and 17C. In the latter the so-called House of Mary Stuart (Maison de Marie Stuart) (**Y E**) with its elegant façade adorned with ogee arches, is noteworthy.

Chapelle Ste-Barbe (**Y**) – *It is best to visit this chapel at high tide. Go round the fishing port and leave the car in the car park on the left. Viewing table.*
In the centre of a pretty little garden sits the tiny chapel dedicated to St Barbara. Its white walls still serve as a landing mark to mariners. There is a beautiful view of the town, the port, the île de Batz, Pointe de Primel and the deep-water harbour at Bloscon, which is the departure point for car ferries to Britain and Ireland.

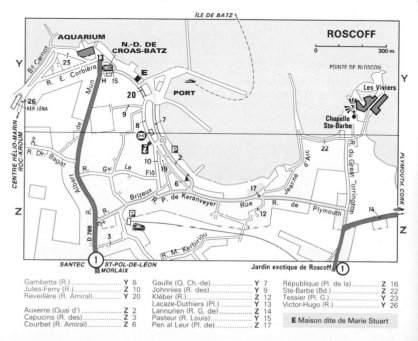

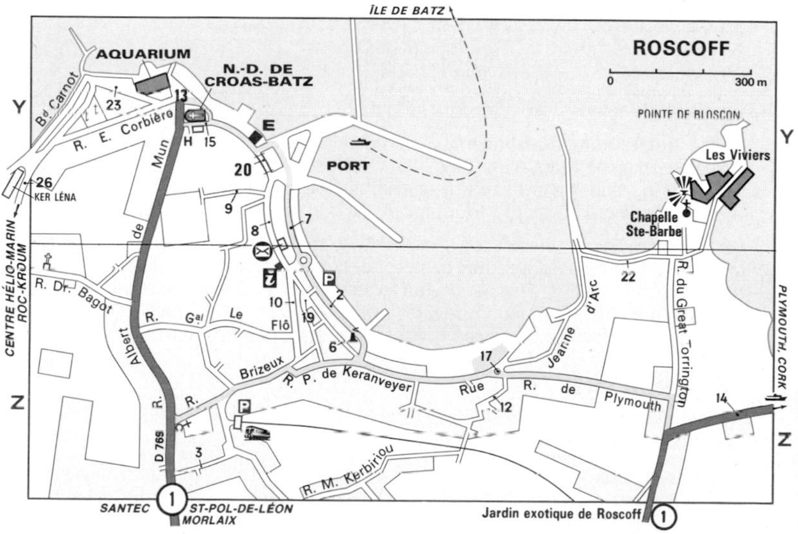

Gambetta (R.) .... Y 8
Jules-Ferry (R.) .... Z 10
Reveillère (R. Amiral) .... Y 20

Auxerre (Quai d') .... Z 2
Capucins (R. des) .... Z 3
Courbet (R. Amiral) .... Z 6

Gaulle (Q. Ch.-de) .... Y 7
Johnnies (R. des) .... Y 9
Kléber (R.) .... Z 12
Lacaze-Duthiers (Pl.) .... Y 13
Lannurien (R. G. de) .... Z 14
Pasteur (R. Louis) .... Y 15
Pen al Leur (Pl. de) .... Z 17

République (Pl. de la) .... Z 16
Ste-Barbe (Bd.) .... Z 22
Tessier (Pl. G.) .... Y 23
Victor-Hugo (R.) .... Y 26

E Maison dite de Marie Stuart

Go round the hill on which the chapel stands.

Viviers (Y) ⓥ – Footbridges lead visitors round the 5 200m² – 55 972ft² fish farm in which lobsters, crawfish and crabs are raised. Thanks to the renewal of the 32 000m³ – 1 130 070ft³ of water with every tide, the shellfish live in conditions which are almost identical with those found in their natural environment.

Go back along the Rue de Great Torrington, then take the road to the deep-water harbour towards St-Pol. Turn left at Keraison.

★**Jardin exotique de Roscoff** ⓥ – This extraordinary garden is wrapped around the Rocher de Roch-Hievec (or Rocher de Maison Rouge). Over one thousand sub-tropical plant species thrive here, producing both blossom and fruit. The footpaths will take you past proteaceous shrubs from Australia, more than 50 varieties of eucalyptus tree, several other southern species and an amazing collection of "succulent plants", in other words, cactuses. A staircase leads to the summit, which commands a nice view of the Bay of Morlaix, Roscoff, Carantec and the Château du Taureau.

EXCURSION

Île de Batz – *Boat trip crossing: 20 minutes. See Île de BATZ.*

ROSPORDEN

Population 6 485
Michelin map 38 fold 16 or 230 fold 33

This little town stands by a pool formed by the River Aven, in which the church's bell tower is reflected. There are many canning factories in the town which is also famous for its mead (*chouchen* in Breton).

Church ⓥ – The 14-15C building, remodelled in the 17C, has a fine square **bell tower**★ with four pinnacles and four windows decorated with tracery framing the octagonal spire. Go through the 14C porch to see, inside, the gilded 17C high altar above an Entombment, a Virgin and Child (15C) and a Mary Magdalene (16C).

EXCURSION

St-Yvi – *9km - 5 miles west. Leave Rosporden by the D 765, the Quimper road.* The town has a small parish close with a simple Calvary-cross with a twisted column and a late-15C ossuary adorned with six trefoil arches. The early 16C **church** ⓥ has an elegant pierced belfry with two galleries. Inside, note the retable at the high altar (17C) and the altarpiece of the Rosary (18C) to the left of the chancel.

ROSTRENEN

Population 3 664
Michelin map 59 fold 11 or 230 fold 21

This pretty little town is situated on a hillside.

Église Notre-Dame-du-Roncier ⓥ – The church was once the castle chapel (set on fire during the League in 1572). It was built in the 14C and remodelled in the 18 and 19C, and has a beautiful transitional Gothic-Renaissance porch. Close by is an interesting 17C sacred fountain. A *pardon* is held on 15 August.

Le Miniou – Take the road towards Pontivy, then a road to the right and up the hill turn left to reach a weather centre *(station climatologique)* situated at an altitude of 263m - 928ft. The panorama extends over Rostrenen and the area round Callac to the northwest and Loudéac to the east; from the terrace, there is a view over the Guéméné region to the south and the Montagnes Noires to the west.

EXCURSIONS

Round tour of 45km - 28 miles – time: about 2 hours 30 min. Leave Rostrenen northeast by the D 790, the St-Brieuc road.

St-Nicolas-du-Pélem – The town includes a 15-16C **church** ⓥ with two fine stained-glass windows depicting the Passion (1470) at the flat east end. Go round the north side of the church to see the 17C fountain of St-Nicolas which abuts onto a house.

Proceed to Lanrivain.

The road crosses the delightful Vallée du Faoudel.

Lanrivain – *See LANRIVAIN.*

Continue to Trémargat and after 1.5km - 1 mile bear left.

★**Gorges de Toul Goulic** – *15 min on foot Rtn.* At the far end of the car park overlooking the wooded valley of the Blavet, take the steep path leading downhill through the woods to the cleft in which the Blavet disappears. The river is still full at the beginning of the cleft (north side) but has completely vanished by the time you reach the middle of the cleft and flows, rumbling, beneath a mass of huge rocks.

Turn back and bear left.

Between Trémargat and Kergrist-Moëlou, the landscape is studded with great boulders.

Kergrist-Moëlou – On the church square, shaded by fine old yew trees, stands a Calvary (1578) with some 100 figures in Kersanton granite resting on its octagonal plinth. The figures were damaged during the Revolution and have been replaced haphazardly. The imposing 16C church has a twin transept and in the chancel the stained-glass windows are decorated with the coat of arms of the Rostrenen family, the church's founders. On the south side is a small ossuary with trefoil arches.

Via St-Lubin return to Rostrenen.

Nantes-Brest Canal – *Round tour of 20km - 12 miles – about 2 hours 30 min. Leave Rostrenen on the road towards Carhaix-Plouguer and after 3.5km - 2 miles, turn left into the Gourin road.*
The road reaches the canal, built between 1823 and 1834, at the summit level (alt 184m - 604ft). Walk along the towpath to the right of the bridge, leading to the canal cutting and affording a view of the forty-four locks through which boats climb or descend 120m - 384ft over 17km - 11 miles to Carhaix-Plouguer.

Proceed to Glomet and then turn right into the road towards Paule; after 1.8km - 1 mile, bear right.

On the canal banks, the former lock keeper's house stands in a pretty **site**★. It is a pleasant walk along the towpath upstream and downstream from the bridge.

Return to the main road and turn right back to Rostrenen.

RUMENGOL

Michelin map 58 fold 5 or 230 fold 18 – Local map under Monts d'ARRÉE

The village, situated in the Château basin, is at its most interesting on *pardon* days *(see the Calendar of Events at the end of the guide)*. People come from all over Brittany to attend these festivals dedicated to Our Lady of all Remedies (Notre-Dame-de-Tout-Remède). The most colourful is on Trinity Sunday and another is held on 15 August. Rumengol dates from the time of King Gradlon (*qv*) who built a chapel here in the 5C.

Church – The church is 16C as shown by the south porch and the magnificent west front in Kersanton granite but significant alterations were made in the 17 and 18C. Inside, a 15C statue of Our Lady stands at the entrance to the chancel on the left. The two **altarpieces**★ and altars date from 1686.
In the centre of the village, near the church apse, is a sacred fountain (1792). On a grassy area surrounded by fir trees stands an oratory where services are held on the two great *pardon* days. Behind the oratory, note the 15C Calvary in the cemetery.

RUNAN

Michelin map 59 fold 2 or 230 fold 7 – 5km - 3 miles west of Pontrieux

Runan, which stands on a plateau in the Tréguier region, has a large church which belonged to the Knights Templar and then to the Hospitallers of St John of Jerusalem.

★**Church** – The 14-15C church is richly decorated. The south side has four gables pierced with broad windows and emblazoned façades. The porch gable is adorned with a sculpted lintel depicting the Annunciation and a Descent from the Cross. The superimposed figures of the twelve Apostles join to form the keystone of the vaulting. The ossuary adjoining the church dates from 1552; the outdoor pulpit from the time of St Vincent Ferrier *(qv)*.
Inside, the building is roofed with panelled vaults resting on multicoloured purlins: signs of the Zodiac to the left of the nave, animals on the right. The Commandery Chapel (right) contains slim sculpted pillars. The furnishings are remarkable: the great stained-glass window depicting the Crucifixion in the east end (1423) is beautifully designed. The old altarpiece of the font chapel of the same period includes exceptionally delicate figures (five scenes from the lives of Christ and the Virgin) made of bluish Tournai stone, Christ and a *Pietà*.

ST-AUBIN-DU-CORMIER

Population 2 040
Michelin map 59 fold 18 or 230 fold 27

This city of the Breton marshland witnessed, in 1488, the decisive battle *(see Introduction: Historical Table and Notes)* waged by Breton troops under Duke François II of Brittany and the army of the King of France led by the Duke de la Trémoille. François II was defeated and signed the *Treaty of Verger* renouncing Brittany's sovereign rights.

Castle ruins – The impressive 13C fortress stands, still an imposing ruin, between the pool and the deep ravine which formed its natural defences.

Rochers Bécherel – Beyond the ruins, a path on the left of the road winds through a mass of rocks in a wooded setting.

The towns and sights described in this guide are indicated in black lettering on the local maps and town plans.

ST-BRIEUC★

Conurbation 83 861
Michelin map 59 fold 3 or 230 folds 8 and 9

The town is built 3km - 2 miles from the sea on a plateau deeply cleft by two water courses: the Gouëdic and the Gouet. Bold viaducts span their valleys. The Gouet is canalised and leads to the commercial and fishing port of Légué.
St-Brieuc is the administrative, commercial and industrial centre of the *département* (Côtes d'Armor). The markets and fairs of the town are much frequented, especially the Fair of St Michael (Foire de la St-Michel) on 29 September and another event in early September. On Saturdays, a market is held on the cathedral's parvis.
An industrial zone has been established southwest of the town. The *pardon* of Notre-Dame-d'Espérance takes place the last Sunday in May.

SIGHTS

★**Cathédrale St-Étienne** (**AY**) ⏱ – This great cathedral of the 13 and 14C has been reconstructed several times and restored in the 19C; its mass bears striking witness to its original role of church fortress. The front is framed by two great towers complete with loopholes and machicolations and supported by stout buttresses. The two arms of the transept jut far out and are protected by towers with pepperpot roofs. The lofty nave with its seven bays was rebuilt in the 18C. The harmonious three-sided chancel has an elegant triforium with quatrefoil balustrade and trefoil arches above the great arcades.
In the south aisle, note the carved wooden altar by Corlay (*c*1745) in the Chapel of the Holy Sacrament. The south arm of the transept is lit by fine 15C stained-glass windows and in the small chapel stands the tomb of St William (died 1234). The stained-glass windows represent the Glorification of Mary. The 16C organ loft, the 18C pulpit and the Stations of the Cross carved in granite by Saupique (1958) are also noteworthy.

★**Tertre Aubé** (**ABV**) – The hill commands a fine **view**★ of the Vallée du Gouet, crossed by the viaduct which carries the road to Paimpol; also of the partly-hidden port of Légué, below, and, to the right, of St-Brieuc Bay. On a hill to the right is the ruined tower of Cesson.

Old houses (**AY**) – The area to the north of the cathedral still retains many 15-16C half-timbered and corbelled houses.
Walk through Place du Martray, Rue Fardel (at the corner of Place au Lin: the Ribeault mansion; at no 15, the house known as the "mansion of the Dukes of Brittany"; nos 17, 19, 27, 29, 31, 32 and 34), Rue Quinquaine (no 9) and Rue de Gouet (nos 6, 16, 22).

Museum (**Musée**) (**AZ M**) ⏱ – Located in renovated rooms, the museum traces the history and development of the Côtes d'Armor *département* (formerly Côtes-du-Nord) during the 19C, when traditional Brittany evolved into modern Brittany. Different themes – St-Brieuc Bay, heathland, cloth and linen trade, village life – accompanied by models, equipment and tools used for fishing, navigation and husbandry, as well as costumes and furnishings, are evoked.

Grandes Promenades (**BYZ**) – These walks encircle the Palais de Justice (Law Courts). Among the statues are a bust by Elie Le Goff Sr. of the writer Villiers de l'Isle-Adam, who was born at St-Brieuc, *Form Arising from Matter* by Paul Le Goff and *La Bretonne du Goëlo* by Francis Renaud.

Rond-Point Huguin (**BX**) – From the roundabout, on which stands a monument to the folklorist Anatole Le Braz *(qv)*, there is a view of the Vallée du Gouëdic and its two viaducts with the village and tower of Cesson perched high above, St-Brieuc Bay and the coast as far as Cap Fréhel.

Fontaine de St-Brieuc (**AY B**) – The fountain, which is sheltered by a lovely 15C porch, stands against the east end of the Chapelle of Notre-Dame-de-la-Fontaine, which was rebuilt in the 19C.

Tour du Saint-Esprit (**AY**) – This tower, an interesting Renaissance structure with a pepperpot octagonal corner tower, was restored in 1962.

ST-BRIEUC

Chapitre (R. du)	**AZ**	3
Charbonnerie (R.)	**AY**	4
Glais-Bizoin (R.)	**ABY**	20
Jouallan (R.)	**AY**	26
St-Gilles (R.)	**AY**	43
St-Guillaume (R.)	**BZ**	46
Abbé-Garnier (R.)	**AX**	2
Corderie (R. de la)	**AX**	13
Ferry (R. Jules)	**AX**	16
Gambetta (Bd)	**AV**	17
Gaulle (Pl. Gén. de)	**AY**	18
Hérault (Bd)	**AV**	23
Le-Gorrec (R. P.)	**AZ**	28
Libération (Av. de la)	**BZ**	29
Lycéens-Martyrs (R. des)	**AZ**	32
Martray (Pl. du)	**AY**	33
Plélo (Bd de)	**BV**	34
Quinquaine (R.)	**AY**	38
Résistance (Pl. de la)	**AY**	39
Rohan (R. de)	**AYZ**	40
St-Gouéno (R.)	**AY**	44
Victor-Hugo (R.)	**BX**	50
3-Frères-Le-Goff (R.)	**AY**	52
3-Frères-Merlin (R.)	**AY**	53

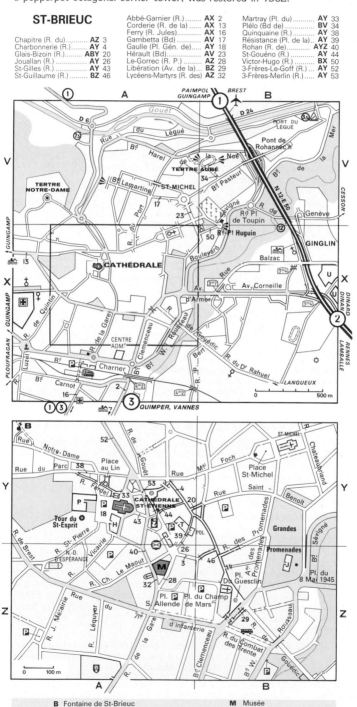

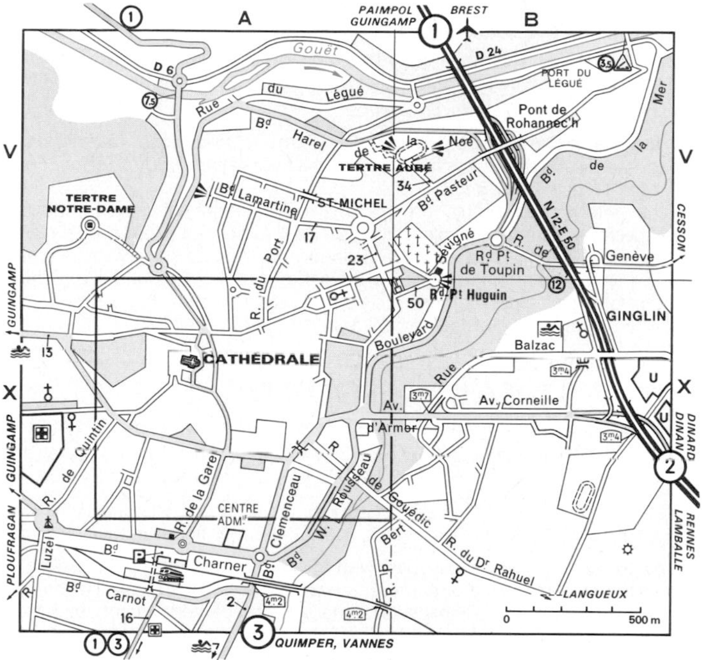

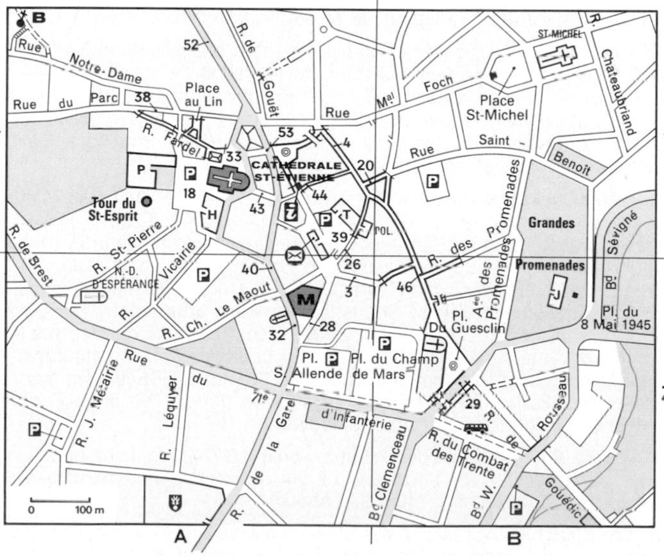

B Fontaine de St-Brieuc **M** Musée

EXCURSION

Round tour of 25km - 15 miles – time: about 2 hours. Leave St-Brieuc north by Légué port, follow the quay on the north bank.

On the right, the ruined tower of Cesson is outlined amid the greenery; as the road climbs there is a good view over Pointe des Guettes at the far end of the bay and the coast as far as Cap d'Erquy.

★ **Pointe du Roselier** – Take a path on the right of the telescope to go round the point. Fine **views**★ extend over St-Quay-Portrieux and the coast; the path passes near an old oven used for turning cannon balls red-hot, and skirts a villa. The view takes in Pointe de Cesson, the far end of St-Brieuc Bay and Pointe des Guettes with its mussel-poles, and the coast towards Le Val-André. Paths cut in the cliffside lead back to the starting point.

Turn back and after 2km - 1mile, bear right.

Martin-Plage – This pretty beach lies between Pointe du Roselier and the Tablettes Reef (Rocher des Tablettes).
The road then climbs steeply and at Ville-Fontaine, bear right into a pleasant little road descending between wooded embankments.

Plage des Rosaires – The beach is framed by wooded cliffs some 100m - 320ft high. The view includes the whole of St-Brieuc Bay from St-Quay Point to Cap d' Erquy.

The road leads straight back to St-Brieuc.

Marinarium de la Baie de St-Brieuc ⏲ – *10km - 6 miles east. Take* ② *on the town plan, then leave the expressway for Yffignac. Take the D 80 to Hillion. Follow the signs to "Maison de la Baie".*
This visitor information centre for the marine environment displays about a hundred species of animal and plant life collected exclusively from the Bay of St-Brieuc, between Plérin and Erquy. Each aquarium illustrates a different type of behaviour: mimicry (plaice and skate on the sandy sea floor); group life in shoals; interrelation of certain species (hermit-crab and sea anemone). Regular excursions are organised in discovery of local bird life or the natural habitat.

ST-CAST-LE-GUILDO

Population 3 093
Michelin map 59 fold 5 or 230 folds 10 and 11
Local map under CÔTE D'ÉMERAUDE – Facilities

This seaside resort is formed by three settlements: Le Bourg, L'Isle and Les Mielles. The port shelters a small fishing fleet which specialises in scallops and clams.

★★ **Pointe de St-Cast** – There is a superb **view**★★ of the Côte d'Emeraude from the point (viewing table – *table d'orientation* – beside the signal station). At the tip of the point a monument to the Escaped Prisoners of France (Monument aux Évadés) can be reached by a cliff path which follows the shore, passes another monument dedicated to the crew of the frigate *Laplace*, mined in 1950, and rejoins the St-Cast road at La Mare Beach (Plage de la Mare).

★★ **Pointe de la Garde** – At the end of this point there is a very fine **view**★★ of the beaches of St-Cast and Pen Guen and the coast as far as Pointe de la Garde; also a statue of Notre-Dame-de-la-Garde by Armel Beaufils. A scenic path goes round the point by way of the Corniche de la Plage near the Hôtel Ar Vro, passes beside the oratory, follows the cliff along the point and, on the south shore, joins the road leading to the slipway near the oratory.

Colonne commémorative – *Follow the signs posted* "Mairie" *and take Rue de la Colonne.*
The commemorative column is surmounted by a greyhound for France, trampling the English leopard. It recalls the failure of a British attack on St-Malo in 1758, during the Seven Years War, when 13 000 British troops returned to embark in warships anchored in the Bay of St-Cast. They were attacked by the Duke of Aiguillon, Governor of Brittany, and lost 2 400 men. The Duke directed the battle from the mill of Anne de la Vieuxville. When La Chalotais *(qv)*, Procurator of the Rennes Parliament, was told that the Duke had "covered himself with glory" he commented sardonically: "Yes, but most of all with flour". This did not improve relations between the Procurator and the Governor.

Church – *At Le Bourg.* The modern church, built 1897-9, contains a 12C stoup and some 17C statues. In the north arm of the transept, a modern stained-glass window depicts the Battle of St-Cast *(see above)*.

Chapelle Ste-Blanche – *At L'Isle.* Above the high altar is an old statue of St Blanche – the mother of St Guénolé, St Jacut and St Venec – which is the object of great veneration.

Chapelle ST-FIACRE★

Michelin map 58 fold 17 or 230 fold 20 – 2.5km - 2 miles southeast of Le Faouët

The chapel is a fine 15C building. The façade has one of the best gable-belfries in Brittany *(details and photograph p 41)*.
Inside, the **rood screen**★★ of lace-like woodcarving is a Flamboyant work of 1480 *(photograph p 43)*. On the nave side, scenes of the Temptation of Adam and Eve, the Annunciation and the Calvary are related. The most curious figures are on the chancel side; they picture theft (a man picking fruit from a tree), drunkenness (a man vomiting a fox), lust (a man and a woman) and laziness (a Breton peasant playing bagpipes and a bombard). The decoration of the panels of the gallery and the corbels is quite varied. The stone altarpiece against the left pillar shows the martyrdom of St Sebastian. There are fine 16C **stained-glass windows** in the chancel and transept: the Passion (chancel), the Life of St John the Baptist (south transept), the Tree of Jesse and the Life of St Fiacre (north transept). The statues of St Apollinia, St Fiacre (in a painted wooden niche) and a Breton duke in court dress date from the 15 and 16C.

ST-GEORGES-DE-GRÉHAIGNE

Population 386

Michelin map 59 fold 7 or 230 fold 13

Before the polders were created, the sea came to within 1km - half a mile of the village. The Benedictine **church** was built in the 15C on the hilltop, on the former site of a chapel, that had been dedicated to St George in 1030. The interior, with its oak roof, is adorned by several large statues, the oldest being one of St Samson (in the nave across from the entrance). The central aisle paved with tombstones leads to the narrower chancel lit by a 15C window showing the Virgin as a Breton peasant. Looking between the trees behind the church one can distinguish Mont-St-Michel beyond a distant row of poplar trees.

EXCURSION

Petit Mont-St-Michel ⏲ – *9km - 5.5 miles north-west on the D 797 towards Le Vivier-sur-Mer and then bear left on the road to St-Marcan.*
On the hillside, in an enclosure, monuments of the region are presented at a 1:50 scale reduction: the Église de Pontorson, Mont-St-Michel, Fougères, etc. Stroll along the pathways from where the views open onto the bay of Mont-St-Michel. Playground.

ST-GILDAS-DE-RHUYS

Population 1 141

Michelin map 63 fold 12 or 230 fold 50 – Local map under Golfe du MORBIHAN

This village owes its origin to a monastery founded by St Gildas in the 6C. The most famous of the abbots who governed it was Abélard in the 12C.

Abélard – It was after the adventures with Héloïse, that the learned philosopher tried to find peace in this Breton solitude. His disillusion was quick and cruel: "I live", he wrote to Héloïse, "in a wild country whose language I find strange and horrible; I see only savages; I take my walks on the inaccessible shores of a rough sea; my monks have only one rule, which is to have none at all. I should like you to see my house; you would never take it for an abbey; the only decorations on the doors are the footmarks of various animals – hinds, wolves, bears, wild boars – or the hideous remains of owls. Every day brings new dangers; I always seem to see a sword hanging over my head."
However, the monks used poison, not a sword, to get rid of their Abbot. It was a wonder he survived and managed to escape through a secret passage in 1132.

★**Church (Église)** – *Time: 30 min.* This is the former abbey church built at the beginning of the 11C and largely rebuilt in the 16 and 17C.
The Romanesque chevet has pure, harmonious lines; it is ornamented with modillions; note a small carving depicting a tournament. Inside, the Romanesque **chancel**★ is remarkable. Behind the Baroque high altar is the tomb of St Gildas (11C). In the north transept lies the 11C gravestone of St Goustan and in the ambulatory, lit by modern stained-glass windows, 13 and 14C gravestones of Breton children and gravestones of abbots and knights. At the end of the nave is a stoup made up from two carved capitals. Another capital is found in the south aisle.
The **treasury**★ ⏲ contains valuable antique objects, well displayed: 14 and 18C shrines, reliquaries (15C) containing the arms and legs of St Gildas, and his embroidered mitre, a 17C silver-gilt cross bejewelled with emeralds, etc.

ST-GONÉRY

Michelin map 59 fold 2 or 230 fold 7 – Local map under TRÉGUIER: Excursions

This little town in the region around Tréguier *(qv)* has a fine 15C chapel.

★**Chapelle St-Gonéry** ⏲ – The chapel has a curiously leaning lead steeple (1612) on a 10C tower.
Inside, the painted wood vaulting depicts scenes from the Old and New Testaments; these **paintings**, which date from the late 15C, were restored in the 18 and 19C. In the chapel on the right of the chancel, there is a 16C **reliquary cupboard**★, a finely carved canopied type of chest. The left chapel contains the 16C **mausoleum**★ of a bishop of Tréguier; the recumbent figure rests on a great marble slab decorated with mouldings and supported on four lions. A 15C Virgin in alabaster stands in the nave. Under the belfry porch are the sarcophagus and tomb (1614) of St Gonery, a hermit who preached in the region in the 6C. An opening in the tomb's arches enabled sailors and soldiers leaving for a long journey to remove a handful of earth which they promised to restore on their return.
A small Calvary and an octagonal 16C pulpit stand in the cemetery.

ST-JEAN-DU-DOIGT★

Population 661

Michelin map 59 fold 6 or 230 folds 5 and 6

This picturesque village owes its name to the relic kept in its church since the 15C. It celebrates its *pardon*, which is attended particularly by people suffering from ophthalmia, on the last Sunday in June.

PARISH CLOSE (ENCLOS PAROISSIAL) *time: 45min*

It has a 16C triumphal gateway and, on the left, a pretty Renaissance **fountain**★ dominated by God the Father blessing the baptism of His Son performed by St John the Baptist. To the right of the church porch is a small chapel (1577) adorned inside with a frieze and sculpted beams.

★**Church** (**Église**) – St John the Baptist's finger, which was brought to the Chapelle St-Mériadoc *c*1420, worked miracles. The construction of a great church was started in 1440, but building went slowly and was finished only in 1513 thanks to the generosity of Anne of Brittany.
The church, built in the Flamboyant style, has a flat east end. The bell tower, which has lost its spire, abuts onto the first bay in the nave, which includes eight bays in all. At its base, abutting onto the buttresses, are two small ossuaries; that on the right is Gothic, the other, Renaissance in style.

★★**Treasury** (Trésor) ⏲ – The treasury contains several reliquaries, one of which holds the first joint of the index finger of St John the Baptist. There is also a **processional cross**★. The finest piece is a silver-gilt Renaissance **chalice**★★.

ST-LUNAIRE

Population 2 163

Michelin map 59 fold 5 or 230 fold 11 – Local map under CÔTE D'ÉMERAUDE

This smart resort, not far from Dinard *(qv)*, has two fine beaches: to the east that of St-Lunaire, which is the more frequented facing St-Malo, and to the west that of Longchamp, which is the larger of the two opposite Cap Fréhel.

SIGHTS

★★**Pointe du Décollé** – The point is joined to the mainland by a natural bridge crossing a deep fissure and known as the Cat's Leap (Saut du Chat); the Décollé promenades are laid out beyond the bridge.

To the left of the entrance to the Décollé Pavilion, take the road leading to the point, on which stands a granite cross.

From here the vantage point affords a very fine **view**★★ of the Côte d'Émeraude, from Cap Fréhel to Pointe de la Varde.

★**Grotte des Sirènes** – From the bridge crossing the cleft through which it opens to the sea, you can see the bottom of the grotto. The wash of the sea at high tide is spectacular.

Vieille église St-Lunaire ⏲ – The church stands among the trees in a former cemetery. The nave is 11C; the side aisles and canted chancel were rebuilt in the 17C. In the middle of the nave lies the tomb of St Lunaire with the recumbent figure of the saint (14C) resting on a Gallo-Roman sarcophagus. The transept contains seven tombs; in the Chapelle des Pontbriand in the north arm, note the tombs of a squire and a lady (15C), in the Chapelle des Pontual in the south arm, the tomb of a lady of the Pontual family (13-14C), richly carved in high relief.

ST-MALO★★★

Population 48 067

Michelin map 59 fold 6 or 230 fold 11 – Local maps under CÔTE D'ÉMERAUDE and Vallée de la RANCE

St-Malo, St-Servan, Paramé and Rothéneuf have joined together to form the municipality of St-Malo. The **site★★★** is unique in France and makes it one of the great tourist centres of Brittany.

The port – Located in the centre of the large roadstead, which once divided the privateer's encampment (St-Malo-de-l'Isle) from the continent (St-Servan, Paramé), the port is developing a wide range of activities. It has four wet docks (Vauban, Duguay-Trouin, Bouvet and Jacques-Cartier) sheltered by a lock, where handling of goods and fish are concentrated. Imported products hold an important position: fertilisers, timber and wood. Its outer harbour is equipped with two shipping terminals for car ferries and boat services; there are daily services between St-Malo and Portsmouth and St-Malo and the Channel Islands (Jersey and Guernesey).
Pleasure boating has not been forgotten: dockage is located at the foot of the ramparts and especially at Bas-Sablons near the Corniche d'Aleth.

HISTORICAL NOTES

Origin – St Malo, returning from Wales in the 6C, converted the Gallo-Roman settlement Aleth (St-Servan) to Christianity and became its bishop. The neighbouring island, on which the present town of St-Malo is built, was then uninhabited. Later, people settled there because it was easy to defend from the Norsemen, and it became important enough for the Bishopric of Aleth to be transferred to it in 1144. It took the name of St Malo, while Aleth put itself under the protection of another local saint – St Servan.
The town belonged to its bishops, who built ramparts round it. It took no part in provincial rivalries. At the time of the League, St-Malo declared itself a republic and was able to keep its independence for four years. This principle was reflected in the device: "Ni Français, ni Breton, Malouin suis" (I am neither French nor Breton but a man of St-Malo).

Famous men of St-Malo – Few towns have had as many famous sons as St-Malo over the centuries.
Jacques Cartier left in 1534 to look for gold in Newfoundland and Labrador: instead he discovered the mouth of the St Lawrence River, which he took to be the estuary of a great Asian river. As the word *Canada*, which means "village" in the Huron language, was often used by the Indians he encountered, he used the word to name the country. Cartier took possession of the land in the name of the King of France in 1534, but it was only under Champlain that the colonisation of Canada began and that Quebec was founded (1608).
Porcon de la Bardinais, who had been charged in 1665 by the St-Malo shipowners to defend their ships agains the Barbary pirates, was captured and taken before the Dey of Algiers. The Dey sent him to Louis XIV with peace proposals on condition that if these were not accepted he would return to Algiers. The Dey's proposals were refused, whereupon Porcon went to St-Malo to put his affairs in order, said farewell to his family and returned to Africa, where he was executed.
Duguay-Trouin (1673-1736) and **Surcouf** (1773-1827; *illustration p 26*) are the most famous of the St Malo privateers. These bold seamen received "letters of marque" from the king which permitted them to attack warships or merchantmen without being treated as pirates, that is, hanged from the main yard. In the 17 and 18C, privateers inflicted heavy losses on the English, Dutch and Spanish.
Duguay was the son of a rich shipowner and had been destined for the priesthood; but by the time he was 16 the only way to put an end to his wild living was to send him to sea. His gifts were such that, at 24, he entered the so-called Great Corps of the French Navy as a commander and at 36 he was given a peerage. When he died, he was a Lieutenant General in the seagoing forces and a Commander of the Order of St Louis.
Surcouf's history is completely different, but just as outstanding. He answered the call of the sea when very young and soon began a prodigious career of fabulous exploits. First as slaver, then as privateer, he amassed an enormous fortune. At 36 he retired, but continued to make money by fitting out privateers and merchantmen.
Chateaubriand and Lamennais brought the flavour of the Romantic Movement to their native St-Malo.
François-René de Chateaubriand (1768-1848) was the tenth and last child of a very noble Breton family who had fallen on bad times. His father went to America in search of fortune and was able, on his return, to set up as a shipowner at St-Malo. In a room on the second floor of a modest town-house (Maison Natale de Chateaubriand – it gives onto the courtyard of the Hôtel France et Chateaubriand and is near the Tour Quic-en-Groigne) René was born. From its window he could look out to sea beyond the ramparts and dream...

Y. Arthus-Bertrand/ALTITUDE

St-Malo

The future poet spent his early years in roaming about the port, then went in succession through schools at Dinan, Dol, Rennes and Brest, dreaming sometimes of the priesthood, sometimes of the sea.
He spent two years in exile at Combourg *(qv)* with his father, mother and sister Lucile. It was through the profession of arms that he began, in 1786, the adventurous career which ended in 1848 in the solitary grandeur of Grand Bé *(qv)*.
Lamennais (1782-1854), another St-Malo shipowner's son, also had a place in the Romantic Movement. He became an orphan early and was brought up by an uncle at the Castle of Chesnaye, near Dinan. At 22 he taught mathematics in the College of St-Malo before entering the seminary of that town.
He was ordained a priest in 1816 and had a great influence on Lacordaire and Montalembert. His writings and violent quarrels got him into trouble with Rome which led him to renounce the Church.
He retired to Chesnay and published, in 1834, the famous *Paroles d'un croyant (Words of a Believer)*. Owing to his advanced political ideas, he was sentenced to a year's imprisonment in 1840 but won a seat in the National Assembly in 1848.
To the famous men of St-Malo, already mentioned, should be added **Mahé de la Bourdonnais** (1699-1753), a great colonist and the rival of Dupleix in the Indies; **Broussais** (1772-1838), who transformed the medical science of his time; **Gournay** (1712-59), the economist to whom the formula *"laissez faire, laissez passer"* (let it be, let it go) is attributed; and finally the saintly figure of **André Desilles**. In 1790 the garrison of Nancy, to which this 23-year-old lieutenant belonged, revolted against the National

Assembly. Troops were sent to subdue it. To prevent the fratricidal struggle, Desilles threw himself in front of the guns and fell, mortally wounded.
As Chateaubriand commented of his home town: "It's not a bad record for an area smaller than the Tuileries Gardens."

Destruction and renaissance of St-Malo – St-Malo and the surrounding area were turned into an entrenched camp by the Germans and became the prize for which a merciless battle raged from 1-14 August 1944. The town was left in ruins. With a great sense of history, its restorers were determined to bring the old city back to life. They have been completely successful in their quest.

★★★ST MALO'S WALLED CITY (The Ramparts) *time: 2 hours*

Leave your car on Esplanade St-Vincent (**DZ**).

The statue near the esplanade, at the entrance to the Casino garden, portrays Chateaubriand by Armel Beaufils. It was erected in 1948 on the centenary of his death. Pass under Porte St-Vincent which consists of twin gates; then take the staircase to the right leading to the ramparts.
The ramparts, started in the 12C, were enlarged and altered up to the 18C and survived the wartime destruction. The rampart walk commands magnificent views, especially at high tide, of the coast and islands.

From Porte St-Vincent to Bastion St-Louis – Directly after Grande Porte (Great Gate), which is crowned with machicolations, the view opens out over the narrow isthmus which joins the old town to its suburbs, the harbour basins and, in the distance, St-Servan.

From Bastion St-Louis to Bastion St-Philippe – The rampart skirts the houses where the rich shipowners of St-Malo lived; two, near the Bastion St-Louis, are still intact but the following walls and façades are reconstructions of carefully-dismantled buildings. This fine group of houses with its high roofs, surmounted by monumental chimneys rising from the ramparts, once more gives this part of town its old look. The view extends over the outer harbour; to Rocher d'Aleth, crowned by Fort de la Cité, and the mouth of the Rance estuary; to Dinard, with Prieuré Beach and Pointe de Vicomté.

From Bastion St-Philippe to Tour Bidouane – A very fine view of the Côte d'Émeraude west of Dinard, and of the islands off St-Malo. To the right of Pointe du Moulinet, you can see part of the great beach at Dinard, Pointe des Étêtés separating Dinard from St-Lunaire, Pointe du Décollé, the Hébihens Archipelago, Pointe de St-Cast and Cap Fréhel; nearer, on the right, are the île Harbour and, further to the right, Grand Bé (*qv*) and Petit Bé Islands; then, in the background, île de Cézembre and Fort de la Conchée. Near Tour Bidouane stands a statue of Surcouf *(qv)*.

From Tour Bidouane to Porte St-Vincent – Having skirted the Ecole Nationale de la Marine Marchande, you can see the Fort National and the great curve which joins St-Malo to Pointe de la Varde, passing through the beaches of Paramé, Rochebonne and Le Minihic.

At the end of the ramparts take the stairway going down near St-Thomas Gate (Porte St-Thomas) – this gate opens onto the immense Paramé Beach.

Cathedral St-Vincent (**DZ**) – The building, started in the 11C and completed in the 18C, was topped by a pierced spire in the 19C, replacing the quadrangular roof. The nave is roofed with quadripartite vaulting typical of the Angevin style; dark and massive it contrasts with the slender 13C chancel. Lit by magnificent **stained-glass windows**★ by Jean Le Moal, the chancel becomes a kaleidoscope of colours. In the transept, restored in the 17C style, the stained-glass windows are muted in colour while in the side aisles the windows by Max Ingrand are brighter (Chapel of the Holy Sacrament). The north side aisle has preserved its original vaulting.
A 16C Virgin, Notre-Dame-de-la-Croix-du-Fief, which comes from a medieval house, is kept in the second chapel north of the ambulatory together with the remains of Duguay-Trouin. The neighbouring chapel houses the head reliquary of Jacques Cartier.

Musée de la Poupée et du Jouet ancien (**DZ M**[1]) ⏲ – The museum is a joy to young and old alike. More than 300 dolls in cloth, wood and felt, surrounded by their furnishings, compose different scenes.
There is a section devoted to the teddy bear, named after Teddy Roosevelt, after he refused to shoot a bear cub during a hunting trip in 1902.

★★CASTLE (CHÂTEAU) (DZ) *time: 1 hour 30 min*

You can enter the courtyard and see the façades of the former 17-18C barracks (now the town hall), the well, the keep and the gatehouse.
The little keep was built as part of the ramparts in 1395. The great keep (1424) dominates the castle while the corner towers were constructed in the 15 and 16C. The chapel and the galley date from the 17C.

★**Musée d'Histoire de la ville et d'Ethnographie du pays malouin** (**M**[2]) – The museum, which is installed in the great keep and gatehouse, records the development of the city of St-Malo and its celebrities (Jacques Cartier, Duguay-Trouin, La Bourdonnais, Surcouf, Chateaubriand, Lamennais and the mathematician Maupertuis). Documents, ship models, paintings and arms trace St-Malo's sea-faring tradition.
To end the visit climb up to the keep's watch towers, from where you will admire an impressive **panorama**★★ of the town, harbour, coast and sea.
A passage leads from the old chapel to the Tour Générale. This tower contains an exhibition laid out on three floors devoted to the economy (commercial fishing, shipbuilding), way of life (headdresses, furniture) and significant historical events in the St-Malo region.

★**Tour Quic-en-Groigne** (**E**) – This **tower** *(65 steps)*, which is located in the left wing of the castle, bears the name Quic-en-Groigne from an inscription Queen Anne had carved on it in defiance of the bishops of St-Malo: *"Qui-qu'en-groigne, ainsi sera, car tel est mon bon plaisir"* (Thus it shall be, whoever may complain, for that is my wish). It contains a **Musée de Cire** (Waxworks Museum) with reconstructions of historic scenes and the celebrities of St-Malo.

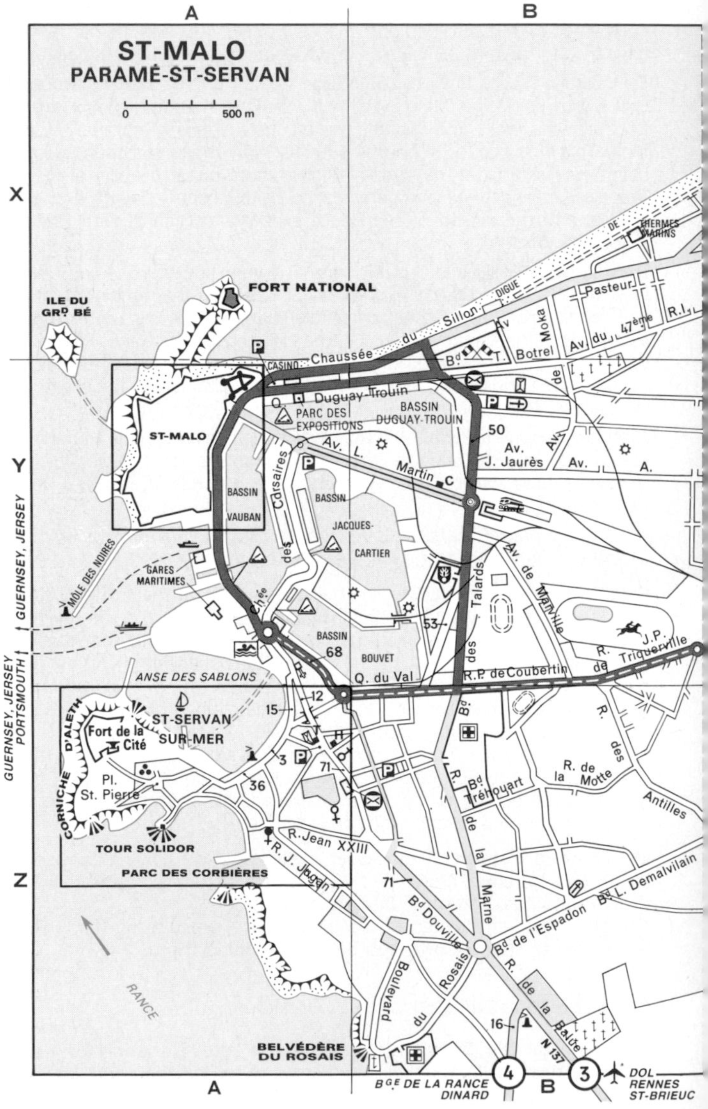

E Quic-en-Groigne **M**[1] Musée de la Poupée et du Jouet ancien

ADDITIONAL SIGHTS

★**Fort National** (**AX** – *town plan below*) ⌚ – *Access by Plage de l'Éventail at low tide, 15 min on foot Rtn.*
Built by Vauban in 1689, the Royal Fort became the National Fort after the Revolution (1789), and then private property. Built on the rock, this stronghold assured the protection of the city. The **view**★★ from the ramparts is remarkable. The fort commands extensive views of the coast and the islands: St-Malo, St-Servan, the Rance estuary, Dinard, the île du Grand Bé, île du Petit Bé, île Harbour, the Grand Jardin Lighthouse, the Fort de la Conchée and in the distance the îles Chausey.
During the tour, one of the events recorded is the fort's resistance in 1692 against the English and Dutch fleet, and Surcouf's memorable duel in which he defended the honour of France against twelve opponents, of whom he spared the last to testify to his exploit. The visit to the dungeon is interesting.

Ile du Grand Bé (**AX** – *town plan below*) – *45 min on foot Rtn. Only at low tide. Leave St-Malo by Porte des Champs-Vauverts and cross the beach diagonally to the causeway. Follow the road that skirts the right side of the island.*
Chateaubriand's tomb is on the seaward side; it is a plain, unnamed flagstone surmounted by a heavy granite cross.

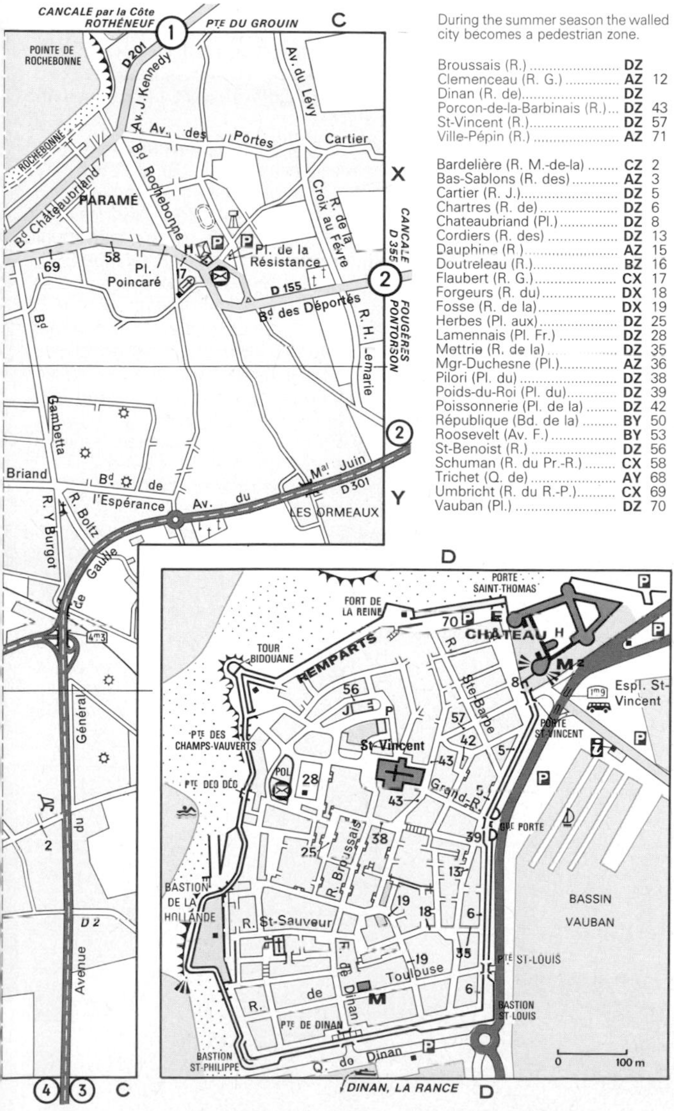

During the summer season the walled city becomes a pedestrian zone.

Broussais (R.)	DZ	
Clemenceau (R. G.)	AZ	12
Dinan (R. de)	DZ	
Porcon-de-la-Barbinais (R.)	DZ	43
St-Vincent (R.)	DZ	57
Ville-Pépin (R.)	AZ	71
Bardelière (R. M.-de-la)	CZ	2
Bas-Sablons (R. des)	AZ	3
Cartier (R. J.)	DZ	5
Chartres (R. de)	DZ	6
Chateaubriand (Pl.)	DZ	8
Cordiers (R. des)	DZ	13
Dauphine (R.)	AZ	15
Doutreleau (R.)	BZ	16
Flaubert (R. G.)	CX	17
Forgeurs (R. du)	DX	18
Fosse (R. de la)	DX	19
Herbes (Pl. aux)	DZ	25
Lamennais (Pl. Fr.)	DZ	28
Mettrie (R. de la)	DZ	35
Mgr-Duchesne (Pl.)	AZ	36
Pilori (Pl. du)	DZ	38
Poids-du-Roi (Pl. du)	DZ	39
Poissonnerie (Pl. de la)	DZ	42
République (Bd. de la)	BY	50
Roosevelt (Av. F.)	BY	53
St-Benoist (R.)	DZ	56
Schuman (R. du Pr.-R.)	CX	58
Trichet (Q. de)	AY	68
Umbricht (R. du R.-P.)	CX	69
Vauban (Pl.)	DZ	70

M² Musée d'Histoire de la ville et d'Ethnographie du pays malouin

From the highest point on the island there is a beautiful **panorama**★★ of the entire Côte d'Émeraude.

Cross the open space, go down a few steps and turn left along a road leading back to the causeway by which you came.

BOAT TRIPS ⏱

☆☆☆**Dinard** – *See DINARD.*

★★★**Cruise to Cap Fréhel** – *See Cap FRÉHEL.*

★★**Vallée de la Rance** – *See Vallée de la RANCE.*

Île de Cézembre – *See DINARD: Boat trips.*

★**Îles Chausey** – *The sights are described in the Green Guide Normandy.*

Channel Islands – *The sights are described in the Green Guide Normandy and the hotels and restaurants are listed in the Michelin Red Guide Great Britain and Ireland.* There are regular boat services ⏱ (car-ferries and various types of catamaran) operating from St-Malo and headed for the Channel Islands.

★ST-SERVAN-SUR-MER

The resort of St-Servan-sur-Mer is cheerful with its many gardens, in striking contrast to the walled town of St-Malo. Its main beach is formed by Sablons Bay, although there are also smaller beaches along the Rance. The town has three ports: the Bouvet dock, a trading and a fishing port, linked with that of St-Malo, the Solidor, a former naval base, and the Saint-Père.

Jeanne Jugan, humble servant of the poor (1792-1879) – The name of Jeanne Jugan (who has a street named after her at St-Servan-sur-Mer) recalls a humble, devoted life, a faith capable of moving mountains and an admirable number of charitable works. Jeanne was the daughter of a Cancale fisherman who lost his life at sea, leaving a widow and seven children. Jeanne found a place as a domestic servant with an old spinster at St-Servan-sur-Mer and, while taking care of her for eighteen years, she helped the poor and lonely old people of the neighbourhood. In 1835 her mistress died, leaving her 400 francs. The great-hearted serving woman bought a hovel in which she sheltered old people with the help of three friends who were also domestics or working women. In 1840 these saintly women formed a sort of religious society of which the Vicar of St-Servan-sur-Mer, Father Le Pailleur, became chaplain. The society, in due course, became the Congregation of the Little Sisters of the Poor. To feed her people Jeanne went out begging every day, regardless of the weather, with her basket on her arm, well received by some, rebuffed by others. One day an angry boor struck her. "The blow is for me, my good man", she said with a smile, "now give me something for my paupers." By the rules of the Congregation, this daily quest was, until the last World War, its only means of subsistence. Jeanne Jugan died at the age of 87. There are now 6 500 Sisters scattered all over the world, in more than 300 establishments, where they house and care for 50 000 old people.

M. Dieu/Association Cotre Corsaire

The *Renard* sailing past St-Malo

ST-SERVAN-SUR-MER

Clemenceau (R. G.)	12
Ville-Pépin (R.)	71
Bas-Sablons (R. des)	3
Cité (R. de la)	10
Dauphine (R.)	15
Fontaine (R. de la)	20
Gaspe (R. de)	21
George-V (R.)	22
Gouazon (Bd)	23
Hauts-Sablons (R. des)	24
Magon (R. A.)	33
Menguy (Espl. du Cdt)	34
Mgr-Duchesne (Pl.)	36
Porée (Bd)	45
St-Pierre (R.)	58
Sébastopol (Quai)	64
Solidor (Quai)	65

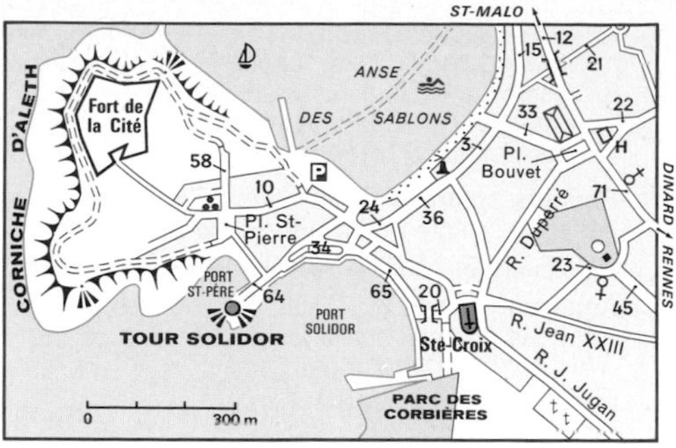

★★Corniche d'Aleth – This walk offers magnificent **views★★**. Leave your car in Place St-Pierre, where the ruins of the former cathedral of Aleth stand in a garden.

Take Rue St-Pierre at the east end of the church and follow on the left the coastal pathway.

First comes a remarkable view of St-Malo. Further to the left can be distinguished the Petit Bé, the Grand Bé and Cézembre Islands. Bear left and skirt the seashore. Go round the fort *(see below)*. The whole harbour is now visible: to the right of the île de Cézembre, in the distance, is the fortified île de la Grande Conchée; on the left, the Grand Jardin Lighthouse, île Harbour and its fort and, in the distance, Cap Fréhel and Pointe du Décollé, followed by a maze of reefs. Finally take a steep downhill path to the right to enjoy a very fine view of the Rance estuary, barred by the Rocher Bizeux, on which stands a statue of the Virgin, and beyond, of the Usine marémotrice de la Rance *(qv)*.

★Tour Solidor – This tower (27m - 88.5ft high), which commands the Rance estuary, was built in 1382 and restored in the 17C. It now houses the International Museum of Cape Horn Vessels.

★Musée International du Long Cours Cap-Hornier ⏱ – The lives of the great navigators (16-20C) who sailed to Cape Horn are recounted in the museum. Throughout the galleries the history, techniques, traditions and life on board are evoked. Among the ship models displayed, note the model of *Victoria*, the first ship which sailed round the world in 1084 days from 1519-22. A succession of exhibits at different levels leads to the wall walk *(104 steps)* which commands a **view★** of the estuary, St-Servan-sur-Mer, St-Malo, Dinard and the Rance.

Parc des Corbières – It is a wooded park with trees of different species. Bear right, follow the cliff path which goes round Pointe des Corbières, affording fine **glimpses★** of the Rance estuary and the tidal power scheme.

Fort de la Cité – The City Fort was built in 1759 on the orders of the Duke of Aiguillon. Around the inner courtyard is a chain of blockhouses joined by over a mile of underground passages, which also serve the barracks, the hospital and all the offices of this little town, laid out on several storeys.

Église Ste-Croix ⏱ – The church is in the Graeco-Roman style. The interior is dec orated with frescoes (1854) and stained-glass windows (1962).

★Belvédère du Rosais (**BZ** – *town plan p 268*) – The viewpoint is near the little marine cemetery on the side of a cliff overlooking the Rance which contains the tomb of Count and Countess of Chateaubriand, the writer's parents. **View★** of Rance Dam, the Rocher Bizeux with a statue of the Virgin on top of it, Pointe de la Vicomté and Dinard.

PARAMÉ

Paramé, a much-frequented seaside resort, possesses a salt-water thermal establishment. It has two magnificent beaches extending for 2km - 1.5 miles: Casino Beach, which continues that of St-Malo, and Rochebonne Beach. The splendid seafront promenade, 3km - 2 miles long, is the chief attraction for the passing tourist.

ROTHÉNEUF *on ① on the town plan on p 269*

This seaside resort has two beaches, which differ widely. That of Le Val is wide open to the sea. That of Le Havre lies on an almost landlocked bay like a large lake surrounded with dunes, cliffs and pines.
Near Rothéneuf is **Le Minihic**, with its own beach and villas.

★Manoir de Jacques Cartier ⏱ – *Rue David Macdonald Stewart.*

After his expeditions to Canada, the explorer, Jacques Cartier, bought a farm which he extended and called *"Limoëlou"* (bald hillock). This 15-16C house and its 19C extension have been restored and furnished in the style of the period. The tour includes an audiovisual presentation on the explorer's expeditions and of the colony "Nouvelle France" otherwise known as Canada.

Rochers sculptés ⏲ – From 1870 onwards, some rocks along the coast were patiently sculpted by a priest, the Abbé Fouré, who spent twenty-five years of his life on the task. There are almost 300 little granite characters.

Aquarium marin ⏲ – This has interesting specimens of live salt-water creatures from the Channel and a large collection of shells.

EXCURSION

Château du Bos ⏲ – *5km - 3 miles. Leave St-Malo on ③ on the town plan then bear right on the D 5.*
The château, built in granite from the îles Chausey, is a perfect example of a *malouinière.* These 18C mansions were constructed by wealthy shipowners, merchants or privateers, who sought the peace of the countryside.
The estate covers 10ha - 24.5 acres and overlooks the Rance. The château's interior, with its great chimneys, typical of the region, can be visited.

Pointe de ST-MATHIEU★★

Michelin map 58 fold 3 or 230 fold 16 – Local map under ABERS

St-Mathieu, which was an important town in the 14C, is now only a village known for the ruins of its abbey church, its site and its lighthouse.

Lighthouse (Phare) ⏲ – The lighthouse has a considerable system of lights; two auxiliary lights are reserved for air navigation. There is also a radio beam. The main light is served by a 600-watt halogenous lamp, giving it an intensity of about 5 000 000 candlepower, with a range of 55 to 60km - 34 to 37.5 miles.
From the top *(163 steps)* there is a superb **panorama★★**; from left to right – the mouth of the Brest Sound, Presqu'île de Crozon, Pointe du Raz, île de Sein (in clear weather), Pierres Noires reef, and the Islands of Béniguet, Molène and Ouessant. Beyond Béniguet, 30km – 18.5 miles away, you can sometimes distinguish Jument Lighthouse.

★**Église abbatiale** – The abbey church ruins are the remains of a Benedictine monastery (6C) which, according to legend, had as a relic the head of St Matthew.

Go inside the lighthouse enclosure.

The 13C chancel, which has pointed vaulting, is flanked by a square keep. The nave with rounded or octagonal pillars has a single aisle on the north side and two 16C aisles on the south side. The church has a 12C façade pierced by a round arched doorway and three narrow windows.
In front of the restored Chapelle Notre-Dame-des-Grâces, note the 14C porch, a relic of the former parish church.

Go round the lighthouse enclosure to reach the tip of the point.

At the tip of the point, a column, erected to the memory of the French sailors who died in the First World War, is the work of the sculptor Quillivic. There is a magnificent **view** from the edge of the cliff.
At a point 300m - just over 300yds from St-Mathieu going towards Plougonvelin are two Gallic **steles** (on the left near a house) surmounted by a cross and known as the Monks' Gibbet (Gibet des Moines).

ST-MÉEN-LE-GRAND

Population 3 729
Michelin map 59 fold 15 or 230 fold 24

In the 6C, St Méen (Mewan), a monk from Great Britain, founded an abbey on this site, which was reconstructed several times from the 11 to the 18C. The abbey buildings now contain flats. The **church** retains a fine 12C square **tower**. Inside, note in the south aisle, the tombstone, and in the south transept, the statue and funerary monument of St Méen, all from the 15C. Some 13 and 14C frescoes recently discovered beneath the plasterwork are currently undergoing restoration.
In the cemetery, beside the church, are the saint's tomb, a basin, recumbent figures and tombstones.
Louison Bobet, the legendary cycling champion who won the famous Tour de France race several times in the early Fifties, was born in St-Méen.

ST-NAZAIRE

Population 64 812

Michelin map 63 fold 15 or 230 fold 52

A visit to St-Nazaire, which is above all a great shipbuilding centre, is particularly interesting. Originally a small fishing port in the 15C, the town developed rapidly in 1856, when large ships, finding it difficult to sail up to Nantes, stopped at its deep water port.

St-Nazaire during the war – The Allied forces landed here during World War I; during World War II the town became a German submarine base. On 27-28 March 1942, a British commando caught the enemy by surprise, while the destroyer *Campbeltown* knocked down the Louis-Joubert entrance lock and the following day neutralised the lock by blowing itself up. A stele, reminding us of this heroic act, faces the sea on Boulevard de Verdun.

An obvious target for aerial bombardment between 1940 and 1945, the town got caught up in the fighting for the St-Nazaire Pocket and consequently was a desolate site when finally liberated.

A monument to commemorate the Surrender of the St-Nazaire Pocket (May 1945) stands west of Bouvron, on the road between Savenay and Blain, 36km - 22 miles from St-Nazaire.

St-Nazaire restored – Rebuilt after the war, the town is now divided into two distinct districts: to the east is the **harbour and industrial zone** and to the west the **residential area** opened with wide avenues following the plans of the architect, Lemaresquier. In the town centre, the town hall (1969) stands amidst a fine square decorated with fountains; the rectangular basin faces Avenue de la République.

Further west Avenue Léo-Lagrange separates the **park**, 50ha – 124 acres of green space enhanced by a lake, from the **sports ground**. Beyond are the hospital centre and schools. Near the coast, modern buildings have been set up in the Kerledé district.

To the east of St-Nazaire, near the mouth of the Brivet, the **Pont-routier St-Nazaire-St-Brévin★** spans the Loire, a distance of more than 3 356m - about 2 miles; it stands 61m - 200ft above mean high water at midpoint. It provides a link between the town of St-Nazaire and the Retz country, the Vendée and the Charentes and promotes industrial development on both banks of the Loire.

THE PORT *time: 1 hour 30 min*

★**Panorama** (**BZ B**) ⏲ – On the submarine exit *(see below)*. This terrace offers a remarkable overall view of the harbour, the Loire estuary, and St-Brévin-les-Pins. Suspension Bridge on the other side of the river.

Harbour installations (**BYZ**) – The **Bassin de St-Nazaire** (St-Nazaire Basin), 10.5ha - 26 acres and reduced to 9ha - 22 acres after the submarine base was built, was established in 1856, when St-Nazaire was only an annexe of Nantes. The port became autonomous in 1879. Two years later **Bassin de Penhoët** (Penhoët Basin: 22ha - 54 acres), one of the largest in Europe with three types of dry dock (the largest measures 226m x 32m - 741ft x 105ft), was opened. The port is governed jointly with that of Nantes by the Autonomous Port Authority of Nantes-St-Nazaire.

Three works deserve attention: the entrance lock, the submarine base and the submarine exit.

The **Louis-Joubert entrance lock** (Forme-écluse Louis Joubert), was built between 1929 and 1932, to allow for the increase in tonnage of great Atlantic liners. The lock is 350 by 50m and 15m deep (1148 x 164ft and 49ft deep). It has three functions: first a dry dock for the repair and careenage of very large ships; second as a lock allowing ships drawing not more than 8.50m - 28ft to pass from the Penhoët dock directly to the Loire estuary at high tide; finally the lock can also serve as a loading and unloading berth. This lock (measurements: 211 x 30m - 692 x 96ft) supplements, for the larger ships, the lock at the southern entrance to the port.

The **submarine base★** (base de sous-marins), which was built during the Occupation, was a very large reinforced concrete structure covering an area of 37 500sq m - 44830sq yds and measuring 300 x 125m - 960 x 400ft. It had fourteen bays, which together could take some twenty submarines. Machine shops were installed at the back of the bays. In spite of much bombing, the base came through the war undamaged and is now the site of various industries.

The **submarine exit** (**BZ B**), opposite the base, is a covered lock. This was to provide shelter from air attack and to allow the German submarines to enter and leave the base in secret (it is no longer used). It adjoins the port's former entrance (53m long by 13m wide – 170 x 42ft), now used for traffic on the River Loire and for fishing craft. It presently houses the submarine Espadon, part of the St-Nazaire Maritime Museum.

Sous-marin *Espadon* ⏲ – From the Augustin Normand Shipyards in Le Havre, this submarine, launched in 1957, was the first French submarine to cruise the polar ice caps. Seventy men lived on board; the torpedo room, engine room, sleeping area and control room can be visited.

Not far from the *Espadon* is a gallery, which presents temporary exhibitions on St-Nazaire's history.

Écomusée de St-Nazaire (**BZ**) ⓥ – On the banks of the Loire, at the heart of the port, a bright yellow building houses exhibits concerned with the St-Nazaire shipyards and the port's development: models of the shipyards, ocean liners *(Normandie, Île de France, France)*, battleships *(Jean Bart)*, dockers' old tools, portraits of people who contributed to the city's development...

The shipyards – Between the Bassin de Penhoët (**BY**) and the Loire lies the Atlantic Dockyard (Chantiers de l'Atlantique), made up of the former Loire workshops and dockyard and the Penhoët Dockyard; these were linked together in 1956 and since 1976 have been incorporated into Alsthom, now forming a subsidiary of the GEC Alsthom group. Among the ships which have come from the Atlantic Dockyard are the battleship *Jean Bart*, and the ocean liners *Normandie* and *France*. Cargo boats, container ships, ore carrying ships and tankers (550 000-ton capacity) and passenger transport ships for French and foreign use are also built in the yards. Since 1987, the year in which *Sovereign of the Seas* (capacity 2 600) was delivered, the Chantiers de l'Atlantique have built a total of 11 cruise liners, including the largest in the world: *Monarch of the Seas, Majesty of the Seas* (capacity 2 770).

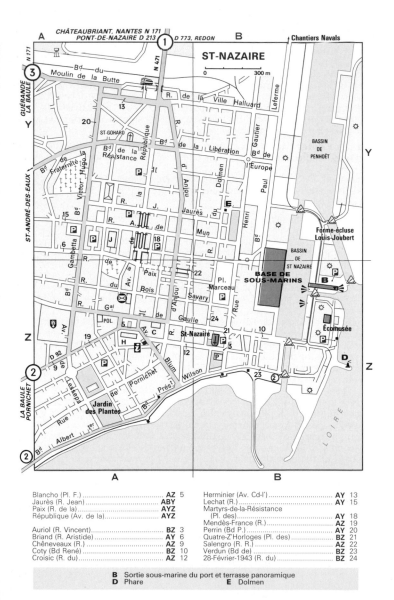

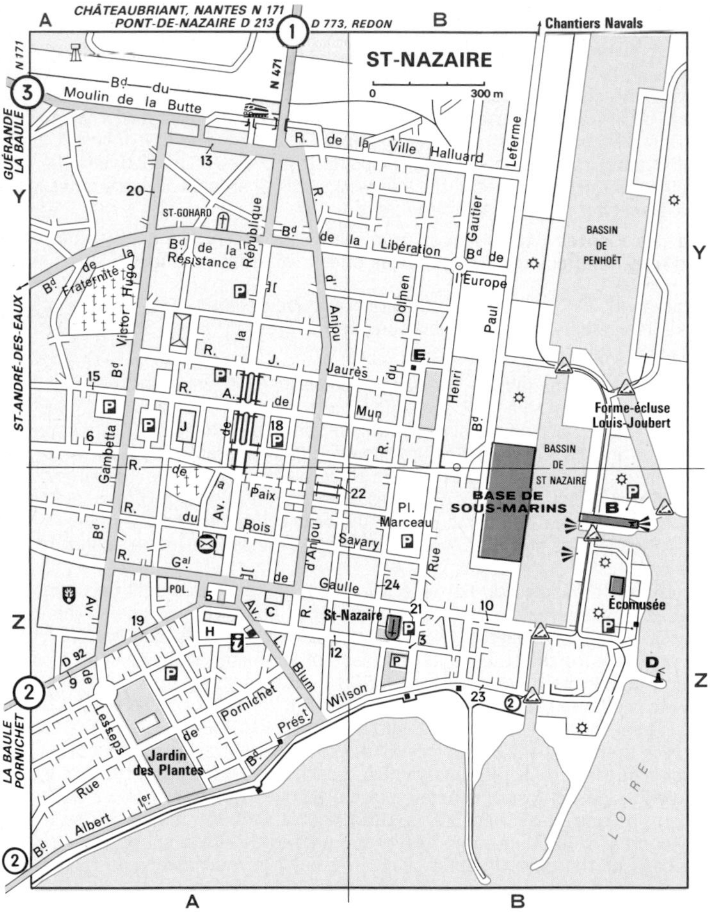

Blancho (Pl. F.)	AZ	5
Jaurès (R. Jean)	ABY	
Paix (R. de la)	AYZ	
République (Av. de la)	AYZ	
Auriol (R. Vincent)	BZ	3
Briand (R. Aristide)	AY	6
Chêneveaux (R.)	AZ	9
Coty (Bd René)	BZ	10
Croisic (R. du)	AZ	12
Herminier (Av. Cd-l')	AY	13
Lechat (R.)	AY	15
Martyrs-de-la-Résistance (Pl. des)	AY	18
Mendès-France (R.)	AZ	19
Perrin (Bd P.)	AY	20
Quatre-Z'Horloges (Pl. des)	BZ	21
Salengro (R. R.)	AZ	22
Verdun (Bd de)	BZ	23
28-Février-1943 (R. du)	BZ	24

B Sortie sous-marine du port et terrasse panoramique
D Phare
E Dolmen

The Atlantic Shipyards are equipped to build several ships simultaneously. This method substitutes for the conventional slipway, a huge dry dock divided into sections in which the ships under construction stand. Launching the completed ship is achieved by filling the section with water and floating her out. A new dock enables ships of 500 000 tons to be built. Near the naval repair dock is a 450 x 95 – 1476 x 312ft dock for battleships.

ADDITIONAL SIGHTS

Lighthouse (Phare) (**BZ D**) – Standing on the old pier, the lighthouse commands a view of the shipyards and the Loire estuary.

Dolmen (**BY E**) – In a square in the town centre, not far from the port, stand a dolmen and menhir, a reminder of St-Nazaire's prehistoric past.

Église Ste-Anne ⏲ – The church (1957) stands between Rue du Soleil-Levant and Boulevard Jean-Mermoz, which you reach via ③ on the town plan. The belfry stands separately to the left of the façade. The entrance is surrounded by great mosaics by Paul Colin depicting work in the St-Nazaire naval dockyard. Inside, the stained-glass windows contrast vividly with the bare concrete walls; to the left, the chapel with blue stained-glass windows contains a statue of St Anne.

Église St-Nazaire (**BZ**) – This vast 19C Gothic style church with its slate-topped belfry, was restored in 1945. Sculpted round the side aisles is a Stations of the Cross with a series of expressive figures. The transept is lit through fine rose windows with modern stained glass. In the transept crossing is a fine modern granite altar. In the chancel is an elegant 18C gilt wooden altarpiece adorned with scenes of the Gospel and statues of the Prophets.

Beaches (Plages) – The Grand and Petit Traict Beaches extend for over 2km - 1 mile between the outer harbour *(avant-port)* jetty, bristling with lift nets, and pointe de la Ville-ès-Martin. They are skirted by Président-Wilson and Albert I Boulevards. The view from the beach extends over the Loire estuary to the south as far as Pointe St-Gildas.

Jardin des Plantes (**AZ**) – Across from the Loire Estuary the gardens with their shaded alleys and colourful flower beds offer a pleasant resting spot near Grand Traict Beach.

Église Notre-Dame-d'Espérance ⏲ – Standing to the south of Place Pierre-Bourdan, near Rue de Pornichet (via ② on the town plan), this 1965 church has a white façade with oblique buttresses and a bare interior showing stonework.

EXCURSIONS

★★**La Grande Brière** – *Round tour of 83km - 51.5 miles. See La GRANDE BRIÈRE.*

Tumulus de Dissignac – *7km - 4 miles west on the N 171, the road to Escoublac.* Built on a hill, surrounded by drystone walls, this tumulus, with two covered burial chambers, dates from 5C BC; two narrow passageways lead to these chambers.

ST-POL-DE-LÉON★

Population 7 261

Michelin map 58 fold 6 or 230 fold 5

This little town, which St Paul, known as the Aurelian, made the first bishopric in Lower Brittany, offers the tourist two of the finest buildings in Brittany: the former Cathedral (the bishopric did not survive the Concordat passed under Napoleon in 1802) and the Kreisker belfry.

From January to September, during the season of cauliflowers, artichokes, onions and potatoes, St-Pol is extremely busy. Numerous lorries, vans and tractors with trailers arrive, bringing these famous Breton products to the market for many transporters and agricultural cooperatives.

★CHAPELLE DU KREISKER ⏲ *time: 30 min*

This 14-15C chapel used to be where the town council met; it is now the college chapel. What makes it famous is its magnificent **belfry**★★, 77m - 246ft high. It was inspired by the spire of St Peter's at Caen (destroyed during the war – see *Michelin Green Guide Normandy*) but the Breton building in granite surpasses the original. The Kreisker belfry has served as a model for many Breton towers.

The upper part of the spire is Norman in style, while the lower part with the squaring of its mullions and railing of the overhanging balcony recalls the English Perpendicular style.

The chapel aisles are formed of a series of gables over fine, tall windows. The west front and the flat east end are pierced with very large bays.

Enter through the north porch.

The 15C gable is surmounted by a statue of Our Lady of Kreisker (11C). The church is roofed with wooden barrel vaulting. The only stone vault joins the four huge uprights which support the belfry at the transept crossing. In the south aisle is a vast 17C carved wood altarpiece (from the Chapelle des Minimes, no longer standing) depicting the Visitation.
You may climb the tower *(169 steps)*. From the platform you will get a superb circular **view**★★ of the town, Batz, the coast as far as the Corniche bretonne and the Monts d'Arrée inland.

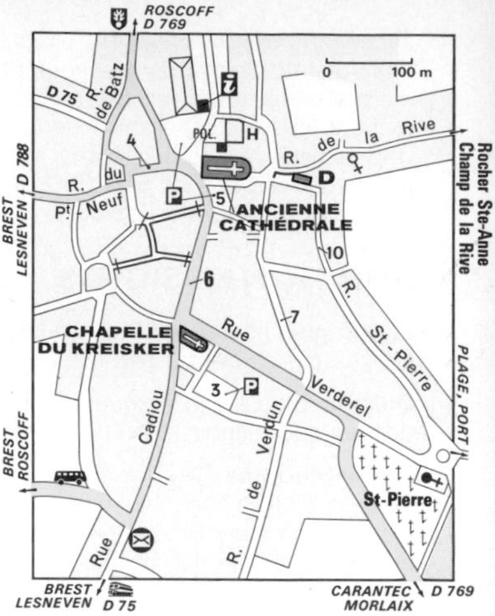

ST-POL-DE-LÉON

Leclerc (R. Gén.) 6
Guébriant (pl. A. de). 5
Colombe (Pl. M.).... 3
Croix-au-Lin (R.)...... 4
Minimes (R. des).... 7
Psalette (R. de la)... 10

D Maison prébendale

ADDITIONAL SIGHTS

★**Cathedral (Ancienne Cathédrale)** – Built on the 12C foundations, the former cathedral was erected in the 13 and 14C (nave, aisles, façade and towers) and in the 15 and 16C (side chapels, chancel, apse and remodelling of the transept). The architects were inspired by the cathedral at Coutances and used Norman limestone to build the nave; the traditional granite was used for the façade, transept and chancel. The Breton influence can be found in the bell turrets on the transept crossing and also in the porches *(see Introduction: Breton Art)*.

Exterior – From a small public garden, on the north side between the church and the former bishop's palace (now the town hall), is a view of the north transept wall with Romanesque characteristics. The south side, which faces Place Budès-de-Guébriant, has a fine porch. The transept contains a remarkable rose window with above it a sort of pulpit from which sentences of excommunication used to be read.
The façade is dominated by two towers each 50m - 160ft high. The terrace which surmounts the porch was used by the bishop to bless the people; the small door under the right tower was reserved for lepers.

Interior – To the left is a Roman sarcophagus which serves as a stoup. Starting the tour from the right, note a Renaissance stained-glass window (1560) and in the transept the 15C rose window. Around the chancel there are tombs of local bishops and two 17C altarpieces. The carved **stalls**★ of the chancel date from the 16C. Over the high altar, a palm tree in carved wood, bent in the shape of a crozier, contains a ciborium for the Host.
In wall niches against the chancel to the right of the ambulatory, 34 wooden reliquaries contain skulls. In a chapel, left of the chancel, kept in a gilded bronze shrine, is the chief reliquary of St Paul the Aurelian.

Rue Général-Leclerc (**6**) – There are interesting old houses in this street: note the slate-faced wooden façade at no 9; a Renaissance house with a corbelled turret at no 12; a mansion with a fine porch and ornate dormer windows (1680) at no 30.

Maison prébendale (**D**) – This was the 16C residence of the canons of Léon. The façade is emblazoned.

Champ de la Rive – *Access by Rue de la Rive.*
A pleasant shaded walk. Take the surfaced path on the right to reach the top of a hillock crowned by a modern Calvary. From the viewing table there is a fine view of Morlaix Bay.

Rocher Ste-Anne – *Access by Rue de la Rive and Rue de l'Abbé-Tanguy.*
As the road descends, there is a **view**★ over Morlaix Bay and its islands. A dike leads to the Rocher Ste-Anne and the Groux pleasure boat harbour. From the rock, which forms a remarkable viewpoint (benches), the **view** extends from Roscoff as far as Pointe de Primel.

Cemetery (Cimetière) – Small arched ossuaries are built into the walls. In one corner is the Chapelle St-Pierre in the Flamboyant style lit by modern stained-glass windows. Opposite the south porch, at the end of an alleyway, is a war memorial by the sculptor Quillivic, backed by a semicircular wall adorned with low reliefs.

EXCURSION

★**Château de Kérouzéré** ⓥ – *8km - 5 miles to the west. Leave St-Pol-de-Léon by the D 788 towards Lesneven, then the road to the right to Plouescat. At Sibiril, turn right towards Moguériec and after 500m - 547yds left towards the castle.*
This granite feudal castle is an interesting specimen of early 15C military architecture. Three of the massive machicolated corner towers remain standing, the fourth having been demolished in 1590 after a siege. A central stone staircase gives access to the three floors which were used by soldiers and include large bare rooms with deep window recesses and stone seats, a wall walk and a guard tower. The castle also retains pepperpot roofs, oratory frescoes, some tapestries and fine Breton furniture, all dating from the 17C.

ST-QUAY-PORTRIEUX

Population 3 018
Michelin map 59 fold 3 or 230 folds 8 and 9 – Facilities

St-Quay-Portrieux, a popular seaside resort, owes its name to an Irish monk – St Ké – who, legend has it, landed on this coast c472. Its beautiful beaches – Casino, Châtelet and Comtesse – are sheltered by a rocky fringe known as the Roches de St-Quay.

The ports – The tidal port at Portrieux used to equip fleets bound for Newfoundland. Nowadays, it is the lively home of a fishing fleet which fishes for mackerel, pollack, bass and, from November to April in particular, scallops and shellfish. The new deep sea harbour, inaugurated in 1990, contains 950 berths for pleasure boats and 100 for fishing boats. There is a regular crossing to the Channel Islands during the summer, and also the opportunity to take a boat out to île de Bréhat *(qv)*.

Chemin de ronde – *1 hour 30 min on foot Rtn, preferably at high tide.*
This former customs officers' path starts at Portrieux port, beyond the town hall, skirts Comtesse Beach, passes in front of the Viking stele and the signal station, affording a fine **view**★ of St-Brieuc Bay, from Bréhat to Cap Fréhel. It then continues along the terrace overlooking Plage du Châtelet *(viewing table)*, round the seawater pool and reaches Casino Beach. The walk may be extended as far as the Grève St-Marc *(add on about 2 more hours on foot Rtn)*.

EXCURSIONS

Étables-sur-Mer – *5km - 3 miles south. Leave St-Quay-Portrieux on the D 786 in the direction of St-Brieuc.*
The road goes towards the coast which it finally overlooks and follows closely.

Chapelle N.-D.-de-l'Espérance ⓥ – Built after the cholera epidemic of 1850, the restored Chapel of Our Lady of Hope, decorated with stained-glass windows in blue tones, two paintings by Jean Michau and a tapestry depicting the Virgin and Child by Toffoli, stands on Étables cliff, overlooking St-Brieuc Bay.

Étables-sur-Mer – The town, built on a plateau and possessing a fine public park, overlooks the quiet family resort on the coast. The two parts of the town are linked by an avenue lined with villas. The two fine sandy beaches, Godelins and Le Moulin, are separated by the Pointe du Vau Burel.

From St-Quay-Portrieux to Paimpol on the coast road – *66km - 41 miles – about 3 hours 30 min. Leave St-Quay-Portrieux northwest on the D 786, the Paimpol road. At the entrance to Plouha, turn right into the road which follows the Corzic.*

Le Palus-Plage – A lovely cove. To the left of the beach, a stairway cut in the rock leads to an upper path from which there are good views of St-Brieuc Bay.

Return to Plouha.

Plouha – This little town has many villas which belong to Navy pensioners.

Port-Moguer – A large rocky creek in a pretty setting. Follow the dike, paved in pink granite, to the rocky islet to enjoy a view of the coast with cliffs up to 100m - 320ft high.

Return to Plouha and bear right towards Paimpol; at a place called "le dernier sou", *bear right.*

Plage Bonaparte – From this beach at the bottom of Cohat Bay, reached by a tunnel cut through the cliff, Allied pilots, brought down on French soil, were taken back to Great Britain. To reach the commemorative monument, take the stairway to the right of the beach car park, then the path up to the top of the cliff or, by car, drive along the road leading off to the right before the beach.

Turn back and bear right towards Lanloup. The rest of the excursion along the Goëlo coast is described in the opposite direction under PAIMPOL: Excursions.

BOAT TRIP

★★**Île de Bréhat** ⓥ – *Boat service in summer.*

ST-THÉGONNEC★★

Population 2 139

Michelin map 58 fold 6 or 230 fold 5 – Local map under Les ENCLOS PAROISSIAUX

This village has a magnificent parish close *(qv)*, the ossuary and the church being the key features of this rich 16-17C Renaissance group.

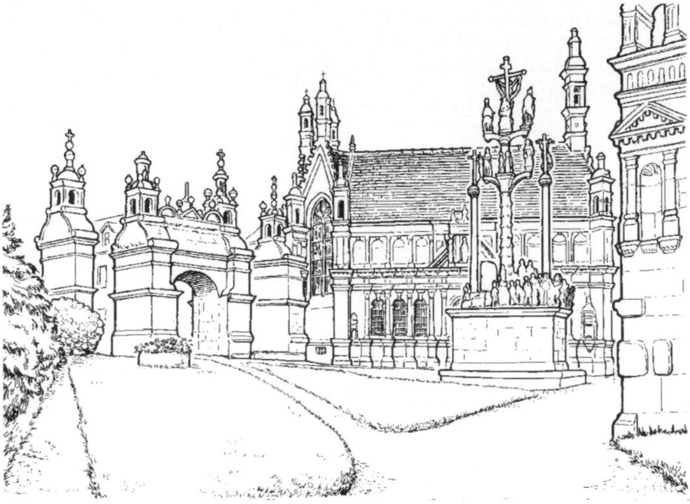

Parish close, St-Thégonnec

★★PARISH CLOSE (ENCLOS PAROISSIAL) *time: 45 min.*

Enter the parish close via the Place de l'Église to the south.

★**Triumphal Arch** (**Porte triomphale**) – A rounded arch surmounted by small lantern turrets (1587).

★**Funerary Chapel** (**Chapelle funéraire**) ⏲ – The chapel was built from 1676-82. Inside is a 17C altarpiece (restored) with spiral columns. In the crypt, under the altar, is a **Holy Sepulchre**★ with figures carved in oak and painted (1699-1702), the work of a Breton sculptor, Jacques Lespaignol.
The treasury which contains gold and silver plate is situated in the ossuary.

★★**Calvary** (**Calvaire**) – The Calvary was erected in 1610. On the base are groups of figures depicting the Passion. Below, a small niche shelters St Thégonnec with the wolf he harnessed to his cart after his donkey had been devoured by wolves.
The platform is surmounted by a double-armed cross bearing figures and two simple crosses for the thieves.

★**Church** (**Église**) – The church has been remodelled several times. The only trace of the old building is the gable belfry (1563) on the left of the tower. The Renaissance tower is crowned with a dome with lantern and corner turrets. A fire in June 1998 caused the roof to collapse and severely damaged the five chapels on the north side. Ten fire companies and local volunteers were able to keep the flames from damaging rood screens, the windows, the organ and the pulpit.
Over the porch is a statue of St Thégonnec; in niches in the corner buttresses there are statues of the Annunciation, St John and St Nicholas; inside the porch, four statues of Apostles.
Inside, the **pulpit**★★ is one of the masterpieces (1683) of Breton sculpture. The corners are adorned with the four Cardinal Virtues, while the Evangelists are depicted on the four panels. On the medallion at the back, God is giving the Tablets of the Law to Moses. The sounding board (1732) decorated with angels and roses, is surmounted by the Angel of Judgment blowing a trumpet.
In the entrance of the Apostles' porch is a statue of the Virgin carrying the Child Jesus, framed in a Tree of Jesse.
The apse and both arms of the transept are covered with **woodwork**★ dating from the 17 and 18C, which has been restored. The panels of the **Rosary altarpiece**★, on the left, represent below and in the centre, the Virgin and the Child, Jesus giving a rosary to St Dominic and St Catherine; above, the Virgin and St Lawrence give Christ a soul saved from the flames of Purgatory.
The organ (1670-6) was restored in the 19C.

STE-ANNE-D'AURAY★

Population 1 630

Michelin map 63 fold 2 or 230 fold 36

Ste-Anne is the outstanding Breton place of pilgrimage. The first *pardon* takes place on 7 March; then, from Easter until Rosary (the first Sunday in October); there are parish pilgrimages (especially Wednesdays and Sundays from the end of April to the end of September). The *pardon* of St Anne on 26 July *(see the Calendar of Events at the end of the guide)* and on 15 August is the most frequented, together with the Rosary *(details on* pardons *p 29)*.
In 1623 St Anne appeared to a ploughman, Yves Nicolazic, and asked him to rebuild a chapel which had been previously dedicated to her in one of his fields. On 7 March 1625, Yves unearthed, at the spot she had indicated, an old statue of St Anne. A church was built there the same year. The present basilica, in the Renaissance style, took its place in the late 19C.

PILGRIMAGE CLOSE

Basilica (Basilique) – Built from 1866-72, it took the place of the 17C chapel. In the south transept is a statue of St Anne (1824); part of the face of the original statue, which was burnt in 1796, is set in the base.

★**Treasury (Trésor)** ⓥ – It contains a relic of St Anne presented by Anne of Austria in thanks for the birth of Louis XIV. There are also gold and silver plate and the cloak of the old statue, and, in a glass case in the centre, ornaments given by Anne of Austria, surrounded by numerous votive offerings.
A Breton art gallery contains old statues (15-19C), small faïence (Quimper, Gien, Nevers) statues and votive offerings.

Scala Sancta – Old doorway from the square with a double staircase which pilgrims climb on their knees.

Monument aux morts – The war memorial was raised by public subscription all over Brittany to the 250 000 Breton soldiers and sailors who died in the First World War. It has become the memorial to all dead during the wars which have occurred in the 20C.
Not far away, on the other side of the road, a Franco-Belgian cemetery contains the graves of 1338 soldiers of whom 370 were followers of the Islamic faith.

Fontaine miraculeuse – The fountain consists of a basin and a column adorned with smaller basins and surmounted by a statue of St Anne.

SIGHTS

Historial de Sainte Anne ⓥ – This retrospective exhibit, which includes wax figures in period costume, brings the visitor into the atmosphere of old Brittany and describes the origins of the annual pilgrimage in twelve tableaux.

Musée du costume breton ⓥ – *To the right of the war memorial.*
A fine collection of old dolls in Breton costume and two small boats offered as ex-votos.

Maison de Nicolazic ⓥ – It was in this house that St Anne appeared to the pious peasant. Inside are a chapel and some old 17C furniture.

Chapelle STE-BARBE

Michelin map 58 fold 17 or 230 fold 20 – 3km- 2 miles northeast of Le Faouët

This Flamboyant-style chapel is built in a rocky cleft on the side of a hill. The **site**★ is very pretty; from a height of some 100m - 300ft, it overlooks the small Ellé Valley. The great stairway *(78 steps)*, built in 1700, leading up to the chapel, is linked by an arch to the St Michael Oratory (Oratoire St-Michel) crowning a rock spur. Nearby, in a small building, is the bell tolled by pilgrims to call down blessings from heaven.
Owing to its position and orientation, the chapel has only a single aisle and a small apse. Inside are Renaissance stained-glass windows and the lords' gallery with finely carved panels. Two *pardons* are held every year *(see the Calendar of events at the end of the guide)*.
Paths lead down to the sacred fountain, below the chapel.
From a rocky platform reached by a path starting on the right half-way along the car park, there is a good view of the sunken, wooded Ellé Valley.

Chapelle STE-MARIE-DU-MÉNEZ-HOM

Michelin map 58 fold 15 or 230 fold 18 – 3.5km - 2 miles north of Plomodiern

The chapel stands in a small parish close at the entrance to Presqu'île de Crozon. The close has a very plain rounded doorway, dated 1739, and a Calvary with three crosses rising from separate bases. The chapel, which has a twin-gabled façade, is entered through a doorway beneath the elegant galleried belfry, topped by a cupola which gives an upward sweep to the massive building. Inside, the ornate **altarpieces★** take up the whole of the east wall, without covering over the window apertures. While both the central altarpiece, with the family and life of the Virgin as its theme, and the north altarpiece, depicting the saints, have figures which are rather heavy and expressionless, the figures of the Apostles on the south altarpiece show life and elegance. The skill with which they were carved marks a step forward in Breton sculpture. The lovely purlins in the north transept, adorned with animals and various scenes, a remarkable St Lawrence and a graceful St Barbara in wood, are also noteworthy.

Île de SEIN

Population 348

Michelin map 58 fold 12 or 230 folds 15 and 16 – Access: Ⓥ

Sein Island makes a picturesque excursion. Off Pointe du Raz, it is less than 1km^2 - half a square mile in area and is very low-lying; the sea sometimes covers it, as it did in 1868 and 1896. The island is bare: there are no trees or even bushes; old fields are enclosed by low, drystone walls.

Men and their work – For centuries the island was the object of superstitious dread. In the 18C, its few inhabitants lived in almost total isolation. The islanders were shipwreck looters. Now they are among the most active lifesavers. The women do all the manual labour, the men are sailors or fishermen. Fishing is the island's only means of livelihood.

A fine page of history (1940-4) – Immediately after General de Gaulle's appeal of 18 June 1940, the men of the île de Sein (altogether 130 sailors and fishermen) put to sea and joined the troops of Free French Forces in England. Moreover, nearly 3 000 French soldiers and sailors also reached the island and embarked for England. When the Germans arrived on Sein they found only women, children, old men, the mayor and the priest. For several months fishing boats brought or embarked Allied officers. Of the sailors from the island who went to England twenty-nine were killed on the battlefields. A commemorative monument stands to the right of the road to the lighthouse. General de Gaulle came in person in 1946 to award the Liberation Cross to the Island.

TOUR

Port – The port provides a good shelter for pleasure craft.

Village – Its small white houses with brightly painted shutters stand along alleys barely a yard wide for protection from the wind. On a hillock near the church, two menhirs rise side by side, hence known as "The Talkers". Beyond the church, the Nifran Calvary is a simple granite cross resting on a tiered plinth. Behind it is the only dolmen on the island.

C. Chevallier

Île de Sein

The **museum** ⓥ commemorates the events of the Second World War by means of photographs, explanatory panels and diagrams: the departure of the men of the île de Sein for England; the activities of the marine Free French Forces; the campaigns in which the activists of the Liberation took part; the losses of the Merchant Navy (45 000 missing, 5 150 ships sunk); and the anti-submarine struggle.

Lighthouse (Phare) – The lighthouse, on the island's western tip, is equipped with a 6 kW light which has an average range of 50km - 31 miles. Left of the lighthouse stands the tiny Chapelle St-Corentin, an old hermitage. Beyond the point lies Sein Reef (Chaussée de Sein), submerged or visible, it prolongs the island some 20km - 12 miles towards the open sea.
On one of these rocks, which is constantly pounded by the sea, the **Phare d'Ar Men** (Ar Men Lighthouse), which took 14 years of superhuman effort to build, was erected in 1881. Its light, with a range of 55km - 34 miles, warns seamen off the rocks.

SIZUN★

Population 1 728

Michelin map 58 fold 5 or 230 fold 18 – Local map under Les ENCLOS PAROISSIAUX

Sizun, a village in the Léon region, has an interesting parish close.

★**Parish Close (Enclos paroissial)** – The most interesting parts of the close are the triple **triumphal arch★**, decorated with Corinthian capitals and topped by a Calvary, and the twin-arched **ossuary-chapel★**; both date from 1585-8.
The ossuary-chapel houses a small local museum with box bed, dresser, head-dresses, costumes and sacred art objects. The 16C **church**, remodelled in the 17 and 18C, is joined by a passage to the sacristy (late 17C) which stands alone. Inside, the decoration of the panelled vaulting is remarkable: a sculpted purlin with, in the transept and chancel, angels presenting the instruments of the Passion, crocodile-headed tie-beams, keystones and fluting. The organ loft, high altar, altarpieces and font canopy are all 17C.

EXCURSIONS

Maison de la rivière, de l'eau et de la pêche ⓥ – *1km - 0.6 miles west.*
Located in Vergraon Mill, water and its importance, fish and their habitat and angling (fishing tackle, flies used in salmon fishing, etc.) are the themes evoked in this small museum. The exhibits are complemented by aquariums containing freshwater fish, explanatory panels, models and films.
Its annexe, the **Maison du Lac** (Fish-Breeding Centre) ⓥ, located at the foot of the Drennec dam *(6km - 4 miles east)*, is an information centre on the world-wide exploitation of rivers, lakes etc.
Both these places aim to help the public understand the importance of preserving the quality of water sources.

Locmélar – *5km - 3 miles north of Sizun.* The 16 and 17C **church** houses imposing altarpieces consecrated to St Mélar and St Hervé and two 16 and 17C **banners★** embroidered in gold and silver.
Purlins and beams adorn the vault.
In the churchyard stands an interesting Calvary (1560), with two crossbars peopled with figures; the sacristy has a keel-shaped roof.

Château de SUSCINIO★

Michelin map 63 fold 13 or 230 fold 50

The impressive ruins of **Suscinio Castle** stand in a wild setting by the seashore, where they are buffeted by sea winds. It was the sea which used to fill the moat. The castle was built in the 13C and modified by the Dukes of Brittany in the 15C, prior to becoming one of their favourite residences. It was confiscated by François I and fell into the hands of the French Crown which used it to house faithful servants and the current Royal favourite. In ruins at the end of the Ancien Régime, the castle was sold to a private individual during the Revolution and was used as a stone quarry. Six of the towers have survived. In 1955, the roofing of the New Tower (Tour Neuve) and the West Pavillion (Logis Ouest) were restored to its former glory. The rooms in the entrance pavilion, also restored, house a small **museum** devoted to the history of Brittany.

TOUR ⊙ *time: 1 hour*

Having crossed the moat, enter the guards' room and the adjoining tower in which the history of the castle and its restoration are explained.
On the upper floors, the history of Brittany is described with the aid of literature, portraits, paintings and locally-produced artefacts (*Scène de pardon* by Camille Chazal, relief depicting Olivier de Clisson on horseback by Fremiet). Several rooms are devoted to splendid 13 and 14C **floor coverings** in varnished ceramic, which came from a chapel outside the castle's curtain wall, on the banks of the moat, which has since disappeared. The variety and quality of the decoration, which has been excellently preserved, make these an eloquent witness to medieval decorative art.
The Ceremonial Hall (Salle des Cérémonies), which opens onto a small chapel, provides access to the north façade and to the terraces, offering a lovely **panorama** of the peninsula and nearby ocean.

TINTÉNIAC

Population 2 163

Michelin map 59 fold 16 or 230 fold 26

This small *commune*, by a lock on the Ille-et-Rance Canal, is set in a charming site. It is the stopping place where canal cruiseboats replenish their water supply.

Church (Église) ⊙ – The church, rebuilt in 1908, has preserved parts of the former structure: on the north wall a small Renaissance door, a gift of Admiral Coligny, is decorated with Ionic columns and a frieze with angels' heads; to the right of the chancel is an odd-looking polygonal 14C stoup, known as the Devil of Tinténiac with grimacing faces carved on it.

Musée de l'Outil et des Métiers ⊙ – The trades and tools museum is located in the old grain store, a wood building near the canal, which used to stock grain, fertilisers and building materials.
Old trades such as the blacksmith, cartwright, cooper, harness maker, shoemaker, etc. are brought back to life with reconstructed workshops and tools and machines in working order.

Zooloisirs ⊙ – *On the Combourg road, the D 20.*
In the **Musée international de la Faune** (International Museum of Fauna), almost 300 stuffed animals brought back from hunts all over the world by the owner are displayed in a series of tableaux reproducing their natural habitat. In this way, visitors see buffalo, ostriches, bears, antelopes, lions, birds, etc. from every continent. A recorded commentary identifies each species.
Nearby, the boundaries of the **Parc naturel de la Faune** (Fauna Nature Park) encompass a vast amount of space for animals and birds, and a variety of children's games. In season the rose garden contains more than 4 000 roses in bloom.

Château de TONQUÉDEC★

Michelin map 59 fold 1 or 230 fold 7 – Local map under LANNION: Excursions.

The ruins of **Tonquédec Castle** ⊙ stand in very fine surroundings on a height overlooking the Léguer Valley. The castle, which was built in the early 13C, was dismantled by order of Jean IV in 1395; rebuilt at the beginning of the 15 C, it was again razed by order of Richelieu in 1622.
The entrance gate is opposite a pool now run dry. Enter a fortified outer courtyard. On the right, two towers connected by a curtain wall frame the main entrance to the second enclosure. Pass through a postern into the second courtyard. Opposite, standing alone, is the keep with walls over 4m - 13ft thick. Go up a stairway *(70 steps)* to a platform to admire the plan of the castle and the local countryside: a wide, fertile and populous plateau intersected by deep, wooded valleys running north and south.

TRÉBEURDEN

Population 3 094

Michelin map 59 fold 1 or 230 fold 6 – Local map under CORNICHE BRETONNE – Facilities

This seaside resort has several beaches; the two main ones are well situated and separated by the rocky peninsula of Le Castel: Pors-Termen Beach, which is a continuation of the Trozoul opposite the harbour and Tresmeur Beach which is much larger and more frequented.

★**Le Castel** – *30 min on foot Rtn. Follow a path along the isthmus (car park) between the two beaches of Trozoul and Tresmeur.*
Le Castel commands an extensive **view**★ of the coast and the Milliau *(access by boat or on foot during low tide)*, Molène, Grande and Losquet Islands.

★**Pointe de Bihit**- *Round tour of 4km - 2.5 miles. The Porz-Mabo road overlooks Tresmeur Beach and offers views of Grande, Molène and Milliau Islands. Take the road to the right.*
From the viewing table there is a fine **view**★ of the coast from the île de Batz and Roscoff right over to the île Grande and Triagoz Lighthouse out to sea with Trébeurden and its beaches down below.

The road, which has covered a quarter of a circle, goes on to Porz-Mabo.

You can see Locquémeau and the Pointe de Séhar in the distance.

Porz-Mabo – A fine sandy beach.

A road goes from the beach to Trébeurden.

TRÉGASTEL-PLAGE

Population 2 201

Michelin map 59 fold 1 or 230 fold 6 – Local map under CORNICHE BRETONNE – Facilities

The resort of Trégastel rivals the neighbouring locality of Ploumanach *(qv)* for the beauty and strangeness of its **rocks**★★, which are characteristic of the Corniche Bretonne *(qv)*.

SIGHTS

Aquarium marin ⓥ – This seawater aquarium is located in caves, which housed a church in the 19C (*Coz Ilis* = the old church) under a mass of enormous rocks, known as the Turtles. In three rooms varieties of fish from Breton waters and tropical seas are exhibited, along with stuffed birds including puffins, herring gulls, guillemots, penguins and gannets, all from Sept-Îles *(qv)*.
At the exit, a stairway *(28 steps)* leads up to a **statue of the Eternal Father** (Père Éternel). From the lookout point, there is a good **view** of the mass of rocks and the pink granite coastline.

Plage de Coz-Porz – This sandy beach is lined with rocks bearing descriptive names: the Turtles, the Witch. At the north end of the beach, beyond the jetty, make for a small beach near two rocks, the Death's Head (Tête de Mort) and the Pile of Pancakes (Tas de Crêpes), both on the right. This last rock, which appears to lie in folds, is a good example of wind erosion. Beyond a sandbank there is a mass of rocks, among which is the Thimble (Dé).

★**Grève Blanche** – *1 hour on foot Rtn.* Rock enthusiasts will go there from Coz-Porz. The path, which starts from

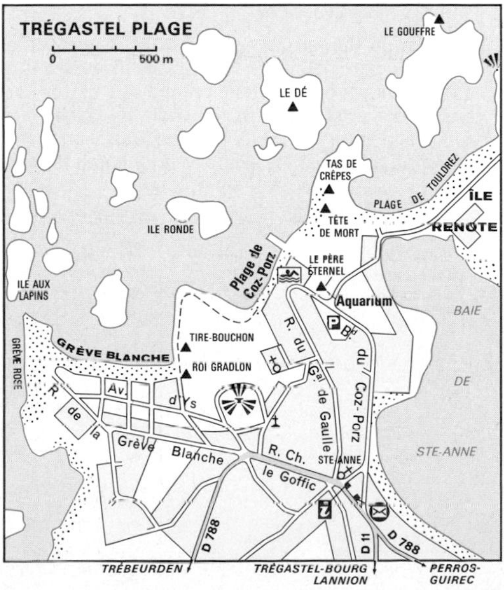

the left end of this beach (Plage de Coz-Porz), follows the cliff edge around a promontory from the end of which can be seen the White Shore, Rabbits' Island (Île aux Lapins) and, out at sea, the Triagoz Islands.
The path continues near the foot of a rock called the Corkscrew (Tire-Bouchon) and reaches the end of the White Shore, dominated by a great rock known as King Gradlon (Roi Gradlon) on account of its resemblance to a crowned head.

Viewing table – *Telescope.* This gives a circular **view★** of the coast: the White Shore, île Grande, the Triagoz lighthouse, Sept-Îles and the hinterland (when weather permits): Clarté, Pleumeur-Bodou (with its distinctive Radôme) and Trébeurden villages.

★★ **Île Renote** – *Northeast.* Leaving the sand bar you will find opposite you Renote Island, formed of huge blocks of granite and now connected with the mainland.

Follow the road that crosses the island.

You pass Plage de Touldrez on your left and approach the Chasm (Le Gouffre), a cavity in the middle of a mass of rocks which can be reached at low tide. As you walk amidst the rocks to the very tip of the peninsula, you get good views of the horizon out to sea and of the Sept-Îles looking north; of the Ploumanach coast to the east and the Baie de Ste-Anne to the south.

Trégastel-Bourg – *3km - 2 miles south towards Lannion.*
The 13C church was remodelled in the 14 and 18C. To the right of the south porch stands a semicircular 17C ossuary adorned with balusters and crowned with a domed turret. At the nave is an unusual 14C stoup, a former grain measure. In the cemetery are a small Calvary, an altar for offerings and the tomb of the Breton author, Charles le Goffic *(qv)*.
Situated 500m - 1/3 mile beyond the village to the south, a modern Calvary rises on a knoll. Steps lead to the top from which there is a fine **view** of the pink granite coastline.

TRÉGUIER★★

Population 2 799

Michelin map 59 fold 2 or 230 fold 7 – Local map under Excursions below

The town (evangelized in the 6C by St Tugdual), a former episcopal city, was built in terraces on the side of a hill overlooking the wide estuary of the Rivers Jaudy and Guindy. The port, which provides a magnificent anchorage for yachts, can receive big ships.
One of the great Breton *pardons* takes place in the town of St Yves on the third Sunday in May *(see Introduction: Traditions and Folklore)*. This is the "*pardon* of the poor", as well as that of advocates and lawyers. The procession goes from the cathedral to Minihy-Tréguier *(see Excursions below)*.

SIGHTS

Leave the car in the harbour car park and enter the town along Rue Ernest-Renan, which is lined with tall half-timbered houses. The two great square towers (**D**) *once framed the town gate.*

Maison de Renan (**M**) ⓥ – This 16C half-timbered house contains memorabilia of Ernest Renan (1823-92). It displays manuscripts and portraits, and one room contains a video presentation on the life of the writer and the places he used to frequent. Visitors can see the room in which he was born, a reconstruction of his study and library at the Collège de France and, on the top floor, the two tiny rooms in which, as a child, he liked to shut himself away to work (lovely view of the town).

TRÉGUIER

Martray (Pl. du)

Chantrerie (R. de la)	2
Gambetta (R.)	3
Gaulle (Pl. du Gén.-de)	4
La-Chalotais (R. de)	5
Le-Braz (Bd A.)	6
Le-Peltier (R.)	8
St-Yves (R.)	12

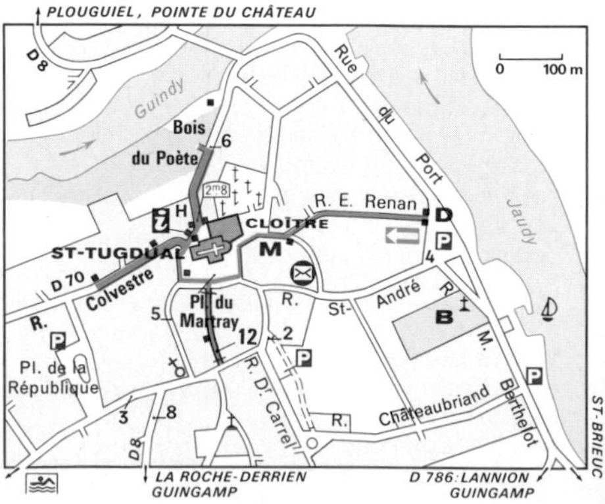

B Calvaire de la protestation
D Tours carrées
M Maison de Renan

★★**Cathédrale St-Tugdual** – The cathedral, which dates from the 14-15C, is one of the finest in Brittany. The transept is surmounted by three towers; the tower of the south arm, topped by an 18C pierced spire, rises 63m - 202ft. At its base is a porch (1438) under a fine Flamboyant **window**★. The Gothic tower of the sanctuary, uncompleted, rises above the crossing. The Romanesque Hastings Tower is all that is left of the 12C church.

Enter through the main porch.

Steps lead down towards the luminous nave with its Gothic arches worked delicately in granite. A sculpted frieze runs under the triforium. The ribbed vaulting in the Tudor style is lit by clerestory windows. The modern stained-glass windows, the work of the master glazier Hubert de Sainte-Marie, portray Biblical themes (to the left scenes from the Old Testament, to the right scenes from the Gospels).

Start from the north aisle.

The tomb of St Yves is an 1890 copy of the monument built by Jean V, Duke of Brittany, in the 15C. The recumbent figure of Jean V, sculpted in 1945, is located in the Duke's Chapel, lit by stained-glass donated in 1937 by American, Belgian and French lawyers. The north arm of the transept is cut off by the Hastings Tower. The doors of the sacristy and cloisters open under handsome Romanesque arches which rise above a heavy pillar, coupled by columns with sculpted capitals and surmounted by an arcature.

In the ambulatory, the third chapel houses a 13C Christ carved in wood. The chancel with slender columns has 15C painted vaulting. It holds 46 Renaissance **stalls**★.

The **stained-glass window**★ brightens the south transept. It recounts the story of the Vine (symbol of the Church) which winds round the founders of the seven Breton bishoprics (among them St Tugdual), around the saints of the land and around the Breton trades. Near the south doorway an interesting 15C **carved wooden group** represents St Yves between the Rich and the Poor. In the south aisle, note the 15C recesses sculpted with knights in armour.

Treasury (Trésor) ⌚ – The sacristy contains the treasure, which includes the head reliquary (19C) of St Yves in gilded bronze placed against the foundation wall of the Hastings Tower (*c*11C). Also of interest are a cupboard reliquary, a vestiary with revolving drawers (1650), old statues and a 15C manuscript.

★**Cloisters** (Cloître) ⌚ – The 15C cloisters abut the former bishop's palace and the cathedral chevet cuts across the north gallery. The Flamboyant arches in Breton granite, roofed with slate, frame a cross rising on a lawn. Under the wooden vaulting with its sculpted purlin, there are 15 to 17C recumbent figures in the ambulatory.

Place du Martray – The shaded square, in the heart of the town, still features picturesque old houses. It contains a **statue** of Ernest Renan, commemorating the writer's birth in Tréguier and his attendance at the local college.

Rue St-Yves (**12**) – A small tower in this pedestrian street gives a view of La Psalette, a residence for young singers, which was built in 1447.

Monuments aux Morts – *North of the cathedral.*

This war memorial is a sober and moving work by F. Renaud, depicting a grieving Breton woman wearing a cape of mourning.

Take Rue Colvestre, almost opposite, which features some lovely old houses and, more particularly, Duke Jean V's house, the Hôtel de Kermorvan and the Hôtel de Coetivy. Turn back and go down, beneath the old bishop's palace, to the Bois du Poète.

Bois du Poète – The wood overlooks the River Guindy and contains a monument to the writer Anatole Le Braz *(qv)*. Pleasant walk.

Notice also the **Calvaire de la Protestation** (Calvary of Protest) (**B**) by the sculptor Yves Hernot, put up in 1904 to reflect the Catholics' objections to the erection of the statue in honour of Ernest Renan in the Place du Martray.

EXCURSIONS *local map overleaf*

Minihy-Tréguier – *1km - half a mile south. Leave Tréguier towards La Roche-Derrien. On leaving the built-up area, turn left.*

The birthplace of St Yves *(qv)* is the scene of a *pardon* on the third Sunday in May. This is called locally "going to St-Yves"; the local priest is even known as the Rector of St-Yves. The 15C church is built on the site of the former chapel of the manor of Ker-Martin, where Yves Helori was born and died (1253-1303). His will is written in Latin on a painted canvas kept in the chapel. A 13C manuscript kept in the presbytery is called the *Breviary of St Yves.* (Bréviaire de Saint Yves) In the cemetery is a 13C monument pierced in the middle by a very low archway, under which the pilgrims pass on their knees. This is called the "tomb of St Yves" (Tombeau de Saint Yves), but is probably an altar belonging to the original chapel.

★1 Jaudy estuary to Port-Blanc

Round tour of 37km - 23 miles – about 2 hours.

Leave Tréguier on the D 8 to the north and at Plouguiel, bear right.

La Roche-Jaune – A small port on the Jaudy Estuary. Oyster farms.
On leaving La Roche-Jaune in the direction of St-Gonéry, you will enjoy a good view of the Jaudy estuary, the oyster-beds and the islands.

St-Gonéry - *See ST-GONERY.*

At St-Gonéry, take the road to Pors-Hir.

Pors-Hir – A small harbour built between great rocks near a little cove.
The road follows the coastline in a beautiful setting; houses built against huge rocks or nestling between tall boulders add a fairy-like touch.

Pointe du Château – From the tip of the headland, there are beautiful views over the îles d'Er, the Heaux lighthouse and Sept-Îles.

★**Le Gouffre** – *15 min on foot Rtn.* A deep cleft in a mass of rocks into which the sea roars furiously.

Turn back and follow the road along the bays, then bear right three times.

From Le Roudour, you can make for **Anse de Pors Scaff** bristling with islands.
After Le Roudour the coastal road affords lovely views.

Buguélès – A small resort fringed by islands, all inhabited. From the harbour there is a good view of Pointe du Château; inland the Plougrescant belfry stands out on the horizon.

Port-Blanc – Facilities. A small fishing port and seaside resort. Under the dunes of the main beach are traces of memorial stones (now covered) which suggest the existence, at one time, of a necropolis.
To reach the **Chapelle Notre-Dame-de-Port-Blanc** ⌚, go to the great esplanade by the sea, turn left before a group of houses built on the rocks *(car park).* At the left corner, take an uphill path and a stairway *(35 steps).* The 16C chapel has a roof that comes down to the ground. Inside, to the right of the chancel, note a group showing St Yves between a rich man and a pauper. There is a Calvary in the close. A *pardon* is held on 15 August. Every year, the small **île St-Gildas** hosts the *pardon aux chevaux,* also known as *pardon de St-Gildas.*

Return to Tréguier by Penvénan.

2 Presqu'île Sauvage – *Round tour of 49km - 30 miles – about 3 hours*

Leave Tréguier towards Paimpol.

After crossing the bridge over the Jaudy, you will see a glass-blower's workshop on the left.

Lézardrieux – The town is built on the west bank of the Trieux, which is spanned by a suspension bridge. The 18C church has an elegant gabled belfry flanked by two turrets and topped by a pinnacle pierced with arcades containing the bells. This particular type of belfry is to be found throughout the peninsula.

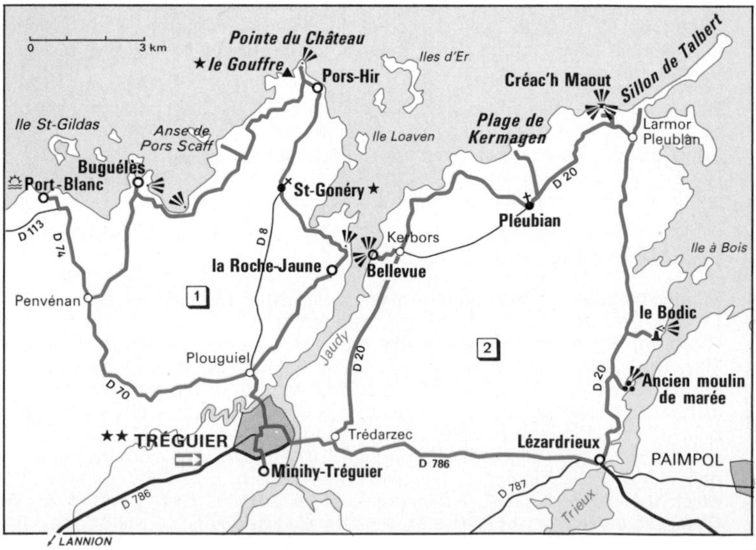

Make for the Talbert Spit (Sillon de Talbert), skirting the large marina on the Trieux. After 3km - 2 miles bear right into a downhill road.

Ancien moulin de marée – The ruined mill was driven by water from a small reservoir upstream. From the dike, there is a good view over the mouth of the Trieux.

Return to Talbert Spit and turn right.

Phare du Bodic – This small lighthouse commands the mouth of the Trieux. A path on the left leads through fields to a lookout point from which the **view★** extends over the Trieux estuary and the île à Bois in the foreground and the île de Bréhat in the distance.

The road then passes near Pommelin Bay, crosses Lanmodez and Larmor-Pleubian.

This stretch of coast (Port-Blanc – Paimpol) can also be explored on foot along the long-distance footpath GR 34

Sillon de Talbert – This long (3km - 2 miles), narrow tongue of land, surrounded by reefs, consists of sand and shingle washed by the currents of the Trieux and the Jaudy; it is possible to go round on foot. Seaweed is collected (the annual local production is estimated at 8 to 10 000 tonnes of algae) and dried on the spot and then sent to a factory nearby for processing. The Sillon de Talbert is now a national preserved site, placed under the protection of the Conservatoire du Littoral.

Return to Larmor-Pleubian and bear right towards Pors-Rand Beach.

Créac'h Maout viewing table – From the viewing table in front of the war memorial and the signal station, there is a wide **panorama★** over Pointe de l'Arcouest, île de Bréhat, Sillon de Talbert, Heaux Lighthouse (built 1836-9, 56m - 184ft high, average range 35km - 22 miles), Pointe du Château and the Jaudy estuary.

Go through St-Antoine to the entrance of Pleubian and bear right.

Plage de Kermagen – This faces Pointe du Château and the îles d'Er.

Pleubian – On the north side of the church with its characteristic belfry, is a fine 16C round **pulpit★** surmounted by a cross and decorated with a frieze depicting the Last Supper and scenes from the Passion: Judas's Kiss, the Flagellation, Christ bearing the Cross.

At Pleubian, take the direction of Kerbors by the coast road.

The road passes near the covered alleyway at Men-ar-Rompet, partly hidden in the greenery, and by the île à la Poule.

At Kerbors, turn right before the church.

Bellevue – It is located on the bank of the Jaudy. On the right the view extends over the Jaudy estuary, on the left over the valley and site of Tréguier dominated by the cathedral towers; opposite, La Roche-Jaune rises in terraces. There are trout and salmon farms along the Jaudy, which is tidal, as fish farming develops in the region.

The road winds through fields growing early vegetables and descends towards the Jaudy Valley and Tréguier.

La TRINITÉ-LANGONNET

Michelin map 58 fold 17 or 230 fold 20 – 13km - 8 miles east of Gourin

This village in the Montagnes Noires possesses a fine Flamboyant-style **church** with a three-sided chevet. The west gabled doorway has twin doors; the south porch added in the 18C is also of interest. Inside, the **timbering★** dated 1568 and decorated with Renaissance designs, shows great craftsmanship and enhances the lofty, well-lit nave. In the richly-ornamented chancel, note the carved recesses, corbels and purlins; and on the left of the chancel, a sacrarium, a fine stone cupboard, placed under a Trinity.

La TRINITÉ-SUR-MER

Population 1 433

Michelin map 63 fold 12 or 230 folds 35 and 49 – Facilities

The village, built on a height, now extends some 800m - 875yds down the slope to the harbour and beaches on the Crach River estuary, which is lined with oyster-beds *(qv)*. A small fishing port, a busy pleasure boat harbour and shipyards add to the activity of this resort which has fine beaches along the Presqu'île de Kerbihan.

Pont de Kerisper – From this great bridge over the River Crach, there is a good **view★** of the estuary, the town and the port installations.

USHANT★★

See Île d'OUESSANT.

Le VAL-ANDRÉ

Population 3 600

Michelin map 59 fold 4 or 230 fold 9 – Local map under CÔTE D'ÉMERAUDE – Facilities

The resort, known officially as Pléneuf-Val-André, has one of the finest sandy beaches on the north coast of Brittany.

★**Pointe de Pléneuf** – *15 min on foot Rtn. From the car park at the port of Piégu starts this walk at the foot of the cliff.*
It leads to a small viewpoint *(bench)* facing the île du Verdelet, a bird sanctuary. Certain spring tides permit access on foot *(apply for information at the Poste des Sauveteurs on the pier or at the Tourist Information Office)*.
By skirting Pointe de Pléneuf it is possible to reach Plage des Vallées *(allow 30 min on foot)*.

Leave from the port of Piégu and go up the steps which end in Rue de la Corniche.

This very pretty walk, on a cliff path overlooking the sea, affords superb **views**★★ of St-Brieuc Bay and the beach and resort of Le Val-André. It is possible to continue to Plage de la Ville Berneuf *(45 min on foot)*.

★**Promenade de la Guette** – *1 hour on foot Rtn. At the southwest end of the quay at the juncture with Rue des Sablons, two arrows point the way to the Guette pathway (Chemin de la Guette), the Corps de Garde and the Batterie.*
Go round the stairs (Anse du Pissot), which go down to the beach, and along the Corps de Garde, which has recently been restored. Soon after, there is an extensive **view**★ of St-Brieuc Bay. From the statue of Our Lady of the Watch go down to **Dahouët**, a fishing port and pleasure boat harbour.

Follow Quai des Terre-Neuvas and take, across from the pool, after the bridge, Mocquelet Path to Val-André Quay.

EXCURSION

Round tour of 19km - 12 miles – Time: about 1 hour 30min. Leave Le Val-André by the D 786 east towards Erquy. After 5km - 3 miles, turn right.

Château de Bienassis ⓥ – At the park entrance take the main tree-lined avenue to the château. Go through an opening in the crenellated wall, all that remains of the 15C enclosure; its corner towers and turrets werre added in the 17C, when the château was rebuilt. The ground floor includes a grand drawing room, the former guardroom and the dining room adorned with porcelain from China, Japan and Bayeux, and furniture in the Louis XIV and Breton Renaissance styles. The north façade overlooking the garden retains two 15C towers.

On leaving the park, bear left in the direction of St-Brieux and after 3km - 2 miles, turn left towards St-Jacques-le-Majeur.

Chapelle St-Jacques-le-Majeur ⓥ – The 13C chapel, restored in the 16C, stands at the crossroads. Its elegant doorway is adorned with clustered columns crowned with carved capitals.
The bare interior, lit by modern stained-glass windows, contains a charming statue of a Virgin and Child (14C) known locally as Our Lady of Safe Return (Notre-Dame-du-Bon-Voyage) and a Stations of the Cross carved in granite by Saupique, a contemporary sculptor from Rennes.

Take the direct road back to Le Val-André.

VANNES★★

Population 45 576

Michelin map 63 fold 3 or 230 folds 36 and 37 – Local map under Golfe du MORBIHAN

Vannes, built in the shape of an amphitheatre at the head of the Golfe du Morbihan, is a pleasant city, very popular in season. It is also a good departure point for boat trips. The old city, enclosed in its ramparts and grouped around the cathedral, is picturesque. It is a pedestrian zone where elegant shops have established themselves in old half-timbered town houses.

HISTORICAL NOTES

During the period of the Veneti, the original settlement was called Darioritum and seems to have prospered well, at least until the Barbarian invasions of the 3 and 4C. In the 4C, Waroc'h, leading the Bretons from the other side of the Channel, took possession of the town.

Nominoé, founder of Breton unity (9C) – Nominoé, a Breton of modest origin, was discovered by Charlemagne, who made him Count of Vannes. Becoming Duke of Brittany (826) under Louis the Pious, he had decided to unite all the Bretons in an independent kingdom. When Louis died, he went into action. In ten years unity was achieved: the Duchy reached the boundaries which were to be those of the Province until January 1790. From the first, Vannes was the capital of the new Breton kingdom, which reverted later to the status of a Duchy.

The union with France (16C) – Anne of Brittany *(qv)*, who married successively Charles VIII *(qv)* and Louis XII, remained the sovereign of her duchy.

When she died in 1514 at the age of 37 without leaving a male heir, Claude of France, one of her daughters, inherited Brittany. A few months later Claude married the heir to the throne of France, François of Angoulême, and after a few months, on 1 January 1515, became Queen of France. The King easily persuaded her to yield her duchy to their son, the Dauphin. Thus Brittany and France would be reunited in the person of the future king.

The last step was taken in August 1532. The States (councils), meeting at Vannes, proclaimed "the perpetual union of the Country and Duchy of Brittany with the Kingdom and Crown of France". The rights and privileges of the duchy were maintained: taxes had to be approved by the States; the Breton Parliament kept its judicial sovereignty and the province could maintain an army.

★★THE OLD TOWN *time: allow half a day*

Start from Place Gambetta.

This semi-circular square, built in the 19C, frames **Porte Saint-Vincent** (Saint-Vincent Gateway), which leads into the old town along a road of this name, lined with beautiful 17C mansions. At the entrance to the road, the most remarkable of these, the Hôtel Dondel, was the headquarters of Général Hoche in 1795.

Morcime/CAMPAGNE CAMPAGNE

Vannes – Wash-houses with the ramparts in the background

Take the little alley on the right and join Rue A.-Le-Pontois via the Calmont tower bridge.

From here there is a very pleasant view of the old Hermine Ducal Castle (rebuilt around 1800) with a pretty flower garden in front of it. The castle houses the Law School.

★**Ramparts (Remparts)** – After crossing a small bridge, go to the left-hand parapet, which overlooks some old **wash-houses★** with very unusual roofing. From Allée des Frères-Jolivel in the Promenade de la Garenne you will get a **view★★** of the most picturesque corner of Vannes, with the stream (the Marle) that flows at the foot of the ramparts (built in the 13C on top of Gallo-Roman ruins and remodelled repeatedly until the 17C), the formal gardens and the cathedral in the background. When you reach the end of the promenade, follow Rue F.-Decker, bordered by the Préfecture's gardens (Jardin de la Préfecture), which leads to the 15C **Porte Prison** (Prison Gate), flanked by a machicolated tower.
On the other side of the gate, the east end of the cathedral comes into view. Going into Rue St-Guenhaël, to the left, the Rue des Vierges and a little passage lead to a section of the ramparts which gives a pretty view of the gardens.

Retrace your steps.

Rue St-Guenhaël, lined with old houses, leads to Place St-Pierre.

★**La Cohue** – This term (literally, a bustling crowd) is commonly used in Brittany to designate the marketplace, the area where traders and the courts of law were found. In the 13C, the market was held in the lower part of the building; the upper floor was reserved for legal affairs. Beginning in 1675, the exiled Parliament of Brittany held its meetings there. Under the French Revolution, the building became a theatre, and functioned as such until the 1950s.
Now, the **musée de la Cohue** ⓥ is located in the beautifully restored building, and offers visitors a permanent collection of paintings.

Galerie des Beaux-Arts – On the first floor, the courtroom (1550), with its fine oak timber ceiling, was the seat of the Presidial court of justice. It has now become a museum, which houses, for the most part, 19-20C works of art by local painters (Jules Noël, Henri Moret, Flavien Peslin, Félix Bouchor), who were inspired by Brittany and its folklore.
Folk art is represented by a collection of polychrome wood statues – note the 16C Christ at the Column.

★**Cathédrale St-Pierre** ⓥ – Men worked on this cathedral from the 13 to the 19C. The only trace of the 13C construction is the north tower of the façade (on Place St-Pierre), which is surmounted by a modern steeple. In the garden next to the north side of the cathedral are the remains of some 16C cloisters. The rotunda chapel, which juts out, was built in 1537 in the Italian Renaissance style, rarely found in Brittany.
Enter the church by the fine transept door (Flamboyant Gothic, with Renaissance niches). In the entrance, on the left, a painting describes the death of **St Vincent Ferrier**, with the Duchess of Brittany present. This Spanish monk, who was a great preacher, died at Vannes in 1419 and was canonised in 1455. On the right is St Vincent preaching at Granada. In the second chapel of the north aisle, a rotunda chapel, is the tomb of the saint. On the walls, a fine tapestry (1615) depicts the miraculous cures made by Vincent and his canonisation.
In the apsidal chapel or Chapel of the Holy Sacrament and nave chapels, you will see altars, altarpieces, tombs and statues of the 17 and 18C. In the Baptismal Chapel there is an altar frontal (16C) in stone depicting the Last Supper. The 15C nave has lost some of its original character as the heavy 18C vaulting has reduced its height and masked the panelled woodwork.
The cathedral **treasure** ⓥ is exhibited in the old chapterhouse, which is ornamented with 18C woodwork. It includes a remarkable 12-13C painted chest, a 12C reliquary cross, an ivory cross and pyx, chalices and other vessels.

★**Place Henri-IV** – The picturesque square is lined with 16C gabled houses. Glimpse down Rue des Chanoines.
Walk along Rue St-Salomon with its old town houses then turn into Rue des Halles, where La Cohue's other entrance is situated.

Musée archéologique de Morbihan ⓥ – This museum occupies 3 floors of Château Gaillard (15C), which once contained the House of Parliament (Parlement de Bretagne).
The museum is rich in prehistoric specimens, most of which come from the first megalithic excavations made in the Morbihan region: Carnac, Locmariaquer and the Presqu'île de Rhuys. Exhibited are a remarkable collection of **necklaces**, bracelets, **polished axes**, swords, etc; another gallery contains a variety of *objets d'art* (13-18C).

On the second floor, there is an unusual display case of 17C paintings, on the theme of "Fathers of the Desert". Collection of weapons used in hand-to-hand combat.

Maison de Saint Vincent-Ferrier (**E**) – *No 17 Place Valencia.*
In this house, remodelled in the 16C, Vincent Ferrier died in 1419. A fine example of a timber framed house with a ground floor in stone.

Maison de Vannes (**D**) – An old dwelling adorned with two carved wood busts of jovial peasants known as "Vannes and his wife".

Go down Rue Rogue.

Place des Lices – This square used to be the tilt-yard, where tilts and tournaments were held in 1532, the year France and Brittany were united under one crown. At one end of the square, set in the niche of a turreted house, is a statue of St Vincent-Ferrier. The saint preached here in 1418.
Returning via the ramparts, you will pass by the Constable's Tower (Tour du Connétable), the Postern (Porte Poterne), and cross the small bridge over the Mairle.

ADDITIONAL SIGHTS

Parc du Golfe – This park is located by the exit to the marina, and is the departure point for boat trips.

★**Aquarium océanographique et tropical** ⏱ – This large building constitutes a "link between the sea and mankind". More than fifty pools, in which the relevant natural environment has been reconstructed, house about a thousand fish from all over the world (cold seas, warm seas, freshwater), which make up an incredible kaleidoscope of colour. In one 35 000l - 7 700 gallon tank, a coral reef has been

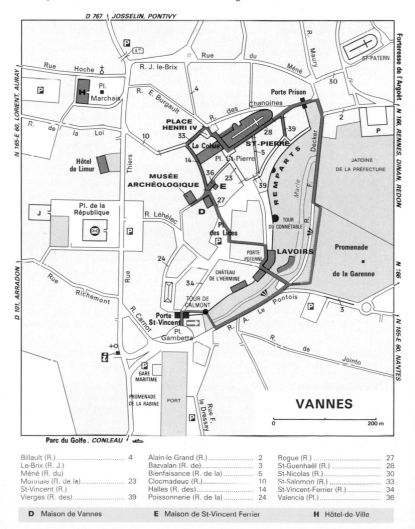

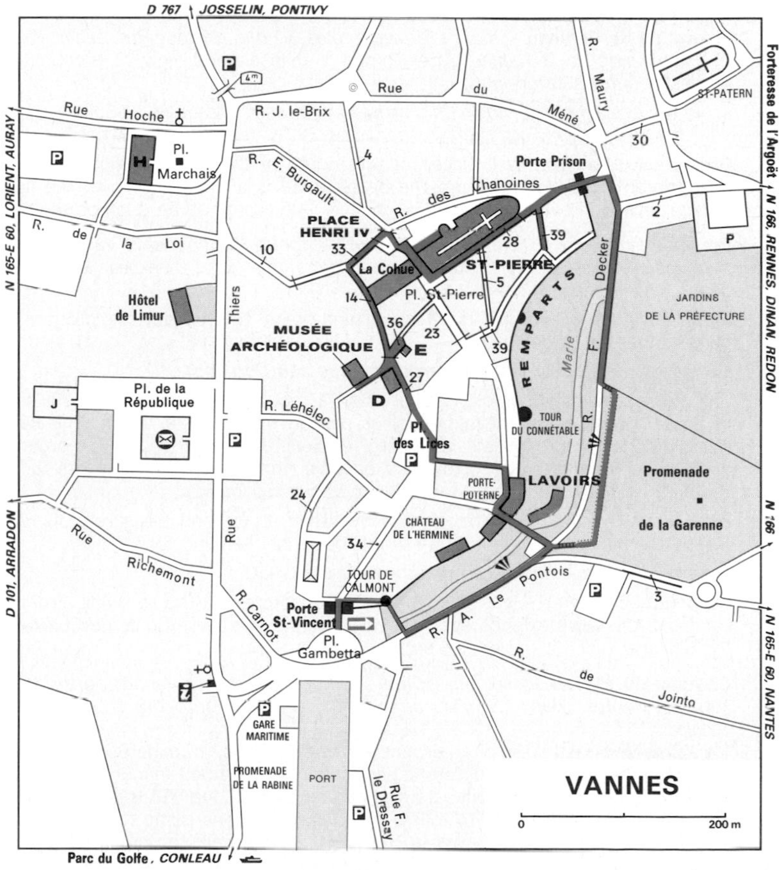

Billault (R.)	4	Alain-le-Grand (R.)	2	Rogue (R.)	27
Le-Brix (R. J.)		Bazvalan (R. de)	3	St-Guenhaël (R.)	28
Méné (R. du)		Bienfaisance (R. de la)	5	St-Nicolas (R.)	30
Monnaie (R. de la)	23	Clocmadeuc (R.)	10	St-Salomon (R.)	33
St-Vincent (R.)		Halles (R. des)	14	St-Vincent-Ferrier (R.)	34
Vierges (R. des)	39	Poissonnerie (R. de la)	24	Valencia (Pl.)	36

D Maison de Vannes **E** Maison de St-Vincent Ferrier **H** Hôtel-de-Ville

recreated and is home to numerous species of fish which habitually frequent this environment. A huge aquarium contains several varieties of shark and an exceptional sight: a huge sawfish 2.5m - 8.5ft long!

Palais des Automates ⓥ – This display includes about 200 automated characters, from the valuable collectors' items from the last century to those used in department store window displays.

Le Jardin aux Papillons ⓥ – Visitors are free to stroll around at will among the many varieties of vibrantly-coloured butterfly that are housed in this environment of tropical trees and floral shrubs. Glass hatching cases illustrate the various stages of development of the chrysalis.

Hôtel de Limur – A late-17C town house with a fine stone staircase.

Town Hall (**Hôtel de Ville**) (**H**) – This building in the Renaissance style, erected at the end of the 19C, stands in Place Maurice-Marchais, which is adorned with the equestrian statue of the Constable de Richemont, one of the great figures of the 15C, for it was he who created and commanded the French army which defeated the English at the end of the Hundred Years War. He became Duke of Brittany, succeeding his brother in 1457, but died the following year.

Promenade de la Garenne – The park of the former ducal castle of Vannes was arranged as a public promenade in the 17C. The view of the ramparts, especially of the Constable's Tower, is attractive. In the upper part of the garden, on a wall, to the left of the War Memorial, a marble tablet recalls the shooting of the Royalists in 1795 *(see Presqu'île de QUIBERON)*.

EXCURSIONS

★**Presqu'île de Conleau** – *5km - 3 miles – plus 30 min on foot Rtn. Leave Vannes by Promenade de la Rabine.* After 2km - 1 mile a good view of the Golfe du Morbihan unfolds before you.

Cross the estuary of the Vincin on a causeway to reach Presqu'île de Conleau. Leave your car (car park). Turn right in the woods on to the path skirting the Vincin.

Conleau – A small port well placed at the mouth of the Vincin; landing stage for boat trip to the île d'Arz. From the beach there is a good view over the île de Boëdic between Pointe de Langle, on the left, and Pointe de Kerguen on the right.

Presqu'île de Séné – *10km - 6 miles south – about 45 min. Leave Vannes by Rue Ferdinand-le-Dressay which skirts the harbour's left shore, then bear left towards Séné.*

Séné – Formerly known for its typical fishing-boats, the **sinagots**, the village maintains its maritime tradition.

On leaving Séné, bear right towards Bellevue and Port-Anna.

The old salt marshes (almost 220ha - 544 acres) have recently become a haven of peace for thousands of migratory or nesting birds of the region. The **Reserve naturelle de la Falguérec-en-Sené** (Falguérec-en-Sené Nature Reserve) ⓥ organises nature rambles and the opportunity to observe (through binoculars) birds such as the black-winged stilt, the elegant avocet or the redshank.

Port-Anna – This little port, frequented by fishing boats and pleasure craft, commands the narrow channel though which boats sail heading for Vannes.

Return to Bellevue and bear right towards the wharf.

Wharf (Embarcadère) – It is used for goods dispatched to the île d'Arz. From the car park, the **view**★ extends over the River Vannes with Presqu'île de Conleau to the left and Séné, at the end of a creek, to the right.

Château du Plessis-Josso ⓥ – *15km - 9 miles east. Leave Vannes on the N 165 towards Nantes. 3km - 2 miles after Theix, turn left onto the D 183 towards Sulniac.*
This charming castle, set in a verdant spot near a lake, is made up of three distinct parts added at three different periods: a 14C fortified manor-house, a 15C main building with a polygonal staircase tower and a Louis XIII-style pavilion.
The visit inside enables you to follow the evolution of the castle's construction. It is easy to imagine how life was in the past, as you walk throught the different rooms: the low reception room, the state rooms and the kitchen (fireplace with counterweight roasting spit, a granite stove with holes used for heating platters). Temporary exhibits are held in the outbuildings.

Grand-Champ - *19km - 12 miles north. Leave Vannes on Rue Hoche and take the D 779. In the nave of the* **church** ⓥ there are two carved wooden panels which come from Notre-Dame-de-Burgo, a ruined chapel in a pretty woodland setting, 2km - 1 mile east of the town.

ROUND TOUR OF LES LANDES DE LANVAUX

55km - 34 miles – time: about 3 hours.

Leave Vannes by Rue du Maréchal-Leclerc and take the N 166. After 14km - 9 miles turn left to the castle.

★**Forteresse de Largoët** – *See Forteresse de LARGOËT.*

After Elven turn left.

Landes de Lanvaux – Contrary to what the name *landes* – moors – implies, this long crest of flaking rock-land, which was not even cultivated last century, is now a fertile region. There remain, however, many megalithic monuments.
On entering **Trédion**, turning left, you go along the banks of a pool which surrounds a most attractive Breton manor-house.

Across from it turn right and cross the built-up area, then left, above the square.

The road drops into the rural Valley of the Claie and its tributary, the Callac stream.

Callac – On the left of the road before a crossroads is a man-made grotto, a copy of the one at Lourdes. To the left of the grotto a path climbs steeply; on either side are Stations of the Cross consisting of groups of figures carved in granite. The path leads to a Calvary from where there is a view on the Landes de Lanvaux.The descent is by another path, which passes near the chapel. On the other side of the road, a stream flows swiftly at the foot of a hillock at the top of which stands a cross; it is a pleasant spot.

Take the left-hand road. When it reaches the Plumelec road, turn left, and 600m - 656yds later bear right. After 2km - 1 mile take the road on the left back to Vannes.

St-Avé – The **Chapelle Notre-Dame-du-Loc** ⏲ rises by the old lie of the Vannes road. A Calvary and a fountain stand before the 15C building. Inside, note the carvings on the purlins and tie-beams which depict angels, grotesques and animals; in the centre of the nave stands a Calvary with figures, surmounted by a wooden canopy. There are alabaster panels on the high altar and 15C granite altarpieces at the right and left-hand altars. The statues, which date from the 15, 16 and 18C, include a 15C Virgin in white stone.

To find a hotel or a restaurant, or to find a garage or car dealer, consult the current edition of the Michelin Red Guide France.

VITRÉ★★

Population 14 486

Michelin map 59 fold 18 or 230 fold 28

This is the best-preserved "old world" town in Brittany; its fortified castle *(photograph p 47)*, its ramparts and its small streets have remained just as they were 400 or 500 years ago and make a picturesque and evocative picture which is long remembered.
The old town is built on a spur commanding the deep Valley of the Vilaine on one side and a railway cutting on the other. The castle stands proudly on the extreme point. From the 15 to the 17C, Vitré was one of the most prosperous of Breton cities; it made hemp, woollen cloth and cotton stockings which were sold not only in France but in England, Germany, Spain and even America and the Indies. Gathered together to form the powerful brotherhood known as "Marchands d'Outre-Mer", the Vitré tradesmen of this period commissioned the building of the highly distinctive houses with half-timbering, many of which can still be seen today.
This prosperity dwindled rapidly in the 18C and revived in the 20C. Knitting mills, shoe and agricultural machinery factories, a factory making metal furniture and food processing industries are developing.

The career of Pierre Landais (15C) – About the middle of the 15C, Pierre Landais, a tailor, was noticed by Duke François II, who made him his wardrobe master. Being clever and enterprising, he worked his way up and became Grand Treasurer of the Duchy (Chancellor of the Exchequer) and Counsellor to the sovereign. But the nobles and the clergy hated this upstart, who encouraged bourgeois representation in the councils and had feudal rights abolished. With the support of the King of France, a plot was hatched which compelled the Duke to sacrifice his Counsellor: Landais was seized in the castle at Nantes. Under torture, he admitted all the charges against him, was sentenced to death and died by hanging in Nantes in 1485.

★★**Arrival at Vitré** – Vitré Castle and the houses at its foot are a fine sight. Motorists should pause before going into the town.

Coming from Fougères: magnificent view of the town on the road coming down the hill.

Coming from Rennes: view of the castle from the bend in the road from Brest.

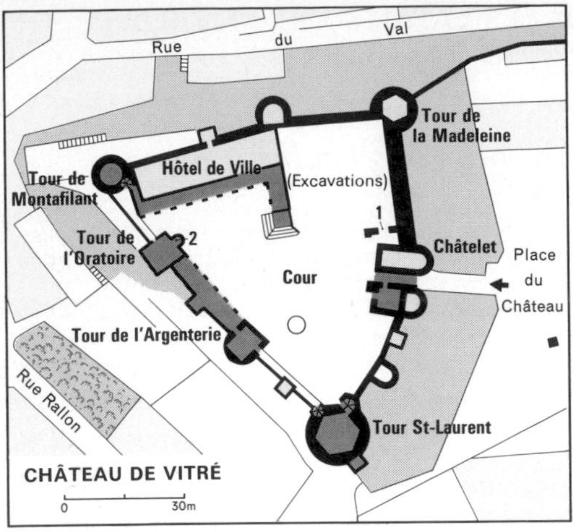

★★CASTLE (CHÂTEAU)

time: 45 min

The castle, rebuilt in the 13, 14 and 15C, was bought in 1820 by the town from the La Trémoille family.
The present square used to be the castle forecourt where the stables and outbuildings were. The fortress is triangular in plan. The entrance is guarded by a drawbridge and entrance fort (Châtelet) flanked by two big machicolated towers. At the south corner stands the main keep or Tour St-Laurent; at the northeast corner stands the Madeleine Tower, and at the northwest corner, the Montafilant Tower. These various works are linked by a wall, reinforced by other towers. As you enter the courtyard you will see, on the right, a Romanesque porch (**1**) with archstones alternating in colour (red granite and black schist), the town hall (1913) abutting on the north front, and before you, the Oratoire Tower with an elegant Renaissance chapel (**2**).
From the platform of the Montafilant Tower *(82 steps)* there is a fine **view**★ of the town, the Tertres Noires and Moines Quarters, the River Vilaine and the old tannery.
Via the curtain wall you arrive at the Oratoire Tower. In its chapel is a beautiful 16C **triptych**★ decorated with 32 Limoges enamels.
The Argenterie Tower presents exhibits of the region's natural history. The St-Laurent Tower houses a **museum** containing 15 and 16C sculpture, which comes from the houses of Vitré (a beautiful chimney has been remounted), the 15C tomb of Gui X (a local lord), a 17C chest, 16C Flemish and 17C Aubusson tapestries and engravings of old Vitré.

★THE TOWN *time: 1 hour 15 min*

Starting from Place du Château, take Rue Notre-Dame and turn right.

★★**Rue de la Baudrairie** (**A 5**) – This, the most curious street in Vitré, gets its name from *baudroyeurs* meaning leather craftsmen. Each house is worth looking at.

Rue d'En Bas (**A 8**) – This street used to lead to the gate (partly destroyed in 1846) of the same name. It is lined with half-timbered houses; note no 10, Hôtel de la Botte Dorée (1513).
Continue along Promenade St-Yves from where a tower, remaining from the ramparts, can be seen.

At Place du Général-de-Gaulle (**B 13**) *take Rue Garangeot.*

Cross Rue Sévigné: note no 9, a 17C mansion known as "Tour de Sévigné" *(qv)*, home to the famous writer.

Turn right.

Rue Poterie (**B**) – Picturesque houses: some half-timbered, some with porches.

Turn right into Rue Notre-Dame.

★**Ramparts (Remparts)** (**B**) – From Place de la République you will see one of the old rampart towers, the 15C Bridolle Tower (machicolations) (**B B**).
On the south side of the town the walls follow the line, at a little distance, of the present Rue de la Borderie and Place St-Yves and then join the castle. Only fragments remain, built into private properties. On the north and east sides the ramparts are still intact.
Old houses line Rue de Paris, which leads into Place de la République.

Go through the gate in Promenade du Val to circle the ramparts. At the end of the alley, after passing a gate, take the ramp to the left which passes under the St-Pierre postern; follow Rue du Bas-Val uphill and turn right in the square, then left into Rue Notre-Dame.

★**Église Notre-Dame** – The church is 15-16C. Outside, the most curious part is the south side, with its seven gables decorated with pinnacles and its pulpit from which preachers addressed the congregation assembled on the small square and its two finely-carved doors.

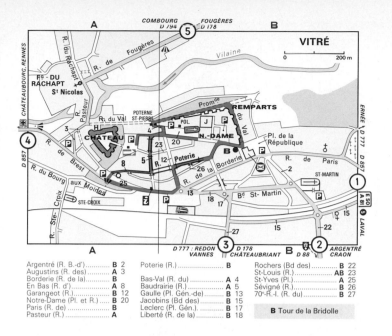

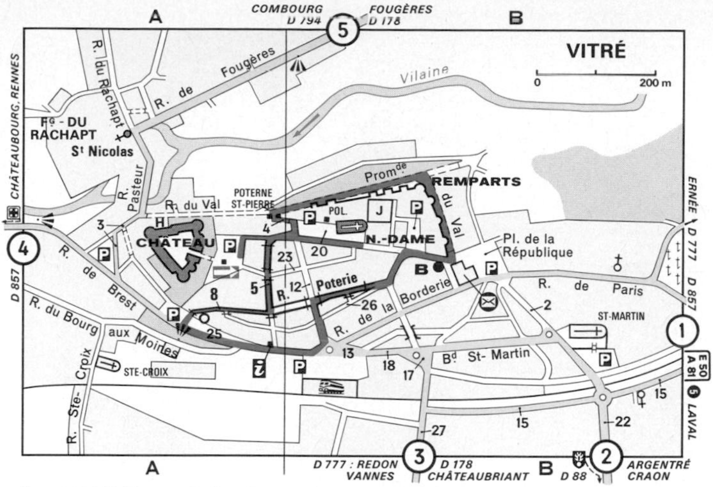

Argentré (R. B.-d')	B	2	Poterie (R.)	B		Rochers (Bd des)	B	22
Augustins (R. des)	A	3				St-Louis (R.)	AB	23
Borderie (R. de la)	B		Bas-Val (R. du)	A	4	St-Yves (Pl.)	A	25
En Bas (R. d')	A	8	Baudrairie (R.)	A	5	Sévigné (R.)	B	26
Garangeot (R.)	B	12	Gaulle (Pl. Gén.-de)	B	13	70e-R.-I. (R. du)	B	27
Notre-Dame (Pl. et R.)	B	20	Jacobins (Bd des)	B	15			
Paris (R. de)	B		Leclerc (Pl. Gén.)	B	17	**B** Tour de la Bridolle		
Pasteur (R.)	A		Liberté (R. de la)	B	18			

Inside, you will see many altarpieces and a fine Renaissance stained-glass window in the south aisle (third bay) depicting Christ's Entry into Jerusalem.
At no 27 Rue Notre-Dame is the former Hôtel Hardy or de la Troussanais (16C) with its finely-carved porches and dormer windows.

Turn round and go to Place du Château.

ADDITIONAL SIGHTS

★★**Tertres Noirs** – *Access by Rue de Brest and Chemin des Tertres Noirs, to the right after the bridge over the Vilaine.*
There is a fine **view**★★ of Vitré, its site and its castle from this shaded terrace.

★**Public garden (Jardin public)** – *Via ③ of the town plan.* A pleasant, well-kept garden.

Faubourg du Rachapt (**A**) – During the Hundred Years War, this suburb was occupied for several years by the English, while the town and the castle resisted all their attacks. The people of Vitré paid the invaders to go away: hence the name of the suburb *(Rachapt = rachat = repurchase)*.
This suburb, lying at the foot of the castle, crosses the Vilaine Valley and rises on the north slope. Rue Pasteur, which affords picturesque views of the town and river, leads to the 15C **Chapelle St-Nicolas** ⓥ which is the museum annexe (in season).

Enter by the little door on the left and skirt the chapel.

At the end, on the right, go through a pretty basket-handle arched door into the chapel where there is an 18C wooden gilded high altar. On the right is St Augustine, on the left St Nicholas and the 3 children (18C); 16C frescoes have been discovered.
Rue du Rachapt is lined with old houses. Lovely view of the castle.

EXCURSIONS

Château des Rochers-Sévigné – *6.5km - 4 miles southeast. Leave Vitré via ② on the town plan. 6km - 4 miles from the town, on coming out of a wood, take the château drive on the left. See Château des ROCHERS-SÉVIGNÉ.*

★**Champeaux** – *9km - 5.5 miles west. Leave Vitré via ④ on the town plan. 2km - 1 mile from the town turn right. See CHAMPEAUX.*

Passage Pommeraye, Nantes

Practical Information

Le Bot/DIAF

Planning your trip

Passport – Visitors entering France must be in possession of a valid national passport. Citizens of one of the European Union countries only need a national identity card. In case of loss or theft report to the embassy or consulate and the local police.

Visa – No **entry visa** is required for US and Canadian citizens as long as their stay in France does not exceed 3 months. Australians and New Zealanders must apply for one at the nearest French consulate. For other countries, check with a French consulate or travel agent.
US citizens should obtain the booklet *Safe Trip Abroad*, which provides useful information on visa requirements, customs regulations, medical care, etc. for international travellers. Contact the Superintendent of Documents, to order. ☎ 202-512-1800. Consult via Internet: www.access.gpo.gov.

Customs – Apply to the Customs Office (UK) for a leaflet entitled *A Guide for Travellers* on customs regulations and the full range of duty-free allowances. The US Customs Service (look in the phone book under Federal Government, US treasury for the nearest office), offers a free publication *Know Before You Go* for US residents. There are no customs formalities for holidaymakers bringing caravans into France for a stay of less than 6 months. No customs document is necessary for pleasure boats and outboard motors for a stay of less than 6 months, but the registration certificate should be kept on board.

French Government Tourist Offices – For information, brochures, maps and assistance in planning a trip to France, travellers should contact the official tourist office in their own country:

Australia – New Zealand
Sydney – BNP Building, 12 Castlereagh Street, Sydney, New South Wales 2000, ☎ (61) 2-231-5244, Fax (61) 2-221-8682.

Canada
Toronto – 30 St Patrick's St, Suite 700, Toronto, ONT M5T 3A3, ☎ 416-593-4723
Montreal – 1981 Av McGill College, Suite 490, Montreal, PQ H3A 2W9, ☎ 514-288-4264, Fax 514-845-4868.

Eire
Dublin – 35 Lower Abbey St, Dublin 1, ☎ (1) 703-40-46, Fax (1) 874-73-24.

United Kingdom
London – 178 Piccadilly, London W1, ☎ (0891) 244-123, Fax (0171) 493-6594.

United States
France On Call Hotline: 900-990-0040 (US$0.50/min) for information on hotels, restaurants and transportation.
East Coast: New York – 444 Madison Avenue, New York, NY 10022, ☎ 212-838-7800, Fax 212-838-7855.
Mid-West: Chicago – 676 North Michigan Avenue, Suite 3360, Chicago, IL 60611-2819, ☎ 312-751-7800, Fax 312-337-6339.
West Coast: Los Angeles – 9454 Wilshire Boulevard, Suite 715, Beverly Hills, CA 90212-2967, ☎ 310-271-2693, Fax 310-276-2835.

Cyberspace
http://www.info.france-usa.org
The French Embassy's Web site provides basic information (geography, demographics, history), a news digest and business-related information. It offers special pages for children, and pages devoted to culture, language study and travel, and you can reach other selected French sites (regions, cities, ministries) with a hypertext link.

Time – The time in France is one hour ahead of Greenwich Mean Time (GMT), except between the end of September and the end of October, when it is the same.
When it is **12noon in France,** it is

3am in Los Angeles	7pm in Perth
6am in New York	9pm in Sydney
11am in Dublin	11pm in Auckland
11am in London	

In France "am" and "pm" are not used and the 24-hour clock is widely applied.

Michelin Route Planning on Internet www. michelin-travel.com.

Michelin, you companion on the road, invites you to visit our Web site and discover European route planning on the Internet.

Wether you just want to know the distance between two points, or need a detailed itinerary, for a holiday or on business, we provide all the information necessary for accurate travel planning.

Getting there

By air – Choose between scheduled flights run by national airlines (Air France, TAT), or commercial and package-tour flights, with rail or coach link-ups or Fly-Drive schemes – contact airlines and travel agents for information.

By rail – British and French Railways (SNCF) operate a daily service via the Channel Tunnel on Eurostar in 3 hours between **London** (Waterloo International Station) and **Paris** (Gare du Nord). From Paris-Gare Montparnasse, the TGV Atlantique (high-speed rail service) leaves for Le Mans, Rennes, Nantes, Quimper and Brest. The SNCF network offers standard rail links for the rest of Brittany. SNCF information in English: ☎ 08 36 35 35 39 (from France) or 33 8 36 35 35 39 (from abroad). In London, the SNCF office is at 178 Piccadilly, ☎ 0891 515 477.

There are rail passes offering unlimited travel and group travel tickets offering services for parties. **Eurailpass, Flexipass** and **Saver Pass** are options available in the US for travel in Europe and must be purchased in the US – ☎ 1-800-4-EURAIL. In the UK, information and bookings can be obtained from French Railways, London and from main Rail Travel Centres and travel agencies.

Tickets bought in France must be validated *(composter)* by using the orange automatic date-stamping machines at the platform entrance.

A useful aid to rail travel is the **Thomas Cook European Rail Timetable,** which gives all the train schedules throughout France and information on travelling by train.

By road – The region described in this guide can be reached **by coach** via Paris. For further information, contact Eurolines:

London: 52 Grosvenor Gardens, Victoria, London SW1W 0AU. ☎ (0171) 730 8235.

Paris: 28 Avenue du Général de Gaulle, 93541 Bagnolet. ☎ 01 49 72 51 51.

Drivers from the British Isles can travel to Brittany **by car.** Numerous cross-Channel services (passenger and car-ferries, hovercraft, SeaCat and via the Channel Tunnel) operate across the English Channel and St George's Channel. For details contact travel agencies or:

Brittany Ferries, The Brittany Centre, Wharf Road, Portsmouth, Hampshire PO28RU. ☎ 01705 827 701. Hoverspeed, International Hoverport, Marine Parade, Dover, Kent CT17 9TG. ☎ (01304) 240241

Irish Ferries, 50 West Norland St, Dublin 2. ☎ (353) 1 6 610511

Le Shuttle-Eurotunnel, ☎ 03 45 30 30 30. Web: www.eurail.com. and www.eurostar.com.

P&O Stena Lines, Channel House, Channel View Road, Dover CT17 9TJ. ☎ (0990 980 980).

Sally Line, Argyle Centre, York St, Ramsgate, Kent CT11 9AS. ☎ (0800) 636465.

To choose the most suitable route between one of the ports along the north coast of France and your destination, use the Michelin Motoring Atlas France, Michelin map 911 (which gives travel times and mileage) or Michelin maps from the 1:200 000 series with the yellow covers *(see page 3).*

J.L. Barde/SCOPE

Hydrangeas

Getting around

MOTORING IN FRANCE

Documents – Nationals of the European Union countries require a valid national driving licence. Nationals of non-EU countries should obtain an international driving licence (obtainable in the US from the American Automobile Association, cost for members: US$10, for non-members US$22). For the vehicle it is necessary to have the registration papers (log-book) and a nationality plate of the approved size.

Insurance – Certain UK motoring organisations (AA, RAC) offer accident insurance and breakdown service schemes for members. Europ-Assistance (252 High St, Croyden CR0 1NF, ☎ (0181) 680 1234) has special policies for motorists. Members of the American Automobile Association should obtain the free brochure *Offices To Serve You Abroad.*

Highway code – The minimum driving age is 18 years old. Traffic drives on the right. It is compulsory for the front-seat passengers to wear **seat belts,** and all back-seat passengers should wear seat-belts where the car is fitted with them. Full or dipped headlights must be switched on in poor visibility and at night; use side lights only when the vehicle is stationary.

In the case of a **breakdown,** a red warning triangle or hazard warning lights are obligatory. Drivers should watch out for unfamiliar road signs and take great care on the road. In built-up areas **priority** must be ceded to vehicles coming from the right. However, traffic on main roads outside built-up areas (indicated by a yellow diamond sign) and on roundabouts has priority. Vehicles must stop when the lights turn red at road junctions and may filter to the right only where indicated by a flashing amber arrow (but give way to any pedestrians crossing the road into which you are turning). The regulations on **drinking and driving** (limited to 0.50 g/litre) and speeding are strictly enforced – usually by an on-the-spot fine and/or confiscation of the vehicle.

Speed limits – Although liable to modification, these are as follows:
– toll motorways *(péage)* 130kph - 80mph (110kph - 68mph when raining);
– dual carriage roads and motorways without tolls 110kph - 68mph (100kph - 62mph when raining);
– other roads 90kph - 56mph (80kph - 50mph when raining) and in towns 50kph - 31mph;
– outside lane on motorways during daylight, on level ground and with good visibility, minimum speed limit of 80kph - 50mph.

Parking regulations – In town there are zones where **parking** is either restricted or subject to a fee; tickets should be obtained from the ticket machines (*horodateurs* – small change necessary) and displayed inside the windscreen on the driver's side; failure to display may result in a heavy fine or even the offending vehicle being towed away. In some towns you can find blue parking zones *(zone bleue)* marked by a blue line on the pavement or a blue signpost with a P and a small square underneath. In this particular case you have to display a "parking disc", which will allow you to stay for 1 1/2 hours (2 1/2 hours over lunchtime) free. You can buy these in supermarkets or petrol stations (ask for a *disque de stationnement).*

Route planning – **www.michelin-travel.com** provides a choice of itineraries, printable maps, travel times and distances, tourist information. **Michelin map 911** shows alternate routes for holiday periods.

The road network is excellent, but roads can be very busy during the holiday period (particularly weekends in July and August) – to avoid traffic congestion it is advisable to follow the recommended secondary routes *(Bison Futé-itinéraires bis).*

Tolls – In France, most motorway sections are subject to a toll *(péage).* You can pay with cash or by credit card (Visa, Mastercard). However, on the major communications routes in Brittany (N 12, N 137, N 165), no tolls are payable.

Car rental – There are car rental agencies at airports, railway stations and in all large towns throughout France. European cars usually have manual transmission, but automatic cars are available on demand (advance reservation recommended). It is relatively expensive to hire a car in France; Americans in particular will notice the difference and should consider booking a car from home before leaving or taking advantage of Fly-Drive schemes.

Central Reservation in France:

Avis: 01 46 10 60 60	Europcar: 01 30 43 82 82
Budget: 01 46 86 65 65	Hertz: 01 47 88 51 51
Eurodollar: 01 49 58 44 44	

Petrol – In France you will find 4 different types of petrol (US: gas):

super leaded *(super)*	super unleaded 95 *(sans plomb 95)*
diesel *(diesel/gazole)*	super unleaded 98 *(sans plomb 98)*

Petrol is more expensive in France compared to the United States and even the United Kingdom.

Tourist Information

Local Tourist Offices – To find the addresses of local tourist offices throughout France, contact the Fédération Nationale des Comités Départementaux de Tourisme, 280 boulevard St-Germain, 75007 Paris. ☎ 01 44 11 10 20.
Locally, you can contact the regional tourist offices where useful brochures and information are available:
Comité régional du tourisme de **Bretagne,** 74 bis, rue de Paris, 35069 Rennes Cedex, ☎ 02 99 28 44 30 or 02 99 36 15 15
Comité départemental de tourisme de l'**Ille-et-Vilaine,** 4, rue Jean-Jaurès, BP 6046, 35000 Rennes, ☎ 02 99 02 97 43
Comité départemental de tourisme de **Loire-Atlantique,** Maison du Tourisme, place du Commerce, 44000 Nantes, ☎ 02 40 89 50 77
Comité départemental de tourisme des **Côtes d'Armor,** 29, rue des Promenades, BP 4620, 22046 Saint-Brieuc Cedex 2, ☎ 02 96 62 72 00
Comité départemental de tourisme du **Finistère,** 11, rue Théodore-Le-Hars, 29104 Quimper Cedex, BP 1419, ☎ 02 98 53 09 00
Comité départemental de tourisme du **Morbihan,** Hôtel du Département, BP 400, 56009 Vannes Cedex, ☎ 02 97 54 06 56
Fédération des pays d'accueil, Vallée des Forges, 22390 Bourbriac, ☎ 02 96 43 44 43
Maison de la Bretagne, Centre commercial Maine-Montparnasse, 17 rue de l'Arrivée, 75737 Paris Cedex 15, ☎ 01 45 38 73 15
Bretagne Infos (24 hour information service), ☎ 02 99 36 15 15, Fax 02 99 28 44 40

Tourism for the Disabled – Some of the sights described in this guide are accessible to handicapped people and are indicated in the Admission Times and Charges section with the symbol ♿. For more information on museum access for the disabled contact La Direction, Les Musées de France, Service Accueil des Publics Spécifiques, 6, rue des Pyramides, 75041 Paris Cedex 1, ☎ 01 40 15 35 88. The **Michelin Red Guide France** and **Michelin Guide Camping Caravaning France** indicate hotels and campsites with facilities suitable for physically handicapped people.
Useful information is also available from the Comité National Français de Liaison pour la Réadaptation des Handicapés, 236 bis, rue de Tolbiac, 75013 Paris, ☎ 01 53 80 66 44, for information and to request a catalogue of publications. Mature travellers, slow walkers and others with special needs will find useful cyber-links at www.access-able.com.

Accommodation

Places to stay – The **Places to stay** map in the Introduction indicates recommended places for overnight stops and can be used in conjunction with the **Michelin Red Guide France,** which lists a selection of hotels and restaurants.
Loisirs Accueil is a booking service that has offices in most French *départements*. For information, contact Réservation Loisirs Accueil, 280 boulevard St-Germain, 75007 Paris. ☎ 01 44 11 10 44, or local offices:
SLA Côtes d'Armor, 29, rue des Promenades, BP 4620, 22046 Saint-Brieuc Cedex 02, ☎ 02 96 62 72 15.
SLA Ille-et-Vilaine, 1, quai Chateaubriand, BP 5093, 35061 Rennes Cedex, ☎ 02 99 78 47 57.
SLA Morbihan, Hôtel du Département, rue de St-Tropez, BP 400, 56000 Vannes Cedex, ☎ 02 97 42 61 60.

Rural accommodation – The Maison des Gîtes de France has a list of self-catering accommodation where you can stay in this region (and all over France). This usually takes the form of a cottage or apartment decorated in the local style where you will be able to make yourself at home. Gîtes de France have offices in:

London: 178 Piccadilly, London W1, ☎ (0891) 244 123

Paris: 59 rue St-Lazare, 75009 Paris. ☎ 01 49 70 75 75

Bed and Breakfast – Gîtes de France *(see above)* publishes a booklet on bed and breakfast accommodation *(chambres d'hôtes)* which include a room and breakfast at a reasonable price.
You can also contact two associations that provide addresses of accommodation throughout the region:
Bed & Breakfast (France), International Reservations Centre, PO Box 66, Henley-on-Thames, Oxon, RG9 1XS, ☎ (01491) 578803, Fax (01491) 410806

Youth Hostels – There are two main youth hostel associations *(auberges de la jeunesse)* in France.

Paris: Ligue Française pour les Auberges de la Jeunesse, 38 boulevard Raspail, 75007 Paris. ☎ 01 45 48 69 84, Fax 01 45 44 57 47.
Fédération Unie des Auberges de Jeunesse, 27 Rue Pajol, 75018 Paris, ☎ 01 44 89 87 27, Fax 01 44 89 87 10; www.fuaj.org.

Holders of an International Youth Hostel Federation card should contact the International Federation or the French Youth Hostels Association to book a bed.
Hostelling International/American Youth Hostel Association in the US (☎ 202-783-6161) offers a publication **International Hostel Guide for Europe**. For the latest hostel news, information on availability, facilities, services and, for some locations, reservations, visit the international web site: www.iyhf.org.

Camping – There are numerous officially graded sites with varying standards of facilities throughout this region of France. The **Michelin Guide Caravaning France** lists a selection of campsites. An international Camping Carnet for caravans is useful but not compulsory; it may be obtained from motoring organisations or the Camping and Caravanning Club (Greenfield House, Westwood Way, Coventry CV4 8JH, ☎ (01203) 694995).

Basic information

Electricity – The electric current is 220 volts. Circular two pin plugs are the rule. Adaptors should be bought before you leave home; they are on sale at most airports.

Medical treatment – First aid, medical advice and chemist's night service rota are available from chemists/drugstores (*pharmacie*, identified by a green cross sign).
It is advisable to take out comprehensive insurance cover as tourists undergoing medical treatment in French hospitals or clinics have to pay for it themselves. Nationals of non-EU countries should check with their insurance companies about policy limitations. Reimbursement can then be negotiated with the insurance company according to the policy held. All prescription drugs should be clearly labelled; it is recommended that you carry a copy of prescriptions. American Express offers its cardholders (only) a service, "Global Assist", for any medical, legal or personal emergency: ☎ 01 47 16 25 29.
British and Irish citizens should apply to the Department of Health and Social Security for Form E111, which entitles the holder to urgent treatment for accident or unexpected illness in EU countries. A refund of part of the costs of treatment can be obtained on application in person or by post to the local Social Security offices ☎ *(Caisse Primaire d'Assurance Maladie)*.

Tipping – Since a service charge is automatically included in the price of meals and accommodation in France, it is not necessary to tip in restaurants and hotels. However taxi drivers, bellboys, doormen, filling station attendants or anybody who has been of assistance are usually tipped at the customer's discretion. Most French people give an extra tip in restaurants and cafés (about 50 centimes for a drink and several francs for a meal). There is no tipping in theatres.

Currency – There are no restrictions on the amount of currency visitors can take into France. Visitors wishing to export currency in foreign banknotes in excess of the given allocation from France should complete a currency declaration form on arrival.

Notes and coins – *See illustration on page 305.* The unit of currency in France is the French franc (F), subdivided into 100 centimes. French coins come in the following values:
5, 10, 20, 50 centimes (all gold coloured except the 50 centime coin which is silver)
1, 2, 5, 10, 20 francs (all silver except the 10 and 20 franc coins which are silver with a gold band).
French notes are available for the values 50, 100, 200 and 500 francs (the old 20 franc note is being phased out).

Banks – Banks are generally open from 9am to 12noon and from 2pm to 4pm and are closed on Monday or Saturday (except if market day). Banks close early on the day before a bank holiday. A passport is necessary for identification when cashing cheques (travellers' or ordinary) in banks. Commission charges vary and hotels usually charge more than banks for cashing cheques for non-residents.
Most banks have **cash dispensers** (ATM) that accept international credit cards. These are easily recognizable by the CB logo. American Express cards can only be used in dispensers operated by the Credit Lyonnais bank or by American Express.

Credit cards – American Express, Visa, Mastercard-Eurocard and Diners Club are widely accepted in shops, hotels, restaurants and petrol stations. In case your card is lost or stolen, call the following 24-hour hotlines:

American Express 01 47 77 72 00
Visa 01 42 77 11 90
Mastercard/Eurocard 01 45 67 84 84
Diners Club 01 49 06 17 90

You must also report any loss or theft to the local police who will issue you with a certificate (useful proof to show the credit card company).

Post – Main post offices open Monday to Friday from 8am to 7pm, Saturday from 8am to noon. Smaller branch post offices generally close at lunchtime between noon and 2pm and at 4pm.
Postage via airmail

UK: letter (20g) 3F
North America: letter (20g) 4.40F
Australia and NZ: letter (20g) 5.20F

Stamps are also available from newsagents and *bureaux de tabac*. Stamp collectors should ask for *timbres de collection* in any post office.

Public Holidays – The following are days when museums and other monuments may be closed or may vary their hours of admission:

1 January	New Year's Day *(Jour de l'An)*
	Easter Day and Easter Monday *(Pâques)*
1 May	May Day
8 May	V E Day
	Whit Sunday and Monday *(Pentecôte)*
	Ascension Day *(Ascension)*
14 July	France's National Day (Bastille Day)
15 August	Assumption
1 November	All Saints' Day *(Toussaint)*
11 November	Armistice
25 December	Christmas Day *(Noël)*

Local Radio stations – These usually give frequent updates on traffic conditions, local demonstrations, etc. as well as information on local cultural events.

Embassies and Consulates

Australia:	Embassy	4 rue Jean-Rey, 75015 Paris, ☎ 01 40 59 33 00, Fax 01 40 59 33 10
Canada:	Embassy	35 avenue Montaigne, 75008 Paris, ☎ 01 44 43 29 00, Fax 01 44 43 29 99
Eire:	Embassy	4 rue Rude, 75016 Paris, ☎ 01 44 17 67 00, Fax 01 45 00 84 17
New Zealand:	Embassy	7 ter rue Léonard-de-Vinci, 75016 Paris, ☎ 01 45 00 24 11, Fax 01 45 01 26 39
UK:	Embassy	35 rue du Faubourg St-Honoré, 75008 Paris, ☎ 01 42 66 91 42, Fax 01 42 66 95 90
	Consulate	16 rue d'Anjou, 75008 Paris, ☎ 01 42 66 06 68 (visas)
USA:	Embassy	2 avenue Gabriel, 75008 Paris, ☎ 01 43 12 22 22, Fax 01 42 66 97 83
	Consulate	2 rue St-Florentin, 75001 Paris, ☎ 01 42 96 14 88

Telephoning

Public Telephones – Most public phones in France use pre-paid phone cards *(télécartes)*. Some telephone booths accept credit cards (Visa, Mastercard/Eurocard; minimum monthly charge 20F). *Télécartes* (50 or 120 units) can be bought in post offices, branches of France Télécom, *bureaux de tabac* (authorised cigarette sales point) and newsagents, and can be used to make calls in France and abroad. Calls can be received at phone boxes where the blue bell sign is shown.

National calls – French telephone numbers have 10-digits: numbers begin with 02 in Brittany and northwest France; 01 in Paris and the Paris region; 03 in northeast France; 04 in southeast France and Corsica; 05 in southwest France; 06 numbers are portable phones; 08 numbers are toll-free. The French ringing tone is a series of long tones and the engaged (busy) tone is a series of short beeps.

International calls – To call France from abroad, dial the country code (33) + 9-digit number (omit the preceding zero). When calling abroad from France dial 00, then dial the country code, followed by the area code and number of your correspondent. For international inquiries dial 00 33 12 + country code (be prepared to wait for up to an hour).
To use your personal calling card dial:

AT&T: 00-0011
MCI: 00-0019
BT: 00-0044
Mercury: 00-00944

Rates from a public phone (1996):

Between France and the UK: 2.97F/min (2.23F/min reduced rate)
Between France and the US: 4.45F/min (3.46F/min reduced rate)
Between France and Canada: 4.45F/min (3.46F/min reduced rate)
Between France and Australia: 8.65F/min (6.92F/min reduced rate)

Reduced rates to the UK: from 9.30pm to 8am Monday to Friday; from 2pm Saturday all day Sunday and public holidays.
Reduced rates to the US and Canada: the lowest rates apply from 2am to noon all week (most expensive time to call is 2pm to 8pm).
Reduced rates to Australia: from 9.30pm to 8am from Monday to Saturday and all day Sunday.

International dialling codes:

Australia: 61	New Zealand: 64
Canada: 1	United Kingdom: 44
Eire: 353	United States: 1

Toll-free numbers: In France numbers beginning with 0 800 are toll-free.

Emergency numbers:

Police: 17
Fire (Pompiers): 18
Ambulance (SAMU): 15

Minitel – France Telecom operates a modern interactive communication service called Minitel, similar to the teletex system, offering a range of services from directory inquiries (free of charge up to 3 min) to 3614, 3615, 3616 and 3617 prefixed numbers (fee charged between 0.37F and 5.57F/min). These small computer-like machines can be found in some post offices, hotels and France Telecom agencies and in most French homes.
Listed below are some of the telematic services offered:

3615 TCAMP (2.23F/min)	camping information
3615 METEO (1.29F/min)	weather report
3615 HORAV (1.29F/min)	general airline information and flight schedules from and to Paris (in English and French)
3615 MICHELIN (1.29F/min)	Michelin tourist and route information
3617 MICHELIN (5.57F/min)	Michelin tourist and route information sent by fax

For information in English dial 0 800 201 202.
Directory inquiries in English on minitel: 3614 ED (0.37F/min).

Shopping

Opening hours

Department stores and chain stores are open Monday to Saturday, 9am to 6.30pm-7.30pm. Smaller, more specialised shops may close during the lunch hour. Food stores (grocers, wine merchants and bakeries) are open from 7am to 6.30pm-7.30pm. Some open on Sunday mornings. Many food stores close between noon and 2pm and on Mondays. Hypermarkets are usually open until 9pm-10pm.

What to take home

Oysters from Cancale, *charcuterie* such as *rillettes* or *boudin noir*, globe artichokes, chestnuts, cider, Muscadet and Gros Plant wine, Breton mead *(hydromel)*, Breton butter biscuits. Local crafts such as carved wood, lace, Quimper pottery.
Travellers from America should note that they are not allowed to take food and plant products home, so this rules out French cheeses and fruit, for example.
Americans are allowed to take home, tax-free, up to US$400 worth of goods, Canadians up to CND$300, British up to £136, Australians up to AUS$400 and New Zealanders up to NZ$700.

Notes and coins

500 Francs featuring scientists Pierre and Marie Curie (1858-1906). (1867-1934)

200 Francs featuring engineer Gustave Eiffel (1832-1923)

100 Francs featuring Post-Impressionist painter Paul Cézanne (1839-1906)

50 Francs featuring pilot and writer Antoine de Saint-Exupéry (1900-1944)

20 Francs

10 Francs

5 Francs

2 Francs

1 Franc

50 Centimes

20 Centimes

10 Centimes

5 Centimes

Conversion tables

Weights and measures

1 kilogram (kg)	2.2 pounds (lb)	2.2 pounds
1 metric ton (tn)	1.1 tons	1.1 tons

to convert kilograms to pounds, multiply by 2.2

1 litre (l)	2.1 pints (pt)	1.8 pints
1 litre	0.3 gallon (gal)	0.2 gallon

to convert litres to gallons, multiply by 0.26 (US) or 0.22 (UK)

1 hectare (ha)	2.5 acres	2.5 acres
1 square kilometre (km^2)	0.4 square miles (sq mi)	0.4 square miles

to convert hectares to acres, multiply by 2.4

1centimetre (cm)	0.4 inches (in)	0.4 inches
1 metre (m)	3.3 feet (ft) - 39.4 inches - 1.1 yards (yd)	
1 kilometre (km)	0.6 miles (mi)	0.6 miles

to convert metres to feet, multiply by 3.28. kilometres to miles, multiply by 0.6

Clothing

Women			
Shoes	35	4	2½
	36	5	3½
	37	6	4½
	38	7	5½
	39	8	6½
	40	9	7½
	41	10	8½
Dresses & Suits	36	4	8
	38	6	10
	40	8	12
	42	12	14
	44	14	16
	46	16	18
Blouses & sweaters	36	08	30
	38	10	32
	40	12	14
	42	14	36
	44	16	38
	46	18	40

			Men
40	7½	7	Shoes
41	8½	8	
42	9½	9	
43	10½	10	
44	11½	11	
45	12½	12	
46	13½	13	
46	36	36	Suits
48	38	38	
50	40	40	
52	42	42	
54	44	44	
56	46	48	
37	14½	14.5	Shirts
38	15	15	
39	15½	15½	
40	15¾	15¾	
41	16	16	
42	16½	16½	

Sizes often vary depending on the designer. These equivalents are given for guidance only.

Speed

kph	10	30	50	70	80	90	100	110	120	130
mph	6	19	31	43	50	56	62	68	75	81

Temperature

Celsius (°C)	0°	5°	10°	15°	20°	25°	30°	40°	60°	80°	100°
Fahrenheit (°F)	32°	41°	50°	59°	68°	77°	86°	104°	140°	176°	212°

To convert Celsius into Fahrenheit, multiply °C by 9, divide by 5, and add 32.
To convert Fahrenheit into Celsius, subtract 32 from °F, multiply by 5, and divide by 9.

Recreation

Weather

For any outdoor activity, on sea or land, it is useful to have reliable weather forecasts. The French weather reporting service, **Météo-France**, can be consulted by telephone: for coastal weather reports on ☎02 36 68 08 followed by the number of the département in question (for Brest in Finistère, for example, you would dial 02 36 68 08 29); for local weather reports and five day forecasts on ☎02 36 68 02 followed by the number of the département in question (for Morbihan, dial 02 36 68 08 56); for weather conditions at sea and five day forecasts for the Channel (Manche), Atlantic or Mediterranean dial ☎ 02 36 68 08 08.

BEAUFORT SCALE

BEAUFORT NUMBER	WIND NAME	WIND SPEED		CONDITIONS	
		knots	mph	Land	Sea
0	calm	1	1	smoke rises vertically	sea like a mirror
1	light air	1-3	1-3	smoke curves slightly upwards	small ripples
2	slight breeze	4-6	4-7	leaves rustle	small wavelets
3	gentle breeze	7-10	8-12	leaves move constantly	large wavelets, some white horses
4	moderate breeze	11-16	13-18	dust and sand rise	small waves lengthening, frequent white horses
5	fresh breeze	17-21	19-24	shrubs sway	moderate waves, many white horses and some spray
6	strong breeze	22-27	25-31	electric cables hum	large waves, white foam crests and spray
7	moderate gale	28-33	32-38	trees sway, walking is difficult	white foam blown in streaks
8	fresh gale	34-40	39-46	walking into the wind impossible	fairly high waves, spindrift, foam blown in marked streaks
9	strong gale	41-47	47-54	damage to buildings	high waves, spray affects visibility
10	whole gale	48-55	55-63	trees uprooted	heavy rolling sea with very high waves and dense spray
11	storm	56-63	64-72	extensive damage	huge waves, sea covered with spindrift
12	hurri-cane	>64	>73	very rare inland	air and sea filled with foam and spray, visibility almost nil

Boating – The Channel and Atlantic coasts lend themselves particularly well to exploration by boat, be it under sail or motor-powered. The main marinas are indicated on the Places to stay map at the beginning of the guide; criteria dictating their selection include number of berths available and range of facilites offered (fuel, fresh water and electricity on the quayside, toilets and washing facilities, elevators or cranes for loading, repair workshops, security guards).

Cycling – For information contact the Fédération Française de Cyclotourisme, 8, rue Jean-Marie-Jégo, 75013 Paris, ☎ 01 44 16 88 88, which will give you the details of its local representatives. Tourist information centres have lists of places to hire bicycles. Main railway stations (Auray, Brest, Châteaulin, Combourg, Concarneau, Dinan, Dol, Guingamp, Lamballe, Lannion, Lorient, Morlaix, Quiberon, Quimper, Rennes, Roscoff, St-Brieuc, St-Malo, St-Nazaire, Vannes) offer three types of bicycle for hire (drop-off can be at a different station).

Deep-sea fishing – From Mont-St-Michel bay to the Loire river estuary, Breton coastal waters offer infinite possibilities to amateur deep-sea fishermen. Contact the local marine authorities (Service des Affaires Maritimes) to find out about regulations governing fishing from boats or underwater. Fishing from the shore is not subject to any formal regulations, apart from the use of nets, which requires permission from the marine authorities. Different areas may however have particular coastal rules; it is advisable to find out what these are from the appropriate local authority.

Freshwater angling – Obey national and local laws. You may have to become a member (for the year in progress) of an affiliated angling association in the département of your choice, pay the annual angling tax or buy a day card, and obtain permission from the landowner if you wish to fish on private land. Special two-week holiday fishing permits are also available.

A leaflet with a map and information called *Pêche en France* (Fishing in France) is available from Conseil Supérieur de la Pêche, 134, avenue de Malakoff, 75116 Paris, ☎ 01 45 02 20 20.

Rambling – A number of long-distance footpaths (sentiers de Grande Randonnée – GR) cover the region described in this guide. Walking holidays and rambles are organised by La Maison du Tourisme, 29, rue des Promenades, BP 620, 22011 St-Brieuc, ☎ 02 96 62 72 00 (Minitel code: 3615 Armor) and ABRI, Maison de la Randonnée, 9, rue des Portes-Mordelaises, 35200 Rennes, ☎ 02 99 31 59 44.
Argoat is criss-crossed by the **GR footpaths 34, 37, 38, 341 and 380**, which offer a range of pleasant rambles to walkers of all abilities.
The Topo-Guides, published by the Fédération Française de la Randonnée Pédestre, give detailed maps of the paths and offer valuable information to ramblers. They are available from the Comité national des sentiers de Grande Randonnée, 64, rue de Gergovie, 75014 Paris, ☎ 01 45 45 31 02.
For short-distance footpaths, enquire at local tourist information centres.

Riding – The possibilities for riding holidays in Brittany are numerous and open to riders of all abilities. For details, contact the following organisations:
Fédération des Randonneurs Équestres de France, 4, rue de Stockholm, 75008 Paris, ☎ 01 42 94 90 94.
Formules Bretagne, 17, rue de l'Arrivée, Centre commercial Maine-Montparnasse, 75737 Paris Cedex 15, ☎ 01 42 79 07 07.
Association régionale pour le tourisme équestre et l'équitation de Loisirs en Bretagne (ARTEB), 7, rue des Écoles, 29710 Plogastel-St-Germain, ☎ 02 98 5 51 95.
CDTE (Comité départemental de tourisme équestre) des Côtes d'Armor, Association des cavaliers d'extérieur des Côtes d'Armor (ACECA), 5, bois l'Abbé, 22970 Ploumagoar, ☎ 02 96 74 68 05.
CDTE de Finistère, contact ARTEB at Plogastel-St-Germain.
CDTE de l'Ille-et-Vilaine, contact ARTEB at Plogastel-St-Germain.
CDTE de la Loire-Atlantique, Le Clos de la Vigne, 44460 Fegréac, ☎ 02 40 91 21 47.
CDTE du Morbihan, 4, rue Georges-Cadoudal, 56390 Grandchamp, ☎ 02 97 66 40 46.

J. Guillard/SCOPE

Sailing school

Sailing and windsurfing – The rugged Breton coastline shelters numerous bays which make an ideal setting for sailing enthusiasts to practise their sport. Many of the Breton yacht clubs have a sailing school attached to them, for example the centre at Glénan. Windsurfing is possible from many beaches, although it is subject to certain rules; contact the yacht clubs for details. Windsurfers can be hired at all the major beaches, as can boats, with or without a crew, in season. For further information, contact the Fédération Française de Voile, 55, avenue Kléber, 75784 Paris Cedex 16, ☎ 01 45 53 68 00 (Minitel code: 3615 FFV), or France Station-Voile, La Corderie royale, BP 108, 17303 Rochefort Cedex, ☎ 02 46 82 07 47.
Regattas are organised throughout the season in all the major resorts.

Skin-diving – This activity is becoming increasingly popular in Brittany. The clear waters of the inlets along Brittany's south coast (Port-Manech, Port-Goulphar to Belle-Ile) are rich in fish and marine plantlife, providing interest for underwater anglers and admirers of underwater landscapes alike. The Iles de Glénan diving centre attracts deep-sea divers, who can practise in the swimming pool during the winter.

Fish auction at Concarneau

Further information can be obtained from the Comité interrégional Bretagne-Pays de Loire de la Fédération Française d'Études et de Sports Sous-Marins (39, rue de la Villeneuve, 56100 Lorient, ☎ 02 97 37 51 51).

Holidays on a theme

ARTISTIC AND HISTORICAL CENTRES

Breton towns designated by the CNMHS as "Villes d'Art et d'Histoire" A (Towns of Art and History) have been regrouped as a special unit in Brittany since 1984. Similarly, smaller towns of particular local character – "Petites Cités de Caractère" – have been administered as a regional association since 1977. These towns regularly hold medieval pageants, *son et lumière* shows, and traditional and modern festivals in their historic town centres. Guided tours accompanied by CNMHS-approved guides are also available *(see the Admission times and charges section)*. Tourists can obtain relevant literature from tourist offices, rest-places alongside main roads and motorways, or from the town hall of the town in question.

Eight Breton towns have been designated as "Villes d'Art et d'Histoire":

Auray (☎ 02 97 24 09 75) **Dinan** (☎ 02 96 39 75 40)
Fougères (☎ 02 99 94 12 20) **Quimper** (☎ 02 98 53 04 05)
Rennes (☎ 02 99 79 01 98) **St-Malo** (☎ 02 99 56 64 48)
Vannes (☎ 02 97 47 24 34) **Vitré** (☎ 02 99 75 04 46).

There are 19 "Petites Cités de Caractère": Bécherel, Châteaugiron, Châtelaudren, Combourg, Le Faou, Guerlesquin, Josselin, Jugon-les-Lacs, Lizio, Locronan, Malestroit, Moncontour, Pont-Croix, Pontrieux, Quintin, La Roche-Bernard, Rochefort-en-Terre, Roscoff and Tréguier.

For details on the above, contact the Associations régionales des Villes d'Art et d'Histoire et des Petites Cités de Caractère de Bretagne, 8, place du Maréchal-Juin, BP 297, 35005 Rennes Cedex, ☎ 02 99 30 38 01.

"Cités en fête" – This festival was set up in 1984 by ARCoDAM, with the blessing of the Conseil Régional de Bretagne, and brings high-quality performances of music and dance to a wide public, in some of the main centres of Brittany's architectural heritage. For details or a brochure, contact ARCoDAM, 1, rue du Prieuré, 35410 Châteaugiron, ☎ 02 99 37 34 58.

CRUISING ON INLAND WATERWAYS

A 600km – 380 mile network of rivers and canals offers the opportunity of discovering inland Brittany by boat. The Channel and Atlantic coasts are linked by the Ille-et-Rance canal and the River Vilaine, passing through Dinan, Rennes and Redon. Leaving from Lorient, a pleasant cruise along the Blavet, the east stretch of the Nantes-Brest canal, and the River Erdre takes visitors through Josselin and Redon before arriving in Nantes.

From the Brest roadstead, the River Aulne and the west stretch of the Nantes-Brest canal lead to Châteaulin and Carhaix-Plouguer.

The main companies handling river cruises are based at Blain, La Chapelle-aux-Filzméens, Châteauneuf-du-Faou, Dinan, Josselin, Messac, Redon, Rohan and Sucé-sur-Erdre.
Helpful publications include the brochures *Tourisme fluvial en Bretagne* (Comité de Promotion Touristique des Canaux Bretons et des Voies Navigables de l'Ouest Bretagne-Pays de la Loire, Place du Parlement, 35600 Redon, ☎ 02 99 71 06 04) and *Formules Fluvial* (Bretagne Nouvelle Vague, Centre commercial Maine-Montparnasse, 17, rue de l'Arrivée, 75015 Paris, ☎ 01 42 79 07 07).
Grafocarte (125, rue Jean-Jacques Rousseau, 92132 Issy-les-Moulineaux, ☎ 01 41 09 19 00) publish nautical maps and guides, also available in English (of particular interest: no 12, which covers from St-Malo to the Arzal dam and from Lorient to Nantes).

HISTORICAL ROUTES

Having been set up in 1975 by the organisations Demeure Historique and Caisse Nationale des Monuments Historiques et des Sites (CNMHS), there are now over 80 historical routes covering France. They explore architectural, archaeological, botanical or geological heritage within a historical context: the Dukes of Brittany, the Painters of Cornouaille etc. These routes are signposted.
Five historical routes run through Brittany, on: Châteaubriand, the regions of Léon and Tréguier, the Painters of Cornouaille, the Dukes of Brittany and the Breton Marches. Most tourist information centres have leaflets on these routes, otherwise contact the Centre d'information de la CNMHS, Hôtel de Sully, 62, rue St-Antoine, 75004 Paris, ☎ 01 44 61 21 50.

M. Guillard/SCOPE

LIGHTHOUSES AND BEACONS

The Breton coast has the highest concentration of lighthouses and beacons on the whole of the coast of France. A route running along the north Finistère coast leads past some of the most important lighthouses in Europe. For details contact GIT de la région brestoise, BP 24, 29266 Brest Cedex, ☎ 02 98 44 17 45.

SET SAIL ON A HISTORICAL SHIP

The last sailing ships (coastal or fishing vessels) were taken out of active service towards the end of the 1960s. Since 1972 the **Fédération Régionale pour la Culture Maritime** (FRCM, 5, quai du Port-Rhu, BP 234, 29172 Douarnenez Cedex, ☎ 02 98 92 36 94) has undertaken the recovery and restoration of these elegant witnesses to Brittany's maritime past. Numerous magnificent old craft have been restored, refitted or simply built according to original plans and can now be hired for anything from a couple of hours up to a long weekend for a trip along the coast or out to sea, or even a brief induction course on old-style sailing techniques.
See the illustrations in the Introduction *(p 21)*. Officially recognised (NUC) associations in charge of hiring out these old ships include:
Gouélia, Breton traditional ships company, 5, rue René-Madec, 29104 Quimper Cedex, ☎ 02 98 95 32 33.

La Recouvrance	(25m - 82ft schooner, Brest)
Le Corentin	(18m - 59ft lugger, Quimper)
Le Dalh Mad	(13.5m - 77ft sloop, Landerneau)
La Belle-Angèle	(14.5m - 47ft coasting lugger, Pont-Aven)

L'Étoile-Marine SARL, 8, avenue Louis-Martin, 35400 St-Malo, ☎ 02 99 40 48 72.

L'Étoile-Molène	(21m - 69ft Dundee tunny boat, St-Malo)
Popoff	(15m - 49ft fore-and-aft ketch, St-Malo)

Association Côtre Corsaire de St-Malo, Tour Ouest, Grande Porte, BP 165, 35400 St-Malo, ☎ 02 99 40 53 10.

Le Renard	(19m - 62ft cutter, St-Malo)

"Une chaloupe pour Dahouët", quai des Terre-Neuvas, 22370 Pléneuf-Val-André, ☎ 02 96 63 10 99.

La Pauline (9m - 30ft pilot lugger, Dahouët)

Association Le Lougre de l'Odet, Parc de Locmaria, BP 1155, 29101 Quimper Cedex, ☎ 02 98 95 59 59.

Corentin (18m - 59ft lugger, Quimper)

THALASSOTHERAPY CENTRES

A seaside setting (with the attendant healthy sea air, seaweed etc.) is well known as an excellent natural restorative for those suffering from fatigue or stress. Thalassotherapy (medical sea treatment, from the Greek *thalassa*, or sea) involves various techniques which maximise the beneficial effects of a seaside climate: algo-therapy (seaweed and sea mud baths), hydrotherapy (spray-jets, sea-water showers or baths), kinesitherapy (massages, gymnastics), saunas, seawater spray treatments etc. The average length of a treatment (recognised as being effective) at one of these thalassotherapy centres is around 7-10 days.

Brittany's major thalassotherapy centres are at La Baule, Belle-Ile-en-Mer, Carnac, Le Crouesty, Dinard, Perros-Guirec, Quiberon, Roscoff and St-Malo. For information and bookings, contact "Formules Bretagne", 17, rue de l'Arrivée, Centre commercial Maine-Montparnasse, 75015 Paris, ☎ 01 42 79 07 07.

Books and films

Brittany by K Spence (George Philip)

Megalithic Brittany: A Guide by Aubrey Burl (Thames and Hudson)

Oysters of Locmariaquer by E Clark (University of Chicago Press)

Pierre Deux's Brittany by L Dannenberg, P Le Vec and P Moulin (Crown)

The Celts by T D E Powell (Thames and Hudson, Ancient Peoples and Places series)

La Route des Peintres en Cornouaille (Groupement Touristique de Cornouaille) – available in English

Le Blé en Herbe (Ripening Seed) by Colette

La Bretagne by J Markale (Sun coll "Voir en France")

Le Recteur de l'Ile de Sein by H Queffélec (Presses de la Cité)

Les Chouans by H de Balzac (Livre de Poche)

Memoirs by F-R de Chateaubriand (trans R Baldick)

Pêcheur d'Islande (Iceland Fisherman) by P Loti (Livre de Poche)

SOME CYBER-RESSOURCES

For general information on France, and links to regional and other sites, the French Embassy is on the Web at **www.info.france-usa.org.**

For information on booking, ferries from England, train passes, and to order brochures: **www.fr.holidaystore.co.uk.**

A wealth of information on travel to Brittany, history, Celtic legends and local events can be found at: **www.bretagne.com,** which provides many links to other sites as well. Another good site with information in English is devoted to the Rhuys peninsula (south Brittany): **www.rhuys.com.**

Regional Nature Parks

Regional nature parks play a different role from national parks, in that they are populated areas which have been selected for development with a threefold aim: promotion of local economy (creation of cooperatives, fostering of local crafts etc.); protection of the natural and cultural heritage of the region (museums, architecture etc.); and education (introduction to the natural environment for visitors). Regional

PARC NATUREL RÉGIONAL D'ARMORIQUE

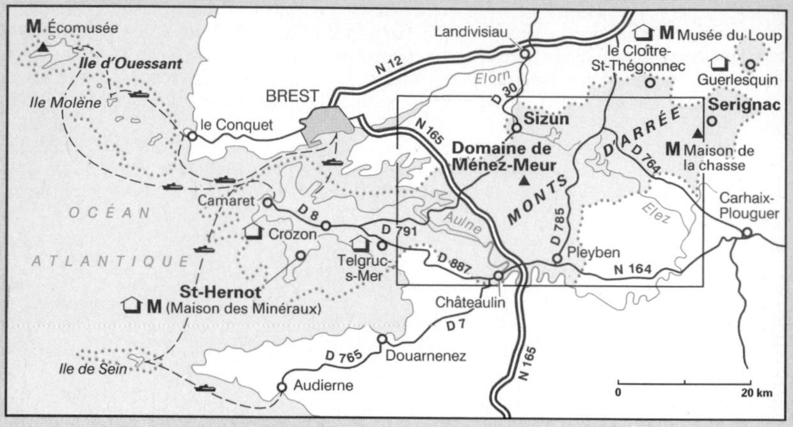

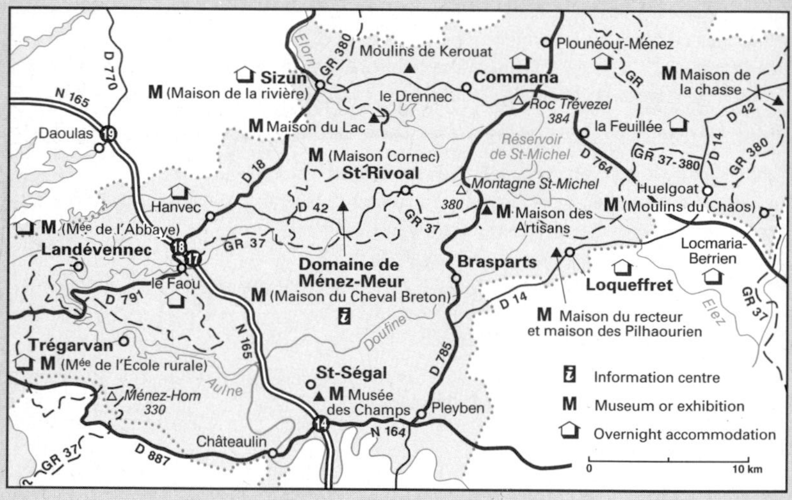

nature parks are administered by an official body (syndicate, association etc.) composed of local councillors, landowners and representatives of various local associations. A charter is set up in agreement with local residents to define the nature and extent of the park's projects.

Parc naturel régional d'Armorique – This park was founded in September 1969 and encompasses 39 communes, covering an area of 172 000ha - 425 021 acres (of which roughly two-thirds is on land and one-third is at sea). The park comprises three zones: the Monts d'Arrée (east and west sections); the Aulne estuary; and the capes and islands (Roscanvel and Camaret peninsulas and Ushant archipelago). The aims of the park are to preserve local countryside, flora and fauna, to improve the economy by fostering local industry (cooperatives, crafts), and to safeguard the traditional lifestyle of the region. Major innovations so far include the setting up of an information centre at Ménez-Meur (29460 Hanvec, ☎ 02 98 21 90 69), the opening of museums in traditionaml houses (in Brasparts, Kérouat, St-Rivoal, Trégarvan and on Ushant), the waymarking of footpaths and the founding of open-air museums (écomusées) on Ushant and in the Monts d'Arrée (which include exhibitions on the Breton horse and minerals).

Parc naturel régional de Brière – *See La GRANDE BRIÈRE.*

Calendar of events

PARDONS

Palm Sunday

Callac.......................... Stations of the Cross

Second Sunday in May

Quintin........................ Pardon of Notre-Dame-de-Délivrance, ☎ 02 96 74 92 17

Ascension Day

St-Herbot..................... Pardon of St-Herbot

Third Sunday in May

Tréguier....................... Pardon of St-Yves, ☎ 02 96 92 30 51

Bubry 230 fold 35 *(1)*. Pardon of St-Yves

Whit Saturday and Sunday

Moncontour................. Pardon of St-Mathurin, ☎ 02 96 73 41 54

St-Gildas Island........... Blessing of the horses

Whit Monday

Carantec...................... Pardon of Notre-Dame-de-Callot

Sunday after Whit Sunday

Rumengol Le Faou...... Pardon of the Trinity

Trinity Sunday and eve

Notre-Dame-du-Crann Chapel Pardon, ☎ 02 98 93 84 78

Rumengol..................... Pardon, ☎ 02 98 81 93 45

Saturday evening and Sunday before the feast of St John the Baptist (24 June)

St-Tugen...................... Pardon, ☎ 02 98 74 80 28

Last Sunday in June

St-Jean-du-Doigt......... Pardon of St John the Baptist, ☎ 02 98 67 30 40

Plouguerneau............. Pardon of Sts Peter and Paul, ☎ 02 98 04 71 02

Le Faouët..................... Summer Pardon of St Barbara

First Sunday in July (and Friday and Saturday before this)

Guingamp.................... Pardon of Notre-Dame-de-Bon-Secours, ☎ 02 96 43 73 59

Second Sunday in July

Locronan...................... Petite Troménie (the Grande Troménie takes place every 6 years; the next one will be on the second and third Sundays in July 2001), ☎ 02 98 91 70 14

Third Sunday in July

Carantec...................... St-Carantec Pardon, ☎ 02 98 67 02 72

25 and 26 July (Feast of St Anne)

Ste-Anne-d'Auray........ Grand Pardon of St Anne, ☎ 02 97 57 68 80

26 July (Feast of St Anne) and following Sunday

Fouesnant.................... Grand and Petit Pardons of St Anne, ☎ 02 98 56 00 91

Fourth weekend in July

Le Vieux Marché 230 fold 6 *(1)*......... Islamic-Christian pilgrimage to the Chapelle des Sept-Saints, ☎ 02 96 38 91 73

Fourth Sunday in July

Le Releg....................... Pardon of St Anne – Breton mass (11am) – Festival of Celtic Music (3.30pm)

Bubry 230 fold 35 *(1)*. Pardon of Ste-Hélène, ☎ 02 97 51 70 38

First Sunday in August

Persquen 230 fold 21 *(1)* Pardon of Notre-Dame-de-Pénéty

15 August (Feast of the Assumption) and eve

Perros-Guirec.............. Pardon of Notre-Dame-de-Clarté

Quelven........................ Pardon of Notre-Dame

Rumengol..................... Pardon of Notre-Dame-de-Rumengol

Porcaro........................ Pardon of the "Madone des Motards" (Our Lady of Bikers)

Bécherel....................... Haute-Bretagne Troménie

Pont-Croix................... Pardon of Notre-Dame-de-Roscudon

Sunday after 15 August

Rochefort-en-Terre ...... Pardon of Notre-Dame-de-la-Tronchaye
Carantec .... Pardon of Notre-Dame-de-Callot, ☎ 02 98 67 07 88
Ploërdut .... Pardon of Notre-Dame-de-Crénenan
Le Releg .... Pardon of Notre-Dame-du-Releg

Last Sunday in August (and eve, and following Tuesday)

Ste-Anne-la-Palud .... Grand Pardon, ☎ 02 98 92 50 17
Le Faouët .... Pardon of St-Fiacre

First Sunday in September

Camaret .... Pardon of Notre-Dame-de-Rocamadour – Blessing of the sea
Le Folgoët .... Grand Pardon of Notre-Dame, ☎ 02 98 83 00 67
Lamballe .... Pardon of Notre-Dame-de-la-Grande-Puissance
Pouldreuzic .... Pardon of Notre-Dame-de-Penhors, ☎ 02 98 54 42 44

Second Sunday in September

Carnac .... Pardon of St-Cornély, ☎ 02 97 52 08 08

8 September

Josselin .... Pardon of Notre-Dame-du-Roncier, ☎ 02 97 22 20 18

Third Sunday in September

Notre-Dame-de-Tronoën Pardon, ☎ 02 98 87 02 80
Pontivy .... Pardon of Notre-Dame-de-la-Joie

Last Sunday in September

Hennebont .... Pardon of Notre-Dame-du-Vœu, ☎ 02 97 36 24 52
Plouguerneau .... Pardon of St-Michel

Sunday nearest 29 September

Mont-St-Michel .... Feast of the Archangel St Michael
Gourin .... Bellringers' Pardon

First Sunday in December

Le Faouët .... Winter Pardon of St Barbara

31 December

Carantec .... Pardon of Notre-Dame-de-Callot, ☎ 02 98 67 07 88

FESTIVALS

End of April

Vannes .... Café-Théâtre Festival, ☎ 02 97 47 24 34

Refreshment Sunday (mid-Lent) and previous Thursday

Nantes .... Carnival, ☎ 02 40 35 75 49

May

Mont-St-Michel .... St-Michel Spring Folklore Festival
St-Malo .... "Étonnants Voyageurs" (Astonishing Explorers), ☎ 02 99 30 07 47

Second weekend in July

Lamballe .... Festival of the Golden Gorse *(Ajoncs d'Or)*
Nantes .... International Summer Festival (music, song and dance), ☎ 02 40 08 01 00
Pont-l'Abbé .... Embroidery Festival, ☎ 02 98 87 02 96
Quimperlé .... "Musiques Mosaïques" Festival, ☎ 02 98 96 04 32
Vannes .... History Festival, ☎ 02 97 47 24 34
Rennes .... "Les tombées de la nuit" (Breton art festival), ☎ 02 99 30 38 01

Third Sunday in July

Paimpol .... Festival of Newfoundland and Iceland, ☎ 02 96 20 83 16

Week before the fourth Sunday in July

Quimper .... Cornouaille Festival, ☎ 02 98 55 53 53
Vannes .... Jazz Festival, ☎ 02 97 01 81 00

Fourth Sunday in July

Guer-Coëtquidan .... "Triomphe des Écoles de St-Cyr-Coëtquidan"

Early August

Erquy	Festival of the Sea, ☎ 02 96 72 30 12
Pont-Aven	Gorse Festival, ☎ 02 98 06 04 70
St-Malo	Jazz Festival

First fortnight of August (including 15 August)

Dinard	International horse jumping event ☎ 02 99 46 19 35
Guingamp	Festivals of Breton Dance and of St-Loup, ☎ 02 96 43 73 89
Lorient	Interceltic Festival, ☎ 02 97 21 24 29
Plomodiern 230 fold 18 *(1)*	Ménez-Hom Folklore Festival, ☎ 02 98 81 57 94
Ile de Fédrun	Festival of the Brière Region – Boat Race
Guérand	Celtic Festival ☎ 02 40 15 60 40
St-Lyphard-en-Brière	Peat Festival
Vannes	Grand Festival of Arvor, ☎ 02 97 47 24 34

Mid to late August

Carnac	Menhir Festival
Concarneau	Festival of the Blue Nets, ☎ 02 98 97 01 44
Lizio	Craft Festival
Moncontour	Medieval Festival
Perros-Guirec	Hydrangea Festival

September

Dinan	Festival of the Ramparts (every two years, even years), ☎ 02 96 85 94 94
Dol-de-Bretagne	Buckwheat Festival
Dinard	British film festival ☎ 02 99 46 94 12

October

St-Malo	Quai des Bulles (Comic-Strip Festival), ☎ 02 99 40 42 50
Redon	"La Teillouse" chestnut Festival. ☎ 02 99 71 06 04.

MAIN MARKETS

Market Day is an important event in the life of local communities, and provides visitors also with an opportunity to meet people, exchange news and views, and find out a bit about the region and local produce from those who live and work there.

MONDAY	Auray, Châtelaudren, Combourg, Concarneau, Guerlesquin, Moncontour, Pontivy, Pontrieux, Redon, Vitré
TUESDAY	Le Croisic, Landerneau, Quintin, St-Malo, St-Pol-de-Léon
WEDNESDAY	Châteaubriant, Guérande, Nantes, Quimper, Roscoff, Tréguier, Vannes
THURSDAY	Châteaugiron, Le Croisic, Dinan, Hennebont, Lannion, Malestroit, Pont-Croix, La Roche-Bernard
FRIDAY	Concarneau, Guingamp, Jugon-les-Lacs, Landerneau, Quimperlé, St-Malo
SATURDAY	Bécherel, Le Croisic, Dol-de-Bretagne, Fougères, Guérande, Guingamp, Josselin, Landerneau, Morlaix, Nantes, Port-Louis, Quimper, Redon, Rennes, Vannes, Vitré

For markets on slightly more unusual themes, try: the **Book Market** at **Bécherel** on the first Sunday of every month; the **Flea Market** at **Dinan** every Wednesday during July and August, otherwise the first Wednesday of the month; the largest **Cattle Market** in the west of France at **Fougères** opens every Friday morning at 5.30am.

FRESH FISH AUCTIONS

The fresh fish auctions which take place on the return of the fishing fleets are certainly lively and colourful affairs. They are generally held every day of the week half an hour after the boats come in, and they last for about two hours. The major ones are to be found at Audierne, Concarneau, Douarnenez, Erquy, Le Guilvinec, Loctudy and Lorient.

(1) Map references are given here for places not described in the main text of the guide

Admission times and charges

As admission times and charges are liable to alteration, the information below is given for guidance only. In cases where it has not been possible to obtain up-to-date information, the admission times and charges from the previous edition of the guide have been given in italics.

The information applies to individual adults. Special conditions for groups are common but arrangements should be made in advance. In some cases there is no charge for admission on certain days, eg Wednesdays, Sundays or public holidays.

Churches are usually closed from noon to 2pm; they should not be visited during services, other than to worship. Admission times are indicated if the interior is of special interest. Visitors to chapels are usually accompanied by the key-holder; a donation is welcome.

Most tours are conducted by French-speaking guides but in some cases the term "guided tours" may cover group visiting with recorded commentaries. Some of the larger and more frequented sights may offer guided tours in other languages. The symbol **A** *indicates that tours are given by lecturers from the Historic Monuments Association (Caisse Nationale des Monuments Historiques et Sites). Enquire at the ticket office or book stall. Other aids for foreign visitors are notes, pamphlets or audio guides.*

Enquire at the tourist office, **i**, *for local religious holidays, market days etc.*

Every sight for which there are times and charges is indicated by the symbol ⓥ in the alphabetical section of the guide. The entries are listed in the order under which they are to be found in the alphabetical section of the guide.

Sights which have comprehensive facilities for the disabled are indicated by the symbol ♿ below.

A

ABERS

Gouesnou: Church – To visit the church, apply to the Town hall. ☎ 02 98 07 86 90.

Chapelle St-Jaoua – To visit the chapel, apply to the farmhouse located right behind the chapel.

St-Jean-Balanant: Chapel – To visit the chapel, apply to the house located right behind the chapel.

Ruines d'Iliz Koz – Open 15 Jun to 15 September 2.30pm to 6pm; the rest of the year, Sundays 2.30pm to 5pm. 10F. ☎ 02 98 04 71 84.

Phare de l'Île Vierge – *Open 1 July to 31 August 11am to noon and 3pm to 6pm. Apply to the caretaker. No admission charge.* ☎ 02 98 04 78 01.

Château de Kergroadès – *Guided tours (30 min) 1 July to 31 August 10am to 12.30pm and 2pm to 6pm. The rest of the year by appointment only. 20F. ☎ 02 98 84 21 73.*

ANTRAIN

Excursion

Château de Bonne-Fontaine – *Open Easter to All Saints' Day Saturdays, Sundays and public holidays 2pm to 6pm (open daily during school holidays). 30F (display of automata + park). ☎ 02 99 98 31 13.*

Monts d'ARRÉE

St-Herbot: Church – Open daily Easter to October; the rest of the year open Sundays only. Apply to the school (école) at St-Herbot.

Loqueffret: Church – Open daily July and August 10am to noon and 2pm to 6pm. If closed, apply to the Town hall.

Lanndern: Church – *Guided tours July and August. Apply to the Tourist Information Office in Pleyben.*

Chapelle St-Sébastien – Access to the chapel interior is temporarily closed to the public owing to restoration work. Apply to the presbytery at Saint-Ségal. ☎ 02 98 73 19 26.

Domaine de Menez-Meur – Open daily 1 June to 30 September 10am to 7pm; during May Sunday to Friday 1.30pm to 5.30pm; the rest of the year open Wednesdays, Sundays and holidays 10am to noon and 1pm to 6pm. Closed January. 20F. ☎ 02 98 21 90 69.

St-Rivoal: Maison Cornec – Open daily July and August 11am to 7pm; in June and September 2pm to 6pm. 15F. ☎ 02 98 81 40 99.

Maison des Artisans (North of Brasparts) – *Open 1 July to 31 August 10am to 7pm; 7 January to 31 March Saturdays and Sundays 10am to 12.30pm and 2pm to 6.30pm; the rest of the year open daily at the same times. Closed Wednesdays (except during school holidays), and 1 January, I May and at Christmas. No admission charge.* ☎ 02 98 81 41 13.

Brennilis: Church – *To visit, apply to the presbytery.*

AUDIERNE

ℹ BP 46, 29770 – ☎ 02 98 70 12 20

Grands Viviers – *Open Monday to Friday, 9am to noon and 3pm to 5pm in the tourist season. The rest of the year, Monday to Friday, 3pm-5pm. Free admission.* ☎ *02 98 70 10 04.*

La Chaumière – ♿ Guided tours (30 min) daily 20 March to 31 October 10am to 1pm and 2pm to 7pm. Closed the rest of the year. 15F. ☎ 02 98 70 13 20.

AURAY

ℹ Place de la République, 56400 – ☎ 02 97 24 09 75

Guided Tour of the City A – *Walking tour (90 min) starts at 10am, Tuesday to Saturday in July and August. 20F. Apply to the Tourist Information Office.*

Golette St-Sauveur – Open daily Easter to September, 10am to 7pm. Guided tours (30 min) also available at the same dates and times. Late closing July and August, weather permitting. 20F. ☎ 02 97 56 63 38.

Boat trip: Auray River – *During the summer season, several companies organise boat trips along the Auray River. Apply to the Tourist Information Office.*

Chartreuse d'Auray – Guided tours (45 min) 2pm to 5pm. Closed Tuesdays, 15 to 31 May and 26 August to 8 September. No admission charge. ☎ 02 97 24 27 02.

St-Degan: Écomusée – Guided tours (1 1/4 hours) 1 July to 31 August 10am to 6pm; 15 April to 30 June and 1 September to 15 October 4pm to 6pm (last admissions 5pm); the rest of the year for groups only by appointment. Closed 1 January, 1 November and at Christmas. 25F. ☎ 02 97 57 66 00.

Ste-Avoye: Chapel – Guided tours daily except Monday mornings 10am to noon and 3pm to 6pm ☎ 02 97 24 02 94.

B

Cairn de BARNENEZ

Tumulus – Free access 1 April to 30 September 10am to 12.30pm (1pm in July and August) and 2pm to 6.30pm (5pm 1 October to 31 March). Guided tours (45 min) also available at the same dates and times. Closed 1 January, 1 May, 1 and 11 November, and 25 December. 25F. ☎ 02 98 67 24 73.

Île de BATZ

Bicycles can be hired all year round. ☎ 02 98 61 77 65.

Boat trips – You can take the Roscoff/Île de Batz crossing from 8am to 8pm once an hour daily from late June to mid-September; 8 departures daily the rest of the year. Tour the island or else visit the Baie de Morlaix: "Compagnie Finistérienne de Transports Maritimes", BP 10, Le Rhû, 29253 Île de Batz. ☎ 02 98 61 79 66 or "Armain excursions" ☎ 02 98 61 77 75.

BATZ-SUR-MER

Église Saint-Guénolé: Ascent to the bell tower – Daily 1 May to 30 September 9am to 1pm and 2pm to 6pm. The rest of the year, the key can be obtained from the address mentioned on the door. 7F. ☎ 02 40 23 99 88.

Musée des Marais salants – ♿ Open daily 1 June to 30 September and during school holidays 10am to noon and 3pm to 7pm; the rest of the year open Saturdays and Sundays only 3pm to 7pm. Closed 1 May. 20F. ☎ 02 40 23 82 79.

BAUD

Vénus de Quinipily – Open 8am to 7pm. 15F. 10F. ☎ 02 97 51 14 93.

Excursions

Chapelle St-Adrien – If the chapel is closed, apply to M. Jean Maho. ☎ 02 97 27 10 50.

Poul Fetan, a typical Breton village of the past – Open 6 June to 20 September 10am to 7pm; 1 April to 6 June and 22 September to 30 October 2pm to 6pm (2pm to 7pm Saturdays and Sundays); guided tours (2 hours) available; the rest of the year guided tours during school holidays, Saturdays and Sundays 2pm to 6pm. Celtic music Sunday afternoon in July and August; old-fashioned fair 15 August, cider fair 4th Sunday in September. Regional specialities (reservations required) in the village inn. Closed 1 January and 25 December. 25F (June to September); 20F the rest of the year. ☎ 02 97 39 72 82.

Château de BEAUMANOIR

♿ *Open daily 29 June to 15 September 2pm to 7pm. 30F. ☎ 02 96 74 90 82.*

Abbaye de BEAUPORT

Open 15 June to 15 September 10am to 1pm and 2pm to 7pm. Guided tours (30 min) also available at the same dates and times. The rest of the year open 10am to noon and 2pm to 5pm. Closed 1 January and Christmas. 25F. ☎ 02 96 20 97 69.

BÉCHEREL

Château de Caradeuc: Park – Open 1 April to 15 September 10am to 7pm; 16 September to 31 October 2pm to 6pm; the rest of the year open Saturdays and Sundays 2pm to 6pm. 15F. ☎ 02 99 66 77 76.

Excursion

Château de Hac – Guided tours (40 min) daily 1 July to 31 August 2pm to 7pm (except Saturdays); in June and September Sundays 2pm to 7pm. 20F. ☎ 02 96 83 43 06.

BEG-MEIL

ℹ ☎ 02 98 94 97 47

Boat trips – *Apply to the Tourist Information Office in Beg-Meil or Fouesnant.*

BELLE-ÎLE

ℹ Quai Bonnelle, Le Palais, 56360 – ☎ 02 97 31 81 93

From Le Palais it is possible to hire cars (without a driver), bicycles, tandems and motorbikes.

Citadelle Vauban – Open 1 July to 31 August 9am to 7pm; 1 April to 30 June and 1 September to 31 October 9.30am to 6pm; the rest of the year open 9.30am to noon and 2pm to 5pm. 32F. ☎ 02 97 31 84 17.

Grand Phare – *Guided tours (20 min) 1 July to 15 September 10.30am to noon and 2pm to 5pm. Access is limited to the tower. No admission charge. ☎ 02 97 31 82 08.*

J. Labbé/PIX

Le Palais.

BÉNODET

🛈 51, avenue de la Plage, 29950 – ☎ 02 98 57 00 14

Excursions

Botforn-en-Combrit: Musée de la Musique mécanique – ♿ Guided tours (1 hour) 1 May to 30 September 2pm to 7pm; the rest of the year Sundays and public holidays only 2pm to 7pm. Closed 25 December. 20F. ☎ 02 98 56 36 03.

Boat trips: Up the Odet River – April to September, up to 10 daily trips are organised by the "Vedettes de l'Odet'; luncheon-cruises daily except Monday. ☎ 02 98 57 00 58.

BERVEN

Church – Open daily July and August from 10.30am to 12.30pm and 2.30pm to 6pm (Sundays 2pm to 6.30pm). ☎ 02 98 69 98 40.

Ferme-Musée du Léon – Open daily 1 May to 30 September 10am to noon and 2pm to 7pm; the rest of the year weekends only at the same times. 25F. ☎ 02 98 29 53 07.

BINIC

Museum – Open 15 April to 15 September 2.30pm to 6pm. Closed Tuesdays. 18F. ☎ 02 96 73 69 54.

Excursions

Trégomeur: Jardin zoologique de Bretagne – Open 1 June to 31 August 10am (11am Saturdays and Sundays) to 6pm; in April, May and September 2pm to 6pm; February, March, October and November Saturdays and Sundays 2pm to 5.30pm (weekdays also during school holidays). 45F; children 30F. ☎ 02 96 79 01 07.

Chapelle Notre-Dame-de-la-Cour – Guided tours 6 July to 28 August 2.30pm to 6pm; open the rest of the year without tours. ☎ 02 96 71 98 20 or 02 96 71 93 93.

BLAIN

Musée des Arts et Traditions populaires – Open all year round 2pm to 6pm. Guided tours (1 hour) all year round 2pm to 6pm. Closed Mondays and public holidays. 20F. ☎ 02 40 79 98 51.

Château de la Groulais – Open 1 April to 30 November 10am to noon and 2.30pm to 6.30pm; daily except Mondays. Guided tours (1 1/4 hours) also available at the same dates and times. 20F. ☎ 02 40 79 07 81.

Forêt du Gâvre

Le Gâvre: Maison Benoist – Open daily 11 May to 15 November, 2.30pm to 6.30pm; 11 April to 10 May and 1 to 11 November Saturdays, Sundays and holidays at the same hours. 15F. ☎ 02 40 51 20 31.

Château de la BOURBANSAIS

Parc zoologique et jardin – ♿ Open daily 15 April to 30 September 10am to 7pm; the rest of the year open 2pm to 6pm. 60F (garden, zoo and château), 50F (garden and zoo), 50F (guided tour of château); children 30F. ☎ 02 99 69 40 07.

Château interior – Guided tours (45 min) 1 May to 15 September at 11am, then every hour from 2pm to 6pm; in April, May and late September at 11.15am, 3pm, 4pm and 5pm; Sundays and holiday from 1 October to late March at 3pm and 4pm. 50F (château only), 60F (garden, zoo and château) children 25F. ☎ 02 99 69 40 07.

Île de BRÉHAT

🛈 22870 – ☎ 02 96 20 04 15

Tour – Bicycles can be hired in Port-Clos.

Boat trips – There are regular ferry services all year round leaving from the Pointe de l'Arcouest. It is also possible to tour the island by boat (6 or 7 departures daily from-April to October). There are day excursions leaving from Binic, St Quay-Portrieux and Erquy in July and August. Estuaire de Trieux: 4 hours. For further information apply to "Les Vedettes de l'Île de Bréhat". ☎ 02 96 55 73 47 or 02 96 55 86 99.

BREST

🛈 Place de la Liberté, 29200 – ☎ 02 98 44 24 96

Guided Tour of the City – *In the summer months, various programmes offered. Apply to the Tourist Information Office.*

Musée de la Marine – Open 9.15am to noon and 2pm to 6pm. Closed Tuesdays. 29F. ☎ 02 98 22 12 39.

Tour of the Dockyard – Guided tours (90 min) on foot are open to French nationals only. 15 June to 15 September daily 9am to 11am and 2pm to 4pm. Report to the Police Station (Poste de Gendarmerie) at the Porte de la Grande Rivière (on Route de la Corniche). For further information apply to the Service de Relations Publiques Amirauté, BP 46, 29240 Brest Naval. No admission charge (donations are welcome for the volunteer guides). ☎ 02 98 22 06 12.

Musée des Beaux-Arts – Open 10am to 11.45am and 2pm to 6pm. Closed Sunday mornings, Tuesdays and public holidays. 25F. ☎ 02 98 44 66 27.

Tour Tanguy – Open daily early June to late September 10am to noon and 2pm to 7pm; October to late May open Wednesdays and Thursdays 2pm to 5pm, Saturdays and Sundays 2pm to 6pm. Closed 1 January, 1 May and 25 December. No admission charge. ☎ 02 98 00 88 60.

Océanopolis – ♿ Open daily all year round 9.30am to 7pm (6pm weekdays 1 October to 14 April). Closed Monday mornings (except during short school holidays). 50F; children 30F ☎ 02 98 34 40 40.

Conservatoire botanique national de Brest – Open in spring and summer 9am to 8pm (the exhibition pavilion is open 2pm-5pm from Sunday to Thursday); in fall and winter open 9am to 6pm (the exhibition pavilion is open 2pm-5pm Wednesday and Sunday). Guided tours of the greenhouses Sunday to Thursday from 1 July to 15 September from 2pm to 5pm; the rest of the year every Sunday at 4.30pm. No admission charge for the garden and information centre; 20F for the greenhouses and guided tour. ☎ 02 98 41 88 95.

Boat trips – *Tours are organised to the naval port and the harbour (1 hour) April to September 5 times a day. For the Presqu'île de Crozon (40 min), there are 3 return trips a day mid-March to mid-October. One may also travel upstream and downstream the rivers Aulne and Elorn, depending on the tides. Apply to the "Compagnie des Vedettes armoricaines", 1er bassin, Port de Commerce. ☎ 02 98 44 44 04.*

Brest roadstead – Compagnie maritime Azénor: military port (90 min); dining cruise (lunch or dinner – 3 hours), reservation required; Brest-Crozon on a speed boat. ☎ 02 98 41 46 23

Tour of the Fortifications – From Brest, Azénor (see above); from Camaret, Vedettes de l'Iroise. 2 hours. Information at the Mémorial Montbarey, allée Bir-Hakeim, 29200. ☎ 02 98 05 39 46.

Excursions

Fort Montbarey – Mémorial du Finistère – Open Monday to Saturday 2pm to 6pm. Guided tours (1 1/2 hours) daily 2pm to 6pm. Closed Sundays and public holidays. 20F. ☎ 02 98 05 39 46.

Fort de Bertheaume – Open daily 1 July to 31 August 2pm to 8pm; opening hours may vary in June and September (inquire). 20F. Sound and light show from 9pm to midnight. 50F. ☎ 02 98 48 30 18 or 02 98 48 30 21.

C

CAMARET-SUR-MER

ℹ 5, quai Kléber, 29570 – ☎ 02 98 27 93 60

Boat trip – Trips to the Ouessant, Molène and Seine islands in July and August. May to October, trip on the "Belle Étoile", a lobster skiff. Information from the Tourist office ☎ 02 98 27 88 71.

CANCALE

ℹ 44, rue du Port, 35260 – ☎ 02 99 89 63 72

Église St-Méen: Ascent to the Tower – Open daily July and August 9am to 7.30pm; 9am to noon and 2pm to 5.30pm (6.30pm in September) the rest of the year. 5F. ☎ 02 99 89 63 72.

Musée des Bois sculptés – Open 1 July to 31 August daily except Monday morning from 2.30pm to 6.30pm; Saturday and Sunday in September from 2.30pm to 6.30pm. 8F40. ☎ 02 99 89 60 15.

La Ferme Marine Musée de l'Huître – ♿ There are guided tours (1 hour) from 16 June to 15 September at 11am, 3pm and 5pm; from 15 February to 15 June and 16 September to 1 November at 3pm. Closed weekends except for school holiday periods. 38F. ☎ 02 99 89 69 99.

Musée des Arts et Traditions populaires – ♿ Open 1 July to 31 August 10am to noon (except Monday mornings) and 2.30pm to 6.30pm; in June Fridays, Saturdays and Sundays 2.30pm to 6.30pm; in September Fridays, Saturdays and Sundays 2.30pm to 6.30pm. 15F. ☎ 02 99 89 71 26.

Maison de Jeanne Jugan – On request only. Apply to M. Charles Ray. No admission charge. ☎ 02 99 45 14 14.

CARANTEC

Musée maritime – Open 15 June to 30 August and 4 to 9 April 10am to noon and 3pm to 6pm. Closed Thursdays. 10F. ☎ 02 98 67 00 30.

Île Callot: Chapelle Notre-Dame – Visiting the chapel or attending religious services depends largely on the tides (times and tidal ranges). If the chapel is closed, apply to Mme L'Hour, who lives in the next-door house. ☎ 02 98 67 07 88.

CARHAIX-PLOUGUER

Maison du Sénéchal: Musée d'Ethnographie locale – Open daily 15 June to 15 September 9.30am to 12.30pm and 1.30pm to 7pm (Sundays 3pm to 6pm). The rest of the year open 9am to noon and 2pm to 6pm. (closed Saturdays and Sundays). Closed on public holidays from 15 September to 15 April. No admission charge. ☎ 02 98 93 04 42.

Locarn: Church – *To visit the church, apply to the Town hall (Mairie).*

CARNAC

ℹ Avenue des Druides, 56340 – ☎ 02 97 52 13 52

Alignements de Kermario – Guided tours organised in July and August, reservations required. 25F. ☎ 02 97 52 29 81.

Musée de Préhistoire J.-Miln-Z.-Le-Rouzic – ♿ Open 1 July to 31 August 10am to 6.30pm (weekends and public holidays 10am to noon and 2pm to 6.30pm); 2 January to 30 June and 1 September to 31 December 10am to noon and 2pm to 5pm (6pm in June and September). Closed Tuesdays (except July and August) and 1 January, 1 May and 25 December. 25F (30F in summer). ☎ 02 97 52 22 04.

Tumulus de Kercado – Open daily 9am to 7pm (5pm 1 November to 31 March). 4F. Information at the crêperie nearby.

CHÂTEAUBRIANT

Castle – Guided tour (1 hour) 15 June to 15 September 10am to noon and 2pm to 6pm. **Gardens**: open year round 9am to 6pm.. 15F. ☎ 02 40 28 20 90.

CHÂTEAULIN

Chapelle Notre-Dame – Open July and August weekdays only (guided tours available) 10am to noon and 4pm to 7pm.. If the chapel is closed, the key can be obtained from the next-door neighbour, the Town hall (Mairie) or the presbytery. ☎ 02 98 86 10 05.

Excursions

Musée de l'École rurale en Bretagne – Open July and August daily from 10.30am to 7pm; 1 April to 30 June and 1 t 30 September from 2pm to 6pm; the rest of the year weekdays only from 2pm to 5pm. Closed 1 January and 25 December. 22F. ☎ 02 98 26 04 72.

Chapelle St-Côme – *Guided tours daily July and August 11am to noon and 4pm to 6pm. The rest of the year apply to Mme Larour. ☎ 02 98 26 54 81 or to the presbytery. ☎ 02 98 26 51 29.*

COMBOURG

Castle and Park – Guided tours (45 min) 1 April to 30 October 2pm to 5.30pm (in summer a single tour at 10.45am). Closed Tuesdays (except July and August) and 1 December to 28 February. The park is open on the same dates, from 10am to noon and 2pm to 4.30pm. 28F (castle and park), 8F (park only). ☎ 02 99 73 22 95.

Excursions

Château de Lanrigan – Tours of the château exterior only Wednesdays, Thursdays and Fridays 1 July to 31 August 9am to noon and 2pm to 6pm. Closed public holidays. No admission charge.

Cobac Parc: Country Park – Open daily April to late September 11am to 6.30pm (July and August 10.30am to 7pm). 58F. ☎ 02 99 73 80 16.

CONCARNEAU

ℹ Quai d'Aiguillon, 29900 – ☎ 02 98 97 01 44

Fresh fish auction – Guided tours (2 1/2 hours). The fish are unloaded Sunday to Thursday nights between 11pm and 5.30am. Fresh fish auction Friday mornings 6am to 9am (depending on the day's catch). ☎ 02 98 97 01 44.

Musée de la Pêche – ♿ (except for the *Hémérica*) Open 4 July to 30 August 9.30am to 7.30pm; the rest of the year open 10am to noon and 2pm to 6pm (5pm from November to Easter). Closed Monday and last three weeks of January. 30F. ☎ 02 98 97 10 20.

Walk round the ramparts – Free access 15 June to 15 September 10am to 9.30pm; Easter to 14 June and 16 to 30 September 10am to 5pm or 6.30pm. Closed 1 October to 31 March. Access to the ramparts may be forbidden in adverse weather conditions or during the Blue Nets Festival. 5F. ☎ 02 98 97 01 44.

Marinarium – ♿ Open 1 July to 31 August, 10am to noon and 2pm to 6.30pm; 1 April to 30 June and 1 to 30 September at the same times, but closed on Saturdays and Sunday mornings. 20F. ☎ 02 98 97 06 59.

CORNICHE BRETONNE

Île Grande: Station ornithologique – Open daily 1 June to 3 September and during school holidays 10am to noon and 2.30pm to 6pm; the rest of the year open Saturdays, Sundays and public holidays only 2.30pm to 6pm. No admission charge. ☎ 02 96 91 91 40.

CORNOUAILLE

Réserve du Cap Sizun – Open daily July and August 10am to 6pm; 1 April to 30 June 10am to noon and 2pm to 6pm. Guided tours (2 hours) available at the same dates and times. Since reproduction takes place between 15 April and 15 July, one can expect to see very few birds in July and August. ☎ 02 98 70 13 53.

Maison de la Baie d'Audierne – ♿ Open daily July to August 11am to 7pm; the rest of the year 2pm to 6pm. Closed 1 January, 1 May and Christmas. No admission charge. ☎ 02 98 82 61 76.

Chapelle de Languivoa – *Open daily July and August 2.30pm to 6.30pm. ☎ 02 98 82 66 00.*

St-Guénolé: Musée préhistorique finistérien – ♿ Open 1 June to 30 September 10am to noon and 2pm to 6pm; the rest of the year by appointment. Closed Tuesdays. 15F. ☎ 02 98 58 60 35.

Phare d'Eckmühl – Guided tours (1 hour) 10am to noon and 2pm to 6pm. At certain times of the year, visits to the lighthouse may be interrupted on account of the weather or for maintenance needs. ☎ 02 98 58 61 17.

Penmarch: Église St-Nonna – Guided tours (SPREV) daily July and August 10am to noon and 2pm to 6pm. ☎ 02 98 58 60 30.

CÔTE D'ÉMERAUDE

Château d'Eau de Ploubalay – *Open 15 April to 15 October. Lift. 5F if you do not order a drink.* ☎ 02 96 27 31 17.

Le CROISIC

ℹ Place du 18 juin 1940, 44490 – ☎ 02 40 23 00 70

Sea trips – *For all information, apply to the local Tourist Information Office.*

Océarium – ♿ Open 1 June to 31 August 10am to 7pm; the rest of the year open 10am to noon and 2pm to 6pm. Closed the last three weeks in January. 46F; children 29F. ☎ 02 40 23 02 44.

Presqu'île de CROZON

St-Hernot: Mineral Collection – Open daily 1 July to 30 September 10.30am to 7pm; in June open 10.30am to 12.30pm and 2pm to 7pm; the rest of the year open 2pm to 5.30pm (except Saturdays). 20F. ☎ 02 98 27 19 73.

D

DAOULAS

Abbey: Cloisters – Open daily 8 May to 11 October 10am to 7pm. Guided tours (30 min) also available at the same dates and times. 40F (during exhibitions). The rest of the year, exclusive of temporary exhibits, open by appointment 9am to noon and 1.30pm to 6pm. Closed November, December, January. 38F to 48F, depending on temporary exhibits. ☎ 02 98 25 84 39.

DINAN

ℹ 6, rue de l'Horloge, 22100 – ☎ 02 96 39 75 40

Guided Tour of the City A – *In July and August, tours focusing on a particular theme are organised at 10am, general tours at 3pm. 30F. Apply to the Tourist Information Office.*

Tour de l'Horloge – *Open daily 1 June to 30 September 10am to 6pm; 1 April to 31 May open daily 2pm to 6pm. Closed the rest of the year. 15F. ☎ 02 96 39 22 43.*

Castle – Open daily 1 June to 15 October 10am to 7pm; 16 March to 31 May and 16 October to 15 November 10am to noon and 2pm to 6pm; 16 November to 31 December and 7 February to 15 March 1.30pm to 5.30pm. Closed Tuesdays (except in summer), January, the first week in February and 25 December. 25F. ☎ 02 96 39 45 20.

Ancien Couvent des Cordeliers – Open July and August 9am to 7pm. No admission charge. ☎ 02 96 39 00 27.

Maison d'Artiste de la Grande Vigne – *Open 1 June to 15 September 10am to 6pm; 1 to 31 May from 2pm to 6pm. 15F. ☎ (Dinan Town Hall) 02 96 87 90 80.*

Excursion

Corseul: Musée de la Société archéologique de Corseul – Open July and August 8.30am to 12.30pm and 2pm to 6pm; the rest of the year daily except Saturday afternoon and Sunday 8.30am to 12.30pm and 2pm to 5pm. Closed on public holidays. 6F (July and August). ☎ 02 99 27 90 18.

DINARD

ℹ 2, boulevard Fart, 35800 – ☎ 02 99 46 94 12

Promenade du Clair de Lune – *Floodlit musical performances June to September, 5 times a week.*

Musée du Site Balnéaire – Because of renovation works, the museum is closed in 1998. ☎ 02 99 46 81 05.

Aquarium et Musée de la Mer – Open 15 May to 15 September 10.30am to 12.30pm and 3.30pm (2.30pm Sundays) to 7.30pm. 15F. ☎ 02 99 46 13 90.

Boat trips – *Apply to the landing stage or the Tourist Information Office.*

Air trips – Apply to the airport at Dinard/Pleurtuit at ☎ 02 99 46 18 46; the "Aéroclub d'Emeraude" at ☎ 02 99 46 76 08; to "Aurigny-Air-Services" at ☎ 02 99 46 70 28; to "Assistance et Loisirs" at ☎ 02 99 46 96 86 or to the Tourist Information Office.

Mont DOL

Musée "Les Trésors du Mariage ancien" – Open daily 1 June to 11 November 10am to 7pm; 1 April to 31 May noon (10am Sundays) to 6pm. Closed 12 November to 31 March (except Sundays and public holidays), All Saints' Day, Christmas and New Year's Day. 25F. ☎ 02 99 48 26 31.

DOL-DE-BRETAGNE

Museum – *Open daily 1 May to late October 9.30am to 6pm; 1 March to 30 April 9.30am to noon and 2pm to 6pm; closed Tuesday (except in summer). Guided tours (40 min) also available at the same dates and times. Closed 1 November to 28 February. 20F. ☎ 02 99 48 09 38.*

Excursion

Baguer-Morvan: Musée de la Paysannerie – ♿ Open daily 1 May to 30 September 9.30am to 7pm. Guided tours (1 hour) also available at the same dates and times. 22F. ☎ 02 99 48 04 04.

DONGES

Church – *To visit the church, apply to 9, rue des Castors (Mondays) or the shop Droguerie-Déco, 33 avenue de la Paix (Tuesday to Saturday).*

DOUARNENEZ

ℹ 2, rue Docteur-Mevel, 29100 – ☎ 02 98 92 13 35

Port-Musée – Open 15 June to 30 September 10am to 7pm; the rest of the year, 10am to 12.30pm and 2pm to 6pm.. Closed Mondays from 1 October to 14 June, A January, 25 December and from 6 January to 5 February. 40F (30F off-season). ☎ 02 98 92 67 30.

Chapelle St-Michel – *If the chapel is closed, apply to the presbytery at 10, rue Ernest-Renan. ☎ 02 98 92 03 17.*

Boat rides – Leaving daily from the fishing port, there are trips to the Cap Sizun bird sanctuary (April to mid-July); fishing expeditions and guided tours of the Bay of Douarnenez (April to mid-September). ☎ 02 98 92 83 83.

Ploaré: Church – Open daily July and August 10am to noon. The rest of the year apply to the presbytery at 2 place Paul-Stéphan. ☎ 02 98 92 05 14.

Pouldavid: Church – *To visit the church, apply to the presbytery.* ☎ 02 98 92 09 41.

Excursions

Le Juch: Church – If the church is closed, apply to Mme Pennanéac'h. ☎ 02 98 74 73 21.

Guengat: Church – Open weekdays only 9.30am to 6.30pm. ☎ 02 98 91 06 59.

E

ENCLOS PAROISSIAUX

Moulins de Kerouat – Open 1 July to 31 August 11am to 7pm; 15 March to 31 May and 1 September to 31 October 2pm to 6pm. Closed Saturdays 15 March to 15 May and 1 September to 31 October. 20F. ☎ 02 98 68 87 76.

Pleyber-Christ: Church – Open late March to late September 8am to 6.30pm. Closed Sundays. ☎ 02 98 78 43 86.

F

Le FAOUËT

Excursion

Chapelle St-Nicolas – Access to the chapel, presently undergoing restoration, is difficult; the rood-screen is partly dismantled.

Le FOLGOËT

Museum – ♿ Open mid-June to mid-September, Monday to Friday 10am to 12.30pm and 2.30pm to 6.30pm. Open Sunday afternoons from mid-June to mid-September. 10F.

FOUGÈRES

ℹ 1, place Aristide-Briand, 35300 – ☎ 02 99 94 12 20

Guided Tour of the City A – *Daily (1 hour 30 min) in summer months at 3.30pm. 27F. Apply to the Service du Patrimoine, Hôtel de Ville, BP 111, 35301 Fougères Cedex. ☎ 02 99 94 88 67.*

Castle: Inner Tour – Open daily 15 June to 15 September 9am to 7pm (guided tours available, 45 min); 1 April to 14 June and 16 to 30 September open 9.30am to noon and 2pm to 6pm; the rest of the year open 10am to noon and 2pm to 5pm. Closed 25 December. 30F (without guide) ☎ 02 99 99 79 59.

Musée Emmanuel de la Villéon – Open daily 15 June to 15 September, 10am to noon and 2pm to 6pm; the rest of the year, Wednesday to Sunday 10am to noon and 2pm to 5pm. Closed January, 25 December. No admission charge. ☎ 02 99 99 19 98.

Cap FRÉHEL

Access to the Site – 1 June to 30 September: 5F for private cars (50 for coaches); no charge the rest of the year.

Lighthouse – *Guided tours (30 min) 1 July to 31 August 2pm to 6pm. No admission charge, donations welcome. ☎ 02 96 41 40 03.*

Boat trips – Departures from Dinard and St-Malo (2 hour 45 min). For all information apply to "Emeraude Lines" in St-Malo. ☎ 02 99 40 48 40 11 11.

G

Cairn de GAVRINIS

Crossing and Tour – Accessible only by boat from the port of Larmor-Baden (landing stage at Penn-Lannic), departure for a maximum of 20 people every half hour. 56F (trip there and back and visit). Guided tours (30 min) daily early June to late September 10am to noon and 2pm to 6pm; in April and May Saturdays, Sundays and public holidays 10am to noon and 2pm to 6pm (weekdays 2pm to 6pm only); in March and October daily 3pm to 6pm. It is advisable to book in advance, especially in summer. ☎ 02 97 57 19 38 or 02 97 42 63 44.

Îles de GLÉNAN

Boat services – There are boat services leaving from Quimper, Bénodet, Loctudy, Beg-Meil, Port-la-Forêt and Concarneau. For information apply to "Les Vedettes de l'Odet". ☎ 02 98 57 00 58.

Château de GOULAINE

Guided tours (1 hour) daily (except Tuesdays) mid-June to mid-September 2pm to 6pm; late March to mid-June and mid-September to early November weekends and public holidays 2pm to 6pm. 30F. ☎ 02 40 54 91 42.

La GRANDE BRIÈRE

Parc naturel régional de Brière: Maison de l'Éclusier – Guided tours (1 hour) 4 to 26 April and 31 May to 30 September 10.30am to 1pm and 2.30pm to 6.30pm; during the February and November school holidays open 2.30pm to 6.30pm; the rest of the year from 2.30pm to 6.30pm Sundays. 18F; combine ticket with parc animalier 22F. ☎ 02 40 66 85 01.

Parc animalier – Open 31 May to the end of the November school holiday, 9am to 6pm (7pm in July and August) 18F. Combine ticket with the Maison de l'éclusier 22F. ☎ 02 40 91 17 80.

Île de Fédrun: Maison de la Mariée – ♿ *Guided tours (30 min) 1 April to 30 September 10am to 12.30pm and 2pm to 7pm. Closed Mondays and from 1 October to 31 March. 10F. ☎ 02 40 91 65 91.*

Chaumière Briéronne – Open daily 31 May to 13 September 10.30am to 1pm and 2.30m to 6.30pm. Guided tours (1 hour) also available at the same dates and times. 12F. ☎ 02 40 66 85 01.

Château de Ranrouët – Open 1 July to 31 August 10am to 7pm; 1 April to 30 June and 1 to 30 September Tuesday to Friday 2.30pm to 6.30pm and Saturdays, Sundays and holidays 2pm to 7pm. 15F. ☎ 02 40 88 96 17.

St-Lyphard: Church's Belfry – Guided tours (20 min) 15 June to 15 September 10.30am to noon and 2.30pm to 6.30pm. 6F. ☎ 02 40 91 41 34.

Kerhinet: Brière interior (Musée du Chaume) – Guided tours (45 min) Easter school holidays 31 May to 30 September 10.30am to 1pm and 2.30pm to 6.30pm; during the February November school holidays 2.30pm to 6.30pm; Sundays in May, October, November and December from 2.30pm to 6.30pm. 12F. ☎ 02 40 66 85 01.

Île de GROIX

Tour – Bicycles, scooters and cars can be hired at Port-Tudy.

Access – Year round, daily departures from Lorient (4 to 8 a day depending on the time of year). Crossing takes 45 min. There and back, 105F. Contact Compagnie Morbihannaise et Nantaise de Navigation ☎ 02 97 64 77 64.

Écomusée de l'Île de Groix – Open 1 June to 30 September 9.30am to 12.30pm and 3pm to 7pm; 1 October to 31 May 10am to 12.30pm and 2pm to 5pm (except Mondays 1 October to 14 April). 24F. ☎ 02 97 86 53 08.

GUÉRANDE

ℹ Tour St-Michel, 44350 – ☎ 02 40 24 96 71

Guided Tour of the City – *July and August (1 hour), Tuesdays and Thursdays at 10.30am. 23F. Apply to the Tourist Information Office.*

Porte St-Michel ("Château-musée") – Open daily 1 April to 31 October 10am to 12.30pm (noon in October) and 2.30pm to 7pm (6pm in October). Closed Mondays, 1 November to 31 March. 20F. ☎ 02 40 42 96 52.

Presqu'île de GUÉRANDE

Saillé: Maison des Paludiers – ♿ Open daily early March to late August 10am to 12.30pm and 2pm to 6pm. 19F. Guided tours (2 hours) of a salt marsh daily July and August at 4.30pm (except in rainy weather). 40F. ☎ 02 40 62 21 96.

Trescalan: Church – Open to the public during religious services only.

Château de Careil – Guided tours (30 min) 1 June to 31 August 10.30am to noon and 2.30pm to 7pm. In summer guided tours by candlelight Wednesdays and Saturdays at 9.30pm. 25F. ☎ 02 40 60 22 99.

La GUERCHE-DE-BRETAGNE

Excursions

Lac des Mottes – Fishing is permitted on Thursdays, Sundays and public holidays.

Château de Monbouan – Guided tours (30 min) 15 July to 31 August 9am to noon and 2pm to 6pm. 20F. ☎ 02 99 49 01 51.

Lac de GUERLÉDAN

In July and August, canoes and kayaks can be hired from the Rond-Pont du Lac at Mur-de-Bretagne.

Boat trips – There are 8 to 10 trips (1 hour) a day mid-June to mid-October. April, May, early June, September and October, inquire. 40F; children 22F. Luncheon cruise (3 hour), reservations required. ☎ 02 96 28 52 64.

St-Aignan: Electrothèque – Open daily 1 July to 31 August 10am to noon and 2pm to 6pm; 1 May to 30 June Saturdays, Sundays and public holidays 10am to noon and 2pm to 6pm; 1 April to 30 October Saturdays, Sundays and public holidays 2pm to 6pm. 15F. ☎ 02 97 27 51 39.

Les Forges des Salles – Guided tours (1 hour) daily 1 July to 31 August 2pm to 6.30pm; Easter to 30 June and 1 September to 1 November weekends 2pm to 6pm. 25F. ☎ 02 96 24 90 12.

Abbaye de Bon-Repos – Open daily Easterto September; the rest of the year Monday to Friday only. ☎ 02 96 24 82 20.

GUINGAMP

Hôtel de Ville – The Town hall is open Mondays to Fridays 8.30am to noon and 1.30pm to 5.30pm (Saturdays 8.30am to noon). No admission charge. ☎ 02 96 40 64 40.

Excursions

Chapelle Notre-Dame-de-Restudo – To visit the chapel, apply to the parish house ☎ 02 96 43 80 83 or M. Hubert in Grâces. ☎ 02 96 43 83 01.

Chapelle d'Avaugour – Open 10am to 5pm. Apply to Mme Mallégol. ☎ 02 96 43 48 08.

H

HÉDÉ

Church – *To visit the church, apply to the presbytery.* ☎ *02 99 45 47 31.*

Excursions

Église des Iffs – *Open Easter to All Saints' Day Sundays and public holidays only 2pm to 6pm; the rest of the year visits by appointment only.* ☎ 02 99 45 83 85.

Château de Montmuran – Guided tours (30 min) daily Easter to All Saints' Day 2pm to 7pm; the rest of the year Saturdays, Sundays and public holidays only 2pm to 6pm. Closed 1 January and 25 December. 20F. ☎ 02 99 45 88 88.

HENNEBONT

ℹ 9, place Foch, 56700 – ☎ 02 97 36 24 52

Tours Broërec'h – Open daily 1 June to 30 September 10.30am to 12.30pm and 1.30pm to 6.30pm; guided tours (45 min) also available at the same dates and times. 15F. ☎ 02 97 36 29 18.

Haras – The stud farm is only open to visitors when all of the stallions are in (mid-July to mid-February). from 15 July to 31 August; guided tours available (45 min) at 10am, 11am, 2.15pm, 3.15pm and 4.15pm daily (except Sundays and holidays); In September, afternoon tours only; from 1 October to 14 February by appointment. No smoking, no dogs. 10F. ☎ 02 97 36 20 27.

Écomusée industriel de Inzinzac-Lochrist – Open daily 1 July to 31 August 10am to 12.30pm (except Saturdays and Sunday mornings) and 2pm to 6.30pm; the rest of the year closed Saturdays and at 6pm. Closed 1 January, 1 May, 14 July, 1 November and 25 December. 23F. ☎ 02 97 36 98 21.

Île de HŒDIC

Access to the Island: Boat Service – One to six daily trips (allow 1 hour) leaving from Quiberon early July to mid-September. The rest of the year no crossings on Wednesday. There and back, 105F. For information apply to the Compagnie Morbihannaise de Navigation. ☎ 02 97 50 06 90.

Château de la HUNAUDAYE

Castle Ruins – Tours with guides in period costume on Sundays in June and daily in July and August (except Saturdays and Sunday mornings) 11am to 12.30pm and 2.30pm to 6pm. 30F; children 15F. Guided tours July and August Saturdays 2.30pm to 6pm, Sundays and public holidays 11am to noon; in April, May and September Sundays and public holidays 2.30pm to 6pm. 15F. ☎ 02 96 34 82 10.

J

JOSSELIN

ℹ Place de la Congrégation, 56120 – ☎ 02 97 22 36 43

Castle – Guided tours (45 min) daily July and August 10am to 6pm; June and September 2pm to 6pm; April, May and October Wednesdays, Saturdays, Sundays, public holidays and during school holidays 2pm to 6pm. 30F or 56F (combined ticket for the Castle and the Musée de Poupées; children 41F. ☎ 02 97 22 36 45.

Musée de Poupées – Open 1 July to 31 August 10am to 6pm; 1 to 30 June and 1 to 30 September 2pm to 6pm; 1 April to 31 May and 1 to 31 October Wednesdays, Saturdays, Sundays, public holidays and during school holidays 2pm to 6pm. 29F; children 21F. Combined ticket for the Castle and the Musée de Poupées: 56F; children 41F. ☎ 02 97 22 36 45.

Basilique Notre-Dame-du-Roncier: Ascent to the Tower – Open 1 June to 30 August 9am to noon and 2pm to 6pm. Guided tours (30 min) available. No admission charge. ☎ 02 97 22 20 18.

Chapelle Ste-Croix – Open daily 10am to noon and 3pm to 6pm in summer months. If closed, inquire at the presbytery. ☎ 02 97 22 20 18.

JUGON-LES-LACS

Excursion

Ferme d'antan de St-Esprit-des-Bois en Plédéliac – Open 1 June to 31 August 10am to noon and 2pm to 7pm (except Monday mornings); 1 April to 30 June and in September Sundays only 2pm to 7pm. 20F. Guided tours (1 1/2 hours) also available at the same dates and times. Closed Sunday mornings and Whit Monday. ☎ 02 96 34 14 67.

K

Manoir de KÉRAZAN

Manor-house, park and gardens – Open 15 June to 31 August 10.30am to 7pm; Easter to 14 June and 1 to 30 September 2pm to 6pm. Closed Mondays. 33F. ☎ 02 98 87 40 40.

Domaine de KERGUÉHENNEC

Contemporary Art Centre, Park and Sculptures – ♿ Open 15 January to 15 December daily except Monday from 10am to 6pm. 25F. ☎ 02 97 60 44 44.

Château de KERJEAN

Open daily July and August 10am to 7pm; open daily (except Tuesday) June and September 10am to 6pm; open daily (except Tuesday) April May and October 2pm to 5pm (6pm May); the rest of the year Wednesdays and Sundays only 2pm to 5pm. 25F; winter rate 18F. ☎ 02 98 69 93 69.

KERMARIA

Chapelle de Kermaria-an-Iskuit – Open 10am to noon and 2pm to 7pm. If closed, apply to the presbytery 22580, Plouha. ☎ 02 96 20 21 31.

KERNASCLÉDEN

Excursion

Château et Forêt de Pont-Calleck – Only the park is open to the public 9am to 7pm. Closed 25 July to 25 August. No admission charge. ☎ 02 97 51 61 17.

L

LAMBALLE

ℹ Place du Martray, 22400 – ☎ 02 96 31 05 38

Haras national – ♿ Open daily July and August and during school holidays 10.30am to 12.30pm and 2pm to 6pm; the rest of the year 2pm to 5pm. 20F. ☎ 02 96 50 06 98.

Collégiale Notre-Dame – Guided tours by the SPREV in July and August. Guided tours are organised by "Les Amis de la Collégiale" Saturdays and Sundays in May and June. For further information call the Tourist Information Office or ☎ 02 96 31 02 55 (presbytery).

Musée du Pays de Lamballe – *Open 1 June to 31 August and spring school holidays 10am to noon and 2pm to 6.30pm (6pm in June),the rest of the year Wednesdays and Fridays 2.30pm to 5pm. Closed Sundays and all public holidays. 15F. ☎ 02 96 31 05 38.*

Musée Mathurin-Méheut – Open 1 June to 30 September and during the Easter school holidays 10am to noon and 2.30pm to 6.30pm (except Sundays and public holidays); the rest of the year Tuesdays, Fridays and Saturdays. Closed January, Sundays and all public holidays. 15F. ☎ 02 96 31 19 99.

LANDERNEAU

ℹ Pavillon Pont-de-Rohan, 29800 – ☎ 02 98 85 13 09

Église St-Thomas-de-Cantorbéry – Guided tours in July and August 10am to 6pm.

LANDÉVENNEC

Ruines de l'ancienne Abbaye – Open daily 15 June to 30 September (except Sunday mornings) 10am to 7pm. The rest of the year open Saturday and Sunday 2pm to 6pm. 25F. ☎ 02 98 27 35 90.

Abbey Museum – Same times and charges as for the Ruines de l'ancienne Abbaye.

LANNION

Excursions

Chapelle de Kerfons – Open June to late August 10am to 12.30pm and 2pm to 6.30pm. The rest of the year, apply to the Town hall (Mairie) at Ploubezre. ☎ 02 96 47 15 51.

Château de Kergrist – Guided tours of the interior (30 min) daily early June to late September: 11am to 6.30pm; May, spring school holidays on weekends from 2pm to 6pm. 30F combined ticket château and gardens; gardens only 20F. ☎ 02 96 38 91 44.

Chapelle des Sept-Saints – To visit the chapel outside the summer season, apply to the Town Hall (Mairie) at Vieux-Marché. ☎ 02 96 38 91 13 or to the address on the chapel door.

Caouënnec-Lanvézéac: Church – Open 9am to 11am and 1pm to 6pm. Apply to M. Yves Mayou, route de Lanvézéac. ☎ 02 96 35 89 96.

Locquémeau: Church – Guided tours July and August 10am to noon and 4pm to 7pm. Closed Thursday. The rest of the year, apply to the Town hall. ☎ 02 96 35 74 52.

Ploumilliau: Church – To visit the church between 2pm and 6pm during the summer season, apply to M. Maurice L'Escop on weekdays only. ☎ 02 96 35 44 44.

LANRIVAIN

Chapelle Notre-Dame-du-Guiaudet – Open daily May to early October; if the chapel is closed, apply to M. Chenu. ☎ 02 96 29 51 65.

Forteresse de LARGOËT

Open daily 1 June to 30 September 10.30am to 6.30pm (1 July to 31 August, guided tours from 2pm to 6pm); 15 March to 31 May and 1 October to 5 November open from 2pm to 6.30pm Saturdays, Sundays, holidays and school holidays. 20F. ☎ 02 97 53 35 96.

Fort la LATTE

Open daily 4 July to 31 August 10am to 7pm; 4 April to 30 June and 1 to 30 September 10am to 12.30pm and 2.30pm to 6.30pm; Guided tours (45 min) also available at the same dates and times. The rest of the year open Saturdays, Sundays and weekdays during school holidays only 2.30pm to 6pm. 19F. ☎ 02 99 30 38 84.

LÉHON

Cloisters, Museum and Gardens – Guided tours (1 hour) daily 4 July to 31 August 2.30pm to 6pm. Closed Monday. 15F. ☎ 02 96 39 07 19.

LESNEVEN

Musée de Léon – ♿ Open July and August 2.30pm to 6.30pm; the rest of the year 2pm to 6pm.. Closed Tuesdays, Easter Sunday, 25 December and from 1 January to 15 February. 10F. ☎ 02 98 21 17 18.

LOCMARIAQUER

ℹ Place de la Mairie, 56740 – ☎ 02 97 57 33 05

Ensemble mégalithique – Guided tours (45 min) 1 June to 30 September 10am to 7pm; 1 April to 31 May 10am to 1pm and 2pm to 6pm. 25F. ☎ Sagemor 02 97 57 37 59.

LOCRONAN

ℹ Place de la Mairie, 29180 – ☎ 02 98 91 70 14

Église St-Ronan and Chapelle du Penity – Guided tours are available July and August. ☎ 02 98 91 70 93.

Chapelle Notre-Dame-de-Bonne-Nouvelle – Open Easter to All Saints' Day 9am to 7pm. If closed, apply to Mme Le Hénaff, rue Moal opposite the chapel.

Museum – Open daily 1 June to 30 September 10am to 7pm; 4 March to 31 May from 10am to 1pm and 2pm to 6pm on weekdays and 2pm to 6pm on Saturdays and Sundays. 15F. ☎ 02 98 51 80 59.

Conservatoire de l'Affiche en Bretagne – *Open 1 July to 30 October (summer exhibit) 11am to 7pm; 4 April to 15 June (spring exhibit) 9.30am to 1pm and 2pm to 6pm. 20F.* ☎ 02 98 51 80 59.

Excursions

Montagne de Locronan: Chapel – *Open only during the "Troménies': the "Petites Troménies" are held every year on the 2nd Sunday in July; the "Grandes Troménies" are held every six years from the 1st to the 2nd Sunday in July (the next one will take place in the year 2001).* ☎ *02 98 91 70 93.*

Ste-Anne-la-Palud: Chapel – Open daily Easter to All Saints' Day; the rest of the year open Sundays only. ☎ *02 98 92 50 17.*

LOCTUDY

Boat trips

Île-Tudy – The peninsula can be reached by CD 144 or by sea, with departures leaving from Loctudy. There are several two-way trips a day (except Sundays mid-September to mid-June). 10F there and back.

LOHÉAC

Manoir de l'Automobile – ♿ Open daily 10am to noon and 2pm to 7pm. Closed Mondays. 30F. ☎ 02 99 34 02 32.

LORIENT

ℹ 6, quai de Rohan, 56100 – ☎ 02 97 21 07 84

Guided Tour of the City – *1 July to 31 August departures from the Tourist Office Mondays at 3pm (2 hours 30 min). Themes include 50's architecture, underground shelters, Mémorial.*

"Ingénieur-Général-Stosskopf" Submarine Base and Dockyard – Guided tours (1 hour 15 min). No longer in active military service, the base and a submarine are open for public tours. Information from the Lorient Tourist Office.

Zoo de Pont-Scorff – Open 1 June to 31 August 9.30am to 7pm; the rest of the year 10am to 5pm. 45F; children 30F. ☎ 02 97 32 60 86.

Boat trips – For information apply to "La Compagnie Morbihannaise et Nantaise de Navigation", Service Transrade, Locmiquélic. ☎ 02 97 33 40 55 (closed Sundays).

LOUDÉAC

Race meetings – *They are held fifteen days before Easter (on Sunday), Easter Sunday and Easter Monday, the following Sunday (Quasimodo) as well as in late May, early June, 14 July and 15 August.*

Excursion

La Chèze: Musée régional des Métiers de Bretagne – Open daily 1 July to 31 August 10am to noon and 2pm to 6pm; in May, June and September open 2pm to 6pm (except Tuesdays); 1 to 30 April Wednesdays and Saturdays 2pm to 6pm. Closed early October to early April (visits by appointment). 19F. ☎ 02 96 26 63 16.

M

MALESTROIT

Excursion

St-Marcel: Musée de la Résistance bretonne – ♿ Open 15 June to 15 September 10am to 7pm; the rest of the year 10am to noon and 2pm to 6pm. Closed Tuesdays 16 September to 14 June. 30F. ☎ 02 97 75 16 90.

La MEILLERAYE-DE-BRETAGNE

Abbaye de Melleray – The abbey is only open during religious services. To visit week-days, apply to the reception service . ☎ 02 40 55 26 00.

MONCONTOUR

Excursion

Château de la Touche-Trébry – Guided tours (40 min) of the château interior 1 July to 31 August 2pm to 6.30pm. 18F. ☎ 02 96 42 78 55.

MONTAGNES NOIRES

Park and Château de Trévarez – Open daily July and August 11am to 7pm; in April, May, June and September 1pm to 6.30pm; the rest of the year open Saturdays, Sundays, public holidays and during Easter and Christmas school holidays 2pm to 6pm. 16F, 22F or 27F depending on the programme. ☎ 02 98 26 82 79.

MONTFORT-SUR-MEU

Écomusée du Pays de Montfort – Open Monday to Friday 9am to noon and 2pm to 6pm; Saturdays 10am to noon and 2pm to 6pm; Sundays and holidays 2pm to 6pm. Closed 1 January. 20F. ☎ 02 99 09 31 81.

Maison natale de Saint Louis-Marie Grignion de Montfort – Open daily 10am to noon and 3pm to 6pm. Guided tours (45 min) also available at the same dates and times. Closed Sunday mornings. No admission charge. ☎ 02 99 09 15 35.

Excursion

La Chapelle-Thouarault: Musée et Atelier d'Art animalier – Guided tour (1 hours) daily 2pm to 6pm. 20F. ☎ 02 99 07 61 90.

MONT-ST-MICHEL

ℹ Corps-de-Garde-des-Bourgeois, 50116 – ☎ 02 33 60 14 30

Car Park – Notice boards, updated on a daily basis, give the times of high tides and warn visitors of possible dangers. These instructions should be followed closely. 15F.

Abbey – Open 2 May to 30 September 9am to 5.30pm; the rest of the year 9.30am to 4.30pm (5pm during school holidays). Guided tours (1 hour) also available at the same dates and times. Closed 1 January, 1 May, 1 and 11 November, and 25 December. 40F. Visit-conferences (2 hours): May to September daily, schedule posted at the abbey; the rest of the year, daily during school holidays or Saturdays and Sundays otherwise (one tour int he morning, one in the afternoon). 65F. ☎ 02 33 60 14 14.

Abbey Gardens – Open to the public in summer only (ask at the abbey entrance).

Archéoscope – 20-min shows daily 17 February to 11 November 9am to 5.30pm (7pm July and August) 45F. ☎ 02 33 48 09 37.

Logis Tiphaine – *Open daily during school holidays and public holidyas 9am to 6.30pm; otherwise closed Fridays, and from 11 November to 10 February. Guided tours (30 min) available at the same dates and times. 30F. ☎ 02 33 60 23 34.*

Golfe du MORBIHAN

The Gulf by boat: Île aux Moines – Departures every 30 min (time: 5 min) 1 July to 31 August 7am to 10pm; the rest of the year 7am to 7.30pm.. 20F there and back. ☎ 02 97 26 34 42 or 02 97 26 31 45.

Guided tour (15 min) June to September 10am to noon and 2pm to 6pm, depending on works underway, keeper's availability and weather conditions. No admission charge, donations welcome. ☎ 02 96 23 92 10.

MORGAT

Les Grandes Grottes – **Boat trips** (45 min) 1 May to 30 September. Departures all day depending on the tide, leaving from the port. 45F; children 33F. Armement Rosmeur ☎ 02 98 27 10 71 or Sirènes ☎ 02 98 96 20 10.

MORLAIX

ℹ Place des Otages, 29600 – ☎ 02 98 62 14 94

Guided Tour of the City – July and August Thursdays at 2.30pm (2 hours); the rest of the year by appointment. Apply to the Tourist Information Office. 20F.

Maison de la Reine Anne – Guided tours (15 min) daily 1 June to 31 August 10.30am to 6.30pm (Sundays 3pm to 6pm July and August); in April and September 10.30am to noon and 2pm to 6pm. Closed Sundays year round and Mondays out of season. *Price not given, previously was free.* ☎ 02 98 88 23 26.

Musée des Jacobins – ♿ Open 10am to 12.30pm and 2pm to 6pm (5pm 1 November to 31 March except Sundays and public holidays). Closed Tuesdays December to Easter, and 1 January, 1 May and 25 December. 25F. ☎ 02 98 88 68 88.

Église St-Mathieu – Open weekdays only 9am to noon and 2pm to 6.15pm during the school term (9am to 6pm during school holidays).

NANTES

ℹ Place du Commerce, 44000 – ☎ 02 40 20 60 00

Every day from April to September, as of 10.15am, a miniature train carries visitors around the centre of town. Departures from in front of the Cathedral, place St-Pierre

Guided Tour of the City A – *There are many tours and theme visits in July, August and September. Apply to the Tourist Information Office.*

Château des Ducs de Bretagne – Open daily 1 July to 31 August 10am to 7pm (castle), 10am to noon and 2pm to 7pm (museums); the rest of the year open 10am to noon and 2pm to 6pm (castle and museums). Guided tours (1 hour) also available at the same dates and times. The museums are closed Tuesdays (except in summer) and all public holidays. No admission charge. Temporary exhibits in the "harnachement" buildings are 20F. ☎ 02 40 41 56 56.

Musée de l'Histoire de Nantes – Closed for renovation.

Cathédrale St-Pierre et St-Paul – The crypts can be visited 10am to 12.30pm and 2pm to 5pm except Tuesdays and during religious services. ☎ 02 40 14 23 00. For guided tours of the cathedral, apply to the Tourist Information Office.

Musée des Beaux-Arts – ♿ Open 10am (11am Sundays) to 6pm. Closed Tuesdays and all public holidays. 20F (free Sundays). ☎ 02 40 41 65 65 and 02 40 41 65 50.

Muséum d'Histoire naturelle – ♿ Open 10am to noon and 2pm to 6pm. Closed Sundays mornings, Mondays and all public holidays. 20F (free Sundays). 30F for some temporary exhibitions. ☎ 02 40 41 67 67.

Palais Dobrée – Open 10am to noon and 1.30pm to 5.30pm. Closed Mondays and public holidays. 20F (combined ticket giving access to the Manoir de la Touche and and Musée archéologique). ☎ 02 40 71 03 50.

Manoir de la Touche – Open 10am to noon and 1.30pm to 5.30pm. Closed Mondays and all public holidays. Renovation works are currently underway. 20F (combined ticket giving access to the Musée archéologique and the Palais Dobrée). ☎ 02 40 71 03 50.

Musée archéologique – Open 10am to noon and 1.30pm to 5.30pm. Closed Mondays and all public holidays. 20F (combined ticket giving access to the Manoir de la Touche and the Palais Dobrée). ☎ 02 40 71 03 50.

Musée de l'Imprimerie – ♿ Open 1 May to 31 July Monday to Friday 10am to noon and 2pm to 6pm; September to late February Tuesday to Saturday 10am to noon and 2pm to 6pm;. Closed August and all public holidays. Guided tours (2 hours) are available at the same dates and times. 20F. ☎ 02 40 73 26 55.

Maillé-Brézé – Guided tours (1 hour or 1 1/2 hours including machinery) daily 1 June to 30 September and during the school holidays 2pm to 6pm; the rest of the year daily 2pm to 6pm during the school holidays; 2pm to 3pm Wednesdays, Saturdays, Sundays and public holidays during the school term. Closed 1 January and 25 December. 30F (45F including machinery). ☎ 02 40 69 56 82.

Église Notre-Dame-de-Bon-Port – Open weekdays only 10am to noon and 2pm to 7pm. ☎ 02 40 69 85 58.

Musée Jules-Verne – Open 10am to noon and 2pm to 5pm. Closed Sunday mornings, Tuesdays and public holidays. 8F. ☎ 02 40 69 72 52.

Planétarium – ♿ Shows (1 hour) at 10.30 (except Sundays), 2.15pm (3pm Sundays), 3.45pm (4.30pm Sundays). Closed Saturdays and public holidays. 26F. ☎ 02 40 73 99 23.

H. Gysselé/DIAF

Old LU biscuit advertisement

Musée de la Poupée et des Jouets anciens – *Open daily 15 April to 15 September 2.30pm to 5.30pm (closed Sundays); the rest of the year open Wednesdays to Saturdays 2.30pm to 5.30pm. Closed Saturdays and public holidays. 20F.* ☎ *02 40 69 14 41.*

Musée de la Poste – Open 9am to noon and 2pm to 4pm. Closed Saturday afternoons, Sundays and public holidays. Free admission. ☎ 02 51 83 39 39.

Chapelle de l'Immaculée – For reasons of security, the chapel is temporarily closed during major restoration work.

Maison de l'Erdre – Open 11.30am to 5.45pm (10am to noon and 3pm to 5.45pm Saturdays and Sundays. Closed Tuesdays. No admission charge. ☎ 02 40 41 90 09.

Boat Trip on the Erdre – Cruises at various times depending on the season; July and August daily at 3pm and 5pm. 55F; children 25F. July and August, by reservation, luncheon cruise (noon to 3pm) 250F; dinner cruise (8pm to 11pm) 285F. For information apply to the "Bateaux Nantais." ☎ 02 40 14 51 14.

Calvaire NOTRE-DAME-DE-TRONOËN

Chapelle – Open 1 July to 15 September 10am to noon and 2pm to 6pm; Easter to 30 June 2pm to 6pm. ☎ 02 98 87 02 80.

Chapelle NOTRE-DAME-DU-CRANN

Open daily in summer 9am to noon and 1.30pm to 6.30pm; open weekdays only in winter 2pm to 5.15pm. ☎ 02 98 93 84 78.

O

Île d'OUESSANT

Regular service from Brest daily, on board the Enez Eussa or the Fromveur (250 to 365 passengers), at 8.30am for Ouessant or Molène via Le Conquet. ☎ *02 98 80 24 68.*
Regular service rom Le Conquet daily on the same ships at 9.45am. From April to September, extra departures are scheduled. ☎ *02 98 70 24 68.*
Summer runs from Brest or Camaret 15 July to 25 August, on board the André Colin (200 passengers). Departure from Brest at 8.15am, return from Ouessant 6pm (does not operate on Sundays).
Access by plane leaving from Brest-Guipavas. ☎ *02 98 84 64 87.*
Bicycles can be hired at Le Stiff during the school holidays (all year round at Lampaul)For all information apply to the Service Maritime Départemental, ☎ *02 98 80 24 68*

Centre d'Interprétation des Phares et Balises – Open daily 1 May to 30 September and during school holidays 10.30am to 6.30pm; the rest of the year open 2pm to 6.30pm; the rest of the year 2pm to 6.30pm (4pm 1 October to 31 March). Closed Mondays except during the school holidays, 1 January and 25 December. 25F. ☎ 02 98 48 80 70.

Écomusée de l'Île d'Ouessant – *Same opening dates and times as for the Centre d'Interprétation des Phares above. 20F; children 12F.* ☎ *02 98 48 86 37.*

P

PAIMPOL

Musée de la Mer – Open daily 15 June to 20 September daily 10.30am to 1pm and 3pm to 7pm. 21F. ☏ 02 96 22 02 19.

Forêt de PAIMPONT

Château de Comper – ♿ Open 1 April to 5 October 10am to 7pm. Guided tours (45 min) also available at the same dates and times. Closed Tuesdays and Fridays in April, May and September. Closed Tuesdays in June, July and August. 25F. ☏ 02 97 22 79 96.

Paimpont Abbey Church: Treasury – ♿ Guided tours daily 15 June to 15 September 10am to noon (except Saturdays and Sunday mornings) and 2pm to 6.30pm; the rest of the year by appointment: apply to Monsieur le Recteur de la Paroisse Saturdays and Sundays 3pm to 6.30pm (except during religious services). No admission charge. ☏ 02 99 07 81 37.

Château de Trécesson – *Access is limited to the interior courtyard, by appointment.*

Tréhorenteuc: Church – ♿ Open daily 2 June to 15 September 9am to 7pm; 2 February to 31 May and 15 September to 31 January 10am to noon and 2pm to 5pm. Guided tours (30 min) also available at the same dates and times. Closed Mondays 15 September to 1 February and 1 December. 5F. ☏ 02 97 93 05 12.

Canton de Guer-Coëtquidan

École de St-Cyr-Coëtquidan: Musée du Souvenir – Open Tuesday to Sunday 10am to noon and 2pm to 6pm. Closed 1 May and from 10 December to 10 February. 20F. ☏ 02 97 73 53 06.

Site mégalithique de Monteneuf – Free access all year round. Guided tours (1 hour) 1 April to 31 October at 11am and 4pm (extra tour at 6pm July and August). 10F. ☏ 02 02 97 93 24 14.

PERROS-GUIREC

ℹ 21, place de l'Hôtel-de-Ville, 22700 – ☏ 02 96 23 21 15

Church – Guided tours daily July and August 10.30 to noon and 3pm to 5.30pm. Presbytère de Perros-Guirec ☏ 02 96 23 21 64.

Musée de Cire-Chouannerie Bretonne – *Open daily 15 June to 15 September 9.30am to 6.30pm; 1 May to 14 June and 16 September to 15 October and during school holidays, 2.30pm to 6.30pm. 18F. ☏ 02 96 91 23 45.*

Boat trips

Sept-Îles: Tour of the Islands – Three companies use a central reservation service at the Trestaou Gare Maritime. Some boats are "glass bottomed". Generally, the excursion period goes from February to early November depending on the type of ship. Trips last from 1 hour 30 min to 3 hours 30 min, some with stopovers, touring various islands. ☏ 02 96 91 10 00.

Île aux Moines: Lighthouse – Guided tour (15 min) June to September 10am to noon and 2pm to 6pm, depending on works underway, keeper's availability and weather conditions. No admission charge, donations welcome. ☏ 02 96 23 92 10.

PLEUMEUR-BODOU

Musée des Télécommunications and Radôme – ♿ Open daily July and August 10am to 7pm; 10am to 6pm April (closed Saturdays), May, June and September; the rest of the year open 1.30pm to 5.30pm except Saturdays and Sunday mornings. 43F. Combined ticket for Musée/Radôme + Planétarium: 65F. Family ticket (2 adults + 2 children) for Musée/Radôme: 100F + 10F for each extra child. Family ticket (2 adults + 2 children) for Musée/Radôme + Planétarium: 200F + 30F for each extra child. An annual pass provides unlimited access to the Musée/Radôme: 100F. ☏ 02 96 46 63 80.

Planétarium du Trégor – ♿ *Astronomy presentations (1 hour) July and August at 11am, 12.15pm, 1.30pm, 2.45pm, 4.15pm and 5.30pm; the rest of the year two presentations in the afternoon at 2.30pm, 3pm, 4pm or 4.30pm depending on the time of year. Closed all January, Wednesday and Sunday off-season. 35F. Combined ticket for Musée/Radôme + Planétarium: 65F. Family ticket (2 adults + 2 children): 200F. ☏ 02 96 15 80 30.*

PLEYBEN

Church – Open daily Easter to 1 October 9am to noon and 1.30pm to 7pm. Guided tours available July and August. ☏ 02 98 26 71 05.

PLOËRDUT

Excursion

Chapelle Notre-Dame-de-Crénenan – To visit the chapel, apply to the presbytery at Ploërdut. ☎ 02 97 39 44 98.

PLOËRMEL

ℹ 5, rue du Val, BP 106, 56804 – ☎ 02 97 74 02 70

Musée du Père Jean-Marie de la Mennais – Open daily Easter to All Saints' Day 9am to noon and 2pm to pm. Guided tours (30 min) available at the same dates and times. No admission charge. ☎ 02 97 74 06 67.

Excursions

Château du Crévy – Guided tours (1 hour 15 min) 1 July to 31 August 10am to 6pm; in April to June and September to 11 November, group visits and by appointment only. 30F. ☎ 02 97 74 91 95.

Lizio: Écomusée de la Ferme et des Métiers – ♿ Open all year round 10am to noon and 2pm to 7pm. Guided tours (1 hour 30 min) all year round at the same times. 23F. ☎ 02 97 74 93 01.

PLOUESCAT

Excursions

Château de Maillé – Tour of the château exterior daily 1 April to 31 October 10am to 6pm. Tour of the château interior 1 April to 31 October afternoons by appointment only (book a few days in advance). No admission charge. ☎ 02 98 61 44 68.

Manoir de Traonjoly – The exterior of the manorhouse can be visited all year round 10am to 6pm. No admission charge. ☎ 02 98 69 40 01.

PLOUGASTEL-DAOULAS

ℹ BP 27, 29470 – ☎ 02 98 40 34 98

Church – Open daily July and August 9am to noon and 2pm to 4pm; the rest of the year 9am to noon "Les Amis du Patrimoine" ☎ 02 98 40 21 18 or Tourist Information Office.

Musée du Patrimoine et de la Fraise – ♿ Open 1 June to 15 September 10am to 12.30pm and 2pm to 6.30pm (Sundays 2pm to 6.30pm); 3 April to 31 May and 16 September to 31 Ocotober 2pm to 6pm. Closed Mondays and public holidays. 25F. ☎ 02 98 40 21 18.

Excursion

Chapelle Ste-Christine – Apply to Mme Le Gall at the next-door house.

PONT-AVEN

ℹ Place de l'Hôtel-de-Ville, 29930 – ☎ 02 98 06 04 70

Museum – ♿ Open daily 1 July to 31 August 10am to 7pm; 1 April to 30 June and in September 10am to 12.30pm and 2pm to 7pm; 10 February to 30 March and 1 October to 31 December 10am to 12.30pm and 2pm to 6pm. Guided tours (1 hour) also available at the same dates and times. Closed 3 to 31 January. The museum closes for a few days between temporary exhibitions (March, June, October). Apply to the Tourist Information Office. 25F (30F off-season). ☎ 02 98 06 14 43.

Excursion

Névez: Chapelle Ste-Barbe – If the chapel is closed, apply to the Tourist Information Office. ☎ 02 98 06 87 90.

PONT-CROIX

Église Notre-Dame-de-Roscudon – Guided tours July and August 9am to 6pm. ☎ 02 98 70 44 52.

PONTIVY

ℹ 61, rue Général-de-Gaulle, 56300 – ☎ 02 97 25 04 10

Castle – Open 1 July to 15 September 10.30am to 7pm; the rest of the year open 10am to noon and 2pm to 6pm. Guided tours (1 hour) available at the same dates and times. Closed Mondays and Tuesdays (excluding public holidays) and from 1 October to 31 May. Exhibits 1 July to 15 September. 8F; 23F with exhibit. ☎ 02 97 25 12 93.

Excursions

Stival: Parish Church – If the church is closed, apply to the presbytery at Pontivy ☎ 02 97 25 14 55 or the Town hall (Mairie) at Pontivy.

Chapelle St-Nicodème – Open daily 1 April to 1 October 8am to 7pm.

Bieuzy: Church – *To visit the church, apply to Mme Marie-Christine Le Courrierec, rue de l'Ermitage. ☎ 02 97 39 57 92.*

Melrand: Ferme archéologique – Open 1 May to 31 August 10am to 7pm; 1 September to 30 April 11am to 5pm (6pm weekends) Guided tours (1 hour) available at the same dates and times. 20F. ☎ 02 97 39 57 89.

Quelven: Chapel – If the chapel is closed, apply to ☎ 02 97 27 73 64.

Chapelle Ste-Noyale – Guided tours daily except Mondays July and August 2pm to 6pm. If the chapel is closed, apply to the Town Hall (Mairie) in Noyal-Pontiny. ☎ 02 97 38 30 66.

Abbaye Notre-Dame-de-Timadeuc – The monastery is not open to the public but it is possible to attend the religious services (Mass Sundays at 11am, 8am weekdays and 11.15am Saturdays). Audiovisual presentation on monastic life at the entrance. ☎ 02 97 51 50 29.

PONT-L'ABBÉ

3, rue du Château, 29120 – ☎ 02 98 82 37 99

Église Notre-Dame-des-Carmes – Open 9am to noon and 2pm to 7pm. If the church is closed, apply to the presbytery. ☎ 02 98 87 02 80.

Musée Bigouden – Guided tours (40 min) 1 June to 30 September 9am to noon and 2pm to 6; from the spring school holidays to 31 May 10am to noon and 2pm to 4.15pm. Closed Sundays and 1 May. 20F. ☎ 02 98 87 35 63.

Excursions

Chapelle Notre-Dame-de-Tréminou – Open daily July and August 2pm to 6pm. ☎ 02 98 82 00 76.

Maison du Pays Bigouden – Open 1 June to 30 September 10am to noon and 2.15pm to 6pm. Closed Sundays and public holidays. 15F ☎ 02 98 87 35 63.

PORT-LOUIS

Musées de la Citadelle – Major renovation is planned to last until 1999. Open 1 April to 30 September 10am to 7pm; 1 October to 31 March 1.30pm to 6pm. Closed Tuesdays (except in July and August) on1 May and 1 December to 15 January. 29F. ☎ 02 97 12 10 37.

Le POULIGUEN

Chapelle Ste-Anne-et-St-Julien – Open 1 July to 30 September 9am to noon and 3pm to 7pm. ☎ 02 40 42 18 51.

Q

QUESTEMBERT

Excursion

Chapelle Notre-Dame-des-Vertus – To visit the chapel, apply to the Town hall (Mairie) in Berric. ☎ 02 97 67 01 37 or to M Grignon, Les Vertus, 02 97 67 03 01.

Presqu'île de QUIBERON

Isthme de Penthièvre: Galion de Plouharnel – Open 1 July to 31 August 9.30am to 7pm; 1 April to 30 June and in September 10am to noon and 2pm to 6pm. Closed the rest of the year. 20F. ☎ 02 97 52 39 56.

Musée de la Chouannerie – Open daily 1 April to 30 September 10am to noon and 2pm to 6pm. 25F. ☎ 02 97 52 31 31.

QUIMPER

Place de la Résistance, 29000 – ☎ 02 98 53 04 05

Guided Tour of the City A – *Guided tours (1 hour 30 min) daily July and August at 11am and 5pm; 1 to 30 June and 1 to 30 September at 3pm. 30F. Apply to the Tourist Information Office.*

Musée des Beaux-Arts – ♿ Open daily 1 July to 31 August 10am to 7pm; the rest of the year open 10am to noon and 2pm to 6pm. Guided tours (1 hour 30 min) available at the same dates and times. Closed Sunday mornings (1 October to 31 March), Tuesdays, and on 1 January, 1 May, 1 and 11 November, and 25 December. 25F. ☎ 02 98 95 86 85.

Musée départemental breton – ♿ Open daily 1 June to 30 September 9am to 6pm; the rest of the year open 9am to noon and 2pm to 5pm. Closed Mondays, Sunday mornings and public holidays 25F (June to September); 20F (October to May. ☎ 02 98 95 21 60.

Musée de la Faïence – ♿ Open mid-April to 31 October 10am to 6pm. Closed Sundays and public holidays. 26F. ☎ 02 98 90 12 72.

Faïenceries de Quimper HB Henriot – ♿ Guided tours (30 min) July and August 9am to 11.15am and 1.30pm to 5.15pm (4.15pm Fridays); the rest of the year Monday to Friday at the same times. Closed from 25 December to 2 January. 20F. ☎ 02 98 90 09 36.

Excursions

Chapelle de Kerdévot – Open daily July to late August 2pm to 6pm. Open Sundays only in May, June and September. ☎ 02 98 59 50 23.

Église de Kerfeunteun – Open weekdays only 9.30am to 6pm. ☎ 02 98 95 13 89.

Chapelle Notre-Dame-de-Quilinen – Open April to October 9am to 7pm. If closed, apply to the Landrévarzec Town hall. ☎ 02 98 57 90 44.

Chapelle de St-Venec – If the chapel is closed, apply to M. Yves Rolland Kerrouzic, 29510 Briec de l'Odet. ☎ 02 98 57 98 59.

Boat trips

Down the Odet – From April to September, there are up to 5 cruises a day (2 hours 30 min). Luncheon cruises Tuesday to Sunday. Stopover in Bénodet, depending on tides, or longer trips out to the Îles Glénan. For information apply to the Tourist Information Office in Quimper or to "Les Vedettes de l'Odet". ☎ 02 98 57 00 58.

QUIMPERLÉ

🅸 Le Bourgneuf, 29391 – ☎ 02 98 96 04 32

Église Ste-Croix – *Guided tours mid-June to mid-September Tuesdays and Fridays at 10am and 3pm.*

Maison des Arhcers: Museum – Open daily 1 July to 31 August 11am to 7m; the rest of the year open depending on temporary exhibits or events.. Guided tours (1 hour) available. 10F. ☎ 02 98 96 04 32.

Église Notre-Dame-de-l'Assomption – If the church is closed, apply to the presbytery. Guided tours July and August 2pm to 6pm. ☎ 02 98 96 03 94.

Excursions

Le Pouldu: Chapelle Notre-Dame-de-la-Paix – Open daily July and August, when volunteers are available.

Moëlan-sur-Mer: Chapelle St-Philibert-et-St-Roch – Open during the spring school holidays and 15 June to 15 September 10am to noon and 3.30pm to 7pm. ☎ 02 98 39 67 28.

QUINTIN

🅸 Place 1830, 22800 – ☎ 02 96 74 01 51

Basilica – Open daily 9am to 7pm (except Wednesday during the school term). In summer the Tourist Information Office organises guided tours which include a visit of the basilica. ☎ 02 96 74 92 17

Château – ♿ (except cellars). Guided tours (1 hour) daily 15 June to 15 September 10.30am to 12.30pm and 1.30pm to 6.30pm; 1 May to 15 June and 15 to 30 September 2pm to 5.30pm; April and October 2.30pm to 5.30pm.. Every summer the château hosts an exhibition on a different theme. 30F. ☎ 02 96 74 94 79.

Château de Robien – Only the park is open to the public, 1 July to 30 September 10am to noon and 2pm to 6pm. No admission charge. ☎ 02 96 74 91 34.

R

Usine marémotrice de la RANCE

Hydro-Electric Power Station – Open daily 8.15am to 8pm. Guided tours (1 hour 30 min) weekdays only by appointment at 8.15am, 10.15am, 2pm and 4pm. Access by the steps situated on the platform of the lock (side giving on to the sea). A terrace commands a general view of the engine room. It is forbidden to take photographs inside the factory. No admission charge. ☎ 02 99 16 37 14.

Vallée de la RANCE

Boat trip – For all information, apply to the "Vedettes" offices or to the Tourist Information Offices of these towns.

Vedettes à St-Malo – ☎ 02 99 40 48 40.

Vedettes à Dinard – ☎ 02 99 46 10 45.

Vedettes à Dinan – ☎ 02 96 39 18 04.

Croisière Gourmande – A dining cruise (3 hours) on board the *Châteaubriand*, leaving from Port de la Richardais – ☎ 02 99 16 35 32.

Pleudihen-sur-Rance: Musée de la Pomme et du Cidre – ♿ Open daily 1 June to 31 August 10am to 7pm; 1 April to 30 May and 1 to 30 September daily except Sundays and holidays 2pm to 7pm. Guided tours (30 min) also available at the same dates and times. 20F. ☎ 02 96 83 20 78.

Pointe du RAZ

Cars must be left in the car park (fee: 20F) 800m away from the point. Allow 1 hour for the visit. Free shuttle service available. Information centre (Maison de la Pointe du Raz et du Cap Sizun) open July and August daily from 9.30am to 7.30pm; late April to end of June and during September from 10.30am to 6pm. ☎ 02 98 70 67 18.

RENNES

Pont de Nemours, 35005 – ☎ 02 99 79 01 98
Information Desk SNCF Station – ☎ 02 99 53 23 23

Guided Tour of the City A – *Guided tours (1 to 2 hours) daily July and August. Apply to the "Rennes Ville d'Art et d'Histoire" service at the Tourist Information Office. 35F.*

Cathédrale St-Pierre – Open daily 9.30am to noon and 3pm to 6pm. ☎ 02 99 30 12 03.

Palais de Justice – *The fire that ravaged the Palais de Justice (Breton Parliament) during the night of 4 to 5 February 1994 makes it impossible to visit the building for the time being.*

Town Hall – ♿ The building may be visited during business hours (8.30am to 5.30pm, Saturdays 9.30am to noon). Closed Sundays and public holidays. ☎ 02 99 28 55 55, extension 339.

Musée de Bretagne – ♿ Open 9am to noon and 2pm to 6pm. Closed Tuesdays and public holidays. 15F. ☎ 02 99 28 55 84.

Musée des Beaux-Arts A – ♿ Open 10am to noon and 2pm to 6pm. Closed Tuesdays and public holidays. 15F. ☎ 02 99 28 55 85.

Excursions

Écomusée du Pays de Rennes – *Open Mondays to Fridays 9am to noon and 2pm to 6pm; Saturdays and Sundays 2pm to 6pm (7pm Sundays). Closed 16 to 31 January, Tuesdays and public holidays. 28F; children 14F. ☎ 02 99 51 38 15.*

Bruz: Church – To visit the church, apply to the presbytery. Closed Sunday afternoons. ☎ 02 99 52 61 17.

Parc ornithologique de Bretagne – ♿ Open daily 1 April to 30 September 10am to noon and 2pm to 7pm; the rest of the year open weekends 2pm to 6pm. 38F; children 22F. ☎ 02 99 52 68 57.

La ROCHE-BERNARD

Musée de la Vilaine maritime – Open daily 22 June to 14 September 10.30am to 12.30pm and 2.30pm to 6.30pm; 7 to 21 June and 15 to 28 September 2.30pm to 6.30pm; 1 October to 30 December and 1 February to 31 May Saturdays, Sundays and public holidays 2.30pm to 6.30pm. Closed January, February and at Christmas. 20F. ☎ 02 99 90 83 47.

Boat Trip on the River Vilaine – Boat services (1 hour 30 min) are available July and August, leaving every hour 2pm to 6pm from the Arzal or dam or La Roche-Bernard. 45F. Luncheon cruises daily July and August departing from Arzal dam at 12.30pm; dinner cruises Fridays and Saturday 8pm. Meal and boat, about 185F (lunch) or 260F (dinner). ☎ 02 97 45 02 81.

Excursions

Parc zoologique de Branféré – ♿ Open daily 1 March to 30 September 9am to 8pm; 1 October to late February from 1.30pm to 6.30pm. The sale of tickets stops one hour before closing time. Closed 1 January and 25 December. 45F; children 25F. ☎ 02 97 42 94 66.

Moulin de Pen-Mur – Guided tours (30 min) daily 1 April to 30 September 10am to noon and 2pm to 6pm (except Sunday mornings in April, May and June); 1 October to 31 March 10am to noon and 2pm to 5.30pm Saturdays and Sunday afternoons. 25F. ☎ 02 97 41 43 79.

Château de Léhélec – ♿ Guided tours (30 min) 13 June to 6 September 2pm to 7pm; 7 to 30 September Saturdays and Sundays 2pm to 7pm. Closed Tuesdays. 20F. ☎ 02 99 91 84 33.

Crowned cranes at Branféré zoo

ROCHEFORT-EN-TERRE

ℹ Town Hall, 56220 – ☎ 02 97 43 33 57

Castle – Guided tours (45 min) daily 1 July to 31 August 10am to 7pm; 1 to 30 June and 1 to 30 September daily 10am to noon and 2pm to 6.30pm; 1 April to 31 May and 1 to 31 October Saturdays, Sundays and public holidays 10am to noon and 2pm to 6.30pm; during the school holidays guided tours daily 2pm to 6pm. 20F. ☎ 02 97 43 31 56.

Excursion

Malansac: Parc de Préhistoire – ♿ Open daily 1 April to 15 October 10am to 8pm; 15 October to 11 November Sundays and public holidays 1.30pm to 6pm; during late October-early November school holidays open daily 1.30pm to 6pm. Closed 12 November to 31 March. 42F; children 22F. ☎ 02 97 43 34 17.

Château de la ROCHE-JAGU

Open 1 July to 31 August 10am to 7pm; 10 February to 30 June and 1 September to 1 November 10.30am to 12.30pm and 2pm to 6pm. Guided tours (1 hour) available at the same dates and times. Closed the rest of the year. 35F. ☎ 02 96 95 62 35.

Château des ROCHERS-SÉVIGNÉ

Guided tours (1 hour) 1 July to 30 September 10am to 12.30pm and 2pm to 6.15pm; the rest of the year open 10am to noon and 2pm to 5.30pm. Closed Tuesdays, Saturdays, Sundays and Monday mornings 1 November to 31 March, and on 1 January, Easter Sunday, 1 November and 25 December. 18F or 26F (combined ticket giving access to the castle in Vitré and the Chapelle St-Nicolas). ☎ 02 99 75 04 54.

Château de ROSANBO

The park is open to visitors and the château is open for guided tours (45 min) 1 July to 31 August 11am to 6.30pm; 1 April to 30 June 2pm to 5pm (tours at 2.30pm, 3.30pm and 4.30pm); 1 September to 31 October Sundays and holidays 2pm to 5pm (tours at 2.30pm, 3.30pm and 4.30pm). 30F. ☎ 02 96 35 18 77.

ROSCOFF

ℹ 46, rue Gambetta, 29680 – ☎ 02 98 61 12 13

Aquarium Charles-Pérez – Open daily 1 June to 31 August 10am to noon and 2pm to 7pm (6pm in June); 8 April to 31 May 10am to noon and 2pm to 6pm; 1 to 10 September 10am to noon and 1pm to 7pm; 11 September to 1 October, first three weekends in October and first weekend in November 2pm to 6pm. 26F. ☎ 02 98 29 23 23.

Viviers – Open Monday to Friday 9am to noon and 2pm to 5pm. Closed public holidays. No admission charge. ☎ 02 98 61 19 61.

Jardin exotique de Roscoff – Open 1 June to 30 September 10.30am to 7pm; 1 April to 31 May and 1 October to 30 November 10am to 12.30pm and 2pm to 5pm; 1 to 30 December and 1 February to 31 March 2pm to 5.30pm. Closed January and Tuesdays off-season. 25F. ☎ 02 98 61 29 19.

ROSPORDEN

Church – Open July and August Monday to Saturday 10am to noon and 3pm to 6pm. The rest of the year, apply to the presbytery. ☎ 02 98 59 21 65.

Excursion

St-Yvi: Church – To visit the church, apply to the presbytery.

ROSTRENEN

Église Notre-Dame-du-Roncier – Open 8am to 6.30pm. ☎ 02 96 29 01 55.

Excursion

St-Nicolas-du-Pélem: Church – Open in summer only 10am to 6pm. Apply to the presbytery at 9, rue du Porz-Koz. ☎ 02 96 29 21 65.

S

ST-BRIEUC

ℹ 7, rue Goueno, 22000 – ☎ 02 96 33 32 50

Guided Tour of the City – *In July and August Monday to Friday at 10.30am and 3pm. Apply to the Tourist Information Office.*

Cathédrale St-Étienne – Guided tours July and August at 10am and 3.30pm. Closed Sunday afternoons. Apply to the Tourist Information Office.

Musée – ♿ Open 9.30am to 11.45am and 1.30pm to 5.45pm. Closed Mondays, Sunday mornings, and on 1 January, 1 May, 1 and 11 November, and 25 December. 20F. ☎ 02 96 62 55 20.

Maison de la Baie de St-Brieuc et Marinarium à Hillion – Open daily 1 July to 31 August 9am to 6pm; the rest of the year daily except Saturdays 9am to noon and 1.30pm to 6pm. 25F. ☎ 02 96 32 27 98.

ST-GEORGES-DE-GRÉHAIGNE

Petit Mont-St-Michel – Open 1 July to 31 August 10am to 7pm; 1 to 30 June and 1 to 30 September and 1 to 30 September Sundays and holidays 11am to 7pm. 20F. ☎ 02 99 80 22 15.

ST-GILDAS-DE-RHUYS

Church: Treasury – Guided tours (1/4 hour) July and August 10.30am to noon and 2pm to 5pm. Closed Sundays and public holidays. 5F.

ST-GONÉRY

Chapelle St-Gonery – Open 9am to noon and 2pm to 6pm. ☎ 02 96 92 50 00.

ST-JEAN-DU-DOIGT

Church: Treasury – Owing to the current restoration work, the treasury is visible only on the day of the Saint-Jean pardon (late June).

ST-LUNAIRE

Vieille église St-Lunaire – Open Easter to September 9am to 7pm. ☎ 02 99 46 30 51 (Town Hall).

ST-MALO

ℹ Esplanade St-Vincent, 35400 – ☎ 02 99 56 64 48

Guided Tour of the City A – Apply to the Musée d'Histoire de la Ville set up in the great keep of the castle. ☎ 02 99 40 71 57.

Musée de la Poupée et du Jouet ancien – ♿ Open daily 1 July to 15 September 10am to 1pm and 2pm to 7pm. 25F. ☎ 02 99 40 15 51.

Musée d'Histoire de la Ville et d'Ethnographie du pays malouin – Open 10am to noon and 2pm to 6pm. Closed Mondays 1 October to 31 March and on 1 January, 1 May, 1 and 11 November, and 25 December. 25F. ☎ 02 99 40 71 57.

Tour Quic-en-Groigne – Open daily 1 April to 30 September 9.30am to noon and 2pm to 6pm. 20F. ☎ 02 99 40 80 26.

Fort National – Guided tours (30 min) daily 15 June to 30 September as well as Saturdays, Sundays and public holidays at Easter, Whitsun, Christmas and New Year's Day: times vary depending on the tide. Closed during high tide, 1 October to 1 April and 15 April to 15 May. 15F. ☎ 02 99 46 91 25.

Boat trips – Apply to the "Gare Maritime de la Bourse", BP 99, 35412 St-Malo Cedex. ☎ 02 99 20 03 00.

Channel Islands – The "Compagnie Maritime Condor Ferries" provides daily services to Jersey, Guernsey, Sark, Alderney and Weymouth by hydrofoil catamaran or conventional car-ferry. ☎ 02 99 20 03 00.

Y. Arthus-Bertrand/ALTITUDE

St-Malo

St-Servan-sur-Mer: Musée international du Long Cours Cap-Hornier – Open 10am to noon and 2pm to 6pm. Closed Mondays 1 October to 31 March and on 1 January, 1 May, 1 and 11 November, and 25 December. 25F. ☎ 02 99 40 71 58.

Église Ste-Croix – Open July and August.

Rothéneuf: Manoir de Jacques Cartier – Guided tours (30 min) daily 1 July to 31 August 10am to 11.30am and 2.30pm to 6pm. Closed weekends in June and September. The rest of the year guided tours Monday to Friday at 10am and 3pm. 25F. ☎ 02 99 40 97 73.

Rochers sculptés – *Open daily 1 April to 30 September 9am to 9pm; the rest of the year 10am to noon and 2pm to 5pm. Closed some days in winter, at Christmas and on 1 January. 14F. ☎ 02 99 56 97 64.*

Excursion

Château du Bos – ♿ Visitors have free access to the landscape garden. Guided tours (1 1/4 hours) of the "malouinière", a typical St-Malo mansion are available at 3.30pm 1 July to 31 August. 30F. ☎ 02 99 81 40 11.

Pointe de ST-MATHIEU

Lighthouse – Apply to the caretaker. ☎ 02 98 89 00 17.

ST-NAZAIRE

ℹ Place François-Blancho, 44600 – ☎ 02 40 22 40 65

Guided Tour of the City – Apply to the Tourist Information Office.

Panorama – Free access; same opening times as for the Sous-Marin Espadon.

Sous-Marin Espadon – Open daily 1 June to 8 September 9.30am to 6.30pm; mid-February to 31 May and 9 September to 2 November 10am to noon and 2pm to 6pm (except Tuesdays); the rest of the year open Wednesdays and Sundays only 10am to noon and 2pm to 6pm. It is advisable to book the day and time of the visit in advance. 45F (combined ticket giving access to the Ecomusée). ☎ 02 40 22 35 33 or 02 40 66 82 16.

Écomusée de St-Nazaire – Open daily 1 June to 8 September 9.30am to 6.30pm; mid-February to 31 May and 9 September to 2 November 10am to noon and 2pm to 6pm (except Tuesdays); the rest of the year open daily (except Mondays and Tuesdays) 10am to noon and 2pm to 6pm. 20F or 45F (combined ticket giving access to the Sous-Marin Espadon). ☎ 02 40 22 35 33 or 02 40 66 82 16.

Église Ste-Anne – Open weekdays only 10am to 11.30am and 5pm to 6.30pm. ☎ 02 40 53 31 95.

Église Notre-Dame-d'Espérance – To visit the church, apply to the presbytery at 2, rue Léon-Jouhaux. ☎ 02 40 70 17 43.

ST-POL-DE-LÉON

Chapelle du Kreisker – Open daily June to September 10am to noon and 2pm to 6pm. ☎ 02 98 69 07 72.

Excursion

Château de Kérouzéré – Exterior: free access all year. Interior: 3 guided tours (45 min) a day 15 July to 31 August (times posted beforehand); 1 to 14 July and 1 to 15 September Wednesdays and Sundays at 5.30pm; 15 May to 30 June and 16 September to 31 October Wednesdays at 5.30pm. 18F. ☎ 02 98 29 96 05.

ST-QUAY-PORTRIEUX

Excursion

Étables-sur-Mer: Chapelle Notre-Dame-de-l'Espérance – *Open daily (except Mondays) July and August 3pm to 6pm. The rest of the year apply to Monsieur le Curé d'Etables-sur-Mer, 22680. ☎ 02 96 70 61 51.*

Île de Bréhat – Details of boat service under Île de BREHAT above.

ST-THÉGONNEC

Chapelle funéraire – Open daily during official Summer Time 9am to 7pm. No admission charge.

STE-ANNE-D'AURAY

Basilica: Treasury – ♿ Open daily 10am to noon and 2pm to 5pm. Closed 1 October to 1 December. 10F. ☎ 02 97 57 68 80.

Historial de Sainte Anne – ♿ Open daily 1 March to 15 October 8am to 7pm. Guided tours (30 min) also available at the same times and dates. Closed 16 October to 28 February, in early November and at Christmas. 15F. ☎ 02 97 57 64 05.

Musée du costume breton – Open 7 March to 7 October 10am to noon and 2pm to 5pm. Closed 8 October to 6 March. 10F. ☎ 02 97 57 68 80.

Maison de Nicolazic – Open 1 April to 7 October 8am to 6pm. No admission charge. ☎ 02 97 57 68 80.

Île de SEIN

Access to the Island by Boat – There are daily crossings leaving from Audierne (Sainte-Evette) 3 July to 6 September at 9am, 11.30am and 16.50pm; 14 July to 25 August leaving from Camaret Saturdays and Sundays at 9am, return at 6.15pm (158F). The rest of the year leaving from Audierne daily at 9.30am, return at 4pm (except Wednesdays outside of the tourist season). 118F. ☎ 02 98 27 88 22.

Museum – Open daily 15 June to 15 September 10am to noon and 2pm to 6pm. 15F.

SIZUN

Excursions

Maison de la Rivière, de l'Eau et de la Pêche – Open daily July and August 10.30 to 7pm; in June and September weekdays 10.30am to 12.30pm and 1.30pm to 5.30pm, Sundays 10.30am to 12.30pm and 1.30pm to 7pm. 20F. ☎ 02 98 68 86 33.

Maison du Lac – Open daily July and August 10.30 to 12.30pm and 1.30pm to 6pm; in June and September weekdays 1.30pm to 5.30pm, Sundays 10.30 to 12.30pm to 6pm. 7F. ☎ 02 98 68 86 33.

Château de SUSCINIO

Open 1 June to 30 September 10am to 7pm; 1 April to 31 May open daily 10am to noon and 2pm to 7pm; the rest of the year open Thursdays, Saturdays, Sundays and public holidays 10am to noon and 2pm to 5pm. Closed Tuesdays and 20 December to 10 January. 25F. ☎ Sagemor 02 97 41 91 91.

T

TINTÉNIAC

Church – Open July and August 10am to noon and 3pm to 5pm. ☎ 02 99 68 03 77

Musée de l'outil et des métiers – *Open 1 July to 30 September 10am to noon (closed Sunday mornings) and 2.30pm to 6.30pm. 10F. ☎ 02 99 68 02 03.*

Zooloisirs – ♿ Open daily 1 April to 30 September 10.30am to 7pm (last admissions 5.30pm). Closed 1 October to 31 March. 47F (children 37F). ☎ 02 99 68 10 22.

Château de TONQUÉDEC

Open 1 July to 31 August 10am to 8pm; 1 April to 30 June and 1 to 30 September 3pm to 7pm. Guided tours (30 min) available at the same dates and times. 20F; ☎ 02 96 47 18 63.

TRÉGASTEL-PLAGE

Aquarium marin – Open July and August daily from 10am to 8pm; Easter to end of June and during September from 10am to noon and 2pm to 6pm; in October and during Christmas school holidays from 2pm to 5pm. 28F. ☎ 02 96 23 88 67.

TRÉGUIER

ℹ Hôtel de Ville – 22222 – ☎ 02 96 92 30 19

Maison de Renan – Open July and August 10am to 1pm and 2.30pm to 6.30pm; the rest of the year 10am to noon and 2pm to 6pm. Closed Tuesdays and Wednesdays (except in July and August). 25F. ☎ 02 96 92 45 63.

Cathédrale St-Tugdual: Treasury – ♿ *Open 1 July to 31 August 10am to 6.30pm except Sunday mornings; 15 to 30 June and 1 to 30 September 10am to noon and 2pm to 6pm. No visits during religious services. Closed the rest of the year and on 15 August. 4F. ☎ 02 96 92 30 51 or 02 96 92 30 19.*

Cloisters – Open daily 6 July to 31 August 9.30am to 6.30pm (Sundays 12.30pm to 6.30pm); 15 April to 30 June and all September 10am to noon and 2pm to 6pm (Sundays 2pm to 6pm). Closed during all religious services. 10F.

Excursion

Port-Blanc: Chapelle Notre-Dame-de-Port-Blanc – Open July and August 10.30am to 11.30am and 3pm to 6pm (except Sunday mornings); the rest of the year call for information. ☎ 02 96 92 67 16.

U – V

USHANT – See île d'OUESSANT

Le VAL-ANDRÉ

Excursions

Château de Bienassis – Guided tours daily except Sundays (45 min) 15 June to 15 September 10.30am to 12.30pm and 2pm to 6.30pm. 23F. ☎ 02 96 72 22 03.

Chapelle St-Jacques-le-Majeur – To visit the chapel, apply to the next-door farm "La Ville Blanche".

VANNES

ℹ 1, rue Thiers, 56000 – ☎ 02 97 47 24 34

Guided Tour of the City A – *Visit of the old town (1 hour 30 min) July and August, 10.30am and 3pm (except Sundays and holidays); 23 April to late June and during September Wednesdays and Saturdays at 3pm. Visits suitable for children are organised on Tuesdays and Thursdays. Apply to the "Animation du Patrimoine", Place St-Pierre. ☎ 02 97 47 35 86.*

Musée de la Cohue – Open daily (except public holidays) 15 June to 30 September 10am to 6pm; the rest of the year open 10am to noon and 2pm to 6pm. Closed Tuesdays, Sunday mornings and public holidays. 26F. ☎ 02 97 47 35 86.

Cathédrale St-Pierre – Guided tours July and August. Apply to the presbytery. ☎ 02 97 47 10 88.

Treasury – Open *July and August 10.30am to 6pm; the rest of the year Mondays, Tuesdays, Thursdays and Fridays 10am to noon and 2pm to 5pm. 14F. Closed in January, February, 1 May, 14 July and 15 August. 14F. ☎ 02 97 42 40 55.*

Bourbansais (Château) *Ille-et-Vilaine* 74
Bourbriac *Côtes-d'Armor* 148
Bourdonnais, Mahé de la 266
Le Bourg 75
Box beds 46
Branféré (Parc Zoologique) *Morbihan* 253
Brasparts *Finistère* 57
Bréca *Loire-Atlantique* 137
Brécun (Île) *Loire-Atlantique* 137
Bréhat (Île) *Côtes-d'Armor* 74
Bréhec-en-Plouha *Côtes-d'Armor* 210
Brennilis *Finistère* 59
Brest *Finistère* 76
Bretagne (Centre Culturel des Métiers) 176
Bretagne (Jardin Zoologique) 72
Bretagne (Musée de l'École Rurale) 92
Bretagne (Parc Ornithologique) 252
Bretesche (Château) *Loire-Atlantique* 253
Breton art 40
Breton climate 23
Breton costumes 30, 235
Breton flag 33
Breton food and drink 48
Breton furniture 46
Breton language 31
Breton legends 28, 210
Breton literature 34
Breton navigators 98, 271
Breton Parliament 251
Breton recipes 49
Breton saints 29
Breton traditions 28
Brézal (Moulin) *Finistère* 124
Brézellec (Pointe) *Finistère* 102
Brière (Parc naturel régional) 27, 135
Brigneau *Finistère* 240
Brignogan-Plages *Finistère* 82
Brittany and painters 35
Brizeux, Auguste 34
Brocéliande 28, 210
Broualan *Côtes-d'Armor* 120
Broussais 266
Brunec (Île) 134
Bruz 252
Bubry *Morbihan* 313
Budoc, Saint 74
Buguélès *Côtes-d'Armor* 286
Bulat-Pestivien *Côtes-d'Armor* 83
Burthulet *Côtes-d'Armor* 87

C

Cabellou (Pointe) *Finistère* 96
Cadoran (Presqu'île) *Finistère* 207
Cadou, René-Guy 35
Cadoudal, Georges 229
Caesar 187
Cairns 40
Calendar saints 30
Callac *Côtes-d'Armor* 87
Callac *Morbihan* 293
Calloc'h, Jean-Pierre 35
Callot (Île) *Finistère* 86
Calvaries 44, 45
Camaret-sur-Mer *Finistère* 83
Camer (Île) *Loire-Atlantique* 137
Camerun (Île) *Loire-Atlantique* 137
Cancale *Ille-et-Vilaine* 84
Canterbury, Knight 113
Caouënnec *Côtes-d'Armor* 166
Cap-Coz *Finistère* 71
Caradeuc (Château) *Ille-et-Vilaine* 65
Carantec *Finistère* 85
Cardinal (Pointe) *Morbihan* 68
Careil (Château) *Loire-Atlantique* 142
Carhaix-Plouguer *Finistère* 86
Carnac *Morbihan* 87
Carnac-Plage *Morbihan* 89
Carnoët (Forêt) *Finistère* 240
Caro (Anse) *Finistère* 219
Carrier, Jean-Baptiste 194, 247
Cartier, Jacques 265, 271
Cassard, Jacques 194
Cast *Finistère* 92
Le Castel *Côtes-d'Armor* 283
Castelli (Pointe) *Loire-Atlantique* 142
Castennec (Site) *Morbihan* 224
Castles 46
Castle: see under proper name
Catell-Gollet 45
Cathedrals 41
Celtic clubs 33
Celtic exodus 24, 75
Centre Océanographique de Bretagne 82
Cézembre (Île) *Ille-et-Vilaine* 118
La Chalotais 246
Champ-Dolent (Menhir) *Ille-et-Vilaine* 120
Champeaux *Ille-et-Vilaine* 90, 295
La Chapelle-des-Marais *Loire-Atlantique* 137
La Chapelle-Thouarault *Ille-et-Vilaine* 181
Chapel: see under proper name
Chapels 41
Charnel houses 44
Château (Pointe) *Côtes-d'Armor* 286
Chateaubriand, François-René de 34, 93, 265, 269
Châteaubriant *Loire-Atlantique* 90
Châteaubriant, Alphonse de 35
Châteaugiron *Ille-et-Vilaine* 92
Châteaulin *Finistère* 92
Châteauneuf-du-Faou *Finistère* 180
Châtelaudren *Côtes-d'Armor* 93
Chatelier (Écluse) *Ille-et-Vilaine* 243
Chats (Pointe) *Morbihan* 139
Chausey (Îles) 118
La Chaussée-Neuve *Loire-Atlantique* 137
Chevet (Pointe) *Côtes-d'Armor* 107
Chèvre (Cap) *Finistère* 112
La Chèze *Côtes-d'Armor* 176
Chouannerie 60, 214, 229, 231, 252
Chouans 128, 229
Church: see under proper name
Churches 41
Church plate 44
Cider 48, 243
Cigogne (Île) 134
Citadelle (Bois) *Côtes-d'Armor* 75
La Clarté *Côtes-d'Armor* 214
Claude of France 289
Cléden-Poher *Finistère* 180
Clisson, Olivier de 60, 155
Coastal fishing 20, 108
Coastal scenery 8
Coatfrec (Château) *Côtes-d'Armor* 166
Cobac (Parc) *Ille-et-Vilaine* 94
Cod fishing 20
Coiffes 30
Cojoux (Landes) *Ille-et-Vilaine* 245
Colbert 76
Combourg *Ille-et-Vilaine* 93
Combrit *Finistère* 238
Commana *Finistère* 125
Comper (Château) *Ille-et-Vilaine* 210

Concarneau *Finistère* 94
Conguel (Pointe) *Morbihan* 230
Conleau 292
Conleau (Presqu'île) *Morbihan* 292
Le Conquet *Finistère* 55
La Corderie *Côtes-d'Armor* 75
Corentine, Saint 231
Corn-ar-Gazel (Dunes) *Finistère* 54
Cornély, Saint 88
Cornic, Charles 190
Corniche Bretonne 97
Corniche de l'Armorique 98
Corniguel (Pont) *Finistère* 238
Cornouaille 100
Corong (Gorges) *Finistère* 87
Corret, Théophile-Malo 86
Corsen (Pointe) *Finistère* 55
Corseul *Côtes-d'Armor* 116
Côte d'Amour 141
Côte d'Émeraude 106
Côte du Goëlo 209
Côte Sauvage 68, 109, 206, 228, 229
Cotriade 49
Coz-Porz 283
Country chapels 41
Country churches 41
Cranou (Forêt) *Finistère* 58
Crapaud (Rocher) *Finistère* 55
Créac'h (Phare) *Finistère* 206
Créac'h Maout (Viewing Table) *Côtes-d'Armor* 287
Crêpes 48
Crévy (Château) *Morbihan* 217
Le Croisic *Loire-Atlantique* 109
Cromlechs 40
Crouesty (Port) *Morbihan* 190
Crozon *Finistère* 110
Crozon (Presqu'île) *Finistère* 110
Crucuno (Dolmen) *Morbihan* 89
Crustaceans 20

D

Dahouët *Côtes-d'Armor* 288
Dahut 28
Daoulas *Finistère* 112
Daoulas (Gorges) *Morbihan* 145
Décollé (Pointe) 264
Deep-sea fishing 20, 307
Desilles, André 266
Diable (Grotte) 152
Diable (Rochers) *Finistère* 239
Diben (Pointe) *Finistère* 100
Dinan *Côtes-d'Armor* 113, 242
Dinan (Pointe) *Finistère* 111
Dinard *Ille-et-Vilaine* 116
Dirinon *Finistère* 112
Dissignac (Tumulus) *Loire-Atlantique* 275
Dobrée, Thomas 202
Dockyards 22, 79, 174, 273
Doëlan *Finistère* 240
Dol (Marais) *Ille-et-Vilaine* 118
Dol (Mont) *Ille-et-Vilaine* 118
Dol-de-Bretagne *Ille-et-Vilaine* 119
Dolmens 40
Donges *Loire-Atlantique* 121
Douarnenez *Finistère* 121
Le Dourduff *Finistère* 100
Drénec (Île) 134
Le Drennec *Finistère* 238
Duc (Étang) *Morbihan* 217
Duguay-Trouin 265
Du Guesclin, Bertrand 24, 60, 113, 246

E

Échelle (Pointe) *Morbihan* 69
Eckmühl (Phare) *Finistère* 105
Economic activity 23
Edict of Nantes 26, 194
Ellé (Vallée) *Morbihan* 127
Elven (Tours) *Morbihan* 168
Enclos Paroissiaux 44, 124
Entombment 44
Épiniac *Côtes-d'Armor* 120
Erdre (River) 204
Er-Grah (Tumulus) 170
Ergué-Gabéric *Finistère* 236
Er Lanic (Île) *Morbihan* 134
Erquy *Côtes-d'Armor* 108
Erquy (Cap) *Côtes-d'Armor* 108
Escoublac *Loire-Atlantique* 64, 141
Espagnols (Pointe) *Finistère* 111
Espinay (Château) 90
Étables-sur-Mer *Côtes-d'Armor* 177
Étel (Barre) *Morbihan* 151
Étel (Rivière) *Morbihan* 150
Étêtés (Pointe) 117

F

Falguéréc-en-Séné (Réserve Naturelle) *Morbihan* 292
Family names 32
Le Faou *Finistère* 126
Faoudel (Vallée) 258
Le Faouët *Morbihan* 126
Fédrun (Île) *Loire-Atlantique* 136
Fer à Cheval (Promenade) *Finistère* 153
Ferme-Musée du Léon *Finistère* 72
La Ferrière *Côtes-d'Armor* 176
Festivals 313-315
Feunteun Velen (Presqu'île) *Finistère* 207
Féval, Paul 34
Feydeau (Île) 195
Fish auctions 315
Fish breeding 20
Fishing 20
Flanders, Jeanne of 150
Foix, Françoise de 90
Foleux *Morbihan* 253
Le Folgoët *Finistère* 53
La Fontenelle 103, 121
Fonts 43
Forest: see under proper name
Forests 22
Forêt (Étang) 63
La Forêt-Fouesnant *Finistère* 128
Les Forges de Paimpont *Ille-et-Vilaine* 211
Les Forges-des-Salles 145
Fort-Bloqué (Plage) *Morbihan* 175
Fortresses 46
Les Fossés-Blancs *Loire-Atlantique* 137
Fouesnant *Finistère* 128
Fougères *Ille-et-Vilaine* 128
Fougères (Forêt Domaniale) *Ille-et-Vilaine* 132
Fougères, Étienne de 34
Fountains 42
Fouquet, Marquis of Belle-Île 66

François I, King 90
François II, Duke 197
Fréhel (Cap) *Côtes-d'Armor* 133
Fréron, Élie 34, 231
Le Fret *Finistère* 111
Fulton 83

G

Gabelle 141
Gabriel, Jacques 246
Galettes 48, 221
Gallery graves 40
Garde (Pointe) 262
Garde Guérin (Pointe) *Ille-et-Vilaine* 107
Garrot (Mont) *Ille-et-Vilaine* 242
Gauguin, Paul 48, 221
Le Gâvre Loire-Atlantique 73
Le Gâvre (Forêt) *Loire-Atlantique* 73
Gavrinis (Cairn) *Morbihan* 134
Giautec (Île) 134
Glénan (Îles) *Finistère* 134
Gloriette (Île) 195
Golden Belt 22
Gorges : see under proper name
Gouesnou *Finistère* 52
Le Gouffre *(Huelgoat)* 153
Le Gouffre *(Tréguier)* 286
Goulaine (Château) 134
Goulven *Finistère* 82
Gourin *Morbihan* 179
Gournay 266
Grâces *Côtes-d'Armor* 148
Gradlon, King 28, 232
Grall, Xavier 221
Grand Bé (Île) 269
Grand-Champ *Morbihan* 292
Grande (Île) *Côtes-d'Armor* 98
La Grande Brière 135
Grand-Fougeray *Ille-et-Vilaine* 138
Grand Phare 68
Grand Rocher *Côtes-d'Armor* 99
Grands Sables (Plage) (Belle-Île) 69
Grands Sables (Plage) (Groix) 139
Graslin 199
Grève Blanche 283
Groix (Écomusée) 139
Groix (Île) *Morbihan* 138
Le Grouanec *Finistère* 53
Grouin (Pointe) *Ille-et-Vilaine* 85, 106
Groulais (Château) 73
Guéhenno *Morbihan* 139
Guengat *Finistère* 124
Guenroc *Ille-et-Vilaine* 65
Guérande *Loire-Atlantique* 139
Guérande (Presqu'île) *Loire-Atlantique* 140
La Guerche-de-Bretagne *Ille-et-Vilaine* 143
Guer-Coëtquidan 212
Guerlédan (Barrage) *Côtes-d'Armor* 145
Guerlédan (Lac) *Côtes-d'Armor* 144, 224
Guerlesquin *Finistère* 193
Le Guerno *Morbihan* 253
Guerzido (Grève) *Côtes-d'Armor* 75
Guette (Promenade) 288
Guilben (Pointe) *Côtes-d'Armor* 209
Le Guildo *Côtes-d'Armor* 146
Guilvinec *Finistère* 105
Guimiliau *Finistère* 146
La Guimorais *Ille-et-Vilaine* 106
Guingamp *Côtes-d'Armor* 146
Gurunhuel *Côtes-d'Armor* 70
Gwaker (Écluse) *Finistère* 179

H

Hac (Château) *Côtes-d'Armor* 65
Halguen (Pointe) *Loire-Atlantique* 59
Le Haut-Pénestin *Morbihan* 59
Headdresses 30
Hédé *Ille-et-Vilaine* 149
Héliaz, Pierre-Jakez 35
Hémon, Louis 35
Hennebont *Morbihan* 150
Hilvern (Rigole) *Côtes-d'Armor* 176
Historical notes 24
Historical routes 27, 310
Hoche, General 229
Hœdic (Île) *Morbihan* 152
Houat (Île) *Morbihan* 152
Huelgoat *Finistère* 57, 152
Huelgoat (Forêt) 153
Huelgoat (Plateau) 86
Hugo, Victor 128
Hunaudaye (Château) *Côtes-d'Armor* 154, 157
Hundred Years War 24
Hydro-electric power 241

I – J

Iffs (Église) *Ille-et-Vilaine* 149
Île-Tudy *Finistère* 173
Iliz Koz (Ruines) *Finistère* 53
The India Company 174, 228
Industry 23
Ingrand, Max 53
Is, Lost City of 28
Isolde 28
Jacob, Max 234
Jaudy (Estuaire) 286
Jean and Jeanne (Menhirs) *Morbihan* 68
Josselin *Morbihan* 155
Jouvence (Fontaine) *Ille-et-Vilaine* 210
Jouvente (Cale) *Ille-et-Vilaine* 243
Le Juch *Finistère* 123
Jugan, Jeanne 270
Jugon-les-Lacs *Côtes-d'Armor* 157
Jument (Pointe) *Finistère* 96

K

Kandinsky, Vasili 199
Karaes (Moulin) *Finistère* 206
Karreg an Tan 237
Keramenez (Panorama) *Finistère* 219
Kerascoët *Finistère* 97
Kérazan (Manoir) *Finistère* 158
Kerbihan (Parc) 150
Kerbourg (Dolmen) *Loire-Atlantique* 137
Kerbreudeur (Calvaire) *Finistère* 178
Kercado (Tumulus) *Morbihan* 89
Kerdéniel (Pointe) *Finistère* 219
Kerdévot (Chapelle) *Finistère* 237
Kerdonis (Pointe) *Morbihan* 69
Kerdruc *Finistère* 222
Kerfany-les-Pins *Finistère* 240
Kerfeunteun (Église) *Finistère* 237
Kerfons (Chapelle) *Côtes-d'Armor* 166
Kergoat (Chapelle) *Finistère* 172
Kergomadeac'h (Château) *Finistère* 218
Kergrist (Château) *Côtes-d'Armor* 166

Kergrist-Moëlou *Côtes-d'Armor* 259
Kergroadès (Chapelle) *Finistère* 55
Kerguéhennec (Domaine) *Morbihan* 15[illegible]
Kerguelen, Yves de 231
Kerguntuil (Dolmen and Gallery Grave) *Côtes-d'Armor* 98
Kerhinet *Loire-Atlantique* 137
Kerhuon *Finistère* 81
Kérity *Finistère* 105
Kerjean (Château) *Finistère* 159
Kerlaz *Finistère* 101
Kerlescan (Alignements) *Morbihan* 88
Kerlud *Morbihan* 170
Kerlud (Dolmen) *Morbihan* 170
Kermagen (Plage) *Côtes-d'Armor* 287
Kermaria *Côtes-d'Armor* 159
Kermario (Alignements) *Morbihan* 88
Kermorvan (Pointe) *Finistère* 55
Kernascléden *Morbihan* 160
Kernisi (Panorama) *Finistère* 219
Kérogan (Baie) *Finistère* 238
Keroman 174
Kerouat (Moulins) *Finistère* 125
Kérouzéré (Château) *Finistère* 277
Kerpenhir (Pointe) *Morbihan* 171
Kerroc'h (Tour) *Côtes-d'Armor* 208
Kersaint *Finistère* 54
Kervalet *Loire-Atlantique* 141
Kervignac *Morbihan* 150
Kerzerho (Alignements) *Morbihan* 89
Kig-ha-farz 49
Kouign-amann 49

L

Laënnec, René 123, 231
Lagatjar (Alignements) *Finistère* 110
Laïta 175, 240
Lambader *Finistère* 160
Lamballe *Côtes-d'Armor* 160
Lamballe, Princess 160
Lamennais, Félicité de 34, 266
La Mennais, Jean-Marie de 217
Lampaul *Finistère* 206
Lampaul-Guimiliau *Finistère* 162
Lampaul-Ploudalmézeau *Finistère* 54
Lancieux *Côtes-d'Armor* 107
Landais, Pierre 293
Landerneau *Finistère* 163
Landévennec *Finistère* 164
Land Formation 18
Landivisiau *Finistère* 164
La Landriais *Ille-et-Vilaine* 243
Landunvez (Pointe) *Finistère* 54
Langon *Ille-et-Vilaine* 138
Langonnet (Abbaye) *Morbihan* 127
Languidou (Chapelle) *Finistère* 103
Languivoa (Chapelle) *Finistère* 104
Laninon 77
Lanleff *Côtes-d'Armor* 159
Lanloup *Côtes-d'Armor* 210
Lanmeur *Finistère* 164
Lannédern *Finistère* 57
Lannion *Côtes-d'Armor* 165
Lanrigan (Château) *Ille-et-Vilaine* 94
Lanrivain *Côtes-d'Armor* 168
Lantic (Chapelle) *Côtes-d'Armor* 73
Lanvallay *Côtes-d'Armor* 243
Lanvaux (Landes) *Morbihan* 293
Largoët (Forteresse) *Morbihan* 168
Larmor-Baden *Morbihan* 188
Larmor-Plage *Morbihan* 168
La Rouërie, Marquis 129
La Latte (Fort) *Côtes-d'Armor* 169
Lauberlach *Finistère* 219
Laz (Point de Vue) *Finistère* 180
Le Braz, Anatole 34
Le Breton, Guillaume 34
Lechiagat *Finistère* 105
Le Goffic, Charles 34, 165
Léguer (River) 166
Léhélec (Château) *Ille-et-Vilaine* 253
Léhon *Côtes-d'Armor* 169
Lemordant 48, 235
Leperdit, Mayor 247
Lesage 34, 189
Lesconil *Finistère* 105
Lesneven *Finistère* 170
Le Letty *Finistère* 71
Leydé (Pointe) *Finistère* 123
Lézardrieux *Côtes-d'Armor* 286
Lighthouses 206, 244
Lindu, Choquet de 79
Livestock 23
Lizio (Écomusée) *Morbihan* 217
Locarn *Côtes-d'Armor* 87
Loc-Envel *Côtes-d'Armor* 70
Loch (Île) 134
Locmaria (Chapelle) (Abers) *Côtes-d'Armor* 53
Locmaria (Chapelle) (Belle-Isle-en-Terre) *Côtes-d'Armor* 69
Locmaria (Belle-Île) *Morbihan* 69
Locmaria (Groix) *Morbihan* 138
Locmariaquer *Morbihan* 170
Locmariaquer (Ensemble Mégalithique) *Morbihan* 170
Locmélar *Finistère* 281
Locminé *Morbihan* 171
Locquémeau *Côtes-d'Armor* 167
Locquirec *Finistère* 171
Locquirec (Pointe) 171
Locronan *Finistère* 172
Locronan (Montagne) *Finistère* 172
Loctudy *Finistère* 173
Loguivy-lès-Lannion 167
Loqueffret *Finistère* 57
Le Logeo *Morbihan* 199
Loguivy-de-la-Mer *Côtes-d'Armor* 209
Lohéac (Manoir de l'AutomobÎle) *Ille-et-Vilaine* 173
Lorient *Morbihan* 174
Loti, Pierre 35, 208
Louannec *Côtes-d'Armor* 214
Loudéac *Côtes-d'Armor* 176
Louvigné-de-Bais *Ille-et-Vilaine* 144
Lower Brittany 32
Lupin (Château) *Ille-et-Vilaine* 106

M

Madec, René 231
Madeleine (Calvaire) *Loire-Atlantique* 222
Madeleine (Fuseau) *Loire-Atlantique* 222
Magdeleine (Chapelle) *Loire-Atlantique* 73

Maillé (Château) *Finistère* 218
Maillé-Brézé (Navire) 202
Maison Cornec 58
Maison de la Baie d'Audierne *Finistère* 104
Maison de la Rivière, de l'Eau et de la Pêche 281
Maison de l'Éclusier 136
Maison des Artisans 58
Maison du Pays Bigouden 226
Malansac (Parc de Préhistoire) *Morbihan* 255
Malestroit *Morbihan* 176
Malouinières 272
Mané-Croch (Dolmen) *Morbihan* 89
Mané-er-Hroech (Tumulus) *Morbihan* 171
Mané-Hellec (Pointe) *Morbihan* 151
Mané-Kerioned (Dolmens) *Morbihan* 89
Mané-Lud (Dolmen) 170
Mané-Rethal (Dolmen) 170
Mané-Verh *Morbihan* 188
Marc'h Sammet (Viewing table) *Finistère* 99
Marie-Morgane 29
Marinarium de la Baie 262
Markets 315
Martin-Plage *Côtes-d'Armor* 262
La Martyre *Finistère* 124
Martyrs (Champ) 61
Maudez (Croix) 75
Megaliths 40, 88, 170, 245
Méheut, Mathurin 162, 236
La Meilleraye-de-Bretagne *Loire-Atlantique* 177
Melleray (Abbaye) *Loire-Atlantique* 177
Melrand 225
Members of Parliament 251
Ménec (Alignements) *Morbihan* 88
Menez Bré *Côtes-d'Armor* 69, 148
Ménez-Hom *Finistère* 92, 177
Menez-Meur (Domaine) *Finistère* 58
Menhirs 40
Merlevenez *Morbihan* 150
Merlin 28, 210
Michael, Saint 118, 182
Millier (Pointe) *Finistère* 101
Minard (Pointe) *Côtes-d'Armor* 210
Mine d'Or (Plage) *Loire-Atlantique* 59
Le Minihic *Ille-et-Vilaine* 271
Minihy-Tréguier *Côtes-d'Armor* 285
Le Miniou 258
Missillac *Loire-Atlantique* 253
Modern towns 47
Moëlan-sur-Mer *Finistère* 240
Moines (Îles) *Côtes-d'Armor* 214
Moines (Île) *Morbihan* 187
Molène *Finistère* 205
Monbouan (Château) *Ille-et-Vilaine* 144
Moncontour *Côtes-d'Armor* 178
Montagnes Noires 178
Montbarey (Fort) *Finistère* 81
Monteneuf (Site Mégalithique) *Morbihan* 212
Montfort, House of 25, 76, 150
Montfort-sur-Meu *Ille-et-Vilaine* 181
Montmuran (Château) *Ille-et-Vilaine* 149
Montoir-de-Bretagne *Loire-Atlantique* 135
Mont-St-Michel *Manche* 182
Mont-St-Michel (Abbaye) 184
Mont-St-Michel (Baie) 186
Morbihan (Golfe) 61, 187
Mordreuc (Cale) *Côtes-d'Armor* 243
Morgat *Finistère* 190
Morlaix *Finistère* 190
Mortas 135
Mottes (Lac) *Ille-et-Vilaine* 143
Mougau-Bian *Finistère* 125
Moulin (Chaos) 152
Moulinet (Pointe) 116
Mountains 22
Mousterlin (Pointe) *Finistère* 71
Mur-de-Bretagne *Côtes-d'Armor* 193
Muscadet 48
Musée des Télécommunications 215
Musée de la Paysannerie 120
Musée de la Résistance Bretonne 177

N

Nantes 194
Nantes-Brest (Canal) 259
Napoléon Bonaparte 223
Napoléonville 223
National Sailing School 230
Névez *Finistère* 222
Niou Uhella *Finistère* 206
Nizon *Finistère* 222
Nominoé 289
Notre-Dame-de-Bon-Voyage (Chapelle) *Finistère* 206
Notre-Dame-de-Confort (Église) *Finistère* 101
Notre-Dame-de-Crénenan (Chapelle) *Finistère* 216
Notre-Dame-de-Kérinec (Chapelle) *Finistère* 101
Notre-Dame-de-la-Clarté (Chapelle) *Finistère* 214
Notre-Dame-de-la-Cour (Chapelle) *Côtes-d'Armor* 73
Notre-Dame-de-la-Joie (Chapelle) *Finistère* 105
Notre-Dame-de-la-Paix (Chapelle) *Finistère* 240
Notre-Dame-de-l'Espérance (Chapelle) *Côtes-d'Armor* 277
Notre-Dame-de-Lorette (Oratoire) 99
Notre-Dame-de-Port-Blanc (Chapelle) 286
Notre-Dame-de-Quilinen (Calvaire) 237
Notre-Dame-de-Quilinen (Chapelle) 237
Notre-Dame-de-Restudo (Chapelle) *Côtes-d'Armor* 149
Notre-Dame-de-Rocamadour (Chapelle) 83
Notre-Dame-des-Vertus (Chapelle) *Morbihan* 228
Notre-Dame-de-Timadeuc (Abbaye) *Morbihan* 225
Notre-Dame-de-Tréminou (Chapelle) *Finistère* 226
Notre-Dame-de-Tronoën (Calvaire) *Finistère* 104, 204
Notre-Dame-de-Tronoën (Chapelle) 104, 204
Notre-Dame-du-Crann (Chapelle) *Finistère* 204
Notre-Dame-du-Guiaudet (Chapelle) *Côtes-d'Armor* 168
Notre-Dame-du-Haut (Chapelle) *Côtes-d'Armor* 178
Notre-Dame-du-Loc (Chapelle) 293

Notre-Dame-du-Tertre (Chapelle) 93
Notre-Dame-du-Tronchet (Abbaye) *Ille-et-Vilaine* 120
Notre-Dame-du-Verger (Chapelle) *Ille-et-Vilaine* 106
Nouë, François de la 160, 178
Nouvoitou *Ille-et-Vilaine* 92
Nova Scotia 67, 26
Noyal-Pontivy *Morbihan* 225

O – P

Odet (River) *Finistère* 238
Old streets and houses 47
Ossuaries 44
Ouessant (Île) *Finistère* 205
Oyster breeding 22, 84
Paimpol *Côtes-d'Armor* 208
Paimpont *Ille-et-Vilaine* 211
Paimpont (Forêt) 210
La Palud (Plage) *Finistère* 111
Le Palus-Plage *Côtes-d'Armor* 277
Paon (Phare) *Côtes-d'Armor* 75
Paramé *Ille-et-Vilaine* 271
Parc Animalier (Grande Brière) 136
Pardons 29, 172
Parish closes 44, 124
Pas-du-Houx (Étang) *Ille-et-Vilaine* 211
La Passagère *Ille-et-Vilaine* 242
Patron saints 29
Pays alréen 61
Pays de Rennes (Écomusée) *Ille-et-Vilaine* 251
Peat bogs 135
Pen-al-Lann (Pointe) *Finistère* 86
Pen-ar-Hoat *Finistère* 58
Pen-Bé *Loire-Atlantique* 59
Pencran *Finistère* 212
Pendille (Île) *Loire-Atlantique* 137
Penfeld (Dockyard) 79
Penfret 134
Pen-Guen *Côtes-d'Armor* 108
Penhir (Pointe) *Finistère* 213
Penhoët (Basin) 274
Penhors *Finistère* 103
Penmarch *Finistère* 105
Penmarch (Presqu'île) *Finistère* 103
Pen-Men *Morbihan* 139
Pen-Mur (Moulin) *Morbihan* 253
Penthièvre *Morbihan* 231
Penthièvre (Fort) *Morbihan* 231
Penthièvre (Isthme) *Morbihan* 231
Percho (Pointe) *Morbihan* 230
Le Perguet *Finistère* 71
Pern (Pointe) *Finistère* 207
Perros-Guirec *Côtes-d'Armor* 213
Perros-Hamon *Côtes-d'Armor* 209
Persquen *Morbihan* 313
Pestivien *Côtes-d'Armor* 83
Petit Mont-St-Michel *Ille-et-Vilaine* 263
Pink Granite Coast 97
Pierres-Plates (Dolmen) *Morbihan* 171
Les Pierres Sonnantes *Côtes-d'Armor* 146
Pies (Île) *Morbihan* 245
Piriac-sur-Mer *Loire-Atlantique* 142
Place names 31
Plateaux 22
Pléhérel-Plage *Côtes-d'Armor* 108
Pléneuf (Pointe) 288
Plessis-Josso (Château) *Morbihan* 292
Plestin (Pointe) 99
Plestin-les-Grèves *Côtes-d'Armor* 99
Pleudihen-sur-Rance *Côtes-d'Armor* 243
Pleubian *Côtes-d'Armor* 287
Pleumeur-Bodou *Côtes-d'Armor* 215
Pleyben *Finistère* 216
Pleyber-Christ *Finistère* 126
Ploaré *Finistère* 123
Ploërdut *Morbihan* 216
Ploërmel *Morbihan* 216
Plogonnec *Finistère* 101
Plomarc'h (Sentier) *Finistère* 123
Plomeur *Finistère* 226
Plomodiern *Finistère* 315
Ploubalay (Château d'Eau) *Ille-et-Vilaine* 107
Ploubazlanec *Côtes-d'Armor* 208
Ploudiry *Finistère* 125
Plouër-sur-Rance *Côtes-d'Armor* 243
Plouescat *Finistère* 218
Plougasnou *Finistère* 99
Plougastel (Presqu'île) *Finistère* 81, 218
Plougastel-Daoulas *Finistère* 218
Plougonven *Finistère* 192
Plouguerneau *Finistère* 53
Plouha *Côtes-d'Armor* 277
Plouharnel *Morbihan* 231
Ploujean *Finistère* 193
Ploumanach *Côtes-d'Armor* 214, 219
Ploumilliau *Côtes-d'Armor* 168
Plourac'h *Côtes-d'Armor* 86
Plouvien *Finistère* 53
Plovan *Finistère* 103
Plozévet *Finistère* 102
Pluneret *Morbihan* 61
Polders 119
Pont-Aven *Finistère* 221
Pont-Aven, School 221
Pont-Callek (Château) *Morbihan* 160
Pont-Callek (Forêt) *Morbihan* 160
Pontchâteau *Loire-Atlantique* 222
Pont-Croix *Finistère* 223
Pont-de-Buis-lès-Quimerch *Finistère* 58
Pontivy *Morbihan* 223
Pont-l'Abbé *Finistère* 225
Pont-Lorois *Morbihan* 151
Pont-Scorff (Zoo) *Morbihan* 175
Pontusval (Pointe) *Finistère* 82
Porches 42
Pornichet *Loire-Atlantique* 227
Pors-Carn (Plage) *Finistère* 104
Pors-Even *Côtes-d'Armor* 209
Pors-Hir *Côtes-d'Armor* 286
Pors Pin *Côtes-d'Armor* 210
Porspoder *Finistère* 54
Pors-Poulhan *Finistère* 102
Pors-Scaff (Anse) *Côtes-d'Armor* 286
Port-Andro *Morbihan* 69
Port-Anna *Morbihan* 292
Port-Bara *Morbihan* 230
Port-Blanc (Belle-île) *Morbihan* 69
Port-Blanc (Tréguier) *Côtes-d'Armor* 286
Port-Clos *Côtes-d'Armor* 75
Port-Coton (Aiguilles) *Morbihan* 69
Port-Donnant *Morbihan* 68
Port-Fouquet *Morbihan* 68
Port-Goulphar *Morbihan* 68

Port-Haliguen *Morbihan* 230
Port-Kérel *Morbihan* 69
Port-la-Forêt *Finistère* 128
Port-Launay *Finistère* 57
Port-Lay *Morbihan* 139
Port-Lazo *Côtes-d'Armor* 209
Port-Lin (Plage) *Loire-Atlantique* 109
Port-Louis *Morbihan* 227
Port-Manech *Finistère* 222
Port-Maria *Morbihan* 69
Port-Melin *Morbihan* 139
Port-Mélite *Morbihan* 139
Port-Moguer *Côtes-d'Armor* 277
Port-Navalo *Morbihan* 190
Portsall *Finistère* 54
Port-St-Nicolas *Morbihan* 139
Port-Tudy *Morbihan* 139
Port-Yorck *Morbihan* 69
Porz Arlan (Crique) *Finistère* 208
Porz Doun (Pointe) *Finistère* 207
Porz-Mabo *Côtes-d'Armor* 283
Porz Yusin (Crique) *Finistère* 207
Poudrantais *Morbihan* 59
Poulains (Pointe) *Morbihan* 68
Poulancre (Vallée) *Côtes-d'Armor* 193
Pouldavid *Finistère* 123
Pouldohan *Finistère* 96
Le Pouldu *Finistère* 240
Poul Fetan (Village) *Morbihan* 63
Pouliguen *Loire-Atlantique* 228
Prehistoric monuments 40
Presqu'île Sauvage 286
Prés salés 48
Primel (Pointe) *Finistère* 100
Primel-Trégastel *Finistère* 100
Proëlla crosses 206
Pulpits 43
Purlins 38-39

Q

Queffélec, Henri 35
Quelven (Chapelle) *Morbihan* 225
Quénécan (Forêt) *Morbihan* 145
Querrien *Côtes-d'Armor* 176
Questembert *Morbihan* 228
Quiberon *Morbihan* 229
Quiberon (Presqu'île) *Morbihan* 229
Quillivic, René 232, 272
Quimerch *Finistère* 58
Quimper *Finistère* 231
Quimper faïence 231, 236
Quimperlé *Finistère* 239
Quinipily (Venus) *Morbihan* 63
Quintin Côtes-d'Armor 241

R

Radôme 215
Raguenès-Plage *Finistère* 97
Ramonette (Plage) *Morbihan* 69
Rance (Usine Marémotrice) *Ille-et-Vilaine* 241
Rance (Vallée) *Ille-et-Vilaine* 242
Ranrouët (Château) *Loire-Atlantique* 137
Raz (Pointe) Finistère 244
Recouvrance (Pont) 78
Redon *Ille-et-Vilaine* 144
Regionalism 32
Regional nature parks 312
Le Releg *Finistère* 125
Religious furnishings 38, 39, 42
Renan, Ernest 34, 284
Renards (Pointe) *Finistère* 82
Rennes *Ille-et-Vilaine* 246
Rennes (Forêt) *Ille-et-Vilaine* 252
Renote (Île) *Côtes-d'Armor* 284
Retiers *Ille-et-Vilaine* 143
Rezé 195
Rhuys (Presqu'île) *Morbihan* 188
La Richardais *Ille-et-Vilaine* 243
Richelieu, Cardinal 79
Rieux *Morbihan* 245
Ris (Plage) *Finistère* 123
Robien (Château) *Côtes-d'Armor* 241
Roc'h Begheor *Finistère* 57
La Roche-aux-Fées *Ille-et-Vilaine* 143
La Roche-Bernard *Morbihan* 252
La Roche Cintrée *Finistère* 154
La Roche du Feu *Finistère* 237
Rochefort-en-Terre *Morbihan* 254
Roche-Jagu (Château) *Côtes-d'Armor* 255
La Roche-Jaune *Côtes-d'Armor* 286
Roche-Longue (Menhir) 241
La Roche-Maurice *Finistère* 255
Le Rocher-Portail (Château) *Ille-et-Vilaine* 56
Rocher Royal *Finistère* 240
Rochers-Sévigné (Château) *Ille-et-Vilaine* 256, 295
Rohan *Morbihan* 225
The Rohans 156
Rondossec (Dolmens) *Morbihan* 89
Rood screens 42
Rood-beams 42
Rophémel (Barrage) *Ille-et-Vilaine* 65
Les Rosaires (Plage) *Côtes-d'Armor* 262
Rosais (Belvédère) 271
Rosanbo (Château) *Côtes-d'Armor* 256
Roscanvel *Finistère* 111
Roscoff *Finistère* 257
Roscoff (Jardin Exotique) 258
Rosé *Loire-Atlantique* 135
Rosédo (Phare) *Côtes-d'Armor* 75
Le Roselier (Pointe) *Côtes-d'Armor* 262
Rospico (Anse) *Finistère* 97
Rosporden *Finistère* 258
Rostrenen *Côtes-d'Armor* 258
Rosulien (Cale) *Finistère* 238
Rothéneuf *Ille-et-Vilaine* 271
Round Table, Legend of the 28
Rouzic 214
Rumengol *Finistère* 259
Runan *Côtes-d'Armor* 259

S

Sables-d'Or-les-Pins *Côtes-d'Armor* 108
Saillé *Loire-Atlantique* 141
Saint: see under proper name
St-Adrien (Chapelle) *Morbihan* 63
St-Aignan *Morbihan* 145

St-Aubin-du-Cormier *Ille-et-Vilaine* 260
St-Avé *Morbihan* 293
St-Briac-sur-Mer *Ille-et-Vilaine* 107
St-Brieuc *Côtes-d'Armor* 260
St-Brieuc (Marinarium de la Baie) *Côtes-d'Armor* 262
St-Cado (Chapelle) *Morbihan* 151
St-Cast (Pointe) 262
St-Cast-le-Guildo *Côtes-d'Armor* 262
St-Côme (Chapelle) *Finistère* 93
St-Cyr-Coëtquidan (Military Academy) *Morbihan* 212
St-Degan *Morbihan* 61
St-Efflam *Côtes-d'Armor* 99
St-Énogat (Plage) 117
St-Esprit-des-Bois en Plédéliac (Ferme d'Antan) *Côtes-d'Armor* 157
St-Fiacre (Chapelle) *Morbihan* 263
St-Georges-de-Gréhaigne *Ille-et-Vilaine* 263
St-Gildas (Chapelle) *Finistère* 86
St-Gildas-de-Rhuys *Morbihan* 263
St-Gildas-des-Bois *Loire-Atlantique* 222
St-Gilles (Pointe) 70
St-Gonéry *Côtes-d'Armor* 264
St-Goustan (Plage) *Loire-Atlantique* 109
St-Guénolé *Finistère* 105
St-Herbot *Finistère* 57
St-Hernin *Finistère* 178
St-Hervé (Chapelle) *Finistère* 179
St-Hernot *Finistère* 111
St-Hubert (Pont) *Côtes-d'Armor* 242
St-Jacques-le-Majeur (Chapelle) *Côtes-d'Armor* 288
St-Jacut-de-la-Mer *Côtes-d'Armor* 107
St-Jaoua (Chapelle) *Finistère* 53
St-Jean (Chapelle) *Finistère* 218
St-Jean-Balanant *Finistère* 53
St-Jean-du-Doigt *Finistère* 264
St-Joachim *Loire-Atlantique* 137
St-Just *Ille-et-Vilaine* 245
St-Juvat *Côtes-d'Armor* 65
St-Léry *Morbihan* 210
St-Lunaire *Ille-et-Vilaine* 264
St-Lyphard *Loire-Atlantique* 137
St-Malo *Ille-et-Vilaine* 265
St-Malo-de-Guersac *Loire-Atlantique* 135
St-Marcel *Morbihan* 177
St-Mathieu (Pointe) *Finistère* 272
St-Maurice *Finistère* 240
St-Maurice (Pont) *Finistère* 240
St-Méen-le-Grand *Ille-et-Vilaine* 272
St-Michel (Chapelle) (Baud) *Morbihan* 63
St-Michel (Chapelle) (Bréhat) *Côtes-d'Armor* 75
St-Michel (Montagne) *Finistère* 58
St-Michel (Tumulus) *Morbihan* 88
St-Michel-de-Kergonan (Abbaye) *Morbihan* 89
St-Michel-en-Grève *Côtes-d'Armor* 98
St-Nazaire *Loire-Atlantique* 273
St-Nic *Finistère* 93
St-Nicodème (Chapelle) *Morbihan* 224
St-Nicolas (Chapelle) *Morbihan* 295
St-Nicolas (Île) 134
St-Nicolas-des-Eaux *Morbihan* 224
St-Nicolas-du-Pélem *Côtes-d'Armor* 258
St-Pern *Ille-et-Vilaine* 65
St-Philibert-et-St-Roch (Chapelle) 240
St-Pierre-Quiberon *Morbihan* 230
St-Pol-de-Léon *Finistère* 275
St-Quay-Portrieux *Côtes-d'Armor* 277
St-Rivoal *Finistère* 58
St-Sébastien (Chapelle) *Finistère* 57
St-Servais *Côtes-d'Armor* 87
St-Servan-sur-Mer *Ille-et-Vilaine* 270
St-Thégonnec *Finistère* 278
St-Tugen *Finistère* 102
St-Uzec (Menhir) *Côtes-d'Armor* 98
St-Venec (Chapelle) *Finistère* 237
St-Yvi *Finistère* 258
Ste-Anne-d'Auray *Morbihan* 279
Ste-Anne-du-Portzic *Finistère* 82
Ste-Anne-la-Palud *Finistère* 173
Ste-Avoye *Morbihan* 61
Ste-Barbe 209
Ste-Barbe (Alignements) *Morbihan* 89
Ste-Barbe (Chapelle) (Le Faouët) *Morbihan* 279
Ste-Barbe (Chapelle) (Névez) *Côtes-d'Armor* 222
Ste-Christine (Chapelle) *Finistère* 219
Ste-Hélène *Morbihan* 151
Ste-Marguerite (Dunes) *Finistère* 54
Ste-Marie-du-Ménez-Hom (Chapelle) *Finistère* 280
Ste-Marine *Finistère* 238
Ste-Noyale (Chapelle) *Morbihan* 225
Salmon fishing 92
Salt marshes 140
Sangliers (Mare) *Finistère* 153
Sarzeau *Morbihan* 199
Sauveur, Mayor 252
Sauzon *Morbihan* 68
Scal (Pointe) *Morbihan* 59
Scorff 175
Sculpture 42
Seafood 48
Seasons 23
Seaweed 22, 52
Second World War 77, 174, 177, 273
Sehar (Pointe) *Côtes-d'Armor* 167
Sein (Île) *Finistère* 280
Séné *Morbihan* 292
Séné (Presqu'île) 292
Sept-Îles *Côtes-d'Armor* 214
Sept-Saints (Chapelle) *Côtes-d'Armor* 166
Sérusier, Paul 180
Sévigné, Madame de 34, 256
Shellfish 22
Shoe-making industry 129
Signal Station 214
Sinagots 292
Sirènes (Grotte) *Ille-et-Vilaine* 264
Sizun *Finistère* 281
Sizun (Cap) *Finistère* 101
Sizun (Réserve du Cap) 102
Skylight houses 192
Slave trade 194
Sordan (Anse) *Morbihan* 145
Stained-glass windows 44
Stangala (Site) *Finistère* 237
Stêr-Ouen *Morbihan* 68
Stêr-Vraz *Morbihan* 68
Stiff (Phare) *Finistère* 207

Stival *Morbihan* 224
Succession, War of 24, 76, 155
Surcouf, Robert 26
La Surveillante 77
Suscinio (Château) *Morbihan* 281

T

Taden *Côtes-d'Armor* 243
Taillefer (Pointe) *Morbihan* 68
Talbert (Sillon) *Côtes-d'Armor* 287
Tanguy, Yves 48
Tas de Pois (Rochers) *Finistère* 213
Térénez *Finistère* 100
Térénez (Pont) *Finistère* 126
Tertres Noirs 295
Thirty, Battle of the 24, 155
Tides 19, 182
Tinténiac *Ille-et-Vilaine* 282
Tobacco 191
Tonquédec (Château) *Côtes-d'Armor* 166, 282
Torche (Pointe) *Finistère* 104
Touche-Trébry (Château) *Côtes-d'Armor* 178
Toul-an-Gollet (Manoir) *Côtes-d'Armor* 148
Toul Goulic (Gorges) *Côtes-d'Armor* 259
Toulinguet (Pointe) *Finistère* 110
Toullaëron (Roc) *Finistère* 179
Tourist information 301
Traonjoly (Manoir) *Finistère* 218
Travelling formalities 298
Trébeurden *Côtes-d'Armor* 283
Tréboul *Finistère* 123
Trécesson (Château) *Morbihan* 211
Trédion *Morbihan* 293
Trédrez *Côtes-d'Armor* 167
Trégarvan *Finistère* 92
Trégastel-Bourg *Côtes-d'Armor* 284
Trégastel-Plage *Côtes-d'Armor* 283
Trégomeur (Jardin Zoologique) *Côtes-d'Armor* 72
Tréguier *Côtes-d'Armor* 284
Tréhiguier *Morbihan* 59
Tréhorenteuc *Morbihan* 211
Trémalo (Chapelle) 222
Trémazan *Finistère* 54
Tremblay *Ille-et-Vilaine* 56
Trémeur, Saint 240
Trépassés (Baie) *Finistère* 102
Trescalan *Loire-Atlantique* 142
Trévarez (Château) *Finistère* 179
Trévezel (Roc) 125
Trévignon (Pointe) *Finistère* 96
Trézien (Phare) *Finistère* 55
Trieux (Estuaire) *Côtes-d'Armor* 75
Trieux (Vallée) *Côtes-d'Armor* 148
Trignac *Loire-Atlantique* 135
Trinité (Chapelle) *Finistère* 103
La Trinité-Langonnet *Morbihan* 287
La Trinité-sur-Mer *Morbihan* 287
Triskell 33
Tristan 28
Triumphal arches 44
Troménies 172
Trou de l'Enfer *Morbihan* 139
Trou du Serpent 62
Tumiac (Tumulus) *Morbihan* 189
Tumuli 40
La Turballe *Loire-Atlantique* 142

U

Upper Brittany 32
Ushant (Island) 205

V

Le Val-André 288
Val sans Retour *Morbihan* 211
Van (Pointe) *Finistère* 102
Vannes *Morbihan* 289
Vauban (Château) 83
Vauban (Citadelle) 67
Vauban 67
Veneti 187
Verdon (Pointe) *Morbihan* 151
Verne, Jules 34, 203
Veuves (Croix) 209
Vicomté (Pointe) 117
Vieille (Phare) 4, 244
Vierge (Phare de l'Île) *Finistère* 53
Le Vieux-Marché *Côtes-d'Armor* 313
Vieux-Moulin (Menhirs) *Morbihan* 89
Vilaine (Vallée) *Ille-et-Vilaine* 252
Villéon, Emmanuel de la 132
Villiers de l'Isle-Adam 34, 260
Vincent Ferrier, Saint 290
Vioreau (Grand Réservoir) *Loire-Atlantique* 177
Les Vire-Court *Finistère* 238
Vitré *Ille-et-Vilaine* 293
Viviane 28, 210
Vivier-sur-Mer 186
La Vraie-Croix *Morbihan* 228

W

Wagner 28
Waves 19
Wine 48

Y

Le Yaudet *Côtes-d'Armor* 167
Yves, Saint 30, 285

Z

Zooloisirs 282

MANUFACTURE FRANÇAISE DES PNEUMATIQUES MICHELIN
Société en commandite par actions au capital de 2 000 000 000 de francs
Place des Carmes-Déchaux – 63 Clermont-Ferrand (France)
R.C.S. Clermont-Fd B 855 200 507

Dépôt légal janvier 1997 – ISBN 2-06-131404-X – ISSN 0763-1383

Printed in the EU 08/98/1
Photocomposition : NORD COMPO, Villeneuve-d'Ascq
Impression et brochage : I.F.C., Saint-Germain-du-Puy

Cover illustration by Dominique BENOIT